The Eagle and the Lion
THE TRAGEDY OF AMERICAN-IRANIAN RELATIONS

The Eagle and the Lion

THE TRAGEDY OF

AMERICAN-IRANIAN

RELATIONS

JAMES A. BILL

YALE UNIVERSITY PRESS
NEW HAVEN AND LONDON

Designed by James J. Johnson
and set in Aster Roman Type by The Composing Room of Michigan, Inc.
Printed in the United States of America by Vail-Ballou Press, Binghamton, New York.

LIBRARY OF CONGRESS CATALOGING-IN-PUBLICATION DATA

Bill, James A.
   The eagle and the lion : The Tragedy of American-Iranian Relations / James A. Bill.
      p.   cm.
   Bibliography: p. 449.
   Includes index.
   ISBN 0–300–04097–0 (cloth)
         0–300–04412–7 (pbk.)
   1. United States—Foreign relations—Iran. 2. Iran—Foreign
relations—United States. 3. United States—Foreign
relations—1945– 4. Iran—Foreign relations—1941–1979. 5. Iran—
Foreign relations—1979– I. Title.
E183.8.I7B5   1988   87–22503
327.73055—dc19   CIP

The paper in this book meets the guidelines for permanence and durability of the Committee on Production Guidelines for Book Longevity of the Council on Library Resources.

10   9   8   7   6   5   4   3

For My Friends, My Family

Contents

Acknowledgments

This book is the result of an education provided by a large number of patient and informed individuals, both American and Iranian, over a period of twenty-eight years. Three leading scholars of Iran and the Middle East at Princeton University directed the formal part of this education—the late T. Cuyler Young, Martin Dickson, and, especially, Manfred Halpern. All three must be counted among those scholars whose greatest contributions reside in the permanent imprints they have left on the hearts and minds of their students. All three understood that the spirit, or *ruh*, of the United States and Iran is often as important as the objective realities that energize these social and political systems. Each in his own quite different way has passed this understanding along to me.

Professor Ervand Abrahamian read this entire manuscript thoroughly and critically, and his comments and suggestions have been indispensable in shaping the final product. Nikki Keddie also read and meticulously critiqued the manuscript. Among the other careful critics who have read sections of this study are Iran specialists Eric Hooglund, Gregory Rose, and especially William Royce, an American with an extraordinary understanding of Iran; accomplished social scientists and scholars Benjamin Page, Thomas Ferguson, Mark Gasiorowski, William Roger Louis, and William Dorman; Iran-seasoned diplomats and government officials Carl Clement, David Long, Michael Metrinko, Charles Naas, Earnest Oney, Henry Precht, John Waller, and John Washburn; and lawyers with firsthand knowledge of Iran and Iranian-American relations William Butler, Stephen Cohen, Cyrus Ghani, and Donald Weadon.

Others who have assisted me in many ways to prepare this book include journalists Kai Bird, Max Holland, and Robin Wright; past American friends in Iran John and Nancy Diekelmann, Walter and Louise Kaiser, Don Linehan, Andrew Mott, John Newton, Terence O'Donnell, Dick and Pat Roloff, and Ned and Nora Snyder; USIS em-

ployees Richard Arndt, William Demyer, Alan Gilbert, Wayne Gled-
hill, Alan Lester, and the late Lois Roth; U.S. Embassy officials Archie
Bolster, Douglas Heck, Michael Michaud, David Patterson, Charles
Rassias, John Stempel, and Donald Toussaint; foreign policy officials
in Washington, D.C., Myles Greene, George Griffin, William Hall-
mann, George Harris, and William Sullivan; experienced former
statesmen and officials George Ball, William Bundy, Richard Helms,
Melvin Laird, and George McGhee; and Iran specialists Amin Banani,
Catherine Bateson, Bill Beeman, Richard Cottam, Gene Garthwaite,
Grace Goodell, Jerrold Green, Michael Hillmann, M. A. Jazayery,
George Lenczowski, John Limbert, John Lorentz, David Menashri,
Rouhollah Ramazani, Hossein Razi, Thomas Ricks, Eliz Sanasarian,
Marvin Weinbaum, Donald Wilber, Sepehr Zabih, and Marvin Zonis.

Other individuals to whom I owe deep thanks include Mohammed
Ali and Reinhild Al-Tajir, Hooshang Amirahmadi, Vernon Aspaturian,
Jim Austin, Stephen Baker, Charles Beardsley, Delphine Blachiowicz,
Carl Brandt, Richard Brown, Mark Bruzonsky, Bruce Buchanan,
Milton and Mimi Buffington, R. M. Burrell, Amon Burton, Denys Cad-
man, Bernard and Mercedes Darbyshire, Paul English, John Esposito,
Tawfic Farah, Hafez Farmayan, John Henry Faulk, Gary Freeman,
Daniel Goodwin, Robert Hand, Lewis Hoffacker, Christos Ioaniddes,
Erik Jensen, Hassan Kamshad, Herb Kress, Carl Leiden, Walter Levy,
David Lilienthal, Jr., William Livingston, Scott Lubeck, Charles
Luellen, Ian Manners, Maury Maverick, Jr., William Millward, George
Nader, Richard Norton, Mansoor Notash, Paul O'Dwyer, Monte Pal-
mer, Marjorie Payne, J. R. Parten, Jim Roach, Archie Roosevelt,
Charles Rudolph, William Scanlan, Karl Schmitt, Gary Silverman,
Harry Snyder, Michael Stoff, David Stronach, Paul Sturgul, Antony
Sullivan, Jack and Rosmarie Sunderland, Micky Takahashi, Peter
Theroux, Everett Titus, Richard Ware, John Wertime, John A.
Williams, and T. Cuyler Young, Jr. A number of talented librarians
provided me with invaluable assistance, including Abazar Sepehri of
the University of Texas, scholar David Painter of the State Department
Library, Martin Elzy and David C. Humphrey of the Lyndon B. Johnson Presidential Library, and Michael Albin and Ibrahim Pourhadi of
the Library of Congress. I also thank cartographer John Cotter for the
excellent drawings and graphics.

Students also contribute much to a book such as this. They constantly hammer away at old ideas and suggest new ones. In the preparation of this book several superb students have provided invaluable
assistance. They include Tura Campanella, Tim Dickey, Manochehr
Dorraj, Ali Eftekhary, Ahmad Farokhpay, Thomas Hartwell, William

Hickman, John Holden, Robert Kitrinos, Pamela Kress-Krikscion, Abbass Manafy, Mehdi Noorbaksh, Farzin Sarabi-Kia, and Robin Stallings. James Hitselberger, a graduate student with the skills of a master librarian, provided especially valuable research aid.

On the Iranian side, I wish to thank hundreds of Iranians from all walks of life. Given the sensitivity of the subject matter, I refer to those to whom I owe special debts only by their first names: three Alis, two Hassans, two Ibrahims, two Gholam Rezas, two Manuchehrs, two Khosrows, Amin, Heda, Abbas, Hushang, Davud, Reza, Mansur, Homayun, Majid, Cyrus, Mariam, Mustafa, Fereshteh, Muhammad Ali, Lili, Fereydun, Ardeshir, Hussein, Parviz, and Farhang. I especially want to thank my old friend Hajji Nafti, an Iranian philosopher who both pumped gas on the street and primed minds in the classroom. Bright, skeptical, generous, and irreverent, he patiently taught me much about human nature, both Iranian and American.

I am also deeply appreciative for the support provided by my editor, Charles Grench, who approached this project with infectious enthusiasm from the very beginning. Throughout the process of preparation, he, with the strong backing of the director and assistant director of Yale University Press, John Ryden and Tina Weiner, displayed a flexibility and understanding rare in today's bureaucratized world of publishing. My manuscript editor, Laura Jones Dooley, has smoothed prose, repaired syntax, and posed numerous questions, all while carefully and sensitively protecting the integrity of the message. Sarah Clark and Jane Levey have marketed the book with gracious zeal. It has been a privilege for me to work with this Yale team.

Finally, the Bill family. My son, Tim, acted as technical expert and computer/word-processing specialist for the project. Puzzled by my slowness to master the intricacies of the computer, he nonetheless provided the repetitious instruction necessary for this tedious process of adult education. Daughter Rebecca generated the sunshine that illuminated the atmosphere in which I worked. In accompanying me on a research trip to Washington, D.C., in early 1987, she proved to me that libraries and boutiques, research and restaurants, are not mutually exclusive. Rebecca and Tim have caused me to cross-examine my ideas and prejudices on matters that go far beyond the subject of this book.

Ann Marie Bachhuber Bill, my wife, accompanied me on my first trip to Iran, a four-week cross-country honeymoon trek from London to Tehran in the fall of 1965. Our life together began with two years in Tehran, years in which we both first came to know and love Iran and its people. Since then, Ann has provided the support and inspiration that have enabled me to complete this book. Her contributions have been varied and rather basic. She nursed me back to health after a severe bout with typhoid fever in 1966. Twenty years later, in 1986, she watched with resigned fascination as books and papers slowly and inexorably crept out of my study and fanned outward into the other rooms of the house, settling in untidy stacks on the dining room and kitchen tables, then on all unoccupied chairs, and finally on the open floor, where they acted as a low-level obstacle course to those who hoped to move from room to room. Ann tolerated this imperial march of the papers quietly, although it undoubtedly had something to do with her constant encouragement that I finish this book. This is her production as much as mine.

Note on Transliteration

The system of transliteration adopted in this study is a modified version of the format recommended by the *International Journal of Middle East Studies*. I have chosen to delete all the diacritical marks with the exception of the *ayn* (') and the *hamzah* (') when they appear in the middle of a word, e.g., Shi'i, Qashqa'i. In this system, the "e" and the "o" are not used but are replaced by the "i" and the "u," respectively. Persian or Arabic words are spelled as they commonly appear in *Webster's Third International Dictionary*, in *Webster's Geographical Dictionary*, or in ordinary English usage. Examples include Islam, Quran, bazaar, Tehran, Ali, Hassan, Hussein, and Tudeh. Well-known Iranian proper names are generally presented as they commonly appear in the English literature, e.g., Muhammad Reza Shah Pahlavi, Ayatollah Ruhollah Khomeini, Sayyid Ziaeddin Tabataba'i, Amir Abbas Hoveyda, Allahyar Saleh, Shapour and Teymour Bakhtiar, Asadollah Alam, Ja'far Sharif-Emami, Sadeq Ghotbzadeh, Ayatollah Hussein Ali Montazeri, and Ayatollah Abul Qassim Kashani. Sharp-eyed readers will note occasional inconsistencies, but such is the nature of transliteration systems and language.

Introduction

Early on the morning of Sunday, May 25, 1986, six men boarded a black Boeing 707 aircraft in Tel Aviv, Israel. They were bound for Tehran, capital of the Islamic Republic of Iran. The six men, a team whose mission had been approved by President Ronald Reagan himself, carried with them a chocolate cake prepared in a kosher bakery in Tel Aviv, six Blackhawk .357 Magnum pistols in presentation boxes, and one pallet of spare parts for Iran's Hawk missiles. Their mission was to exchange the badly needed spare parts for four Americans being held hostage in Lebanon. When they landed in Tehran an hour and a half ahead of schedule that morning, they found themselves immediately embroiled in controversy and tense diplomatic conflict.

Carrying Irish passports, the six official adventurers included former National Security Council head Robert "Bud" McFarlane, Lt. Col. Oliver North, NSC official Howard Teicher, Central Intelligence Agency Iran specialist George Cave, a CIA communications expert, and Amiram Nir, an Israeli counterterrorist expert and a confidant of Prime Minister Shimon Peres of Israel. Nir made the trip disguised as an American named Miller.

Delicate diplomatic negotiations in Tehran were marked by distrust, fright, and misunderstanding. The head of the U.S. delegation, Robert McFarlane, described his Iranian counterparts in the following terms: "It would be best for us to try to picture what it would be like if after a nuclear attack a surviving Tartar became Vice President; a recent grad student became Secretary of State; and a bookie became the interlocutor for all discourse with foreign countries." He referred to the first group of Iranian representatives as "bush leaguers." The Iranians, on the other hand, were very skittish and feared both the Soviet Union and the United States. As one adviser to the Iranian Ministry of Foreign Affairs noted, "It is not easy to sleep next to an elephant that you have wounded."[1]

When the six flew away three days later, the pallet of arms remained in Tehran. The four American hostages remained in Lebanon. United States-Iranian tensions had deepened, not relaxed. A secret, risky mission that Colonel North had expected to go "peachy keen" had failed ignominiously. Yet it was on the return trip to the United States that North confided to Robert McFarlane that the escapade had not been a "total lost cause," since funds received from the Iranians for arms had been applied to Central America.[2]

On May 29, the day after their return to the United States, McFarlane, North, and Teicher solemnly reported on the failed mission directly to the president of the United States at the White House. Vice President George Bush, NSC head John Poindexter, and White House Chief of Staff Donald Regan were also present at this important briefing.

This bizarre incident occurred at a time when President Reagan had been publicly proclaiming Iran a terrorist state and when his secretaries of State and Defense were pursuing a decidedly anti-Iranian foreign policy. It also occurred only five weeks after the president had ordered an air attack on Mu'ammar Qaddafi's living quarters in Libya, another country the administration charged with the promotion of international terrorism. This flight to Tehran was only one dramatic episode in what is known as the Iran-Contra arms affair, an affair described by Alabama senator Howell Heflin on the first day of Congressional Hearings in May 1987 as one dominated by "rogue elephants, rug merchants, loose cannons, soldiers of fortune, privateers, profiteers, hostages, and contras."

The Iranian-U.S. arms affair capped a long period of confused and confusing U.S. policy toward an ancient Middle Eastern country of great strategic significance in the international community of nations. It demonstrated forcibly that American foreign policy toward postrevolutionary Iran reflected many of the flaws that had dominated U.S. policy before the revolution: Flaws of massive ignorance, bureaucratic conflict, Sovietcentricity, economic obsessions, and the prevalence of informal or privatized decision making all transcended the revolution as America carried past mistakes into the future. The situation was exacerbated by an inexperienced, beleaguered, and paranoid leadership in the Islamic Republic that formulated policy based on its own misperceptions and misunderstandings of the United States.

Informed Iranians often wrote and spoke about America's lack of knowledge of their country. They murmured quietly about the naïveté of Americans. On the other hand, these same Iranians insisted that the United States was intimately acquainted with everything that transpired in their country. In the Iranian view, the CIA was omnipresent in Iran; what Americans did not know for themselves, they found out through their connections with the omniscient British or the stealthy Israelis.

In the United States itself, leading policymakers through the years were consistently confident that they knew Iran very well indeed. This confidence was shared in varying degree by every U.S. president from Eisenhower through Reagan. It was so deeply ingrained that even during the great Iranian-American tensions following the revolution of 1978–79, Presidents Carter and Reagan attempted to confront the crises with no serious Iran expertise on their all-important National Security Councils. Before the revolution, this sturdy confidence was reinforced for twenty-five years by the reporting that came out of the American embassy in Tehran, by the close personal ties that dominated the relationship between the Iranian political elite and American decision makers, and by the American mass media, whose often shallow and orthodox reporting lent a kind of public legitimacy to this deceptive mind-set. After the fall of the Pahlavis, this false confidence increasingly rested on the fragile foundation of arrogance, individual ambition, and a certain reckless flamboyance emanating from NSC offices that had plotted aggressive adventures in places like Nicaragua, Grenada, Libya, and Lebanon.

Over the years a tiny group of American diplomats, Peace Corps volunteers, and scholars were anything but confident about America's understanding of Iran. These individuals were themselves baffled by the shifting depths of the Iranian personality, but all agreed that the Iran that they observed in the villages and mosques throughout the country was significantly different from the Iran described in Washington, D.C., and in the American mass media. Their voices, however, were drowned out by the loud cries of acclamation and praise stressing the strength and stability of the Pahlavi-led government in Iran. Prerevolutionary Iran was labeled alternately an "island," an "oasis," and a "pillar" of stability. A Department of State semiannual report on Iran in September 1969 typified this attitude when it referred to Iran's "almost monotonous domestic political stability."[3] This opinion was promoted and protected through the Nixon-Ford-Kissinger years until December 12, 1978, when President Carter stated: "I fully expect the Shah to maintain power in Iran, and for the present problems in Iran to be resolved. . . . I think the predictions of doom and disaster that came from some sources have certainly not been realized at all. The Shah has our support and he also has our confidence."[4] One month later, Muhammad Reza Shah Pahlavi fled his country never to return. By mid-February 1979, a violent revolution had swept through Iran, leaving an indelible imprint on both the United States and the entire international system.

Under the Reagan Administration, the United States once again stumbled clumsily into the Iranian political minefield in a way that proved counterproductive professionally, debilitating domestically, and embarrassing internationally. Whereas the Carter Administration had relied on uninformed professional advisers, the Reaganites gathered their information from international businessmen with private motives, third country specialists with questionable credentials, and NSC consultants who had never visited Iran and could not speak Persian. The era of the Kissingers, Siscos, Brzezinskis, and Sicks gave way to an era of Ghorbanifars, Ledeens, Teichers, Norths, Secords, Nirs, and Nimrodis.

Few international relationships have had a more positive beginning than that which characterized Iranian-American contacts for more than a century. The United States stood aloof from the great power rivalry of Britain and Russia over Iranian territory. For decades, Iran managed to maintain its independence as a nation-state by playing the two superpowers against one another. Whenever the two rivals came to an understanding, Iranian leaders saw their country's independence and identity in serious jeopardy. Such was the case, for example, in 1907, when the two great powers signed the Anglo-Russian Agreement, effectively dividing Iran into zones of influence—the Russians in the north, the British in the southeast, and a neutral zone in between.

Even more dangerous to Iranian independence was the scenario in which either great power gained clear ascendancy over the other. This occurred in 1825–28 when a Persian-Russian war resulted in a treaty that not only cost Iran all of its territory west of the Caspian Sea but also forced it to grant extraterritorial privileges to Russian citizens resident in Iran. One British example was the Reuter Concession of 1872, which granted a British subject a monopoly over virtually all of Iran's economic and financial resources. As Lord Curzon stated, it was "the most complete and extraordinary surrender of the entire industrial resources of a kingdom into foreign hands that has probably ever been dreamed of."[5] Another case in point was the Anglo-Persian Agreement of 1919, which was concluded in secret and which gave Great Britain enormous political, military, and economic control over Iran. Although these last two agreements were ultimately rejected, they stood as stark reminders of the external threats to Iran's independence.

As Iran zigged and zagged its way through a political thicket inhabited by such interested and predatory creatures as Russia and Britain, its leaders constantly looked for third forces to exercise a neutralizing influence. Along with Germany and, to a lesser extent, France, the United States represented a major hope in this respect. Until 1953, American statements and activities convinced Iran's leaders that this hope was well placed. As early as 1919, for example, the United States had strongly protested to Britain about its secret agreement of that year. And in the mid-1940s, the United States took the forward position in pressing the Soviet Union to withdraw its forces from Azarbaijan following World War II. For motives both national and personal, Iranian political leaders sought "to use America as a political balancer and an economic Santa Claus."[6] Partially because the United States played this role quite well, Americans were liked and admired in Iran.

After its part in the overthrow of Muhammad Musaddiq in 1953, the United States found itself the object of growing Iranian criticism. Both the moderate, nationalistic opposition forces as well as the more radical voices on the left began to refer to the United States as an imperialistic, oppressive external force. At the same time, the Shi'i religious leaders began to condemn America and American policy. Iranians of all political persuasions increasingly formed a negative image of the United States. They no longer saw America as an external, liberating force whose influence would protect Iran from its traditional enemies, Britain and Russia. Instead, they developed a perspective in which the protector had become the exploiter. In the view of many Iranians, the first significant move in the American turnabout occurred with the fall of the nationalistic movement of Musaddiq. Here, according to Iranian nationalists, the United States chose to ally itself with the imperial interests of Great Britain and in the process rescued the shah, a man who had fled ignominiously from his own country. As Britain retreated from its preeminent role in the Persian Gulf, the United States replaced it as the new, obtrusive, and intervening external power.

Throughout the 1970s the United States increased its influence in Iran to levels highly reminiscent of the direct interventions of Britain and Russia during the heyday of colonialism. The traditional Persian paranoia and accompanying resentment were increasingly transferred from Great Britain and the USSR to the United States, especially as America entwined itself more and more with the governing regime in Iran. By the time of the Iranian revolution in 1978, America's reservoir of historical goodwill had been drained dry. The violent, antimonarchical revolution had a sharp anti-American edge that became even sharper in reaction to policies developed in Washington in response to the revolution. In the years following the revolution, Iran-American relations reached an all-time low. When the Carter Administration admitted the shah to the United States for medical treatment on October 22, 1979, a group of extremist Iranian students took over the American embassy in Tehran and held over fifty U.S. citizens hostage for almost fifteen months. During this time the two countries engaged in practically every form of conflict short of all-out war.

What happened? How could two allies and longtime friends reach such a state of estrangement that their confrontation had come to harm seriously the national interests of both parties? What forces at work in Iran, the United States, and the world contributed to this conflict? Can damaged Iranian-American relations be repaired? What does the future hold for these relations—relations that are of great significance to both countries?

Iran is a country of approximately fifty million people, a number almost twice that of all the other Persian Gulf countries put together. Sharing a 1,600-mile border with the Soviet Union in the north and fronting the important Strait of Hormuz to the south, Iran is a nation of special geostrategic significance. Iran has 10 percent of the world's proven reserves of petroleum (about 65 billion barrels), and throughout the 1970s Iran was the world's second largest oil exporter. It also possesses the world's second largest reserves of natural gas. Conservatively estimated at 500 trillion cubic feet, these reserves are the energy equivalent of another 82 billion barrels of oil. In these circumstances, the state of Iranian-American relations assumes a special importance to every American. Is there any relationship acceptable to the peoples and governments of both countries?

What general policy lessons does the tragic history of Iranian-American relations teach? As a case study in U.S. foreign policy, what might this history indicate about the strengths and weaknesses of such policy-making? How might it affect American relations with other Middle Eastern and Third World countries? What does it indicate about the future of the United States in a world caught in the midst of revolutionary change? Can we avoid similar imbroglios elsewhere as we navigate ourselves through stormy international waters toward the year 2000?

These are among the questions I will seek to answer in this book. In so doing, it is necessary to examine both English and Persian sources; reasons for the dramatic developments in Iran-U.S. relations are to be found as much in the complex context of internal Iranian politics as in the American policy-making environment. The story is elusive and multifaceted, involving the vested self-interest, ambitions, and ideals of personalities like Muhammad Reza Shah Pahlavi, Amir Asadollah Alam, Amir Abbas Hoveyda, Muhammad Musaddiq, Ayatollah Ruhollah Khomeini, Ali Shariati, Abol Hassan Bani Sadr, Mehdi Bazargan, Ali Akbar Hashemi-Rafsanjani, and Hussein Ali Montazeri in Iran and John Kennedy, Lyndon Johnson, Kermit Roosevelt, Richard Nixon, Henry Kissinger, David Rockefeller, Zbigniew Brzezinski, Jimmy Carter, Robert McFarlane, Oliver North, John Poindexter, and Ronald Reagan in the United States. It also concerns such social forces as the religious, commercial, and professional classes that spearheaded the Iranian revolution. It is a story that focuses on petroleum prices, arms sales, intelligence capers, international public relations, and a great deal of political misunderstanding and human suffering.

I have observed the Iran-American tragedy firsthand for over twenty-five years. I first began to study Iranian society and politics in 1961, writing a master's thesis entitled "Social Structure and Political Power in Iran" at Pennsylvania State University in 1963. During the next two years I studied the Persian language and Iran's history and politics at Princeton University before leaving for my first two-year research stint in Iran itself. My honeymoon consisted of the overland trek from Western Europe to Iran. This fieldwork resulted in a doctoral dissertation completed in 1968 and titled "The Iranian Intelligentsia: Class and Change." I made other extended research visits in 1970 and 1974 and briefer fact-finding trips in 1975, 1977, and November–December 1978, during the height of the revolution itself.

In Iran I was fortunate enough to be able to travel widely and to live in many corners of the land, including with the Turkoman and Qashqa'i tribes in northwest and south-central Iran. I traveled for a week with the governor-general through the villages of Fars province and later spent two weeks with the people of Ahwaz as they prepared for an upcoming visit by the shah. On another occasion, I accompanied several district governors (*bakhshdars*) as they went about their development duties deep in the Iranian countryside. My wife and I also shared the hospitality of young American Peace Corps volunteers in their modest but friendly homes in Shiraz, Mashhad, Hamadan, and Ahwaz.

In 1970 I visited four Iranian prisons and witnessed the grinding poverty in villages in Fars province, where on two occasions I saw starving children eating grass and roots in fields near their villages. I joined the religious pilgrims in the holy Shi'i shrines in Qum and Mashhad and spent many hours with Shi'i mullahs both in their *hujrah*s (cells) and homes and at my apartment. Although my best Iranian friends were students, teachers, poets, physicians, journalists, and midlevel bureaucrats, I also maintained close contact with taxi drivers, teaboys, money changers, carpet dealers, barbers, tribesmen, and bus drivers. I had extensive private interviews with Empress Farah and Prime Minister Hoveyda. I also had close friends among the members of various opposition groups, many of whom had been imprisoned and some of whom had been tortured by the Pahlavi regime. My goal while in Iran was to immerse myself as completely as possible in the society and, in the process, to come to better understand it. Any such understanding that I may have gained is primarily because of the hospitality and warmth that the Iranian people showed me as a guest in their country for so many years.

My contact with Iran inevitably brought me into close touch with many Americans, both official and unofficial, who also had Iran interests. In the mid-1960s, for example, I studied an American university's attempt to build a major school of excellence at Pahlavi University in Shiraz. In 1970 I carried out an in-depth study of the U.S. Embassy in Tehran, interviewing the ambassador, the various Foreign Service and Foreign Service Information officers, many staff members, and several local Iranian employees as well. A view of the American military establishment was provided through friends in the armed forces stationed in Iran and through the U.S. Air Force hospital in north Tehran, where my wife was employed as a registered nurse. Over the years I became acquainted with Ambassadors Armin Meyer, Douglas MacArthur II, Richard Helms, and William Sullivan as well as with several different deputy chiefs of mission, political counselors, and political officers who served in Iran. I made presentations to Peace Corps volunteers in Tehran and Hamadan and stayed for a time with the American consul in Tabriz.

In the United States I consulted with the lower and middle levels of the Department of State concerning Iran and made a number of presentations at the Foreign Service Institute. It was here that I became acquainted with a number of diplomats who were later taken hostage. In 1970 I spent several days at the Iran desk at the Department of State while participating in the scholar-diplomat seminar program, and in 1974 I worked on a project concerning district governors for the United States Information Agency. My contacts with the White House were limited, although I did meet with George Ball in December 1978 the day before he presented a special report on the Iran crisis to President Carter.

In all, I have had considerable interaction with the Americans who made our Iran policy over the past two decades. As a minor, outside participant in that policy-making process, I had the opportunity to gain some unusual insights into the official system that related America to Iran. By observing it in action in both the United States and Iran, I was able to see what went into the system, what came out, and how the latter influenced the former. And, very importantly, I witnessed firsthand how this policy affected Iran and how it was received by Iranians of all classes. In April 1966, for example, an influential but uneducated Turkoman mullah asked me over tea in a tent on the Gorgan plain why America kept bombing "Saigoon." Was America intending to do the same to Tehran? America's policy in Vietnam, which the shah permitted to be sharply criticized in the Persian press, was one factor that slowly twisted Iranian public opinion against the United States. The Iran-America story clearly needs to be told in terms relating domestic and international politics.

The following study does not always make pleasant reading, since it documents many instances of the politics of greed, misunderstanding, oppression, and suffering. Mistakes and misperceptions abounded on all sides, and policy conflict was present at all levels both in the United States and in Iran. Many of the players in the drama have already published their interpretations of the events; the only common denominator in all these accounts is the claim by each that their actions were correct and that all the others were badly mistaken and misguided. The writers seem to need to rewrite history in order to rationalize and defend their role in it. At times this is done not only for posterity but also to help the writers achieve future political ambitions. Henry Kissinger and Zbigniew Brzezinski are only the most obvious cases in point. Among the Iranian actors, the members of the former Pahlavi regime write defensively and with understandable bitterness, since their political futures are now nonexistent and their ambitions in ashes. Like Kissinger and Brzezinski's writings and statements, the widely distributed memoirs of the shah and his twin sister, Princess Ashraf, are transparently self-serving. To my knowledge, few have conceded making mistakes. But mistakes were many.

In this book, I attempt to present the story as I witnessed it. Since any interpretation is likely to be challenged by someone somewhere in either country, I have made a special effort to document my interpretation. The analysis is, of course, mine and is subject to my biases. I can only attempt to be sensitive to these prejudices and to play them down whenever possible. Like all Iran-watchers, I have often been wrong in my own observations and prognoses. Just as I will on occasion document the accuracy of my predictions, I will also make a special effort to admit some embarrassing mistakes of interpretation of my own. All serious students of Iran soon learn that it is best to be modest about one's understanding of that country. Like politicians, professors have a difficult time with modesty. In the case of Iran, most scholars quickly learned this lesson one way or another, but the highest American decision makers learned it either slowly or not at all.

Although a healthy dose of modesty mixed with some self-skepticism was always evident at the Department of State, it was seldom apparent in the presidential inner circle or in the National Security Council. As a result, Iranian actions were always surprises that could only be explained as irrational, fanatical, unpredictable, aberrant, or "oriental" behavior. This mind-set carried severe consequences for the American national interest. As one retired Foreign Service officer who served for years in the Middle East noted: "The more serious the international crisis, the less expertise that is brought to bear on it. This is because these crises are handled at the very highest level." The lack of expertise combined with supreme confidence is a deadly combination and one that is often encountered in this book.

The Iranian social and political process is extremely difficult to penetrate, understand, and explain. The processes of power and decision making are usually hidden within the deepest recesses of society, where they exist in a state of constant flux. The eminent British writer and authority on the Middle East Gertrude Bell wrote in 1891 that Iranian social and political life was "a life into which no European can penetrate."[7] Many of the shrewdest and most influential political figures in Iran have intentionally avoided the blinding sunlight of publicity and have sought to exert power in the more shadowy corridors of the political system. Here they presented no targets to potential enemies and their influence often transcended that of those who have held ministerial portfolios. These quiet influentials heeded well the Persian proverb: "The camel rider cannot duck out of sight."

The American political structure is also riddled with nooks and crannies that are not easily entered or observed. Here, key unofficial actors and informal power brokers help fashion policy. A complex, informal network of powerful American personalities played a critical role in shaping U.S. policy toward Iran. The sinews of this network must be traced and studied. In the mid-1980s, after the revolution, foreign policy became "privatized" in a different way as outsiders, including foreign nationals, became the actual proponents and managers of the process. The Iran-U.S. relationship cannot be understood without analyzing this dimension of the politics of both countries because the points of interaction between these informal actors were also the decisional junctures that largely determined policy. Despite

Gertrude Bell's admonition, serious understanding is possible. In this study I attempt to expose and analyze this level of interaction and I discuss the Iranians and Americans who operated most effectively here.

Former Supreme Court Justice William O. Douglas once stated that "Persians are spiritually close kin to Americans."[8] This book presumes to analyze the personal, social, and political forces that challenged and severely damaged that kinship.

PART I

1 America and Iran: Early Entanglements

Americans developed divided attitudes toward Iran from the start. Their first contacts with Iranians on Iranian soil were spurred by a humanitarianism heavily tinged with ethnocentric strains of superiority and proselytization. In 1830, Harrison Gray Otis Dwight and Eli Smith traveled into northwestern Iran to reconnoiter the area for future missionary purposes. They were the first Americans known to have set foot in Iran. Five American missionaries took up residence in Urumiyeh in the present-day province of Azerbaijan in 1835. From this base, they worked among the twenty thousand Nestorian Christians who then inhabited that area. The Americans also periodically attempted to carry their Christian messages to the masses of Shi'i Muslims, although they were consistently greeted with cool rejection.

During their first twenty-five years in Iran, the American missionaries made fundamental contributions to the health, education, and overall social well-being of the Iranians they served. When the Americans arrived in 1835, fewer than twenty men and but one woman were literate in the entire northwestern region. By 1860, more than fifteen hundred Iranian students were enrolled in the American missionary schools. These early Americans in Iran were hardy, courageous individuals who paid a heavy personal price for their dedication. Of the four dozen adults who lived in Iran before 1860, ten died prematurely in the field, while critical illness forced eight others into early retirement. In 1840, all but one of the children of the five American families in Iran were killed by a plague that devastated the countryside.[1]

The first contingents of Americans looked down on their Iranian brethren and quietly discussed among themselves strategies to achieve their foremost goal: conversion. A special contempt and condescension was reserved for the Muslim majority. Even Rev. Justin Perkins, a distinguished and dedicated man who identified himself with the everyday lives and customs of the Nestorian Assyrians among whom he lived, strongly disliked those whom he termed "savage

Muhammedans."[2] According to Perkins: "Yes; Muhammedism, proud, exclusive, corrupt, revengeful and bloody, as it is, is tottering in its dotage, and ready to fall. . . . Like a mighty polar iceberg, breaking away from its dreary moorings and floating gently downward into a kindlier zone, so Muhammedism, amid the growing light and warmth of civilization and Christianity, that are kindled up around it, is silently and harmlessly melting away."[3]

A century and a half later, Americans in Iran still felt both admiration and dislike for Iran and Shi'i Islam. A number of Peace Corps volunteers and scholars, as well as some diplomats and occasional businessmen, exhibited genuine respect and love for the Iranian people while working to achieve both their own goals and those of Iranians with whom they came in contact. Many of the American diplomats held hostage in Iran after the revolution of 1978–79, such as John Limbert, Barry Rosen, Charles Scott, Ann Swift, and Kathryn Koob, while condemning those responsible for their captivity, publicly praised the Iranian culture and people long after their release. Other American diplomats felt differently. One official who returned to the United States in 1979 after five years' residence in Iran described Shi'i Islam as a "dirty, bloody, and thoroughly evil force."[4] This latter-day Justin Perkins represented the many Americans who considered Iran and Iranians uncivilized, fanatical, and corrupt.

Between 1860 and 1940, Americans had little official contact with Iran. Throughout the nineteenth century Britain and Russia intrigued in Iran, each state jealously seeking to draw Iran into its sphere of influence. Pursuing its basic policy of isolation and nonentanglement, the United States carefully avoided entering this field of European confrontation. Although official contact was established in 1851 and modest treaties were negotiated in 1851 and 1856, it was not until 1883 that Iran and the United States exchanged diplomatic representatives. From that time until World War II, American influence in Iran was minimal and was overshadowed by the deep and persistent influence of the British and the Russians. During these years, the United States developed a positive, benevolent image in the eyes of the Iranian people, who increasingly resented British and Russian intervention. The anti-British paranoia that developed over those 150 years remains in Iran even today despite the strident anti-Americanism that surfaced with the revolution of 1978–79.

The reservoir of goodwill between Iran and the United States was deepened during the pre-1940 period by the impressive activities of individual Americans who lived and worked in Iran, including such missionary-teachers as Howard Baskerville and Dr. Samuel Martin Jordan and such diplomat-humanitarians as Louis G. Dreyfus, Jr., and his wife, Grace. Howard Baskerville, a young teacher at the American Memorial School in Tabriz, was killed in April 1909 while fighting with the revolutionaries in support of the Iranian constitutional movement. Baskerville was sometimes referred to as "the American Lafayette in Iran," and he became a national hero to many Iranians. Perhaps the most famous American in the minds of Iranians was the influential educator Samuel Jordan. An extraordinary American pioneer in Iran from 1898 to 1941, he was principal both of the American High School in Tehran and, beginning in 1925, of the American College in Tehran. Jordan was responsible for the education of thousands of Iranians and was in many ways the father of modern education in Iran. Of all the American missionary-teachers in Iran, "none did America higher service in Persia than Dr. Samuel M. Jordan."[5] A female counterpart of Jordan was Jane E. Doolittle, an extraordinary woman who first entered Iran in 1921 as a missionary and who dedicated her life to furthering the education and health of the Iranian people. After her retirement in 1964, Jane Doolittle chose to remain in Iran, where she continued her work right up to the revolution in 1979. Other American missionary families deeply respected in Iran over the years were the Gurneys, Youngs, Wrights, and Wilsons.

Louis G. Dreyfus, Jr., served as the American minister plenipotentiary to Iran during the difficult war-torn years of 1940–44. Despite the Allied occupation of Iran, Dreyfus and his wife, Grace, remained popular in Iranian society. Unlike the overwhelming majority of American diplomatic mission heads in Iran, the Dreyfus influence directly touched the lives of the Iranian lower classes. Grace Dreyfus, who had been a volunteer nurse in World War I, opened both a typhus clinic and an orphanage in the poor districts of south Tehran. According to financial adviser A. C. Millspaugh: "Mr. Louis G. Dreyfus, who presided over the Legation at the time of my arrival, was generally considered the best as he was the most popular and effective, of the men who had represented the United States in Teheran. The Minister's wife had captured the hearts of the Persians, not only as a charming hostess, but also as a sympathetic and tireless worker in the slums of south Tehran."[6]

These Americans and hundreds like them established over the years a reputation for America that was positive and warm. As the Iranians sought to free themselves from the crushing embrace of the British and the Russians, they beckoned to America, which they saw as a powerful potential ally. The many Americans who had lived in their midst had given them good reason to place their hope and trust in the United States.

The Early 1940s: Patterns of the American Presence

Between 1925 and 1941 Iran was ruled by Reza Shah Pahlavi, a shrewd and ruthless dictator who eliminated all rivals while at the same time working to protect his country's independence and modernize its military. A pragmatic nationalist, Reza Shah applied the time-honored Persian technique of protecting Iran's national integrity by balancing such powerful predatory countries as Britain and the Soviet Union with a third-party alliance. In the case of Reza Shah, this third force was Germany, a country whose ideology greatly impressed him. Over one thousand German advisers, businessmen, and officials were stationed by 1941 in Tehran alone. This deeply disturbed the Allies, who considered Iran a crucial geostrategic actor in the coming confrontation with Nazi Germany. Great Britain and the Soviet Union invaded and occupied Iran on August 25, 1941, driving the proud shah into exile. Reza Shah's highly touted military crumbled in the face of the invasion, and the United States joined the USSR and Britain in occupying the country. Throughout World War II, Iran served as an important supply bridge to the beleaguered Soviet Union, which was under German attack from the west.

Reza Shah was replaced as king by his twenty-two-year-old son, Muhammad Reza Shah. Holding his position at the sufferance of the external Allied powers and confronted by explosive domestic forces that had been bottled up for fifteen years by his father, the young shah found himself in a tenuous political position. The Soviet Union and the United Kingdom joined Iran in January 1942 in signing the Tripartite Treaty, which guaranteed the territorial sovereignty and political independence of Iran in line with the Atlantic Charter, but did not allay the fears of the new shah or his advisers, who saw the real possibility of their country's dismemberment. In this context, the experienced Iranian aristocrats and statesmen decided to push for heavy American presence and influence in their country.

In Washington, American foreign policymakers agreed that the United States should become involved in Iran as part of the Allied war effort. On March 10, 1942, Iran was declared eligible for lend-lease aid. American decision makers realized immediately that Iranian independence was of major long-term interest to the United States. In January 1943 an extremely thoughtful memorandum that analyzed

America's developing role in Iran had been prepared in the Department of State. This document decried British and Soviet interventionism in Iran: "Although Russian policy has been fundamentally aggressive and British policy fundamentally defensive in character, the result in both cases has been interference with the internal affairs of Iran, amounting at times to a virtually complete negation of Iranian sovereignty and independence."[7] Noting that Iran had appealed desperately and persistently to the United States, the January 1943 memo responded to these representations thus: "So far, we have rested our response to this appeal primarily upon our interest in winning the war. I wonder if we should not also begin, privately, to base our response upon our interest in winning the peace? The United States, alone, is in a position to build up Iran to the point at which it will stand in need of neither British nor Russian assistance to maintain order in its own house."[8] In August 1943, Secretary of State Cordell Hull summarized the American interest in Iran even more pointedly in a communication to President Franklin D. Roosevelt. After discussing the moral and humanitarian reasons for an American presence in Iran to offset British and Soviet ambitions, Hull stated: "Likewise, from a more directly selfish point of view, it is to our interest that no great power be established on the Persian Gulf opposite the important American petroleum development in Saudi Arabia."[9]

In response to the various requests from the Iranian government and with the encouragement of the British, the United States began to send advisory teams and missions to Iran in 1942. By 1943, six major American missions and centers of influence were located in Iran. The first was the diplomatic legation headed by Louis Dreyfus, Jr., who held the rank of minister. Although four ambassadors served in Iran in the 1940s after the departure of Dreyfus (Leland Morris, 1944–45; Wallace Murray, 1945–46; George Allen, 1946–48; John Wiley, 1948–50), Dreyfus's tenure was especially important since it was then that America first became deeply involved in Iran. The legation was the coordinating center of the American presence and was the direct line to the Department of State. Three other missions were noncombatant military-related teams. A mission to the Iranian army was headed between 1942 and 1947 by Gen. Clarence Ridley as intendant general to the Iranian Armed Forces. Ridley, who had replaced Gen. John Greely, attempted to strengthen the organization and forces of the badly weakened Iranian army.

A second military mission was the Persian Gulf Service Command (PGSC), headed by Gen. Donald Connolly. The PGSC consisted of nearly thirty thousand noncombatant American troops who aided the Allied cause by providing the USSR with badly needed wartime supplies over the Iranian land bridge. These troops, who began arriving in Iran in December 1943, played a vital role in supplying the Soviet Union with more than 5½ million tons of goods during the war.[10] The PGSC represented the first major American presence in Iran. The third American military mission to Iran was the team of Col. H. Norman Schwarzkopf and twenty-four police experts who served as advisers to the Iranian gendarmerie, or rural police force. Schwarzkopf, a 1917 graduate of the U.S. Military Academy who had formerly been head of the New Jersey police, worked in Iran until 1948. His mission, known as GENMISH, was extended three times between 1942 and 1948, and, American advisory missions to the gendarmerie continued until the late 1970s.

In January 1943, A. C. Millspaugh arrived in Iran to begin his second financial advisory mission to that country. Millspaugh had already served as financial administrator-general in Iran from 1922 to 1927. Millspaugh's task, which was to reform the confused system of Iranian public finances, was deeply political in nature and put him immediately into direct conflict with a wide range of Iranian groups. His work was also hampered by persistent Soviet opposition.

The sixth major center of American influence in Iran in the early 1940s was more informal and personal in nature. It consisted of the fact-finding and advisory trips of Gen. Patrick J. Hurley, who visited Iran in 1943 and 1944 as the personal representative of President Roosevelt. In 1942 Hurley had served as Roosevelt's personal envoy to Stalin, and in the mid-1940s he evinced a special interest in Iran. His reports and recommendations to the president were presented both orally and more formally in written reports. Diplomacy by personal envoy was also represented in the 1940s by two visits by W. Averell Harriman, the inveterate presidential envoy and master diplomat.

The American presence in Iran in the early 1940s included many individuals and actors other than the six missions listed above. L. Stephen Timmerman served as an urban police expert, while Joseph Sheridan functioned in the role of food and supply adviser. Besides these missions, the United States maintained two small but significant intelligence-gathering organizations in Iran. Office of Strategic Services (OSS) employees were stationed in Tehran along with a new military intelligence team directed by a Colonel Baker, the U.S. military attaché affiliated with the embassy in Tehran. The latter group had individuals resident in the crucial rural areas of Kurdistan, Azerbaijan, and in the Qashqa'i area between Isfahan and Shiraz. By the end of the war, an Office of War Information and a press and information office attached to the embassy had also been established.

From the beginning, the various official American missions to Iran operated in a tense and complex network of rivalry. A major line of tension existed between the Department of State and the Department of War. On the ground in Iran this was expressed by conflict between Minister Dreyfus and Intendant Generals Greely and Ridley. Even greater tension existed between Dreyfus and General Connolly of the PGSC. Millspaugh's financial mission enjoyed State Department support while Dreyfus was minister; this support later evaporated in the face of growing Iranian opposition. Millspaugh found himself in direct conflict with both Ridley and Connolly, who aggressively sought financial resources for their military-related goals. Struggling to avert a total Iranian financial collapse, Millspaugh was less than sympathetic to these entreaties. Schwarzkopf, in the meantime, while enjoying cordial enough relations with the legation, found his mission in conflict with Ridley's. Both the Iranian army and the gendarmerie competed for resources and national control. Finally, presidential envoy Patrick Hurley had little confidence in the State Department and worked to undercut the authority of Dreyfus in Tehran.

The many lines of tension and rivalry that marked the American missions to Iran in the early 1940s were complex and intertwined. Although divisions and differences of opinion existed between the military and police missions, the major focus of attention was the diplomatic legation itself headed by Minister Dreyfus and his small staff of a half-dozen. The legation was not upgraded to the status of embassy until August 27, 1944, shortly after Dreyfus's departure.

Louis Dreyfus was a shy, sensitive individual and perhaps one of the best minister/ambassadors that the United States ever sent to Iran. He was extremely popular among Iranians of all classes, who respected his sincere commitment to understanding and communicating their concerns to his government in Washington. Dreyfus's approach is best summarized in a statement taken from a despatch he sent to Secretary of State Cordell Hull on April 14, 1943.

> Our policy should be firm but kind, forceful but friendly, insistent but considerate. The Prime Minister, a few days ago in a conversation concerning the delay in granting Millspaugh's powers, remarked smilingly that foreigners are apt to forget that Iran is an oriental country and that things here are not done in a day. This is a statement of fact which is too often overlooked by foreigners who think of Iranians as westerners simply because they have adopted western clothing and strive to emulate us in things material.[11]

Despite his effectiveness with Iranians, Dreyfus was removed from his position in early 1944 and was appointed ambassador to Iceland. Within the web of rivalries that marked U.S. missions to Iran, three were responsible for the fall of Dreyfus and the general weakness of the Department of State in determining Iran policy: the three major military missions to Iran.

Both Gen. John Greely and Gen. Clarence Ridley clashed with Minister Dreyfus over the question of authority and responsibility. When he suspected that Dreyfus was not sharing information with him, Greely reported that he "intended to have as little as possible to do with him."[12] Ridley also resisted suggestions from Dreyfus and the Department of State. He wanted military issues to take precedence over political considerations and sought to strengthen the place and role of the Iranian military while ignoring the political context.

General Patrick Hurley was an aggressive and ambitious man who had little respect for career diplomats. A colorful character who would let go with native Oklahoman war cries in the middle of diplomatic receptions in Tehran, Hurley had his eye on the ambassadorship to Iran in 1944. As a special representative of President Roosevelt himself, he carried considerable clout wherever he went. In his trips to Iran, Hurley concluded that more direct and forceful American intervention was needed. Although his recommendations were generally approved by the Department of State, his methodology and emphasis on American interventionism concerned the diplomats. In undercutting the authority of Dreyfus, Hurley also struck at the State Department. In a crisp exchange between Hurley and Cordell Hull's undersecretary Dean Acheson and his assistant, Eugene Rostow, the latter officials criticized Hurley for risking American long-term interests in Iran through a clumsy, stumbling interventionism. Rostow argued that indiscriminately flooding Iran with American advisers could be termed a "classic case of imperial penetration" and labeled Hurley's schemes as "innocent indulgence in messianic globaloney."[13]

Even more detrimental to the career of Dreyfus and the credibility of the U.S. diplomatic mission in Iran was the opposition stance taken by General Connolly. "His low regard for civilians caused him to treat Dreyfus disdainfully. In turn, Connolly's arrogance embittered Dreyfus and led to a feud between the Legation and PGSC that made the State Department's role more difficult."[14] Connolly, however, backed this alleged arrogance with important political clout at the White House. He was a personal friend of Harry Hopkins, President Roosevelt's most trusted adviser, and he used this channel to discredit Dreyfus. Connolly's damning assessment of Dreyfus was passed to Roosevelt through Hopkins. This occurred despite Dreyfus's consistent defense of the PGSC troops, who were often and severely criticized for their behavior in Iran by the Iranian government.

The immediate introduction of intense rivalry among Americans in Iran weakened the authority and credibility of U.S. policy. The seriousness of this situation can be seen in the words of a February 1944 OSS report: "The apparent clumsiness and lack of unified policy among the American group is leading an increasing number of thoughtful Iranians to believe that they eventually will have to look to the Soviet Union for aid."[15] President Roosevelt's policy of using trusted envoys who operated outside the official diplomatic context is best seen in Patrick Hurley. Roosevelt made himself clear on this matter in a statement to his son Elliot: "I wish I had more men like Pat [Hurley], on whom I could depend. The men in the State Department, those career diplomats . . . half the time I can't tell whether I believe them or not."[16] Although Hurley's credibility with the president was such that he was able to convince the president of the fundamental significance of Iran and to get executive action on the Iranian question, such diplomacy carried two heavy costs.

First, Hurley was an instant expert on Iran whose recommendations were not always informed and prudent. His strong appeal for an overwhelming and immediate American presence is a case in point. More importantly, perhaps, such visits badly undercut the credibility of the official diplomatic establishment in Iran. The presence of presidential envoy Hurley, who clearly ignored Dreyfus, weakened Dreyfus's capacity to deal with his Iranian counterparts. The Iranians were well aware of the conflict and divisions that marked the American presence in their country, and they soon began to use these for their own purposes. The same is true of the British and the Russians, who had their own agendas in Iran. Great Britain's actions are especially instructive.

Louis Dreyfus maintained deep reservations concerning British policy in Iran. Because of his contacts with a broad cross-section of Iranian citizens, he sensed their deep dislike of the British. He concluded that this animosity resulted from British imperial arrogance and often sent reports critical of the British to Washington. He was particularly critical of Britain's direct intervention in internal Iranian affairs as well as its failure to deliver badly needed grain supplies to the Iranian government when many Iranians were going hungry in 1942. On the latter point, he reported: "The press takes the view that

Iran has been pillaged by the allies, who now look blandly on while Iran starves. British propaganda in this matter of food, has, in true style, tripped itself up and smashed its nose on the curb stone."[17]

Back in Washington, American officials shared Dreyfus's concern about British freewheeling interventionism in internal Iranian affairs. Wallace Murray, then in the Office of Near Eastern Affairs, was extremely upset that despite a major American advisory commitment to Iran, Britain and the USSR continued to intervene unilaterally in domestic Iranian politics. In his words: "In light of these developments it seems to me odd indeed that the British and Soviet Ambassadors in Tehran should be picking over the lot of Iranian politicians and deciding 'whose man' should be put in power without prior consultation with our Legation."[18]

Both Murray and Dreyfus were particularly concerned that the United States would gradually find itself in the same unpopular position as Britain and the Soviet Union in Iran. In October 1942, for example, Dreyfus wrote in a dispatch that "there is a growing tendency on the part of the Iranians to classify the United States with the British and Russians and, at least by inference, to blame us increasingly for Iran's woes."[19] The U.S.-British tension in Iran stemmed partly from this concern by such American diplomats as Louis Dreyfus. These diplomats criticized British interventionist policy for three reasons: first, on idealistic moral grounds; second, because Britain failed to consult the United States, which had by now committed considerable funds and manpower to the Iranian scene; and third, because British policy could implicate the United States through guilt by association, thereby tarnishing America's image in Iran.

Although bureaucratic rivalry neutralized the effect of the professional American diplomatic mission in Iran and unannounced British and Russian manuevers in the country presented numerous challenges to the legation, the mission was at the same time baffled by the intricacies of domestic Iranian politics. The second Millspaugh mission aptly demonstrated this situation.

Like the first Millspaugh financial reform expedition of the 1920s, the second mission soon became deeply embedded in an Iranian political quagmire. Unlike the other American missions discussed above, Millspaugh's mission did not represent any department of the U.S. government but rather was hired by the government of Iran itself. An enormous opposition soon developed against the financial reforms that Millspaugh hoped to implement, and he found he needed both American diplomatic support as well as extraordinary powers from the Iranian government. Crucial support from the American legation at critical points during the first months of his mission enabled Millspaugh to survive early crises. He was also granted special powers, which ultimately only fueled the vociferous opposition to his mission.

Millspaugh was a crusty campaigner and crusader who sought to introduce reforms into the Iranian financial and economic systems. He had failed to develop any more tact since his first stay in Iran, when he ultimately lost his position both because of Russian intrigue and because of a clash with Reza Shah over financial allocations for the military. Some of this single-minded idealism was shared by Louis Dreyfus, who at one point wrote with barely disguised glee that when Millspaugh "begins to tread on the toes of the entrenched classes, who consider themselves as 'untouchables,' the day of his supreme test will have come. He is ready for the fray."[20]

Millspaugh failed this supreme test. As that rare adviser who genuinely hoped to introduce reform into the Iranian economic system, he failed to understand the internal political forces arrayed against him and in the process dealt the American image in Iran a severe blow. Rather than wield the rapier of political finesse, he drove an American-made bulldozer into the Iranian labyrinth. The results were predictable, given the alignment of Iranian social forces and personalities.

Iran in the 1940s was an exploding cauldron of political forces and issues. After sixteen years of repressive control, the country erupted when the Allies removed the lid of Reza Shah. Political parties and publications representing all shades of the ideological spectrum proliferated, spreading their social ideas and political messages.[21] A large and vociferous group of extreme nationalists decried external imperial intervention in the affairs of their country. Within this coalition were committed groups who demanded the destruction of the old aristocracy and an end to internal corruption and exploitation. On the other hand, strongly entrenched landed and bazaar interests sought to protect their power and privilege. Some of these forces were willing to cooperate with external forces in order to protect the domestic status quo in which they thrived.

Arthur Millspaugh quickly found himself trapped between these two powerful Iranian millstones. The profiteers and monied classes were horrified by Millspaugh's attempts to impose progressive income taxes and to introduce reforms that directly threatened their personal wealth. His proposals to cut back on military expenditures also alienated entrenched interests. On the other hand, the nationalists resented Millspaugh's interventionary powers in their country's internal affairs. They also disliked the high-handed manner in which he seemed to operate and his Iranian allies, such as Sayyid Ziaeddin Tabataba'i, who were considered by many to be British sympathizers. Both forces combined in the figure of a nationalist aristocrat, Muhammad Musaddiq, who took it upon himself to lead the attack against the Millspaugh mission.

Millspaugh's only allies were in Sayyid Zia's camp. This group argued that Iranians should support the Millspaugh mission in order to guarantee a strong and certain American presence in Iran, which would in turn promote reform while protecting Iran from a takeover by either the British or the Soviets. The climate of opinion in Iran, however, was increasingly anti-Millspaugh. The Soviets, of course, helped promote this atmosphere. Musaddiq's arguments and rhetoric against the mission were particularly forceful and effective.

Among other things, Muhammad Musaddiq argued that Millspaugh's team of Americans was composed of third-raters whose performance was poor and unguaranteed by the U.S. government. He stressed that this external mission was, in any case, in no position to dictate Iran's best interest. "The Iranian himself is the best person to manage his house."[22] Musaddiq went on to point out that Millspaugh's drive for extraordinary power violated the letter of the Iranian constitution and the authority of the Iranian parliament (Majlis).

Musaddiq's major concern, however, centered on America's increasing presence and influence. He believed that this influence only reinforced the British position, thereby tipping the delicate political balance that had traditionally marked British-Russian relations within Iran. He was convinced that the Soviets were being increasingly alienated and could easily be goaded into a direct intervention into northern Iran because of the growing American-British nexus. Musaddiq was clearly not anti-American, but he did not want an American presence to become overwhelming to the point of destroying the protective balance that he referred to as "negative equilibrium." Musaddiq's careful differentiation between the Dreyfus mission and the Millspaugh venture is seen in his statement to the Majlis on August 12, 1944:

> I am sure that the Americans do not want one of their citizens [Millspaugh] who is employed and paid by this country to treat us the way he does. Iranians will never forget that America defended Iran in 1919 and they will always appreciate that help. The popularity of Mr. Dreyfus and his respected (*muhtaram*) wife within the Iranian community is an indicator of the warm feeling that Iranians have for Americans. There is no hard feeling, therefore, between me and the American advisors. But Dr. Millspaugh does not

want anyone to discover what he is doing. He wants to act always in secret.[23]

In the face of this political situation, the U.S. government began to withdraw support from Millspaugh in late 1944. This was made easier by the fact that Dreyfus had departed Iran as U.S. minister plenipotentiary. On January 8, 1945, the Majlis stripped Millspaugh of all his economic powers. On February 15, he tendered his resignation. The American bulldozer plated with ideals of reform and piloted by a tough and tactless driver had been easily untracked by the Iranian political terrain in which it sought to operate.

While the American missions attempted to carry out their assignments in Iran in the 1940s, still other central considerations influenced their goals and activities. One major factor was the struggle for access to Persian oil. This issue was one in which domestic Iranian politics and international political rivalries intersected. Its outcome presaged the dramatic events that were to occur in the early 1950s.

The 1940s and the Politics of Oil

World War I had proven to the world that petroleum was a critical resource for any nation that aspired to greatness. Such a realization called special attention to the countries of the Middle East in general and to Iran in particular. Although the British had had a firm foothold in Iran since the Anglo-Persian Oil Company began operations there in 1909, the other great powers were also intensely interested in the oil of Iran. This was clearly the case in the United States, and already in the 1920s American oil companies began to seek concessions there.

The giant Standard Oil Company of New Jersey (today's Exxon) began to negotiate for an oil concession in northern Iran in 1920–21, as did Sinclair Oil two years later. Further efforts were made by Amiranian Oil, a subsidiary of the Seaboard Oil Company, in 1937 and by Standard-Vacuum Oil (today's Mobil) in 1940. Although these efforts failed, they demonstrated the deep American interest in Iranian oilfields. American companies failed to land concessions during this twenty-year period in large part because of British opposition. British foreign secretary Earl Curzon referred to Standard Oil in 1920 as "that omnivorous organization endeavoring to secure a foothold on Persian soil." In a conversation with the Iranian foreign minister, Curzon "warned him very strongly against any attempt to introduce the Standard Oil Company in Persia, assuring him that this would mean a competition which would be a source of certain trouble in the future and which the British Government could not be expected to regard with any favour."[24]

The growing American presence in Iran in the early 1940s sharply increased tension between the United States and Britain. In response to Winston Churchill's questions about America's interest in Iranian oil, Franklin Roosevelt wrote in March 1944 that "I am having the oil question studied by the Department of State and my oil experts, but please do accept my assurances that we are not making sheep's eyes at your oil fields in Iraq or Iran." Churchill responded: "Thank you very much for your assurances about no sheep's eyes at our oil fields in Iran and Iraq. Let me reciprocate by giving you the fullest assurance that we have no thought of trying to horn in upon your interests or property in Saudi Arabia."[25]

Standard-Vacuum, with the encouragement of the Iranian government and the Department of State, now began actively to seek a concession in Iran and throughout 1943 was deeply involved in negotiations toward this goal. The British nervously monitored this American initiative. One Shell board director put it bluntly when he advised that Britain keep "up our end before the Americans get all there is left."[26] In order to check Standard-Vacuum's advance, Royal Dutch-Shell sent two London representatives to Iran in November 1943 to seek the same concession that Standard was after. The rush for concessions in Iran was complicated in early 1944 when Sinclair joined the hunt.

Among those pushing hard for American economic intervention in Iran was Gen. Patrick Hurley, who was a close friend of Harry Sinclair's who received $108,000 in 1942 as a consultant to Sinclair Oil.[27] In the words of one observer: "Anxious because Russian communism and British imperialism threatened Iran, Hurley believed that a good dose of American capitalism would cure Iran's ills."[28] In mid-1944, the State Department assisted the Iranian government in hiring two well-known petroleum consultants, Herbert Hoover, Jr., and A. A. Curtice, who were to advise on the granting of concessions.

These activities alarmed both the Soviet Union and many Iranian nationalists. The Soviets sent their influential vice commissar for foreign affairs, Sergei Kavtaradze, to Iran in September 1944 in a major bid for an oil concession in the north. This action, coming on the heels of strong American and British representations, placed Iran, already an occupied country, under enormous pressure. Iranian leaders found themselves in the unenviable situation of having powerful occupying forces struggle with one another for the rich spoils of oil. Iranian domestic forces now began to play a determining role in the political and economic struggle.

Majlis member Muhammad Musaddiq took the initiative and criticized Iranian prime ministers Ali Soheili and Muhammad Sa'ed for encouraging the United States in its search for oil concessions in Iran. He believed that this directly precipitated the Soviet demand for a concession of their own. In his words: "When from the other side of the world the American government asks for a concession, why should the Soviet government, which is our neighbor not do so?"[29] On October 8, 1944, the Iranian cabinet voted to postpone all oil concessions. This action infuriated the Soviet Union and its proxy political organization in Iran, the Tudeh party. While the Soviets applied pressure from without, the Tudeh organized wild demonstrations from within. Iranian nationalists like Musaddiq were concerned that a new prime minister or cabinet might yield to pressure and grant further concessions.

On December 2, 1944, Musaddiq suddenly proposed an oil bill in the Majlis that forbid the government from granting any oil concessions without legislative approval. Masterfully presented, this proposal caught the Tudeh party members off guard and passed overwhelmingly. In effect, it guaranteed that no further oil concessions would be granted while Iran was an occupied country; when the occupation ended, the Majlis would determine the issue of concessions.

The Soviets were infuriated by this proposal and argued that the moratorium on concessions only favored the British, who already possessed a petroleum position in Iran. If Musaddiq sought equilibrium, then the only way to balance British influence in the south was to grant the Soviet Union a concession in the north. Musaddiq responded that this was like recommending that a man who had already lost one hand should have his other hand cut off in order to establish a balance![30] Musaddiq found himself on the defensive when a bill was introduced in the Majlis on December 3, 1944, to cancel the British oil concession in the south. He refused to support this proposal, arguing that it would contravene international law and that, in any case, it was not the time to attempt to redress past wrongs. The Soviet Union subsequently labeled Musaddiq as pro-British, and the Tudeh party launched a major propaganda attack against him. Despite this, the actions taken by the Iranian government effectively terminated the American and Soviet drive for oil concessions.

The United States was ill prepared to deal with the oil struggle and stumbled somewhat clumsily into an unfavorable situation. Although the Department of State and such envoys as Hurley, Hoover, and Curtice worked together to encourage American entry into the Iranian oil scene, this was done ineffectively. The State Department did not, for example, attempt to coordinate the competing bids of Standard-Vacuum and Sinclair. Besides competing with the British and the Soviets for concessions, the Americans found themselves in competition with one another. The British blocking maneuver of sending Shell out to Iran also seriously hampered the American effort. At the same time, American attempts at penetration, even though neutralized by the British, alarmed both the Soviet Union and the Iranians, who saw clear evidence of American-British collusion.

This competition in Iran over oil in the mid-1940s represented the earliest origins of the Cold War between the United States and the Soviet Union.[31] Revisionist historians have argued impressively that U.S. interests in Iran were primarily economic in nature and that policy was largely determined by major petroleum corporations.[32] Although the data provided above lend considerable support to this thesis, it is doubtful that U.S. entry into Iran was motivated only by economic factors. Richard Cottam argues the other extreme: "Even in those which see oil as a primary determinant of foreign interest there is virtually no evidence advanced that American oil interests, acting independently or as part of an international trust, were significant in determining either major detail or the general color of American policy in Iran." Cottam postulates that the overriding factor in American foreign policy toward Iran was an anticommunist, anti-Soviet preoccupation of U.S. leaders. In his words, American interest in Iran was "overwhelmingly defensive."[33] Yet there was clearly also an offensive component. A reexamination of the record demonstrates that American oil interests were heavily entwined in the complex process of U.S. foreign policy-making toward Iran in the 1940s.

American attempts to penetrate into the Iranian oil fields were matched by a Soviet drive to do the same in Iran's northern provinces. This economic competition overlapped with an increasing political rivalry that had begun with the arrival of both countries' troops on Iranian soil. In the meantime, Britain, the only country with a major concession in Iran, was anxious to see that neither the United States nor the Soviet Union gained access to the rich Iranian oil fields. In the end, the British emerged from this early oil crisis with their petroleum position in Iran intact. United States petroleum attaché Col. John Leavell, who was appalled at the rivalry between Standard and Sinclair and at the high profile of the various American advisory missions, reported that "by opposing the Russians, we are assisting the British to cut our own throats."[34] Herbert Hoover, Jr., suspected that the British might have been behind the Iranian policy of concession cancellation.

Politically, however, Great Britain and the United States cooperated in an alliance against the Soviet Union. This cooperation increased significantly as the Soviets responded by pursuing a heavy-handed policy of lengthened military occupation and direct intervention in northwestern Iran. Thus the economic competition for Iranian oil that marked the early and mid 1940s quickly and directly blended into political rivalry. It was this economic and political competition involving the United States, the Soviet Union, and Great Britain that marked the earliest manifestations of the Cold War.

Iranians themselves significantly shaped the outcome of the economic and political rivalry that dominated Great Power relationships in Iran in the 1940s. Iran's leaders shrewdly developed the policy that blocked Soviet movement into the Iranian oil fields by temporarily turning back the American drive for Iranian oil. In so doing, they were aided by American inexperience and the noticeable lack of enthusiasm of the British for an American oil presence. The rejection of American projects made it diplomatically possible to deny Soviet requests. Iranian statesmen like Muhammad Sa'ed and Muhammad Musaddiq played key roles in assuring this outcome.

The United States misunderstood the internal political forces of Iran and clearly underestimated the role that these forces played in determining events. In his excellent study of these events, Mark Lytle summarizes this point well: "The failure of American diplomats to recognize the Iranian contribution was symptomatic. The Americans frequently assumed that Allied actions determined the results, both for good or ill, of events in Iran. With their big power bias, the Americans ignored the vital role Iranians played for themselves."[35] This attitude was to dominate American policy toward Iran for years to come and was a major contributor to the dramatic foreign policy failures of the Carter and Reagan administrations toward Iran in the 1970s and 1980s.

Iran, America, and the Crisis of Soviet Withdrawal of 1946

As World War II neared its end, the government of Iran sought to develop a policy that would ensure its postwar independence and political autonomy. The most important step to this goal was to convince the three great occupying Allied powers to withdraw their troops from Iranian soil. Early in 1945 the British had recommended a gradual withdrawal *pari passu* of Allied forces from Iran. In five major Allied conferences that took place between February and December 1945, the issue of troop withdrawal was discussed on both a formal and an informal basis. Although the British suggested an early gradual withdrawal, the Soviet Union was unenthusiastic. The United States took a generally passive position during the early meetings. The Allies finally agreed that all their forces were to be out of Iran by March 2, 1946, six months after the Japanese surrender.

The Soviet Union was in no rush to remove its troops from Iran. There were many reasons for this reluctance. First, the Soviets were concerned about the security of their rich oil fields in Baku on the Caspian Sea. They were uneasy about the unpredictable policies of the various unstable Iranian governments that seemed linked to the British and Americans. Second, the Soviet Union sought to maintain its protective military umbrella in Iran in order to help promote indigenous Iranian communist movements, which were thriving both in Tehran and in the important northwestern province of Azerbaijan. Third, the Soviets hoped to offset the British presence and oil concession in the south by establishing something similar in the north. Finally, the USSR undoubtedly thought that it could use military presence as leverage to achieve future favorable political and economic accommodations with Iran.

Throughout the months of 1945, the United States scrupulously avoided direct confrontations with the Soviets on this issue. At the same time, Great Britain lacked the will and capacity to do much. There is evidence that the British were not excessively concerned about the Soviets in the north as long as British influence in the south remained unchallenged. In addition, Britain clearly lacked the power and credibility to alter the Soviet position. In the perhaps overstated words of an American correspondent in London, Great Britain was an "exhausted" and "second rate power" whose only hope in confronting a "dynamic, expanding Russian imperialism" was "international action and control."[36] British scholar Peter Avery makes the same point in more measured terms: "This plain sailing for Russia was little marred by a Great Britain exhausted and faced by many problems more pressing than Persia."[37]

In fact, the Soviet Union did not have "plain sailing" in Iran in the postwar years. Just as the American bulldozer had become badly lost and damaged in trying to negotiate the quicksands of the Iranian landscape in the early 1940s, the heavy Soviet political warship soon found itself disoriented in the unpredictable violent hurricanes of the Iranian social and political system of the later 1940s. Again the key actors were not the British, the Americans, or the Russians; they were the Iranians themselves.

Although the Iranian social system was a kaleidoscope of fluctuating and fractionating political groups, there was general agreement that Iran must be independent of external domination. The sole exception to this common goal was the Tudeh party, which was the only organized political party in Iran and which maintained close ties with the Soviet Union. Between September 1944 and January 1948, Iran had eleven cabinets under seven prime ministers—Muhammad Saʿed (1944), Murtiza Quli Bayat (1944–45), Ibrahim Hakimi (1945), Muhsin Sadr (1945), Ibrahim Hakimi (1945–46), Ahmad Qavam (1946–47), and again Ibrahim Hakimi (1947–48). The philosophies of these experienced Iranian politicians reflected the current political struggle. Saʿed and Sadr were considered to be staunchly conservative and pro-British in outlook, while Bayat and Qavam were acceptable to the Russians. Hakimi was an honest court physician whose personal fragility made him an ideal transition figure. Whenever the domestic and foreign pressures became too severe and the political scale too imbalanced, Hakimi would step in as caretaker.

Despite rumors to the contrary, these statesmen were patriots who sacrificed themselves politically for their country's independence. As aristocrats, they represented the privileged ruling class that had dominated Iranian society for years. The most important of them was Ahmad Qavam, known by his aristocratic title as Qavam al-Saltanah. It was Qavam who played the central role in the dramatic events that marked the international crisis involving the Soviet refusal to withdraw its troops from northwestern Iran following World War II. Just as Muhammad Musaddiq had entered the scene to oppose external intervention by blocking oil concessions in 1944, so Qavam moved to center stage in 1946–47.

Ahmad Qavam was born in 1878 into the most powerful aristocratic family in modern Iranian history. Eight individuals from this extended family served as prime ministers in nineteenth- and twentieth-century Iran, including Qavam's brother Hassan Vusuq (Vusuq al-Dawlah) and his second cousin Muhammad Musaddiq. Qavam entered politics at age twelve when he was chosen as personal attendant to Nasir al-Din Shah, who ruled Iran between 1848 and 1896. By the time he became prime minister in 1946, he had already served as prime minister over five cabinets in 1922–23 and 1942. Sent into exile in Europe by Reza Shah in 1923, he returned to Iran in 1929 through the intercession of his elder brother, Hassan Vusuq. He bided his time on his tea plantations near Lahijan in Gilan Province until the abdication of Reza Shah in 1941. He then rushed back into the vortex of Iranian politics, a subject he lived and breathed for almost fifty years.

Ahmad Qavam was the quintessential old-school Persian statesman who shuffled back and forth between the British and the Soviets as he sought to preserve Iran's independence. As a result, both the British and the Russians alternately worked with him and against him; they seldom trusted him. In dispatches in the 1930s, for example, the British labeled him "a clever man, but sly, intriguing and unreliable. Has generally been friendly to His Majesty's Legation."[38] Called "one of the most remarkable men in the history of modern nations" by an astute analyst of Iranian politics,[39] Qavam in 1946 found himself facing a formidable political task.

By the time that Qavam became prime minister on January 26, 1946, the domestic situation had deteriorated badly, and political violence had increased in the streets of Tehran. The fall of 1945 was marked by explosive conflict between the Soviet-backed Tudeh party and a new Marxist Democratic Movement in Azerbaijan on one side and the wide assortment of non-Marxist nationalists, right-wing aristocrats, religious groups, liberal professionals, and monarchists on the other. Tudeh party groups and government forces regularly attacked one another. In Azerbaijan, Ja'far Pishevari established a separatist government backed by occupying Soviet troops.

With a radical communist government established in Azerbaijan and clear signs from the Soviets that they would keep their occupying forces in northern Iran as long as it suited their interests, the United States became seriously alarmed. This concern deepened when Iranian statesman Hussein Ala arrived in Washington on November 11, 1945, and immediately began a vigorous campaign to gain American support against the Russian occupation. The United States soon began to send notes of mild protest to the USSR, and at the Allied conference in Moscow in December 1945, Secretary of State James Byrnes protested to Stalin about the situation in northern Iran. In January 1946, just before Qavam's accession to prime minister, Iran put its case before the United Nations Security Council.

Qavam's election to prime minister was opposed by the young shah, by Sayyid Ziaeddin Tabataba'i and his followers, and by the British. The shah feared Qavam, who had always held the Pahlavis in low regard. Sayyid Zia and the British did not trust Qavam either and feared he would accommodate the Soviets. Qavam, however, did have supporters. Although there was little love lost between the two cousins, Muhammad Musaddiq supported Qavam here because he felt that the Soviets and Iran must settle their differences bilaterally and directly. He strongly opposed any agreements that involved collusion among the three Allied powers. The Soviets themselves favored Qavam because they considered him a political realist who had deep differences both with the British and with the shah. They were convinced that they could deal effectively with him. The United States also quietly backed Qavam's premiership, since already in the early 1940s Qavam had indicated his support for an American presence in Iran. Unlike Musaddiq, Qavam was willing to rely on a third external force to help keep the other two under a modicum of control.

Shortly after becoming prime minister early in 1946, Qavam made a number of friendly gestures to the Soviet Union and the Tudeh party in Iran. Since he kept the important portfolios of foreign minister and minister of the interior for himself, he guaranteed a minimum of interference from members of his own government. He removed a few powerful right-wing Iranian Anglophiles from their jobs and permitted a carefully controlled number of Tudeh sympathizers to take positions in his government. On February 19, 1946, he left for Moscow.

During his two weeks in Moscow, Qavam met with both Foreign Minister Vyacheslav Molotov and Stalin himself. It soon became clear that the Soviets had no intention of withdrawing their troops from Iran by the agreed date. Indeed, the March 2 deadline came and went while Qavam was in the Soviet Union. While in Moscow, however, Qavam presented a proposal that indicated Iran's willingness to entertain favorably a Soviet oil venture in northern Iran. In return, the Soviet Union would promise to withdraw its troops.

While Qavam put together a political package deal with the Soviet Union, the case of Iran was under active consideration at the United Nations. The Soviets attempted to have the issue removed from the agenda. This failed, and with American encouragement Hussein Ala presented a strong case against the Soviet Union in the newly formed international body. While dealing directly with the Soviet Union in Iran, Qavam quietly backed Ala's actions in New York. In early April 1946, Qavam concluded an agreement with the USSR that provided for all Soviet troops to evacuate Iran by May 6, 1946. In return, the Soviet Union would receive an oil concession in concert with a public Iranian company with the Soviets owning 51 percent and Iran 49 percent of the stock. The latter was contingent on elections for the Fifteenth Majlis, whose members were required to ratify the accord within seven months. At the same time, the United Nations Security Council resolved to defer further action on the Soviet-Iran matter until May 6, when it was expected that the Soviet troops would withdraw from Iran.

The United States increasingly lent support to Iran during these events. Notes of inquiry were sent to the Soviet Union in February and March 1946, and President Harry Truman refused to heed Andrey

Gromyko's request to have the case dropped from the United Nations agenda. In April, George Allen arrived as the new U.S. ambassador to Iran, and he immediately began to support the Iranian position. The overall Iranian strategy developed by Qavam and other Iranian leaders was to draw the United States directly into the political conflict. This, of course, represented a continuation of the policy initiated in 1942–43 and is described well by an Iranian politician of the time: "Our policy then was to bring as many Americans as possible to Iran, to be witnesses of the Soviet political encroachments and by their presence act as a deterrent for the more open violations of our independence and interference in our internal affairs."[40]

By mid-May 1946, Soviet troops had withdrawn from Iran. Qavam then sanctioned a six-month period of increased Tudeh activity; Tudeh political influence reached new heights when three of the party's members took cabinet portfolios. This temporary policy put the Soviet Union and its allies in Iran at ease and assured the departure of Russian troops. It also guaranteed a counter trend. And such there was. The political surge to the left was suddenly stifled when a Qashqa'i tribal uprising took place in the south. This revolt was undoubtedly supported by the British and a number of influential Iranian political leaders. It provided Qavam with the pretext that he needed to dismiss the three Tudeh ministers and to crack down severely on the Tudeh party itself in October and November 1946. Then, on November 21, Qavam announced the government's intention to send Iranian troops to free Azerbaijan from its separatist occupation.

Qavam now found both the shah and the United States to be key allies. Ambassador George Allen made a strong statement of support, and the shah used his influence with the Iranian military to implement this drive. On December 12, 1946, the two communist separatist regimes in Azerbaijan and Kurdistan collapsed in the face of internal disaffection and the military challenge from Tehran backed by American political support. Meanwhile the wily old statesman Ahmad Qavam had neutralized the threatening power of the neighboring Soviet Union.

Having recently withdrawn its troops from Iran amid great international publicity, the Soviet Union was extremely reluctant to move them south once again. More important, the Soviets had an agreement with Qavam that an important oil concession was to be theirs after troop withdrawal. The USSR did not want to jeopardize this opportunity, which it had sought for many years. Therefore, the Soviet Union gritted its teeth and watched the Iranian government dismantle and destroy its surrogate political forces in northwestern Iran.

In early 1947, the elections for the Fifteenth Majlis were finally held. In no way were they free and fair in nature. Not surprisingly, the elected legislative body consisted of a membership sympathetic to Qavam, to the shah, and to the British. Although all three groups were in conflict with one another, they shared strong opposition to the Soviet Union and the Tudeh party. While the small pro-Soviet group still active in Iran engaged in a strident campaign in favor of the passage of the oil agreement, the overwhelming majority of Iranian groups bitterly opposed it. The latter forces were bolstered in their position by Ambassador George Allen, who on September 11, 1947, publicly stated: "Patriotic Iranians, when considering matters affecting their national interest, may therefore rest assured that the American people will support fully their freedom to make their own choice. Iran's resources belong to Iran. Iran can give them away free of charge or refuse to dispose of them at any price if it so desires."[41] On October 22, 1947, Prime Minister Qavam submitted the Soviet-Iranian oil proposal to the Majlis. It was rejected by one hundred deputies with two abstentions. Not a single vote was cast in favor.

The coalition of Iranian groups that had held together temporarily to reject the Soviet oil concession immediately fell to pieces. Two weeks after the Majlis rejected the Soviet-Iranian oil agreement, Ahmad Qavam was forced to resign. A coalition that supported the shah feared Qavam's power and was able to turn the Majlis against Qavam. The United States supported this move, as did the shah's twin sister, Princess Ashraf, who lobbied quietly and effectively with her Majlis contacts against Qavam. But before he was forced to resign, Qavam had tamed a complex and unpredictable array of internal Iranian political forces while also manipulating powerful external actors like the Soviet Union in a way that protected Iran's independence.

After a heavy commitment in finances, troops, and national prestige, the Soviets had come up empty-handed in Iran. In the words of one observer, "They were in fact the victims of one of the biggest pieces of double-dealing in Persian history."[42] The central figure in bringing about this result was neither Britain nor the United States, although both played important supporting roles, but rather the 68-year-old Iranian politician Ahmad Qavam. He was the coordinator, the maneuverer, and the expediter.

Historians of the period tend to take two extreme positions concerning America's role in this early Cold War confrontation. For years it was assumed that the Soviets retreated from Iran only because of President Harry Truman's forceful position, which involved an "ultimatum" warning the USSR to withdraw or else. Researchers have now demonstrated that there was no such ultimatum, although the U.S. clearly supported Iranian independence. American support was exhibited in two telegrams sent to the Soviet Union on March 5 and 8, 1946, expressing grave concern about Soviet intentions in Iran. These messages were sent because U.S. intelligence reports from Tabriz indicated that the Soviets planned to move troops further south in Iran.[43]

Another more recent position holds that the Iranians "sucked" America into a deep involvement in their country, that American officials "took up Iranian causes too readily and committed many anti-Soviet acts in Iran," and that "American diplomats failed to heed signs of Iranian complicity in creating the perception of a Soviet threat and to recognize the continuity of Iranian politics."[44] This position focuses all attention on Iran and understates the strength of the Soviet challenge.

In reality, the outcome of the stormy events in Iran in 1946–47 was determined by Iranian political forces and such actors as Ahmad Qavam, who was cast in the central role. The United States did, of course, play a key supporting role. It is true that the Iranians effectively manipulated American intervention and support on their behalf. It is also true that the Soviet and Tudeh challenges were real and that Iran did face the possibility of dismemberment. Most important, the 1946–47 crisis in Iran represented a continuation of American-Iranian relations begun in the early 1940s when Americans first entered Iran in significant numbers. The United States was now directly involved in the internal political affairs of Iran.

British influence in this episode was minimal. The British lacked credibility both in Iran and with the Soviet Union. This enabled the United States to move into the partial vacuum and to play the role of external balancer. Nonetheless, the British remained active behind the scenes and backed American activities whenever they could. A prime example is the British complicity in the tribal uprisings in the south that helped precipitate the government's moves against the Tudeh party in September and October 1946. This pattern of the United States moving out front with the British following and pushing in the background became an important part of the Iranian political scene in the years that followed.

It was during the episode of Soviet occupation that the United States began to develop a close personal and professional relationship with the shah—primarily through the efforts of Ambassador George Allen, who nurtured close ties with the shah. The two played tennis together every Saturday afternoon, after which, in Allen's words, "the

Shah usually asked me to stay for a cup of tea or a whiskey, when he would discuss the local situation in an informal and, at times, intimate manner."[45] In addition, Allen dined with the shah and his family on Mondays, when the two would share information on the domestic political situation. In this way the United States began a long and special relationship with the shah that consistently bypassed the formal governmental apparatus of Iran. Experienced, aristocratic, and highly nationalistic statesmen like Qavam and Musaddiq not only did not spend much time on the tennis courts but were leery of associating themselves too closely with any external power.

As Ambassador Allen tightened his relationship with the shah, American policy slowly moved in support of autocracy in Iran. Qavam, himself no democrat, nonetheless became the first important casualty of this newly forming policy. The two precipitants for this change were Qavam's alliance with the Qashqa'i tribe, which frightened the shah, and his recommendation of an air agreement with the Soviet Union, which frightened the United States and Britain. "Ironically, as Qavam proceeded systematically to weaken the Tudeh party and to strengthen his own Democrat party, George Allen decided that it was time to join forces with the court and oust the prime minister."[46] On October 14, 1946, Allen informed the shah that he had "finally reached the conclusion that he [the shah] should force Qavam out and should make him leave the country or put him in jail if he caused trouble."[47]

With the Soviet threat to Iran now defeated, with the independent, wily statesman Qavam forced into retirement, and with the young shah increasingly asserting himself, the United States in the late 1940s began to increase its activities in Iran and to tighten its relationship with the shah. On October 6, 1947, General Ridley's small advisory mission was succeeded by a major U.S. Army mission, hereafter known in Iran as ARMISH. The U.S. Air Force became part of the ARMISH arrangement in 1949, as did the Military Assistance Advisory Group (MAAG) in 1950. The ARMISH-MAAG mission was to be an important part of the Iran-American connection until the revolution of 1979. The Gendarmerie mission (GENMISH) was also continued after Colonel Schwarzkopf left in 1948.

Although the United States failed to provide Iran with oft-requested economic and financial assistance until the early 1950s, a number of influential American economic missions were already established in Iran in the late 1940s. Iran signed a contract with Morrison-Knudsen International to prepare a study of Iran's economic potential on December 17, 1946. Another, more important contract was signed on October 8, 1948, this one between Iran and Overseas Consultants, Inc. (OCI), also to survey Iran's economic capacities in line with the establishment of a seven-year plan. The central figure in both contracts was Max Weston Thornburg, an influential American petroleum executive and a consultant to the Department of State. Thornburg and others like him played critical roles in shaping Iran-American relations during these formative years.[48]

Another early personal contact that was to bind Pahlavi Iran and America for many years was established when the shah's twin sister, Princess Ashraf, made her first trip to the United States at the invitation of the American Red Cross in August–September 1947. The mayor of New York met her at the airport. In Washington she talked politics with President Truman and met many powerful Americans for the first time at a reception given for her by Secretary of State George Marshall. Princess Ashraf's first trip to America predated that of her brother by over two years.

In November–December 1949, the shah made his initial visit to the United States. This lengthy visit included stays in Washington and New York as well as time in Michigan, Ohio, Kentucky, Arizona, California, and Idaho. The shah was the guest of honor at numerous dinners given by such organizations of the American political and industrial elite as the National Press Club, the Council on Foreign Relations, the Metropolitan Museum of Art, General Motors, and Lockheed. He was given twenty-one-gun salutes at both the U.S. Naval Academy in Annapolis and the U.S. Military Academy at West Point. And he visited universities like Princeton and Michigan; he was even selected as "honorary captain" of the George Washington University football team before witnessing his team do battle against crosstown rival Georgetown University. Although disappointed at not receiving the financial aid that he sought, he did manage to establish new ties while strengthening old relationships with influential Americans across the country.

An important technical aid agreement was negotiated between Iran and America in October 1950 under the Point Four program. Although the sums of money involved were limited at the beginning, this agreement was significant because it was in keeping with Iran's "long-standing objective of deepening American involvement in Iran for ultimately political ends."[49]

The late 1940s saw the United States and Iran continue to tighten their relationship. In the view of American officials, this strengthening connection was to be soldered around the personality and office of the shah. In so doing, primary emphasis was placed on military aid and advisers. The underlying goal of this relationship, therefore, was to strengthen the monarchy against internal challenges. In the words of John C. Wiley, U.S. ambassador to Iran from 1948 to 1950: "Iran needs an army capable primarily of maintaining order within the country, an army capable of putting down any insurrection—no matter where or by whom inspired or abetted."[50]

Political Patterns and the Formative Stage of U.S.-Iran Relations

> Our failures in Persia may be explained by poor organization; by defective or inadequate informational services; by lack of co-ordination among the departments in Washington; by disagreements among officials of the State Department, causing confusion of purpose, delays, compromises, or total paralysis; by personal jealousies and intrigues; and by incapacity or laziness.
> —A. C. Millspaugh, *Americans in Persia*

In a very few years in the 1940s the United States entered the Iranian political arena and became deeply involved in the dramatic geopolitical events that took place there. The situation was politically explosive and highly unpredictable, yet there were significant American successes. The United States played a vital role in assisting the Allied war effort, it joined Britain and Russia as a force to be reckoned with in this part of the Middle East, and it contributed to the successful containment of the Soviet Union, helping to deflect a Soviet drive to occupy sections of northern Iran after the war.

In more specific terms, the various military missions did an impressive job given their difficult task. Over five million tons of materials were transported almost one thousand miles from the Persian Gulf to the Soviet Union during a three-year period. Credit for this accomplishment must go largely to Maj. Donald Connolly and the PGSC. The most successful mission was that of Colonel Schwarzkopf. Although his advisory mission to the gendarmerie began with little support from anyone, Schwarzkopf managed to instill an impressive esprit into this poorly provisioned rural police force—a force that moved quickly into northern Iran to take up positions as the Soviets withdrew in 1946. Schwarzkopf understood Iranian society better than his American counterparts and was the only American official in Iran who really appreciated the political tactics of Ahmad Qavam.

American presence and policy were considerably less successful in other ways. United States policy was as yet unformed, confused, and ad hoc in nature. Competing policy centers and missions clashed with one another, neutralizing their effect and damaging their credibility.

American ignorance of Iran was embarrassingly evident at all levels, from President Roosevelt down to the GI stationed in Abadan. United States decision makers in both Washington and Tehran overemphasized their control over events and deemphasized the role played by Iranian personalities and social forces. The introduction of American power into Iran was such that it began to appear to many Iranian citizens to be not unlike that wielded for years by Britain and Russia. Finally, it was at this time that the United States clearly elected to choose sides with the shah and thus begin a long, intimate relationship with an absolute monarch whose career was marked by persistent challenges from his own people.

As the opening chapter of major American involvement in Iran, the decade of the 1940s already reflected many of the persisting, intractable problems and dilemmas that would mark U.S. policy for the next thirty-five years. The problem areas can be analyzed in four categories: (1) the United States and Britain: cooperation and conflict; (2) the American mission and internal conflict; (3) the mixed profile of the American in Iran; and (4) general policy dilemmas.

The United States and Britain: Cooperation and Conflict

There is little doubt that America and Britain shared the same overall goals in Iran in the 1940s. These involved a common commitment to the Allied war effort and a sensitivity to the need to keep Iran in the Western camp by blocking the Soviet challenge to Iranian independence. Yet tension underlaid the relationship between the two Western allies. Great Britain quietly questioned American idealism, blaming it on the enormous inexperience that the United States had in the Middle East. The bright American image then prevalent among the Iranian population also provoked resentment. Finally, the British were suspicious of American intentions toward the rich Iranian oil fields, which were the monopoly of the Anglo-Iranian Oil Company.

The United States, on the other hand, was unimpressed by British policy in Iran; many American representatives believed it overly heavy-handed and imperialistic. American diplomats were determined not to repeat the experience of the British in Iran, which they felt had unnecessarily alienated the Iranian people. The latter, of course, encouraged this attitude among the Americans in Iran and constantly criticized the British and their policies to newly arrived U.S. officials. The British felt that they were better informed and more knowledgeable about Iran than the Americans, while many Americans, although recognizing Britain's greater experience, felt that they could easily improve on the British record in Iran.

The difference in field representation of the two Allies is evident when one examines the comparative qualifications of the leading American and British officials then involved directly in Iran. British minister (later ambassador) Sir Reader Bullard served in Iran from 1939 to 1944. He had many years of experience in the Middle East and had studied Persian, Arabic, and Turkish. His understanding of Iran was greatly furthered by his studies with one of the greatest Western scholars of Iran, Edward G. Browne. In Tehran, Bullard was assisted by another eminent Western Iranologist, Ann Lambton, then press attaché to the British legation. Colonel G. D. Pybus, assistant military attaché and a head of British intelligence, was a scholar of Iran who wrote and recited Persian poetry. Although Bullard worked closely with his American counterparts, he was unimpressed. In his words: "The fact that the State Department are so ill-informed about the situation here confirms my impression that the United States Ambassador [then Leland Morris], though honest, frank and ready to help, is himself ill-informed as well as inert."[51]

American representatives did not question British expertise on Iran. In 1944, for example, the oss reported that "the British have, during these last 25 years, built up an unequalled organization for the collection and coordination of information about every aspect of Iran."[52] Still, U.S. officials considered Britain's attitude toward Iran condescending and its policy manipulative. Minister Louis Dreyfus, for example, described Bullard as "a real old-school British Middle Eastern specialist, with the virtues and the faults that characterized that breed. He looked upon the Iranians as grown-up children, not to be trusted very far but to be protected against themselves and guided in the way they should go."[53] Bullard resented this attitude and scoffed at American idealism. He later wrote that American missionaries and their "humanitarian impulses" had in fact "functioned behind a barrier which was kept in constant repair mainly by Britain."[54]

American representatives in Iran in the early and mid-1940s were generally unprepared and uninformed. Still, individuals like Louis Dreyfus, Wallace Murray, and John Jernegan, despite their weak background in matters Persian, were generally sensitive and successful diplomats. In the field, such diplomats as Robert Rossow (Tabriz) and intelligence gatherers like Bob Rigg (Tabriz), Archie Roosevelt (Kurdistan), and Edward Kennedy (the Qashqa'i territory) were effective representatives. In general, though, Americans in Iran lacked the experience and expertise of the British. This clearly annoyed the latter, who had great difficulty taking U.S. suggestions seriously. This situation was aggravated by the Persian press's often shrill condemnation of the British while praising the Americans and warning them against British intentions.

British representatives watched with some satisfaction when America's high-handed approach, which criticized British imperialism, was contradicted by its own policy of political interference. Well-meaning but tactless reformists like A. C. Millspaugh and hard-headed realists like George Allen drove for this interventionist policy. In Millspaugh's words: "It is precisely the internal affairs of Persia that must be interfered with if she is to achieve the stability that comes from political freedom and a rising standard of living."[55] Sir Reader Bullard wrote that "there is still a tendency to attribute to Britain an unteachable imperialism, and to assume that the United States has a blameless record in this respect. . . . We have seen that the United States Government, far from protesting against the Anglo-Russian invasion of Persia in 1941, defended the action and hastened to take advantage of it even before becoming a belligerent, co-operating with one 'aggressor' to carry aid to the other through the territory of the 'victim.' "[56]

Finally, underlying the relationship was a tension born of raw economic self-interest. The British were quietly nervous about a possible American penetration into the oil fields of Iran. They recognized that increasing American activity in Iran could only maximize the chances for an early end to their monopoly over Iranian oil. Yet they realized that American power was essential to the protection and control of Iran, given the aggressive actions of the Soviet Union in northern Iran and Britain's decreasing ability to project power into the Middle East.

The American Mission and Internal Conflict

The main cause of the intramural political conflicts between American missions in Iran in the 1940s was the willy-nilly manner in which they became involved in Iran. Both the Iranians and the British lobbied for different missions at different times for different reasons. In Washington, the various relevant governmental departments had differing objectives. The result was an evident lack of coordination and communication. This was especially the case with the two government agencies most directly involved, the Department of State and the Department of War. Millspaugh, who had firsthand knowledge of each although he was employed by neither, stated bluntly that "a part of our difficulty in Persia arose from a failure during the war to effect full and consistent co-ordination between the State and War Departments."[57]

The leaders of the various military missions tended to view Iran as one gigantic supply route, as a society to be crisscrossed by rural police, as the home of a crippled and undisciplined army badly in need of a major salvage operation. The diplomats, by contrast, sought to sort out a complex political situation in which a strange mélange of Iranian politicians was operating within a larger international arena in which the British and the Soviets were the critical actors. The key decisions here involved British influence, Soviet imperialism, Iranian self-determination, and conflicting economic interests.

The early tension between military and diplomatic goals in Iran was to endure for the remaining years of prerevolutionary Iran. After World War II, both missions expanded in relative isolation from one another. Although each was hampered by its own internal divisions and rivalries, the major cleavage was that between ARMISH-MAAG and the diplomatic officers at the embassy.

Finally, the White House had its own agenda, which did not necessarily accord with that being worked out in the State Department. President Roosevelt therefore sent to Iran personal emissaries and envoys who clearly undercut the authority of the U.S. mission. The key envoy, of course, was Patrick Hurley. What is more, when President Roosevelt and his entourage traveled to Iran in November–December 1943, the American minister, Louis Dreyfus, was cut out of the deliberations. At an important state dinner given by the British legation on November 30, 1943, Dreyfus was conspicuously absent. Instead, influential confidants such as Harry Hopkins, W. Averell Harriman, and Col. Elliot Roosevelt were in attendance.

This pattern of informal advisers and influentials whose power rested outside official diplomatic channels became a major part of the Iranian-American relationship. Besides the presidential envoys already mentioned, these came to include private individuals representing consulting firms and business interests. Many of those who first arrived in the 1940s later returned for many years to Pahlavi Iran, where they maintained their ties at the highest levels. These individuals were well connected both in Washington and in Tehran and were major influences in the development of America's Iran policy. Petroleum-related advisers such as Herbert Hoover, Jr., Walter Levy, and Max Thornburg were among those who first arrived in the 1940s.

The internal conflict that marked the American missions in Iran had an important impact on policy. Since each mission had slightly different goals, the leaders of each sought to emphasize their goals over those of other U.S. organizations. The military groups, for example, saw their primary role as one of support and defense of the political status quo. As such, their view of Iran was that shared by the local military establishment with which they worked so closely. Military officials sent reports highly supportive of the shah and his government. These reports were reinforced by the opinions voiced by the informal influentials from their view at the top. Although the diplomatic staff may or may not have shared these particular opinions at any particular time, they were not locked into them in the same manner as was the military. The diplomats generally had the opportunity to adopt a broader perspective.

These internal rivalries were carefully noted by both the British and the Iranians, who made appropriate adjustments in their own political dealings with American officials. In general, Iranian politicians adopted a tack that reinforced and deepened existing rivalries. As a result, the lines of tension etched from the beginning into the operations of the American mission to Iran deepened and hardened over time.

Finally, the intramural competition and confusion that often marked the American presence called attention away from the central role played by the Iranians in determining their own affairs. This and the preoccupation with the British and the Russians resulted in a situation in which Iran itself was "seen only through the small end of the telescope, diminutive and incidental."[58]

The Mixed Profile of the American in Iran

The United States began the 1940s with a very positive image throughout Iranian society. As the Iran-American entanglement increased through the decade, however, that image was somewhat tarnished. By 1950, Iranians had a mixed view of America and Americans. This change resulted directly from the sudden influx of Americans into Iran and the increasing influence of U.S. policy on Iranian affairs.

Many of America's early difficulties in Iran resulted from ignorance and misunderstanding, evident even at the highest echelon of the American political structure. President Franklin Roosevelt managed to insult the shah and the Iranian people in late 1943 when he was in Tehran for the Tehran Conference. While there, he refused to return a visit from the shah. This contrasted sharply with the special effort made by Stalin, who called on the shah for a lengthy meeting. Iranians were baffled and upset by this diplomatic omission. Roosevelt also exhibited his surprising lack of knowledge of Iran and the geopolitics of the region when he recommended a scheme whereby there would be international control of the Trans-Iranian railroad with a free port to be constructed on the Persian Gulf. Such a move, of course, would have provided an open highway to Soviet influence into Iran for years afterwards. Although the Department of State managed to lay this idea to rest, it is one example of the misunderstanding of Iran that existed in high places in the United States.

In Iran itself, the American presence was a mixed story. The sudden injection of thirty thousand American troops into Iran could understandably be a source of difficulty. That these Americans had little preparation for their mission and that most had never been out of their own country only guaranteed problems. Incidents abounded. Although drinking and brawling prevailed, a recurrent problem involved traffic accidents in which Iranian citizens were injured and killed. There were hundreds of such accidents, and the Iranian government constantly, if quietly, protested to the American minister, Louis Dreyfus. Dreyfus would then consult with Gen. Donald Connolly, who would issue memos, but to little avail. In June 1943, Dreyfus cabled Washington that "there is no doubt that the numerous accidents and the rather frequent incidents of drunkenness and rowdyism have had an adverse effect on American prestige in Iran."[59] Dreyfus's explanation of the traffic situation, however, indicates as much about his knowledge of Iran as about the actual incidents: "It is impossible, however, to expect the oriental Iranian pedestrian to behave when alarmed by an approaching automobile in the same manner that similar person would in the United States. The reflexes of the Iranian, to whom the automobile is still a comparatively recent innovation, are relatively slow, and by the time the pedestrian endeavors to get out of danger it is apt to be too late."[60]

Throughout the war, the American troops in Iran enjoyed de facto extraterritorial rights and were immune from prosecution under Iranian law. Iranian leaders consistently protested this status, which they felt constituted a serious infringement of Iran's sovereignty. In the case of the United States, this was an especially sensitive issue, since, unlike the British and the Russians, America was officially a nonoccupying power. During the 1940s, this thorny but emotional issue was never legally resolved, and the United States simply ignored the Iranian legal system and proceeded to operate according to its own civil and criminal codes. This issue later came back to haunt the United States in the 1960s and 1970s.

The technical missions, both official and unofficial, were also fraught with serious problems. The bickering and personal animosity that marked Millspaugh's mission were clearly evident to Iranian observers. Millspaugh's own tactlessness was revealed when he reportedly brought his son with him to Tehran. "Of military age, his son appeared to be dodging the draft and his drunken rowdy behavior scandalized many Iranians."[61] Another head of an important mission died of alcoholism and was described by the head of the British Persian-Iraq Force as "a perfectly dreadful man doing much harm to the United States of America's prestige. It is common talk by everyone that he is never sober, and his nose suggests the truth of this accusation."[62]

Although it is impossible to generalize from these examples, they do indicate that some Americans harmed the U.S. cause in Iran. Many others, of course, earned the respect and gratitude of the Iranians with whom they dealt. Still, the presence of many unsuited American soldiers and officials provided material for Persian journalists and writers of differing political and ideological perspectives. Those opposed to the United States and Britain and friendlier toward the Soviet Union used these incidents for their own purposes. The truth of these criticisms clearly compromised American interests.

On the other hand, in the 1940s many Americans familiarized themselves with Iranian society and politics and in the process developed an important sensitivity to the culture. Some were active in Iranian affairs for many years to come, including such scholars and writers as Edwin Wright, F. Taylor Gurney, T. Cuyler Young (all of missionary background), George Lenczowski,[63] Donald Wilber, and Joseph Upton. Americans in Iran in the 1940s included all kinds. If general ignorance and ugly Americanism were present, also present was an important group of sensitive, friendly Americans who became students and scholars of the country and its people. Although these individuals were to divide sharply in their recommendations on American policy, they shared an abiding interest in Iran and its people.

General U.S. Policy Dilemmas

In the early 1940s, the United States felt compelled to enter the Iranian picture in order to protect America's perceived interests, which focused primarily on the Allied war alliance. In addition, the United States had a clear but secondary interest in gaining access to the petroleum wealth of Iran while also protecting America's economic interests in Saudi Arabia. Paralleling these interests, the United States had a strong commitment to the ideals of national independence and self-determination of the peoples of all nations. This belief was rooted in democratic principles, and the official cables and correspondence of the time indicate that it was widely shared by American leaders. In an important memorandum of August 16, 1943, to President Roosevelt in which Secretary of State Cordell Hull bluntly spoke of the need to protect American oil interests in Saudi Arabia, Hull first wrote: "Since this country has a vital interest in the fulfillment of the principles of the Atlantic Charter and the establishment of foundations for a lasting peace throughout the world, it is to the advantage of the United States to exert itself to see that Iran's integrity and independence are maintained and that she becomes prosperous and stable."[64]

The central contradiction in America's general goals in Iran was that the United States had both real political and economic interests as well as a genuine commitment to democratic principles. Already in the 1940s U.S. officials spoke earnestly about the latter while developing policies based on the former. It became increasingly difficult to defend U.S. commitments to democracy in the face of activities implemented in Iran itself. These included American actions taken against such politicians as Muhammad Musaddiq and Ahmad Qavam while throwing full support behind the shah and other controversial political actors like Prime Minister Ali Razmara. This contradiction increasingly upset both the British and, more importantly, large groups of Iranian nationalists and patriots.

The official U.S. military historian of the period concluded his well-researched document by raising a central question that he then proceeded to answer. "Had America come to the madhouse of Middle Eastern politics as visitor, doctor, or inmate? In undertaking to strengthen Iran the United States became a doctor, one who may only prescribe and hope for the best."[65] In this case, the patient's view of the doctor changed as the physician increased the time of his attendance, the size of his staff, and the number of his prescriptions. The United States had clearly moved beyond a policy of "hoping for the best" by the late 1940s. During these years, deep new tensions had begun to develop between America and Iran.

A crucial long-term cause of tension developed when the United States chose to throw its support behind the shah within the internal context of Iranian politics. American diplomats never felt comfortable with the other major actors of the Iranian political scene. Shrewd, experienced statesmen such as Musaddiq and Qavam seemed terribly unpredictable and in many ways anachronistic. Other active politicians, such as Hussein Makki, Muzaffar Baqa'i, Hassan Arsanjani, Hussein Fatemi, and Khalil Maliki, maintained views far too radical and nationalistic for American policymakers. In addition, the shah himself did an excellent job of lobbying for his own position. America chose sides in the internal Iranian political game by selecting the royal alternative.

Already in the late 1940s Iranian nationalists began to criticize American policy on the grounds that the United States supported monarchical authoritarianism through a heavy emphasis on military aid. After the United States had provided Iran with $10 million in military aid, one influential Iranian writer responded in a March 1948 publication, "Why should a poor nation such as ours that has gone through years of poverty be armed to defend the selfish interests of the millionaires of American and England? This is the story of the wolf and the lamb. Why doesn't the United States give us aid to help us improve our education, agriculture, and health. . . . This is a $10 million baited trap (*dam*) that we must jump away from."[66]

The more the United States became involved in Iran, the more exposed it became to charges of intervention and imperialism. The dearth of prior U.S. experience in the country aggravated this situation—U.S. officials lacked the ability to interact smoothly in Iran's highly charged political milieu. Unprepared American officials and missions were pulled into the political whirlpool of Iranian domestic politics while attempting to follow an experienced British policy about which they maintained many nagging reservations. A thorny situation in which America had both successes and failures resulted. These early successes and failures set the stage for the increasing Iran-American interactions of the next three decades.

2 Petroleum Politics and the American Intervention of 1953

The forces of nationalism and anticolonialism that developed throughout the Third World following World War II expressed themselves in dramatic form in Iran.[1] These forces were promoted and encouraged by the numerous social and political movements that burst into prominence with the withdrawal of the occupying Allied troops. The focal point of the deepening nationalist attacks in Iran quickly became the Anglo-Iranian Oil Company (AIOC), Iran's largest industrial unit and employer. In July 1946, a general strike of Iranian workers in the oil fields shook the country, and the British responded by anchoring warships off Abadan. The many political factions and parties that sprung into prominence represented a wide ideological cross section from the extreme religious right to the radical communist left. In the center existed a mixed but influential assortment of liberal nationalists represented most importantly by a loose conglomeration of political groupings formed in October 1949 and known as the National Front.

Political magazines, newspapers, and pamphlets proliferated, and the atmosphere became highly charged with the electricity of political extremism. On February 4, 1949, the shah survived an assassination attempt at Tehran University, and on November 5 of that year, his minister of court, Abdul Hussein Hazhir, died after being shot by an assassin the day before. Prime ministers and ministers appeared, disappeared, and reappeared in a strange and sporadic political dance. Debate in the Fifteenth Majlis was marked by political acrimony and personal accusation. Much of the discussion focused on the position of the Anglo-Iranian Oil Company and, in more general terms, the role of the British in Iranian political and economic affairs. Most Iranian factions condemned the terms of the agreement through which the AIOC did business in Iran and demanded the immediate rejection of this arrangement.

These rapidly moving events left U.S. diplomats baffled, uncomfortable, and confused. Although the United States still relied heavily on British intelligence and interpretation, American officials became increasingly concerned about the communist challenge and were especially troubled by the political strength of the communist Tudeh party. The opinion slowly gained prevalence among certain U.S. representatives in Tehran that the shah needed to be backed by a strong military figure who had the personality and clout to pull the situation together. Such a man would carry proven anticommunist credentials, would be willing to use force whenever necessary to achieve his aims, and would be well known to American officials. General Ali Razmara seemed the ideal personality to assume this role. Razmara was a wiry, tough, no-nonsense soldier and had played a central role in moving Iranian government forces into Azerbaijan as the separatist movement there collapsed. He greatly impressed U.S. officials. With American support and despite natural reluctance and distrust on the part of the shah, Razmara became prime minister on June 26, 1950. Less than nine months later, on March 7, 1951, Razmara was assassinated. Clearly he had been the wrong man at the wrong time for the wrong job.

The key American diplomat in Iran and the man who pushed ceaselessly for the Razmara appointment was a diplomatic officer named Gerald Dooher. Dooher directly involved himself in Iranian political affairs and was widely viewed both by many Iranians and by some of his American diplomatic colleagues as an intriguer and manipulator. His fellow diplomats considered him bright but an adventurer. During the ambassadorship of George Allen, Dooher's political escapades were limited by Allen, who in fact acted as his own political officer. When Allen left as ambassador in February 1948 and was replaced by John C. Wiley two months later, Dooher's ideas came to dominate. Wiley was a distinguished foreign service officer with no prior Middle Eastern experience. In his words, working with Iranians was "like eating soup with a fork."[2] Dooher played a key role in convincing Wiley that Razmara was the man to take charge. Wiley then urged the shah to make the appointment. This position was not shared by all members of the U.S. embassy staff, some of whom were deeply concerned about this kind of direct meddling in Iranian politics and who themselves questioned the Razmara choice. According to one official: "We were playing with fire here"; Razmara was unpopular and was a man "heady for military dictatorship."[3]

Thus, after first having thrown its support behind the shah, the United States moved in behind General Razmara. Even the shah was more popular than Razmara, who was viewed as oppressive, ambitious, and as the puppet of both the Americans and the British. Dooher's activities were a constant source of comment and criticism in the Iranian press. Informed Iranians knew that Dooher played a central role in promoting Razmara to the premiership; they could read about it in their newspapers.[4] And once Razmara became prime minister, Dooher openly and actively supported him, even going so far as to castigate members of the Iranian press corps for their written criticisms of the prime minister.[5] The Dooher-Wiley-Razmara episode was "when the United States first got its feet wet in the world of political intrigue in Iran."[6] It was also an early example of America placing itself squarely in the path of the gathering forces of Iranian nationalism.

General Razmara's personality and policies quickly alienated the leaders of the budding Iranian nationalist movement. The major figure in this movement and an outspoken opponent of Razmara was Muhammad Musaddiq, who had already in the mid-1940s criticized foreign intervention in Iran. With Musaddiq's rise to power, the United States entered the Iranian political arena, where it was to remain a central influence for twenty-five years.

Muhammad Musaddiq: Profile of a Nationalist

Muhammad Musaddiq (known for years by his aristocratic title, Musaddiq al-Saltanah) was born in Tehran on May 19, 1882, into arguably the most prominent Iranian political family of the past century.[7] The son of an important scribe and intellectual in the Qajar court, Mirza Hidayatullah Vazir-i Daftar, Musaddiq had six brothers and two sisters. His cousins Mirza Hassan Mustawfi al-Mamalik and Ahmad Qavam alone served as prime ministers on over twenty occasions in the twentieth century. Other family members accounted for hundreds of ministerships over the years, while many other powerful political personalities in Iran married into this elite family. The familial and social roots of Muhammad Musaddiq were part of the tree that gave sustenance to the politicians who guided Iranian political affairs for a century and a half.

Like his second cousin Ahmad Qavam, Musaddiq began his political career before the turn of the century while still in his teens, receiving positions associated with the ministry of finance in the provinces. In the early years of this century, Musaddiq traveled to Europe, where he studied in France and Switzerland and acquired a doctorate in law. After a brief return to Iran, he traveled again to Europe, returning to Iran in 1920 to become governor general of Fars Province. In 1921–22, he served briefly as minister of finance in Qavam's first cabinet. During this period he was also governor general of Azerbaijan and in 1923 was minister of justice for four months. Musaddiq was elected as deputy to the Fifth and Sixth Majlises. It was as deputy to the Fifth Majlis in 1925 that Musaddiq, very much in the minority, spoke and voted against Reza Khan's accession to power as the first Pahlavi shah. Reza Shah saw to it that Musaddiq was not elected to the Seventh Majlis.

During the Reza Shah period (1926–41) Muhammad Musaddiq was frozen out of politics and spent most of his time at his estate in Ahmadabad, near Tehran. He also spent short periods of time abroad for medical reasons, in exile in Birjand, and in jail for political reasons. His family ties and national contacts protected him from a worse fate during these difficult years. With the Allied occupation of 1941 and the accession of Muhammad Reza Shah to the throne, Musaddiq was released from prison and began his second and stormiest political career.

Musaddiq was elected to the Fourteenth Majlis in 1944 when two political actions gained him national recognition. The first was his successful political battle against the granting of further oil concessions. The second was his long speech and attack on Sayyid Ziaeddin Tabataba'i in March 1944. In this speech, Musaddiq bluntly condemned what he termed the tyranny of Reza Shah, praised the democratic form of government, and attacked Sayyid Zia's credentials. He characterized Sayyid Zia, who had participated in the 1921 coup that brought Reza Shah to power, as the harbinger of dictatorship. He argued, in short, that by again entering politics Sayyid Zia was setting the stage for a new dictatorship: "He is establishing the foundation for another dark period."[8] This hard-hitting speech captured the imagination of many in Iran who now recognized the name "Musaddiq."

In October 1949 at the age of sixty-seven, Muhammad Musaddiq was the moving force behind the establishment of the National Front. This loose coalition of political groups professed liberal democratic goals and strongly opposed all forms of foreign intervention into the internal affairs of Iran. Musaddiq and the National Front mounted a major challenge to the traditional style of politics in Iran and to the forces that supported this system.

Musaddiq has been one of the least understood political figures of this century. Diplomats and scholarly observers have badly misinterpreted him. Much of the literature has mistakenly focused on his physical characteristics—his age, his dress, his health, his walk, his manner of speech, his etiquette, his hearing. Writer Gerard de Villiers described Musaddiq as "a pint-sized trouble-maker" who had "the agility of a goat" and who "pranced before a group of journalists."[9] Both Villiers and Leonard Mosley described Musaddiq as having a "yellow" face and a running nose that he did not bother to wipe.[10] Western observers continually commented on Musaddiq's pajamas and proclivity for weeping. In its obituary of Musaddiq, the *New York Times* tastelessly belittled him, emphasizing the fact that the old statesman had "held cabinet meetings while propped up in bed by three pillows and nourished by transfusions of American blood plasma. He favored pink pajamas, occasionally covered by a fawn-colored jacket, during these sessions."[11]

These images distorted and seriously hindered an understanding of Musaddiq and contributed greatly to the political confrontation and conflict of the early 1950s. A closer examination of Musaddiq's background and politics indicates that he was a shrewd statesman, a man of principle, and an individual who contained within himself the hopes of most of his Iranian contemporaries. He was also an individual of great success and enormous failure.

From an early age, Muhammad Musaddiq never seemed to tire of tilting at windmills in Iran. While still a young and relatively inexperienced finance official in the early years of this century, he attempted single-handedly to implement massive reform measures. In their secret profile of Musaddiq the British claimed, undoubtedly with considerable accuracy and with some satisfaction, that the young administrator "destroyed indiscriminately the good with the bad, and at the end the organization was worse off than before, as he proved himself entirely incapable of making reforms."[12] Within his own extended family, Musaddiq had a reputation of inflexibility and unwillingness to extend favors to kinfolks. Quite the opposite. He consciously attempted *not* to extend any special assistance to relatives. A grandson points out that relatives simply did not count when Musaddiq made political and economic decisions. "When the person with whom he was dealing was a relative, that person was considered last."[13] In the words of U.S. ambassador Henry F. Grady, "Mossadegh is not to be discounted. He's a man of unusual ability, well educated at European universities, and of great culture. He is a Persian gentleman."[14]

Musaddiq was a beloved figure of enormous charisma to Iranians of all social classes. His wry sense of humor was infectious, although it was not understood in the West. His very emotionalism and physical frailty (he was in constant poor health) endeared him to his people, who saw in him the embodiment of a weak and embattled Iran. In the words of one observant scholar of Iran who was not sympathetic to Musaddiq: "In thus behaving, Mossadeq was, perhaps very consciously, presenting the antithesis of the stern, authoritarian figure common to traditional Iran. Instead, he substituted the figure of tragedy, the man of sorrow who took upon himself burdens and obligations to be resolved by self-sacrifice."[15]

An old-fashioned liberal, Muhammad Musaddiq believed neither in ideological dogma nor in the use of coercion in government. On several occasions he stressed to the people that democracy was the best form of government. If not, he liked to ask, then why had the most powerful Western countries adopted such a system? In his own words in 1944: "If the ship captain is one individual only, whenever that individual becomes incapacitated or whenever he dies the ship is doomed to sink. But if there are many captains, the illness or death of one particular man has no effect on the safety of the ship. . . . No nation goes anyplace under the shadow of dictatorship."[16]

Forced to resort to extraordinary means to maintain his premiership when Iran began to fall to pieces in 1952–53, Musaddiq became visibly uncomfortable and unhappy. In the end he was overthrown because he would not risk widespread bloodshed in his land. He failed as a statesman because he refused both to compromise with Iran's external opponents and to annihilate his enemies at home. As his followers insisted for years afterwards, Musaddiq lacked the killer instinct. Or, as a perceptive Iranian feminist and physician noted, "Politically, Dr. Musaddiq had a slipped disc."[17] Twenty-five years later, Iranian revolutionaries swore that they would never make "the Musaddiq mistake."

Throughout his political career, Muhammad Musaddiq had one preeminent political preoccupation: a thorough opposition to foreign intervention and interference in Iran. While deputy to the Fourteenth Majlis, he stated, "The Iranian himself must administer his own house."[18] As a French newspaper noted: "The opposition called him an Anglophile. The Russians entitled him the servant of American imperialism. The British labelled him a Communist. But, in the end, it was clear that Musaddiq was a national champion who without any foreign support whatsoever fought for the independence and freedom of his homeland."[19]

Since the primary means through which external influence was exerted in Iran involved oil and the exploration and exploitation thereof, the ultimate clash between Musaddiq and the foreign-controlled oil industry was inevitable. After successfully deflecting an American-Soviet drive for oil concessions in 1944, Musaddiq next prepared himself to confront the powerful Anglo-Iranian Oil Company, which had been active in Iran for four decades. Musaddiq entered this fray with a large body of newly awakened Iranian support at the core of which were the deeply nationalistic middle classes. Articulate, well-informed, and angry, these groups rallied around Musaddiq as they sought to take control of their most valuable natural resource—petroleum.

The Political Background of the Anglo-Iranian Oil Company in Iran

The Anglo-Iranian Oil Company (known as the Anglo-Persian Oil Company until 1935) began operating in Iran in 1909, a year after a major oil field was discovered at Masjid-i Sulaiman in the southwestern province of Khuzistan.[20] In May 1914, the British government acquired 51 percent ownership of the company and thus became a direct partner in running the affairs of the sixty-year concession that had been signed by the W. K. D'Arcy group in 1901. Ten weeks later, the British Admiralty signed a thirty-year contract with the company to provide fuel for the oil-burning Royal Navy. In Great Britain, individuals such as Admiral John Fisher and First Lords of the Admiralty Lord Selborne and Winston Churchill played major roles in the conversion of the navy from coal- to oil-burning vessels. Thus the Anglo-Persian Oil Company immediately began to play a critical role in the service of British national interests as Iranian oil helped to fuel the allied victory in World War I. As Winston Churchill stated: "And so it all went through. Fortune rewarded the continuous and steadfast facing of these difficulties by the Board of Admiralty and brought us a prize from fairyland far beyond our brightest dreams."[21]

The original D'Arcy concession was a sixty-year exclusive privilege to explore for and develop petroleum over a 500,000-square-mile area of Iran. Only the five provinces that bordered on the Soviet Union in the north were exempted from this concession. The Persian government was required to protect the facilities and personnel of the company as it operated in Iran. In return, the government was to be paid a modest amount of cash, but most important it was to receive 16 percent of the company's net profits.

Early disagreements over the terms of this concession resulted in hard negotiations between Iran and Great Britain, and in 1920 the Armitage-Smith agreement was reached. Iran was dissatisfied with the financial terms, while Britain argued that tribal lawlessness had damaged facilities and had cost the company large amounts of money. The Iranians held that the 16 percent profit-sharing principle applied to all companies under the Anglo-Persian Oil Company umbrella. In the end, the company accepted this principle. In so doing, however, it exempted profits from the refining and distribution of Iranian oil out-side of Iran. As one eminent Iranian oil economist wrote:

> In practice, with great flexibility in accounting procedure which an integrated company such as APOC enjoyed, the company was able to allocate the largest portion of its profits to downstream activities and the balance to the producing end of the operations. In this way the Armitage Smith Agreement limited the profit-sharing of the Persian government in the concession, to the producing activities of the companies within Persia.[22]

The Armitage-Smith agreement was never formally ratified and in the end satisfied neither side. It occurred at a time both of great political upheaval in Iran and of extensive foreign interference into the domestic affairs of the country.

Despite a declared policy of neutrality during World War I, Iran was quickly overrun by Turkish, Russian, and British forces, while German agents were also active everywhere. Social and political chaos prevailed, and economic devastation resulted in famine in 1918. Then an agreement negotiated in secret between Great Britain and Iran's political elite was signed in August 1919 in Tehran. Money changed hands, and in return for a loan Iran was required to accept a large contingent of British advisers who would direct Iran's civil and military affairs. An uproar ensued, and the agreement was eventually canceled, but it left in its wake a deep, permanent scar of distrust on the Anglo-Iranian relationship.[23]

The agreement horrified the United States and France, and they protested loudly and publicly. In the United States, commentators argued that the Anglo-Persian agreement violated the covenant of the newly formed League of Nations. President Woodrow Wilson himself responded angrily. But this anger was nothing compared to the hostility that swept through Iran. Revelations of the agreement certainly did not further the kind of understanding necessary to the continued smooth operations of the Anglo-Persian Oil Company.

In February 1921 a dramatic coup d'état that led to the overthrow of the Qajar dynasty took place through the cooperation of journalist and political activist Sayyid Ziaeddin Tabataba'i and an illiterate military officer known only as Reza Khan. In the first year of the new regime, the 1919 agreement was canceled and a Soviet-Iranian friendship agreement was signed. With the formation and solidification of the new Pahlavi dynasty in 1925–26, it was inevitable that the terms of the oil agreement would be challenged again. The new Iranian leadership, headed by Reza Shah Pahlavi (the former Reza Khan), argued that the concession had been obtained through misrepresentation and under duress by a regime now deposed and irrelevant. The leaders, moreover, were supported by widespread antagonism toward Britain for its political dealings. Thus, already in the late 1920s, the Iranian government began to pressure for fundamental changes in the terms of the oil concession.

Sir John Cadman became chairman of the Anglo-Persian Oil Company in 1927. Originally a professor of mining and petroleum technology at the University of Birmingham, Cadman came to the chairmanship with considerable governmental and international experience. As a young man, he had served, for example, as inspector of mines for three years in Trinidad, West Indies. Cadman was an extraordinary personality—that rare scientist with a special talent for personal relations, sensitive to the always critical surrounding political environment, and with the capacity to understand change. As chairman designate of the APOC, in 1926 he had attended Reza Shah's coronation, where he consciously worked for "the establishment of a more friendly spirit and to the creation of the necessary machinery whereby much closer contact could be maintained with the Persian Government than had hitherto been possible."[24]

Cadman knew the disaffection within Iran, and he recognized the explosive nature of the sociopolitical milieu. The situation in the late 1920s was not unlike the situation that was to prevail during the late 1940s. As the official historian of the company noted: "The Company had become a double scapegoat. On ideological grounds it was caricatured as an imperialist bogey, a capitalist bloodsucker. In religious circles it was characterized as being a partner in an unholy alliance with the Government in overturning traditional values and introducing alien principles."[25] Cadman developed his own sources of information about Iranian society, relying heavily on such individuals as Dr. M. V. Young, who had years of experience among Iranians of all social classes and who was respected for his medical service throughout the countryside. At one point Cadman sent his sons' former housemaster at Harrow, the Reverend D. B. Kittermaster, out to Iran to observe and report.[26]

Besides improving educational facilities and living conditions for Iranian employees, Cadman attempted to negotiate a groundbreaking agreement with the Iranian government in 1928–29. This arrangement, painfully put together by Cadman and Reza Shah's talented minister of court, Abdul Hussein Teymurtash, would have given the government of Iran 25 percent of the company's shares. This was a revolutionary idea, but despite severe opposition from much of British officialdom it was approved by Winston Churchill, then chancellor of the Exchequer. The accord failed because the Iranians refused to approve it and kept driving for a better bargain. Mustafa Fateh, the leading Iranian employee for the oil company for thirty years, later argued strongly that this was the greatest mistake that Iran ever made with respect to the oil industry.[27] In his last trip to Iran at the beginning of World War II, Cadman sadly reminisced in a private discussion: "Note the important place that our Company holds in the world today. . . . It has a huge apparatus for the transportation and sale of oil throughout the world. My regret in all this is that ten years ago the government of Iran turned down our proposal which would have enabled it today to be a partner and shareholder in this great international company."[28]

In the early 1930s, anti-British feeling in Iran built steadily among the educated classes. The Iranian press launched a sharp campaign against the APOC that the British minister in Tehran in 1932 described as "absurd in its unanimity and unanimous in its absurdity."[29] Then, early in 1932, the company informed Iran that its royalties for 1931 would be down by 76 percent from the previous year (from £1,288,000 to £306,872).[30] Reza Shah unilaterally canceled the D'Arcy Concession on November 26, 1932. The APOC's profits had been slashed due to the worldwide depression, this at a time when Reza Shah had begun massive development projects based on expanding oil revenues.

In a sharp confrontation of diplomacy and personal style, Sir John Cadman and Reza Shah went head to head in negotiations that ultimately resulted in the agreement of 1933. Cadman traveled to Tehran, where he headed the negotiations himself, and in the end he successfully outbargained and outbluffed the shah.[31] There is little consensus about how much of an improvement the new agreement represented for the Iranian position. The Iranians witnessed a modest improvement in terms of revenues per ton received but were guaranteed a minimum annual payment. The company promised to move more Iranians into supervisory and technical positions and not to interfere in internal Iranian affairs. The original concession area was cut back to 100,000 square miles. In return, the company was exempted from all taxes other than those provided in the original concession, and, most importantly, the concession was extended for another sixty years—to 1993.

An objective position would indicate that neither side scored a victory in these negotiations. On the other hand, unlike the original concession, where there was considerable doubt about the availability of the resource, this time the company was betting on a proven proposition—and for another sixty years. Most important, however, is that after all the diplomatic infighting and political confrontation, the agreement temporarily blunted the nationalist drive in Iran. This force resurfaced, however, with a vengeance in the early 1950s.

When the Anglo-Iranian Oil Company again became the target of Iranian nationalist ire in the late 1940s, the 1933 agreement was heavily criticized. One of the foremost nationalist leaders, Hussein Makki, argued forcefully that the old D'Arcy agreement had in fact been better than the deal negotiated by Reza Shah in 1933.[32] The eminent Iranian statesman Hassan Taqizadeh, who had headed the delegation that signed the agreement, came under heavy attack. He responded by arguing that it had been signed under duress. Sensing the seriousness of the situation, the AIOC, under the chairmanship of Sir William Fraser, began to develop a new program of response.

The Politics of Nationalization

As the forces of nationalism slowly awoke in the 1940s, Third World countries increasingly attempted to gain greater control over their natural resources. In Venezuela by the early 1940s officials had begun to demand a higher percentage of the profits from their oil resource, and by 1948 a revolutionary new fifty-fifty agreement had been signed. In Saudi Arabia, much closer to Iran, similar negotiations were carried on during the later years of the decade. These discussions resulted in Aramco (Arabian American Oil Company) agreeing to a fifty-fifty division of profits with the Saudi government on December 30, 1950. In Iran, whose own forces of nationalism were catching fire, these external developments were well known and contagious. The fundamental worldwide challenges to the old arrangements of control over and profit from valuable natural resources resulted in a political clash in Iran in the early 1950s that shook the world.

Amid domestic turmoil that included strikes in the oil fields, nationalist and communist upheaval in the streets, and hard-hitting newspaper campaigns, in 1948 the Iranian government presented the AIOC with a document listing twenty-five areas of concern. This document reflected Iranian dissatisfaction in six major areas: (1) the amount of revenues accruing to the government of Iran; (2) the supplying of the British Royal Admiralty and Royal Air Force with Iranian oil at an advantageous price; (3) the demand that Iran receive its share of the profits from the company's operations outside of Iran; (4) the need to have access to the accounts and ledgers of the company since these figures affected Iran; (5) the improvement of the status of the Iranian employees of the company; and (6) the revision of the length of the concession.

In response to these and other pressures developing within Iran, the AIOC sent Neville Gass to Iran on negotiating trips in both 1948 and 1949. The result was the Gass-Golshayan Agreement (also known as the Supplemental Agreement), which was signed by the government of Iran on July 17, 1949. This compact provided increased revenues to Iran by raising the royalty from twenty-two cents to thirty-three cents per barrel. Although the chairman of the AIOC argued strongly that this arrangement was the best offered to any Middle Eastern country by any oil company, it was not viewed as such in Iran. Nor elsewhere. In 1949, for example, the devaluation of sterling had a direct negative impact on the company's revenues to Iran. This and numerous other factors, including the failure to adequately provide for the improvement of the conditions of Iranian workers, were not seriously addressed by the agreement.

In the frank words of the official historian of the AIOC: "The official failure to mitigate their impact, in spite of requests, at the least, showed an insensitivity to Iranian susceptibilities and a lack of appreciation of the exposed position of the AIOC. It contrasted with the American Treasury which facilitated the adoption of the 50:50 Agreements in the Middle East in 1950." The AIOC historian continued: "The Company, more concerned with the efficiency and cost of its operations in Iran, was over cautious in admitting the suitability of a growing number of Iranians to a widening range of posts. This was doubtless an error of judgement similar to the assessment by the Suez Canal Company of the competency of Egyptian pilots."[33]

Sir William Fraser and a number of his associates in the company did not understand the social and political forces in Iran. They seemed genuinely astonished when the agreement was condemned by a wide cross section of Iranian society. In both the Fifteenth and Sixteenth Majlises, the agreement was the subject of much fiery and emotional criticism. While a number of Iranian political polemicists castigated the agreement without even bothering to read it, many responsible and eminent political leaders, some with sensitivity to the British position, also opposed the arrangement. That the oil commission members voted unanimously to reject the Supplement Agreement is an important indicator of the degree of its unpopularity in Iran.

In an important memorandum of September 10, 1950, the leading petroleum analyst for the Department of State summarized the situation in Iran. After discussing the provisions of the Supplemental Agreement, he wrote:

> The Iranian Majlis, however, refused the agreement in a 1949 session marked by emotional excesses and have [sic] since shown no

disposition to sign. AIOC and the British are genuinely hated in Iran; approval of AIOC is treated as a political suicide. Iranians have since made miscellaneous requests for additional benefits including: Increased employment of Iranians, government right to audit books, 5–10 year renegotiation, increased role of Iranians in AIOC management.

The Prime Minister has asked AIOC to begin payments at the new rate and make installment payments of back sums due under the unratified Supplemental Agreement. Since the Majlis is not in session, the agreement cannot be submitted for ratification for months: meanwhile, Iran urgently needs this money for its 7-year Plan. Both U.S. and U.K. Governments believe it important that AIOC comply with this request because of the economic, political and strategic considerations involved. AIOC, however, refuses to pay until the agreement is ratified.[34]

In 1951, Iranian nationalist official Allahyar Saleh told the United Nations Security Council that in 1950 the Anglo-Iranian Oil Company had earned a profit approaching £200 million from its oil enterprises in Iran. Of this, Iran had received only £16 million as royalties, share of profits, and taxes. The company's profits that year alone, after deducting the share paid to Iran, amounted to more than the sum of £114 million paid to Iran during the entire past half-century.[35] The Iranians were fond of quoting the fact that Iran received considerably less in royalties than the sums paid in taxes to the British government. In 1948, for example, Iran received £9 million in royalties compared to the £28 million paid in taxes to the government. In 1949 and 1950, the figures were £13.5 and £16 million in royalties and £23 and £50.5 million in taxes, respectively.[36] Foreign Secretary Anthony Eden of Britain later revealed his understanding of the Iranian position when he wrote, "I understood their feelings, for it must seem to them ingenuous that His Majesty's Government, as a large shareholder, should take increasing sums in taxation, and refuse the increased dividends from which the Iranian Government would have benefited."[37]

Far more intolerable to Iran than the financial considerations was the question of national sovereignty. The institution of a concession by which large foreign corporations had complete control of resource exploration and exploitation over large areas of land for long periods of time galled the nationalists. The AIOC refused to allow Iranian officials to examine their accounts and announced the amounts of payments unilaterally. Within the country, they did not always live up to contractual obligations to employ increasing percentages of local employees at all levels. About 70 percent of the unskilled and semiskilled labor force was Iranian, while the increase in the proportion of salaried Iranian personnel rose only slightly between 1935 and 1948. The

AIOC's operation in Iran "remained a classic example of an enclave organization—a foreign-oriented industry superimposed on an entirely different economy, without any real economic linkages between it and the rest of the economy."[38]

In general, the British failed to understand these gathering nationalist forces in Iran. In the late 1940s, for example, the Imperial Bank of Iran (renamed the British Bank of Iran and the Middle East in 1949) blithely expanded its activities and improved its properties in Iran. Its officers ignored the obvious. According to the bank's commissioned historian: "In the climate of post-war Iran, however, the decisions acquire an element of the bizarre, or, at least of the imprudent. . . . In retrospect, it can be seen that the Bank's judgement was characteristic of a wider British misunderstanding of the nature and strength of Iranian nationalism."[39] After sixty-two years of operation in Iran, the bank, under great pressure, closed its Iranian offices on July 30, 1952.

The expansion of the chasm between Iran and Great Britain is evident in the distorted perceptions that dominated the thinking of each side. The British felt that their influence in Iran was benign and that without English technological support Iran would have remained a backward desert land. Their many interventions in the past had served to protect Iran from its aggressive Russian neighbor to the north. Therefore, even some of the most learned of "old Persian hands" in Britain professed horror at the ingratitude displayed by Musaddiq and the Iranian nationalists.

After praising AIOC's "genuine benevolence," which "far exceeded any contractual or legal obligations," Brigadier Stephen Longrigg wrote, "The whole of this effort, the whole of a half-century of generous and enlightened treatment of its own workers and the public was, in the final destiny of the Company in Persia, not only treated as of no account, but attacked in terms suggesting not mere neglect but the crudest exploitation."[40] Even talented Iranologist Peter Avery, after critically describing the nationalization of AIOC, approvingly quoted a correspondent's observation about the "innate national yearning" of Iranians for "self-immolation." Avery explained the facts of power politics to Iran: "The heyday of national self-assertion, however, was to have its price; the squeeze, administered by the more powerful to the weaker, had inevitably to begin."[41]

The Iranian viewed Britain as a nation of satanically clever and shrewd maneuverers who acted to bring power and prosperity to the British Isles while smilingly and secretly planting seeds of decay and impotence elsewhere. For a century Iranians tended to blame any negative occurrence on "the hidden hand of the English." Musaddiq described the British to Special Envoy W. Averell Harriman in Tehran in 1951 in the following terms: "You do not know how crafty they are. You do not know how evil they are. You do not know how they sully everything they touch." When Harriman responded that the British were pretty much like most other people, some good, some bad, and most in between, Musaddiq responded: "You do not know them. You do not know them."[42]

In Iranian politics, everyone's political opponent was automatically considered to be a tool of the British. The charge traditionally emanated loudest from the weaker party in any competitive relationship. Generations of Iranian political leaders carry the reputation of being British agents. Despite the mutual distrust and intense dislike between Musaddiq and the British (in the 1930s the British had already tagged Musaddiq as a "demagogue and a windbag"),[43] even Musaddiq was accused of being pro-British by Muhammad Reza Shah. In this environment, it would have been impossible for the AIOC to convince the Iranians that it was seriously engaged in a program designed to protect the interests of Iran just as much as those of England—even if that were true.

In mid-1950, politics in Iran began to move rapidly. An eighteen-member oil commission was established in the Majlis, and, after meeting through the summer and fall of 1950, it voted on November 25, 1950, to reject the Supplemental Agreement. Muhammad Musaddiq chaired this commission. He and other nationalist political leaders increased their demands to nationalize the oil company. One month later, the Saudis publicly announced their fifty-fifty agreement. Although the AIOC now hinted that it might also be willing to consider a fifty-fifty agreement, the company insisted that it would not negotiate as long as Iran was considering the option of nationalization. But by now, "the 50-50 sharing of profits from oil had come too late—several years too late to stem the tide of nationalization."[44] As an American journalist then in Tehran noted: "Now, as previously, Anglo-Iranian seems to suffer from the time lag which has caused it to miss not only one bus but a whole series of busses."[45]

Prime Minister Razmara spoke before the Majlis on March 3, 1951, in support of the Supplemental Agreement and in opposition to the idea of nationalization. His assassination four days later only hardened the respective positions. On March 15, the Iranian Majlis passed a bill to nationalize the oil industry; the Senate ratified this action five days later. After a two-month transitional premiership by Hussein Ala, Muhammad Musaddiq became prime minister of Iran on April 29.

The nationalization of the AIOC was described by one observer as "the most traumatic experience to afflict the international oil industry in the past forty-five years."[46]

During the eventful months of 1951, many of the key political players on all sides changed. Besides Musaddiq's accession to power in Iran, the Sixteenth Majlis ended its tenure in May. In Great Britain Ernest Bevin resigned in March as foreign secretary and was replaced by Herbert Morrison, while in October, the Conservatives replaced Labour as the party of power, and Winston Churchill succeeded Clement Atlee as prime minister. Anthony Eden became Britain's foreign secretary. In Iran in September, Loy Henderson became the new U.S. ambassador, replacing Henry Grady. In the United States, the Democratic administration of Harry Truman and Secretary of State Dean Acheson was replaced in March 1953 by Republican Dwight Eisenhower with John Foster Dulles as secretary of state. Dulles's brother, Allen, took over the directorship of the Central Intelligence Agency.

Throughout 1952, although there were flurries of proposals and counterproposals, the positions of the two protagonists remained essentially static. The AIOC backed its tough position, opposing nationalization by seeing to it that Iran was unable to sell its oil on the international market. This boycott was effective: Iran's oil export income dropped from more than $400 million in 1950 to less than $2 million in the two-year period from July 1951 to August 1953.[47]

Within Iran, Musaddiq desperately worked to hold together a fragile and unwieldy alliance. In July, in a struggle with the shah over the control of the military, Musaddiq temporarily stepped down as prime minister and was replaced by his second cousin Ahmad Qavam. This time wily and experienced Qavam had misjudged the political winds, and after four days of turmoil and street politics, Musaddiq was called back. His alliance, which included elements of the radical left and extremist right, held together on this occasion. It did not last, however, and after the old prime minister began to assume an increasingly authoritarian position in an attempt to preserve his position and his programs, his alliance began to splinter. In October 1952, Iran severed diplomatic relations with Great Britain.

Prime Minister Musaddiq faced a deteriorating economic and political situation in 1953. As he sought to extend the period during which he exercised extraordinary powers, he lost the support of the religious right. The major blow to his coalition was the defection of Ayatollah Abul Qassim Kashani and his supporters in the early months of 1953. Even members of Musaddiq's National Front coalition began to turn against him. The key defection here was that of Dr.

Muzaffar Baqa'i and his Toiler's party. Musaddiq was forced to rely more heavily on the radical left and the communist Tudeh party. In April his police and security support suffered a serious blow when Chief of Police Muhammad Afshartus was found brutally murdered. General Afshartus had been Musaddiq's key military-police supporter; he was not replaceable. The economic situation became more desperate and the political environment more unpredictable, and on May 28 Musaddiq wrote to President Eisenhower requesting American economic assistance. The president did not respond for over a month; when he did, the answer was negative.

In a series of wild political events in mid-August 1953, involving an embarrassing flight from Iran by the shah on August 16, Musaddiq and his government were overthrown on August 19 in an operation planned and carried out with the direct assistance of Britain and the United States. On August 22 the shah returned to Iran and the monarchy was reinstated. The new Iranian government of Gen. Fazlollah Zahedi approached the United States for economic aid on August 26, and on September 5, President Eisenhower announced that the United States was providing Iran with $45 million for immediate assistance on an emergency basis. America and Great Britain then began discussions of how to establish the next oil agreement.

Much of the cause of the confrontation in Iran rests with the AIOC; much of the reason for Musaddiq's fall can be found in the Iranian domestic situation. It is also true, of course, that Iran carried some responsibility for the conflict and that the AIOC, backed ultimately by the governments of Great Britain and the United States, played a key role in the overthrow of Musaddiq. Yet the internal social and political factors have been most often overlooked by analysts.

Musaddiq and Nationalization: The Major Internal Political Forces

During the short but critically important Musaddiq political era all the political forces that had surfaced in the 1940s after fifteen years of suppression interacted in a complex and changing political drama. A steadying of the political kaleidoscope reveals the following configuration of major forces:

On the far left was the communist Tudeh party, a well-funded and developed organization that maintained political ties with the Soviet Union. This party tended to draw its membership from the middle and working classes of society and was extremely active in such industrial cities as Isfahan and in the oil fields of Khuzistan province. Officially formed in 1941, the Tudeh party expanded rapidly in the mid-1940s, suffered a decline in the late 1940s, and revived again during the early 1950s. At its peak in mid-1953, the party had over 25,000 members and some 300,000 sympathizers.[48] Although the Tudeh party for a time supported Musaddiq in an effective alliance of convenience, its leaders later broke sharply with him, and its press consistently portrayed him as a feudal landlord and a stooge of the United States.[49] Throughout his premiership, Musaddiq was under Tudeh pressure.

On the right, Muhammad Reza Shah and the Pahlavi court sought constantly to choke Musaddiq's drive to power and to defeat him in any way possible. This conflict came to a head in the 1952 struggle for control of the Iranian military. Because of his own contacts in the military and because especially of his close relationships with the Western powers then involved in Iran, the shah had substantial power resources of his own. His twin sister, Princess Ashraf, worked closely with him, and there was strong personal dislike between all Pahlavis and Musaddiq, whose biting criticisms of their rule went back twenty-five years. Ashraf labeled him a demagogue and fanatic and even went so far as to compare him to Sen. Joseph McCarthy. She also admitted the strong personal grudge that she and Musaddiq maintained toward one another. For his part, the shah's deep dislike for Musaddiq distorted his understanding to the extent that he even referred to the elderly statesman as a "British agent."[50]

Despite a tight squeeze from both left and right, Musaddiq captured power for a brief period through the creation of a coalition of political groups that hung together because of a common antipathy toward both the Pahlavi monarchy and the British. Although most of these groups were loose members of the National Front coalition, each had independent personalities and interests. On the basis of social background, there were two clusters of four groups each. The first political cluster drew its support from the traditional middle class, whose base of operations was found in the traditional business community of the bazaar and in the mosque. The second cluster was rooted in the professional middle class of liberals, moderates, and those with modern educations.

The four traditional middle class groups were: (1) the Toiler's party; (2) the Society of Muslim Warriors (Jamah'i Mujahidin-i Islam); (3) Ayatollah Abul Qassim Kashani and his closest followers; and (4) the Devotees of Islam (Fidayan-i Islam). Aside from the Toiler's party, the groups tended to be extremist religious organizations. The key figure in the other three groups was Ayatollah Kashani, although he always maintained a small but distinct distance between himself and the other, more formal, religious-based organizations. The Fidayan-i Islam was implicated in a number of assassinations, including that of Prime Minister Razmara, and never became part of the National Front.

The Toiler's party was headed by Muzaffar Baqa'i, an idiosyncratic and ambitious politician from the southeastern city of Kirman. This party, whose original membership also included Khalil Maliki, a former Tudehi and gifted intellectual, had an estimated five to seven thousand members. Its membership bridged the gap between bazaar and university even though its basic constituency was rooted more in the former. Its platform stressed constitutional monarchy, political equality, and an end to imperialism. The Toiler's party was highly personalistic, and its primary purpose increasingly reflected the political ambitions of its leader, Muzaffar Baqa'i.

Other than Musaddiq himself, the most important political figure opposed to the British and the AIOC was Ayatollah Kashani. Born in 1885, Kashani was a charismatic personality in the line of leading Shi'i Muslim mujtahids who command huge personal followings. Kashani spent much of his life in active opposition to British influence in the Middle East. In Iraq in 1915–19, for example, Kashani led uprisings against the British. In 1941 the British arrested him in Iran and exiled him to Kirmanshah, charging him with collaboration with the Germans.

Kashani's main supporters included distinguished clerics who had worked with him against the British in Iraq. One such man was Ayatollah Muhammad Taqi Khunsari in the important religious center of Qum; Khunsari acted as Kashani's mentor and confidant. Despite his private connections with Khunsari, Kashani stood virtually alone among leading Iranian mujtahids in supporting the nationalist movement. This was because the preeminent personality of Shi'i religious leader, Ayatollah Sayyid Muhammad Hussein Burujirdi, passively supported the political system of the day. It was rumored that other religious leaders, including Ruhollah Khomeini, Haj Aqa Ruhollah Khurramabadi, and Muhammad Reza Gulpayigani, urged Burujirdi to support the nationalist movement. Burujirdi resisted this advice, however, primarily because he felt able to promote Shi'ism within the context of Pahlavi political rule.

Kashani's religious credentials, along with his strident opposition to the British, provided him with solid political credentials in these days of nationalist upheaval. A knowledgeable Western observer of the time described Kashani in the following terms:

> Through him speaks the democracy of Islam, the elimination of bars of class and colour, the fellowship with millions of other Asians

and Africans from Nigeria to the Malay States. Like others of his class, he is completely fearless, completely unscrupulous, completely free from self-interest. With these qualities he combines humility and ready accessibility, kindness and humour, wide learning and popular eloquence.[51]

Kashani was in many ways a personality in the genre of Ayatollah Khomeini, whose later, more lasting platform to power contained many of the same planks as those fashioned by Ayatollah Kashani for his political foundation in the early 1950s.

Despite his religious and political commitment, Kashani was more of a political pragmatist than was the Fidayan-i Islam. This resulted in a rupture of relations between the two forces in mid-1951. Kashani saw little place for the politics of terrorism in the Musaddiq coalition, and he stepped aside and watched as the leaders of the Fidayan-i Islam were arrested and the organization was gradually neutralized.

These forces of the traditional middle class were an important part of the Musaddiq coalition; their commitment to the antiimperialist cause was intense, and they maintained direct linkages with the masses of Iranian people. Although much of the religious hierarchy in Qum remained relatively uninvolved politically, Kashani and a number of lesser known mujtahids rallied to the nationalist cause and brought with them large numbers of lower-class and lower-middle-class Iranians. This support was also to become critical during the revolutionary movement twenty-five years later.[52]

The modern middle-class supporters, on the other hand, directed the political administration during the Musaddiq period. This cluster of supporters included the following four groups: (1) the Iran party; (2) the National party; (3) the Third Force (Niru-yi Sivvum); and (4) the independent supporters.

The intellectual core of the National Front was the Iran party, an organization whose origins went back a decade and whose membership included such well-known political figures as Allahyar Saleh, Mehdi Bazargan, Karim Sanjabi, Ahmad Zirakzadah, Abdullah Mu'azimi, and Shapour Bakhtiar. These liberal nationalists had modern higher educations (mostly in Europe) and provided the ideological infrastructure for the National Front. They favored liberal democracy and preferred nationalism and reform to violent revolution.[53] Musaddiq's own political ideas more closely approximated those of this group than those of any other segment of the coalition.

Much less important than the Iran party was an offshoot of the Pan-Iran party known as the National party of Iran, which was formed and headed by a bright and politically active law student named Dariush

Furuhar. The membership of the National party consisted primarily of high school and university students who shared Musaddiq's ideas and who provided important street and organizational support for the movement. The Third Force was an important liberal group headed by a brilliant former member of the Tudeh party, Khalil Maliki. Maliki and his followers broke from Baqa'i's Toiler's party when the latter turned against Musaddiq. Advocating socialism and liberalism, the Third Force had much more in common with the ideologues of the modern middle class than with the extremist thinking of the religious leadership of the traditional middle class.

A number of independent individuals were also important figures in the National Front and were extremely close to Musaddiq himself. Hussein Makki and Hussein Fatemi are two prime examples. Makki was a forty-year-old bureaucrat from a bazaar background in Yazd. He was an animated speaker and was especially active in the campaign against the AIOC. A man of modest intelligence, he was one of the first of the liberal nationalists to break with Musaddiq and the National Front. Hussein Fatemi, on the other hand, stood with Musaddiq to the very end—and paid for it with his life when he was executed two months after the fall of the Musaddiq government. Fatemi edited the National Front newspaper, *Bakhtar-i Imruz*, and served as Musaddiq's foreign minister. Like Makki, he was a fiery and outspoken critic of the British. In public speeches he fearlessly condemned the shah and called for an end to the Pahlavi dynasty.[54]

This complex coalition of political forces was fragile—bound together by little more than Musaddiq's personal charisma and a common opposition to the perceived external interventionary politics of Great Britain emphasized in the activities of the AIOC. Most groups opposed Pahlavi authoritarianism but were willing to live with a benevolent constitutional monarchy. The major fault line in the coalition was that between the religious traditional middle-class group and the liberal modern middle-class group. Since Musaddiq's own ideas were more in accord with the latter, it is not surprising that the former broke away from the coalition when tough, controversial political decisions had to be made.

Musaddiq and his secular, liberal government represented alien thinking to the traditionalists. The Kashani group distrusted Musaddiq because of his class background and because of his bland and somewhat cavalier approach to Islam. As Musaddiq began to seek extraordinary political powers for himself, and as the Tudeh party (considered a major atheistic and imperial threat by the traditionalists) increasingly asserted itself, the bazaar and religious groups angrily departed the coalition. This was, of course, encouraged by the shah and the royalists, who succeeded in bringing to their side some of the traditional middle-class forces. Even Kashani began to quietly cooperate with the court. The loss of the traditional middle class was a serious blow to Musaddiq; it effectively cut his connections with the lower middle classes and Iranian masses.

As the nationalist coalition began to collapse, Musaddiq increasingly resorted to authoritarian tactics. He was also forced for a time to rely more heavily on the communist Tudeh party. The increasing authoritarianism slowly alienated the liberal members of his modern middle-class support base. These fissures were widened and deepened by the shah, the court, the large landowners, and the rightist military officers. External forces also played an important role in encouraging the breakup of the coalition: by the end of 1952, the United States had joined the British in opposition to Musaddiq and his weakening nationalist movement in Iran.

The United States and the Musaddiq Movement

By the late 1940s the United States had become deeply concerned about events in Iran, especially about the position that the Anglo-Iranian Oil Company had taken regarding Iranian demands. State Department officials argued that the Iranian position was not without merit and that unless a compromise was reached nationalization could easily become a reality. In the words of the petroleum adviser to Assistant Secretary of State George McGhee in 1951:

> A year before nationalization, in May 1950, the State Department sent out a cable saying that we took the threat of nationalization seriously and recommended that others do the same. In September George McGhee was asked by the British Foreign Office to discuss the problem with the board of directors of the Anglo-Iranian Oil Company. He walked into the room, told them how seriously we took the threat of nationalization, also told them that the American companies who had been apprized of the situation in Iran felt Sir William Fraser could give in on the terms Razmara was asking. There were four terms, nonfinancial terms. The American companies, when we presented these terms to them, were amazed that no more money was involved, at least in the short run. The terms were that Iran should get prices as low as AIOC sold anyone else; they should have a program of "Iranization," which is constantly a source of friction—more Iranians in the higher jobs; they also wanted a check on the books because they got 20 percent of the general reserves and the profits.
> Sir William Fraser, in a masterful statement, said, "One penny more and the company goes broke." We felt that was unrealistic.[55]

Early American disagreement with the British was exemplified in the crackling tension that existed between George McGhee and British officials. McGhee was born in Waco, Texas, was educated at the University of Oklahoma, and attended Oxford University as a Rhodes scholar. A self-declared Anglophile, over the years McGhee developed many close friendships with influential British personalities. In June 1949 he was appointed assistant secretary of state to Dean Acheson, with whom he had a strong personal and professional relationship. Despite his respect for Great Britain, McGhee had serious reservations about Britain's policy in Iran. He felt that the British were forcing nationalization on themselves, and on more than one occasion he bluntly told them so. In return, the British referred to him as "that infant prodigy" who was recommending a policy of "appeasement" in the face of Iranian pressure.[56]

McGhee was a powerful official in a Democratic administration that was relatively sensitive to the gathering tides of nationalism in Asia and the Middle East. His views were shared in large part by Henry Grady, whom he recommended as America's ambassador to Iran to replace John Wiley. Grady, who served in Iran from July 1950 until September 1951, was experienced in administering American aid programs in the region, having competently directed the huge U.S. aid program in Greece after the war. An Irish-American sympathetic to the principle of national self-determination, Grady had little respect for British foreign policy. Like McGhee, he was unpopular in England. One leading scholar of British imperialism noted that "he had developed a substantial reputation in British circles for meddling in the affairs of the British Empire. He sympathized with nationalist aspirations."[57] Grady was a hard-headed, short, baked-potatolike figure who is still sardonically criticized in the hallways of British Petroleum. He did, however, understand the strength of the nationalist urge in Iran and foresaw the explosive consequences of AIOC policy.

According to Grady's associates at the American embassy, the ambassador sensed trouble, and in a trip to London six months before nationalization he attempted to explain this to high-ranking officials at the AIOC. Grady's pleas fell on deaf ears, and on his return to Tehran he held a country team meeting in which he emotionally recounted in critical language the response his arguments had received in London. Another important American diplomat then stationed in Tehran described the attitude of the AIOC as "high-handed." The AIOC had a "piggy-wiggy" attitude towards their profits and "they didn't seem to realize that the world had changed."[58]

In Great Britain, the inflexible hard-line approach was best exemplified by the attitude of Sir William Fraser, who, unlike his predecessor, Sir John Cadman, was relatively insensitive to changing times. Although Fraser had been a protégé of Cadman's, he had the background of an accountant and the mindset of a ledger and failed to understand the intricacies of the social and political relationships of the Middle East. Fraser and his colleagues seemed to American officials to be unaware of the situation of Iran. A State Department official stated:

> In December [1951], we had a meeting of the chiefs of mission from all of our Near East posts, and as a final problem in the oil picture, they discussed what we should do in the case of nationalization of AIOC property. Unfortunately AIOC didn't take the hint; they felt they didn't have to give in. Harriman in his comments following his Tehran trip said he never in his entire experience had known of a company where absentee management was so malignant. Walter Levy says Harriman spent more time in Tehran than the total combined time of the board of directors of AIOC. They didn't know what was going on or the needs and demands of the Iranian people.[59]

In Britain several high officials generally supported the Fraser school of thought. These included Geoffrey Furlonge, head of the Eastern Department of the Foreign Office, Minister for Defence Emmanuel Shinwell, and especially Labour party foreign secretary Herbert Morrison, all of whom favored an active, even interventionary approach. Britain's ambassadors to Iran, Sir John Le Rougetel and especially Sir Francis Shepherd, also shared this view. Shepherd was clearly contemptuous of Iranians and seemed to belong to the "give them a whiff of grapeshot" school of diplomacy. It is not surprising that he reported that U.S. ambassador Grady was "by temperament quite unsuited to dealing with Persian deviousness and intrigue."[60] Morrison and Shepherd may not have disagreed sharply with a writer in the *Daily Telegraph* who assessed the British capacity in the following words: "We have only for one moment to stretch out a terrible right arm and we should hear no more from Persia but the scampering of timid feet."[61]

Labour party leaders like Prime Minister Clement Attlee and Foreign Secretary Ernest Bevin, on the other hand, were opposed to any direct intervention into Iran and favored a more prudent, conciliatory approach. British governmental officials did privately and strongly criticize the AIOC and its ownership. In an October 1951 memorandum to Morrison, for example, Minister of State Kenneth Younger wrote: "The principal reason why our advance information was inadequate was the short-sightedness and the lack of political awareness shown by the Anglo-Iranian Oil Company. They were far better placed than anybody to make a proper estimate of the situation but, as far as I am aware, they never even seriously tried to do so."[62] Even within the AIOC, there was no unanimity. Sir Frederick Leggett, the AIOC's experienced labor adviser in Iran, criticized his own company, which in his opinion "still seemed to be thinking in terms of offering a little money here and another sop there, but all this . . . was entirely beside the point. What was required was a fresh start, on the basis of equal partnership."[63]

In the early years of the crisis, the American leadership agreed with the Attlees, Bevins, Youngers, and Leggetts. Secretary of State Acheson stated in March 1951 that "We recognize the right of sovereign states to nationalize provided there is just compensation."[64] In a meeting between British and American officials in Washington in April 1951, the Americans also made it clear that they recognized the Iranian right to nationalize. The British, for their part, seriously considered a military response. They were finally dissuaded from doing so because of the unsettled political situation in newly independent India, the Indian-Pakistani conflict over Kashmir, and ongoing political crises in Egypt that severely challenged British interests. An even more important reason for Britain's decision not to intervene militarily rested in the strong opposition of the United States.

In a September 25, 1951, meeting between Secretary of Defense Robert Lovett and Sir William Elliot (British air marshal), Lovett warned Elliot that the British were operating on the basis of poor intelligence and that they would fail in Iran the same way they had failed in the Arab-Palestinian situation. Lovett asked Sir William what better tool could be given the Soviets than for the British to move troops into Iran. This, he argued, would give the Soviet Union the excuse they needed to occupy Azerbaijan and to support a Tudeh party takeover. Lovett later informed Secretary of State Acheson that he felt there was definite need for a little more "give" on the part of the British.[65]

The Truman administration's policy as developed by Secretary of State Acheson was to attempt to placate the British while trying to convince Musaddiq to agree on a compromise. American leaders were convinced that any British military attack was not only unwarranted but also might serve as a pretext for Soviet intervention. As Acheson put it in mid-May 1951: "Only on invitation of the Iranian Government, or Soviet military intervention, or a Communist *coup d'état* in Teheran, or to evacuate British nationals in danger of attack could we support the use of military force."[66] Anthony Eden later admitted that "the temptation to intervene to reclaim this stolen property must have been strong, but pressure from the United States was vigorous against any such action."[67]

While holding off the British military urge, President Truman sent troubleshooter and special envoy W. Averell Harriman to Iran in July 1951. Harriman and his team, which included oil expert Walter Levy and diplomat-linguist Vernon Walters, were greeted on arrival in Tehran on July 15 by wildly rioting crowds. Harriman and Levy made a concentrated effort to instruct Musaddiq in the realities of international oil economics and politics. They managed to convince him to receive another British negotiating mission, which arrived in Tehran on August 4, 1951, under the leadership of Richard Stokes. Stokes, a wealthy businessman but somewhat clumsy negotiator, also failed in his mission although he felt that a good deal could be arranged.

Harriman, Levy, and Walters established excellent personal rapport with Musaddiq but were unable to break the impasse. At one point when Levy was attempting to convince the old prime minister that it would be in Iran's interest to accept a negotiated settlement, Musaddiq responded by asking Levy about the Boston Tea Party when America was struggling desperately against British colonial control. What, he asked Levy, would American independence leaders have responded if some Persian mediators had come aboard the ships anchored in Boston harbor and asked the colonists not to throw that tea overboard?[68]

While the American negotiating team was in Iran, Hussein Makki took its members on a tour of the oil fields and facilities in the southwest. There they were shown the separate facilities and superior quarters enjoyed by the British staff. Much was made of drinking fountains marked "Not for Iranians." In the discussions, the Harriman team pointed out that the Iranian employees of the AIOC were immeasurably better off than their compatriots who worked for local industrialists. The response was that the comparison must be made with British counterparts, who enjoyed superior salaries and living conditions. At one point, the Americans even asked Musaddiq about the working and living conditions of the peasants who lived on his estates. Despite this, the Harriman team recognized the Iranian labor grievances and considered them legitimate.

Musaddiq visited the United States between October 8 and November 18, 1951. During this visit he presented Iran's case before the U.N. Security Council and engaged in intensive discussions with high-level American diplomats, including President Truman and Secretary of State Acheson. Most negotiations were carried on between Musaddiq and George McGhee, who estimated that he spent over seventy-five hours in discussions with Musaddiq. Painstakingly, McGhee and Musaddiq worked out a proposal to solve the impasse, and then Musaddiq delayed his return to Iran while the British elections took place on October 25, 1951.

The main points of the McGhee-Musaddiq proposal included the following: (1) a national Iranian oil company would be established and would be responsible for the exploration, production, and transportation of crude oil; (2) the Abadan refinery would be sold to a non-British firm that would select its own technicians; (3) the AIOC would establish a purchasing organization to buy, ship, and market Iranian oil; (4) the contract would be in effect for fifteen years and would provide for a minimum of thirty million tons of oil a year; and (5) the price of petroleum would be determined through negotiations between Iran and Great Britain and would not exceed $1.10 per barrel. The final result of this pricing scheme would have closely approximated the fifty-fifty profit-sharing arrangement then in effect in Saudi Arabia. American officials were very hopeful that these terms would be an acceptable foundation for negotiations with the new British government.[69]

Immediately after the elections, Britain's new Conservative government with Anthony Eden as foreign secretary met on five occasions with American officials to discuss the proposal. In the end, the British refused to accept the compromise. Eden found the nationalization principle unacceptable. The exclusion of British technicians from Iran also upset the British government. Acheson telephoned the Department of State from Paris after his final meeting with Eden and asked the department to inform the waiting Musaddiq that the British had rejected the proposal. George McGhee, who had worked so hard to hammer out the details of the proposal, was shaken by the news. In his words: "There was silence as we grasped the fact that we had failed. To me it was almost the end of the world—I attached so much importance to an agreement and honestly thought we had provided the British a basis for one."[70]

McGhee then went to see Musaddiq, who was staying at the Shoreham Hotel. The old man "merely said, 'You've come to send me home.'" "Yes," McGhee responded, "I'm sorry to have to tell you that we can't bridge the gap between you and the British. It's a great disappointment to us as it must be to you." McGhee concluded, "It was a moment I will never forget. He accepted the result quietly with no recriminations."[71]

Musaddiq had made the best offer in his power during those days in

Washington in late 1951. Walter Levy has indicated that, given the political situation in Iran at the time, Musaddiq had little room to maneuver. John Foster Dulles himself stated in a National Security Council meeting in February 1953 that Musaddiq "could not afford to reach any agreement with the British lest it cost him his political life."[72] Levy points out that not only did Musaddiq not trust the British, he did not trust many Iranians. He did not know whom he could count on. And this was before his coalition had begun to fall apart and many of his supporters, cutting their own deals, deserted him.

The United States, meanwhile, had taken important actions to placate Britain. The Department of State issued a press release on May 1, 1951, that stated: "Those United States oil companies which would be best able to conduct operations such as the large-scale and complex industry in Iran have indicated to this Government that they would not in the face of unilateral action by Iran against the British company be willing to undertake operations in that country."[73] This effectively helped the British impose a collective boycott on Iranian oil operations and exportation. George McGhee himself played an important role in this policy and has written that "I am not sure that my British friends ever quite understood the strong efforts I had made to keep American oil companies from taking advantage of AIOC's difficulties."[74] Special attention was given to independent American companies, who had every incentive to attempt to penetrate the rich Iranian market at this time. But they, too, ultimately agreed to stay away from the Iranian scene. For this they would claim their reward in 1955.[75]

The Truman administration was also concerned about the contagious nature of the nationalization act in Iran. If Iran could nationalize the powerful British oil company in Iran, then why couldn't the other oil-producing countries do the same thing to American companies? On May 24, 1951, only days after the release of the important State Department memorandum quoted in the paragraph above, Arthur Krock reported the following revealing conversation with President Truman:

> But these foreign oil countries have a good case against some groups of foreign capital. The President said he thought Mexico's nationalization of oil was "right," even thought so at the time; but it was regarded as "treason" to say so. If, however, the Iranians carry out their plans as stated, Venezuela and other countries on whose supply we depend will follow suit. That is the great danger in the Iranian controversy with the British.[76]

The Iranians were quite aware of this position. The deputy minister of court, for example, bluntly told the second secretary of the U.S. Embassy in Tehran that America's position in Iran "was primarily motivated by commercial interest." He argued that the United States would not permit any oil agreement that would completely benefit Iran because if this occurred "the Saudi Arabs would ask for a similar deal."[77]

Despite this, the British were highly suspicious of American intentions. Their own Iran specialists in the field hinted of evidence that Musaddiq and Kashani were receiving significant financial support from an external source and that it "was not impossible" that America was that source.[78] The British also suspected that the United States was attempting to use Musaddiq as a wedge to help drive American oil interests into their Iranian preserve. When American oilman George McGhee recommended that AIOC come to an accommodation with Iran, British suspicions deepened. They became even more concerned when Harriman and Levy openly suggested that the AIOC's former dominant position in the country would almost certainly have to be changed. The U.S. provision of Iran with economic and military aid in 1951 and early 1952 did not allay British suspicions.

As the oil crisis dragged on, as politics in Iran became increasingly stormy, and as the British applied diplomatic pressure, the United States began to shift its position. American decision makers gradually came around to the British idea that the best way to confront the situation was to actively seek the overthrow of the Musaddiq government and to assure its replacement with a regime more amenable to compromise. Before Eisenhower took office in early 1953, there had been discussion in Washington (especially in the CIA) about planning a covert political intervention into Iran. In general, however, officials at higher-level policy positions did not entertain such ideas until 1953.[79]

The United States changed its policy from one of diplomacy and conciliation to one of intervention and confrontation for four reasons. Two can be classified as immediate causes and two can be termed contributing causes. The two immediate political causes were the U.S. preoccupation with the communist challenge in Iran and American concerns about the accessibility of the rich Iranian oil reserves to the Western world. The two tactical contributing causes were both positive and negative in character. The first was Britain's successful campaign to bring the United States to accept their approach to the crisis. The second was Musaddiq's own political methodology, which ultimately proved to be counterproductive and self-defeating.

As the early 1950s unfolded, the U.S. government became increasingly obsessed with the challenge of communism. China had recently adopted a communist government; the Korean War was in progress; the Chinese had invaded Tibet, where they imposed a humiliating treaty; and Ho Chi Minh and the Vietminh were driving for control in Vietnam. At home, ideologues like Sen. Joseph McCarthy who had built their political careers on the foundations of hysterical threats of communist infiltration were in the ascendancy. American policymakers had great difficulty throughout this period distinguishing nationalist movements from communist movements in the Third World. This distinction was especially hard to see in Iran, where there was in fact a strong, well-organized national communist movement in the Tudeh party. Ignorance of things Iranian also prevented American leaders from drawing such critical distinctions. The mass media only reinforced the confusion by portraying Musaddiq himself as a communist and his movement as communist inspired or communist controlled.[80] *Time* magazine went so far as to refer to the Musaddiq national movement as "one of the worst calamities to the anti-Communist world since the Red conquest of China."[81] This massive national preoccupation with communism as a direct and immediate threat to the United States was a powerful force behind the American decision to support a move against Musaddiq and his government.

The politics of oil provided the second major reason for the dramatic change in American policy. Many knowledgeable analysts believe that Musaddiq was used as an American wedge to break the AIOC's monopolistic grip on Iran's oil resources. According to Mustafa Fateh, the best-informed Iran oil economist long employed by the AIOC, there is no doubt that American and British oil interests reached an entente on this issue. In exchange for American support in overthrowing the Musaddiq government, the British grudgingly permitted U.S. companies a 40 percent interest in Iranian oil. Fateh pointed out that American companies had made several attempts to penetrate the Iranian fields but had failed until the appearance of Musaddiq.

As early as October 1943, James Byrnes, then director of the Office of War Mobilization, wrote a letter to President Roosevelt decrying Britain's control over Iran's oil. According to Byrnes, the government should request Britain to assign the United States one-third of its interest in Iranian oil as compensation for American contributions to the war effort.[82] Although the president took no action on this recommendation, it was clear that the United States had an eye on Iranian oil. While Roosevelt denied to Winston Churchill early in 1944 that America had "sheep's eyes" on the Iranian oil fields, it is probably true that the United States had at least one eagle's eye on these reserves. The British certainly thought so in the early 1950s. Not only did they believe that American wanted access to Iranian oil, but they also thought that the United States was attempting to push an agreement in order to weaken the AIOC vis-à-vis the large multinational American companies. In August 1950, for example, the British Foreign Office reported that "the State Department may have been over much influenced by the American oil companies, who wish to see our companies driven into an uncompetitive position by constant pressure to raise their royalties and labor conditions."[83]

There is little doubt that petroleum considerations were involved in the American decision to assist in the overthrow of the Musaddiq government. Clearly the oil companies (both American and European, both majors and independents) all cooperated in boycotting Iranian oil and thus succeeded in putting enormous pressure on the Iranian economy. In addition, the U.S. government seriously entertained a plan for a consortium of American oil companies to purchase oil from Iran and then sell it to other international companies, including the AIOC. Secretary of Defense Robert Lovett and Gen. Omar Bradley favored this plan, which also captured the interest of Secretary of State Acheson. The Justice Department, however, opposed it on the grounds that it ran counter to antitrust litigation then underway against the oil companies. Another U.S. plan considered at somewhat lower levels was proposed by Charles Rayner of the Department of Interior. The Petroleum Administration of Defense at Interior suggested that the British government withdraw immediately from its position in AIOC and that the company be placed "preferably under Dutch or American leadership."[84] These proposals indicate that the United States clearly had an interest in gaining entry to the Iranian oil business.

Although many have argued for America's disinterest in Iranian oil, given the conditions of glut that then prevailed, Middle Eastern history demonstrates that America had always sought such access, glut or no glut. In 1921–22, for example, the United States struggled for access to the rich Iraqi oil fields then controlled by British and Dutch interests. Despite a heavy glut of oil on the world market, America fought for a share of the action "in order to ensure that her citizens were given equal economic participation in the development of the former Turkish Empire. The underlying objective, made absolutely clear, was that the U.S. would not accept the prohibition of her citizens' participation in the economic development of areas hitherto barred to American capital."[85]

Thus both the politics of oil and the preoccupation with the communist threat were major reasons for the American policy change.

Furthermore, both factors were interrelated and were mutually reinforcing; ironically, when one branch of the U.S. government (the Department of State) was in constant contact with the oil companies concerning the Iranian crisis, another branch of the government (the Department of Justice) was vigorously pursuing an antitrust campaign against the companies.

On January 23, 1952, President Truman sent a memorandum to the secretaries of State, Defense, Interior, and Commerce and to the Federal Trade Commission that stated: "I have requested the Attorney General to institute appropriate legal proceedings with respect to the operations of the International Oil Cartel. I should like for you to cooperate with him in gathering the evidence required for these proceedings."[86] Throughout 1952 the Department of Justice pursued this investigation, charging among other things that the oil cartel used the mechanism of joint companies to eliminate competition in both price and production. Early in the proceedings, a district court ruled that the AIOC was an instrumentality of the British government and was therefore immune from investigation. Also in early 1953, President Truman moved the investigation from a grand jury format to a civil action proceeding. In the process, the Department of Justice found itself confronted politically by the Departments of State and Defense and the Joint Chiefs of Staff. In the last days of the Truman administration, a major debate took place in Washington over whether this antitrust campaign should be pursued. It is important to recall that at this time the U.S. government had enlisted the cooperative support of oil companies in the struggle against Musaddiq.

Given the difficulties in Iran and the growing concern about the spread of communism, arguments stressing national security neutralized the Department of Justice's anticartel case. Both Acheson and then Dulles used the national security argument to encourage cooperative relations between U.S. foreign policymakers and the leaders of the oil companies. As one Department of Justice official noted: "The pressures were continuous from month to month, sometimes from week to week, to downgrade the importance of prosecution of the cartel case."[87] The White House issued a statement to John Foster Dulles summarizing the American position on this important issue: "It will be assumed that the enforcement of the antitrust laws of the United States against the Western oil companies operating in the Near East may be deemed secondary to the national security interest."[88] There was, in the end, little doubt among decision makers in the executive branch of government in Washington "that the global battle against Communism must take precedence against any complications about anti-trust."[89] These concerns about communism and the availability of petroleum were thus interlocked. Together, they drove America to a policy of direct intervention.

Within this general political context, Musaddiq himself unwittingly adopted a political tactic that only reinforced U.S. decisions. In order to encourage desperately needed financial and moral assistance from the United States, he began to raise the specter of a communist threat to his country. He argued that American assistance was essential if Iran were to stay out of the communist camp. This approach had exactly the opposite effect from the one desired by the elderly prime minister. Rather than attracting aid, it provided further justification for those U.S. policymakers who agreed with the British that intervention and overthrow were the only realistic alternatives.

The American drift to the British position was hastened by the enigmatic nature of Musaddiq himself, whose negotiating techniques were enormously frustrating to the best American diplomats. George McGhee, W. Averell Harriman, and Vernon Walters all failed, despite weeks of intensive discussions with the Iranian prime minister.[90] Musaddiq zigged and zagged, advanced and retreated, hurried and stalled until the American negotiators were hopelessly confused. Vernon Walters, who enjoyed an excellent personal relationship with Mussadiq, stated:

> It seemed to me that he reversed Lenin's adage that one must take a step backward in order to take two forward. Dr. Mossadegh had learned to take one step forward in order to take two backward. After a day's discussions, Mr. Harriman would bring Mossadegh to a certain position. The next day when we returned to renew the discussion, not only was Mossadegh not at the position where he was at the end of the previous day, he wasn't even at the position where he had been at the beginning of the day before that. He was somewhere back around the middle of the day before yesterday.[91]

According to Secretary of State Acheson: "It was like walking in a maze and every so often finding oneself at the beginning again."[92] Although Musaddiq was no more stubborn than the British, he repeatedly insisted that the days of British exploitation in Iran were over, that nationalization would stand, and that Iran would determine the compensation to be paid by the AIOC.

Besides his personal convictions in these matters, Musaddiq's unyielding position was essential within the context of the social forces then at work in Iran. The communist left, the growing nationalist middle, and the xenophobic religious right exerted continual fierce pressure. Economic rationality models and cool financial reasoning made little sense in this climate of political upheaval and nationalist fervor. Also, Musaddiq was a magnificent negativist: he had the courage to challenge but lacked the capacity to construct. In a secret meeting of the Majlis Oil Commission in 1951 he argued that in order to defeat communism, reforms were necessary. In order to implement reforms, money was essential. In order to obtain money, nationalization was vital. When questioned how he proposed to convert oil into money by a nationalization that made it impossible to sell and market that oil, he responded: "I have no intention of coming to terms with anyone. Rather than come to terms with the British, I will seal the oil wells with mud."[93] In this situation, the United States ultimately found Britain to be a more congenial and predictable party to deal with.

The British understood this and applied diplomatic pressure on the United States throughout the period. In Anthony Eden's terms, the principal goal here was to "align" American policies with those of Great Britain. Other British diplomats spoke of the need to "stiffen" the American resolve. George McGhee found himself in negotiating disagreement with old British friends, including his former tutor and dean at Oxford, Sir Oliver Franks, then British ambassador to the United States. Anthony Eden and Dean Acheson constituted a two-person mutual admiration society, and both were conscious of the fact that they even resembled one another physically. In Eden's words, Acheson was "a loyal colleague. I would never hesitate to go tiger-hunting with him."[94] Ultimately, the hunt was not for tigers but rather for Musaddiq and his government in Iran.

American foreign policymakers were somewhat awed by British experience and expertise in Iran. Eden, for example, had read Oriental languages at Oxford and had emphasized Persian and Arabic as his languages of study. He was extremely knowledgeable about Iranian history and culture, and his diplomatic experience with Iran dated back to 1933, when he was under-secretary in the Foreign Office during the tense negotiations with Iran over the oil agreement. With few exceptions—primarily American citizens from missionary backgrounds who had lived in Iran—the United States was still largely illiterate in matters Iranian. The personal connections that American and British officials maintained with one another in conjunction with the aura of Britain's special knowledge of Iran combined to pull America to the British position. Anthony Eden himself stated that he knew "that the United States Ambassador took the view that the United States ought not to intrude its views too much in a matter where large British interests were at stake."[95]

Although the Truman-Acheson Democratic administration became increasingly exasperated and impatient with the situation in Iran, it was the Republican administration of Eisenhower-Dulles that decided to intervene. Kermit Roosevelt, the field commander of the American intervention, stated that the plan was deliberately withheld from the Democrats since the latter were considered too sympathetic to Musaddiq. According to Roosevelt:

> Acheson was absolutely fascinated by Dr. Mossadegh. He was in fact sympathetic to him. I didn't feel like raising the matter with him. Neither did Allen Dulles, because we knew that Foster Dulles was going to be taking Acheson's place. We saw no point in getting the outgoing administration involved in something we thought they might be less enthusiastic about than the Republicans. . . . Allen Dulles said, "Let's not get this thing evolved until the Republicans and my brother Foster take over."[96]

The change in administrations in Washington in January of 1953 occurred fourteen months after the Conservative government of Winston Churchill and Anthony Eden came to power in Great Britain. David Bruce, U.S. ambassador to France, had been meeting with the British in Paris about the oil crisis and stated that the new British government was quite different from its predecessor. It had a new attitude "which starts from Churchill with the roar of a wounded lion, becomes more articulate with Eden, as he remembers twitting the Laborites for weakness during the campaign, and is fully rationalized by the civil servants."[97]

Both new governments were more susceptible to the arguments of the oil industry and were considerably more paranoid about the communist threat. Furthermore, they both had little patience or sympathy for nationalist movements in areas of the world where they had vested economic and political interests. Thus, both were more willing than their predecessors to conduct an operation of direct intervention into Iran.

The intersection of interventionary ideas occurred in November 1952, when the British approached the United States both in Washington and London concerning a covert operation. In Washington, the primary British operative, C. M. "Monty" Woodhouse, met with American officials at the State Department and the Central Intelligence Agency and made his proposal for what the British termed Operation Boot. Meanwhile in London Kermit "Kim" Roosevelt, head of CIA operations in the Middle East, was approached with the same plan by Woodhouse's colleagues. In his discussions with American officials in Washington, Woodhouse chose to use the threat of communism as his basic argument:

> Not wishing to be accused of trying to use the Americans to pull British chestnuts out of the fire, I decided to emphasize the Communist threat to Iran rather than the need to recover control of the oil industry. I argued that even if a settlement of the oil dispute could be negotiated with Musaddiq, which was doubtful, he was still incapable of resisting a *coup* by the Tudeh Party, if it were backed by Soviet support. Therefore he must be removed.[98]

Given the mentality of the American administration, this tactic was to prove highly successful.

The Methodology of the American Intervention

The American intervention of August 1953 was a momentous event in the history of Iranian-American relations. This direct covert operation left a running wound that bled for twenty-five years and contaminated America's relations with the Islamic Republic of Iran following the revolution of 1978–79. From Iran's perspective, the manner in which the United States intervened in Iran's internal affairs was at least as reprehensible as the decision to intervene itself. For years, Iranians harshly condemned the Central Intelligence Agency and Britain for coordinating the activities of royalist Iranians and distributing money to hired demonstrators. These actions were recalled in the anti-American chants and speeches of the 1978–79 revolution.

After the fall of Musaddiq the acronym CIA became the most pejorative political term in the vocabulary of Iranian nationalists. It implied a particularly vulgar type of imperialism that was increasingly associated with U.S. policy. The sullen buildup of resentment toward America was born of severe disillusionment—Iranians believed that an ally and respected friend had deserted them for the enemy. Given these feelings, it is essential to take a brief look at the intervention itself.

American intelligence organizations had been active in Iran since the late 1940s, when numerous operatives were stationed there. These agents focused their attention on Soviet activities in Iran and sought to neutralize the appeal of the local communist organization, the Tudeh party. American agents forged letters and books allegedly written by Tudeh leaders, planted articles in the Iranian press to discredit Tudeh political programs, and made direct payments to Iranian politicians who opposed the local communist movement. They also developed a program against the National Front and, among other things, placed articles in the press portraying Musaddiq as a cryptocommunist.[99]

The 1953 CIA intervention was well known in Iran but was never publicized in the United States until the revolution of 1978–79. Except for mentions in scattered magazine articles and occasional books that specialized in the history of the CIA itself, this intervention was ignored in most of the major scholarly accounts of the period.[100] With the publication of books by the two intelligence agents who oversaw the operation, it is now possible to understand the extent of American involvement.[101]

The new administration, in control in Washington and with a new ambassador in Tehran, now prepared a dramatic covert operation to overthrow the Musaddiq government. The key actors in Washington were Secretary of State John Foster Dulles, his brother, Allen, head of the CIA, Gen. Walter Bedell Smith, Allen Dulles's predecessor at the CIA and then under secretary of State, and Frank Wisner, then CIA director of operations. Wisner's assistant was Richard Helms, although Helms was not involved in the 1953 intervention. The key link in the operation and the man who connected Washington and the field was Kermit Roosevelt.

In the middle levels of the Washington bureaucracy, many individuals were less than enthusiastic about the project. Within the CIA itself, the two Iran analysts in Washington were not informed of the operation until it was underway. When told of the plans, they predicted imminent failure.[102] Despite these reservations, the CIA–State Department establishment, solidified by the Dulles brothers, committed itself to the operation.

Allen Dulles, Frank Wisner, and Richard Helms had all worked together in the OSS, sharing a house while operating out of Germany. Having struggled against communist infiltration in Eastern Europe following World War II, they were deeply preoccupied with the communist threat whenever and wherever it appeared. Dulles, Wisner, and Roosevelt were intelligence activists who believed strongly in the efficacy of covert operations. Their personalities are well summarized in the following passage:

> All were gregarious, intrigued by possibilities, liked to do things, had three bright ideas a day, shared the optimism of stock market plungers, and were convinced that the CIA could find a way to reach it. They also tended to to be white, Anglo-Saxon patricians from old families with old money, at least in the beginning, and they somehow inherited traditional British attitudes toward the colored races of the world—not the pukka sahib arrogance of the Indian Raj, but the mixed fascination and condescension of men like T. E.

Lawrence, who were enthusiastic partisans of the alien cultures into which they dipped for a time and rarely doubted their ability to help, until it was too late.[103]

The central figure in Iran was Ambassador Loy Henderson, who replaced Henry Grady in September 1951. Born in Arkansas in 1892, Henderson earned bachelor's and law degrees from Northwestern University. He had a long career as a foreign service officer and had worked on Soviet and East European affairs through the 1920s and 1930s. He served as American ambassador to Iraq in 1943–45, preceded George McGhee as assistant secretary of State for Near Eastern and African affairs in 1945–48, and served as ambassador to India and Nepal before moving to Iran. Henderson was a smooth diplomat who was viewed by his associates as a thorough professional. One of Henderson's colleagues has compared Henderson and Grady in the following terms:

> Henderson was a diplomat's diplomat, extremely popular and admired by his staff. He was able to establish the personal relationships with Iranians which Grady found difficult to do. Henderson and Musaddiq had really a very good personal relationship until the crisis which unseated him. Henderson's emphasis was more political than economic, perhaps because the times demanded it. Henderson was a team player inside the bureaucracy. He gracefully accepted Kim Roosevelt's role and cooperated completely, although his instincts and style may have been quite different and he may have had doubts about the wisdom of this course of action.
> On balance, I feel that Henderson is the better pro—versatile and charming, hard-boiled and a good leader. But Grady must be given credit for taking on the British when he realized they (and we with them) were heading for disaster.[104]

Despite his diplomatic polish, Henderson's own political views were deeply colored by what he considered the omnipresent threat of Soviet communism. He subordinated any possible personal sensitivity to local social forces to this overriding consideration. According to his friend Kermit Roosevelt, Henderson played a prominent role in the June 25, 1953, meeting at the Department of State during which U.S. leaders made the final decision to go with Operation Ajax, as the intervention into Iran was known on this side of the Atlantic. Henderson had flown in from Tehran to attend this crucial meeting and weighed in with the following words: "Mr. Secretary, I don't like this kind of business at all. You know that. But we are confronted by a desperate, a dangerous situation and a madman who would ally himself with the Russians. We have no choice but to proceed with this undertaking. May God grant us success."[105]

In the end, the men involved in the American decision to intervene came from similar political backgrounds and maintained the same mind-set. In most cases, this involved past experience in Eastern Europe or in the Soviet Union. General Walter "Beetle" Smith, for example, a strong supporter of the intervention, was an intelligent military man who nursed a deep hatred for anything that reminded him of communism. He had served as ambassador to Moscow following World War II and "had come away with a deep suspicion of Marxist philosophy, a hatred of Soviet cruelty, deception, and hostility, and a contempt for any 'parlor pinks,' as he called them, in the United States who believed that communism was the salvation of the people."[106] Smith strongly supported Operation Ajax in the June 1953 meeting.

Wisner and Henderson were lawyers from Mississippi and Arkansas, respectively; the Dulles brothers had grown up in New York state, and both held law degrees. Such individuals maintained the lawyer mentality of addressing problems on a case-by-case basis and not seriously considering the long-term ramifications of solutions to immediate crises. Furthermore, both Dulles brothers had been employed by the powerful Wall Street law firm of Sullivan and Cromwell, whose numerous clients in the field of oil included the Anglo-Iranian Oil Company. In 1926 Foster had become the senior partner. The Dulleses first, overriding concern was to get rid of Musaddiq; as John Foster Dulles said when he looked through Kim Roosevelt's plans for the operation, "So this is how we get rid of that madman Mossadegh!"[107]

Kermit Roosevelt was a major U.S. intelligence officer in the Middle East for years. A quiet, soft-spoken, true believer, he seemed the complete antithesis of an intelligence operative and activist. At parties in elegant Middle Eastern homes, he was the ruddy-faced quiet little man standing in the corner in subdued conversation with whomever happened along. His contacts were monotonously the same and consisted of the upper-class elites wherever he went. Unlike his British counterparts, he spoke no Middle Eastern language, and his understanding of these societies was clearly superficial. Nonetheless, Roosevelt was accomplished at what he did and in this sense was a very successful professional. He loved his work and the flair and adventure that went with it. Although he had a strong mind of his own, he worked smoothly with his associates and linked up well with individuals like Allen Dulles and "Beetle" Smith.

As the British and Americans prepared the final plans for the intervention, an ironic situation developed because of Anthony Eden's reluctance to approve such a direct, blatant, and risky operation. Eden may have been outraged by the Iranian act of nationalization, but he was clearly not willing to approve this kind of intelligence adventure. Ultimately, he did not have to. In April he underwent the first of three operations related to a serious gall bladder problem and did not return to the Foreign Office until October. By that time the meddlesome Musaddiq problem had been disposed of; Winston Churchill had no reservations whatsoever about the joint American-British intervention and enthusiastically approved it. As Monty Woodhouse put it: "Churchill enjoyed dramatic operations and had no high regard for timid diplomatists. It was he who gave the authority for Operation Boot to proceed."[108] Eden heard the news of the final result when on a cruise of convalescence between the Greek islands. In his words, "I slept better that night."[109]

Using the pseudonym James F. Lochridge, Kermit Roosevelt slipped across the Iraqi border and into Iran on July 6, 1953. In hiding in Tehran, he orchestrated the countercoup that overthrew Musaddiq and replaced him with the shah. Although Ambassador Loy Henderson remained out of Iran during most of the clandestine operation, he coordinated affairs closely with Roosevelt. In Iran, Roosevelt had two highly competent CIA country heads, both of whom were attached to the embassy with diplomatic cover. The one who played an important planning role left the country soon after Roosevelt arrived and was replaced by the second. The British agent who had done so much to plan the operation and to convince the Americans to cooperate, Monty Woodhouse, also left the country long before the actual operation went into effect. Meanwhile, attached to the embassy were other CIA employees whose more extended residence in Iran provided important continuity and intelligence.

Also involved in the overall operation were Gen. Norman Schwarzkopf (former U.S. adviser to the Iranian Gendarmerie), who flew into Iran in full public view on August 1, 1953, and the shah's omnipresent twin sister, Princess Ashraf, who had arrived in Iran on July 25. The visits of Princess Ashraf and Schwarzkopf, though brief, were important. Both met with the shah and worked hard to reinforce his flagging self-confidence. Furthermore, Schwarzkopf met with "old friends" in the military. In Beirut and Cyprus, meanwhile, other American officials and Iran experts were monitoring events and proferring advice.

Roosevelt and his team bucked up the confidence of the shah, made important contacts with the military and Gen. Fazlollah Zahedi, and developed ties with the lower-middle-class rent-a-crowd leaders of south Tehran. Two clusters of Iranian brothers served as a medium and provided the key links between Roosevelt and Iran. One set of brothers was America's own and provided contact with the military.

The other set, of more critical importance to the operation, were British contacts introduced and loaned to the United States for purposes of implementing Operation Boot/Ajax. The latter set is especially noteworthy because its role in linking Iran and America through the influence of Kermit Roosevelt continued long after the Musaddiq period.

These important linkage figures were the Rashidian brothers, Seyfollah, Asadollah, and Qodratollah. Like their father before them, they had strong ties with the British and had worked with them in Iran in the 1940s. Seyfollah, the eldest and a musician and philosopher, was the brains of the triumvirate and a superb conversationalist and host. He was a student of political history and liked to quote verbatim from Machiavelli. Asadollah was the organizer, political activist, and confidante of the shah, while Qodratollah was the businessman and entrepreneur. It was Seyfollah and Asadollah who helped coach Kermit Roosevelt through the escapade in 1953.[110]

The first act of Operation Ajax failed when Musaddiq got word that he was to be ousted. Colonel Nimatullah Nassiri, the officer who tried to serve him with political eviction orders signed by the shah, was arrested on the spot, and the shah made a hasty flight out of the country on August 16, 1953. Rather than cancel the operation at this point, Roosevelt took it upon himself to move forward with plans to call into the streets his paid mobs from south Tehran along with the royalist military officers led by Gen. Fazlollah Zahedi. The Iranian brother teams played a crucial role in the implementation of these plans. After much confusion and street fighting, the royalists won the day, and on August 19, Muhammad Musaddiq was forced to flee his residence and was arrested soon thereafter. On August 22, the shah flew back to Iran in triumph.

The outcome of the coup was in doubt until the very end. The Tudeh-directed mobs controlled the streets for a time on August 16–17 but were attacked on August 18 by the Iranian army on Musaddiq's orders. The following day, when the paid royalist "countermobs" appeared, the Tudeh stayed off the streets. Aside from internal division and vacillation within the ranks of the local communists, the Soviet Union at no time indicated any external support for the Tudehis. Not only was there uncertainty in Moscow because Stalin had died on March 5, but the Soviet Union was itself unable to judge clearly the strength and nature of the Musaddiq movement. If the Soviets had chosen to get involved, the outcome might have differed greatly.

Although the operation ultimately succeeded, it had its seamy side, and this helped cripple American credibility in Iran for years afterwards. Few analysts mention, for example, that at least three hundred

Iranians died in street fighting and many more were wounded. Also, when Ambassador Henderson flew back to Tehran from Beirut after the first part of Operation Ajax had failed, he met immediately with Kermit Roosevelt. The two discussed what Henderson should say to Musaddiq when the latter asked about American support for the shah. Roosevelt recommended that Henderson lie. Henderson agreed, stating, "I will make it quite plain that we have no intention of interfering in the internal affairs of a friendly country." To which Roosevelt responded, "To this noble sentiment I made no comment. Diplomats are expected, if not required, to say such things."[111]

The duplicity of the venture extended to other Americans then in Iran and conversant in its language and culture. The most noteworthy example is "Professor Roger Black," an eminent American scholar who is alleged to have unwittingly assisted Roosevelt by introducing him to several of his Iranian contacts.[112] This distinguished gentleman knew Iran intimately and believed that it was in America's national interest to work with the moderate middle-class nationalist groups. His sympathetic interpretations of Musaddiq and the National Front upset Roosevelt, who later explained Black's nationalist leanings in terms of the professor's "sense of guilt" for having been used so crudely—even though Roosevelt admits that "Black" had nothing to do with the operation.[113] The episode with Professor Black demonstrates well a symbolic crossover point between the time when American missionaries, scholars, and knowledgeable diplomats who had been central to Iran-American relations since the 1930s were replaced by the Dulles school of thought in Washington and the intelligence and military operatives in the field.[114]

A summary analysis of the American intervention into Iran known as Operation Ajax reveals the following fifteen conclusions:

1. The Democratic administration of President Harry Truman was reluctant to adopt the threatening tactics contemplated by key British officials to counter the nationalization movement in Iran.
2. The Eisenhower administration, with the full knowledge and support of Secretary of State John Foster Dulles, CIA Director Allen Dulles, and Under Secretary of State Walter Bedell Smith, decided to intervene directly to overthrow the Musaddiq government.
3. Opinion was deeply divided in both Great Britain and the United States over the wisdom of such a course of action. Administration changeovers in both countries narrowed these divisions.
4. The idea of the intervention originated with the British (SIS/MI6), who used the threat of a possible communist take-

over as their major tactic in attracting American involvement. The British and the Americans cooperated fully in the venture. Noted one American expert who helped devise the plan: "It was a joint effort."[115]

5. The coup could not have succeeded without substantial Iranian participation. Yet the Iranians would not or could not have acted without American/British direction and the psychological support that this involvement carried with it. In the informed view of Monty Woodhouse: "There may be reasons for not being dogmatic in claiming that the revolution of August 1953 in Tehran was planned and executed by our Anglo-American team. Still, I think it was. We may have done no more than mobilize forces which were already there, but that was precisely what needed to be done, and it was enough."[116]

6. The action succeeded because of the deep fragmentation of the social and political forces in Iran, the tenuous nature of the economy, the organizational skills of the handful of leading Iranians involved, the liberal and idealistic nature of both Musaddiq and his followers in the National Front, the conscious decision of the Soviet Union not to intervene, and the element of good luck.

7. The communist Tudeh party in Iran was relatively small and lacked the support of either the nationalist middle classes or Iranian masses. As a State Department intelligence report prepared in January 1953 stated, Musaddiq himself was neither a communist nor a communist sympathizer; he was in fact hated by the Iranian communist leadership. The report indicated that Musaddiq's nationalization had "almost universal Iranian support" and that the Tudeh party deemed Musaddiq's overthrow "a high priority." It carefully listed thirteen ways in which Tudeh objectives differed from those of the National Front.[117] In the end, the Tudeh party's strategy proved itself weak, indecisive, and self-defeating during the political showdown in August 1953.

8. The intervention bought twenty-five more years for the Pahlavi dynasty and enabled the international oil industry to export at favorable terms 24 billion barrels of oil during this period. Western consumers paid very low prices for this precious resource during these years. The average posted price of Iranian crude was about $1.85 between 1954 and 1960 and $1.80 between 1960 and 1971.[118]

9. The American action in Iran was followed by a general purge of any remaining elements of the Tudeh party, whose influence was almost completely annihilated in the country. One U.S. congressman summarized a view shared by a number of key decision makers in Washington when he, in somewhat exaggerated terms, stated: "We saved Iran for the free world when the rest of that area had gone over to the Communists."[119]

10. By crushing the Musaddiq move to nationalize, the United

States and Great Britain discouraged further movements toward unilateral nationalization of the oil industry in the Third World. Although the Suez Canal was nationalized in 1956, it was almost two decades before any more major oil industries were nationalized.

11. Washington policymakers for years considered the operation in Iran a great success story in direct covert intervention. As such, the Iran escapade acted as a catalyst that bred other CIA interventions—beginning with Guatemala in 1954.

12. Operation Ajax locked the United States into a special relationship with the shah and signaled the powerful entrance of American intelligence and military activity into Iran.

13. The U.S. intervention alienated important generations of Iranians from America and was the first fundamental step in the eventual rupture of Iranian-American relations in the revolution of 1978–79.

14. The intervention damaged the image of the United States in the eyes of the nationalists who swept to power in the Middle East in the 1960s and 1970s. As Justice William O. Douglas wrote: "When Mossadegh in Persia started basic reforms, we became alarmed. That man, whom I am proud to call my friend, was a democrat in the LaFollette-Norris sense of the term. We united with the British to destroy him; we succeeded; and ever since our name has not been an honored one in the Middle East."[120] Historian David Painter has concluded that the costs of intervention were high: "The necessity of providing U.S. oil companies with a compatible international environment ultimately led the United States, in the case of Iran, to violate the principle of nonintervention in the affairs of other nations."[121]

15. The 1953 intervention aborted the birth of revolutionary nationalism in Iran that would burst forth twenty-five years later in a deeply xenophobic and extremist form.

The United States and Muhammad Musaddiq: The Political Legacy

American intervention in Iran ensured that no communist takeover would take place and that Iranian oil reserves would be available to the Western world at advantageous terms for the next two decades. It also deeply alienated Iranian patriots of all social classes and weakened the moderate, liberal nationalists represented by such organizations as the National Front, thereby paving the way for the incubation of both leftist and rightist extremism. This extremism, already in its embryonic stages, became unalterably anti-American.

Both the Tudeh party on the left and Ayatollah Kashani and others on the right condemned American intervention with that of the British and the Soviet Union. Kashani repeatedly criticized American links with Great Britain. In November 1951 he stated that "we don't want any outside government interfering in our internal affairs. . . . The United States should cease following British policy otherwise it will gain nothing but hatred and the loss of prestige in the world in general and in Iran in particular."[122] In his contacts with the American embassy in Tehran, Kashani sharply criticized U.S. policy. On one occasion, he told embassy counselor A. R. Richards that the U.S. aid program was useless because it emphasized military priorities rather than the improvement of the living conditions of the deprived masses. He asked Richards, "What good could a well-equipped and well-trained army of even 250,000 do against 18 million hungry people in Iran?"[123] By its actions in Iran in 1953, the United States guaranteed the unremitting future opposition of the nationalist extremism of the religious right while at the same time effectively undercutting the strength and credibility of the liberal, nationalist center.

This distrust deepened in the years following the fall of Musaddiq; the United States bound itself increasingly tightly to the shah and his policies, which in turn only increased the doubt and distrust of the Iranian middle and lower classes. The central figures of the American intelligence team that carried out the intervention was crucial to the tightening American-Pahlavi relationship. The key connection here was a Roosevelt-Rashidian economic and political alliance that supported Muhammad Reza Shah Pahlavi. The Rashidians became wealthy entrepreneurs and financiers with international business ventures.[124] Kermit Roosevelt's public relations firm represented the shah's interests in the United States. The Rashidians spoke often of their friend "Kim," who stayed with them during his many subsequent trips to Iran, which in the 1960s averaged five or six a year. Roosevelt maintained a parallel path to the shah, with whom he had closer relations than did any American diplomat posted to Tehran. Although this upset leading members of the U.S. diplomatic mission in Tehran, they were unable to do anything about it. Roosevelt's line to the shah was through the Rashidians to the commander of the Imperial Guards, Gen. Muhsin Hashimi-Nijhad, to the monarch himself. Back in Washington, Roosevelt had personal connections that led directly to the White House.

In this way, certain American agents involved in the 1953 intervention continued to exert influence on America's Iran policy long after 1953. The Rashidians' elegant home in the north Tehran suburb of Kamraniyah and their bank near Firdawsi Square became centers for continued Roosevelt-Rashidian collaboration. This was only one connection that bound the United States tightly with the British and the shah until the revolution. However significant, this particular link existed as a constant and grating reminder to the growing body of informed Iranian nationalists that the shah remained in power only through American and British intervention.

The fall of Musaddiq marked the end of a century of American-Iranian friendship and began a new era of intervention and growing hostility for the United States among the awakened forces of Iranian nationalism. A sense of the spirit of the American establishment during this period is captured in an article that appeared in the *Reporter* in November 1953. In a long discussion of the Musaddiq movement, the American author warned new Iranian prime minister Fazlollah Zahedi, "Like other leaders with empty treasuries, he [Zahedi] will learn that the sun rises and sets according to the schedule laid down by our Constitution for the sitting of the United States Congress." And the writer ended his analysis and advice by predicting that the new government in Iran "won't be with us long unless it can prove that being nice to the West is more profitable for Iran than being as consistently nasty as Old Mossy was."[125] This crude message was not lost on educated Iranians who read its translation in the leading Iranian weekly news magazine shortly after it appeared in the *Reporter*.

The Musaddiq movement of 1951–53 shared certain similarities with the Khomeini-led revolution that shook the world twenty-five years later. Fiercely nationalistic, the movement of the 1950s was anti-Western in tone with special antipathy reserved for the British. But even in 1953 signs of strident anti-Americanism were visible. Slogans such as the one labeling the U.S. embassy a "nest of spies" were already shouted in the streets of Tehran in 1953. Musaddiq, like Ayatollah Khomeini after him, was designated as *Time* magazine's Man of the Year and was presented throughout as enigmatic, irascible, and even insane. In its cover story on Musaddiq in January 1952, *Time* presented the old man as fanatical and chided the West for lacking the "moral muscle" to deal with him. Although he discussed and debated with American representatives, Musaddiq ultimately refused to compromise and became a political casualty as a result.

The experiences of 1951–53 also influenced the revolution of 1978–79. Khomeini and the other leaders of the revolution vowed not to allow a repetition of what they termed "the Musaddiq debacle."[126] Convinced that the United States through the auspices of the CIA would attempt to replay the Kermit Roosevelt record, they took every precaution to keep this from happening. Anti-American rhetoric was kept at a fever pitch; every word, act, or signal from Washington was thoroughly scrutinized; Khomeini himself remained aloof from American diplomats; Iranian civil and military officials with close ties to the United States were executed, imprisoned, or retired; and, finally, when a Pahlavi restoration attempt seemed imminent, American diplomats were taken hostage.

Despite these similarities and influences, the American intervention of 1951–53 did not determine the revolutionary events of 1978–79. Although the American image was tarnished severely by its actions against Musaddiq, the United States had numerous opportunities to rethink and revise its policy towards the shah's Iran in the quarter-century before the revolution. Instead, however, America slowly tightened its relationship with the Pahlavi regime. Increasing numbers of Iranians thus came to view American actions as policy extensions of the 1953 intervention. In the streets of Tehran in 1978 a constantly repeated slogan was "Death to the American shah!" In short, American policy between 1953 and 1978 emphasized a special relationship with the shah and his political elite while largely ignoring the needs and demands of the Iranian masses.

In the quarter-century between 1953 and 1978, much happened in Iran to keep history from repeating itself. Besides the internal social dynamics that included the explosive growth of an alienated professional middle class, the clumsy political miscues of the shah and his inner circle, the widening gap between the haves and the have-nots, and the adamant opposition of the popular Shi'i religious leaders, the external ingredient also contributed to the developing revolutionary equation. An increasing American presence and an interventionary American policy became integral parts of the Iranian political process after 1953.

3 The Politics of Reaction and Pahlavi Retrenchment, 1954–1961

Muhammad Reza Shah's brush with disaster during the Musaddiq upheaval convinced the thirty-four-year-old ruler that it was time to take firm control of the situation and to crush whatever opposition existed to his leadership. He appointed Maj. Gen. Fazlollah Zahedi as prime minister and announced Zahedi's cabinet on August 20, 1953. One third of its members were military generals. Martial law was declared, and the shah chose to rule by the bayonet rather than by the ballot.

The centerpiece and dreaded symbol of the shah's new system of control was formed in 1957. Known as SAVAK (Sazman-i Ittili'at va Amniyat-i Kishvar), this intelligence and internal security organization is best translated as the Intelligence and Security Organization of the Country. It was established with the full assistance of the United States, which put its own intelligence forces at the shah's disposal in SAVAK's formation. Israeli intelligence also played a major part in the creation and operation of SAVAK. Over the years the United States, Iran, Israel, and Turkey were to cooperate closely in intelligence matters. Domestically, SAVAK was viewed as a police-state monster, and as its tactics became more extreme and ruthless over time, it acquired an unsavory reputation not only in Iran but throughout the world.

SAVAK was organized by function into eight departments. The four most important departments were the Second Department (foreign intelligence collection), the Third Department (internal security), the Seventh Department (foreign intelligence analysis), and the Eighth Department (counterintelligence). It was the Third Department that gave SAVAK its black reputation, since this section focused its efforts on internal political surveillance and control. As one informed American observer noted: "SAVAK became notorious for the brutality of the prisons operated by the Third Department. It does not excuse the organization to note that it was no worse than similar organizations operating in most of the world."[1]

The first head of SAVAK was a thirty-nine-year-old military general trained at St. Cyr whose origins, like those of Queen Soraya, were of the powerful Bakhtiari tribe. Teymour Bakhtiar was a strong, ruthless, and ambitious individual—the ideal personality to direct the shah's new policy of political control. Bakhtiar formed SAVAK in his own image and rapidly became a feared and unpopular figure. His two political preoccupations were a deep desire to destroy any form of socialism in Iran and to develop a power base that would carry him to the pinnacle of political power in the country. In many ways he was a taller, louder, and more ruthless version of General Razmara. And he was a much more dangerous man both to the opposition groups and to the shah himself.

While the military was his prime instrument of power, the shah permitted elections in 1954 and then 1956 for the Eighteenth and Nineteenth Majlises, respectively. The elections of January 1954 were blatantly rigged: a number of the same mob leaders who had been active in the streets in the overthrow of Musaddiq roamed the polling places, where they attacked and intimidated voters. The results were two parliaments dominated to unprecedented degrees by landlords and wealthy Iranian aristocrats who were unconditional Pahlavi supporters. Sixty percent of the Eighteenth Majlis, for example, was made up of landed elements, while landlords composed 59 percent of the Nineteenth Majlis. Deputy names like Ardalan, Ibrahimi, Bushihri, Panahi, Hikmat, and Khalatbari demonstrate the unrepresentative nature of these representative bodies. Three members of the Bakhtiari tribe alone sat in the Nineteenth Majlis. The Senate was even more aristocratic in composition but also included military figures like Major Generals Ahmad Amir-Ahmadi and Amanullah Mirza Jahanbani and Lieutenant Generals Hassan Baqa'i and Majid Firuz.[2]

The shah built his new foundation of political support on an old alliance of the wealthy landed elite and the traditional bureaucratic and bazaari middle classes. He managed to fashion this alliance through the methodology of political and economic bribery. Those who had stood by him throughout the Musaddiq period now stumbled over one another in the stampede for rewards, while those who had remained neutral came off the fence and rushed to embrace the shah's new system of control. The shah then moved to deal with those who had been part of the determined opposition to his rule.

Muhammad Reza Shah and Prime Minister Zahedi developed a three-pronged political policy to dispose of any actual or potential opposition. The three prongs included coercion and destruction, repression and control, and surveillance and accommodation. Each policy prong was directed toward a different opposition element: the communist Tudeh party, the National Front, and the religious hierarchy, respectively. The first order of business was the Tudeh party.

In a major frontal attack on the Tudeh party, the new regime captured, arrested, tried, or executed the bulk of the leadership of the movement. Although the party had infiltrated the military, it was generally much weaker than many had imagined. Uncertainty, internal conflicts, indecision, and ideological confusion marked the party. The committed Tudehis either fled the country or were jailed or executed; the doubters recanted, and a number of them took positions in the government as salaried bureaucrats. The party sustained a major blow when, in the summer of 1954, an extensive network of nearly 600 Tudeh members was uncovered in the Iranian armed forces. The government brought over 450 of these individuals to trial, and the leaders were sentenced either to death or to life imprisonment. After the mid-1950s the Tudeh party survived primarily through its organization outside Iran; within the country, the party barely managed to maintain a clandestine presence.

The post-Musaddiq government dealt with the National Front in a less draconian manner. Many of its leaders were jailed but later released. The regime carefully monitored the activities of all National Front members, who were subject to harassment and political pressure. Despite this, the leaders of the National Front continued in varying ways to keep their movement alive through private meetings and discussions. They spent the 1950s walking a political tightrope. They quietly stressed democratic values and liberal ideals while existing in what they privately termed a political tyranny. Front veterans like Karim Sanjabi, Ali Shayegan, Kazem Hasibi, Ghulam Hussein Sadiqi, and younger members like Shapour Bakhtiar and Dariush Furuhar professed secular, liberal goals while directing their appeal to the educated middle classes. Other influential leaders such as Mehdi Bazargan and Sayyid Mahmud Taliqani also shared such ideals but were more interested in developing communications with the lower-class masses through the medium of Shi'i Islam. All tiptoed carefully along the political fringes of Iranian society while struggling to preserve their political vision and identity.

Musaddiq himself did much to preserve the spirit of the National Front through his performance at his last public political appearance—his trial, which was held in a military court over a forty-day period in November and December 1953. Musaddiq gave a premier performance at the trial; he defended his political actions, condemned the shah's rule, criticized what he termed British and American imperialism, and praised democratic values throughout. He was clearly in charge of the courtroom, and his words provided inspiration for Iranian nationalists for years afterwards.

> He wept, laughed, shouted, went on hunger strike, and—once or twice—fainted. And all that the British and American mass media saw in all this heroic as well as skilled conduct by a man of seventy-two was, on the whole, the antics of a broken old fool. The Iranian people, however, saw it in an entirely different light: Musaddiq had lost some popular support before the coup. . . . But his unfair and illegal trial, and, especially, his conduct both at the trial and in the appeal tribunal won him more support and admiration than he had ever enjoyed.[3]

Musaddiq was given a three-year jail sentence, after which he spent the last decade of his life under house arrest in his village of Ahmadabad. From here he quietly maintained contact with his family and followers throughout the country.

With the Tudeh party essentially destroyed and the National Front badly crippled by the regime's policies, the final element, the religious right—potentially the most dangerous opposition force of all—was neutralized with relative ease. Here the shah built a policy of cooptation around the person of the leading ayatollah, Sayyid Muhammad Hussein Burujirdi. Burujirdi maintained cautious contact with the regime but was too religious an individual to work directly with the shah. Instead he indicated the need to keep religion and politics in separate compartments. The shah did, however, hold the active cooperation of such clerics as Ayatollah Muhammad Musavi Bihbihani, who had proven Pahlavi credentials, having actively helped to mobilize mob opposition to Musaddiq in August 1953. An influential cleric stationed in Iraq, Ayatollah Sayyid Hibat al-Din Shahrastani, also indicated his support for the shah and even traveled to Iran, where he carefully spread this message. Finally, the shah had his own cleric-in-court, Sayyid Hassan Imami, the Imam Jum'ah of Tehran, who was educated in Switzerland and provided constant if questionable public legitimation for the shah's rule.

In the face of this alignment of clerical support for the shah and military rule, the other clerics pursued a policy of political quiescence. As long as they were able to carry out their religious mission in relative peace, they did not challenge the system. The fiery old campaigner Ayatollah Kashani had lost the support of the Musaddiqists, and as his own political constituency slowly melted away he slipped into political obscurity. The regime solidified its support with the Shi'i religious establishment in 1955 when it acted slowly in dispersing mobs that attacked Baha'i centers in Tehran. Meanwhile the shah busily emphasized his own personal commitment to Islam and was careful to make public visits to mosques and holy shrines throughout the country.

This system of political control maintained order through the decade, but as 1960 approached, growing numbers of Iranians became increasingly restless and disaffected in an oppressive political environment within which corruption thrived and spread. Zahedi and his coterie were especially tainted and were heavily criticized in this regard. In April 1955 the shah replaced Zahedi with loyal standby Hussein Ala, who was in turn replaced by Manuchehr Eqbal a year later. Eqbal served out the rest of the decade. During these years, he watched political and social pressures increase until the shah opened a political safety valve. In 1957 he announced the formation of a two-party system in which Prime Minister Eqbal's "party," the Milliyun, or Nationalist, party, would be challenged by an "opposition party," the Mardum, or People's, party, headed by landed aristocrat and courtier, Asadollah Alam.[4]

It was in the 1950s that three of the shah's closest political advisers and troubleshooters came into their own. This revolving triumvirate of Asadollah Alam, Manuchehr Eqbal, and Ja'far Sharif-Emami played a critical role in the shah's system of political rule over the next two decades. They helped to shape political policy in Iran into the 1970s and, although completely subservient to the shah, wielded arbitrary power over others in the political system. As royal troubleshooters, they moved in and out of such critical positions as university chancellorships, ministerships, prime ministerships and such economic and financial guardianships as leadership of the National Iranian Oil Company (NIOC) and the Pahlavi Foundation. In order to comprehend the Pahlavi political system during its last twenty-five years, it is essential to understand the personalities and politics of these three men.

Manuchehr Eqbal was born into an important Khurasan family in 1909. A French-trained medical doctor, Eqbal returned to Iran in 1933 and began government service as a physician in the Health Department in Mashhad. In the 1940s he became deputy minister of Health. Eqbal was then called to the attention of the Royal Court and from then on never looked back, holding hundreds of important social, economic, and political positions. Besides serving as prime minister, he held a half-dozen different ministerships, was both a Majlis representative and a senator, and served as governor-general, chancellor of Tabriz and Tehran universities, and head of the Plan Organization. Eqbal ended his career as the powerful chairman and managing director of the National Iranian Oil Company, a position that he held for fifteen years. In the presence of the shah, Eqbal was an obsequious nonentity. This characteristic was already general knowledge in Iran in the 1950s when Eqbal publicly described himself as his majesty's *ghulam* (house servant). In the presence of an old friend, he once pointed to a glass of water and said: "I won't drink that glass of water without the permission of His Imperial Majesty."[5] With the exception of his relationship to the Pahlavis, Eqbal was a strong, dominant personality and a man of relative integrity in circles where such integrity was rare.

The same age as Eqbal, Ja'far Sharif-Emami was a Swedish-trained engineer who married the sister of Dr. Abdullah Mu'azzami, a prominent Iranian liberal and nationalist. He started in public service in 1931 when he began work for the Iranian State Railways. He served as minister of roads, minister of industries and mines, and senator in the 1950s, becoming prime minister in 1960–61. Besides these political posts, Sharif-Emami was deeply involved in financial pursuits and banking. His most influential and self-enriching position was as head of the Pahlavi Foundation, which was the gigantic repository of Pahlavi wealth. Toward the end of the Pahlavi regime in the mid-1970s, Sharif-Emami was widely rumored in Tehran to be in close collaboration with SAVAK head Nimatullah Nassiri in financial arrangements in which Nassiri applied the pressure and Sharif-Emami collected the rewards. Like Eqbal, Sharif-Emami was self-effacing in the presence of the shah; but while Eqbal used this relationship to wield professional and political influence, Sharif-Emami reportedly used it for financial gain. Sharif-Emami was for years a leading member of the Chamber of Mines and Industries in Iran as well as a central figure in the Association of Engineers and in the Masonic movement. He took governmental posts when asked to do so by the shah but preferred to avoid formal political affiliations and positions.

Although ten years the junior of Eqbal and Sharif-Emami, Asadollah Alam was more powerful than either. For years he was an especially close adviser to the shah and was the only one in the shah's own generation who would on occasion cautiously and privately make political suggestions to the king. Nonetheless, his subservience is seen in his own public description of the shah: "I cannot say that he is faultless. Everyone, as you say, has faults. . . . his fault to my mind is that he is really too great for his people—his ideas are too great for we people to realize it."[6] Alam was an extremely wealthy landed aristocrat from the eastern province of Birjand and was the shah's most trusted political troubleshooter. He served as prime minister, minister of interior, governor-general, university chancellor, Majlis deputy, secretary-general of the Mardum party, and minister of court. It was in the last position with constant and close proximity to the shah, where he wielded special influence and was effective in controlling the access routes to Muhammad Reza Shah. Alam was quietly ruthless and was described in Tehran by a close associate as a man "who could cut your throat with a feather." When asked at a dinner party in 1963 about a dissident who had been criticizing the regime, Alam stopped filling his plate long enough to say, "Oh him; I hanged him."[7] Although he lacked any formal education, he was an impeccably charming host who invariably impressed foreign dignitaries and ambassadors. His loyalty to the shah was total.

The Eqbal–Sharif-Emami–Alam triangle of power remained in place until the Pahlavi dynasty neared its fall in the late 1970s. Although there was quiet tension among the three, they never let this destroy their influence at court. All nurtured friendships with Western dignitaries, and all carefully built international contacts. Sharif-Emami's relationships were strongest with Europe; Eqbal's contacts spanned Europe and the United States; and Alam was consistently close to the British embassy and ambassadors like Sir Denis Wright, although in the 1970s he developed close working relationships with such leading American diplomats as Richard Helms. Alam was the ruthless politician; Sharif-Emami was the aggrandizing financier-banker; and Eqbal was the faithful bureaucrat and oil company head. By the late 1970s both Eqbal and Alam had died, and Sharif-Emami, the weakest and least-respected of the three, was disastrously moved into a key political post at the end. But times had changed, and this appointment only hastened the fall of the dynasty.

The system of guided democracy instituted from above by the shah, Eqbal, and Alam in the late 1950s backfired badly when the Iranian people began to take the matter seriously and a number of independents with serious political ambitions entered the electoral fray. When it became clear that there was to be no genuine political participation, there was a massive and indignant public outcry that ended in the dissolution of two parliaments and the dismissal of two prime ministers. As matters began to veer out of control internally, political upheaval in neighboring countries increased the alarm of the shah and his political elite. The bloody revolution in Iraq in July 1958 was followed in 1960 by a military takeover in Turkey in which the army seized power from a corrupt and unpopular civilian regime. The growing political discontent at home and the political upheaval in the region together resulted in the major policy changes that would take place in Iran in the early 1960s.

The Politics of the Oil Agreement of 1954

The stability of the Iranian political system following the fall of Musaddiq depended to a large extent on the health of the economic system. This health in turn depended on an immediate return of Iranian petroleum to the international market. During the effective embargo imposed by the British and supported by the United States, Iran (actually the AIOC) had lost its markets to neighboring oil-producing states such as Kuwait, Iraq, and Saudi Arabia. Also, new arrangements had to be made with respect to the ownership, exploration, production, and overall administration and control of the petroleum industry in Iran. Soon after Musaddiq fell, American and British officials began in-depth discussions about these fundamentally important issues.[8] Later the leaders of the new political regime in Iran were brought into the negotiations.

Between August and October of 1953, British and American government officials and petroleum executives met in Washington to discuss a new arrangement for the exploitation of Iranian oil. The persisting differences of philosophy between the United States and Great Britain concerning the politics of oil plagued these discussions. One distinguished Iranian observer and participant noted that these talks were "a tug of war between the avarice of William Fraser and the acquisitiveness of the major oil companies."[9] Nevertheless, in December 1953, the heads of the major U.S. oil companies met with the leadership of the AIOC at Britannic House in London, and a cooperative consortium idea was eventually accepted. In February 1954, a team of twenty oil company experts toured the Iranian oil fields and Abadan where they found the facilities to be in excellent condition. This Western team admitted its surprise in noting that the Iranians had done an impressive job with the industry despite the absence of British technicians during the Musaddiq period. Then in April the consortium of Western company representatives began negotiations in Tehran with the Iranian government. These very difficult negotiations continued through August, when an agreement was announced. It took effect that October.

The negotiators quickly recognized that three conditions had to be met if an agreement was to be forthcoming: (1) the nationalization of Iranian oil was a fait accompli and had to be allowed to stand; (2) the British single-company control of the Iranian oil industry had to be replaced by a multicompany U.S.-British arrangement; and (3) satisfactory compensation had to be paid to the Anglo-Iranian Oil Company both for its losses and for the transference of its facilities to the Iranian government. Within this context, it was essential that the overriding presence of the AIOC be shaded, its influence diluted, and that the Iranians be allowed to save face.

The American government and the leading negotiators for the American oil companies successfully prevailed on a somewhat reluctant AIOC leadership to agree to these terms. Sir William Fraser was at first less than anxious to come to terms with Iran but was convinced to do so; the British media later alleged that Fraser deserved great credit for the final consortium agreement, and he was created baron Strathalmond of Pumpherstone. To which oil magnate Calouste Gulbenkian is reported to have said that a more appropriate title might have been Lord Crude of Abadan.[10] In the crisp summary of experienced petroleum engineer Charles Hamilton: "Largely because of American persistence at governmental level [sic], the Anglo-Iranian wreck was salvaged to live again as British Petroleum (with greater assets and more vigor than ever before), while Iran 'saved face' and kept her nationalized oil properties."[11]

The two major negotiators on the American side were Herbert Hoover, Jr., and Howard Page. Hoover oversaw the negotiations and was the coordinating leader of the American delegation. Page, a shrewd and experienced international negotiator from Standard Oil of New Jersey, worked out the details of the agreement. He replaced Jersey Standard vice president Orville Harden, who had been the first head of the consortium delegation. Page took a hard look at the Iranian position and, well understanding the climate of bargaining and negotiation that dominated in Iran, correctly concluded that that there was room to chip out an agreement. This view was shared by the British counselor in Tehran, Sir Denis Wright, an intelligent and well-informed diplomat whose opinions reinforced the Page position.

Herbert Hoover, Jr., was not unfamiliar with Iran; in the mid 1940s he had acted as a consultant to the Iranian government. Hoover had personal and professional roots in the oil industry. His father had been not only president of the United States but secretary of Commerce and had played a key role in bringing about American participation in the Iraqi Petroleum Company. Hoover, who was a director of Union Oil of California and was chairman of the board of United Geophysical Company, acted as Secretary of State Dulles's special petroleum adviser. A conservative engineer, Hoover was convinced that he could help work out an agreement that would benefit both the United States government and the American oil companies. He let it be known early on that his efforts would not be derailed either by British obstinacy or by Iranian emotionalism. Although some authors have given Hoover the credit for the idea of establishing a consortium, this option had already been discussed by other American international oil experts such as Walter Levy when he accompanied W. Averell Harriman to Iran and England in 1951.

Howard Page put the package together. Page, who Sen. Frank Church once referred to as "the Kissinger of the oil industry," was a California-born chemical engineer who had been employed by Standard Oil of New Jersey since 1929. As Jersey Standard's representative in London beginning in 1949, he also became a director of the Iraqi Petroleum Company and was directly involved in the difficult oil negotiations in Iraq in 1950–51. Page was an oil man through and through, and his loyalty was to his company and to the industry. This commitment went so far that in public testimony he condemned the very idea that anyone would purchase Iranian oil during the AIOC boycott. To him, this oil was stolen goods, belonging not to Iran but to the AIOC. When asked how AIOC could bring lawsuits against those who might purchase Iranian crude, Page responded: "Because it was their property and it had been stolen from them. They had a right of action, no question about that. We don't deal with stolen property and people who do sometimes get lawsuits."[12]

Distinguished-looking yet crusty and hard-talking, Page was best captured in the 1974 Church Senate Hearings during which he abrasively, cuttingly, and disdainfully attacked his questioners. His performance here has been described by one writer as "a dazzling exposition of control, method, concealment—of hypocrisy, ultimately."[13] Page's understanding of Iranian society and politics was modest. His understanding of international oil politics, by contrast, was genuine and deep. Not surprisingly, he was well-thought-of by the AIOC leadership and was able to hold the major American companies together to present a united front in the negotiations with the Iranians.

The Iranian delegation was led by Ali Amini, who was minister of finance in the Zahedi cabinet. Amini's advisers and assistants were distinguished and competent technocrats from aristocratic families, men such as Murtiza Ghuli Bayat, Fatollah Naficy, and Fatollah Nouri-Esfandiary. Amini himself was a fifty-year-old French-educated economist of personal integrity and independence. His father, Muhsin Amin al-Dawlah, was the son of famous Qajar statesman Mirza Ali Khan Amin al-Dawlah, and his mother, Fakhr al-Dawlah, was the influential daughter of Muzzafar al-Din Shah, who had ruled

Iran from 1896 to 1907. Amini had strengthened his personal pedigree by marrying a daughter of Hassan Vusuq al-Dawlah and was therefore an important appended in-law to the powerful family cluster that included such individuals as Vusuq's brother, Ahmad Qavam, and Musaddiq himself. The British and Americans both maintained some respect for Amini; the British referred to him in their secret files as "an agreeable, and usually very helpful, representative of the younger school."[14] Throughout the difficult negotiations, Amini took a thoroughly professional position and exhibited patience and firmness.

The basic features of the consortium agreement were as follows: The ownership rights of the National Iranian Oil Company (NIOC), already claimed in 1950, were finally recognized by all interested parties. The NIOC was charged with the management of the internal distribution of petroleum products, with the operation of the Kirmanshah Refinery and the Naft-i Shah oil field, and with nonbasic operations, such as the housing, education, and medical care of oil industry employees. It passed along to the consortium operating companies the remaining assets it owned within the agreement area, which was basically the former concession area of the AIOC. The consortium companies were charged with the task of running the operations, making use of the land and the assets now recognized as owned by the NIOC. The trading companies bought the oil produced (in excess of that needed by Iran for internal consumption) at cost and sold it to their customers at full posted price. The NIOC received $12\frac{1}{2}$ percent of the crude oil produced in kind as royalty at the posted price and the government received as income tax an amount which when added to the $12\frac{1}{2}$ percent royalty would make 50 percent of the net profit. Iran agreed to pay the AIOC approximately $70 million (£25 million) over a ten-year period while the other participant foreign companies were also to make substantial payments to the British company.

The Iranian Oil Participants, a British holding company, was set up to hold the shares of two operating companies known as the Iranian Oil Exploration and Producing Company and the Iranian Oil Refining Company. The operations of each company were to be overseen by a board of seven directors. Two of the seven were to be selected by the NIOC. These companies, incorporated in the Netherlands, carried out operations for the NIOC. The actual buying and selling of oil, however, was carried on by trading companies that bought the crude oil from NIOC and then shipped it and sold it on the world markets. The Iranian government was to receive one half of the net profits resulting from oil exports.

In brief, this complex agreement meant that Iran now clearly owned its own oil reserves and industry while a foreign consortium of companies had the de facto power of operation. "In no case could the host country interfere in the running of the concession."[15] Iran now received royalties on the fifty-fifty profit basis enjoyed by other producing countries, and the AIOC received compensation for the nationalization of its assets. From the shah on down, the Iranians were not pleased with this agreement. Even Ali Amini often admitted that the consortium arrangement was not what Iran deserved or needed, since control still existed in the hands of foreigners. On the other hand, it was the best agreement Iran could have gotten given the time and circumstances. In the words of Fatollah Naficy, "Iran had to choose between the devil and the deep blue sea, between chaos and humiliation. What happened is they chose humiliation rather than chaos, leading possibly to communism."[16]

Although the Iranian Majlis and Senate ratified the consortium agreement in October 1954, nationalist groups throughout the country quietly criticized and condemned the arrangement. The regime responded with political pressure and force. When a dean and a dozen leading professors at Tehran University signed a petition criticizing the agreement, the chancellor of the university was called to the royal court and ordered to expel these faculty members from the university. When the chancellor, a respected and distinguished educator who had led the university since 1942, refused, he was removed from his position.[17] His replacement was Manuchehr Eqbal. In the end this resentment was stifled and went underground, where it bubbled into other grievances, gradually forming a widening pool of subterranean political disaffection.

Analysts and scholars differ in their interpretations of the consortium arrangements. Most diplomats and oil executives and occasional scholars view it as clear political and economic success for everyone concerned. Others view it as a boon for the American oil companies and a disaster for Iran. One writer goes so far as to state that "the Iranian Consortium, viewed from any standpoint, represented a resounding triumph for the British and the International Petroleum Cartel and a catastrophic defeat for the national aspirations of Iran."[18] Another analyst simply concludes that "the A.I.O.C. came out of the dispute victorious."[19] Iranian economist Fereidun Fesharaki's assessment seems the most informed and best balanced and is, therefore, worth quoting at length.

> The Consortium Agreement did not bring any extra benefits for Iran, at least in the short run. It brought Iran essentially the same type of contract as Iran would have obtained anyway. Insofar as the

Iranian objections against a single monopoly (AIOC) was concerned, the monopolistic structure did not really change. Indeed, Iran was in a weaker position facing eight majors rather than facing a single major oil company. As to the nationalization principle accepted by the Consortium, this did not change the picture at all. The assets belonged to NIOC, but were exploited as any other concession by the Consortium. As far as the provisions of the agreement with regard to NIOC's control of the Consortium operations were concerned . . . , Iran was unable to exercise any effective control. Important decisions on the level of production, the expansion of domestic reserves, and purchase prices were left to the Consortium members.

Although the Iranian nationalization brought no immediate extra benefits for Iran, it proved to be of great help to the Iranian oil industry in the long run. Whether this would make up for the material losses, the political turmoil, and the individual suffering that accompanied the nationalization may never be established. A lesson Iran learned was how dependent her economy was on oil; the mistake was never repeated again. Perhaps the most significant consequence of the nationalization was the creation of the NIOC. NIOC was the first national oil company in a major oil-producing country. Its immediate task of taking over the domestic distribution of the oil products in Iran, . . . contributed greatly to the material well-being of the country and its economic development by providing cheap energy and expanding its distribution network. As a young company, it observed the operations of the Consortium and gradually obtained a great deal of experience and knowhow.[20]

Regardless of such scholarly assessments, the United States government was extremely pleased with the outcome of the consortium negotiations. The Department of State had been deeply involved in the discussions and was so anxious to secure an agreement that it supported united activities by the five major international oil companies, which the Department of Justice had been seeking to prosecute on grounds that they constituted a cartel. The most important internal decision facing the American government concerned which American companies would participate in the Iranian consortium arrangement.

The independent oil companies strongly desired positions in the consortium. They originally requested 36 percent of the shares. They saw this as their right given their boycott of Musaddiq when the major companies, supported by the American and British governments, implemented a strangling embargo on Iranian oil. For their part, the major American companies denied that they wanted to do business in Iran and pointed to the surplus of oil on the world market. In the words of Howard Page, as "a straight business deal, it was for the birds."[21] In fact, Page and his associates were very interested in using the rich Iranian market for some corporate nest-feathering. In November

1953, the British Foreign Office assessed that the United States "want[s] an agreement with Persian for political reasons. The oil companies want access to Persian oil reserves."[22] The majors did indeed work to acquire what they could of the Iranian market. As a result, the independents, organized into what was known as the Iricon group, received only a 5 percent share of the consortium. There is evidence that even this was resented by the majors. Howard Page, for example, testified before the U.S. Senate that the majors received the lion's share of the consortium because only they had the marketing outlets to move the Iranian oil. The independents did not deserve a piece of the action, "but when you got a nice gravy train like Iricon did with getting their percentage of 5 percent without having to have done any backing up or anything like that, well, sure you make the most of it."[23]

Just as the American major companies entered the consortium to dilute the concentrated influence of the AIOC, the independents were brought in to dilute the obvious strength of the American majors. The original consortium agreement provided the following lineup: British Petroleum-AIOC (40%), Royal Dutch-Shell (14%), Compagnie française des petroles (6%), and the five American companies of Standard Oil of New Jersey (later Exxon), Mobil, Texaco, Gulf, and Standard Oil of California (8% each). Finding themselves completely frozen out of the agreement, the independent oil companies immediately began an intensive lobbying campaign with the Department of State. This campaign was led by Ralph K. Davies, president of the American Independent Oil Company (Aminoil), which was composed of interests held by nine independents, including Phillips Petroleum, Signal, and Ashland. In letters to both Secretary of State Dulles and Attorney-General Herbert Brownell, Jr., on October 15, 1954, Davies reminded the government of the mutual agreement reached when they had accepted the State Department's request not to do business with Musaddiq's Iran.[24] Davies, a former official of Standard Oil of California and the petroleum administrator for war (PAW), was an influential figure whose career had transcended private industry and government service. His representations were effective.

The five American majors each relinquished 1 percent of their shares, and the Iricon group was brought in for 5 percent ownership. The two largest Iricon participants were Richfield and Aminoil. The others were Signal, Hancock, Sohio, Getty, Tidewater, Atlantic, and San Jacinto. Mergers and business shifts later narrowed the Iricon group to Atlantic-Richfield, Reynolds, Charter, Getty, Continental, and Sohio.

When all the haggling and politicking finished, the oil agreement of 1954 brought the five major American oil companies directly into the Iranian petroleum picture. Through their own political efforts, a number of American independents also succeeded in obtaining a small piece of this very profitable business. Meanwhile, the British had succeeded in dodging the nationalization bullet and had obtained 40 percent of the shares in the newly created agreement. Furthermore, the AIOC, long hated by many Iranians, now found its influence camouflaged in a complex coalition that included other Western oil companies.

On the Iranian side, the consortium agreement resulted in dramatically larger revenues, which increased from $10 million in 1954 to $91 million in 1955 and to $285 million by 1960.[25] More importantly, the agreement opened the way for increased Iranian control over its own natural resources. This new state of affairs was seen in 1957 when the government of Iran passed a new comprehensive petroleum act that broadened and deepened the functions of the NIOC. In brief, the 1957 law empowered the NIOC to enter into agreements for petroleum exploration and production in areas other than the districts bound by the consortium agreement. This act opened up the offshore areas of the Persian Gulf to the NIOC and gave rise to joint venture agreements. Shortly after the 1957 act was promulgated, Enrico Mattei of the Italian state oil company, Ente Nazionale Idrocarburi (ENI), entered into negotiations with NIOC and signed a revolutionary new agreement through an ENI subsidiary known as AGIP. The new Iranian-Italian oil company, SIRIP, provided that both companies would share the profits *after* the taxes to the Iranian government had been deducted. In effect, this meant that Iran would receive 75 percent of the profits of the venture.[26]

Following the SIRIP breakthrough, Iran signed another joint venture agreement in June 1958 with Pan American International, a subsidiary of Standard Oil Company of Indiana. Then, in the mid-1960s, in a flurry of activity, NIOC signed further joint venture agreements with such American companies as Shell Oil, Tidewater, Skelly, Sunray DX, Kerr-McGee, Cities Service, Atlantic-Richfield, Superior Oil, Phillips Petroleum, Murphy Oil, and Union Oil. Such agreements were highly advantageous to Iran but were viewed with deep concern by both the U.S. government and the major international oil companies. Iranian leaders, on the other hand, praised these agreements and described them as indicators of their country's increasing independence. The shah took full credit for these joint ventures. He also felt, however, that these agreements helped turn the international oil companies against him and that, from then on, the oil companies sought to destroy him. In his own words:

> The international oil companies were long-time adversaries. After Mossadegh's defeat I roused their anger by negotiating an agreement with Italy's Enrico Mattei. . . . Our agreement, in and of itself, was not large but its terms were significant. Instead of splitting profits fifty-fifty as we had been doing, Mattei agreed to take only 25 percent for himself with Iran receiving 75 percent. Shortly afterwards I made the same arrangements with Standard Oil of Indiana. The fifty-fifty principle had been broken and Big Oil never forgave me. By 1959, two years after the ENI agreement, the first student demonstrations against me were orchestrated in, of all places, the United States. I suspected that Big Oil financed the demonstrations and that the CIA helped organize them.[27]

Although this fascinating interpretation explains much about the shah's political views, it also indicates the importance that Iranian leaders gave to the new joint venture agreements begun in 1957–58. In the eyes of many Iranians, these agreements were evidence of the injustice of the entire 1954 consortium accord. That, too, would one day have to be renegotiated and revised. Meanwhile it stood as a constant reminder to Iranian nationalists of continuing foreign influence and control in their country.

The Solidification of Pahlavi-American Relations in the 1950s

With the Pahlavi throne restored and an oil agreement signed, the Eisenhower-Dulles administration chose to pursue a policy of regime reinforcement in Iran. American foreign policymakers implemented this policy through a strong emphasis on economic and military aid. This aid was designed to strengthen the shah's government both against internal threats and against any threats that may have emanated from outside Iran's borders. Aid was also very shrewdly used as a reward for Iranian political actions with which the United States strongly approved. Only four days after the shah returned to Iran after his unplanned flight to Baghdad and Rome, Prime Minister Zahedi dashed off a letter to Washington urgently requesting emergency economic aid. In this August 26, 1953, letter, the general wrote:

> The assistance which the United States is already rendering Iran, helpful as it is, is unfortunately not sufficient in amount and character to tide Iran over the financial and economic crisis which I find it to be facing. The treasury is empty; foreign exchange resources are exhausted; the national economy is deteriorated. Iran needs

immediate financial aid to enable it to emerge from a state of economic and financial chaos.[28]

In sharp contrast to the month-long delay in responding to Musaddiq's urgent request for aid earlier that year, President Eisenhower responded immediately to Zahedi's letter. The President replied that "your request will receive our sympathetic consideration and I can assure you that we stand ready to assist you in achieving the aspirations for your country which you have outlined."[29] On September 3, the Foreign Operations Administration (FOA) announced that the United States would provide Iran with $23.4 million for technical assistance purposes. Two days later, President Eisenhower issued a press release announcing a $45 million grant for immediate economic assistance to Iran. The president concluded the press release by stating that "it is hoped that, with our assistance, there will be an increase in the internal stability of Iran which will allow the development of a healthy economy to which an early effective use of Iran's rich resources will contribute."[30]

The Eisenhower administration continued to give financial transfusions to the Pahlavi government throughout the decade. Between 1953 and 1960, these transfusions amounted to $567 million in economic aid and another $450 million in military aid. In short, over $1 billion of American aid was provided to Iran in this crucial seven-year period. Despite this largesse, neither the Iranian government nor the controlled and besieged opposition was pleased—for several reasons.

First, the shah and his advisers wanted an even greater commitment from the United States. They felt that the United States was dragging its feet in support of their government; both the shah and his ambassadors in Washington privately complained about this. The shah himself considered this policy to be an extension of what had occurred in 1949 when he felt that his desperate arguments for increasing aid fell on deaf ears in Washington. Still, the Iranian political elite's discontent here was muted and was part of the traditional Iranian style of always bargaining for more favorable outcomes. The tightening American commitment to Iran was understood.

More serious discontent came from the Iranian middle classes and from those who passively and sullenly opposed the rule of the shah, Bakhtiar, and Zahedi. Their complaints were threefold. First, throughout the decade they argued that the United States was using its aid program to gain control over policy-making in Iran. Several times the United States granted aid as a reward for favorable actions taken by Iran. Initial aid announcements were made, for example, immediately after Musaddiq was overthrown and the shah was restored to his throne. Those who opposed the shah clearly saw this as part of the payment for Musaddiq's defeat. In addition, a major aid package of $127 million was announced on November 2, 1954, just after Iran had grudgingly agreed to the consortium agreement. Many Iranians saw this as the payoff for their country's acceptance of the new oil arrangements; the consortium agreement had been signed on September 19, passed by both the Majlis and the Senate in October, and promulgated as law by the shah on October 29. The timing of the early November aid package was not lost on the Iranians, nor should it have been. A National Security Council report of late 1953 stated that "granting of other than emergency aid prior to an oil settlement may make Iran less interested in coming to an early settlement and at the same time harm our relations with the U.K."[31]

The United States made other important gestures of financial assistance in 1955 after Iran had joined the Baghdad Pact and in 1958 after Iran continued to support this Western alliance system when it became CENTO (Central Treaty Organization) following the dramatic revolution in Iraq. This pattern of American influence whereby badly needed economic aid was offered as a political reward was thus established in the 1950s and was strongly resented by many Iranians over the next two and a half decades.

A second complaint of Iranian middle- and lower-class nationalists was America's contribution to increased corruption in Iranian society. After the fall of Musaddiq, the 1950s came to be known in Iran as a decade of decadence. The huge infusions of American aid into Iran were administered by an inexperienced and suddenly bloated American bureaucracy. As we will see later, this contributed to conspicuous corruption of many different kinds and alienated many Iranians. Aid was seen as benefiting the rich and, despite the best of American intentions, seldom dribbled down to the poorer echelons of society.

Finally, Iranian critics severely criticized the heavy military and security emphasis of the U.S. aid program. Besides the funds targeted for internal security purposes, there was a special concern in Washington about possible Soviet aggression against Iran. This concern translated into an increasingly heavy emphasis on the military dimensions of aid, especially following the overthrow of Iraq's rulers in July 1958. This event shook the shah, who used it in his representations to the United States for increased military assistance. Within Iran, many groups argued that aid was being wasted in the construction of a police state while the social, educational, and economic conditions of the Iranian people remained primitive.

Despite these doubts and disaffections that existed beneath the surface of the Iranian political system, American diplomats were optimistic, almost exuberant, about the situation in Iran. In Washington in December 1953, Assistant Secretary of State Henry Byroade paraphrased the poet Nemazi, saying, "out of the black cloud of the severance of diplomatic relations between Iran and the United Kingdom white rain has descended." He went on to state that "now, from the bitter drug of the past, His Majesty the Shah and Prime Minister Zahedi are producing sweet remedies."[32] The United States increasingly helped concoct these remedies as Iranian-American relations increased and deepened in all areas and at all levels.

The highest-ranking American and Iranian officials began increased official migrations to one another's country. Vice President Richard Nixon and Pat Nixon traveled to Iran in December 1953 for an important official visit. The Nixon visit was a strong sign of American support for the shah's regime. This was Nixon's first visit to Iran, and while there he strengthened his personal relations with the shah while familiarizing himself with a country he saw as an American ally and bastion against communism. Both Nixon and the shah viewed this visit as the initial step in a treasured friendship. This friendship was to have deep implications for Iranian-American relations as they developed over the next twenty-five years.

One year after the first Nixon visit, the shah and Queen Soraya traveled to New York and spent two months visiting the United States. During this "unofficial visit," the shah met with President Eisenhower and numerous other influential Americans with whom he renewed old friendships and built new ones. Since his country had only recently received a large American grant of assistance, the monarch pressed somewhat less for aid on this occasion than he had done in his 1949 visit.

In 1955 the United States supported the formation of the Baghdad Pact, an economic and political alliance cobbled together by Great Britain and including the northern tier countries of Turkey, Pakistan, Iraq, and Iran. Although the United States did not become a formal member of the pact, it contributed financial assistance and had representation on three of the standing committees. The Baghdad Pact was in complete line with Secretary of State John Foster Dulles's policy of forcing as many Afro-Asian countries as possible to commit themselves to pro-Western treaty agreements and formal defense pacts. Although this policy ran against the strong currents of neutralism and nonalignment then prevalent in the Third World and alienated leaders such as Gamal Abdel Nasser in Egypt, Dulles pressured for such commitments wherever he could. The shah of Iran came aboard, although he was clearly a bit piqued that the United States itself refused to make the same kind of official commitment to the Baghdad Pact.

American leaders wanted Iran as a central member of the Baghdad Pact primarily for strategic and military reasons having to do with the Soviet Union. An important memorandum prepared by the Joint Chiefs of Staff Joint Intelligence Committee on April 13, 1955, graphically describes the position that dominated the thinking of key Washington policymakers through the 1970s concerning the importance of Iran to United States interests.

> From the viewpoint of attaining U.S. military objectives in the Middle East, the natural defensive barrier provided by the Zagros Mountains must be retained under Allied control indefinitely. Because Western Iran includes the Zagros Mountain barrier, geographically, Iran is the most important country in the Middle East, excluding Turkey. Iranian participation in a regional defense organization would permit the member countries to take full advantage collectively of the natural defensive barrier in Western Iran and would permit utilization of logistical facilities of the area. The relative importance of Iran in relation to other countries of the Middle East would be significantly increased if she became a partner in a regional defense organization which included Turkey, Iraq and Pakistan.[33]

In the fall of 1955, Congressman Clement Zablocki led a special study mission of six members of the House of Representatives to the Middle East. During its stay in Iran, the mission noted the strong opposition to the alliance that existed in the country. "Arguments against adherence were based partly on nationalistic appeals, partly on reliance on the traditional Iranian policy of neutrality, and partly on fears of possible Soviet countermoves which might endanger the political and economic security of Iran." The American delegation therefore urged increased U.S. military assistance to Iran. It argued that the shah had taken a personally dangerous position; in fact, "he has staked his own life as well as that of his country in making this choice."[34]

When revolution swept through Iraq in July 1958, the Baghdad Pact lost Baghdad; the old agreement now became the Central Treaty Organization (CENTO) with the same membership minus revolutionary Iraq. The Baghdad Pact-CENTO alliance was never popular in Iran. The shah himself questioned its value, given both America's reluctance to join and the fact that the United States had done little to impede the revolution in Iraq. Iranian nationalists, middle-class progressives, and the religious lower middle classes all opposed this alliance, which was in their eyes just the latest example of Western imperial control.

The fact that England was the central member of the agreement and that the United States stood silently behind the British reminded them of the style of Western intervention that had prevailed since the 1940s.

Dulles's goal here was to build a solid bar of allied countries along the southern borders of the Soviet Union while at the same time isolating Nasser's Egypt from other important Arab countries. Many Iranians well understood this strategy; it gave them more reason than they already had to admire Nasser's independent policies. The shah's adherence to CENTO was both a cause and an effect of his rivalry with and strong dislike for President Nasser. Because of his own doubts about the strength and significance of this pact, the shah worked to develop other more reliable ties with the United States. Between 1957 and 1959, there was a flurry of intense American-Iranian political activity.

In 1957 Iran announced its enthusiasm for the Eisenhower Doctrine, which was designed to protect the territorial integrity and independence of nations requesting aid when threatened either by armed communist invasion from without or by subversion from within. To reinforce support of this doctrine, former chairman of the House Foreign Affairs Committee, James P. Richards, led an American congressional delegation to the Middle East in the spring of 1957. In Iran the delegation was assured of Iranian support for the Eisenhower Doctrine, and in return Iran was promised increased economic and military assistance. Iran was one of the first and one of the few Third World countries that publicly endorsed the Eisenhower Doctrine.

In January 1958 Secretary of State Dulles visited Iran; he met with the shah and the prime minister on his way to Turkey for meetings of CENTO (then called the Middle East Treaty Organization). This visit was especially significant because in his 1953 tour of the region Dulles had indicated his disapproval of the Musaddiq government by pointedly omitting Tehran from his itinerary. Six months after the Dulles trip to Iran, in late June and early July of 1958, the shah made his third trip to the United States. Muhammad Reza Shah had divorced Soraya in March and was accompanied by his powerful sister, Princess Ashraf. Both Pahlavis worked the Washington political and social circuit. According to the *Washington Post*, the shah "gave a dinner at the Mayflower Hotel, in which 20 pounds of caviar was served on gold, and he also gave a little party for Iranian students here. His sister's diamonds knocked everybody's eyes out."[35] Meanwhile, at the request of the Iranians themselves, over forty leading American businessmen met with the shah. He strongly urged them to make major investments in Iran, maintaining that the only industries that the Iranian state would continue to own were petroleum and steel.

The shah's visit coincided closely with the July 14, 1958, revolution in Iraq. The revolution accelerated the American aid program to Iran, and military considerations began to dominate U.S. thinking on Iran. In October 1958, the secretaries of Treasury and Defense visited Tehran, and on March 5, 1959, the United States and Iran signed a bilateral defense agreement that strongly guaranteed an American military commitment to Iran: "In the case of aggression against Iran, the Government of the United States of America, in accordance with the Constitution of the United States of America, will take such appropriate action, including the use of armed forces, as may be mutually agreed upon and as is envisaged in the Joint Resolution to Promote Peace and Stability in the Middle East, in order to assist the Government of Iran at its request."[36]

This agreement, following on the heels of the Baghdad Pact, alienated the Soviet Union, which had been actively courting Iran and had been seeking to sign a fifty-year nonaggression pact of its own with Iran. The shah had in fact encouraged the Soviet Union in this quest by maintaining close diplomatic contact with the USSR. In June–July 1956 the shah and Queen Soraya had made a state visit to Moscow, and over the next two years there was considerable diplomatic and economic interaction between the two countries. The Soviet Union and Iran signed a half-dozen treaties and trade agreements in this period of especially warm relations. The Soviets were obviously attempting to neutralize the threat of the Baghdad Pact. The shah, for his part, was pursuing a policy designed to build bargaining power with the West so that his support would not be taken for granted. He stated confidentially to private American visitors that he communicated with the Soviet Union in order to increase America's political, military, and economic commitment to his government

The 1959 bilateral defense agreement with the United States ended the thaw in Iran-Soviet relations. The Soviet Union accused the United States of attempting to convert Iran into its own military base from which it could exploit Iran's petroleum resources and threaten the independence of other Middle Eastern countries.[37] The United States, on the other hand, was delighted with the new agreement, since it represented the culmination of five years of tightening Iranian-American relationships.

The decade ended with a visit on December 14, 1959, to Tehran by President Eisenhower, who was in the midst of an eleven-nation tour. Although in Iran for only six hours, the president made two important public statements, one at the airport on arrival and one to the Majlis. Besides stressing the special partnership and togetherness that marked Iranian-American relations, Eisenhower also emphasized the need for peace, justice, freedom, and genuine economic and social development. And he warned the Iranian leaders that "military strength alone will not bring about peace and justice."[38] In this message in his last days as president, Eisenhower provided a remarkable preview of the new emphasis that would distinguish the foreign policy of the successor administration of President John F. Kennedy.

Patterns of Corruption and American Developmental Aid

With the fall of Musaddiq, the United States began to pour men, money, and machines into Iran at unprecedented rates. This was the heyday of the American belief in enabling allies in Asia, Africa, the Middle East, and Latin America to solve their national problems through massive doses of financial assistance. The panacea to all problems was considered to be the drive to reach take-off points to self-sustaining economic growth. American leaders emphasized the need for economic planning and rational administration. In the process, little attention was paid to human considerations, social reform, or political development. For the policymakers in Washington, the key political determinant was negative: Aid recipients were expected to be strongly anticommunist; if so, they qualified for assistance.

American private and public economic and aid missions to Iran in the 1950s were numerous and varied. Privately sponsored projects included expanded activities of the Near East Foundation; the Ford Foundation/Harvard University advisory group attached to the Plan Organization; the American Friends of the Middle East; the Iran Foundation, which funded the Shiraz Medical Center; and the Lafayette College consortium, which was charged with the development of a technical college in Abadan. Western banking and investment firms also entered the Iranian financial market in ever increasing numbers. Chase Manhattan Bank and Lazard Brothers became partners in a development bank in early 1958. The major private entrepreneurial venture was a project signed in 1957 between the Development and Resources Corporation of New York and the Plan Organization in Iran. This project was a massive plan to develop Khuzistan province through the construction of a series of dams and a complex new irrigation system. The American corporation was headed by David Lilienthal and Gordon Clapp, the two dynamic entrepreneurs who had directed the huge Tennessee Valley Authority project. Their Iranian counterpart was Abol Hassan Ebtehaj, a forceful and knowledgeable banker-economist who had become managing director of the Plan Organization in Iran in 1954.

David Lilienthal was a liberal visionary who truly believed in an entrepreneurial capitalism that would result in improving the living standards of the masses. Ebtehaj shared these goals and was a tough, hard-driving, uncompromising man. He refused to tolerate incompetence, delay, or professional mediocrity. He was particularly opposed to the intervention of other officials or offices into his projects. It was Ebtehaj who took issue in 1946 with Arthur Millspaugh's activities and who was primarily responsible for Millspaugh's dismissal. After his first meeting with Ebtehaj in Istanbul in September 1955, Lilienthal described him as "intense, cultivated, and utterly sincere. He is positively incandescent, impetuous, full of feeling. Without this kind of missionary zeal, I wonder if anything can be done to change the present conditions of what was once a great country."[39] Together, Ebtehaj and Lilienthal formed an impressive team of technical missionaries. Between them, they convinced the shah of the value of the project, and with royal support they immediately began this mammoth task.

Because the shah initially backed the Khuzistan project and because Lilienthal himself became an American appendage to the technocratic elite of Iran, David Lilienthal developed a strong loyalty to Pahlavi rule and became an extremely effective voice for the shah in the United States. His idealism and dynamic commitment to technocratic success blinded him to the realities of power, poverty, and corruption in the Iranian bureaucracy. As time passed, political and bureaucratic rivals in the bureaucracy slowly, quietly, and effectively undermined the work of the Plan Organization and especially of the Lilienthal-Ebtehaj Khuzistan development scheme. The more that Ebtehaj fought and thrashed in the bureaucratic snare, the more entangled he became. He resigned in 1959 after the Plan Organization was put under the direction of the prime minister's office and its budget was cut sharply. After a time of employment as a private banker, he was arrested and imprisoned for a period in 1961. Despite construction of the enormous Dez Dam and other hard-earned, expensive accomplishments, the Khuzistan project had mixed success, and the project gradually ground to a halt after Ebtehaj's fall.

Ebtehaj's forceful, prickly personality had helped to destroy him politically and in the process had nullified many of his programs. Like other strong political figures in Iran, Ebtehaj's increasing influence began to alarm the shah, who quietly withdrew his support for Ebtehaj and his projects. The American team that had been attached to Ebtehaj was obviously also weakened and discredited. Muhammad Reza Shah himself, when asked about what happened to Ebtehaj, said "I don't understand this man. Iran has been good to him, yet he doesn't like Iranians. He calls us all thieves. He doesn't seem to believe in what we are doing. The worst thing is that he doesn't seem to like his country."[40] In the end, the shah softly but effectively undercut Ebtehaj both because of his attacks on corruption and because his popularity had begun to rival that of the shah himself. His close ties with the United States also troubled the insecure monarch.

Lilienthal, an extraordinary, dedicated man who made eleven working trips to Iran between 1956 and 1962, stayed with the project. Unaware of the subtle but deadly political game that was being played around him and his project, he ceaselessly defended the shah and the Pahlavi regime to key American decision makers in Washington and New York. He lobbied for the shah with influential and somewhat skeptical friends such as Edward R. Murrow, Walter Lippman, and Henry Luce. He continued to play this role even though it was the shah who engineered the dismissal and destruction of Ebtehaj. After others had cautioned him about the shah and his policies following Ebtehaj's defeat, Lilienthal stubbornly stated in his diaries that "I really believe this man."[41] When the shah made a successful presentation to the Council on Foreign Relations in New York on April 19, 1962, Lilienthal was ecstatic. He described the ruler's performance as "an absolute knockout, a smash hit and no mistake. I have just this moment returned from the late-afternoon meeting and am still bubbling with the excitement and I confess, the pride that his performance gave me. He impressed that group as no Prime Minister or intellectual has in my experience."[42]

In Iran, however, the shah, always using other personalities, had undercut the project in which Lilienthal and Clapp had invested so much of their lives. He orchestrated the appointment of Plan Organization heads most opposed to Ebtehaj and the Khuzistan project. One of the most implacable of these enemies, Ahmad Aramesh, publicly stated to the Majlis in April 1962 that under Ebtehaj the Plan Organization had paid Lilienthal and Clapp 7 billion rials ($100 million) since 1956 without their having accounted "for even a single rial."[43] These unfounded but damaging charges were contagious, and soon American congressmen also began to question and criticize Lilienthal and Clapp's Development and Resources Corporation.

This episode demonstrates several points very well. First, it indicates the increasing involvement of the United States with Iran. In this case, the Khuzistan project was international in scope, but its leadership and vision were American. Second, the American leadership linked itself directly to the shah, whom Lilienthal met during each of his numerous visits to Iran. The Iranian people viewed this association as elitist and exclusionary. Third, the American advisers and their project inevitably became caught up in the web of Iranian politics, and, although they had the greatest technical expertise in the world at their disposal, they lacked even the most fundamental understanding of Iranian personalities and politics. Fourth, as a result, their technical effectiveness was necessarily limited, and they became pawns in the complex game of personal politics and power in Iran. Finally, the American project leaders, who were generally enlightened, dedicated individuals, were unwittingly used by the shah to present his policy views and to polish his image back in the United States.

David Lilienthal and Gordon Clapp were experienced, sensitive, and humanitarian in their perspectives. In many ways their mission represented the best that America had to offer. Although their program met with limited technical success, it was also very costly economically, politically, and personally. The fact that they met with many problems and some considerable failure (not the least of which was the political career and reputation of Abol Hassan Ebtehaj) indicates what the experience of other American missions must have been like.

The Development and Resources Corporation's Khuzistan project found itself in rivalry with the technical assistance program of the American government. This tension was especially prevalent during the ambassadorship of Selden Chapin, who represented the United States in Iran during the three years between July 1955 and June 1958. Given the situation that had obtained among U.S. agencies in Iran in the 1940s, this intra-American rivalry was not surprising. Lilienthal and Clapp had their own direct line to the shah. Their program was not dependent on American government largesse or subject to American bureaucratic regulation. The embassy, by contrast, was skeptical about Ebtehaj's position, which it saw as politically exposed and personally tenuous. Diplomats were also somewhat more realistic about the shah's internal political game plan. Lilienthal resented this embassy position, and he put his complete trust in Ebtehaj and the shah and the strong support that he felt the latter had committed to the former.

Furthermore, the Lilienthal-Clapp team differed decidedly with the U.S. government approach on two grounds. First, they felt that American economic aid programs were spread too thinly across the

Iranian landscape. Such programs, they reasoned, might generate visibility but only visibility linked with superficial success. Secondly, they disagreed with the American government policy of providing its aid through the serpentine, corrupt local bureaucracy. By feeding economic aid through the Iranian ministries, they argued, it was inevitable that inefficiency, ineffectiveness, and an increasing level of corruption would result. There is considerable evidence that these concerns were well founded.

The primary American technical and economic aid program to Iran was the Point Four agreement, which began as a result of a memorandum of understanding signed in October 1950. This was expanded in January 1952 during the Musaddiq period, and with the Pahlavi restoration it became a central part of the American presence in Iran. Point Four in Iran was part of the International Cooperation Administration (ICA), or U.S. Agency for International Development (AID), and was also administered under the titles of Technical Cooperation Administration (TCA) and United States Operations Mission (USOM) in Iran. This complex American organization, the largest of its kind in the world, focused on technical aid in the fields of agriculture, health, and education, and its activities were spread throughout the Iranian countryside. In the 1950s American financial commitment to these aid programs increased rapidly (see table 1).[44] Between 1952 and 1956 unprecedented numbers of American technical advisers moved into Iran. According to published Foreign Service lists, in January 1952 fewer than 10 technical advisers were attached to the U.S. Embassy. By October 1952, the number had increased to 26, but it was after the fall of Musaddiq that the major increases occurred. In October 1953, the number of ICA advisers listed by name reached 133, and by January of 1956 the number had ballooned to 207. The actual number of the ICA

Table 1   U.S. Technical Aid to Iran,   1951–1956   (Millions   of Dollars)

Fiscal Year	Aid
1951	1.3
1952	23.6
1953	23.2
1954	84.8
1955	75.5
1956	73.0

staff at the beginning of 1956 was 308 technicians and support personnel, including almost 100 local nationals. Another 100 technicians were employed under contracts with American educational and professional organizations. Above and beyond this were another 3,800 Iranian employees working for American missions and programs.[45]

Yet even these numbers were insufficient to direct and control the millions of dollars of aid that were pumped into Iran. The result was waste, uncertainty, equipment failure, logistical disaster, social disruption, and financial corruption. In 1956 the House Committee on Government Operations carried out an extensive congressional investigation of U.S. aid programs to Iran. The proceedings of these hearings, which were printed in a 1,268-page document, are revealing.

Congressional and administrative critics of the aid to Iran program charged financial irregularities and the misuse of funds, citing numerous cases in point. Irregularities had begun by 1952 and continued in various forms as time went by. The comptroller of the mission had written a series of detailed memorandums to his superiors in Washington, documenting a number of serious charges. He had soon afterwards been relieved of his duties by the head of the mission in Tehran. The entire mission was torn by dissent and internal rivalry, aggravated by the fact that the U.S. Embassy provided little support for the aid missions and hindered rather than helped their operation. The fluid state of the Iranian social and political scene only made matters worse. In an attempt to move responsibilities more to the Iranian side, much of the decision-making power of the aid program was transferred to Iranian agencies in 1956. This proved to be disastrous as the post-Musaddiq governments set new records for bureaucratic corruption.

In January 1957 the investigating congressional committee produced its conclusions in a document containing nineteen points of criticism. The first four points capture the nature of these conclusions:

1. United States aid and technical-assistance programs in Iran which, between 1951 and 1956, totaled a quarter billion dollars, were administered in a loose, slipshod, and unbusinesslike manner.
2. The so-called expanded technical-assistance program which began in January 1952 and resulted in United States obligations of over $100 million in a 5-year period, was neither technical assistance nor economic development, but an ad hoc method of keeping the Iranian economy afloat during the years of the oil dispute.
3. The expenditure of technical-assistance funds during these years

was undertaken without regard to such basic requirements of prudent management as adequate controls and procedures, with the inevitable consequences that it is now impossible—with any accuracy—to tell what became of these funds. The resulting opportunities for waste and loss of funds were considerable, but the extent to which loss and waste actually occurred cannot be determined since management practices and control procedures were so poor that records of the operation, especially in the early years, are not reliable.

4. Amounts requested for United States aid to Iran seem to have been picked out of the air. There is no evidence that they were based on advance study of what the Iranian economy needed, the amount it could absorb, or programs which could be intelligently administered by the United States personnel available at the time to expend the funds.[46]

Although these conclusions demonstrate the real problems that American technocrats and technicians were having in Iran, they were a bit harsh. In such areas as medicine and agriculture the American advisers had tangible success. Also, the Washington bureaucracy had little understanding of the Iranian bureaucracy and therefore failed to comprehend the flexibility and independence essential to any successful aid mission in Iran. The American advisers inevitably found themselves trapped within the labyrinth of traditional Iranian bureaucratic politics. And in this labyrinth they lost their sense of direction and began to turn on one another. In the words of the chief of the Health Division of the American mission: "Are we not fiddling while Iran burns?"[47]

The central problem was the lack of experience and understanding of the working context that was Iran. Washington provided little preparation. If Lilienthal and Clapp, with their experience, personal commitment, and direct connections at the very highest level of the Iranian political system, only met with limited success, it was not surprising that the American government advisers were confused, disoriented, and generally ineffective. The sudden transfusion of American dollars and advisers into Iranian society, coming after the overthrow of Musaddiq and the signing of the 1954 consortium agreement, understandably alienated many Iranians. That the aid was being administered through and by a particularly corrupt government (and one that many believed was put in place by the British and the Americans) only deepened the alienation. The intramural rivalries, the ignorance of subjects Iranian, and the close association of the Americans with the Iranian regime and its administrative arms all combined to decrease further the popularity of the official American in Iran.

Even Congressman Zablocki's study mission of 1955, which was extremely praiseworthy of the new Iranian-American link and which uncritically defended the shah's government, sensed an increasing resentment of Americans in Iran. In its report summary, the team wrote that these growing resentments were such that "we simply have to do a better job with our human relations in our various aid programs. The key thing is not the amount of aid, it is the manner. It is not enough to analyze figures; we must do a better job of analyzing people."[48]

The Political, Economic, and Military Entanglement of the 1950s

The large reservoir of goodwill for America in Iran began to dry up in the 1950s. After playing a direct, dramatic role in the overthrow of Muhammad Musaddiq, the United States joined the British in championing an oil agreement that was very coolly received by most Iranians. Then the United States moved in behind the new government of Iran with unprecedented amounts of economic and military aid. The introduction of these aid programs coincided with an increase in political oppression and economic corruption in the country.

As the decade continued, the United States began to take the place of the British in the eyes of Iranian nationalists. Now America was considered to be the primary external force rearranging the Iranian political landscape. An excellent example of this occurred in 1958. As the decade progressed, the shah's new tactics of control generated increasing opposition. The government of Iran in 1958 accused Gen. Valiullah Qarani, the chief of military intelligence, of planning a coup. Among those rumored to have been aware of the alleged plot were a number of National Front sympathizers and Ali Amini, who had become Iranian ambassador to the United States after playing a critical role in fashioning the 1954 consortium agreement. Arrested early in 1958 along with over two dozen associates, General Qarani was quickly brought to trial before a military court and sentenced to three years' imprisonment. Given the serious nature of the charge, this sentence was relatively light.

General Qarani apparently had become critical of corruption in the regime and had prepared a sixty-page report implicating leading military-security figures such as SAVAK head Teymour Bakhtiar, Chief of Police Alavi-yi Muqaddam, and Gen. Alavi Kia as being at the center of the ring of corruption. The shah simply passed the confidential report along to the accused three after he had himself been told by informants that Qarani was plotting a coup. Qarani's opponents, which reportedly included the British, also managed to plant the rumor that Qarani enjoyed American support. When the U.S. Embassy made the strongest possible denials of these clearly fictitious charges, Qarani was quietly released from prison.[49]

The Iranian intelligentsia bought the message in the rumor mill and was convinced that the United States had been involved in the Qarani incident. The evidence they used for their position was the fact that the general received such a light sentence. The strength and persistence of this conspiracy theory is seen in the fact that, despite Qarani's own denials of American complicity, well-informed Iranian observers as late as 1979 were still arguing American involvement. Their arguments were based on little more than speculation and the relatively mild sentence.[50] In fact, Qarani was personally deeply critical of the regime's policies and corruption.

This episode reveals the willingness of Iranians to believe in American involvement in whatever political activities that now took place in Iran. In their eyes, the United States had become the primary external interventionist force in Iran. Although the British were still considered cleverly influential, they were viewed as the manipulators behind the scenes, while America was clearly considered to be the force out front. The hundreds of economic and military advisers now present in Iran provided continual visual reinforcement of this position.

In some ways the Americans, professionally competent but ill-prepared for their tasks in the Iranian context, were not unlike the British who had worked for years for the Anglo-Iranian Oil Company in Iran. Although the U.S. advisers carried a certain refreshing enthusiasm to their work, they were somewhat more naive and clumsy than the British. Both Western groups, however, suffered from superiority complexes. In a sensitive article written in 1958, a Britisher with long-time experience in Iran stated that "it is the misfortune of so many foreigners in Iran that they have gone there in a superior, even patronizing role. The business man with his glossy Western products, the technical expert with his higher knowledge, even the missionary with his unspoken condemnation of the country's faith, all run the risk of evoking in those with whom they have to deal the reaction of the 'underdog.'"[51] It was in the 1950s that the Iranians began to view themselves as the underdog confronted by an American imperial giant.

Although the religious establishment in Qum remained politically quiescent, numerous younger Shi'i religious leaders were opposed to the shah's style of rule and now began to resent growing American presence and U.S. policy. These included mujtahids such as Ayatollah Ruhollah Khomeini in Qum and the more scholarly and renowned

Ayatollah Hadi Milani in Mashhad. Through their religious teachings, which always carried significant social and political content, they profoundly influenced a generation of younger members of the *ulama* (Islamic clerics) against the rule of the shah and the American backing for this rule. This deep-seated opposition went deeper than that of the middle-class intelligentsia since it was based on more than an opposition to oppression and corruption. It rested on a fundamental distrust of the Western model of politics and the Western way of life.

The religious-guided Iranian masses (and even some significant groups within the intelligentsia) were already deeply critical of the Western alternative. This view rested on "the apparent wholesale collapse of morality in the West, revealing itself in two world wars, the rise of totalitarian states, both Fascist and Communist, the wave of genocide, the threat of the atom and hydrogen bombs, as well as the (to Iranians) vulgarity of so much popular Western culture as displayed in magazines and films."[52] The sudden presence of Americans everywhere in Iran placed Western culture before the eyes of all Iranians. At times, the exhibit was garish, even obscene in the conservative environment of Iranian mosques and villages.

The perceived American alliance with the shah, which coincided with increasing levels of corruption in the society, confirmed this critical view. As the 1950s ended, Iran scholar T. Cuyler Young perceptively summarized the state of affairs between Iran and America:

> During the last decade . . . , the United States has furnished Iran more than a billion dollars in economic and military aid. Like it or not, justly or unjustly, this has served to identify the United States with the Shah's regime, together with responsibility for what that regime has done, or failed to do. Also, however unjustly, popular opinion holds that the sums have been wasted as far as helping the common people of Iran is concerned.
>
> For this reason the United States is distrusted, if not indeed thoroughly disliked, by all those who have come to distrust the Shah and oppose his policies. Among these anti-Western, anti-United States groups are those who still think and feel in the neutralist tradition, who deplore such complete alliance with, but especially dependence upon, the United States. This is not so much because of fear of what Russia may do by way of reaction, though this is real; it is rather their fear of becoming so beholden to, and identified with, the United States that the nation loses its independence and freedom of action. Fiercely patriotic and nationalistic, they are suspicious of any policy that might give any great power undue hold upon them.[53]

Young's sharp conclusions were supported by Abol Hassan Ebtehaj in a speech before the International Industrial Conference in San Francisco in September 1961. This speech contributed to Ebtehaj's arrest and imprisonment a few months later. Ebtehaj seriously criticized the concept of bilateral aid programs, using the Iranian-American example as the major case in point. In his words: "I can think of no better summary of all the disadvantages and weaknesses of the bilateral system than the modern history of my own country. Not so very many years ago in Iran, the United States was loved and respected as no other country, and without having given a penny of aid. Now, after more than $1 billion of loans and grants, American is neither loved nor respected; she is distrusted by most people, and hated by many."[54]

The 1960 American presidential elections were closely monitored by Muhammad Reza Shah, whose sympathies, not surprisingly, were for Richard Nixon and a Republican victory. When Democrat John F. Kennedy won the close contest, the shah became deeply concerned. Domestic unrest and opposition were growing. His attempt to tighten control through the use of a growing contingent of security forces seemed only to deepen burgeoning opposition. The attempt to coopt the opposition through the artificial creation of political parties from above had backfired. Even President Eisenhower, in his short visit to Tehran, had publicly advised Iran against an overemphasis on military solutions and expenditures and had stressed the importance of social justice and reform. The shah and his advisers were nervous about their political future. And they were especially apprehensive about the position that the new Democratic administration would take toward Iran. As events were to indicate, the Pahlavi elite had good reason to be apprehensive—on both counts.

4 An Interlude of Reform: John F. Kennedy and Iran, 1961–1963

In his inaugural address of January 20, 1961, John F. Kennedy summarized in somewhat idealistic terms the new Democratic administration's policy toward the Third World:

> To those people in the huts and villages of half the globe struggling to break the bonds of mass misery, we pledge our best efforts to help themselves, for whatever period is required—not because the communists may be doing it, not because we seek their votes, but because it is right. If a free society cannot help the many who are poor, it cannot save the few who are rich.[1]

Although an element of altruism in the Kennedy program was evident, Kennedy's main reason for supporting political reform and economic development in the Third World was to increase American influence while nullifying the appeal of Soviet communism. The Kennedy administration particularly sought to cut back on military aid programs and to replace them with economic development funds. In fact, the New Frontier years effectively altered the pattern of the priority of military aid established over the previous four years.[2]

John F. Kennedy adopted a foreign policy designed to encourage peaceful reform from above in order to forestall violent revolution from below. The centerpiece of this program was the Alliance for Progress (Alianza para Progreso), announced on March 13, 1961, and directed toward Latin America. This dramatic program sought to pressure decrepit, unpopular Latin regimes to introduce reform in order to avoid revolution. The driving force behind the Alliance for Progress was Fidel Castro's victory in Cuba. Kennedy and his advisers considered that economic programs focusing on agrarian reform and improved housing, health, and educational systems were the best way to head off future Cubas in Latin America.

Besides the policy of reform from above, the Kennedy administration adopted a second tactic in its attempt to deflect the communist thrust into the Third World. If reform failed, then friendly elites were to employ military force to smother popular uprisings. A significant counterinsurgency program came into being during the Kennedy years, and friendly elites were encouraged to adopt these methods when in difficulty. In Latin America, the key example was President Romula Betancourt of Venezuela, whose widely published agrarian reform in the service of preserving the traditional power structure led ultimately to mass demonstrations that resulted in the gunning down of many Venezuelans in the streets of Caracas.

John F. Kennedy's emphasis on economic development, agrarian reform, and democratic revolution was ultimately an attempt to preserve the political status quo in countries challenged by communism. In Latin America, the threat was seen to be communist Cuba; in Vietnam, the challenge emanated from China; and in Iran, it was the Soviet Union itself that worried the American administration.

The Kennedy Presidency and the Shah of Iran

President John Kennedy's policy toward Iran was a clear and consistent application of his general program—reform from above ultimately buttressed by the military might of besieged Third World regimes. In this sense, Iran policy was a direct if unspoken application of the Alliance for Progress program developed for Latin America. If and when mass disruption occurred, then the principles of counterinsurgency were to be used as they had been in Venezuela.

Kennedy first became concerned about the political stability of Pahlavi Iran in April 1961, less than one month after he had first announced the idea of the Alliance for Progress. This was when Kennedy heard the results of Walter Lippmann's discussions with Premier Nikita Khrushchev at Khrushchev's Black Sea villa on April 10, 1961.

In these discussions Khrushchev singled out Iran as an example of a country headed for revolution despite its very weak communist party. In his words, the misery of the masses and the corruption of the government added up to certain revolution. "You will assert that the Shah has been overthrown by the Communists, and we shall be very glad to have it thought in the world that all the progressive people in Iran recognize that we are the leaders of the progress of mankind."[3] Summarizing his talks with Khrushchev about Iran, Lippmann not only emphasized the nature of the threat but also reinforced Kennedy's policy predispositions.

> In his [Khrushchev's] mind, Iran is the most immediate example of the inevitable movement of history in which he believes so completely. He would not admit that we can divert this historic

movement by championing liberal democratic reforms. Nothing that any of us can say can change his mind, which is that of a true believer, except a demonstration in some country that we can promote deep democratic reforms.[4]

John Kennedy rose to the challenge by selecting Iran as precisely that country in which the United States could and would help promote such reforms.

That Iran in the early 1960s was the scene of considerable political turmoil lent urgency to Kennedy's decision to push for reform. Kennedy relied heavily on Supreme Court Justice William O. Douglas as well as on his own brother, Attorney General Robert Kennedy, for information and advice on Iran. Douglas had a long association with Iran; he had traveled and lived among the villagers and tribesmen there. Having seen the society from the bottom up, he was skeptical about the shah's style of governance. Robert Kennedy had been intrigued by the opinions of the young Iranians studying in the United States and was the rare example of a high-level American official who took the time to listen carefully to their position. In one incident, the Iranian ambassador in Washington asked Secretary of State Dean Rusk to have twenty Iranian students deported because they were communists. When Rusk approached the attorney general, Kennedy spoke with Douglas and ordered an FBI investigation that cleared all the students of the charge of communism. When Douglas asked Kennedy about the final resolution of the matter, the attorney general said "I just told Rusk to go chase himself."[5]

In the early months of 1961, a chorus of influential voices both inside and outside the new administration warned of possible trouble in Iran. At the Department of State, Iran analyst John W. Bowling wrote two thoughtful nine-page analyses of Iran's internal political situation. In the first paper, prepared in early February, Bowling carefully analyzed the gathering opposition forces in Iran and recognized the unpopularity of the shah's regime among the burgeoning middle classes. After discussing the advantages of a Western policy shift of support for a nationalist, more popularly based, Musaddiqist coup, Bowling dismissed it as too costly since it would carry with it the following "probable" disadvantages: (1) the breakup of CENTO; (2) the withdrawal of the U.S. military mission from Iran; (3) the abandonment of the current economic stabilization program; (4) undetermined moves to extract more money from the oil consortium; (5) a great blow to the global prestige of the U.S.; (6) an opportunity for communist infiltration into the regime; (7) the loss of Iran's friendly United Nations vote; (8) Neutralism as a positive policy; and (9) the acceptance of Soviet aid. In conclusion, Bowling argued: "These probable short-range costs would have to be balanced against the long-range advantages of a more popularly based regime in Iran. The cost does not appear to be worth the advantages, but a proper appreciation of the choice could only be made in the light of global national security considerations."[6]

In his second paper, prepared on March 20, 1961, Bowling listed fourteen specific suggestions that would enable the shah to deflect the serious challenge of the urban middle class. This important list became in some ways the blueprint of the shah's reform program and is therefore worth citing. The shah should:

1. Channel current resentments against his Ministers rather than against himself.
2. Dump his family, or most of it, in Europe.
3. Abstain from state visits abroad and discourage state visits to Iran.
4. Reduce his military forces gradually to a small, tough force of infantry and artillery capable of internal security and guerrilla activities.
5. Remove gradually most U.S. advisers from the Iranian government except those few engaged in health, education, and welfare work in the field.
6. Publicly excoriate the traditional ruling class for its lack of social responsibility.
7. Withdraw from his openly pro-Western international posture with as little damage as possible to free world morale and to his own prestige.
8. Ostentatiously reduce his personal standard of living and the pomp and panoply of his life.
9. Proceed loudly with at least a token land distribution program against the big landlords.
10. Make menacing gestures against the Oil Consortium and "extract" concessions from it in such a way as to make it appear that the consortium was reluctantly bowing to his power and determination.
11. Make public scapegoats of scores of "corrupt" high officials, whether or not the "corruption" could be proved.
12. Appoint respected moderate Mussadiqists to positions such as those of minister of Finance and head of the Plan Organization, where they could assume responsibilities without being able to reverse policy.
13. Make public all details of the operations of the Pahlavi Foundation, and appoint as its supervisors a few moderate Musaddiqists.
14. Employ his personality to make constant personal contact with the members of the middle class.[7]

Bowling's Fourteen Points became an important part of the shah's reform program of the next two years. Bowling admitted that "many of them would be demagogic in nature and would be hard for the West to swallow. But it is still possible that the Shah could turn the trick. He has the brains, the personality, and the cunning to do it."[8]

Meanwhile, at other levels of the U.S. government, Iran specialists were warning of trouble in Iran. On April 2, 1961, one week before Khrushchev's discussions with Walter Lippmann, Professor T. Cuyler Young of Princeton University communicated his reservations to W. W. Rostow in the Kennedy White House. In a letter of April 19 written shortly after he had arrived in Iran for a research visit, Young reiterated that he viewed "the general situation in Iran with considerable concern, if not indeed alarm." He went on to write:

> This regime is considered by most aware and articulate Iranians as reactionary, corrupt, and a tool of Western (and especially Anglo-American) imperialism. The fact that the U.S. economic and military aid has been used to buttress the current regime is ample evidence for the people that the U.S. generally approves and supports the regime.
>
> Moreover, since the regime has ruthlessly eliminated almost all genuine opposition, even of a fairly conservative nature, an increasing number of Iranians are beginning to think of communism as the only means to effect basic change in Iran. The majority of Iranians for historical reasons are anti-Russian and for ideological reasons pro-Western; in most cases, they are very pro-American. The U.S., however, already has overdrawn this valuable capital of goodwill accumulated in Iran during half a century of genuine friendship and cooperation in the cause of Iranian independence and freedom.

In his letter to Rostow, Young included some policy recommendations that bore an uncanny resemblance to those suggested by John Bowling. In his opinion, the shah should: (1) reduce the pomp and ceremony surrounding himself and court; (2) ostentatiously cultivate the middle class and related public; (3) exile or hold in check those members of the royal family who are the center of corruption; (4) open the Pahlavi Foundation to public inspection and its books to public audit; (5) appoint some popular and trustworthy Musaddiqists to important government posts, such as in the ministry of Finance and the Plan Organization; (6) reduce his state visits and absences from the country; and (7) espouse vigorously reforms in the judiciary, the armed forces, the civil service, planning, land tenure, taxation, education, and foreign policy.[9]

These analyses and policy considerations took on special relevance in May when violence erupted in many cities of Iran. In Tehran, up to fifty thousand teachers marched to protest their wages and working conditions. The police was assisted in quelling the demonstrations by two companies from infantry divisions of the regular army as well as by a special forces parachute battalion, which was used for this purpose for the first time. When these forces killed one of the demonstrators and seriously wounded two others, the situation threatened to veer out of control. The shah reacted by dismissing the cabinet of Sharif-Emami and, with strong U.S. encouragement, appointed Ali Amini to head a new government. The instability in Iran deepened the concern of American policymakers, and in June influential voices in the United States Senate joined the chorus of criticism.

Although the shah had friends in the U.S. Congress, a number of senators from the Democratic party questioned the monarch's capacity to rule his country. Those most outspoken included key members of the Senate Committee on Foreign Relations such as Hubert Humphrey, Frank Church, and William Fulbright, the committee chairman. The committee met in executive session on June 15, 1961, to discuss the political situation in Iran. After Senator Humphrey indicated that Khrushchev had also emphasized to him that revolution was imminent in Iran, Senator Church responded: "I just want to say this. What worries me so is I think Khrushchev is right. I just think it is going to be a miracle if we save the Shah of Iran. All I know about history says he is not long for this world, nor his system. And when he goes down, boom, we go with him."[10] Senator Humphrey then seconded Church's assessment and argued that the United States should be building vocational schools in Iran rather than a huge military establishment. Referring to the shah and his political colleagues, Humphrey argued that "they are dead. They just don't know it. I don't care what revolution it is. Somebody is going to get those fellows. They are out. It is just a matter of time."[11] In a powerful and prescient statement, Senator Humphrey described the situation of the Pahlavi regime in Iran:

> There is a limit to the amount of money that this country can give to those people who are unwilling to do what they ought to do. They ought to just get out before it is too late, Khrushchev or somebody like him is coming just as sure as you and I are around this table, or somebody like him. The same thing happened to Cuba. We did not pay any attention to it. Nobody from the executive branch ever came into this committee and told us one thing about the illiterate Cubans or the sick Cubans or the poor Cubans or the worker Cubans. All we ever heard about was the Hilton Hotel or the nice big

golf course or something else. Now we have Castro. He is there for quite a while; I'm afraid far too long. That is what we are going to get in Iran. And all that military aid is never going to save him, not one bit.[12]

Privately, the shah of Iran was worried about the Kennedy administration; he had quietly supported the Nixon candidacy and feared criticism and pressure from the Democrats. He was particularly disturbed by Kennedy's constant use of the word "revolution" during the presidential campaign. The shah was extremely allergic to this word and felt that Kennedy might have Iran specifically in mind whenever he used it. In early March 1961, one month before Khrushchev warned Walter Lippmann of probable revolution in Iran, the shah himself warned of the communist threat to his regime in a interview with *U.S. News and World Report:* "I am somewhat worried that the new United States administration may not have a proper appreciation of this fact." He concluded this interview with a clear warning: "We hope you in the United States don't forget who your friends are."[13] In the end, warning of possible communist threats only played into the hands of the Kennedy administration, whose reform emphasis was developed precisely on the basis of this threat.

There is little doubt that the shah resented the American concern about the possible instability of Iran. In 1969, after he had improved his image and solidified his position in Washington, the shah told an American interviewer that "your worst period was in 1961 and 1962. But even before that, there were your great American 'liberals' wanting to impose their way of 'democracy' on others, thinking their way is wonderful."[14] The shah also later stated that "he regarded Kennedy's message as more or less an American coup directed against him."[15]

The shah's disagreements with the United States during this period ran much deeper than his visceral disapproval of any policy that stressed major reform. He nurtured a personal dislike for John F. Kennedy and was not displeased when he heard the news of Kennedy's assassination.[16] He was envious of Kennedy's popularity and charismatic appeal among the masses of Iranian people and strongly resented the fact that Kennedy, who was two and half years younger than he, would attempt to advise him on how to run his kingdom. Kennedy was equally unimpressed by the shah, whom he considered a corrupt and petty tyrant. It now appears that Kennedy's doubts about the shah were so strong that he even considered forcing his abdication in favor of rule by regency until his young son came of age.[17]

The American Drive for Reform in Iran

President John F. Kennedy made his first direct official contact with the government of Iran on March 1, 1961, when he met with Lt. Gen. Teymour Bakhtiar in Washington. Bakhtiar, then the forceful, ambitious head of SAVAK, delivered a letter from the shah to Kennedy and took the opportunity to request increased American economic and military aid for Iran. Bakhtiar argued that such aid was essential for Iran's security since, in addition to the Soviet Union, Iran had two other neighbors, Iraq and Afghanistan, that were receiving aircraft more modern than those in the Iranian inventory.

During this meeting, Kennedy indicated that the United States was sympathetic to Iran's needs, that the foreign aid issue was under consideration, and that he was sending Ambassador W. Averell Harriman to Iran to speak with the shah. He also politely indicated that he was unaware that Iran faced any serious threats from either Afghanistan or Iraq. In this session the president was courteous but noncommittal. In a meeting with the shah in Tehran on March 13, W. Averell Harriman and the shah reiterated the similar positions discussed by Kennedy and Bakhtiar in Washington. The shah was not reassured. On March 17, Secretary of State Dean Rusk informed President Kennedy that American ambassador to Iran Edward T. Wailes "has reported that the Shah fears that the new administration may not support Iran; our Ambassador has recommended that everything possible be done to reassure the Shah as to considering United States interest and support."[18]

The memorandum of a conversation between the Iranian ambassador to Washington and an American official and old friend on March 22, 1961, indicates the growing tenseness of relations between the Kennedy administration and the Iranian political establishment. At this meeting, Ambassador Ardeshir Zahedi "discussed Mr. Harriman's recent visit to Iran and with particular bitterness described how Mr. Harriman had avoided making any commitments to support Iran, while only a few days later in New Delhi he publicly stated that the United States would continue to support Pakistan's army." Zahedi also indicated that General Bakhtiar had complained to the shah about the shoddy treatment he had received in Washington, since it took him some three weeks to get to see the president. In the course of this frank and private litany of complaint, Zahedi said that "General Ayub Khan of Pakistan advised the Shah that the only way to deal with the United States is to insult and threaten; if this is not done the United States takes its allies for granted and concerns itself only with countries threatening to join unfriendly blocs."[19]

From February 10 to 14, 1962, presidential envoy Chester Bowles visited Iran and met with numerous high-ranking government officials, including Minister of Agriculture Hassan Arsanjani. Bowles focused his attention on village issues, land reform, and economic planning. Among other things, he recommended that Iran familiarize itself with the civil development work being done by the U.S. Army Corps of Engineers with a view to implementing a similar program in Iran. In a 4½-hour private session attended only by the shah, Iran's foreign minister, the American ambassador, and himself, Bowles stressed repeatedly the primary importance of economic and social progress over military considerations.[20]

In April 1962 Muhammad Reza Shah made his fourth official visit to the United States. Accompanied by Empress Farah whom he had married in 1959, he visited, among other places, New York, Hollywood, and Cape Canaveral; in Philadelphia, the University of Pennsylvania awarded him an honorary doctorate of law. His most important business, however, was conducted in Washington, where he carried his requests for increased military and economic aid directly to President Kennedy. The Kennedy-Pahlavi visits were cordial enough on the surface. The royal couple visited the Bronx Zoo, where the empress fed potatoes to an elephant and the shah confessed his aversion to snakes. The two first ladies spent considerable time together, with the empress visiting the grave of four-year-old Caroline Kennedy's canary and playing with John, Jr. An underlying tension, however, permeated the meetings as the shah pressed hard for military assistance while Kennedy and his advisers recommended economic and social reform instead. In a speech before a joint session of Congress on April 13, the shah warned of the communist threat to his north while at the same time assuring the American administration that his government was attempting to "give a firm foundation to our reform activity by evolving a government of the people, by the people."[21]

The shah heard the message from the Kennedy administration and slowly began to alter temporarily his priority of demands from military to economic emphases. As will be indicated below, he also began to take dramatic steps toward the introduction of social and economic reform at home. The Kennedy administration's careful shift in America's Iran policy was further reinforced by an important official visit made by Vice President Lyndon B. Johnson to Iran on August 24–26, 1962.

Although Lyndon Johnson had little experience in foreign affairs, President Kennedy sent him on numerous overseas official visits. Johnson posed a constant problem for the Kennedy White House staff:

with his huge ego, enormous energy, and driving ambition he attempted to interfere in a raw, embarrassing, and bumbling way in all possible presidential business. Kennedy's close staff determined that one way to keep the vice president busy in a nonharmful manner was to encourage him to travel—the farther from Washington the better. Thus during his vice presidency Lyndon Johnson made eleven foreign trips and visited thirty-three countries. In August 1962, President Kennedy and National Security Adviser McGeorge Bundy prevailed on a reluctant Johnson to make an official trip to several Mediterranean countries and Iran.

Iran's domestic political situation was in turmoil, and a dramatic change in prime ministers had just occurred: reformer Ali Amini had been replaced by conservative aristocrat Asadollah Alam. A Central Intelligence Agency summary paper prepared just before Johnson's trip warned of serious trouble in Iran: "We reiterate our earlier estimate that profound political and social change appears virtually inevitable in Iran."[22] Johnson's charge was twofold: to reassure a nervous shah of continuing American support and to encourage him to modernize through an emphasis on socioeconomic reform rather than military might. Given the change in prime ministers, Johnson was to see that the reform momentum in Iran was not lost. In a briefing paper he was advised "to steer [the] shah on to our desire he continue pressing internal development and reform. . . . In our view, Iran's internal problems [are] far more pressing than [any] external threat."[23]

Lyndon Johnson and his entourage arrived in Tehran at noon on August 24, 1962. Over the next two days, Johnson met constantly with Iranian leaders, and in a memorable cavalcade through Tehran dashed into the crowds, talking, hugging, shaking hands, and distributing small gifts. Always curious and appreciative of a good show, the Iranians responded with warmth and good-natured greetings. Johnson's style baffled the Iranian aristocrats who accompanied him, and as American ambassador Julius C. Holmes wrote: "The Vice President's effect on the people whom he greeted along the way with handshake and a friendly wave favorably impressed even the hard-bitten commanding general of the Imperial Guard who obviously had never seen anything quite like it."[24]

The shah was less favorably impressed with the vice president's clear message. During his visit, Lyndon Johnson made five public statements, and in each he stressed the importance of reform and the need for social justice. He attempted to convince the shah that military strength must be balanced by economic development. At a small, informal state dinner on August 25, Johnson was particularly blunt.

Noted Ambassador Holmes: "The Vice President laid great stress on the proposition that the ultimate strength, prosperity and independence of Iran would lie in the progress made in the fields of economic well-being of the population and in social justice. . . . He cited the fact that we had recently demobilized two divisions which had been called up following the Berlin emergency in order to lessen defense costs. This point was not lost on the Shah."[25]

In his departure speech, Lyndon Johnson left no doubt about the thrust of the American message to the shah's government. "We realize the extent to which our views and those of your farsighted leaders are parallel. We all agree on the necessity for programs of responsible change. We all have seen that the status quo alone provides no safeguard for freedom." Johnson then quoted from John Kennedy's inaugural address: "If a free society cannot help the many who are poor it cannot save the few who are rich."[26]

Lyndon Johnson left Iran with euphoric feelings about Iranians and with a strong personal respect for the shah. True to form, Johnson appreciated and admired strong men of the Third World whoever they were and wherever they ruled. The shah, on the other hand, took his measure of Johnson and, smothering him with Persian hospitality, convinced Johnson that he was a firm, reliable, anticommunist ally who would stand by the United States. Although he disapproved of the reform aspects of Johnson's message, he listened and developed an important rapport with the vice president. This strategy later paid major dividends.

Many other important Iranian-American high-level official and unofficial contacts were made during the Kennedy administration. Important Americans visiting Iran during these years include, in chronological order: Secretary of Agriculture Orville Freeman, Sen. Stuart Symington, Sen. Barry Goldwater, David Rockefeller, Edward R. Murrow, Secretary of State Dean Rusk, oil authority Howard Page, Sen. Ernest Gruening, John J. McCloy, Gen. Maxwell Taylor, Chief Justice Earl Warren, and presidential envoy Alexis Johnson. More privately, David Lilienthal and Kermit Roosevelt maintained close and continuing touch with the shah and his government. Despite the new thrust of its policy, the United States continued to entangle itself in Iranian affairs in line with the policy established following the overthrow of Muhammad Musaddiq.

Political Instability and the Strategy of Reform from Above

Political unrest and upheaval shook Iran in the early 1960s. Between January 1960 and January 1963, a dozen serious incidents took place in Tehran's streets. In 1961 the National Front attempted to resuscitate itself, organizing rallies, establishing clubs, and publicly issuing political proclamations. One symptom of the front's resurgence was the appearance on May 7, 1961, of Muhammad Musaddiq's picture in the Iranian press for the first time since 1953. Beginning in October 1961, violent demonstrations and political protests again marked Tehran University, culminating in January 1962 in an invasion of the campus by the regime's specially trained commandos. As the regime introduced carefully apportioned doses of reform, the explosive social and political broth of long-simmering grievances began to bubble over. It was in this tense situation that a major change in high-level political leadership took place.

Despite much Western commentary to the contrary, the peasant and lower classes of Iranian society were not strong supporters of the Pahlavi regime. As one American scholar who spent more time in the villages of provincial Iran than in the salons of Tehran noted: "In all the years I have been carrying out research in Iranian villages, I never encountered any genuine enthusiasm for the shah or his government on the part of the majority of villagers."[27] Although the lower classes did not strongly support Pahlavi rule, throughout the 1950s the religious establishment, led by Ayatollah Muhammad Hussein Burujirdi, had exerted a calming influence. The younger fiery and disaffected clerics had not yet made their political appearances. Burujirdi's death on March 30, 1961, opened the way to the politicization of the deeply religious classes. The growing professional middle classes led the opposition and expressed it in their writings, especially poetry, which was most successful in avoiding the suffocating effects of the regime's censors.

Following the May 1961 teachers' riots, the shah replaced ineffective caretaker Ja'far Sharif-Emami with tough aristocrat reformer Ali Amini. Amini, who as minister of Finance in the first post-Musaddiq government had negotiated the 1954 consortium agreement and who more recently had served as ambassador to the United States, had a reputation for personal integrity. Although the shah disliked Amini, about whom he had an inferiority complex, he was willing to use him to dissipate the growing crisis. Amini was well aware that the shah feared a diminution of his own power, and upon becoming prime minister Amini frankly stated: "I only want to serve him and the country because I believe a king is necessary here. He *must* let me carry out his desires, and not intervene directly in government matters. He must trust me."[28]

The Kennedy administration encouraged Amini's appointment. According to former U.S. ambassador Armin Meyer:

> The Kennedy administration was very concerned about Iran and immediately set up a task force. There was a fear that Iran's demise was about to take place. Some of us felt that Iran had been around for 2,500 years and it might last a few more. However, the general belief was that it was about to go down the drain, unless America took some drastic action.
>
> The result of that task force activity was to instruct our ambassador that we would provide $35 million in aid to Iran in return for which we would expect from the Iranians various steps which we considered necessary for progress, including even a suggestion as to the prime ministerial candidate we considered best qualified to administer the proposed reforms.[29]

On May 9, 1961, the shah dissolved the Twentieth Majlis and gave Amini extraordinary powers to govern the country. In choosing to shift tactical gears of political control from repression to reform, the shah undoubtedly had the assistance of an American hand on the gearshift.

During his fourteen-month tenure as prime minister, Ali Amini oversaw the introduction of many reforms. These included economic austerity measures, a highly visible campaign against corruption, and the demise of many hated and reactionary political personalities. In an important symbolic move, the shah severed his formal personal connection with the Pahlavi Foundation in October 1961. General Teymour Bakhtiar, the feared head of SAVAK, was relieved of his duties in March 1961 and was forced to leave the country on January 26, 1962. Also, loyalist royalist Manuchehr Eqbal took an unexpected vacation from Iran beginning on May 16, 1961. The most critical personnel changes, however, occurred in the cabinet, where Amini's appointments included not only American-trained reform-minded technocrats but also two unexpected revolutionary personalities—Minister of Agriculture Hassan Arsanjani and Minister of Education Muhammad Derakhshesh.

Derakhshesh had been organizing Iranian teachers since the late 1940s. With the demonstrations in May 1961 that had ended in violence, he was brought into Amini's cabinet in a move to placate the challenging teachers' organizations. Derakhshesh moved immediately and actively to improve the situation of the thousands of teachers throughout Iran, and during his tenure as minister he was a courageous force for reform. The man who fought for radical social and political reform at the heart of the system, however, was Hassan Arsanjani. Far more than any other man, he made a lasting mark on the

Iranian polity, and the policies he began in the early 1960s did much to pave the way for the explosive revolution of the late 1970s.

In policies similar to those promoted in Latin America—in which the Kennedy administration sought to foster controlled agrarian reform programs that would ultimately give the dispossessed masses a stake in the ongoing system—the shah and his political elite agreed to attempt the same general scheme in Iran. The major difference between Iran and Latin America, however, was in the individuals selected to lead the land reform efforts. From the beginning, Arsanjani's goal was to awaken the Iranian peasantry, to initiate class conflict, to improve the lives and power base of the peasants, and, having awakened this slumbering force, to bring about a massive revolution in Iranian society.

Hassan Arsanjani was born in 1922 in Tehran. His father, Sayyid Muhammad Hussein Arsanjani, a religious leader who participated in the constitutional movement, was originally from the town of Arsanjan in Fars Province. He died when Hassan was only nine years old, and Hassan was brought up by his mother, who was from a merchant family. Arsanjani spent his formative years in the bazaar, where he developed a firsthand understanding of politics and trade. While studying law at Tehran University in 1940–41, he worked part-time at the Agricultural Bank, where he developed a detailed knowledge of rural Iran and even introduced revolutionary peasant cooperative systems in the villages of Damavand, Savah, and Najafabad. On graduating, he went into private law practice while editing the influential and critical leftist newspaper *Darya*. In the 1940s he associated himself closely with the politically experienced Ahmad Qavam, from whom he learned some valuable lessons in the realities of Iranian politics. When only twenty-five years old, Arsanjani, through the assistance of Qavam and others, managed to maneuver himself electorally into the Fifteenth Majlis, from which he was soon ejected. In 1953–54 he worked informally with Ali Amini on the oil consortium agreement. Between 1954 and 1961 he practiced law and formed a political party known as Hizb-i Azadi (the Freedom party). During Eqbal's premiership in 1958 Arsanjani spent six weeks in military prison after being accused of attempting to overthrow the government of Iran.

Arsanjani was appointed to the ministership of agriculture because he combined considerable knowledge of rural Iran, a reform-radical political commitment, and a history of past cooperation with establishment figures like Qavam and Amini. Once he became minister, however, he struck out on his own. A feisty, five-foot two-inch campaigner, Hassan Arsanjani nourished a genuine and deep hatred for the aristocratic landlords, whom he consistently referred to as "reactionary sons-of-bitches." He held both the Soviet Union and the United States in contempt and viewed the shah as a lackey of the superpowers. He began the land reform program in Maraghah in the northwestern province of Azerbaijan for three reasons: first, Arsanjani himself was closely acquainted with this region; second, in Azerbaijan the large landlords were the most powerful, visible, and repressive; and third, because of the landlords' reactionary image here, he would be better able to rally public opinion against them when he initiated the confrontation. Arsanjani's logic was that if he could break the power of the landlords in Maraghah, then it could be done anywhere in the country.

Arsanjani moved quickly. In a series of lightning moves that included press conferences, congresses, seminars, and announced distributions in May, June, and July 1961, he not only caught the landlords by surprise but also outflanked Prime Minister Amini and the shah. Constantly confronted by Arsanjani fait accomplis, they had no choice but to accept them in order to maintain their own credibility with the Iranian people. In Arsanjani's own words:

> I knew that I had to act with *qudrat* (power) and *surat* (speed) since I had no social revolution upon which to base the reform. Even the Iranian constitution justified feudalism and the Pahlavis were the biggest feudals of all. If the program were to be introduced slowly, it would never get off the ground. The entire Iranian government in its heart of hearts was against serious land reform. By appointing study groups and seeking to carefully implement agrarian reform over a number of years, the program would be effectively destroyed. This is what happened in countries like the Philippines, Syria, and Egypt. I was not going to let this happen in Iran.[30]

Arsanjani argued that the Soviet Union, the United States, and the shah all opposed fundamental land reform since they did not support genuine revolutionary change in Iran. He claimed that the Soviet Union contacted him frequently to complain that collectivization was the only path to land reform. The Americans reportedly urged him repeatedly to slow down the process and to implement it cautiously and incrementally. A great landlord himself, the shah was only willing to see land reform implemented selectively. He supported the land reform program so long as he was given the credit for its creation and so long as it weakened only those landlords whose power and influence competed with his own. He deeply resented the national reputation that his minister of agriculture was receiving and waited quietly until he could remove the ambitious little man from his increasingly influential post.

Arsanjani eventually lost his position. But before he did, he had managed to awaken the Iranian countryside. A land reform program did take hold, and, although it eventually ground to a halt, it had achieved precisely what Arsanjani wanted it to achieve. It had politicized the masses, sharpened their expectations, and brought them into the political process as self-interested observers. Hassan Arsanjani had plowed the ground and prepared the way for the mass mobilization that occurred under the direction of the religious leaders fifteen years after the fiery *rahbar* (leader)—as he called himself—had been forced from his position on March 7, 1963.

A measure of Hassan Arsanjani's acumen and cunning is that his cabinet tenure was eight months longer than that of Prime Minister Amini, who resigned from his post on July 18, 1962. Although supported by the United States, which contributed important sums of aid to his coffers, Amini did not receive the larger amounts of financial assistance that he considered necessary. Also, he was locked in a basic disagreement with the shah over the latter's commitment to heavy military expenditures. In the end, however, Amini was trapped in an untenable political position. Because of Arsanjani's land reform fait accompli and his own anticorruption drive, Amini was opposed by the landed and industrial aristocracy, who labeled him a traitor to his own class. The alienated middle-class intelligentsia, represented primarily by the National Front, became his implacable opponents because of his refusal to call elections or to form a Majlis. As opposition grew to the reforms that were being accelerated by members of his own government, Amini was forced to adopt more authoritarian techniques. These in turn were resented and resisted by the intelligentsia, who increased their opposition. Paradoxically, it was the members of the intelligentsia who should have been Amini's natural allies. This scenario was not unlike the one that had confronted Muhammad Musaddiq a decade earlier.

The incident that demonstrated Amini's inability to handle the disaffection of the middle classes took place at Tehran University on January 21, 1962, when the shah approved a brutal military attack on unarmed demonstrating students. While on campus the commandos went beserk, and in numerous bloody and violent episodes they desecrated the institution in a way that was never forgotten by Iranian intellectuals. In his letter of resignation to Prime Minister Amini, Dr. Ahmad Farhad, the distinguished chancellor of Tehran University, wrote: "I have never seen or heard so much cruelty, sadism, atrocity, and vandalism on the part of the government forces. Some of the girls in the classrooms were criminally attacked by the soldiers. When we inspected the University buildings we were faced with the same situation as if an army of barbarians had invaded an enemy territory."[31]

The National Front, meanwhile, contributed significantly to Amini's fall and to the shah's continued dominance. Accepting support from all quarters (except the court itself), the front embarked on what one analyst described as "an unmitigated suicide mission." The same analyst attributed this disaster to the fact that the National Front then combined "analytical feebleness, political misjudgment, absence of a decisive leadership, lack of internal democracy, and organizational chaos."[32]

Meanwhile, the shah, who had been using Amini as a shield to deflect criticism from himself, cut the ground out from under his prime minister in order to pave the way for the appointment of a less independent, more loyal, political lieutenant. From the shah's point of view, it was time to gain royal control over the reform program, which had begun to veer into unpredictable directions. Two days after Amini's resignation, the shah appointed his reliable, ruthless old friend, tribal aristocrat Asadollah Alam, to the premiership. Alam could be counted on to stand faithfully beside the shah at the bridge of the Iranian ship of state as it sought to negotiate the treacherous waters that lay ahead. With Alam came a number of new cabinet crew members who reflected the return to conservative pre-Amini days. With the temporary exception of Arsanjani, who did not fit the mold, the new cabinet was the one that the shah wanted in charge of the implementation of the coming White Revolution.

The United States did not protect Amini for two reasons. First, Amini himself had failed to demonstrate any greater popular base of support than had any of his immediate predecessors. Second, his reform program had been unpredictable, straying in revolutionary directions led by Iranian Napoleonic figures like Arsanjani on the one hand while failing to meet even the most basic demands of the intelligentsia on the other. Furthermore, American policymakers saw the possibility that increasing violence in Iran might well require a repressive and ruthless response best understood by an Alam rather than an Amini. In this instance, the Kennedy administration was looking to the second track of the foreign policy it had established with respect to Third World countries: reform first but tough repressive counterinsurgent measures second.

The moment for the backup tactic occurred during the first week of June 1963, when riots and demonstrations opposing the rule of the shah spread across the country. This political rebellion was multiclass in complexion and cut across ideologies. It included religious leaders, students, bazaaris, teachers, workers, writers, and professionals of all kinds. The demonstrations were put down viciously; the imperial military forces killed thousands in the streets of Tehran. Among those involved in stirring up the demonstrations was an individual little known in the West. He was identified by one American Iran specialist as "Abdullah" Khomeini.[33]

Six months before, on January 9, 1963, the shah of Iran outlined the principles of his six-point reform program. On January 26, this program was supported by a referendum and the White Revolution came into existence. Besides land reform, which was the core of the campaign, the program included the nationalization of forests, the public sale of state-owned factories, profit sharing in industry, electoral power for women, and a literacy corps. Despite the fanfare and the referendum results, the White Revolution was greeted skeptically by the major Iranian opposition forces. The old aristocracy opposed the land reform, the clerics and lower middle classes resented the attack on their power bases, and the middle-class professionals criticized the reforms for failing to deal with the central issue of political participation and social justice. Referred to in Persian as the Revolution of the Shah and the People, the White Revolution was called by many intellectuals the Revolution of the Shah *against* the People.[34] The middle classes saw it as a political palliative designed to impress foreigners while Pahlavi power continued absolute. One controversial and widely known book of poems that resulted in the arrest and imprisonment of its author, Firaydun Tunakabuni, satirically and sarcastically described the January 1963 (Bahman 6, 1341) inauguration of the reform program in a poem entitled "The Historical Day":

> Faces are frowning.
> Fists are clenched.
> Faces are disappointed.
> Heads are bowed.
> Hearts are trembling.
> Steps are quick.
> Flags are faded.
> Lights are dim.
> People gather in groups.
> Groups gather within groups.
> What's the news?
> People are celebrating.
> Bah![35]

In the months before President John Kennedy was assassinated on November 23, 1963, the situation had swung back to normal in Iran. Martial law was declared and then lifted; more importantly, controlled elections were held for the Twenty-first Majlis, which was seated on October 6. With the opposition gravely wounded by the machine-gun fire of early June and with a trusted hard-line government in control, the shah felt free to pursue reform measures at his own pace and according to his own tastes. The death of President Kennedy guaranteed the shah this power.

The Kennedy Period Analyzed

In January 1963, at about the same time that the shah had announced his six-point White Revolution, the United States government expressed its delight at what was transpiring in Iran. The State Department indicated its confidence that the shah had "made a clean and irreversible break with the traditional moneyed, land-owning, and religious elites on whom he had relied so heavily in the past." In a secret memorandum dated January 21, 1963, the executive secretary of State summarized America's role in "the Shah's politico-economic experimentation" in the following words:

> A new and positive U.S. course of action has emerged since early 1961. Steps were taken to head off the threatening financial crisis, to encourage the Shah to move back into a more constitutional role, to reduce the size of Iran's military forces and improve its efficiency and public image, to work toward a moderate political synthesis, and to rely on a program of carefully planned social reform and economic development to avert what appeared to be an eventual certain overthrow of the regime followed by chaos and ascendancy to power of demagogic, anti-Western forces.[36]

There is little doubt that during the Kennedy presidency the United States pressured the shah's regime to begin a program of dramatic selective and controlled reforms. Many of the reforms in fact adopted by the shah were identical to those recommended by the U.S. Department of State and contained, for example, in J. W. Bowling's Fourteen Points.

President Kennedy's innovative Peace Corps program reinforced the new American reform emphasis. This program had a strong, positive impact in Iran since it was targeted at a different constituency, the lower and middle classes. The first forty-three American Peace Corps volunteers arrived in Iran in September 1962. These and nearly two thousand others after them moved out into the Iranian countryside, where they lived and worked with the Iranian people. In Iran the American Peace Corps volunteer was generally the antithesis of the "ugly American" and gained the United States some badly needed credibility.

Although the shah responded to American suggestions, he resented the pressure. He harbored hidden suspicions that the United States was planning a revolution against him. Julius Holmes, Kennedy's tough and forthright ambassador to Iran, told David Lilienthal in October 1961 that what had really upset the shah were Kennedy's speeches that "the U.S. was for 'revolution'—that was the word and the theme. The Shah interpreted these words to mean just one thing: we were going to support a revolution in Iran."[37] The shah questioned the wisdom of even deep-seated reform programs, and he had always resented external intervention in the affairs of his country. The humiliating exile of his father at the hands of the British and the Soviets in 1941 was a vivid, unpleasant memory that remained with him throughout his life. Insecure in his power, he was particularly paranoid about the responsibilities he was forced to turn over to individuals such as Amini and Arsanjani.

In this context, it is noteworthy that in 1962 the shah arranged a rapprochement with the Soviet Union. The crucial event in this reconciliation was Iran's unilateral pledge on September 15, 1962, to prohibit the basing of foreign missiles on its soil. The Soviets, anxious themselves to repair and improve relations with Iran, greeted this announcement warmly. It was the first time the Soviet Union had received a formal assurance of nondeployment from a country allied with the West. The State Department's Bureau of Intelligence and Research interpreted the USSR's enthusiastic acceptance of the gesture in the following way: "In recent months, the Soviet Union has been seeking to establish better relations with the new Iranian government headed by Prime Minister Alam. . . . The precise timing of the Soviet action appears to have been intended to offset the effects of Vice President Johnson's visit to Tehran, and to pave the way for further Soviet efforts at cultivating better relations with Iran."[38]

From the shah's perspective, the rapprochement with the Soviet Union was partially intended as a not-so-subtle warning to the United States not to take him for granted or to push him too far. The Iran-Soviet rapprochement was solidified by an official visit to Tehran by President and Madame Leonid Brezhnev on November 16–23, 1963. The Brezhnevs left Tehran the very day President Kennedy was assassinated in Dallas, Texas.

American policy toward Iran during the Kennedy presidency carried four political results that profoundly influenced U.S.-Iran relations in the years ahead. First, the Kennedy administration managed to assist the shah to open the doors of social and economic reform; second, the opening of these heavy doors was intended to preserve rather than to transform the Iranian political structure; third, the attempt to introduce selective reform without an accompanying political transformation resulted in awakened expectations and sharpened aspirations that would one day have to be confronted and satisfied; and fourth, even though its policy reflected a new reforming thrust, the United States during the Kennedy period found itself entangled more deeply than ever in Iranian affairs.

Although opposition elements have often attempted to deny it, there was indeed a reform program implemented in Iran in the early 1960s. In the areas of land tenure and literacy there was a great deal of activity. It is certainly true that the effectiveness of these reform programs left much to be desired, but there was change. In brief, the shah attempted to carry out a reform program from above in which he sought to build an alliance with the nation's peasantry against the growing and challenging middle classes. But by circumnavigating the middle classes, he alienated the very forces necessary for any successful implementation of the reforms. The White Revolution failed ultimately because it was intended to protect the shah by preserving the political system. This was the second result of American policy.

The Kennedy administration with its Alliance for Progress sought to introduce just enough reform from above in order to guarantee the political status quo of Third World countries. Evidence for this can be seen in the heavy emphasis on counterinsurgency and internal police control. Kennedy and his advisers thought the best way to combat communism was to mix reform with repression. If and when the former failed, then it was time to call in the troops. "For Latin America, as for the rest of the Third World, the Kennedy Administration's tool for combatting communist subversion would be its new military specialty—counterinsurgency."[39] The Iranian equivalent to America's Green Berets were known as the Red Berets. Well aware of this American support, the shah did not hesitate to call out the commandos and special forces as well as the regular army to crush the demonstrations at Tehran University in January 1962 and in the streets of Tehran in June 1963.

The long-term consequences of such selective reform ineffectively administered in the service of protecting a political status quo that allowed for no genuine popular participation were to be severe. The countryside was awakened, and the expectations of the masses for a better life were aroused. The alienation of the middle classes increased as they found themselves frozen out of the reform programs. The shah himself ensured that the reforms were to be limited; it is no accident that reforming prime minister Amini's tenure lasted little more than a year and that his premiership was bracketed by conservative royalists Sharif-Emami and Alam. It was in this kind of social and political environment that a revolutionary brand of political opposition began to incubate. One case will suffice.

The influential Shi'i religious leaders that had begun to replace the deceased Ayatollah Burujirdi opposed both the policies of reform and those of repression. Although it remains a debatable question whether their opposition to the White Revolution resided primarily in their unhappiness with the substance of the program or in their condemnation of the methodology of its implementation, there is little doubt that they lined up against the shah, whose actions they considered illegitimate and based on collusion with a foreign country. Throughout early 1963, Ayatollah Ruhollah Khomeini spoke out against the tyranny of the shah's government. On June 3, 1963, on the day commemorating the martyrdom of Imam Hussein at Karbala, Khomeini delivered a fiery speech denouncing the shah and the corruption of his rule. Two days later he was arrested by the shah's police and taken to Tehran, where he was placed in confinement. The next day the country broke into massive rebellion. In the words of a leading scholar of Iran and biographer of Khomeini:

> The date on which this uprising began, Khurdad 15 according to the solar calendar used in Iran, marked a turning point in the modern history of Iran. It established Imam Khomeini as national leader and spokesman for popular aspirations, provided the struggle against the Shah and his foreign patrons with a coherent ideological basis in Islam, and introduced a period of mass political activity under the guidance of the religious leadership instead of the secular parties that had been discredited with the overthrow of Musaddiq. In all of these ways, the uprising of Khurdad 15 foreshadowed the Islamic Revolution of 1978–1979.[40]

The final result and irony of Kennedy's reform policy is that it entangled Americans more deeply than ever into Iran's internal affairs. Because of its support of reform policies and programs such as the Peace Corps, it improved the American image among certain groups within the professional middle classes. This, however, was offset by the violent repression of the shah's regime as it shot down thousands of unarmed but demonstrating Iranian citizens in the streets and alleys of cities throughout the country. Just as America could take some of the credit for the reform, it also had to take some of the blame for the repression. In the end, the balance was tilted severely. The religious leaders and the awakening masses questioned the value of the reforms while at the same time condemning the brutality of the shah's military intervention against his own people.

With the death of John F. Kennedy, the government of Asadollah Alam in firm control, and the reform program in place but ineffective and lacking momentum at the end of 1963, the shah of Iran began another period of entrenched and repressive political rule. As he did so, he found an American ally at his side who more closely resembled the one he had known following the countercoup against Musaddiq in 1953. The shah looked forward to the administration of Lyndon Baines Johnson.

5 Counterreform, Lyndon Johnson, and Pahlavi Retrenchment, 1963–1970

Lyndon B. Johnson came to the presidency with considerably more Iran experience than any American president in history. His vice-presidential trip to Iran when he had leaped from motorcades to shake hands with hundreds of Iranians from all walks of life had convinced him that he knew the Iranian people very well indeed. Furthermore, he had developed a personal relationship with the shah both during the Tehran visit and during the shah's 1962 visit to the United States. In the end, it was his relationship with the shah and not his understanding of the Iranian people that determined Johnson's foreign policy toward Iran.

Johnson had partially bought into John Kennedy's foreign policy framework, which included both a concern for human rights and a commitment to the use of military and police force to guarantee stability in those Third World countries governed by American allies. As an old Texas New Dealer and populist, Johnson often spoke of the need to promote the well-being of the masses. Thus his unprecedented Great Society program in America. He professed the same principles with respect to the non-Western countries of the world, many of which he had visited as vice president of the United States.

After returning from an extensive visit to Asia in early 1961, Johnson stressed the importance of understanding the pressing need for reform in these developing societies. "Either these economic and social reforms are pushed or we shall find that our military men have built iron fortresses on foundations of quicksand." He snorted in derision at those American representatives who travel abroad where they "fly over in an air-conditioned plane, jump into an air-conditioned limousine, ride to an air-conditioned palace to talk to an air-conditioned prince and then flit home pretending to have conquered the world." In his opinion, American diplomats must "run the risk of getting some Homburgs dusty. They have got to walk the streets and the dusty footpaths in a personal effort to ensure that the image of

America as a dynamic land dedicated to change, to the achievement of social justice, is not dead." Such were the words of Lyndon Johnson.[1]

Despite these sensitive words, Johnson was deeply impressed by and supportive of every Asian dictator he met, including Ngo Dinh Diem of South Vietnam, Chiang Kai-shek of Taiwan, Thanarat Sarit of Thailand, Muhammad Ayub Khan of Pakistan, and Ferdinand Marcos of the Philippines. Above all else, he was affected by their personalities and friendliness toward him, Lyndon Johnson. At the same time, he felt that both these leaders and the United States must brook no opposition, no nonsense. Threatened by communism, they must not hesitate to use force to maintain their power and privilege, and America must back them to the hilt. "I have seen as a boy and a man that when you start running from a bully he keeps you running, and if he doesn't respect the line you draw out in the pasture he isn't going to respect the line that you draw at your front yard. He is going to wind up chasing you right out of your own house."[2] "The American people knew what they were voting for in 1964. They knew Lyndon Johnson was not going to pull up stakes and run."[3]

Although President Johnson spoke of the need for social and economic reform, of the need to lighten the burdens of the poverty-stricken masses throughout the world, he did not follow through with foreign policies that would implement such goals. His trips abroad were partly ego trips. In the words of one longtime expert on the American presidency:

> He wanted the roaring adoration of great crowds. He sought motorcades through jammed streets and the homage of important people. This was the one major flaw—so soon apparent—that marred his Asian exploration. Somehow the spirit of adventure was not in him. The sheer joy of going to foreign lands and seeing what others look like, what they do and what they say, never moved LBJ. He went, as he did everything, to get something. He was sadly, mainly interested in Lyndon Johnson and what it all meant for him. When he did not feel that he was getting proper return on his investment, when he had only a handful of natives around him and there was nothing for him to do but inspect their simple homes or view their handicraft, Johnson's interest waned rapidly.[4]

Johnson basked in the spotlight of power and was always impressed by those who maintained power monopolies in their own lands. The more power, pomp, and circumstance, the more impressed Johnson was. The shah of Iran, therefore, was an extremely attractive and important figure to Johnson. Furthermore, the shah was knowledgeably smooth, an ally, and a tough one at that. "Toughness" was important to LBJ, whose foreign policy rested ultimately on a mythical Alamo Syndrome[5] that guided America's actions in places like the Dominican Republic and Vietnam. Johnson carried with him a special Alamo spirit and went so far as to repeat publicly the fabricated story that his own great-great-grandfather had died at the Alamo. In his words: "Nobody can accuse us of a soft attitude. If anyone doubts the basis of our commitment, they will find that we have more troops in Vietnam than there are words in the new Webster's Dictionary."[6]

Lyndon Johnson approved of the shah's highly touted reform program and White Revolution. He approved even more of the shah's brutal treatment of demonstrators throughout Iran in June 1963. To LBJ, the shah was a defender of American interests—a "good guy" manning the barricades for America in the Persian Gulf region. He was defending the Persian Alamo while America was busy working within such other larger Alamos as South Vietnam. President Johnson and his advisers felt that the shah could not be tough enough and that he deserved American support down the line.

In this political situation, it is not surprising that in 1964 a series of events occurred that made a lasting impact on Iranian-American relations. Along with the American involvement in the overthrow of Musaddiq in 1953, the events of late 1964 represented a crucial signpost along the road leading to the ultimate rupture of Iranian-American relations after the Iranian revolution of 1978–79. They involved the imposition of special privileges for Americans living in Iran and an ayatollah named Ruhollah Khomeini.

The Status of Forces Agreement and an Ayatollah Named Khomeini

On October 13, 1964, the Majlis approved a law that provided American military personnel and their dependents stationed in Iran with full diplomatic immunity. This action effectively exempted Americans serving in military advisory positions in Iran from Iranian law; American military officials could no longer be held accountable in Iranian courts for any crimes that they may have committed in that country. The U.S. Department of Defense had been pushing hard for such an agreement for some time, but the United States had been having great difficulty in convincing the Iranian government to accept a policy that clearly represented an assault on Iranian national sovereignty. Recognizing that there would be strong and widespread condemnation of such a policy within Iran, the shah and his advisers in the Ministry of Foreign Affairs sought to deflect the American pressure.

The pressure nonetheless continued, and in the end Iranian officials reluctantly approved what has come to be known in America as the Status of Forces Agreement (SOFA) and in Iran as the Capitulations Agreement. Even the docile and Pahlavi-picked Majlis barely passed the measure; the final vote was 70–62 with the large bloc of remaining deputies intentionally absenting themselves from the session. The reaction throughout Iran was instantaneous, and outrage was expressed by Iranian nationalists regardless of their political predilections.

This outrage widened and deepened when, twelve days after the Majlis had approved the SOFA, the parliament voted to approve a bill authorizing the Iranian government to accept a $200 million loan provided by private American banks and guaranteed by the United States government. This money was to be used to purchase the most modern kinds of military equipment from the United States. It was clear to Iranians that this money was the Iranian government's payoff for accepting the new law of capitulations.

In March 1962 the American Embassy in Tehran had already formally approached the Iranian government to request that U.S. military personnel receive the privileges and immunities specified for "Members of the Administrative and Technical Staff" in the annex to the final act of the United Nations Conference on Diplomatic Intercourse and Immunities signed at Vienna on April 18, 1961. The embassy had then broadened its request by suggesting "that in the interest of uniformity and ease of administration the foregoing principle be made applicable to any other United States military personnel or civilian employees of the United States Department of Defense and their families forming part of their households whose presence in Iran is authorized by the Imperial Iranian Government."[7] After repeated American representations, Iran's Ministry of Foreign Affairs had responded one year later that it was in the process of carrying out studies of the request. Recognizing the explosiveness of this issue, Iranian officials had attempted to stall in response.

After buying time for over a year, the Iranian government had responded in a long diplomatic note on November 17, 1963. In this note, the Iranians had explained that special legal authority was needed to make the Vienna agreement applicable to the Iranian Ministry of War, which was in fact the employer of American military advisers. This then had to be approved by the Iranian parliament at the same time it voted to extend or deny the privileges, immunities, and exemptions to those advisers who could indeed be defined as the "administrative and technical employees" referred to in the 1961 Vienna accord.

A month later the U.S. Embassy had indicated its satisfaction with this action but had reminded Iran that military missions were to be defined as "those United States military personnel or civilian employees of the Department of Defense and their families forming part of their households who are stationed in Iran in accordance with agreements and arrangements between the two Governments relating to military advice and assistance."[8] Iran had again attempted to stall, but in late 1964 the government agreed to go with the American requests, requests that had now been broadened to include immunity for dependents as well as for military personnel themselves.

The format for standard American Status Forces agreements had been established in the early 1950s and referred to American troops stationed in NATO countries. In these agreements, jurisdiction was concurrent in that both the United States and the receiving country exercised legal control. If the United States chose not to prosecute, then the country in which the offense was committed could do so. "Unlike the Status of Forces Agreements (SOFAS) that govern most American servicemen overseas, the arrangement in Iran allows the United States exclusive criminal jurisdiction over all personnel at all times. Iran has waived its right to prosecute, even if American authorities choose not to do so."[9] With the partial exception only of an agreement with West Germany, the Iranian-American SOFA was unprecedented. It was a particularly severe application of the concept since it nullified any and all Iranian legal control over the growing American military colony stationed in that country. And it broadened the idea to include all dependents.

The issue of immunity and extraterritoriality had long been a sensitive issue for Iranians, who considered their country the victim of capitulations to the British and Russians from 1828 to 1928. As one professional explained to me in Tehran in early 1966: "Isn't this part of the reason why you Americans fought the British? The redcoats refused to abide by local law and did as they wished in the colonies. Why do you Americans insist on being above the law here in Iran?"[10] Recognizing this fact, officials in the Department of State attempted to soften the Defense Department's demands but were singularly unsuccessful in doing so, given both congressional pressures and the mindset in the White House.

Few political observers or scholars of Iran then understood the long-term significance of what was happening. One notable exception was T. Cuyler Young of Princeton University, who witnessed firsthand in Iran the explosive anti-Americanism that rose in reaction to the SOFA. In a powerful paper delivered at Harvard University in April

1965, Young described the situation: "The news was met by a bitter and vehement public reaction, which was reflected in the press; this must have been condoned by the government, such is the close and continuous surveillance accorded the press. The depth and breadth of the bitter resentment among the people was highly disturbing to one visiting the country a few weeks after the event."[11] Early in 1969, Young told his students at Princeton that the SOFA was a catastrophic mistake for American interests in Iran, that such a heavy-handed act was being interpreted as a mark of crass imperialism, yet that "we pushed it through."[12]

The secular and the religious intelligentsia of Iran bitterly opposed the immunity bill. On October 26, 1964, one day after the Majlis approved the $200 million loan for military equipment and the date of the shah's forty-fifth birthday, a religious leader stood up and publicly condemned the immunity agreement. The speaker's name was Ayatollah Ruhollah Khomeini. His fiery speech stands as one of the most important and moving political statements made in Iran in this century. In it, Khomeini powerfully and frontally attacked the shah and America for attempting to destroy the dignity, integrity, and autonomy of Iran. Alternating between anger and pathos, at times almost pleading in frustration, Khomeini began by emphasizing the great sadness in his heart. "Our dignity has been trampled upon; the dignity of Iran has been destroyed." He went on to explain why:

> A law has been presented to the Majlis according to which we are to accede to the Vienna Convention, and a provision has been added that states that all American military advisors, together with their families, technical and administrative officials, and servants—in brief, anyone in anyway connected with them—are to possess legal immunity concerning any crime they may commit in Iran.
>
> If the servant of some American or some cook of some American assassinates your *marja'* [the leading religious leader] in the middle of the bazaar or runs over him, the Iranian police do not have the right to apprehend him. Iranian courts do not have the right to try him. The files must be sent to America so that our masters over there can decide what is to be done.
>
> The previous government approved this measure without telling anyone. The present government recently introduced a bill in the Senate and settled the entire matter without breathing a word to anyone. A few days ago, the bill was taken to the Majlis and with a few deputies voicing some opposition it was passed. They passed it without any shame, and the government shamelessly defended this scandalous action.
>
> They have reduced the Iranian people to a level lower than that of an American dog. If someone runs over a dog belonging to an

American, he will be prosecuted. Even if the shah himself were to run over a dog belonging to an American, he would be prosecuted. But if an American cook runs over the shah, the head of state, no one will have the right to interfere with him.

Appealing frequently to Islam and the members of the ulama, Khomeini chastised the secular leaders of Iran for selling their country and roundly condemned them as traitors. The United States was singled out for special criticism for its activities in Iran; but Great Britain and the Soviet Union also came in for sharp criticism.

> Are we to be trampled underfoot by the boots of America simply because we are a weak nation and have no dollars? America is worse than the British; the British are worse than the Americans; the Soviet Union is worse than both of them. Each is worse than the other; they are all despicable. But today our business is not with all these forces of evil. It is with America.
> The President of the United States must know that he is the most obnoxious person in the world in the eyes of our people. He stands obnoxious before our people because of the crime he has committed against this nation of Islam. Today, the Quran opposes him. The people of Iran oppose him. . . .
> The American advisors get immunity (*masuniyyat*) and some of our poor Majlis deputies have cried out: "Ask these friends of ours, please don't force this on us. Don't sell us. Don't colonize us." But who listened? No one is able to understand one article of this Vienna Agreement. Article 32 does not exist. I don't know what this article is. I don't know. Nor does the Speaker of the Majlis know. Nor do the deputies. I don't know why they accepted it. Why did they sign it? Why did they approve it?[13]

The shah's government responded quickly to Khomeini's speech. Already under government surveillance and under considerable pressure for the role he had played in igniting the June 1963 demonstrations, this time Khomeini was picked up and exiled in Turkey on November 4, 1964.

Ayatollah Khomeini never forgot the 1964 immunity agreement and never forgave the United States for it. In a declaration shortly after he went into exile, he asked: "Are Iranians aware of what is going on in the Majlis these days? Are they aware of the fact that, unknown to them, a crime has occurred through deception? Do they know that the Majlis approved a document of enslavement for Iran?"[14] According to Khomeini in this pronouncement, the United States tried to force immunity agreements on the governments of Pakistan, Indonesia, Turkey, and West Germany. But while all these countries rejected the suggestion, Iran meekly agreed to it. In a widely circulated declaration addressed to Prime Minister Hoveyda in April 1967, Khomeini personalized his opposition to the immunity bill, stating: "I have been in exile all this time because I have disagreed with the immunity of Americans which is antithetical to the sovereignty of Iran. It is against the independence, religion, and constitution of the country. . . . The granting of immunity to strangers (*ajanib*) is testimony to our weakness and unconditional surrender."[15]

Even after his return to Iran following the revolution, Ayatollah Khomeini recalled the humiliation of this event and often referred to it in his speeches. In December 1982 in a major speech before the Revolutionary Guard Corps and their leaders, he condemned the hollowness and corruption of imported values and cultures. In pointing out how such values undercut Islamic principles, he specifically explained how these outside ideas had been forced on Iran by outside powers. In particular, he discussed the special protection given Americans who had carried such values into Iran and how they had been protected by an imported law and system of "capitulations" that overrode Iranian and Islamic tradition. Khomeini had quietly vowed that such a surrender of national sovereignty would never again occur in Iran.

Although of particular importance because of Khomeini's role in the episode, the SOFA was only one part of the overall tightening of Iranian-American relations in the 1960s. This tightening was itself accompanied by the gradual hardening of the shah's system of control. Domestically, the Iranian political system began to harden in a way that brought moderate critics to the surface while forcing radical and extremist opponents underground. The machine-gun fire of June 1963 followed by the passage of the hated immunity bill accelerated this process.

The Politics of Police Control and Controlled Reform

On January 21, 1965, the twenty-one-year-old son of an ironworker named Muhammad Bukhara'i shot Prime Minister Hassan Ali Mansur just outside of the Majlis building. Mansur died five days later. He had been prime minister for only ten months before his assassination. Mansur's assassination occurred at a time of general economic crisis and after the government, with the shah's strong personal support, had unilaterally declared stiff price increases for such basic commodities as bread, rice, and kerosene. As Iran scholar Marvin Zonis, who was in Tehran at the time, has stated, the reasons for the assassination had to do with a "milieu of discontent and malaise permeating all Tehran, but especially the poorer sections surrounding the bazaar."[16]

Mansur's assassination led immediately to major shakeups in the country's security and police organizations. The main change was the shah's decision to replace SAVAK head Hassan Pakravan with Lt. Gen. Nimatullah Nassiri. Pakravan, a man of civility and relative moderation, had replaced the more ruthless Teymour Bakhtiar. His replacement by Nassiri represented a reversion to Bakhtiar days and worse. A thoroughly brutal officer who had proven his devotion to the shah when he led the royalist forces against Prime Minister Musaddiq in 1953, Nassiri began a period of secret police control that made him one of the most feared and detested officials in Iran. Nassiri, in turn, was replaced as chief of police by another hard-line practitioner of punishment, Maj. Gen. Muhsin Mubassir. During those few days in late January 1965, a military officer with secret police connections, Col. Abdul Azim Valian, was named to head the Land Reform Organization. The significance of placing a SAVAK man in charge of the primary reform program was not lost on Iranians.

Despite these dramatic moves to bolster and harden the Iranian security forces, another major act of political violence occurred only two months later. On April 10, 1965, a twenty-two-year-old member of the shah's own imperial guards opened fire with a submachine gun on the monarch and his bodyguards as the shah entered his Marble Palace office. Although the shah escaped unscathed, the attempt badly shook the political system. The would-be assassin was one of Muhammad Reza Shah's trusted guardsmen and was considered to be a completely loyal and religious young man. Many now speculated about the levels of discontent and alienation that might be present throughout the country.

The assassination of Mansur and the attack on the shah himself represented the growing breadth and depth of the opposition to the Iranian political leadership. The plot against Mansur was found to be rooted in the religious right associated with the old Fidayan-i Islam group and known as the Islamic Nations party (Hizb-i Millat-i Islami). Assassin Muhammad Bukhara'i and the three associates that were executed with him for their role in the killing were all young religious extremists of lower middle-class bazaar background. In October 1965, fifty-five members of the Islamic Nations party were arrested, and in early 1966 they were tried, sentenced, and jailed. This little-known clandestine group, composed of very young men and deeply embedded in the hidden recesses of lower-class Iranian society, was a clear early indicator of the opposition that was to effectively overthrow the Pahlavi regime in the next decade. In fact, one cleric reportedly referred to the arrested members of this group as only "one branch of a very large tree."[17] This tree would grow both below and above ground in the years that followed.

While the religious opposition briefly showed itself in the Mansur plot, the secular intelligentsia was also quietly organizing against the regime. In the Marble Palace plot, the government arrested and tried fourteen young men on charges of masterminding the attempt on the shah's life. Although the regime never proved a direct link between these individuals and the young assassin, there is little doubt that they had been actively criticizing and condemning the Pahlavi government in meetings held in such places as the Tehran Palace Hotel. The accused averaged twenty-seven years of age, and all were members of the professional middle class; half were either teachers or students. Most were highly intelligent and believed in Marxist-Leninism. One member, Parviz Nikkhah, for example, a twenty-six-year-old teacher at Tehran Polytechnic, was an individual of enormous intellectual talent who had written a manuscript on revolution. After serving a prison sentence, he went to work as an ideologue for the shah's government in the Ministry of Information.[18]

Taken together, the two groups charged with the two assassination plots of 1965 represented the major opposition that would ultimately spearhead the Iranian revolution: the religious lower-class and the cluster of liberal and left-wing middle-class intelligentsia. It was in the mid-1960s, therefore, when opposition began to develop covertly and informally in Iran. During this period were formed the two major guerrilla organizations that would play significant roles in the revolution, the Sazman-i Mujahidin-i Khalq (the Organization of the Crusaders of the People) and the Sazman-i Chirikha-yi Fidayan-i Khalq (the Organization of the Guerrilla Crusaders of the People).[19] The heavy buildup of police power in Iran coincided with the spreading formation of dedicated opposition groups in the country.

Along with its reemphasis on coercive control, the Pahlavi regime decided to continue with its reform program, but in whittled-down form. The Majlis, which had been dissolved during Amini's premiership, was revived and inaugurated in the fall of 1963. In this, the Twenty-first Majlis, the regime promoted the candidacy of new educated professional middle-class members—individuals who represented a growing salariat that was increasingly challenging the system of monarchical rule. The percentage of college-educated representatives burgeoned to 62 percent of parliamentary membership, a larger percentage than any time in the political history of Iran. In this

Majlis, 121 of 196 representatives possessed modern higher educations, and of these 57 had been educated abroad. At the same time, landlord representation fell to its lowest proportion since 1909.[20]

As the regime slowly moved to shift its base of support from the old landed aristocracy to the growing, pushing, professional middle class, it continued and expanded its six-point reform program. Land reform and the literacy corps received special emphasis, and the shah added six new points: the establishment of a health corps, a reconstruction and development corps, and rural courts of justice, the nationalization of waterways, a program of national reconstruction, and an educational and administrative revolution. Reform activity did indeed take place as the shah shrewdly sought to preempt the political program of the intelligentsia while attempting to draw this class into his system of control. Despite this, it is clear that the shah's overriding goal was the preservation of Pahlavi rule. That the reforms took place in a climate of repression and increasing personal insecurity was a reminder that economic growth and measured social change were surrogates for any form of political development.

A major plank in the shah's informal platform of political control in the mid- to late 1960s involved coopting the Iranian professional intelligentsia. Middle-class Iranian observers referred to this process as *rushvah dadan bi-rawshanfikran* (bribery of the intellectuals). Because the shah needed the professional intelligentsia to guide and implement his reform program, because many members of this class were viscerally opposed to repressive politics, and because these educated forces were viewed most favorably by the United States, a concerted effort was made to suck them selectively into the political elite. The primary vehicle for this program of cooptation was the establishment of the Iran Novin party in 1964. Formed from the Progressive Club (Kanun-i Taraqqi), at the center of which were such intellectuals as Amir Abbas Hoveyda and Hassan Ali Mansur, the Iran Novin party became the central political instrument of Pahlavi control until 1975, when the shah himself suddenly dissolved it. This party provided the main channel through which educated professionals joined the shah's system.

This new technocracy was carefully handpicked from above and was screened by both SAVAK and the shah himself. The principal criterion for membership was complete loyalty to the person of the shah and subservience to his system of rule. Although occasional independent-minded professionals were able to survive for a time in this system, the overwhelming majority of high-ranking political professionals were individuals with secret police connections, insatiable personal ambitions, and intense unpopularity among the Iranian population who knew them. Key examples include Manuchehr Shahqoli (Iran Novin party member and minister of Health, 1965–74), Mrs. Farrukhru Parsa (Iran Novin party member and deputy to Twenty-first Majlis, minister of Education, 1968–74), and Hushang Ansary (minister of Information, ambassador to the United States, minister of Economy, minister of Economy and Finance, head of National Iranian Oil Company, 1966–78). Two members of the professional intelligentsia who best represent the kind of individual who joined the Pahlavi system in the 1960s were Hushang Ansary and Amir Abbas Hoveyda. The former operated quietly in the shadowy habitat of Iranian politics while the latter was a highly visible, public political figure from the 1960s until the revolution.

Ansary, considered by many Iran watchers to be a shifty-eyed, ambitious maneuverer, was certainly one of the most powerful figures in Iran during the last fifteen years of the shah's rule. With close contacts to the American business elite, Ansary labored in the financial shadows while shrewdly working his way into the shah's confidence. He first impressed the shah when the latter traveled to Japan in 1958 when Ansary was Iranian commercial attaché there. During the shah's stay, Ansary made sure he served him obsequiously but effectively. From that time on, he never looked back as he spun webs of personal contacts that drew him ever closer to the center of power. He was an undersecretary in the Ministry of Commerce, ambassador to Pakistan and Ceylon, minister of Information, Ambassador to the United States, minister of Economy, minister of Economy and Finance, and chairman of the National Iranian Oil Company. Although Ansary was a good administrator who surrounded himself with competent people, his greatest strength was in building and nourishing personal connections with the powerful.

While serving as ambassador to the United States in the late 1960s, he "assiduously cultivated high-ranking contacts,"[21] and he did so effectively. An American embassy profile summarized his style well: "He is apt to curry favor with the Shah, just as he appreciates judicious flattery from his own subordinates, but he makes sure he also has the facts and figures on whatever matter is discussed."[22] Hushang, as his friends called him, was a troubleshooter for the king while carefully establishing and protecting financial and political links with American foreign-policy figures like Henry Kissinger.

An even better example of the coopted professional was Amir Abbas Hoveyda, who held the premiership of Iran longer than any other man in Iranian history. He became prime minister on the assassination of his close friend and brother-in-law, Hassan Ali Mansur, on January 26, 1965, and remained in this post until July 1977. He then served as minister of Court until September 9, 1978. Hoveyda was both an intellectual and a political actor of great talent. Educated in Belgium and Lebanon, he was the son of a middle-class professional of Baha'i persuasion and a woman of aristocratic background, Afsar Khanum, the granddaughter of the powerful Qajar princess Ezzat Al-Dawlah. Hoveyda liked to stress his own humble middle-class origins, choosing to ignore his mother's background.

Hoveyda and the shah complemented one another very well; the shah was the aloof, unreachable figure of monarchy while Hoveyda played the role of folksy, smiling, friendly politician. In fact, one might refer to the Hoveyda premiership as a "quipocracy" because he constantly deflected questions with clever quips and one-liners. The shah used him to balance the influence of other powerful members of the political elite such as Ardeshir Zahedi, who engaged in a bitter personal feud with Hoveyda. In the presence of the shah, Hoveyda was always properly obsequious, but he presented himself to outsiders as personally independent.

A balding, pipe-smoking wit with a carnation in his lapel and walking stick in his hand, Amir Abbas Hoveyda projected the image of a warm, friendly political figure. In fact, he was very tough, and, and as one of his close associates put it, he used his subordinates like pomegranates, squeezing them dry and then discarding them. He was formally in charge of SAVAK and had a private budget that he tapped at will for purposes of political control. As his tenure as prime minister lengthened, he became increasingly ruthless and turned on the members of the intelligentsia, once referring to them as "little cry-baby communists trained at the London School of Economics."[23] Hoveyda and Hushang Ansary were among the best examples of the educated intelligentsia coopted into the system. There they joined such old, faithful politicos as Alam, Eqbal, and Sharif-Emami. With the coming of the revolution, Ansary quietly slipped away to the United States with a personal fortune; Hoveyda, steadfastly refusing to leave his country, was imprisoned and executed by the revolutionary regime in 1979.

The educated intelligentsia who bought into the system were in many ways more ruthless, ambitious, and corrupt than the old aristocracy, who had for so many years provided the political support for the shah. Their new professional educations provided them with an arrogance bred of a kind of *nouveau éducation*. This was summarized well by one astute Middle Eastern observer:

Every country east of the Mediterranean is torn to bits by some kind of inheritance. . . . But I can envisage the day when these countries will be even worse, torn by degree-holders more self-interested and sycophantic than their predecessors, and far, far less charitable. If you think the sheikh grinds the faces of his tribesmen you should wait and see the Ph.D. grind the faces of all and sundry, without even a touch of the magnanimity we pride ourselves on.[24]

In Iran this argument became reality in the 1960s with the rise of the Iran Novin party. The Western-educated professionals were the most ruthless members of SAVAK, the most ambitious bureaucrats and ministers, and the most avaricious businessmen. In order to institute his policy of cooptation and bribery, the shah enlarged his bureaucracy so that more challengers could be appended to his political elite. During the 1960s, for example, the number of ministries increased from twelve to twenty-two. By 1970 the highest echelon of the civil bureaucracy alone counted almost 500 persons, including 22 ministers, 111 deputy ministers, and 331 directors-general. Other powerful inspectors, experts, and advisers were omnipresent in the civil service. That these individuals were important to the shah's modernization program was only part of the reason for this expansion.

As the shah maneuvered middle-class technocrats into his political elite, he accomplished four interrelated goals. First, he succeeded in recruiting to his team many potential disenchanted young professionals and political activists who now acquired a stake in the system. Second, he effectively divided the professional middle class and sapped its power through dissension and infighting. Third, he demonstrated to outside critics that he was not ruling by repression but was in fact widening political participation in his country. American statesmen and the U.S. media were especially impressed by this activity. Fourth, he provided the government with badly needed expertise necessary to the implementation of the selective reform programs.

The third result of this program is especially worthy of note. The Hoveyda-Iran Novin governments were extremely popular in America, where Pahlavi supporters used them constantly to indicate the shah's commitment to reform and progress. This attitude was strengthened by the fact that of the twenty-three members of Hoveyda's first cabinet, nineteen spoke English and sixteen had either studied or traveled in the United States. This group frequented the social circles of high-ranking official Americans posted to Tehran and were those who hosted the numerous U.S. dignitaries who visited Iran. This pattern continued right up until the revolution.

Despite this policy of cooption, serious flaws in the strategy were already observable in the late 1960s. Significant numbers of the professional middle-class refused to be coopted. They scoffed at the system's obvious methodology of political bribery. When they objected, they were harassed and their dissent was suppressed through the increasingly active Secret Police. Also, as membership in this salaried class exploded in size, it was simply impossible to absorb all of them into the ruling system. Many members of the intelligentsia scathingly criticized the October 1967 coronation ceremonies, where, in the midst of international dignitaries, the shah crowned himself and the empress king and queen of Iran. This costly spectacle, a preview of an even more extravagant coronation ceremony four years later, was described by guest George Ball in words reminiscent of those used at the time by many members of the Iranian middle-class intelligentsia: "What an absurd, bathetic spectacle! The son of a colonel in a Persian Cossack regiment play-acting as the emperor of a country with an average per capita income of $250 per year, proclaiming his achievements in modernizing his nation while accoutered in the raiments and symbols of ancient despotism."[25]

Meanwhile, the White Revolution proceeded with great fanfare. Yet without the cooperation and commitment of the bulk of the technicians and professionals, the reforms remained mostly plans on paper. This alienated the lower and lower-middle classes, who were constantly bombarded with promises, few of which were met. The religious leaders, who had lived and worked for years in the villages with the people, developed an attitude of sullen resentment as they themselves were largely cut out of any participation in the programs promulgated from Tehran.

The real failure of the reform programs through the 1960s was privately recognized by United Nations reports and by a few independent Western scholars then doing research in Iran. By 1970, for example, over two-thirds of Iran still had no access to any medical facilities; development was seriously slowed by severe shortages of trained engineers and skilled workers; income distribution remained badly skewed with millions of villagers as poor as ever; unemployment and underemployment were on a constant rise through the 1960s; only one-fifth of the total irrigated land was adequately irrigated; one-third of the land under the huge dams had no distribution system whatsoever; agricultural production was growing at only 2 percent per year while the population was increasing by 3 percent and the cost of living at 6 percent; in 1968, Iran began for the first time to import wheat in large amounts to help feed its people; and the administrative system was a morass with five different government ministries competing for control over agricultural policy.[26]

In sum, the Pahlavi policies of the late 1960s, while impressive and energetic on the surface, were clearly lacking in many ways. Both prongs of the policy of reform and repression had inherent flaws. In particular, they carried longer-term negative consequences. Ultimately, the central problem was the failure to match the economic emphasis with fundamental political reform of any kind. The shah and his closest advisers concluded that programs such as land reform and industrial growth made political development quite unnecessary. Thus a little-known and greatly ignored Department of State intelligence report on the political dynamics of Iran could conclude that "Iran remains basically a weak and vulnerable country. . . . In sum, the Iranian political climate is fundamentally unhealthy."[27]

Lyndon Johnson, Personal Politics, and Tightening the Connection

During the administration of Lyndon Johnson, American-Iranian relations tightened considerably. The shah made official visits to Washington in July 1964, August 1967, and June 1968; he also stopped briefly in New York in May 1965. In addition, other high-ranking Iranians visited America, including Prime Minister Hoveyda, who made a one-week, highly publicized visit in December 1968. Meanwhile, important American financial and political emissaries traveled constantly back and forth between the United States and Iran. Both David and John D. Rockefeller III traveled to Iran during this period, as did a high-level presidential delegation on Human Rights led by Roy Wilkins, executive director of the National Association for the Advancement of Colored People. The conference on human rights was held in Tehran in April 1968, and Wilkins was chosen to lead the delegation in order to help deflect any criticism that might be raised by liberal Americans wondering about a human rights conference being held in a country recognized by the U.S. government itself to be one in which the secret police maintained order through repression.[28]

The link between Lyndon Johnson and the shah, between the United States and Iran, was maintained in good part by W. Averell Harriman, who undertook four important presidential missions to Iran between May 1965 and November 1967. Harriman's constant appearances in Tehran indicated the growing strength of the Iranian-American connection. It was also during this period, on May 25, 1967, that Hushang Ansary presented his credentials as Iran's ambassador to the United States. In the White House, such individuals as Special Assistant for National Security Affairs W. W. Rostow pressed for policies in support of the Pahlavi regime.

During the Johnson presidency, the American president and the Iranian shah developed a close professional relationship—one in which the shah inexorably came to exert a stronger and stronger influence. Still smarting from American pressures applied during the Kennedy administration, the shah determined that he would use all means at his disposal to win the Johnson administration to his personal cause. He viewed Johnson as a somewhat crude but kindred spirit, as a consummate politician who understood the realities of political power and manipulation. One could bargain and bluff with him, and in such contests the shah was confident that a Persian king could consistently outbargain and outpolitick a Texan rancher.

Friction existed between the United States and Iran, especially over weapons and oil. The shah had an insatiable appetite for military supplies and always sought the best and the latest weapons (especially aircraft) as they came off the American production line. He made it his business to know what these weapons were and avidly read such periodicals as *Aviation Week and Space Technology*. In the mid-1960s, the shah also chose to confront the oil consortium about production levels allotted to Iran. He argued that increased production was essential in order that Iran receive the revenues necessary for his modernization program. And, of course, he needed the funds in order to purchase the highly priced military equipment that he was also demanding. The shah's pressures were so great that the U.S. government intervened to convince the oil companies in Iran to increase their production.

In 1965 and 1966, the shah began to use his powerful informal connections in America to pressure the United States and to gain the attention of the Johnson administration, which was then preoccupied by the Vietnam War. In a three-hour private meeting in Tehran with the omnipresent Kermit Roosevelt in July 1966, the shah fumed at the United States for ignoring him and for charging him "discriminatory" fees for military equipment. The shah indicated that he was "tired of being treated as a schoolboy" and warned in the best Iranian bluffing technique that Iran and America were very near the end of their relationship. Roosevelt rushed back to Washington and immediately transmitted his messages through his grid of high-level contacts. On July 27, 1966, he relayed the shah's arguments directly to Walt Rostow and then sought a meeting with Assistant Secretary of State Ray Hare. His contact to the president himself was through George Carroll, a former CIA agent who had worked with Roosevelt in Operation Ajax, which had helped overthrow Musaddiq in 1953. Carroll now worked for Vice President Hubert Humphrey and reported Roosevelt's message in a memorandum that began: "You know Kermit Roosevelt. He is Vice President, Gulf Oil Company. He is also President, Middle East Institute. No American knows the shah of Iran as well as does Kim."[29]

In his meeting with his friend "Kim" Roosevelt, the shah listed numerous reasons why he was indispensable to America. These included the following: (1) Geostrategically, Iran, with its long border with the Soviet Union, served as a buffer against Soviet expansionism; (2) the shah had faithfully supported the United States position on Vietnam; (3) Iran was willing to fill the vacuum left in the Persian Gulf when the British finally began to withdraw their forces; (4) Iran stood as a strong regional antidote to the radicalism of President Nasser of Egypt; and (5) the shah's regime was one of the few Middle Eastern governments willing to support and assist the state of Israel. In providing the United States with these kinds of critical services, the shah indicated that he was shocked by the "indifference of his American friends." Because of "maltreatment," the shah concluded that "America does better by its enemies than it does by its friends."

This kind of informal, personal pressure was reinforced by a number of general public actions that indicated an Iranian rapprochement with the Soviet Union. In June 1965 the shah made a state visit to the Soviet Union; in April 1968 Soviet premier Aleksey Kosygin traveled to Tehran for a five-day state visit; and in September 1968 the shah and empress went to Moscow for a ten-day visit. In January 1966, Iran and the Soviet Union signed a major commercial agreement that provided for the establishment of a steel mill and gas pipeline. Then the shah dramatically agreed to purchase $110 million in Soviet arms supplies. In 1966 the shah also began a flurry of commercial activity with the communist countries of Eastern Europe. He visited Rumania, Yugoslavia, Bulgaria, Hungary, and Poland, while Prime Minister Hoveyda also traveled to Rumania. Return visits to Tehran were made by the leaders of Rumania, Bulgaria, Yugoslavia, and Poland. Through these means, the shah let it be known to America that he was not to be taken for granted.

Throughout 1966 the shah pressured the United States unrelentingly for increased arms supplies. He lobbied especially for two F-4 squadrons of sixteen planes each, while the United States had agreed to provide only one such squadron. He also insisted that the United States was overcharging him, pointing out that the price of a Soviet MIG was only $600,000 to $700,000, while the cost of a F-4 was well over $3 million. Furthermore, he resented the American policy of annual review whereby the United States reserved the right to limit its arms sales to Iran on the basis of an assessment of Iran's general economic well-being. Muhammad Reza Shah and Prime Minister Alam bluntly let the United States know that Iran was no longer to be "taken for granted" and that the shah was not America's "lackey." The shah bluffed hard to get his way. At one point, referring to his apparent willingness to turn to the Soviet Union, he said that it would be a shame if this disagreement on arms supplies should result in "another steel mill business." Alam smoothly told American diplomats that surely it was unthinkable that the shah would "sleep with the devil," but then again maybe he would if he were desperate enough. At one point the shah even went so far as to tell U.S. ambassador Armin Meyer that he might have to divert some of his security officials from watching the Soviets and have them instead begin monitoring U.S. actions in Iran.

The shah eventually got his two squadrons of F-4s and much more. After some resistance and bargaining, the U.S. Embassy adopted the shah's position. In a supplement to a long report on military sales, the embassy presented thirty reasons for continued military sales to Iran on terms favorable to Iran. These were organized under six headings: the shah remains an important friend; a new and healthier relationship between Iran and America is developing; Iran has legitimate defense reasons for this arrangement; Iran's economy is stronger than is generally thought; there would be adverse reactions in Iran and the region if the American response should be inadequate; and increased sales are economically practical for all concerned.[30]

The Johnson administration finally heard the shah's message. Hemmed in by a series of international crises, U.S. foreign policymakers decided to meet the shah's requests for increased military aid. The response was immediate and generous and, in the words of one observer, was "made in strange haste."[31] Although scattered objections were raised by the International Security Agency in the Department of Defense and by Sen. William Fulbright, chairman of the Senate Committee on Foreign Relations, the White House rammed through the sharply increased military sales to Iran. In a communication to the president, Fulbright wrote that he was "disturbed" by the F-4 sale, which was then the most advanced aircraft in operational squadrons and which had not been sold to any country except Great Britain. Walt Rostow immediately drafted a response to Fulbright justifying the sales because the USSR was selling MIG fighters to Iraq and because such sales would "bolster our balance of payments."[32]

The economic argument for increased American arms sales to Iran in the 1960s was strongly reinforced by other high-ranking members of Johnson's entourage like Robert S. McNamara. In a memorandum to President Johnson in 1967, McNamara wrote: "Our sales have created about 1.4 million man-years of employment in the U.S. and over $1 billion in profits to American industry over the last five years." He further wrote that "the military sales program involves less than seven percent of U.S. military production and is not carried on for the purpose of generating business for American industry, but the fact is that a large number of jobs and substantial profits are attributable to U.S. military sales abroad."[33] According to one U.S. diplomat, President Johnson "pressed corporations like McDonnell Douglas and Boeing to sell more. The companies worked in tandem with the Pentagon, which sought to improve the U.S. balance of payments through such purchases."[34]

In 1967–68, the United States sold Iran on credit somewhat less than $96 million worth of military equipment; the figure for such sales during 1969–70 was $289 million. Nearly $250 million worth of F-4 Phantom aircraft alone were delivered to Iran between 1967 and 1970. During the same period, Iran took delivery of 768 Sidewinder and Sparrow air-to-air missiles as well as forty AB205 Iroquois helicopters, two 1,100-ton general purpose naval fighters, and three motor gunboats. The increasing sales of military materiel to Iran took place within a general atmosphere of American-sponsored official praise for the shah and his regime summarized well by National Security Council aide Harold Saunders who was himself a consistent supporter of pro-Pahlavi policy: "We are trying to broaden our public praise of the Iranian Government."[35]

A network of influential U.S. policymakers both in Washington and Tehran consistently worked to promote this pro-Pahlavi policy. In Tehran, the key actor was Armin Meyer, who replaced Julius Holmes as ambassador in the spring of 1965. A career foreign service officer from the Midwest, Meyer had previously served as U.S. ambassador to Lebanon. While Holmes had encouraged his officers to report Iranian affairs objectively, Meyer revised this policy noticeably. He and his influential political counsellor, Martin Herz, presented the shah's rule in glowing terms, and young foreign service officers were often discouraged from contacting the opposition and from presenting critical political reports.[36] The pressure was so great that at least one talented officer left the foreign service after this Tehran experience. A silver-haired, friendly man of modest talent, Armin Meyer was manipulated by the shah, and for four years his actions approached those of a public relations officer for the Persian king.

Back in Washington, influential national security adviser Walt Rostow performed much the same role. When the shah was scheduled to visit Washington on a private visit in June 1967, Rostow convinced President Johnson to break protocol and to meet twice with the shah, keeping the second session off the printed schedule. Rostow stated in a memorandum to the president: "Normally, I would stand firm against a second meeting on any but a State visit. However, in this case there is a great deal to talk about. Moreover, the Shah is a person you can talk seriously with."[37] The June trip was canceled due to the outbreak of the Arab-Israeli war, but the shah's visit was rescheduled for August. On this occasion, two important meetings were held at 5:30 P.M. on the consecutive days of August 22 and 23. Both during this visit and in June 1968, when he again traveled to Washington, the shah was promised military weapons and complete American support for his rule.

Armin Meyer and Walt Rostow formed an informal team to promote the shah in official America. In unofficial correspondence both in 1967 and 1968, Rostow and Meyer congratulated one another about the successes achieved in strengthening American-Pahlavi relations. In a letter of October 21, 1967, to Rostow, Meyer stated that these relations had been "revivified" as a result of the shah's visit to Washington that August. In a revealing letter to Rostow on July 15, 1968, Meyer urged the administration to respond favorably to the shah's requests for military aid. He ended with his "heartfelt thanks to you, to Hal Saunders, and of course, to our mutual boss (to whom I am writing separately) whose Texas hospitality and understanding make it possible for us both to be proud and lucky." In his response, on July 22, Rostow revealed his own role in the continuing "revivification": "Believe me, we handle your business here with much pleasure. A relationship like this is a welcome relief. We all recognize and appreciate the contribution you have made to this relationship." When Meyer was in Washington for the shah's visits there, Rostow arranged meetings for the ambassador with President Johnson himself. Meyer worked hard to keep these channels open by sending Iranian pistachios and caviar to the president and his immediate staff, including special assistant Marvin Watson. On June 27, 1968, Johnson wrote Ambassador Meyer in Tehran that "my relationship with His Majesty has been one of the real pleasures of my Administration."[38]

Although the Johnson administration embraced the shah and praised his policies, there were voices of caution and criticism. Many Iranian students and nationals living in the United States flooded the State Department and the White House with telegrams and letters condemning the corruption and repression of the shah's regime. These communications were routinely filed and smothered by such individuals as Benjamin Read, who was then executive secretary at the Department of State. In the case of particularly important Iranian critics, McGeorge Bundy, Walt Rostow, and other White House staffers personally saw that the letters went nowhere and that they received little serious consideration.

One such example was Dr. Ali Sheikholislam, founder and president of the National University in Iran, who was forced into exile by the shah. Because of his former position in Iran, he had met with Lyndon Johnson on two occasions when the then vice president visited Tehran in 1962. On February 12, 1966, Sheikholislam wrote a strong letter to Johnson criticizing the shah's rule. In it, he condemned the shah's government as a police state and wrote that he himself had been "threatened to death by the Shah's gunmen and secret police called Savak." Sheikholislam indicated his horror at hearing former U.S. ambassador Julius Holmes publicly praise the shah and compare him to American Founding Fathers like Jefferson. And he warned: "Mr. President, with the present situation in Iran, I have not the slightest doubt that you will have, in the near future, another Vietnam or worse."[39] Sheikholislam's communication was intercepted by McGeorge Bundy, who refused to acknowledge it and turned it back to Benjamin Read at the State Department.

It was more difficult to deflect criticism by such individuals as Supreme Court Justice William O. Douglas. Douglas knew more about Iran than anyone in the White House, and he was deeply concerned about the political situation there. In a letter to the president on November 8, 1965, Douglas indicated his concern about the trials of the fourteen Iranian students accused of complicity in the Marble Palace plot. Douglas argued that these trials were "really trials of the political opposition, not of criminals." After working through a number of drafts, Robert W. Komer, deputy special assistant for national security affairs, sent a carefully worded response to Douglas defending the shah's system of justice. In this letter Komer lectured Douglas on the finer points of law and pronounced that according to Iranian law those convicted were in fact "culpable."[40]

Another individual who knew considerably more about Iran than anyone in the White House was Princeton professor T. Cuyler Young. Young had been communicating his views about the fragility of the shah's rule since the early 1960s. He was particularly concerned about growing repression and corruption as well as increased American military assistance to Iran. Young's views were brushed aside by the American foreign policy establishment, and the Council on Foreign

Relations chose not to publish his excellent manuscript on Iran, which had been commissioned a decade before. In a letter of rejection on July 23, 1970, the head of the council's Middle East program assured Young that "no one on the staff or at the Council raised any question about the manuscript because of disagreement with your opinions and conclusions." He went on: "I think it only honest to say, however, that there were some of us who felt that you stressed the issue of the royal dictatorship fairly close to the point of a political polemic and at the expense of other issues."[41] And the hard-hitting paper that Young presented at Harvard in April 1965 received more attention in Iran than in the United States.

Finally, a small number of sensitive Iran specialists employed by the U.S. Department of State recognized serious difficulties in Iran and attempted to caution their superiors of the long-term consequences of these problems. Several of these younger diplomats had served in Iran during the ambassadorship of Julius Holmes, who permitted them considerably more reporting latitude than did later ambassadors. These doubts were clearly expressed in a State Department political dynamics study of December 1966. Its three primary authors were William Miller, who actually began the study years earlier, Larry Semakis, and Archie M. Bolster. All three were fine foreign service officers and accomplished Iran specialists, but their views flew futilely in the face of their foreign policy superiors.

Thus, although pro-Pahlavi policy and support came to dominate the very highest levels of the American foreign policy establishment in the latter 1960s, some voices always dissented. That those who questioned the establishment interpretation were among the leading and most astute observers of Iran made little difference; they had negligible impact on policy-making. This pattern marked the American-Iranian relationship over the next decade and was only broken by the explosive events of 1978–79.

Lyndon Johnson, the Shah, and Growing Anti-Americanism in Iran

The Johnson administration shifted American policy into decidedly pro-Pahlavi directions. Coming immediately after Kennedy's program of enforced reform and involving a number of the personalities responsible for that program, this shift represented a crossover in Iranian-American relations. Several things explain Lyndon Johnson's Iran policy. First, Johnson himself believed strongly in the efficacy of force. Although he spoke of economic development, social justice, and political reform, he believed much more fervently, particularly in the area of foreign relations, in the reinforcement of order through military might. In his thinking, the Alamo must be manned, and those who hold the high ground must never relinquish it. Over the years, Johnson's views were reinforced by such close and influential advisers as W. W. Rostow, McGeorge Bundy, Robert Komer, and a generally very hard-line National Security Council staff.

Second, and perhaps most important, Johnson was preoccupied in an ugly, demoralizing military venture in Vietnam that was slowly dividing and draining his country. He was grateful to those friendly Third World countries whose governments appeared stable. Not only did Iran seem to have such a government, but its leader was one of the few Third World supporters of America's Vietnam policy. The shah knew this and used it continually to enlist Johnson's support for Pahlavi projects of all kinds. In his meetings with W. Averell Harriman, the shah liked to emphasize his approval of American actions in Vietnam. On occasion, he also indicated that he backed Lyndon Johnson's invasion of the Dominican Republic. Lyndon Johnson appreciated this and told the shah so.

The shah also cleverly reiterated his own support for American policies in the Middle East. American and Iranian interests obviously coincided in the region; the shah feared and hated President Nasser of Egypt, and he criticized and condemned Nasser's radicalism whenever he spoke with American officials. More importantly, and less obviously, the shah stressed his support for Israel, a country that Lyndon Johnson supported with a special fervor.[42] The Johnson administration's special commitment to and belief in Israel influenced its entire Middle East policy. That the shah's Iran was that rare Muslim regime to quietly but clearly maintain a de facto recognition of Israel impressed Johnson and many of his key advisers. Furthermore, the shah indicated his willingness to help fill the political vacuum when the British withdrew their forces from the Persian Gulf. He argued that this would guarantee regional stability without the United States, already deeply burdened in Vietnam, having to commit troops to the Middle East as well.

Finally, the shah's rich oil deposits and growing wealth promised economic opportunities for the United States. This became especially evident when Iranian oil revenues increased to such a degree that on November 30, 1967, the Agency for International Development (AID) closed its doors in Tehran after many years of extensive activity in Iran. The previous year President Johnson's Cabinet Committee on Balance of Payments had declared Iran a "developed" country. American industry flooded into Iran, and the leading U.S. military firms competed for lucrative contracts. American government officials recognized what was happening and provided approval and encouragement. For its military supplies, the shah's government now began to pay premium prices, what the shah irritably called "exorbitant" prices. There were good balance-of-payment reasons not to alienate such an important client.

The sinews of the American-Pahlavi connection were reinforced in the 1960s by numerous relationships on both sides. On the Iranian side, Ardeshir Zahedi and Hushang Ansary played prominent roles, while on the American side, such businessmen as David Lilienthal, David Rockefeller, and Kermit Roosevelt and politicians such as W. W. Rostow and Armin Meyer were active. David Lilienthal, for example, presented his zealous, uncritical views of the shah to Walt Rostow and McGeorge Bundy and directly to Lyndon and Lady Bird Johnson. After a meeting on June 16, 1964, with Lilienthal, the president stated simply: "Dave, what is going on in Iran is about the best thing going on anywhere in the world."[43]

These relationships were solidified by constant exchanges of gifts of all kinds. The heaviest flow of gifts came from the Iran side; a stream of caviar, pistachios, and orchids poured into the Johnson White House. The champion of generosity was Ardeshir Zahedi, who seldom forgot a birthday or overlooked an illness in the life of America's first family. Whether in London as Iran's ambassador to Great Britain or in Tehran as minister of Foreign Affairs, Zahedi managed to send remembrances to relevant American policymakers. Ansary was a close second to Zahedi in the gift-giving sweepstakes.[44]

While the shah was publicly supporting America's Iran policy on the international stage, back home in Iran he permitted his press to criticize this policy sharply. Popular periodicals such as *Firdawsi*, *Bamdad*, *Tawfiq*, and the newsweekly *Khandaniha* condemned America's role in Vietnam in graphic articles. In 1965 Mihdi Bahar wrote a critical attack describing the United States as a colonial power bent on promoting the interests of the American economy and the multinational oil companies. Bahar's book, *The Heir of Colonialism*, was published as a 650-page paperback and created a minor sensation when it appeared in Tehran bookstores. Although the government pretended to censor it and to keep it off the market, the book was easily obtainable. Nearly twenty thousand copies were sold in the first few months. Then in 1966 Bahar wrote a hard-hitting series of five articles that were published in the weekly *Tehran-i Musavvar*. This series also castigated U.S. foreign policy and emphasized the theme of petroleum imperialism.

Bahar was permitted to publish his ideas since he pitched his attack against the Western oil companies—companies that he implied had even been responsible for Mussadiq's movement against the shah. It is instructive to note that Bahar's attacks came as the shah was pressing the oil company consortium for greater production and higher prices and when the Pahlavi government was turning to the Soviet Union and Eastern Europe in an effort to pressure the United States to increase supplies of sophisticated arms. This particular offensive against the United States and the oil companies was carefully framed in the argument that the oil industry sought to destabilize the shah in order to control Iran. Regardless of Bahar's motives, his research and writing seriously undercut America's reputation in Iran.[45]

In the Persian press, therefore, the seeds of anti-Americanism were being planted deeply into the subconscious of the Iranian citizenry. The shah allowed this to occur in order to placate the challenging middle class, to put some distance between himself and his American patron in the eyes of the growing numbers of educated critics at home. He also did it to gain leverage in his drive for American arms and aid. The unintended consequences of this policy were disastrous for America's long-term interests in Iran. In Washington and Tehran, American Middle East officials never seriously bothered to follow the Iranian press. If they had, they might have been shocked at the bitter nature of the criticism of U.S. foreign policy in Southeast Asia. Thus, while the Johnson administration was gratefully applauding the shah for his courageous backing on Vietnam, in Iran the shah slyly watched his own government-controlled press blast the United States. The Meyers, Rostows, and Bundys had no idea what the shah was doing in this respect. Meanwhile, many members of the Iranian younger generation spent their formative years reading and hearing about a brutal, militaristic, imperialistic America. These young people were among those who took to the streets in the revolution a decade later.

Large numbers of the Iranian population sullenly and cynically watched the increasingly close connections between the United States and Iran. When the United States proclaimed Iran a "developed" nation, many Iranians were furious. In their eyes, the United States had first forced a humiliating immunity agreement on them and had ever since been pouring huge supplies of military equipment into the shah's arsenal. They viewed the announcement of Iran as "developed" as a ploy to force Iran to pay America premium prices for these weapons. In a 1967 article published in the weekly *Bamshad*, one writer protested that "we are still a developing country and not a developed one. . . . We hope to be able to announce our development some day.

Although it is possible that this day is not far off, it is certainly not today. We can diagnose our own interests better than others."[46]

In December 1966, a distinguished member of the moderate opposition in Iran, Allahyar Saleh, described U.S. policy in Iran in uncharacteristically bitter terms. Although a Musaddiqist, Saleh was a mild-mannered individual who rarely spoke in sharp or exaggerated tones. He stated that "one can no longer place any hope in the Americans because they, too, are following the British in the policy of colonialism. There is one difference, however—the British were flexible, but the Americans are a symbol of harshness." Saleh, whose brother, Ali Pasha, had worked for years for the U.S. Embassy, argued that "the Americans insist on working with infamous elements, oppressors or men endowed with oppressive qualities, and that they support only those elements who enjoy the dislike and hatred of their society." And he complained that "unfortunately whoever refuses to cooperate with the Americans is accused of collaborating with the communists." He concluded: "Therefore, one must not cherish any hopes in them. I, too, have become a supporter of the opinion of the clergymen—hope in God and in forthcoming developments."[47]

The depth of the growing anti-American sentiment was starkly conveyed in Firaydun Tunakabuni's *Memoirs of a Crowded City*, published in early 1970:

> If I were a cartoonist, I would sketch the American in complete military uniform. He has one of his heavy, hobnailed boots on the back of Latin America while the other boot stands on the back of Southeast Asia. His left hand has a black man by the throat. On the other side of the page I would draw the Russian with Rumania and Czechoslovakia as two small children. The Russian is pulling their ears while they whimper. The American is pointing at the Russian and saying: "Hey folks, look at how this savage is behaving, ignoring all principles of humanity, transgressing the sovereignty of nations, and trampling upon the freedom of the people.[48]

David Rockefeller and Muhammad Reza Sa'idi

On May 17, 1970, a group of thirty-five leading American industrialists and investors began a six-day conference in Iran. Known as the Tehran Investment Seminar, this event represented a major attempt by American industry to pursue opportunities in Iran, whose increasing oil wealth made it one of the most attractive business centers on the international scene. James A. Linen of Time, Inc., and David Rockefeller of Chase Manhattan Bank were the two leading organizers of the project. The seminar was billed as having attracted the largest group of influential American businessmen ever gathered in a Third World society. Besides Linen and Rockefeller, the investment contingent included H. J. Heinz, chairman of H. J. Heinz, Donald Kendall, chairman of PepsiCo, Frederick Bissinger, president of Allied Chemical, Donald Burnham, chairman of Westinghouse, Najeeb Halaby, president of Pan American World Airways, and Howard Clark, chairman of American Express. Also present were David Lilienthal of the Development and Resources Corporation and Eugene Black, past president of the International Bank for Reconstruction and Development.

The Iranian political and economic elite greeted these American industrial giants with open arms, and many sessions were held with leading members of the Iranian banking community. In a session with the shah himself, the investors heard that they were most welcome but that they must understand that they would have to make their money as minority shareholders. The American delegation traveled around Iran and were wined and dined wherever they went. They left Iran feeling that Iran in fact was a country that represented very real investment opportunities.

Not all Iranians welcomed the American delegation. Middle-class nationalists and religious groups strongly condemned the conference, and political demonstrations broke out, including an attack on the Iran-America Society offices in Tehran. Nationalists immediately labeled this Conference of Investors either the Conference of Imperialists or, on occasion, Rockefeller's Conference. Throughout the presence of this high-powered group in Iran, anti-American opinion seethed beneath the surface of Iranian society. From his exile in Najaf in Iraq, Ayatollah Khomeini issued a statement in which he condemned the conference: "Any agreement that is concluded with these American capitalists and other imperialists is contrary to the will of the people and the ordinances of Islam."[49]

In Iran, one of Ayatollah Ruhollah Khomeini's students, a forty-one-year-old cleric named Muhammad Reza Sa'idi, stood up publicly and sharply criticized the American investment group. He termed the shah's regime treasonous for attempting to sell its country to American imperialism. Although at times a troublemaker in class, Sa'idi was one of Khomeini's favorite students, and the young cleric revered the Ayatollah. A bespectacled, bearded man of tense, nervous disposition, Sa'idi had a history of resistance against the shah's government and had been arrested and imprisoned on several occasions for his opposition. SAVAK knew him well and considered him a stubborn true believer and religious fanatic. His followers viewed him as fearless and portrayed him as an individual destined for martyrdom.

On June 10, 1970, Muhammad Reza Sa'idi was tortured to death by the shah's police. The gruesome details of this deed spread like electricity across the human grid that is Iran's communication network, and Iranians from all walks of life exhibited both great sorrow and suppressed anger. The regime permitted Sa'idi's remains to be transported for burial to Qum, where other leading Shi'i religious leaders vowed that his death must one day be avenged. Sa'idi became an instant hero and martyr. Legend has it that as he faced his torturers, he said: "I swear to God if you kill me, in every drop of my blood you can see the holy name of Khomeini."[50]

Just as Khomeini's exile stemmed from his opposition to the SOFA, Sa'idi's martyrdom resulted from his opposition to the visit of the American investment group. These two events dealt crippling blows to the image of the United States among rank-and-file Iranians. Furthermore, the killing of Sa'idi represented the first real assault on religious leaders by the shah's regime. Thus began the stormy decade of the 1970s.

6 Iran, America, and the Triumph of Repression, 1971–1977

On October 11, 1971, the shah of Iran inaugurated a week-long social celebration and political extravaganza in commemoration of 2,500 years of Persian monarchy. The celebration was held at the ancient capital of Persepolis, where three enormous tents surrounded by fifty-nine smaller ones were imported and erected especially for the ceremonies. These air-conditioned tents, furnished with Baccarat crystal, Limoges china, and Porthault linens, became the center of what *Time* magazine described as "one of the biggest bashes in all history."[1]

Present for the festivities were high-ranking officials from sixty-nine countries, including twenty kings or shaykhs, five queens, twenty-one princes and princesses, sixteen presidents, three premiers, four vice presidents, and two foreign ministers. The notables included Presidents Nikolay Podgorny of the Soviet Union, Marshal Tito of Yugoslavia, Yahya Khan of Pakistan, V. V. Giri of India along with King Hussein of Jordan and Emperor Haile Selassie of Ethiopia. Vice President Spiro Agnew represented the United States. Besides these and other dignitaries and their entourages, several hundred selected world figures in the fields of industry, education, the arts, and the mass media, along with the cream of Iranian society, were also in attendance.

Nothing was spared in the preparation and execution of this Persian pageant, which cost an estimated $200 million.[2] The special lighting in Tehran and Shiraz alone required over sixty miles of cable and twenty miles of garlands from which were hung 130,000 bulbs. At the formal banquet attended by five hundred guests, the menu included quail eggs stuffed with caviar, crayfish mousse, roast lamb with truffles, and roast peacock stuffed with foie gras. Dessert included fresh raspberries flown in from France for the glazed fig and raspberry special. Master hotelier Max Blouet came out of retirement to supervise a staff of 159 chefs, bakers, and waiters, all of whom were flown in from Paris ten days in advance of the banquet. Maxim's of Paris catered the event, for which 25,000 bottles of wine (including a 1945 Château Lafitte-Rothschild) were shipped to Iran a month early to rest.

The ceremonies at Persepolis were covered by over six hundred journalists and camera operators from all over the world. According to a leading government spokesman in charge of the public relations, these journalists sent out over 10 million words describing the event to people in every corner of the world. In the United States, NBC-TV beamed coverage of the colorful ceremonies via satellite to an estimated ten million American viewers.

With this 2,500-year celebration, Muhammad Reza Shah Pahlavi began a new phase of his monarchy, one of increasing megalomania. At Persepolis, many of the most powerful and famous figures in the world came to praise his country, but, more importantly, they came to praise him. The shah favored a select few with private audiences, while personally welcoming an even smaller number as they arrived in Iran. He was somewhat amused when they quarreled about who received the more ostentatious living quarters, who had the more honored places at the banquet tables, and who received helicopter service rather than travel by Mercedes limousine.

At Persepolis, the shah linked himself directly to Cyrus the Great when he ceremoniously read the following words:

> O Cyrus, Great King, King of Kings, Achaemenian King, King of the Land of Iran!
>
> I, the Shahanshah of Iran, offer thee salutations from myself and from my nation.

And Muhammad Reza Shah concluded his statement to Cyrus the Great as follows:

> Cyrus! Great King of Kings, Noblest of the Noble, Hero of the history of Iran and the world! Rest in Peace, for we are awake, and we will always stay awake.

On October 17, 1971, the masses of Iranian people were asked to recite a short prayer for the "nation." This prayer mentioned the Shahanshah or monarchy six times and began with the following line:

> O, God Almighty, Creator of Universe and Man, The bestower of intelligence, wisdom and thought on Man, The Creator of countless blessings in our Noble Land, Thou who has appointed the Just Aryamehr as the Custodian of the Land of Iran!

The events of 1971 not only placed the shah in the line of Cyrus the Great but also identified him as the Appointed One of God Himself.

The Just Aryamehr was otherwise identified in the official prayer as Our Great Shahanshah.

But the masses of Iranian people were not all praying for their leader. They had not been invited to Persepolis. The participants in the ceremonies totaled somewhat fewer than three thousand persons, and of these the overwhelming majority were foreigners. The people of Iran were sealed out of the festivities by a tight military-security ring. Thousands of suspected troublemakers had been rounded up and detained by the police during the celebrations. United Press International slipped into print the following report: "If the pageant dramatized Persia's past and showed some of the armed strength of the present, there were reminders of some of the dangers still facing the country in the helicopters ceaselessly patrolling hills on guard against urban guerrillas who threatened a bloodbath during the celebrations."[3] Indeed, while the foreign dignitaries feasted on caviar, peacock, and Maxim's raspberries, a serious famine was in progress in the provinces of Sistan and Baluchistan as well as in areas of Fars Province itself, the very province in which Persepolis is located.

Even *Time* and *Newsweek*, perennial admirers of the shah, both carried somewhat critical accounts of the events at Persepolis. The criticism left the shah indignant. "So what are people complaining about? That we are giving a couple banquets for some 50 Heads of State? We can hardly offer them bread and radishes, can we? Thank heavens, the Imperial Court of Iran can still afford to pay for Maxim's services. Be assured, however, that Maxim's won't make a killing here. It will be, after all, the greatest gathering of Heads of State in history."[4]

Much more serious criticism emanated from Iraq, where the exiled Ayatollah Ruhollah Khomeini issued an appeal to the Iranian people to demonstrate against what he termed the plundering Pahlavi regime. Referring to demonstrating Iranian students who had been attacked and beaten by the shah's police, Khomeini stated: "Their only crime was to show their opposition to these 2,500th celebrations. They said, we do not want these celebrations, do something about the famine, we do not want you to celebrate over our people's corpses."[5] When asked whether Khomeini's words would have any effect in Iran, the shah answered: "None at all. The Iranian people have nothing but scorn for a man like Khomeini, who is of foreign extraction—he was born in India—and a traitor to his country of adoption in the bargain. Some say he is a paid agent of the British. He is also in the service of the Iraqi Government."[6]

The Politics of Confrontation and Repression

With the June 1970 murder of Ayatollah Saʿidi and the party at Persepolis sixteen months later, the shah initiated a new methodology of internal politics. He abandoned his past policy of balancing coercion with cooptation, repression with reform. It is true that the reform pole in this dialectic of control had shriveled considerably in the decade since 1963, but it had nonetheless carried enough meaning to serve as a safety valve for dissent. After October 1971, the shah hardened his position further and indicated that he would no longer tolerate any internal dissent or political opposition. In his view, such voices emanated from the misguided and the ignorant, communistic, or crazy malcontent. By giving his security forces a blank check, the shah for the first time in his thirty-year rule sought to rest his throne solely on a brittle policy foundation of repression and coercion.

The new policy resulted in a reign of terror. The systematic use of the ugliest forms of torture became the order of the day. People disappeared from their homes without explanation, the prisons rapidly filled, and political trials and executions increased sharply. By the mid-1970s, the shah himself began to admit that torture was being used in his country. He at one point said: "I am not bloodthirsty. I am working for my country and the coming generations. I can't waste my time on a few young idiots. I don't believe the tortures attributed to SAVAK are as common as people say, but I can't run everything."[7] In an unguarded moment in 1974, Prime Minister Hoveyda admitted bluntly that torture was being practiced in Iran's prisons. The following is a verbatim exchange between Hoveyda and this writer in a private interview at the Prime Ministry on June 30, 1974.

> Q: Mr. Hoveyda, the shah in an interview in *Le Monde* a few days ago indicated that torture was being used in the prisons of Iran.
> A: I don't believe he said that. . . .
> Q: Yes, he said exactly that . . . in an interview published in *Le Monde.*
> A: No, I believe he said that Iran only did what other nations of the world do.
> Q: He said that other nations tortured psychologically and that Iran was now beginning to use this kind of torture as well, implying that Iran had been practicing physical torture all along. Mr. Prime Minister, is torture going on in the prisons of Iran?
> A: [weak laugh] You mean like pulling out nails and breaking fingers . . . that kind of torture? No [laugh] of course not.
> Q: What would you say if I told you I know of individuals personally who had been tortured in Iranian prisons, friends who had been whipped, beaten, and had their fingernails pulled out?
> A: Perhaps. But that is not our business. This is police business. I

have nothing to do with their activities. The work of police is different. Some university students asked me the same question that you have asked me. Do you know what I told them?

Q: No.

A: I said: "Look, police are trained to be police. What do you think they should do when they move in to break up disturbances, hand everyone a flower? No, they are trained to move in with clubs!"

Q: Well, I find all this torture business depressing.

A: [shouting] Well you taught us how! You trained us! You Americans and British!

Q: *I* didn't train anybody.

A: You Americans did.

By 1974 the shah's regime maintained five major prisons with heavy concentrations of political prisoners. Four new penitentiaries were in the process of construction. As General Nassiri and SAVAK increasingly dominated the Iranian political process, infamous torturers with names such as "Drs." Husseinzadah, Rizvan, Rassouli, Husseini, and Mustafavi plied their trade in the quiet, yet screaming, caverns of the prison system. In a carefully documented study published in 1976, the International Commission of Jurists reported that "there can be no doubt that torture has been systematically practiced over a number of years against recalcitrant suspects under interrogation by the SAVAK." And in the words of Martin Ennals, secretary general of Amnesty International in 1974: "No country in the world has a worse record in human rights than Iran."[8]

Between 1972 and 1974 the shah's security apparatus systematically began an all-out attack on the Shiʻi religious establishment. Although they were also engaged in conflict with small, secular, guerrilla groups that had become an annoyance to the regime, the one major pocket of opposition left in the Pahlavi system was religious. The regime made a conscious decision to collapse this pocket. The Saʻidi affair had been the earliest indicator of this policy.

The government took charge of the wealthy Endowments Organization (Sazman-i Awqaf), and the Prime Ministry began to control this important religious and economic sphere in the early 1970s. Secular leaders, some with SAVAK connections, were put in positions of authority over this sacred network. Many religious Iranians interpreted this move as an obvious attempt by the government to take control of all the mosques and religious properties throughout the country and to steal the wealth of the people and the imams. In the words of Iran scholar Michael Fischer, the perception in Iran was one of a government "noose being tightened around the independent ulama."[9] The noose was tightened even more in the summer of 1974, when Gen. Abdul Azim Valian was named governor of Khurasan and was appointed *Na'ib al-Tawliyah* (sacred guardian) of the holy shrine of Imam Reza in Mashhad. This appointment was a special affront to all practicing Shi'ites in Iran, who knew Valian as a military man with SAVAK ties. People from all levels of society bitterly criticized this political decision privately. The fact that Valian later began a "modernization" project that involved razing the traditional buildings and businesses surrounding the holy shrine only increased the resentment.

This government broadside against the Shi'i religious organizations put the masses of believers in a difficult position. The time-honored practice of donating monies for the purchase of *vaqf* (Islamic endowment) properties and for the construction of mosques was placed in serious jeopardy. Shi'ites began to refrain from donating to their religion because they knew that their contributions would now be appropriated by the shah's government. This disruption of traditional religious practices was viewed as an intolerable attack at the very roots of the relationship between Shi'ism and the people.

In July 1972 the director of Endowments and several high-level associates sent an extraordinary memorandum to Prime Minister Hoveyda concerning a plan of action designed to destroy the credibility of Ayatollah Khomeini, who was then in exile in Iraq. This memorandum was part of the overall plan to crush the influence of the clerics. By bribery, force, and rumormongering, the government was urged to isolate and discredit Khomeini, whose critical declarations from Iraq were becoming troublesome. The plan was to present Khomeini as a foreign agent in the employ of the Iraqis and to attempt to turn the religious leaders in Iran against the ayatollah. Those who refused to denounce Khomeini were to be immediately arrested. According to the memorandum, even the Boy Scouts organization of Iran was to join the campaign against Khomeini.[10]

The summer of 1973 saw the government close down the Husseini-yi Irshad and the subsequent arrest and imprisonment of its leading lecturer, Dr. Ali Shariati. The Husseini-yi Irshad was a large religious building and lecture hall in Tehran where thousands upon thousands of Iranians of all social classes had been gathering to hear lectures by leading scholars and religious figures. Although primarily religious in focus, these presentations inevitably carried heavy sociopolitical messages and were thinly disguised statements of popular opposition to the government.

Ali Shariati was the most eloquent and popular speaker at the Husseini-yi Irshad; he smoothly combined social, political, economic, and religious analysis in his stirring public presentations. A brilliant, charismatic, chain-smoking intellectual who was then thirty-seven years of age, Shariati had studied sociology, history, and philosophy in Mashhad and at the University of Paris, where he earned his advanced degree. He developed a synthesis between Islam and modern Western social thought, and as such his work served as an important intellectual bridge for the modernized Iranian middle classes. Born in a Khurasan village the son of Shi'i cleric Muhammad Taqi Shariati, Ali Shariati later became a leading ideologue of the Iranian revolution. Although he died an untimely death in London in June 1977, Shariati was a revolutionary hero whose image outshone all except Ayatollah Khomeini himself.

Shariati argued that true Islam was a revolutionary, populist Islam and not an Islam that encrusted itself about an oppressive ruling class. In a powerful lecture at the Husseini-yi Irshad entitled "Religion against Religion" on August 14, 1970, he used many examples from Shi'i social history to demonstrate the point that corrupt regimes throughout Muslim history had attempted to use Islam as a means of control. They had borrowed religious symbols, had bought and corrupted weak religious leaders, and had distorted and twisted religious ideals for their own narrow, self-interested purposes. There is no doubt that such arguments represented direct and effective attacks on the Pahlavi regime. By 1974, Shariati was arrested and placed in solitary confinement; his father and young son were also imprisoned that year.[11]

In their crushing attack on Shi'ism, the shah's government closed down the publishing houses that produced books on religion and social problems. SAVAK infiltrated mosque meetings and prayer sessions and disbanded religious student organizations on campuses throughout Iran. The government arrested, interrogated, imprisoned, tortured, and even executed large numbers of clerics. Those imprisoned included important figures and later revolutionary leaders such as Ayatollah Hussein Ali Montazeri, Ali Akbar Hashemi-Rafsanjani, and Ali Hussein Khamene'i.

In December 1974 the regime tortured to death a fifty-four-year-old cleric named Ayatollah Hussein Ghaffari. In the tradition of the Shi'i ulama of the day, he had spoken out against corruption and repression in his sermons and Quranic commentaries, even comparing the Pahlavi government to that of the Egyptian pharaoh. More significantly, perhaps, he was a follower of Ayatollah Khomeini, with whom he maintained contact while Khomeini was exiled in Najaf. Iranian security forces had imprisoned Ghaffari on three different occasions between 1962 and 1965. In July 1974 he was arrested again, and he died under torture on December 28. Police report number 22304 stated merely that he had died accidentally from thrashing around on a bed while resisting having his beard shaved. This incident evoked the death of Ayatollah Sa'idi four years before, and it provoked an angry reaction across the country. SAVAK had provided the opposition with another important martyr.[12]

Under great pressure from the shah's regime, the leading religious leaders increasingly blamed the United States. In a long personal interview at his home in north Tehran in September 1970, Ayatollah Muhammad Burghe'i, a distinguished and widely respected cleric, softly but sharply argued that the government was attempting to destroy Shi'i institutions. He indicated that the United States was committing a "sad mistake" by associating exclusively with the shah's political elite. He argued that Americans did not even understand that elite since they failed to see the elite from below, from the eyes of the Iranian people. Burghe'i suggested that if the United States hoped to understand the spirit and heart of Iran, it should send representatives to visit the city of Qum. He expressed deep concern and controlled anger at the increasing political repression directed against the Shi'i leaders and suggested that the United States was playing an important role in this repression.[13]

The shah's rule by repression helped establish a vicious circle of violence as the opposition moved in desperation to increasing activities of greater extremism. The Mujahidin-i Khalq and the Fidayan-i Khalq guerrilla organizations attracted more and more followers to their causes. As SAVAK tightened the screws of control, the incidents of anti-regime violence increased proportionately. The period of guerrilla activities began on February 8, 1971, when thirteen armed young men attacked a gendarmerie post in the village of Siakal near the Caspian Sea. After killing three gendarmes, the small band escaped into the forests; the thirteen were later apprehended and executed on March 27. In early April another fifty young persons accused of plotting "anti-state activities" were arrested by the government's security forces. Also that year Prince Shahram, the son of Princess Ashraf, was attacked and almost kidnapped, and Gen. Ziaeddin Farsiu, the powerful military prosecutor who had just sentenced to death several young Iranians, was assassinated in the streets of Tehran. In 1972 guerrillas assassinated the deputy chief of police, and in late 1973 other political plotters attempted to kidnap and assassinate the shah, the empress, and the crown prince.

Throughout the country the universities were the scene of constant upheaval. In spring 1973, several demonstrating students were seriously injured when troops attacked Tabriz University. An even more violent incident occurred in June 1974, when military commandos, in a rampaging raid reminiscent of the 1962 attack on Tehran University, invaded Pahlavi University in Shiraz, beating and arresting hundreds of students. Between 1971 and 1975, Iran witnessed approximately four hundred bombing incidents.[14] According to the careful calculations of Ervand Abrahamian, 341 guerrillas and members of armed political groups lost their lives battling the shah's regime between 1971 and 1977.[15]

Americans in Iran now became for the first time serious targets of antiregime violence. On November 30, 1971, opposition guerrillas boldly attempted to kidnap the U.S. ambassador to Iran, Douglas MacArthur II, as he returned late in the evening from a party at the home of Asadollah Alam. Terrorists killed Lt. Col. Lewis Hawkins, a military adviser in Tehran, on June 2, 1973, and on May 21, 1975, U.S. Air Force colonels Paul Shaffer and Jack Turner were assassinated as they rode to work in a U.S. military staff car. Finally, in August 1976, three American civilians working on a sophisticated electronic surveillance system (IBEX) were killed in the streets of Tehran. Americans in Iran were increasingly subject to surveillance, harassment, and physical attack. Thirty-one bombings and threatened bombings alone were directed against American organizations and facilities in Iran between 1971 and 1975. Opposition groups bombed the facilities of the U.S. Information Service and its subsidiary, the Iran-America Society, six times, while they hit the U.S. Embassy in Tehran twice and the Peace Corps offices once during these years.[16]

The regime's policy of applied force and increased repression was counterproductive. In 1974 a young leftist poet and writer named Khosrow Golesorkhi publicly refused to recant and condemned the regime before millions of Iranians on national television. Before this, under SAVAK pressure and the threat of more torture, opposition intellectuals had admitted their errors and had apologized to the shah and the nation on Iranian television. Parviz Nikkhah, accused for complicity in the Marble Palace plot of 1965, was only one of those who publicly recanted. But, despite his wife and two young children and knowing that he would pay for it with his life, Golesorkhi refused to yield and publicly denounced the Pahlavi government as corrupt, repressive, and illegitimate. He was duly executed and thus became an instant martyr and hero to Iranians across the country. The Golesorkhi phenomenon was something new to the regime, which slowly came to the realization that its own policy had transformed a little-known writer into an instant hero and rallying point for the opposition. In a powerful commemoration, poet and Pahlavi prisoner himself Reza Baraheni wrote:

> we too have spies among the policemen
> the sergeants and the agents of SAVAK
> —you have killed Khosrow Golesorkhi
> that has nothing to do with your glories in the Iranian press
> nothing to do with oil your money and the royal entourage aloft
> on the shoulders of the SAVAK priests
> nothing to do with the raven-pattern silk
> woven by the hungry Baluch laborers to cover
> the symmetrical carcass of the Queen
> nothing has anything to do with anything
> but the news of the shooting is everywhere
> without the news of the shooting being anywhere
> which confirms only one thing
> you have killed Khosrow Golesorkhi[17]

In the summer of 1974, a Tehran taxi driver described Iran as a valley of tears and warned emotionally that these tears would become a flood that would wash away the repressive and unpopular Pahlavi government.[18] This deep feeling and hardening opposition was the clear response to the shah's repressive policies. Why then in 1971–72 did the shah of Iran depart from his proven political strategies and resort to sole rule by repression? The answer must begin with Muhammad Reza Shah himself.

The Flawed Genius of Muhammad Reza Shah Pahlavi

For thirty-five years, the Iranian political system had been directed and shaped by the personality and policies of one man, Muhammad Reza Shah Pahlavi. By the 1970s, the shah had become one of the most visible and influential political leaders on the world stage. He appeared frequently on American television and gave hundreds of interviews to the international mass media, offering the world free advice on everything from oil conservation to child rearing. He gathered information on military technology, energy economics, and nuclear science and spoke knowledgeably about all three. He lectured the United States on its need for increased "social discipline" and told Great Britain that it had become "lazy, undisciplined, and permissive." At the same time, the shah confidently stated his belief that his country would soon be one of the top five industrial powers in the world.

A true enigma, the shah of Iran was bold and timid, knowledgeable and uninformed, prescient and short-sighted, courageous and cowardly, kind and cruel, patient and restless, resolute and uncertain. He ruled as a lion and a fox and could show both loyalty and ingratitude to his associates. In other aspects of his personality, the shah's character traits were quite clear; he was insecure, humorless, and egocentric. And he never acquired the ability to seek and consider criticism of any kind. Yet Muhammad Reza Shah worked extremely hard at his job and seemed to live for little else. Political affairs kept him so occupied that he had little time for his family. After the revolution, former crown prince Reza indicated, for example, that in eighteen years his father devoted an average of only fifteen minutes a day to his eldest son.

To his enemies, the shah of Iran was the incarnation of evil, a petty tyrant, a cruel and selfish dictator, and a traitor to his own country. To his admirers, he was a great leader, a reformer designed to lead his people to the good life, a storybook monarch busy at work polishing a democracy in the rough. Given his own contradictory internal traits and these conflicting external assessments, it is difficult to evaluate the shah as a political leader. Yet it is essential to do so in order to assess Iran, its revolution, and its relations with America.

Born on October 26, 1919, Muhammad Reza Shah was the eldest son of Reza Khan, an unlettered military man who crowned himself king in 1925, thus beginning the Pahlavi dynasty. Reza Shah was tall, tough, intimidating, and determined to modernize his country—by force if necessary. He subdued Iran's tribes and brought central control to his country. Meanwhile, he worked hard to establish a military and a modern educational and administrative system in Iran. A proud man and a nationalist, he brooked no political opposition and systematically eliminated political rivals. Yet in 1941 he was ignominiously forced to abdicate and to leave his country in the face of Allied British and Soviet military intervention. The Iranian army self-destructed, and, after a period of discussion, the Allies determined that his son, Muhammad Reza, would be allowed to continue the Pahlavi tradition.

Having taken the throne at the sufferance of foreign powers, the young twenty-two-year-old shah was understandably resentful and insecure. He picked his way gingerly through the political minefields of the 1940s, when his country lay helpless before the Allied occupation. In 1949 he survived an assassination attempt at Tehran University. When his bodyguard dove for cover, the shah survived by "shadow-dancing and feinting."[19] Dodging and weaving his way through the 1940s, the shah learned important tactics of maneuver and manipulation that were to become a part of his political repertoire.

As he staggered out of the 1940s with a bullet wound in his cheek and deeper psychological scars inflicted by wide-ranging political threats, the shah ran directly into the Musaddiq movement. This stormy challenge, which at one point forced a humiliating flight from his country, reinforced all of his earlier prejudices and insecurities. He returned to the throne partly through the intervention of another foreign power, the United States.

Through the 1950s and 1960s, the shah survived further political and personal threats, including rioting students, recalcitrant clerics, bitterly critical intellectuals, jealous aristocrats, reactionary provincial landlords, corrupt family members, wily veterans of Persian politics, and liberal democrats seeking reform. In the process, he developed a political approach that enabled him both to protect himself and to extend his power and influence. This approach combined reform and repression, favor and force, cooptation and coercion. As part of the first ingredient, he introduced selective reforms through the mechanism of the White Revolution, coopted into his political system members of the challenging professional middle class, and refined and implemented an effective strategy of divide-and-rule.

Since his primary motivation was "the ruler's imperative"[20]—the first and foremost need to maintain power—the shah sought to build a system that would first, promote complete loyalty to his person and second, effectively achieve administrative goals. Muhammad Reza Shah stood in the center of a gigantic personal network through which power emanated only from his own person. The political elite that clustered about him was there only at his sufferance, and all members of this elite remained vulnerable to his will. Standing as he did at the center of the system, the shah received information provided to him independently by each personal node in the network. And he especially sought to insure that no single node would grow too large, influential, or independent. Thus he encouraged rivalry among all his associates as well as among the various organizations that they headed.

Rivalry and balanced tension permeated this kind of personalistic political system, and the shah proved himself a master at playing key subordinates off against one another. He managed to keep all the lines of personal rivalry in fine tune. In the shah's Iran bitter rivalry even marked the Royal Family—powerful Princess Ashraf was constantly locked in conflict with the empresses, especially Soraya and Farah. Prime Minister Hoveyda and confidant-minister-ambassador Ardeshir Zahedi spent the 1970s engaged in a bitter personal conflict that approached a vendetta. In the National Iranian Oil Company, perennial elite member Manuchehr Eqbal conflicted with Reza Fallah, a competent, ambitious oilman with an enormous appetite for personal wealth and also a confidant of the shah. And even SAVAK's feared General Nassiri found his power checked by Gen. Hussein Fardust, who headed the shah's intelligence office (Daftar-i Vizhah). Twelve military-security organizations provided further balanced tension, and a half-dozen ministries competed to formulate agricultural policy in Iran.

This system enabled the shah to maintain effective control over his own political elite and provided him with detailed information about the comings and goings of each of them. It also promoted insecurity, encouraged corruption, and absorbed the valuable time of all elite members. It encouraged sycophancy and servility among the shah's associates, who became mere extensions of his own personality. Those who dared challenge the shah's ideas were quickly and unceremoniously cut out of the system. Individuals of integrity and independence had no place in the shah's polity. Muhammad Reza Shah destroyed the political futures of such individuals and privately and sarcastically referred to them as individuals of idées fixes or as *gardan-i shak* (stiff-necked ones). Those with stiff necks had an understandably difficult time kissing the shah's hand.

Muhammad Reza Shah directed this system brilliantly. He left in his wake powerful, experienced, challenging Persian politicians by the dozens. They included shrewd maneuverers like Sayyid Ziaeddin Tabataba'i and Ahmad Qavam, popular leaders like Muhammad Musaddiq and Khalil Maliki, and later challengers like Ali Amini and Hassan Arsanjani. As he used, discarded, or defeated such individuals, he became increasingly accomplished in the politics of elite control. His capacity to manipulate personalities was vast.

Challenging social classes provided a more serious challenge to the shah. The professional middle class, for example, although splintered and divided against itself, represented a strong threat. Some members of this class were susceptible to cooptation and political bribery; other more recalcitrant professionals retreated into apathy as they saw their symbols appropriated through the shah's dramatic reform program; still others refused to accept the shah's rule, which they saw as corrupt and repressive. The masses who had been awakened by the loud talk of reform developed little commitment to the shah. Instead, their expectations were heightened and their aspirations sharpened by the constant governmental propaganda. When the White Revolution failed to deliver, they sought the succor and support of their religious leaders, many of whom lived in their midst. And these Shi'i clerics were almost completely ignored in the shah's reform calculations. He viewed them with contempt; at best, he avoided dealing with them, and at worst, he had his police attack them. Ayatollahs were generally immune from tactics of political cooptation and bribery and were therefore especially difficult to control.

The second half of the shah's political strategy involved the application of force. He preoccupied himself with police and military matters and sought to maintain direct and complete control over these forces. He handpicked all military leaders above the rank of major and monitored their every action. Close relatives and trusted friends occupied the highest ranks in his military organization. The shah prided himself on his knowledge of military science and considered himself the quintessential military man because of "my father's examples *and* because I am a soldier."[21] An accomplished pilot, he had a special interest in his air force and ceaselessly sought the most advanced aircraft for his country. No expense was spared in his military build-up, and by the mid-1970s Iran was spending approximately $5 billion a year on arms and materiel. In the end, the shah rested his power on the pillar of military might, a pillar of which he himself was an integral part. As he said: "I am the army."[22]

As long as the shah balanced military might with reform and astute political manipulation, his system seemed politically impregnable. He never wavered in his commitment to the force of arms. In the early 1970s, however, he began to deemphasize the reform-manipulative component of his rule. This coincided with an increasing personal megalomania. Short in height but large in ego, he came to see himself as both omniscient and omnipotent. The delicate politics of reform no longer interested him. He proceeded make important political decisions unilaterally and arbitrarily. In 1975, for example, the shah suddenly announced the establishment of a new one-party system. Beginning that March, every Iranian adult would be required to join the National Resurgence (Rastakhiz) party. As the shah bluntly put it:

> A person who does not enter the new political party . . . will have only two choices. He is either an individual who belongs to an illegal organization, or is related to the outlawed Tudeh Party, or in other words is a traitor. Such an individual belongs in an Iranian prison, or if he desires he can leave the country tomorrow, without even paying exit fees and can go anywhere he likes, because he is not an Iranian, he has no nation, and his activities are illegal and punishable according to the law.[23]

The shah accompanied this kind of arbitrariness and tough talk by cutting the lines of communication and information with political realities in his country, surrounding himself only with ambitious and servile servant-advisers like Ja'far Sharif-Emami, Hushang Ansary, and Amir Abbas Hoveyda. The old, wily advisers who had been carryovers from the days of his father and who would on occasion speak frankly to him had by now all passed away. Empress Farah was his only line to reality, and even her influence was minimal. In short, the shah of Iran lost touch. He could genuinely believe what he had told *U.S. News and World Report* in January 1969: "In this country, the word 'King' is almost magic. The people accept almost anything from the King."

At his core, Muhammad Reza Shah was insecure and resentful of foreign influence. When he embarked on his political ego trip in the early 1970s, he did so with a vengeance, muffling his insecurities and resentments with the trappings of imperial power. He blamed everyone but himself whenever difficulties arose. This tendency was to be exhibited most vividly after the revolution when the shah blamed the oil companies, the communists, the British, the American Democratic party, the CIA, and the international mass media for his demise.

Muhammad Reza Shah's dramatic change of political pace in the early 1970s did not occur in and of itself. It occurred in the context of a changing constellation of regional arrangements and international events, all of which came together at this time in history. It was in the area of foreign policy that the shah excelled, and it was here that he increasingly placed his political emphasis.

The Shah as a Leading Actor on a Changing International Stage

With the 2,500-year celebrations at Persepolis in October 1971, the shah of Iran announced his intention to undertake major international political and economic responsibilities. Earlier that year, in January and February, he had helped orchestrate a breakthrough in the determination of oil prices when he hosted Organization of Petroleum Exporting Countries, or OPEC, company meetings in Tehran. Through his minister of Finance, Jamshid Amuzegar, the shah forced acceptance of the principle that henceforth the producing countries would have the deciding voice in setting oil prices. The February 14 Tehran agreement stands as a landmark in the transformation of the system of petroleum pricing.

An even more significant part of the shah's game plan was the British military withdrawal from the Persian Gulf. This decision had been announced back in 1968, and ever since then the shah had been busy planning to move Iran into the power vacuum as soon as it developed in late 1971. He pounced on the opportunity by arranging for the establishment of an independent Bahrain and then militarily occupying Abu Musa and the Tunbs, three small islands then under the de facto control of Britain but belonging to the shaykhdoms of Sharjah and Ras al-Khaimah. This military move took place only three days before the formation of the United Arab Emirates (UAE). The Bahrain, Abu Musa-Tunb, UAE developments were all related and reflected the shah's goal of making Iran the preeminent force in the Persian Gulf.

The Iraqis well understood this intention and registered strong objections. Diplomatic relations between Iran and Iraq were severed on December 1, 1971, the day after Iran took the three islands. Throughout the next year, Iran and Iraq fought a sporadic war along the Iran-Iraq border.

Several other events in 1971 also reflected the impact of the inter-

Major Political Events

1971

OPEC Tehran meetings (Tehran agreement)	January 28–February 14
Siakal guerrilla incident	February 8
British military withdrawal from Gulf (formal confirmation)	March 1
Iran recognizes independent Bahrain	August 14
Iran establishes diplomatic relations with China	August 17
2,500-year celebration of Persian monarchy	October 11–17
Iran occupation of Abu Musa and Tunbs	November 30
Iran and Iraq sever diplomatic relations	December 1
Formation of United Arab Emirates	December 2
Third Indo-Pak war (creation of Bangladesh)	December 3–17
U.S.-Bahrain agreement for American naval base	December 23

1972

Soviet-Iraqi treaty	April 9
Nixon-Kissinger visit to Tehran	May 30–31
Empress Farah on official visit to China	September 18–October 2
Shah/Empress official visit to Soviet Union	October 10–31
Soviet-Iranian treaty	October 12
Shah states Indian Ocean vital to Iran's security	November 11
Shah sends Iranian troops to Oman	Fall
Nixon recommends Helms as ambassador to Iran	December 21
Ardeshir Zahedi named Iran's ambassador to United States	December 29

national arena on the shah's domestic political strategy. In August Iran recognized the People's Republic of China, and soon thereafter the two countries exchanged ambassadors; a year later Empress Farah made a two-week official visit to China. In December 1971, the third Indo-Pakistani war broke out, resulting in the creation of the independent state of Bangladesh. The shah watched this event with great dismay and was deeply upset by the dismemberment of a neighboring Muslim ally. He vowed that he would not let any such thing happen in Iran and became even more determined to develop a dynamic, aggressive foreign policy.

Throughout 1972 the shah moved sharply on the political offensive in the international arena. This offensive was catalyzed by an event of April 9, 1972. On this date, the Soviet Union and Iraq signed a historic treaty of friendship that involved a fifteen-year Soviet military and economic commitment to Iraq, which was then engaged in a series of bloody border conflicts with Iran. In October the shah and the empress traveled on an extended official trip to the Soviet Union, where on October 12 the shah signed a treaty of friendship. A month later, he let it be known that he now considered the Indian Ocean to be vital to Iran's national security and thus indicated that Iran's power was no longer limited to the gulf. Late in the fall, he sent his first contingent of fighting troops to Oman, whose sultan was engaged in a civil war with Dhofari insurgents. Thus in 1971–72 the shah made a series of lightning international moves that put Iran into a preeminent position in the region.

As he maneuvered his country into a dominant position in the Persian Gulf, the shah became the prime example of the Nixon Doctrine in action. Under Pahlavi direction, Iran now provided stability in the area while promoting the mutual interests of itself and the United States.

Deeply preoccupied with these regional and international issues, Muhammad Reza Shah clearly could not be troubled by unpleasant and destabilizing incidents at home. As he opened Iran's front door to international influences, he slammed the interior trapdoor on those compatriots who were criticizing his rule within the Iranian house. The shah and his advisers were incredulous that thirteen young men would take up arms against the powerful Pahlavi forces, as had occurred in Siakal in February. Through the spring and summer, internal political upheaval and violence occurred throughout the country as the October date for the 2,500-year extravaganza at Persepolis approached. Students demonstrated constantly on university campuses, laborers challenged the government, and bank robberies and gun battles broke out sporadically in downtown Tehran. In the week before the Persepolis celebrations, at least three gun battles occurred in Tehran alone.

Enormously annoyed and embarrassed by these dissident activities, the shah was only too happy to turn matters completely over to his secret police. To him, critics were dissidents and dissidents were traitors. When a reporter asked him in 1971 for the number of political prisoners in Iran, the shah snapped: "The number of political prisoners is exactly the same—no more and no less—as the number of traitors."[24]

Due to unprecedented security precautions and the protection provided by two divisions of troops, the 2,500-year celebrations took place without major incident. After this, the shah provided his police forces with a carte blanche. SAVAK now had total control of the internal political and security system. The shah had the complete support of the United States in instituting this policy. This official support was reinforced by an admiring American mass media. *Time* magazine led the applause. In a special cover story on November 4, 1974, *Time* began its adulatory piece with an "old Persian proverb" that "The Shah is the Shadow of God." The shah was described as having "brought Iran to a threshold of grandeur that is at least analogous to what Cyrus the Great achieved for ancient Persia."

Nixon, Kissinger, and Tightening the Pahlavi Connection

On May 30–31, 1972, President Richard Nixon and National Security Adviser Henry Kissinger visited Tehran on their way back from a summit meeting in Moscow. During these meetings with the shah the Nixon administration made the unprecedented promise to the Pahlavi king that he could purchase any conventional weapons he wanted from the American inventory. Among other military goods, this included the extremely sophisticated F-14 and F-15 aircraft. "He'll buy anything that flies," stated one U.S. official.[25] According to a U.S. Senate staff report, this extraordinary executive decision

> effectively exempted Iran from arms sales review processes in the State and Defense Departments. This lack of policy review on individual sales requests inhibited any inclinations in the Embassy, the U.S. military mission in Iran (ARMISH-MAAG), or desk officers in State and DOD to assert control over day-to-day events; it created a bonanza for U.S. weapons manufacturers, the procurement branches of three U.S. services, and the Defense Security Assistance Agency.[26]

On June 15, 1972, Henry Kissinger sent a memorandum to the secretaries of State and Defense outlining the military sales commitments that President Nixon and he had made to the shah during their May meetings. Then, in an extraordinary follow-up memorandum of July 25 addressed to the same officials, Kissinger concluded:

> The President also reiterated that, in general, decisions on the acquisition of military equipment should be left primarily to the government of Iran. If the Government of Iran has decided to buy certain equipment, the purchase of US equipment should be encouraged tactfully where appropriate, and technical advice on the capabilities of the equipment in question should be provided.[27]

In a letter to the minister-counselor in Tehran that concluded with a "keep the flag flying" salute, Jack Miklos, Iran desk officer at the Department of State, could hardly contain his personal delight with Kissinger's pronouncement. Miklos, who was an exceptionally strong supporter of Pahlavism in the Department of State, wrote that "we now have what I consider a very satisfactory memorandum from Dr. Kissinger which gives everyone his marching orders as to what should be done in following up the President's talk with the Shah."[28] These "marching orders" in effect indicated that from then on decisions concerning the Iranian purchase of conventional weapons from the United States were the business of the government of Iran.

Nixon and Kissinger gave the shah this blank military check against the best advice of the Department of Defense. On May 18, 1972, the Pentagon sent President Nixon briefing papers recommending that the United States not commit itself to selling Iran either the F-14 or the F-15, that the shah not be provided with laser-guided bombs, and that there be no further increase in uniformed American technical personnel in Iran.[29] Despite this, Nixon and Kissinger went ahead with their unprecedented commitment. The Department of State and, especially, the Department of Defense were deeply troubled by this fait accompli. In making the argument that the primary motive for the May 1972 commitment was strategic in nature, one scholar has even described it as "shortsighted and almost criminally careless."[30]

A major emphasis of the 1972 military agreement was the Grumman F-14 Tom Cat aircraft manufactured for the U.S. Navy. Then the most sophisticated jet fighter in the world, it was also one of the most expensive at $17 million per unit. When Grumman faced severe financial difficulties, it began to search for wealthy overseas purchasers. After a bitter intramural struggle between Grumman and McDonnell Douglas, which was promoting its F-15 with the support of the U.S. Air Force, Iran surprised many observers by signing a contract to purchase eighty F-14s. Grumman won the contest after an intensive struggle that involved middlemen, commissions, and an extraordinary amount of personal and political manipulating. Among other things, it resulted in Iran providing Grumman with a $75 million loan and paid commissions worth several million dollars. On January 23, 1976, the first three F-14s left the United States for Iran. An F-14 training base was established near Isfahan, and plans called for a ten-thousand-person American settlement there in the heart of Iran.

Between 1972 and 1978, the transfer of arms from America to Iran took place at levels never before known in international political history. Between 1972 and 1977 alone, the value of U.S. military sales to Iran amounted to $16.2 billion.[31] The Iranian defense budget increased from $1.4 billion in 1972 to $9.4 billion in 1977—an increase of 680 percent. By 1977 the military and security establishments in Iran were absorbing over 40 percent of the Iranian budget.

A Senate Committee on Foreign Relations staff report of July 1976 presented an unusually critical and prescient report on these huge arms transfers. Among the problems listed in this study were those associated with the growing numbers of Americans in Iran. "Anti-Americanism could become a serious problem in Iran, as it has elsewhere, if there were to be a change in government in Iran." The report went on to state that if there were a crisis, then "United States personnel in Iran could become, in a sense, hostages." It also pointed out that Iran could not absorb these weapons, which were among the most sophisticated in the world. The Grumman F-14 Tom Cat fighter, for example, was so electronically complex that even the U.S. Navy was having difficulty keeping it operational. Furthermore, sending hundreds of these planes to Iran only increased the chances that the Soviets could somehow gain access to the technology.[32]

The price of oil quadrupled in the fall of 1973, and Iran's oil revenues suddenly increased from $4 billion to nearly $20 billion per year. The shah immediately went on a gigantic military spending spree, and Tehran became the center of a Middle Eastern gold rush as arms dealers, contractors, and representatives from virtually all American manufacturers of military-related materiel descended on the city on droves. General Ellis Williamson, chief of the Military Assistance Advisory Group (MAAG) from 1971 to 1973 testified that he was swamped by approximately thirty-five visitors a week from the United States. According to Williamson: "So I was constantly seeing people coming in with something to sell. Iran was a good business deal. It was called the commercial man's smorgasbord. It was good, very, very good, and commercial interest was running extremely high."[33] General

Williamson, who indicated that his two-year assignment in Iran seemed more like two hundred years, stated that in these two years his office negotiated about seven hundred contracts for almost $4 billion.

The Nixon-Kissinger justification for the shah's military carte blanche rested ultimately on the perceived American need to have a trusted local power protect U.S. interests in the Persian Gulf. This foreign surrogate deserved to receive whatever military goods it deemed necessary to carry out its responsibilities. This was the application of the Nixon Doctrine with a vengeance. The fact that the littoral power policing American interests in the gulf was willing and able to pay hard cash for these goods only reinforced the decision. In effect, much of the increased income that Iran was now receiving for its oil was turned around and sent back to the United States in the huge prices the shah was paying for his weapons.

Both Nixon and Kissinger viewed American and Iranian interests as coterminous. In Kissinger's words: "On all major international issues, the policies of the United States and the policies of Iran have been parallel and therefore mutually reinforcing."[34] The shah was, from Kissinger's perspective, "that rarest of leaders, an unconditional ally, and one whose understanding of the world situation enhanced our own."[35] Kissinger's power arched across the Nixon and Ford administrations. During this time, he openly and continually promoted the shah's interests, which were, by his definition, America's interests.

On January 10, 1972, Minister of Economy Hushang Ansary and Vice President Spiro Agnew delivered addresses at the second Iranian-American investment conference, convened this time in New York City. Those attending the lavish dinner in the Grand Ballroom of the Plaza Hotel included such influential American Pahlavites as David Rockefeller and Joseph Reed of the Chase Manhattan Bank, James A. Linen of Time, Inc., David Lilienthal of Development and Resources Corporation, and Kermit Roosevelt. Also present were the following chief executives, all of whom had been in Tehran for the 1970 investment conference: Donald Kendall of PepsiCo, Frederick Bissinger of Allied Chemical, Donald Burnham of Westinghouse, Russell DeYoung of Goodyear, John Drick of the First National Bank of Chicago, John Harper of Alcoa, Najeeb Halaby of Pan American World Airways, Edgar Kaiser of Kaiser Industries, Ralph Lazarus of Federated Department Stores, Henry Wingate of International Nickel, and George Woods of the First Boston Corporation. Many other leading American industrialists were also in attendance as testimony to the widening commercial ties between the two countries.

The shah of Iran made his tenth trip to Washington in July 1973.

His productive discussions with Nixon and Kissinger in effect restated and enlarged the commitments made the year before in Tehran. He made a pilgrimage to Andrews Air Force Base, where he indicated personal enthusiasm for both the F-14 and the Phoenix missile. Nixon and Kissinger reaffirmed their unconditional support for the shah and in return asked the king to hold the line against increasing oil prices. The shah's role in the OPEC councils' demands for higher oil prices was the only major point of contention between America and Iran. The shah constantly used this issue as a bargaining chip.

In a communiqué on November 2, 1973, Iran and the United States agreed to establish a joint economic commission to accelerate further commercial relations of all kinds between the two countries. Between January 1973 and September 1974, United States companies signed contracts and joint ventures with Iran that totaled $11.9 billion. Henry Kissinger and the shah met on February 18, 1975, in Zurich, where the monarch agreed to provide the Israelis with additional Iranian oil if they acceded to Kissinger's retreat plan from Egyptian oilfields in the Sinai. Here the shah worked closely with the United States in a way that promoted America's more general perceived interests in the Middle East. In return for unconditional American support, the shah usually responded sympathetically to U.S. diplomatic requests. Two weeks after the Zurich meeting, Henry Kissinger (now secretary of State) and the everpresent Hushang Ansary (now minister of Economy and Finance) signed a $15 billion economic agreement.

The March 1975 economic accord committed Iran to the expenditure of $15 billion on American goods and services over the next five years. The largest agreement of its kind ever signed by two countries, it emphasized the construction of eight large nuclear power plants, which were to provide Iran with some eight thousand megawatts of electricity. By April 1975 American officials were privately estimating that Iranian-American nonmilitary and nonoil trade could reach $23 to $26 billion over the next six years. When added to the unprecedented level of U.S. military sales to Iran, this highly publicized agreement seemed to weld the two countries into one huge, commercial, binational conglomerate.

Iran and America were also cooperating very closely politically. An excellent example of the intimate Iranian-American political relationship sponsored by Nixon and Kissinger involved Iran, Iraq, and the Kurds. A hardy tribal people who inhabit the mountains of Iran, Iraq, Turkey, and the Soviet Union, the Kurds had been fighting a costly war for autonomy against the Iraqi government since 1961. Led by a venerable elderly leader, Mulla Mustafa Barzani, who had guided their fortunes for forty years, the Kurds had fought the Iraqi military to a standstill. After the Ba'thist regime in Iraq signed a treaty of friendship and cooperation with the Soviet Union in April 1972, both the United States and Iran became seriously concerned about Iraqi power and Soviet influence. Israeli interests also dictated anti-Iraqi views in Washington. In that important meeting in May 1972 of the shah, Kissinger, and Nixon, more was involved than a blank check for military purchases. The shah also asked for joint American-Iranian aid to the Kurds.

Although professionals in the Department of State and the CIA recommended against surreptitious U.S. aid to the Kurds, they were overruled by Kissinger and Nixon, who once again chose to cooperate with the shah. In June President Nixon sent Texan Republican John Connally to Iran to inform the shah that the United States would support his plan. As a favor to the shah, the United States funneled $16 million in CIA funds to the Kurds between 1972 and 1975. Iran also provided the Kurds with considerable military aid. The Israelis had also been assisting the Kurds in Iraq. In 1973–74, the Kurds and Iraq fought to a military stalemate, but the cost was especially high for the Iraqis, who had the bulk of their military forces tied down in Kurdestan.

Neither the United States nor Iran were anxious to see a Kurdish victory, which would encourage Kurdish autonomy movements elsewhere; the shah was, of course, especially concerned about his own Kurdish population and problem. The goal was to keep Soviet-supported Iraq occupied and on the defensive. Barzani and his Pesh Merga Kurdish troops were considered to be expendable. The Kurds themselves realized that they were an exposed people with few allies. In their own words: "The Palestinians have 18 Arab countries to help them. Bangladesh has India to help it. We have no one. The Kurds have no friends."[36] It is clear that the shah and Kissinger planned to use the Kurds for their own geostrategic purposes. And so they did.

According to a House Select Committee on Intelligence report (Pike Report): "The President, Dr. Kissinger and foreign head of state [the shah] hoped our clients [the Kurds] would not prevail. They preferred instead that the insurgents simply continue a level of hostilities sufficient to sap the resources of our ally's neighboring country [Iraq]. This policy was not imparted to our clients, who were encouraged to continue fighting. Even in the context of covert action, ours was a *cynical* enterprise." In the words of one U.S. official, purportedly Kissinger,

"Covert action should not be confused with missionary work."[37] In 1975 it became clear that neither the shah nor Kissinger were missionaries.

In March 1975 the shah met with his Iraqi nemesis, strongman Saddam Hussein, in Algiers, where they established the framework for the Algiers agreement, eventually signed in Baghdad on June 13, 1975. This agreement provided that the Iraqis now recognize the thalweg (deepest channel) principle concerning sovereignty over the Shatt al-Arab waterway. This replaced the traditional agreement whereby the Iraqis had controlled the waterway all the way to the Iranian shoreline. Also, Iraq would cease supporting dissident anti-Pahlavi activities in the Iranian province of Khuzistan. In return, the shah promised to end all aid to the Kurdish insurgents in Iraq. The Kurds were not consulted about this sudden volte-face. After fighting a costly and painful fifteen-year campaign against the Soviet-backed Iraqi army, they suddenly found themselves trapped in a political-military squeeze between Iran and Iraq.

Between March 13 and April 1, when the shah promised to seal the border with his troops, the Kurds were promised a cease-fire period. But the Iraqi troops advanced almost immediately, and in the pandemonium the Kurds—men, women, and children—fled across the mud and snow-covered Zagros mountain range. Thousands, many barefooted and with little more than the clothes on their backs, crossed into Iran, where they subsisted in varied conditions in twelve refugee camps established by the Iranian Red Lion and Sun organization. In April the shah kept his latest promise, sealed the border, and terminated all aid to those Kurds still fighting in Iraq. One of the refugees to Iran was Mulla Mustafa Barzani, who lived briefly in Tehran as the shah's "guest" and then emigrated to the United States, where he lived in McLean, Virginia, before he died a demeaning and little-noticed death in March 1979.

The United States had in fact been slowly withdrawing its aid to the Kurds in late 1973 and through 1974. Although the shah had remained active in support of the Kurds until the Algiers accord, Kissinger and his associates only wanted the Kurds to drain strength from the Iraqis and to keep them occupied. At one point, in a futile attempt to improve his standing with Kissinger, Barzani reportedly sent him three valuable Oriental carpets and a gold and pearl necklace as a wedding gift for Nancy Kissinger. This failed to move Kissinger, who simply chose to cooperate with the shah and to ignore the plight of the Kurds. With the Iranian defection, Barzani desperately called on the United States for assistance, fearing the specter of genocide. He sent numerous pleas for assistance to Kissinger. On March 10, 1975, the CIA chief of station in the region cabled CIA Director William Colby in Washington: "Is headquarters in touch with Kissinger's office on this; if U.S.G. (U.S. Government) does not handle this situation deftly in a way which will avoid giving the Kurds the impression that we are abandoning them they are likely to go public. Iran's action has not only shattered their political hopes; it endangers thousands of lives."[38] Neither Secretary of State Kissinger nor President Gerald Ford responded to the call of the Kurds. In this way, the United States acquiesced in the shah's betrayal of the Kurds.

The shah abandoned the Kurds for several reasons. First, he was nervous about his own Kurdish population, which also aspired to autonomy. Kurdish successes in neighboring Iraq could have had contagious consequences. Second, he was displeased by Barzani's lack of success against the Iraqi army and found that Iranian troops were increasingly necessary to support and buttress the Kurdish forces. The shah was not ready for an all-out war with Iraq. Finally, and most importantly, the Iranian king saw the opportunity to gain a cease-fire that would provide Iran with very attractive terms. These terms were provided in the Algiers agreement.

Columnist William Safire, who had access to the unexpurgated version of the Pike Report, strongly condemned Kissinger and Ford in two articles in February 1976 for what he termed the "unconscionable sellout" of the Kurds: "If the President wants to defend this sellout of the Kurds at the command of the Shah, let him do so; if he wants to disavow this act of American dishonor, let him fire the adviser [Kissinger] who urged this dishonorable act upon him."[39] Barzani had never completely trusted the shah. He did, however, believe that the United States would support him and, at a minimum, protect his people. It was the American component in the shah-Kissinger agreement that the Kurds were counting on. In a personal interview in September 1976, Barzani summarized the situation as follows: "We wanted American guarantees. We never trusted the shah. Without American promises we wouldn't have acted the way we did."[40] In the end, American policy was the same as Iranian policy. Nixon, Kissinger, and Ford chose to accept the shah's judgment concerning Iraq and the Kurds.

Although the American role in the collapse of the Kurdish government was never widely publicized in the United States, it was known and condemned in much of the Third World. It also alienated the Kurds, perhaps permanently, and radicalized the Kurdish movement as anti-American fringe elements filled much of the vacuum left by the destruction of Mulla Mustafa Barzani. Already deteriorating rapidly, America's image was further tarnished by this unfortunate saga. The Nixon-Kissinger-Ford tightening of the Iranian-American connection clearly took precedence over the interests and well-being of a tribal people, a people who were now considered to have served their purpose.

In his voluminous political memoirs, Henry Kissinger devotes one short paragraph and one footnote to the Kurdish issue. In his footnote, he defended the 1975 decision to withdraw aid from the Kurds by arguing that "the Kurds were about to be overwhelmed; they could not have been saved without the intervention of two Iranian divisions and $300 million in assistance from us."[41] He failed to mention that the shah sacrificed the Kurds on the altar of an Iran-Iraq rapprochement and that the United States once again moved in behind the Pahlavi position. Just before he died, Barzani was asked what he considered the biggest mistake of his career. The old man immediately responded: "My judgement about the American government that betrayed us."[42]

On August 6, 1976, Secretary of State Henry Kissinger met for more than four hours with the shah at the king's summer palace at Noshahr on the Caspian Sea. At a press conference afterwards, both Kissinger and the shah belittled the recently publicized Pike Report. Arms sales between the two countries were not only to continue but were to be accelerated. "Do you have any choice?" the shah asked rhetorically. He pointed out that "if the United States does not help its friends," its only alternatives were either nuclear holocaust or more Vietnams.[43] Kissinger agreed and often used the same Pahlavi phrases in seconding the shah's point of view. As he later wrote, "we have a better chance of assuring our future if we remember who our friends are."[44] The shah would remind America who its real friend was; Kissinger would then reinforce that reminder.

As Iranian-American commercial and military agreement discussions gained momentum, Kissinger and Hushang Ansary met in Tehran on August 7 and announced that Iran was to purchase another $10 billion worth of American arms. The shah was now interested especially in acquiring some three hundred F-16 planes and two hundred F-18 aircraft along with the most sophisticated airborne-warning systems being developed by American electronic arms manufacturers. These expenditures were to be part of a $50 billion trade program that was to run from 1975 to 1980. The era of billion dollar deals had arrived.

During both the Nixon and Ford administrations, Kissinger continually asked the shah for political favors. In return for granting these favors, the shah would ask Kissinger to sign his most recent shopping list of sophisticated and expensive military equipment and jet aircraft. As the list grew longer, the F-4s and F-5s were supplemented by F-14s and F-15s, which were in turn replaced on the list by F-16s and F-18s. Kissinger was pleased to approve the lists, often pointing out that the shah was a paying customer whose credit was good. The secretary of state never concerned himself with the questions pertaining to the stability and popularity of his royal friend's regime. At the Noshahr news conference of August 6, he stood by in great disinterest as the shah publicly denied that Iran had any political prisoners— other than some 3,500 Marxists and terrorists, who were perhaps prisoners but certainly not *political* prisoners.

The Nixon-Kissinger-Ford policy toward Iran had powerful support from the major U.S. arms, electronic, and telecommunication industries. By the fall of 1975, thirty-nine such companies had contracts and representation in Iran. They included such giants as Bell Helicopter International (of Textron), General Electric, Grumman Aerospace, International Telephone and Telegraph, Litton, Lockheed, McDonnell-Douglas, Northrop, Page Communications, Philco-Ford, Raytheon, Stanwick, Sylvania, and Westinghouse.[45]

The Iran market was a bonanza for these industries, and the competition for contracts was sordid, involving bribery, huge commissions, and payoffs of all kinds. The situation brought out the worst elements in both countries. In a June 20, 1972, U.S. Embassy report on corruption in Iran, a section entitled "American Companies and Influence Peddlers" listed seven U.S. companies that were "to the Embassy's certain knowledge, buying the influence of the persons listed with them." The companies listed included General Electric (Allison Engine), Northrop, Boeing Aircraft, Cities Service, McDonnell-Douglas, Radio Corporation of America, and Neill-Price.[46] These allegations, which represented the U.S. diplomatic assessment of the situation, reflected the business climate of the time.

Grumman Aerospace was implicated in a scandalous episode in 1976 involving an agreement to pay $28 million in commissions to Iranian officials in order to expedite a $2.2 billion contract to supply Iran with eighty F-14s. This episode received wide publicity in the Persian press. According to the *New York Times*, the president of Grumman International admitted that he had written a personal note to Gen. Hassan Toufanian, the shah's deputy-minister of War and head procurement officer, pledging the $28 million payment.[47] When confronted with this admission, Toufanian responded in righteous indignation, threw the blame back on Grumman, and angrily stated: "This shows that the foreign countries want to loot us. We will not allow this and we will pull the extra money out of their throats."[48] Toufanian was an air force officer with forty-six years of military service. He enjoyed the shah's complete confidence, and he remained in his position until the end of the shah's rule even though the shah was jettisoning dozens of his other closest advisers.

The situation had already deteriorated so badly by 1973 that Secretary of Defense James Schlesinger sent a retired army colonel named Richard Hallock as his unofficial representative to Iran. Hallock's charge was to provide Toufanian and the shah with some independent analysis on weapon procurement and at the same time to keep Schlesinger informed of problems as they developed. In this situation, it is easy to understand how Hallock could have ended up working for both sides. Such was the charge. By the time Erich von Marbod, another Defense Department troubleshooter, got to Tehran in September 1975, Hallock "was employed as a private citizen, by General Toufanian. He was apparently advising the General on weapons procurement matters."[49] Colonel Hallock had allegedly been "in the enviable position of advising the shah on what to buy, advising the United States government on what to recommend to him, helping the arms-supply companies close the deals, and overseeing the program under which all these transactions were being made."[50]

In the mid-1970s, the terrain of Iranian-American commercial relations had become a swamp crowded with international entrepreneurs and arms salesmen of all kinds seeking to make a fortune for themselves and for their clients. The seamier side of American capitalism was especially visible to the Iranian people, who suddenly saw thousands upon thousands of American military advisers and commercial adventurers spread throughout their country. The Nixon-Kissinger-Ford triumvirate encouraged and expanded this situation; in seeking to wed America's national interests with those of the shah, they never stopped to ponder the actual strength of the Iranian leader. They ignored the domestic forces brewing within Iran and failed to question the results of their policies on Iranian society itself.

The United States anchored its national interests to this small, non-Western, absolute monarchy on a scale unprecedented in American diplomatic history. The period between 1972 and 1977 saw the two countries increasingly fused, beginning at the top of their respective power structures. The CIA and SAVAK penetrated one another. In 1976, for example, the shah admitted publicly that SAVAK was active within the United States itself. Meanwhile, in Iran, America had expanded its electronic listening-post capacities along the Russian border. The feared head of SAVAK, Gen. Nimatullah Nassiri, was referred to by Kermit Roosevelt as "our General Nassiri."[51] With the increasing political upheaval in Iran in early 1978, a respected American journalist put together a television special entitled "Our Crisis in Iran."[52] In its lead editorial on November 11, 1979, which discussed the shah's presence in the United States, the *Washington Post* defended "giving asylum to a used-up Middle Eastern potentate and dictator who was—and is—one of 'ours.'" By 1977 an estimated sixty thousand Iranian students resided in the United States. In Iran the number of Americans had increased from eight thousand in 1970 to nearly fifty thousand by the end of 1977.

One revealing index of the dramatic increase in Iran-American relationships is the pattern of telephone communication between the two countries. In 1973 a total of 53,597 telephone calls were completed from the United States to Iran. This number increased to 122,477 in 1975, but by 1977 the number of calls had exploded to an astonishing 854,382. In these five years, the number of calls completed from the United States to Iran had increased by over 1,600 percent. In 1973 the 50,000 calls totaled almost 9,000 hours of conversation; four years later the annual hours of conversation had risen to over 134,000. In response to an unprecedented demand, the telephone company had increased the number of U.S.-Iran circuits from six in January 1973 to ninety in December 1977. By 1978 Iran had become the fourth largest revenue producer in the world for AT&T Long Lines.[53]

American policy in Iran did not go entirely unchallenged during the 1970s. In 1975 and 1976, a handful of Senate Democrats such as Edward Kennedy, William Proxmire, Gaylord Nelson, and John Culver began to question the huge arms sales to the shah. The considerations raised in the Senate Committee on Foreign Relations staff report of 1976 represent this minority view. Also, on August 3 and September 8, 1976, a House subcommittee of the Committee on International Relations under the chairmanship of Rep. Donald M. Fraser held hearings on human rights in Iran. These sessions produced alarming evidence of torture and repression. In 1975 a National Intelligence Estimate warned of serious internal problems in Iran and analyzed various opposition groups in considerable detail. Meanwhile, a handful of American Iran scholars documented in articles and books the fundamental instability of the Pahlavi regime. All such doubts and warnings were futile before the overwhelming rush of acclaim of official and unofficial America for Pahlavi Iran.

In the United States, the shah had the best of all possible worlds.

Professional and diplomatic ties were reinforced by a network of durable personal relationships. Richard Nixon's ties with the shah were extremely close; the two leaders maintained deep personal admiration for one another and supported one another in every possible way. On Nixon's shortlist of great world leaders, the shah was always included as one of the top three or four. In the summer of 1974, rumors abounded that the shah had poured money into the Nixon campaign by way of Mexico. When columnist Jack Anderson began to investigate, he received several calls from former Secretary of State William Rogers categorically denying these unsubstantiated charges. Nonetheless, many observers believed them to be accurate. The reason was the extraordinarily close relationship that existed between Nixon and Muhammad Reza Shah. Kissinger and Ford also enjoyed similar relationships with the shah.

Nixon had first visited the shah in Tehran in December 1953, sixteen years before he became president of the United States. In referring to that first meeting during a 1969 state visit of the shah to Washington, Nixon stated that the shah had already then "made a very deep impression on me and on my wife." He pointed out that "there were those who thought Iran in 1953 might not make it. When I left Iran, I knew it would make it." This was "particularly because of the personality and the strength and the character of the man who is our honored guest tonight."[54] The Pahlavi-Nixon relationship continued right up until the shah's death in exile in Egypt on July 27, 1980. The shah kept Nixon constantly supplied with an ample supply of caviar. When the shah was exiled in Cuernavaca, Mexico, in July 1979, Nixon flew down to visit him and to cheer him up. "Don't fade away," he exhorted the shah, "you've got to keep fighting." When the shah died, Richard Nixon flew to Cairo to attend his funeral. While there, he bitterly told reporters that Jimmy Carter's handling of the shah was "one of the black pages of American foreign policy history." In a brief and emotional eulogy to the deceased monarch, Nixon concluded that the shah "was a real man."[55]

The dozens of American politicians in charge of Iran-U.S. relations between 1971 and 1977 could not have been more sympathetic to the shah. Besides Nixon, Kissinger, and Ford they included individuals embedded in the bureaucratic structure, such as Assistant Secretary of State Joseph Sisco and the director of the Defense Security Assistance Agency, Lt. Gen. Howard M. Fish. Sisco, a minor emanation of the personality of Henry Kissinger, was a shallow but persistent spokesman for the shah's rule and defended the Pahlavi regime even after he left the Department of State. Fish was chief procurements officer during these years, and in 1977 he boasted publicly that during his tenure in this position he had handled $36 billion in arms sales. He indicated that sixty congressional bills had been written opposing such sales, and he proudly said that not one had gotten out of committee.[56]

In the U.S. Senate, the shah's most ardent and consistent supporters included Jacob Javits, Abraham Ribicoff, Charles Percy, and Barry Goldwater. This alliance cut across liberal-conservative and Democrat-Republican divisions. Senator Goldwater spent a week in Iran in 1973 at the invitation of the shah himself and was so enthusiastic on his return that he profusely praised both the shah and Iran on the Senate floor. He concluded: "The strength of its leader, his understanding of his nation's problems, his burning desire to solve them are the marks of good leadership and the results, in my opinion, will be spectacular."[57] On September 11, 1974, Goldwater had read into the Senate record an address given on August 31 at Kent State University by Ardeshir Zahedi, the Iranian ambassador to the United States. Goldwater described Zahedi as "one of the best personal friends that all of us has here in Washington." The House of Representatives was also filled with dozens of Pahlavi admirers. John Brademas of Indiana, for example, had a week before read the same Zahedi speech into the House proceedings.

The last American ambassadors in Iran were men of military and security background who had strong proshah proclivities before they arrived there. This was especially true of former CIA director Richard Helms, who had known the shah for years. The Helms appointment was viewed by middle-class Iranians as a blatant public admission that the CIA, which had in their view been covertly controlling events in Iran since 1953, now intended to call the plays formally and officially. In the words of one influential Iranian writer in 1974: "Why else has Helms been sent here? Why has the United States sent its head spy as ambassador to our country? Could not your country have had the decency to at least remain out of sight while you help the shah pull the strings?"[58] When Helms was replaced in 1977 by former U.S. ambassador to the Philippines William Sullivan, an official associated with the extensive American intelligence operations in Southeast Asia, Iranian nationalists only nodded knowingly.

Thus, while the shah's regime increasingly resorted to repression, including the systematic use of torture to maintain control, the United States sent to Iran ambassadors with intelligence backgrounds and flooded the country with military advisers and arms of all kinds. American firms like Rockwell International began work on sophisticated electronic surveillance systems, such as the half-billion-dollar IBEX system, which could be used to gather information about dissidents within Iran as well as about the activities of other nations on the Persian Gulf. Many of the Americans recruited for this project were former employees of the National Security Agency and the Air Force Security Service. When I expressed my horror at the methods being used by the shah's security apparatus in a meeting with Ambassador Helms in Tehran in June 1974, there was a long, clumsy silence before Helms muttered, "Seems quite unnecessary."[59] In reaction to a similar observation on my part, the embassy's best political officer simply stated: "A police state is a police state." This American official indicated that there was little that the United States could do. In his words: "All the dirty linen will be aired, of course, when the regime does eventually fall."[60] Two years later, the vicious circle of regime repression and opposition violence had spun out of control.

Early in 1976 the shah himself came to this realization. Two facts convinced him of the seriously counterproductive nature of the hardline, repressive policy that he had implemented in 1971. First, young guerrillas increasingly demonstrated their willingness to sacrifice their lives to fight the system of political rule in Iran; the Golesorkhi case was the major case in point. Second, opposition guerrillas were beginning to infiltrate even SAVAK, usually through SAVAK employees who were relatives of the young people in the opposition. Several such incidents occurred in 1974–75. This kind of increasing opposition deeply concerned the shah and forced him finally to reconsider his political methodology.

He decided first to begin shrugging off more of the responsibility from his royal shoulders over to those of the United States. This scapegoat strategy became so blatant that even the U.S. government noticed it and in mid-1976 began to be alarmed. A Bureau of Intelligence and Research of the Department of State report of May 4, 1976, began: "In recent months the Shah has permitted unusually severe criticisms of the United States in Iranian media. He has lent his own name to sweeping charges against the U.S., raising public questions about the bases of the alliance and U.S. reliability."[61] The shah had used the tactic in the mid-1960s, and, as in the 1960s, he reinforced the emphasis by encouraging increasing anti-Americanism in the government-controlled Iranian press. Although this approach certainly deepened anti-Americanism in Iran, it did not succeed in deflecting criticism away from the shah. In the eyes of the growing opposition forces, the shah and America were one.

The shah's second tactic was more notable. On the brink of the revolution, he decided suddenly to reintroduce some selected but visible reform into his formula for control. In this way, he sought to break the deadly cycle of violence. This effort had just begun when on January 15, 1977, Jimmy Carter took the oath of office as thirty-ninth president of the United States.

7 America and the Iranian Revolution, 1977–1979

Two years into his presidency, Jimmy Carter watched in helpless disbelief as Iran exploded in revolution and one of America's major political allies in the shifting terrain of the Middle East collapsed like a pillar of sand. On January 16, 1979, the shah himself, with a few members of his family and inner circle, fled his country for the final time. Ayatollah Ruhollah Khomeini, the stern, charismatic leader and inspiration of the revolution, arrived in Tehran from his Paris exile on February 1. And on February 9–11, the last remnants of the shah's once proud and loyal army fought their last stand at Dushan Tappah Air Force Base in east Tehran; a contingent of the Royal Guards, the Immortals were crushed in a confrontation with rebelling air force cadet-technicians assisted by thousands of civilian guerrillas. American officials and observers considered the fall of the Pahlavi dynasty as a foreign policy catastrophe of tremendous proportion.

The year 1977 set the stage for the revolution. These critical twelve months contained, in retrospect, all the signs of imminent political collapse. Although few read these signs at the time, they were visible in the economic system, which was in the midst of a sharp retrenchment; in the religious revival, where hundreds of thousands of Iranians returned to the fundamentals of Shi'i activism; and in the political realm, where the Pahlavi regime attempted to cope with growing dissent in an inconsistent and ineffective manner.

The phenomenal economic growth rate of 1973–75 came to a sudden halt as oil revenues leveled off between 1975 and 1978. This "superboom," in which the economy had veered "virtually out of conventional control,"[1] had brought into Iran plans to create a herd of economic white elephants that included turbotrains, nuclear power plants, heart transplant centers, and a multibillion dollar naval base at Chah Bahar on the Indian Ocean. Meanwhile, by 1977, the agricultural growth rate had stagnated to less than 3 percent, and the rural-urban migration had shifted into a pattern of all-out flight. At the same time, a huge rural-urban income distribution gap became visible, careful observers indicated that this gap had tripled since the mid-1960s. Government studies reportedly documented the severe shortage of skilled laborers, who were replaced by a foreign work force that numbered over 300,000 and included Indian and Pakistani physicians, Filipino nurses, Korean truck drivers, U.S. military and industrial advisers, and Afghan laborers. While bad weather and migration had cut wheat, rice, and barley production in the country, the peasants lacked incentive to grow grains since they could not compete with imports that were being sold at subsidized prices. Meanwhile, the situation in the cities was aggravated by a severe recession in the construction industry.

Although the economy cooled off and a serious retrenchment policy took hold, the runaway corruption that had accompanied the boom showed little signs of abating. The enormity and visibility of this corruption, which involved huge bribes, fraudulent land schemes, and extravagant commissions on contracts, hurt the country both economically and politically. As the creeping corruption accelerated into a mad dash for instant wealth, the shah's family and closest associates ran at the head of the pack. In August 1978, for example, Court Minister Hoveyda complained to Iran's ambassador to England that "corruption at the top is rampant on a shameless scale." According to Hoveyda, it was so embarrassingly visible that when the shah indicated his intention to announce publicly an anticorruption campaign, Hoveyda dissuaded him from doing so because "people will laugh."[2]

In an attempt to cool the overheated economy, the regime inaugurated a heavy-handed anti-inflation policy that involved sending groups of zealous young inspectors, recruited mainly from the Rastakhiz party, through the bazaars seeking price gougers and merchants suspected of overcharging their customers. This policy wreaked havoc in the traditional business community; many of its leaders were arrested, exiled, and punished in a variety of ways. The arbitrary nature of this action alienated the bazaar, the heart of the Iranian economy. As part of this drastic austerity campaign, the regime terminated its subsidies to the Shi'i religious establishment, further alienating the already aggrieved ulama.

The technocracy, Western-educated and enormously confident, brushed aside the criticisms of informed observers who warned of the great fragility of the economic system. In 1975, for example, internationally known petroleum analyst Walter Levy had warned the Iranian technocrats that they had overextended themselves, that they had substituted "black gold," which was in fact "manna from heaven," for any fundamental, lasting economic system.[3] Bright, enthusiastic, and ambitious young planners such as Minister of State in Charge of Industries Farokh Najmabadi, Plan Organization head Abdolmajid Majidi, and Deputy Minister of Economic Affairs Hassan Ali Mehran responded glibly and confidently using technocratic jargon they had learned in Western universities. In fact, rhetoric and jargon substituted for meaningful action and effective policy.

This was a time of conferences, seminars, and long discussions about "infrastructures" and "bottlenecks." First used by the technocrats, these terms soon found their way into the vocabulary of Prime Minister Hoveyda and the shah himself. Once the shah began speaking about the need for a *zirbana* (infrastructure) in order to alleviate the *tangna* (bottlenecks), then every planner increased his own use of these terms. In his budgetary message to the Majlis in February 1977, Hoveyda went so far as to list a major budget objective as the "accelerated alleviation of bottlenecks and infrastructure shortages."[4] Although several economic problems existed, many of the bottlenecks were social and political in nature as the lack of nationwide institutions of genuine political participation increased disaffection among Iranian masses, many of whom now returned to the fundamentals of Islam.

Throughout 1977 thousands of young Iranians continued their movement to Islam as a force of liberation and a refuge from the oppressive secular politics of Pahlavi rule. This revival, unprecedented in recent Iranian history, was most visible in secondary schools and universities, where large numbers of young women reveiled themselves and attended classes completely clad in the black veils (*chadurs*). When police authorities forbade them to wear the veil on the streets of certain provincial cities, the women carried them to campus, where they put them on upon arrival. When university authorities attempted to forbid their use on campus, the women wore them to and from campus. At Isfahan University in August 1977, one veiled young lady explained very simply why she had returned to the veil: "I am making a statement."[5]

Men and women flocked to religious study centers, where they discussed social and political matters in terms of the lives of the infallible religious leaders (*Imams*) of Shi'i Islam. The explosive strength of this religious revival was seen at Tehran University on October 9, 1977, when two dozen masked students, demanding the segregation of women on campus, went on a rampage, smashing windows and burning buses. That fall also saw numerous religious demonstrations in the holy city of Qum.

This return to Islamic activism was not completely unnoticed by U.S. embassy officials in Tehran. In a report of July 25, 1977, signed by Ambassador William Sullivan, the embassy indicated that religious forces were "stirring" and explained that the "religious restiveness" was being reinforced by an Islamic revival in neighboring Muslim countries such as Pakistan, Turkey, and Saudi Arabia. Although American diplomats admitted their lack of knowledge about this religious resurgence and stressed instead opposition from the secular left, they could not help but sense that some kind of religious force was gathering in Iran.[6]

Politically, 1977 was the year in which the shah and his political elite announced dramatic plans to implement a new policy. The key phrase used to describe this new political program was "the year of liberalization." The core of this "liberalization" program was called *musharikat* (participation). Like the economic buzzwords "bottlenecks" and "infrastructures," however, the new political vocabulary did not necessarily indicate a fundamental change in political reality.

The Partial Path to Liberalization

By mid-1976, the shah and his closest advisers decided that it was essential that the vicious cycle of violence, regime repression, and opposition terrorism had to be broken. Despite the conventional argument that the shah began to liberalize his political system solely in response to Jimmy Carter's human rights policy, the reasons for the liberalization, which in fact began months before Carter became president, were far more complex. Barry Rubin makes an important point when he writes: "Complaints after the revolution by the shah and his defenders that Washington forced him to become too soft, and thus encouraged the upheaval, seem, simply, to have no basis in fact."[7] The shah chose to modify dramatically his policy of control for five reasons.

First, the shah was shrewd enough to recognize that the repressive policy of the past five years had been counterproductive. The evident commitment of the young guerrillas to their cause and their increasingly suicidal missions troubled him. Furthermore, close security advisers such as Gen. Hussein Fardust, who despised the ruthless, crude techniques of SAVAK head Nassiri, reportedly convinced the king to take matters again into his own hands and to lighten his political touch.

Second, during these few years the shah began to consider seriously the long-term future of his dynasty. He was particularly concerned about the accession to power of his eldest son, sixteen-year-old Crown Prince Reza. At this time he was also well aware that he had cancer, a fact diagnosed by French physicians a few years earlier. He wanted a strategy that would maximize the chances for his son to succeed him without incident. He also wondered privately about the method of governance that would be most congenial to his son. As American officials judged it, the shah had come to believe that a more liberal, open style might be the best for the future and for his son.

Third, the repressive tactics had been gaining increased international attention. Both the terrorist acts that occurred in the streets of Tehran and the growing chorus of world criticism bothered the shah very much. He wanted as much international mass media coverage as possible for his country and for himself. Sharp bursts of criticism, especially in the form of exposés in the European press, increasingly appeared along with the paeans. This criticism embarrassed the shah, who had worked hard to assume a central position on the world stage.

Fourth, in jettisoning a number of his older advisers in line with coopting younger voices into his ruling establishment, the shah in 1976–77 brought in a number of bright young technocrats of more liberal disposition. Many were former opponents of Pahlavi rule and had associations with the National Front. These included individuals such as Fereydoun Mahdavi, who first joined the cabinet in 1974 as minister of Commerce, and Daryoush Homayoun, who in 1977 became minister of Information and Tourism. Other bright young stars who joined the shah's system at somewhat lower but influential levels late in the game included individuals such as Amir Taheri, a particularly astute observer of the political scene, and Ahmad Qoreishi, an American-trained political scientist who joined the system with a vengeance. During these years the empress also assumed more political influence, and her circle consisted of young professionals who counseled political reform.

Last and least, the shah's commitment to liberalization was reinforced by the election of Jimmy Carter to the presidency of the United States. The shah was betting on his friend Gerald Ford to win the election and was clearly upset when the Democrat Carter was elected. He immediately sent two of his best "America-watchers" to Washington to gather information about Carter, a little-known figure to the Iranian political elite. The shah feared that Jimmy Carter might prove to be another John F. Kennedy, whom he had disliked immensely, partly for reasons of personal envy and partly for the pressure that Kennedy had put on him to reform his political system. In the end, the shah determined to see for himself and arranged a meeting with the new American president late in 1977. Meanwhile, he moved to deflect any possible criticism of his rule by publicizing the liberalization policy that he had initiated earlier in 1976.

The shah's liberalization policy was multipronged. He emphasized the success of his White Revolution and constantly quoted the material changes this program had brought to Iran. Throughout 1977 his spokesmen emphasized that Iran's per capita income had increased 1,100 percent since 1963, while the shah himself confidently predicted that within a dozen years Iran would be as developed as Western Europe and that it would soon after be one of the five most powerful countries in the world. In August 1977, the shah attempted to keep the seventeen points of the White Revolution alive and visible by proclaiming two additional reforms: the control of land prices and the requirement that government officials make public their personal earnings.

American officials were particularly fond of using this argument when they testified before congressional committees investigating human rights violations in Iran. Rather than confront the issue of such violations, they repeated the progress made by the shah's White Revolution. The details of this reform program, many of which were quite accurate and did indeed represent material advances and economic growth, seldom failed to impress American audiences. In 1974, a high-ranking member of the U.S. Embassy in Tehran indicated that a visiting Unitarian group had asked about human rights in Iran. When I asked the official if he had mentioned the torture going on in the prisons, he responded, "Of course not." He went on to say that he spent an hour and a half telling the delegation about the impressive achievements of the White Revolution.[8] On September 8, 1976, Assistant Secretary of State Alfred Atherton and Director of Iranian Affairs Charles Naas testified before a congressional committee investigating human rights violations in Iran. The committee was chaired by Congressman Donald Fraser of Minnesota. In their testimonies, Atherton and Naas sidestepped the issue of human rights by focusing attention on the White Revolution. Atherton's testimony was packed with data purporting to demonstrate the great success of the White Revolution.

A second tactic, resuscitated and expanded in 1976–77, was the emphasis on a party system that promoted a variant of democracy in Iran. In this case, it was the single Rastakhiz party, which had been created from above in 1975. Government spokesmen stressed that this party enabled everyone to participate in the political process. When the question of forced membership in a single party was raised, they responded that there were in fact two wings to the party, the Constructive Wing, headed by Hushang Ansary, and the Progressive Wing, led by Jamshid Amuzegar. Pahlavi ideologues thus argued that Iran had the best of both worlds, a one-party system and a two-party system all rolled into one!

The new twist in 1976–77 was a strong emphasis on participation. The justification for this mass institution, referred to in Persian as an "all-encompassing party" (*hizb-i faragir*), was provided by American-trained social scientists who had become the shah's latest political brain trust. Educated in the school of developmental politics taught by scholars such as Harvard University's Samuel Huntington, these Iranian professionals argued that development was best defined in terms of participation manifested in the process of institutionalization. And the best form of institutionalization was a strong party system. This theoretical approach maintained that the fundamental goals of politics in the developing world were the protection of authority, the priority of capacity, and the preeminence of political order. In Huntington's own words: "Today in much of Asia, Africa, and Latin America, political systems face simultaneously the needs to centralize authority, to differentiate structure, and to broaden participation. It is not surprising that the system which seems most relevant to the simultaneous achievement of these goals is a one-party system."[9] The American-trained Iranian social scientists had little difficulty in selling such ideas to the shah, a man who appreciated the need for strong central authority.

Besides the continuing emphasis on the White Revolution and the mass political party, the shah's government in 1977 introduced a number of other policies that highlighted the attempt to release the social and political pressures that had been building in the system. These included several highly publicized and selected releases of political prisoners, a loosening of the tight system of censorship, and the establishment of various study groups and commissions to hear the complaints and grievances of the people. Furthermore, during the first ten months of 1977, the regime invited three major international human rights groups—the International Red Cross, Amnesty International, and the International Commission of Jurists (ICJ)—into the country for a firsthand examination of social and political conditions. Although the efforts of Amnesty International received most world attention, the activities of the ICJ were especially effective since the shah took its recommendations most seriously. The ICJ was a commission of thirty-six distinguished jurists that presented itself as an apolitical organization with a deep concern for international human rights. In Iran's case, the ICJ placed special emphasis on procedural due process. The shah, in response, agreed to reform the Military Justice and Penal Code in a number of important respects involving the processes of detention and trial.

The ICJ's small but notable success in Iran was due primarily to the energetic efforts of William J. Butler, a Harvard-trained New York lawyer who was chairman of the executive committee of the ICJ. A bright, refreshingly blunt, and well-connected political realist, the silver-haired Butler was a pragmatic campaigner who worked directly with national leaders in pursuing ICJ's goals. He had already begun to study Iran with a vengeance in 1975 and had visited there that October, ultimately producing the important ICJ report entitled *Human Rights and the Legal System in Iran.* Butler was able to develop an impressive rapport with the shah during personal meetings in Tehran on May 30, 1977, and in Shiraz on May 2, 1978. During these sessions, the shah and Butler discussed in detail various reforms of Iran's penal code and overall system of justice.[10] Although Butler's efforts did not result in any substantive changes, they did reinforce a process of procedural reform from which there was to be no return.

Along with these policy changes, the shah shuffled the membership of his political elite. On August 6, 1977, he relieved Hoveyda from his longtime position as prime minister and named him minister of court. The next day he appointed Jamshid Amuzegar as prime minister. Amuzegar's cabinet included ten new faces, all educated technocrats. Jamshid Amuzegar was the supreme technocrat, and his appointment indicated that the new political strategy was to be reform by technocracy. But not just any technocracy; it was clearly an American-style program with the various cabinet members holding college degrees from such American universities as Colorado, Nebraska, Kentucky, Utah, Columbia, and California. The appointment of Amuzegar himself represented the strengths and weaknesses of the Pahlavi political strategy just before the revolution.

Unlike many of his associates, Jamshid Amuzegar reflected a rare degree of personal independence and integrity. He had been feuding with Hoveyda and, to a lesser extent, with Hushang Ansary for years. After graduating from Tehran University in 1943, Amuzegar traveled to the United States, where he did graduate work for seven years. He earned an M.A. in sanitary engineering and a Ph.D. in hydraulics at Cornell University. Back in Iran, he worked for the Agency for International Development (AID), held the posts of deputy minister of Health, minister of Labor, minister of Agriculture, minister of Finance, and was for years the head of Iran's delegation to OPEC. In some ways, he was Iran's answer to Shaykh Ahmad Zaki Yamani of Saudi Arabia. The shah later explained his appointment of Amuzegar in terms of Amuzegar's integrity and his friendships in the United States. Most importantly, "his appointment could serve as a springboard for a new liberalization drive that would promote democracy within Iran."[11] Despite this reasoning, the Amuzegar appointment was a serious mistake within the context of the time.

The new prime minister was above all else a technocrat who consciously avoided addressing basic political issues. Yet it was precisely the political situation that was the critical issue of the day. One keen observer of Iranian politics summarized it well: "Hoveyda is too political, Amuzegar not political enough."[12] Furthermore, Jamshid Amuzegar was impatient and occasionally clumsy; he immediately announced policies that alienated many Iranian professionals and merchants. His known American connections and isolation from the Iranian masses also severely damaged his national credibility. The religious leaders, for example, resented what they privately referred to as one more American technocrat and shah-worshipper (*shah-parast*).[13]

One further significant personnel change took place on November 30, 1977, when the shah moved Hushang Ansary from the ministry of Economy to head the National Iranian Oil Company. Here Ansary immediately began, for the last time in Iran, to build another small empire for himself. Amuzegar and Ansary became the shah's major means of publicizing his liberalization program. They did so primarily in their capacities as leaders of the two wings of the Rastakhiz party. In his first news conference as prime minister, Amuzegar stated, for example, that "the Government expects the people to express their views on all matters and frankly discuss problems and present solutions." Ansary was more outspoken. In September 1977, his Constructive wing of the Rastakhiz party issued a statement calling for political liberties, the free flow of information, and wider public participation in politics. The free flow of information "like the flow of blood in the body, contributes to life and better living and the strength of the Iranian political system." And in January 1978, Ansary told a Rastakhiz party congress that greater openings in political freedoms were the logical culmination of the achievements of the White Revolution. He was careful to stress that the liberalization process was the wish of the shah himself, whom he claimed enjoyed the support of all the Iranian people.[14]

The liberalization process struck a responsive chord in Iran. As the regime slowly lifted its lid on society, pent-up political pressures escaped immediately and explosively. When the newspaper *Kayhan* asked "what is wrong with Iran," it received over forty thousand letters in response. During the last six months of 1977, several highly critical open letters were sent directly to the shah and other high-ranking government leaders. These included a courageous two-hundred-page analysis of social and political problems by A. A. Haj Sayyid Javadi, a shorter but incisive critique signed by three former National Front leaders, a letter by forty writers asking for freedom of expression, and a declaration signed by sixty-four lawyers and judges calling for a return to the rule of law in Iran. It is important to note that during this period of relative liberalization, there was little violence in the streets. The nation and the guerrilla leaders were watching and waiting to see how serious the reforms would be. Their verdict was negative. The liberalization was partial; the reforms were superficial; the political system was to remain fundamentally the same.

In fact, the shah pursued an inconsistent policy. This is revealed through an analysis of twenty-three major speeches and interviews he gave between May 1976 and December 1977. While stressing liberalization and, in the shah's words as reported in an Iranian newspaper, attempting to "loosen the reigns [*sic*] a little,"[15] at the same time he argued for maintaining a strong centralized regime with his own role preeminent and predominant. In the words of scholar Homa Katouzian, he insisted on continuing to rule arbitrarily and despotically.[16] The shah viewed opponents and dissidents as either "red" or "black"—communists or reactionary mullahs. He would lead the nation to the Great Civilization (*Tamaddun-i Buzurg*) by force if necessary. Those Iranians who did not support the Rastakhiz party were "suffering from mental imbalance." A strong monarchy was essential in Iran, which would never see any other kind of political system. Western societies suffered from a severe lack of social discipline, sloth, and indolence and, as permissive societies, were destroying themselves. The Iranian monarchy was on the way to becoming the major political model for the world.

That the shah introduced his policy of liberalization arbitrarily from above and politically through Pahlavites such as Amuzegar and Ansary convinced many Iranians that it was clearly a palliative developed to buy the regime more time while satisfying the new Democratic administration in Washington. SAVAK was still extremely powerful and was still headed by General Nassiri. Shuffling faces did little to change the fundamental actors. Corruption continued to percolate outward from the core of the Pahlavi family. Liberal critics such as Muhammad Musaddiq's grandson, Hedayatollah Matin-Daftary, criticized the regime's new policy on the grounds that the same old individuals and the same "old circles" still had complete control over political affairs. In the words of other Iranian observers, the shah had only rearranged the garbage cans. William Butler of the ICJ described the shah's efforts at legal reform as simply "too little, too late."[17] In the eyes of most, despite all the verbiage, the shah had introduced little political change. In sum, he had opened the political door slightly, had sought to hold it there, and, when necessary, had instructed his police to slam it shut again.

Jimmy Carter: Human Rights and Political Wrongs

The Carter administration determined from the beginning that it would continue past American policies toward Iran with a special sensitivity to the importance of that country as a major military force for stability in the Persian Gulf and as a moderating force in the pricing of petroleum. America's special strategic relationship with Iran was to be protected at all costs. At the same time, the new Democratic administration concluded that it would promote human rights policy in the international arena. In his inaugural address on January 20, 1977, President Carter had stated: "Our moral sense dictates a clear preference for those societies which share with us an abiding respect for individual human rights." An emphasis on human rights, it was argued, would be in the American national interest since it was both morally right and politically expedient. The administration argued that American allies in Third World societies would in fact strengthen themselves politically by the promotion of human rights policies. One important part of the emphasis on human rights was a careful reexamination of American arms sales.

Iran was centrally important to the fledgling Carter administration. Iran accounted for over half of all American arms sales. Carter's foreign policy team of Secretary of State Cyrus Vance and National Security Adviser Zbigniew Brzezinski were well aware that the shah's policies directly benefited the United States. Vance himself listed five such positive policies: (1) the shah provided important economic assistance to countries in the area; (2) he helped reduce tensions in southwest Asia; (3) his forces had helped to defeat an insurgency in

Oman; (4) he was "a reliable supplier of oil to the West"; he had, in fact, refused to join the 1973 Arab oil embargo; and (5) he was Israel's primary source of oil. Thus, "we decided early on that it was in our national interest to support the shah so he could continue to play a constructive role in regional affairs."[18] Although human rights was a genuine concern for the Carter administration, this issue was certainly not to take precedence over security and economic issues.

The shah was nervous about Carter's presidency, not only because of the general issue of human rights but also because of his own close past associations with the Nixon-Ford-Kissinger group. Ford had been a friendly and malleable political ally. Carter was an unknown. Furthermore, the shah's old friend Richard Helms had departed as U.S. ambassador to Iran in December 1976 and was not replaced until June 1977 by William Sullivan. The absence of a U.S. ambassador in Tehran during these critical months troubled the shah, who was busily trying to read every little sign out of Washington.[19] The shah therefore determined to meet the new Democratic president as soon as possible in order to size him up and to make certain that he could count on the United States's unwavering support for his regime. He thus began a quiet lobbying campaign for an exchange of official visits.

In May 1977, Secretary of State Vance traveled to Tehran, where he held important meetings with the shah. During a 2½-hour meeting on May 13 at Niavaran Palace, Vance invited the shah to Washington in November, informed him that the United States had decided to go ahead with the pending sale of 160 F-16 aircraft, promised that the president would seek congressional approval for the shah's request for the sophisticated airborne warning and control system (AWACS) and explained America's plans for convening a Geneva peace conference focusing on the Arab-Israeli dispute. In general terms he also indicated that the United States supported principles of human rights and praised the shah's recent policies of liberalization. The shah gave Vance a pointed lesson in the significance of human rights through 2,500 years of Iranian history and indicated that he had no trouble with America's emphasis on human rights as a general principle—as long as this policy was not directed at Iran and did not threaten Iran's security. As a U.S. embassy official noted afterwards, "Vance only mentioned the issue of human rights to the shah; there were many more important issues to be discussed."[20]

When Vance left Tehran, the shah was somewhat more confident about his capacity to deal politically with the Carter administration. Vance had been appropriately impressed by the policy of liberalization begun a year before; he had promised to deliver the F-16s; he had even indicated Carter's willingness to support the controversial AWACS request. But while the shah had one interpretation of the Vance visit, the gathering opposition had quite another interpretation.

After Vance's visit, the word spread quickly through the extensive Iranian grapevine that the shah had just been given his orders from Washington: either liberalize or be removed. This fanciful interpretation of the Vance visit, based on a heavy portion of wishful thinking on the part of the opposition intelligentsia, was repeated until it soon became accepted fact in Tehran.[21] The gap between what Vance had in fact said and what the growing Iranian opposition groups said he had said carried severe political consequences. The shah interpreted the visit as an important preliminary sign of Carter's support for his policies and autonomy. He now became somewhat less concerned about liberalization, and his police began again to take sporadic harsh actions against suspected opposition groups. The opposition, on the other hand, concluded that they could now operate under an American protective umbrella that had been raised by Cyrus Vance. When this protective umbrella failed to appear and the shah's police cracked down, the political situation in Iran began to deteriorate rapidly.

Although the Carter administration did not put any serious human rights pressure on the shah, the support of Carter's government for human rights more generally made it easy for the Iranian opposition, with its exaggerated belief in American influence over the shah, to conclude that the shah had been given his human rights marching orders. When the shah cracked down, the opposition forces, in line with their obsession with foreign influence, drew the reverse conclusion—the United States had now ordered the shah to reestablish a policy of repression.

Throughout the summer and early fall of 1977, President Carter sent numerous signals of support to the shah. The most important example was the administration's campaign to sell the shah the technologically advanced $1.23 billion AWACS. This political battle clearly indicates a strong early commitment by the Carter administration to the shah's government—a commitment that ran against the very principles that Carter had announced from the onset of his presidency. Despite his public determination to reduce American arms sales across the board, early in 1977 Carter chose to make Iran an exception. In so doing, he suddenly ran into surprising opposition from a number of influential senators and representatives who questioned the wisdom of this policy. Cyrus Vance wrote, "The subsequent debate in Congress and the administration's handling of this controversial issue became a major test in convincing the shah that the president was serious about continuing a special security relationship with him."[22]

During his campaign for the presidency, Jimmy Carter had sharply criticized the Nixon and Ford administrations for their record of enormous arms sales throughout the world. He had stated: "I am particularly concerned by our nation's role as the world's leading arms salesman. How can we be both the world's leading champion of peace and the world's leading supplier of the weapons of war?" On May 19, 1977, he announced a new restrained arms transfer policy and a tough set of sales restrictions relevant to all countries except those with which the United States had major defense agreements. The exceptions included the NATO countries, Japan, Australia, New Zealand, and Israel. Iran was not mentioned. Two months later, on July 7, Carter presented Congress with a proposal to sell Iran seven highly sophisticated flying radar systems consisting of Boeing 707 jet airplanes equipped with thirty-foot diameter mushroomlike radar scanners sprouting from their bodies. It was at the time the most expensive aircraft system the United States had ever developed. This proposed AWACS package represented an astonishing presidential aboutface and shocked Carter's liberal allies in Congress. It also contributed to Carter's growing image of inconsistency and unpredictability.

Under considerable pressure from the shah and his friends in Washington, Jimmy Carter provoked a confrontation with the Congress of such severity that old-timers such as Hubert Humphrey and Clifford Case saw a major governmental crisis in the offing. Congressional questions resulted in several hearings before two subcommittees of the House Committee on International Relations in June and July 1977. Concerned about runaway arms sales to Iran, Sen. John Culver of Iowa and Sen. Thomas Eagleton of Missouri, joined later by Majority Leader Sen. Robert Byrd of West Virginia, opposed the sale. Supported by a General Accounting Office (GAO) study filed on July 15 and a CIA statement by Admiral Stansfield Turner that indicated the danger of such a sophisticated system possibly falling into Soviet hands, the challenging congressmen managed temporarily to deflect the sale. Their arguments were powerful and convincing.

Senator Eagleton stated that "this is not an ordinary arms deal. It was born in the atmosphere of secret deals of prior administrations which this committee has done much to expose. It violates the tenets of restraints in the arms sales policies which are being developed by the new Carter administration." He went on to specify presciently the particular problems, which he outlined as an increased American presence in Iran and a serious security risk since Iran's government, "centered on a mortal leader, is fragile and subject to radical change. To endorse this sale is to take an imprudent risk to American national security."[23] Senator Culver argued that the sale carried dangerous risks to America's own technology and to its national security. He summarized it in the following terms:

> The painful fact is that the sale of AWACS to Iran goes contrary to the President's own expressed principles. It makes an exception right out of the starting blocks for our biggest single arms purchaser. It introduces a highly advanced system with great offensive capacity into the region. . . . If we are to have a policy that approves sale only in exceptional cases, as the President announced, it makes little sense to me to turn around, before the ink is dry on that piece of paper, and exempt Iran from these guidelines.[24]

After continuing to push stubbornly for the sale, Carter and Secretary of State Vance finally withdrew the proposal on July 28. They did so in the face of a House International Relations Committee vote of disapproval and an impending Senate vote that was also sure to go against the president.

Through the good offices of Hubert Humphrey, a compromise was worked out that ultimately resulted in the approval of the sale in the fall. Carter reintroduced the AWACS proposal on September 7. The administration had continued to press relentlessly, and with the help of Secretary of Defense Harold Brown, Secretary of State Vance, and a number of senators sympathetic to the Pahlavi government such as Barry Goldwater they finally succeeded in pushing through this major arms agreement. On October 5, Howard Fish, Department of Defense point man for promoting America's arms sales, privately and triumphantly told a small group in Washington that "this time we've got the votes!"[25] Between the July retreat and the fall political offensive, the administration had agreed to six minor modifications in the proposal that permitted the sale to pass and allowed all sides to save face. The AWACS sale was approved when by October 7 the congressional committees lacked the votes to kill the proposal.

Meanwhile, the Carter administration, so publicly committed to slowing arms sales, also approved the $1.8 billion sale of an additional 160 General Dynamics F-16 fighters to Iran and immediately began considering a further Pahlavi request for 140 more F-16s. Thus, contrary to the assertions of many observers, Jimmy Carter hardly slowed the flow of American arms to the shah. He did this for several reasons.

First, Carter appeared to accept the arguments of his advisers concerning Iran's needs for this advanced radar system for important reasons of security and stability in the Persian Gulf. But this could not have been the deciding factor, since Carter was clearly leery of such justifications for arms sales. In later explanations for his aggressive support for this sale, he does not even mention this. Second, and more convincing, Carter bought the argument of Secretary of State Vance and others that the United States could not afford to alienate the shah. Vance himself explained the reason why: "We were trying to persuade the shah to moderate increases in oil prices, which were causing major dislocations in the international economy."[26]

Another economic factor was emphasized by R. K. Ramazani, who argued that the key reason was the size of the $1.2 billion contract that enabled the U.S. Air Force to spread its own research and development costs.[27] Senator Goldwater presented another economic argument: "This further refusal to continue in the engagement of the sale of aircraft, whether it is military or airliners, to other countries will in my opinion just continue to destroy this country's ability to meet its balance of payments. It is only through the aircraft industry that we have met our balance of payments."[28] It was in an attempt to counter these persistent if quiet arguments that Senator Eagleton reminded his colleagues of a September 1977 Committee on Foreign Relations resolution that stated "the foreign arms sales policy of the United States should be guided exclusively by considerations of the overall foreign policy interests of the United States and not by considerations of commercial advantage."[29]

When Jimmy Carter became president, the flow of arms from the United States had gained enormous momentum. The flow seemed to have a life of its own. Many of the technocrats who had been long promoting this arms flood were still embedded in the bureaucracy, where they had been expertly polishing arguments supporting the flow of aid to the shah. Ardeshir Zahedi, the influential Iranian ambassador in Washington, constantly reinforced Iran's demands for more and more weapons. In July 1977, Empress Farah visited the United States by herself and developed a rapport with the influential Rosalynn Carter, who was deeply impressed by Farah.

Most importantly, the shah himself bluntly let Carter know what his arms expectations were. When difficulties with Congress led to a delay of the AWACS sale, the shah sent an angry message to Carter on July 31, 1977, threatening to withdraw his AWACS request and, employing the tactic that had proven so successful with other American presidents, implying that he might take his radar business elsewhere. Carter was not particularly pleased with this threat but hastened to placate the shah. In Iran, Ambassador Sullivan hurriedly flew to the shah's small marble palace at Ramsar on the Caspian, where he reassured the king that the AWACS sale would be approved with only very minor modifications.

In sum, early in the Carter administration the shah had effectively convinced the new president that the Pahlavi regime was exceptionally important to the United States. And the United States reacted accordingly. The issue of human rights did not figure heavily in the political equation; it was far down on Carter's list of issues concerning the United States and Iran. The outcome of the shah's visit to Washington that November reinforces this conclusion.

On November 15, 1977, while Jimmy and Rosalynn Carter and the shah and empress of Iran stood on the White House lawn in a welcoming ceremony, thousands of shouting students were demonstrating just outside the gates. The police resorted to tear gas in an attempt to control the demonstrators, but uncooperative breezes carried the gases directly into the faces of the presidential party. With tears running down their faces, the Carters and Pahlavis cut the formalities and pleasantries short, but they never forgot this embarrassing event. In their books, Jimmy Carter would refer to it as "a memorable moment" while Rosalynn would term it "an unforgettable event." President Carter later referred to this incident as an "augury"; it had created "the semblance of grief," and almost two years later "there would be real grief in our country because of Iran."[30] The demonstrations in Washington were paralleled by similar demonstrations in Tehran against the shah and his American supporters. These public events should have alerted the world to the seriousness of the situation in Iran, whose political system would soon begin to unravel.

Meanwhile, the tear gas incident notwithstanding, the shah's twelfth and last official visit to the United States proceeded smoothly. The Carters impressed the Pahlavis, and the Pahlavis impressed the Carters. In the first bilateral meeting of the delegations in the Cabinet room, the shah made an especially effective presentation that led presidential adviser Hamilton Jordan to term it a *tour d'horizon;* "it was more than a presentation—it was a performance." Jordan went so far as to argue that of the more than forty heads of state that Carter had met during his first year of office, "the shah was easily the most impressive."[31] The shah, in turn, was impressed with Carter, and the two developed both a close personal rapport and political understanding.

The November 15–16, 1977, meetings paralleled those the shah had with past presidents. In fact, Carter's behavior and decisions concerning Iran were not unlike those of Johnson, Nixon, and Ford, all of whom the shah considered very special friends. There was a brief private chat between the two heads of state about the general issue of human rights, but the monarch firmly pointed out that Iran's laws had to be enforced and that these laws were designed to combat communism, which was the real threat to his country. He assured Carter that the troublemakers were in any case only a tiny minority. Carter did not push his argument and understood quite well that his own "expression of concern would not change the policies of the Shah."[32] The issue of human rights was not among the three objectives of the Carter administration concerning the shah's visit. They were (1) to convince the shah of the president's commitment to the special relationship between Iran and America, (2) to work out a systematic understanding of Iran's important defense needs, and (3) to convince the shah to take a moderate position on oil prices at forthcoming OPEC meetings.[33]

The major issues actually discussed during the Washington visit were oil prices, arms purchases, nuclear power plants, the Arab-Israeli issue, and Soviet influence in Somalia and Ethiopia. In general, the shah agreed to continue a moderating posture on the issue of petroleum prices and offered to assist in persuading his friends, King Hussein of Jordan and President Sadat of Egypt, to follow the American lead in working for a Middle East peace settlement. In return, he pushed very hard for more arms, specifically 140 F-16s and 70 F-14s, which he argued were absolutely essential for his air defenses. Carter indicated that he would do his best to carry these requests to Congress. Muhammad Reza Shah left Washington confident and reassured of the strong support of the Carter administration for his policies and his regime. The gas-induced tears at the opening of the meetings had been replaced by smiles of understanding. When the shah shook hands with the Department of State's Charles Naas in the White House receiving line, he beamed and said: "Everything is wonderful."[34] Both leaders looked forward to President Carter's forthcoming New Year's visit to Tehran.

Revolution and the Collapse of a Political System

Iran under the great leadership of the Shah is an island of stability in one of the more troubled areas of the world. This is a great tribute to you, Your Majesty, and to your leadership, and to the respect, admiration and love which your people give to you.
—President Jimmy Carter, Tehran, December 31, 1977

In order to acquire name and fame, Ruhollah Khomeini became a tool for the red and black colonialists who have sought to discredit the revolution of the shah and the people. . . . Actually, Khomeini is known as the Indian Sayyid

(*Sayyid Hindi*). . . . He lived in India for a time where he was in touch with British colonial circles and it is said that when young he composed love poems under the pen name of Hindi.

—*Ittili'at*, Tehran, January 7, 1978[35]

These two ill-conceived statements, both presented within one fateful week, helped light the fuse that led directly to the revolutionary explosion that was to tear Iran asunder over the next fourteen months. During his short visit to Tehran on New Year's Eve and New Year's Day of 1978, President Carter only reinforced the pro-Pahlavi posture that he had adopted throughout 1977, including his positive response to the shah's long-term $10 billion military shopping list. After a year of protest and upheaval, Iran was strangely quiet; millions of Iranians watched and waited for the American president and the shah to state their strong joint support for a new, open political system in which "liberalization" would become a reality. In this lull before the storm, President Carter's concern for human rights was publicly suffocated by his effusive, almost obsequious praise for Muhammad Reza Shah Pahlavi. The Persian press reported that as he boarded his plane to leave Tehran, Carter in fervently friendly terms told the shah "I wish you were coming with us." One year later the shah may have wished he had accepted the president's offhand invitation.

Well aware of Carter's somewhat contradictory policy, the opposition religious leaders in Iran concluded that the president was a dangerous hypocrite. On February 19, 1978, Khomeini himself sharply and directly put it in the following terms:

> [Carter] says human rights are inalienable, and then he says, "I don't want to hear about human rights." Of course, he's right from his own point of view; he uses the logic of bandits. The head of a government that has signed the Declaration of Human Rights says, "We have military bases in Iran; we can't talk about human rights there. Respect for human rights is feasible only in countries where we have no military bases."[36]

Carter's unquestioning support for the shah signaled to the Pahlavi regime that it could continue to pursue its policy of alternating reform and repression. Pahlavi functionaries immediately adopted a new aggressive strategy. They underestimated the depth and intensity of the opposition, which was seething after Carter's unfortunate visit. The major tactical error was a direct, vicious personal attack on Ayatollah Ruhollah Khomeini in an article entitled "Iran and Red and Black Colonialism" published in the newspaper *Ittili'at* on January 7, 1978. Cleverly picking up the shah's old argument about the foreign-inspired attacks on his modern and progressive ideas by red leftist intellectuals on the one hand and black religious reactionaries on the other, the writer carelessly put Khomeini's finger on this double-barreled political shotgun. He then assailed Khomeini's character directly, accusing him of being a foreigner, a writer of love sonnets, an opponent of the shah's great reform program, a tool of the British, and responsible for the deaths of many Iranians in the June 1963 riots.

Allegedly written by Daryoush Homayoun, the bright recently appointed minister of Information, the article was probably prepared by a lower influential propagandist in the ministry named Farhad Nikukhah.[37] Nikukhah was a fifty-year-old under-secretary in the ministry who had a degree in political science from Tehran University and a long history of service to the Pahlavi dynasty, including positions as head of public relations for the Pahlavi Foundation and as a planner of the 2,500-year celebrations at Persepolis. In any event, the attack certainly represented the thinking of the regime and had the explicit or implicit support of the shah himself.

The next day, January 8, the clerics and religious students in the holy city of Qum staged massive demonstrations and protest marches. With the American president back in Washington after his enthusiastic embrace of the shah, the government was scarcely restrained by concerns of liberalization and human rights. The police opened fire on the crowds in Qum, killing two dozen people and wounding many more. Religious leaders were among those killed. This event set off a long series of demonstrations and violent incidents throughout Iran that gained momentum with time. The protest marches grew in size and spread in number as the year passed. The shah's police and military forces responded forcefully, but their bullets ultimately only stitched together the fragmented protesting organizations until the bloodstained patchwork quilt of opposition forces covered the entire nation.

The violent events of 1978–79 have been chronicled in great detail in several sources. In brief, they included major riots in the city of Tabriz in Azerbaijan on February 17–21, 1978, renewed violence in Tabriz in early March, contagious rioting in Tehran, Mashhad, Khomein, Isfahan, Miyanah, Rizaiyah, and Zarand on March 30–April 2, demonstrations and violence in Shiraz, Tehran, Tabriz, and Qum during the first two weeks of May, a general strike in Qum along with peaceful demonstrations in Isfahan, Tabriz, Ahwaz, Khurramshahr, Yazd, and Zanjan on June 16–18, violent riots in Mashhad on July 25 and in a dozen other cities during the last week of July, particularly bloody confrontations in Isfahan on August 10–12, over four hundred deaths in the Cinema Rex fire in Abadan on August 19 and subsequent demonstrations in that city, rioting in fifteen cities during the first week of September, the bloody massacre in Tehran on September 8, afterwards known as Black Friday, violent riots in Babul and a dozen other cities on October 8–9, large demonstrations in Mashhad, Qum, Tehran, and Hamadan on October 16–25, opposition groups' control of the city of Babul on October 27–30, huge demonstrations and considerable bloodshed in thirty-six cities during the last three days of October, and thousands of strikes, demonstrations, and riots during November and December 1978 as well as in the early months of 1979. The country was literally afire. From January 1978 to February 1979 not a month passed without major antiregime demonstrations.

The opposition and violence spiraled throughout 1978 as the traditional Shi'i forty-day tradition of mourning brought further opportunities for demonstrations and killings. The death of one family member radicalized other relatives, who then joined the active opposition; this extended-family phenomenon added to the cumulative nature of the revolution.

Although a number of influential observers have argued repeatedly both that the shah lost his will to control the situation and that he did so partly because he was ill and partly because he was concerned about pressure from President Carter, this position fails the test of historical fact. Surrounded by trusted hard-line military advisers such as Gens. Manuchehr Khosrowdad, Hassan Toufanian, Gholam Ali Oveissi, and Amir Hussein Rabi'i and SAVAK chief Nassiri, the shah initially gave orders à la 1963 to put down the disturbances with as much force as necessary. The bloodshed in Tabriz in February, Tehran in September, Isfahan in December, and Mashhad in early January 1979 bear witness to this forceful policy. During these bloody months, troops fired on funeral processions, invaded homes of religious leaders, and, on a number of documented occasions, fired directly into unarmed crowds of men, women, and children.

Careful research indicates that an estimated 10,000 to 12,000 persons were killed and another 45,000 to 50,000 injured during the fourteen-month revolutionary upheaval.[38] Whatever the exact number, it is indisputable that the casualties far exceeded those of any previous crisis in modern Iranian history. The ultimate futility of trying to put down in blood a revolt by millions slowly became clear to the shah himself before it did to a number of American officials who even now, a decade after the revolution, continue to perpetuate the myth that more force and more deaths could have salvaged the Pahlavi regime. In late fall 1978, the shah came to the conclusion that he would not and could not rule a country in which he had to stand in the flowing blood of his people. In short, he understood that he could not militarily occupy his own country. He repeatedly told American ambassador William Sullivan that the events of 1953 and 1963 could not be repeated and that it was impossible this time to quell the massive rebellion by military force alone. In the informed words of Britain's last ambassador to Pahlavi Iran, Anthony Parsons: "Above all he [the shah] was right to reject the advice of his rash and foolish loyalists to unleash the armed forces against the people. . . . It is to the eternal credit of the Shah that, right up until January 16th, he refused to contemplate a greater bloodbath which both he and I knew would have availed him nothing."[39]

One could reasonably argue that the massive application of force only exacerbated the situation. The regime struck repeatedly at both the most revered religious leaders and at the more vulnerable and respected secular opposition leaders. On May 10, 1978, for example, three busloads of imperial commandos arrived in Qum to quell large demonstrations in that city. During this operation, the commando leader, Brig. Gen. Abbas Shafaʻat, burst into the home of Ayatollah Kazem Shariatmadari with a group of his troopers. After Shafaʻat lectured the clerics present, a follower of Shariatmadari, Shaykh Sattar Kashani, protested. He was shot to death on the spot. This act effectively furthered the deepening alienation of Shariatmadari, a learned cleric from Azerbaijan who many believed had quietly collaborated with the regime for years. A natural competitor of Ayatollah Khomeini, this elderly leader represented the moderate wing of the ulama. The hardline police tactics of the regime forced the religious moderates to the side of the extremists.

The same occurred with the liberals and the secular leaders. Although never admirers of Pahlavism, many members of the intelligentsia were not interested in actively confronting the system. Yet the government left them little choice. Special SAVAK committees sent intimidating letters to individuals involved in human rights issues, kidnapped and beat prominent writers, bombed the offices of moderate National Front leaders, and established vigilante groups of thugs that moved into action against students. According to a report of June 1, 1978, prepared by the U.S. Embassy in Tehran: "Among the methods most outraging liberal opinion, both in Iran and elsewhere, are the bombings and the beatings of respectable opponents who are able professionals (lawyers, writers, doctors, engineers, businessmen), and the use of strongarm squads against students or oppositionists."[40] These actions only drove moderate secular professions into alliance with the religious right, with which they had little in common other than an opposition to the Pahlavi government. Through 1978 the opposition solidified under the hammer blows of Pahlavi police and military forces.

Meanwhile, the guiding inspiration of the revolution, Ayatollah Khomeini, kept the pressure on, pushing relentlessly to end the Pahlavi dynasty. From the holy Shi'i city of Najaf in Iraq until October 6 and then from a small home near Paris, Khomeini directed the burgeoning opposition movement. He did so through an extensive personal network, the nodes of which were a large number of key religious and bazaari followers. It is reliably estimated that over the years Khomeini helped educate hundreds of mujtahids and that during his last years at Qum over twelve hundred students (*shagirdan*) had taken courses from him.[41] The Khomeini network had been in place ever since his exile fourteen years earlier, and over the years it had absorbed and then distributed millions upon millions of dollars among the ayatollah's followers and the impoverished masses who were his constituents. The Khomeini net was also used as a flexible communications grid to constantly transmit his ideas and teachings. When the revolutionary sparks ignited, this network was firmly in place and served as an extremely effective organizational medium for the movement.

Ayatollah Ruhollah Khomeini was born on September 24, 1902, in a small town approximately sixty miles from Tehran. His father, Mustafa, suffered a violent death shortly after the birth of Ruhollah, who also lost his mother when he was in his teens. Like many earnest religious young men from small towns in the Iranian heartland, Khomeini had little material wealth but considerable natural talent; he chose to study the religious sciences. He studied for many years in Arak and then in Qum under the guidance of some of the leading religious Shi'i scholars of the day, such as Shaykh Abdul Karim Ha'iri and Mirza Javad Aqa Maliki Tabrizi. Eventually, he developed considerable expertise of his own and became a popular lecturer and teacher of ethics and Islamic philosophy. Through the 1930s and into the 1940s, he spoke to thousands of religious students, becoming their teacher and guide. Himself a follower of the very learned, if apolitical, Shi'i grand ayatollah, Sayyid Muhammad Hussein Burujirdi, Khomeini nurtured strong feelings about the Pahlavi political system, which he considered illegitimate, corrupt, and repressive. It was after the death of Burujirdi in March 1961 that Khomeini began his career as political activist.

Ruhollah Khomeini's first serious public protests against the government occurred late in 1962 when he opposed the repeal of the requirement that local assembly officials be male Muslims. His active public political career, therefore, began when he was sixty years of age. In 1963 he stepped up his opposition by challenging aspects of the shah's White Revolution. This led to his arrest in June and helped precipitate the 1963 national uprising. He was released from prison and again confronted the system in October 1964 over the American-supported status of forces agreement. This in turn led to his expulsion and exile. Khomeini's thirty months of confrontational politics then gave way to an extended period of lower-key, persistent opposition from exile in Iraq. The thirty-month spurt of political activity had given him the image of a fearless, uncompromising champion of the oppressed, and he became a Shi'i folk hero, a temporal imam who was both absent but present, persecuted but powerful.

Whether he is judged a man of unshaking morality and principle or one of vindictive religious-lined tunnel vision, there can be no doubt that Khomeini pursued his goals with single-minded determination and total dedication. From the early 1960s onward, he sought the destruction of the Pahlavi dynasty, which he felt had sold Iran's soul to the West while promoting corruption, immorality, and oppression in Iran. His early dispositions were reinforced by the regime's actions against him in the 1960s and against his followers and student-disciples in the early 1970s. He argued that the United States had forced "the American shah" to create the White Revolution and that therefore America was to blame for the massive casualties of the fifteenth of Khurdad. He also blamed the United States for pushing the SOFA on "the puppet shah." It was quite clear to him then that it was America that banished him.

Throughout 1978, Ayatollah Khomeini issued proclamations from Najaf condemning the shah, praising Islam, castigating the United States for its support of the shah, and honoring those Iranians who were demonstrating and rebelling against Pahlavi rule. His speeches were emotional and politically astute. He spoke the language of the Iranian masses and sensitively highlighted their everyday problems and suffering. And he did so through the idiom of religion. He spoke as a radical religious populist. He constantly encouraged the people of Iran to challenge the ruling class, not to "swallow the poison the holders of authority wish to force down our throats." He exhorted them to die if necessary in their resistance, "to water the roots of the tree of Islam with their blood." And he cleverly turned the tables on the regime by arguing that "the shah and his government are in a state of armed rebellion against the justice-seeking people of Iran, against the constitution, and against the liberating decrees of Islam." In the words of Khomeini and his growing mass constituency, the shah was a rebel against both his own people and his own religion. This rebellious regime had to be overthrown at any cost.[42]

As Iranians increasingly rallied to the cries of Khomeini and as hardline tactics yielded counterproductive results, the shah desperately attempted to resort again to proven political moves. He continually shuffled the deck of political actors close to him, arbitrarily discarding those he considered dispensable and retaining others. As time passed, he merely shuffled the personalities more rapidly. On June 19, 1978, he replaced notorious SAVAK head Nassiri with his deputy, Gen. Nassir Muqaddam, a less draconian version of Nassiri. Nassiri was named ambassador to Pakistan and remained there until October 7, when he returned to Iran; he was later arrested and jailed. On August 27, the shah replaced Prime Minister Amuzegar with his old standby, troubleshooter Ja'far Sharif-Emami. That same day four high-ranking army officers, including his longtime personal physician, Abdul Karim Ayadi, widely known to be of the Baha'i faith, were retired. Two weeks later, on September 9, Amir Abbas Hoveyda resigned as minister of Court, ending an era of Hoveydan political influence in Iran. Two days after that, the shah had several former ministers and businessmen arrested for corruption. As the political situation worsened, the shah made a number of other changes, including the replacement of Sharif-Emami as prime minister by Gen. Ghulam Reza Azhari, who oversaw a period of martial law beginning November 6. This lasted only until December 29, when the shah replaced Azhari with Shapour Bakhtiar. Azhari left the country the next day.

These personality shifts were too little, too late. As the shah's last ambassador to the United Nations stated, "So, where immediate surgery was required, the Shah used first aid."[43] Like the entire liberalization program, these policies were half-hearted and poorly implemented. A number of those considered to be among the most corrupt and who were anathema among the opposition escaped unscathed. These included such powerful political and economic figures as Gen. Hassan Toufanian, Ambassador Ardeshir Zahedi, Princess Ashraf Pahlavi, and numerous high-ranking military personalities. Although the shah had scapegoated a few members of his inner circle, most remained in place until the end, when they made their hurried exits. In a private interview at Niavaran Palace on November 29, 1978, Gen. Hassan Pakravan, former head of SAVAK and close adviser returned to influence at the end, stated that the only remaining solution would be for the shah to arrest and execute the band of thieves that still surrounded him. In Pakravan's words, "the shah should do what they did in Qajar days. He should hang a number of these scoundrels from the city's gates."[44]

The shah's most glaring error was appointing Sharif-Emami as prime minister. Certain American officials viewed this as an astute decision, and the Western press presented Sharif-Emami as a religious man who could dissipate the opposition. Even Barry Rubin has referred to Sharif-Emami as "a man with a pious reputation."[45] In fact, Sharif-Emami had quite a different reputation in Iran; in the words of Ambassador William Sullivan, he "was regarded as personally corrupt."[46] It was common knowledge in Tehran that he was the leading ceremonial figure in the Iranian Masonic organization, not a position that commanded much respect in the days of quickening Islamic revivalism. Sharif-Emami's attempts to liberalize the system were referred to by Sullivan and other American policymakers as "feeding the crocodiles." In fact, in this case, Sharif-Emami, the prime feeder, was in the eyes of the "crocodiles" himself contaminated, and they only renewed their attacks on him and those who stood behind him.

I lived for two weeks in November–December 1978 among the so-called crocodiles in southeast Tehran on a small alley behind a gas station near Jalah Square, where the Black Friday massacres had taken place. Here the masses of Iranian people, crowded in line for their kerosene and rationed meat, shouted slogans against the shah. Taxi drivers spit in the direction of the shah's soldiers, and students combed the city for pictures of the royal family to tear down and deface. Luxury hotels, cinemas, and liquor stores stood silent as dark, windowless, bombed-out hulks. Anti-Americanism was intense, and a wild, powerful sentiment pervaded the crowded sidewalks, markets, and streets. This was the heartbeat of the revolution, and the people's anger swelled out of south Tehran. Young bearded representatives of "Aqa" (as they then referred to Ayatollah Khomeini) hurried constantly to the key homes and mosques where they organized the opposition and dispensed Aqa's latest directives.

Meanwhile, twenty miles to the north, in Niavaran Palace, an unreal, eerie atmosphere prevailed. The shah sat silently at his desk, while the empress nervously greeted guests from whom she earnestly, almost desperately, sought advice. As the shah sat stunned and suspicious, even Farah was unable to get him to follow her advice. In her words, "the husband does not always listen to the wife." But both resisted the fact that this time the masses were laying full blame for their plight at the feet of the Pahlavis—and those who backed the royal family. The cultural and political distance between Jalah Square in southeast Tehran and Niavaran Palace to the north was much greater than the geographic reality. Meanwhile, the growing clouds of revolutionary anger, containing the thundering shouts of the huge crowds, slowly and inexorably encompassed the shah and his diminishing group of loyal followers.

In another part of Tehran, four miles west and slightly north from Jalah Square, the American embassy bustled with activity around Ambassador William Sullivan. Sullivan's staff had recently been bolstered by the arrival of a few hands who had served with some distinction in Iran in the past. As they monitored the deteriorating situation, they talked of crocodiles (or alligators, depending on who was speaking), privy councils, evacuations, Pahlavi political acumen, successor governments, alternative political leaders, and military force and crowd control. One veteran foreign service officer indicated that he was certain that there were Tudeh party members in the Iranian political "woodpile"; another said that he had found no remaining support whatsoever for the shah in the bazaar; several diplomats mumbled about public statements from Washington that only exacerbated an already tense situation. In the end, America's representatives in Iran were left with little to do but monitor every moment of the collapse of a political system.

The shah's grip slipped in the face of increasing turbulence and the flight of many of the leading members of the Pahlavi elite. It loosened despite constant advice and moral support from individuals such as Empress Farah and Ardeshir Zahedi and from the American and British ambassadors. Those who met with the shah at the end of 1978 reported that he seemed listless, depressed, baffled, and shaken. Some have concluded that if he had acted with firmness and resolution, he could have faced down the revolution. They have attributed his indecision to a number of factors, blaming everyone and everything from Jimmy Carter to the shah's cancer. But the fact is that times had changed. The shah's early mistakes had been institutionalized over the years. In late 1978, he stood in the path of millions of Iranian citizens in revolt against him. He did take actions, both forceful and accommodating. Nothing worked. It is no wonder that his grip weakened and his mind wavered.

On January 16, 1979, the shah and empress of Iran and a small entourage boarded a silver-and-blue Boeing 707 bound for Egypt. As the shah flew out of the country for the final time, masses of people rushed to the streets of the major cities and held frenzied celebrations. On February 1 Ayatollah Ruhollah Khomeini arrived in Tehran from

France, and the Iranian revolution became a reality. The United States, a country that had confidently rested its vital interests in the Middle East on the Pahlavi pillar, watched in shock and alarm as that pillar collapsed with a roar heard round the world.

The United States in the Iranian Revolution

When the shah's regime collapsed, American officials, policymakers, and friends of the Pahlavi regime reacted in shocked disbelief but quickly recovered in order to begin sustained and elaborate efforts to absolve themselves of any responsibility for this foreign policy debacle. The methodology adopted for this purpose has been to call attention to the culpability of others, thereby deflecting blame away from oneself. This has given rise to an increasing proliferation of articles and books written by most of the major political, economic, and academic actors involved with Iran. A survey of this literature of apologetics and an analysis of the events indicates a positive correlation between those who blame others most vehemently and those most responsible for the foreign policy failure.

Perhaps the two most accusatory have been President Carter's adviser for national security affairs, Zbigniew Brzezinski, and Brzezinski's adviser on Iranian affairs, Gary Sick. Brzezinski's memoirs are obviously self-serving, while Sick's account, while more subtle and scholarly, is also slanted. Slightly less dogmatic but still bitterly blaming others are former president Jimmy Carter and first lady Rosalynn Carter and such advisers as Hamilton Jordan. A third, less dogmatic level of self-justification is practiced by former ambassador William H. Sullivan and embassy political officer John Stempel. This elaborate screen of interpretive underbrush makes it particularly difficult to ascertain what really happened. Yet it is essential to attempt to acquire an overall objective understanding of the roles performed by key American players.[47]

The American foreign policy establishment was badly divided over the Iranian situation, and the major actors were involved in a tangled web of personal and policy rivalry. One perceptive and informed Washington political reporter noted, "The fall of the shah involved a bitter though collegial contest among the president's key advisers, contending for control over foreign policy."[48] The struggle was clearly more bitter than collegial. The primary fault line was the institutional conflict between the U.S. Department of State, directed by Secretary of State Cyrus Vance, and the National Security Council, headed by Adviser for National Security Affairs Zbigniew Brzezinski. In descending order of influence, the following organizations (with their respective heads listed in parentheses) were also deeply involved in the formation of Iran policy: Department of Defense (Harold Brown), Department of Energy (James Schlesinger), Central Intelligence Agency (Stansfield Turner), and Department of Treasury (W. Michael Blumenthal). Other input was provided briefly by special adviser George Ball and, in a private and unsolicited manner, by the Rockefeller group, which included Nelson and David Rockefeller, John J. McCloy, and Henry Kissinger. The major decision maker, and the one on whom ultimate responsibility must rest, was President Jimmy Carter himself, who also sporadically sought the advice of such close associates as Charles Kirbo, Walter Mondale, and Hamilton Jordan.

To complicate the picture further, many of the above groups were deeply divided within themselves in the recommendation of policy. This was true of both the State Department and the CIA. Also, several individuals changed their positions constantly throughout the crisis. In order to understand the ultimate policy outcomes, it is essential to provide profiles of the most important Washington decision-making centers. The most complex of these was the Department of State.

The Department of State: Expertise, Division, and Impotence

The chief State Department official, Cyrus Vance, was a thoroughly professional and faultlessly loyal official. Cautious and judicious in approach, he mistakenly assumed that other high-level officials shared similar orientations. He was deeply preoccupied by the Camp David negotiations and the strategic arms limitation talks with the Soviet Union and had little time to devote to events in Iran. Instead, he relied heavily on his major assistants, Deputy Secretary of State Warren Christopher, Under Secretary of State for Political Affairs David Newsom, and Assistant Secretary of State for Near Eastern and South Asian affairs Harold "Hal" Saunders. Christopher, Newsom, and Saunders all reflected Vance's own personality; each was a highly professional, somewhat dry, and exceedingly cautious individual. All were involved in Carter's priority Camp David initiatives but took time to fill in for Vance on important Iran meetings when Vance was absent.

Given his long experience in Washington and his responsibilities for Middle Eastern affairs, Saunders was a particularly important deputy. A veteran of the Arab-Israeli imbroglio, where he had learned to survive in situations of intense bureaucratic conflict, Saunders was a soft-spoken gentleman with a long history of high-level government service. After three years with the Air Force and three more with the CIA, he served as a junior member of the National Security Council staff from 1961 to 1966 and as a senior member from 1967 to 1974. He then transferred to the State Department, where he headed the Bureau of Intelligence and Research (INR), among other posts. Saunders subscribed to the conventional wisdom on the stability of the Pahlavi regime and, as an ultracautious diplomat, was slow to accept the reality of the situation. Later, however, Saunders, along with Christopher and Newsom, fought gamely and loyally alongside Vance in a futile attempt to educate both President Carter and National Security Adviser Zbigniew Brzezinski about the political realities in Iran.

At lower levels at State, two individuals rested at the center of a growing group of officials who increasingly questioned the prevailing Pahlavi stability thesis. Henry Precht, Iran desk officer, and George Griffin, principal officer responsible for Iran at INR, were deeply concerned about the growing political violence in Iran, and by midsummer 1978 they both sensed real trouble. They were supported in their analysis by Carl Clement, a quiet, knowledgeable foreign service officer who had served for years in Iran and who had excellent Persian language capabilities. These midlevel specialists consistently sought the advice of the small group of American scholars of contemporary Iran. Generally, these scholars expressed views of great concern and brought considerable evidence to bear in support of their feelings that this time the shah was in very deep trouble.

In a paper presented on March 10, 1978, to a group of midlevel government foreign-policy officials, for example, I wrote that time did not favor the shah:

> It is true that he [the shah] has run a few steps out ahead of the forces of political disaster. He is obviously an experienced runner who knows the track. But the pace of the race continues to pick up and those who are chasing him are more numerous, more dedicated, and more prepared. . . .
>
> The government can now only respond with more and more coercive force and military control and repression. The large groups of individuals already alienated by the regime will in turn become more demanding and desperate in their response. And they will be joined by others—the only common denominator to their cooperation being opposition to the regime. As this occurs, the shah will have lost the will and capacity to use his traditional tactics of political control. Unless something is done again to break this wildly spinning vicious circle, the future of the current actors in the Iranian political drama can only be a grim one. And the American future in Iran can in no way be considered bright.[49]

Seven months later, on October 27, 1978, I presented another paper to the Department of State that ended with the following:

> The killing of unarmed demonstrators by the shah's troops and the subsequent rule by martial law will only provide a temporary respite for the regime. These deaths in the streets have added an element of fanaticism in the resolve of the opposition. The months ahead will almost certainly be violent ones for Iran. Against this backdrop of conflict and death, the shah's clear attempts to keep his program of liberalization going will only be viewed with cynicism and distrust by both the moderate and extreme opposition. Passive opposition and resistance along with social sabotage will increase. The economy, already in a serious trouble, may grind to a halt and the specter of a rebellious society at a standstill is not at all beyond credibility.
>
> The shah cannot occupy his own country forever. Nor can be continue to resort to his traditional methods of rule by calculated reform. Perhaps his only serious chance is to back off of the tiny plateau of absolute power. Nothing less than his survival and that of his dynasty are at stake.[50]

It was at this October meeting that Professor Marvin Zonis and I engaged in a spirited debate over whether political events in Iran could be likened more to an avalanche (Zonis) or to a raging forest fire (Bill). This discussion apparently shook the officials present, most of whom maintained much milder and less alarming views of the situation.

Henry Precht, however, took such analysis seriously, and although he later became the scapegoat of such writers as Gary Sick and Zbigniew Brzezinski, he was one of the few in Washington who understood the fragility of the shah's power. After two years as deputy chief of mission in Mauritius, Precht had been posted to Iran, where he served as political-military affairs officer between 1972 and 1976. At times somewhat stiff and formal, Precht had long held conventional conservative views about the Pahlavi regime. But through his careful and honest analysis of day-to-day events in Iran, he gradually came to believe that the Pahlavi regime was collapsing. Precht was one of the first American officials to realize this, and he spent the latter half of 1978 and early 1979 attempting to pass along this realization both to his superiors in the State Department and to the White House, where Iran policy was in fact being made.

In Tehran, America was represented by a tough career foreign service officer who had arrived as ambassador there in June 1977. William H. Sullivan was a distinguished white-haired, ramrod-straight man who spoke quietly and directly. He exuded personal strength and confidence. Sullivan had just served for four years as ambassador to the Philippines, and before that he had held posts in Washington and in Laos and Vietnam, where it was widely rumored that he directed a wide range of American intelligence operations. He had no experience in the Middle East. Sullivan was not pleased with the Tehran appointment, but he had a reputation as a man who knew how to deal with authoritarian leaders. Yet as one foreign service officer confided after Sullivan had been briefed by State Department oficials, "the shah likes to deal with tough guys. He'll have Sullivan eating out of his hand the same way he did Helms and MacArthur. The shah is no Marcos."[51]

Sullivan did his homework before he left for Iran. The American Pahlavi supporters weighed in with praise for the shah, with special emphasis on the stability of his regime. But Sullivan carefully listened to the other side when he was briefed by academics and middle-level State Department Iran specialists. These advisers strongly recommended that Sullivan would do well to break out of the old circle of Iranian hangers-on who encircled and encrusted the U.S. Embassy in Tehran. They warned him that all was not as it appeared on the surface in Iran and that the Pahlavi regime had a number of soft spots. Sullivan spent a day listening in apparent boredom to the State Department team. But his questions and comments made it clear that he had indeed listened well.

As expected, Bill Sullivan was enormously impressed by the shah. He developed an excellent rapport with the monarch, and they quickly established a close working relationship. He was also duly impressed with Asadollah Alam, who had made a career of gaining the favor of American and British ambassadors. Sullivan was professional enough to realize, however, that the United States did not really understand the intricacies of Iranian politics. Even John Stempel, who had served as political officer in Iran since 1975, admitted that "America did not realize what was happening in Iran."[52] Sullivan attempted to improve American intelligence in Iran but never really succeeded. By the time he made a serious effort to do so, the most extreme members of the Iranian opposition refused to have anything to do with American officials.

Although Ambassador Sullivan may have personally supported a human rights policy, he strongly disagreed with the vigor of the approach pursued by the Bureau of Human Rights in the Department of State. Sullivan and Charles Naas, his deputy chief of mission, preferred an indirect, quiet approach, and as a result significant tension developed between the mission in Tehran and the bureau in Washington. Although Sullivan, like Carter himself, failed to push the shah seriously on this issue, he did cooperate to an extent with the International Commission of Jurists and the Butler missions, whose legalistic approach he preferred to the more frontal political tack of Amnesty International. In a letter of December 1977 to William Butler, Sullivan compared the two approaches as follows:

> You both come to more or less the same conclusions, but Amnesty's approach is that of looking at a glass half empty while yours can be described as looking at a glass half full. It would be my judgment that the Amnesty paper will be poorly received here merely because of its tenor, rather than because of its contents. On the other hand, your observations, while they amount to the same thing, would be considered constructive and therefore might be more persuasive.[53]

Sullivan's major concern was economic in nature, and he focused his most serious analysis on the Iranian industrialization program. In the process, he underestimated the social and political fragility of the Pahlavi regime, and it was not really until November 1978 that he realized that the shah was in serious trouble. As late as May 5, 1978, Sullivan signed off on a memorandum prepared by his deputy Jack Miklos that contained the following assessment: "In a major sense Iran has now reached the position of a stable and moderate middle-level power well-disposed toward the United States which has been a goal of our policy since the end of WWII. There are no outstanding issues of such serious magnitude that they need be identified in this memorandum."[54] Sullivan had been so confident in the shah's control of the situation that he had taken an extensive home leave during the middle of the revolution, from June to late August 1978. On November 9, 1978, he wrote his now famous cable entitled "Thinking the Unthinkable" in which he cautiously but seriously indicated that the United States had best begin preparing contingency plans in case the shah did not survive politically.

Sullivan was enough of a professional to admit that he had been much too optimistic and that it was now time to face facts. Although he had come very late to the realization that the shah was unlikely to make it, he became increasingly sure of it through November and December 1978. He attempted to get the message to Washington, even recommending that the United States establish direct contact with Ayatollah Khomeini in Paris. But Sullivan found his increasingly desperate messages ignored in Washington. Not only had Zbigniew Brzezinski and his staff taken charge of Iran policy, but Secretary of State Vance himself refused to believe that the shah was in serious trouble. As David Newsom noted, "Vance was among the very last to admit, even to himself, that the shah might collapse."[55] The fact that

Sullivan received no response to his important cable of November 9 was symptomatic of the misunderstanding and lack of communication that henceforth marked Carter foreign policy toward Iran.

The National Security Adviser and Staff: Politics of Power and Ignorance

National Security adviser Brzezinski had consistently argued that only a hard-line, no-nonsense policy from the shah could save the day. Although he had been particularly slow to recognize the shah's difficulties, he always felt that tough action by the shah's military forces would scatter the opposition, which he believed consisted of communists on the left and a few reactionary religious leaders on the right. Brzezinski was reinforced by his deputy David Aaron, a humorless, steely-eyed bureaucrat who had become an instant expert on the Middle East. Naval captain Gary Sick represented Brzezinski's Iran expertise. Sick was a bright, sensitive individual, but he had very little background in Iranian affairs, and, as a consummate loyalist, he simply reinforced Brzezinski's distorted views. Brzezinski's major understanding of Iran came from his friend, Iranian ambassador Ardeshir Zahedi, with whom he maintained close contact throughout the crisis. Brzezinski and Zahedi spent the last half of 1978 reinforcing one another's opinions on the situation in Iran.

Policy conflict between the national security adviser and his staff on the one hand and the Department of State on the other hand was inevitable. Old foreign policy hand George Ball was horrified by Brzezinski's bureaucratic imperialism. Ball stated: "He was operating in a free-wheeling manner, calling in foreign ambassadors, telephoning or sending telegrams to foreign dignitaries outside State Department channels, and even hiring a press adviser so he could compete with the Secretary of State as the enunciator of United States policy." In describing Brzezinski's pompous justifications for policy recommendations, which were always framed in some grand global context, Ball quoted his father, who described this tactic as "a flair for making little fishes talk like whales."[56]

In the bureaucratic infighting that swirled about U.S.-Iran policy during the Carter administration, Brzezinski, a shrewd and slashing competitor, consistently bested Secretary of State Vance, who although principled and loyal presented an inviting target for Brzezinski's thrusts. One Carter confidant noted that Brzezinski "never accepted a defeat as final or a policy as decided if it did not please him. Like a rat terrier, he would shake himself off after a losing en-

counter and begin nipping at Vance's ankles, using his press spokesman and chief deputies as well as himself to tell the world that he had
won or that only he, Zbigniew Brzezinski, hung tough in the national-
security game as a foreign-policy realist."[57]

By the time Vance belatedly understood what was going on in Iran,
he found that Brzezinski had preempted him and had the ear of the
president. Sullivan was another matter. He was at least as tough as
Brzezinski. Furthermore, Sullivan was on the ground in Iran and had
received some difficult on-the-job education in Iranian politics. When
Brzezinski failed to respond to Sullivan's suggestions or merely took
contradictory actions to those Sullivan recommended, Sullivan responded with increasingly caustic cables. Brzezinski used these to
turn President Carter against Sullivan. Only Vance's intervention kept
Carter from firing Sullivan on the spot. This type of confrontation
occurred up and down the U.S. policy-making hierarchy.

In early November 1978, for example, State Department officials
Carl Clement, George Griffin, and Stephen Cohen (Bureau of Human
Rights) traveled to Tehran, arriving there on November 4. That day
Clement and Cohen visited the Tehran bazaar, which was partially
closed since many bazaaris had gone to meet Ayatollah Taliqani, who
had just been released from prison. Major riots that resulted in heavy
casualties also erupted at Tehran University that day—a day that
would be commemorated one year later by the taking of American
hostages. While in Iran, these three officials split up and traveled
widely, visiting such cities as Tabriz, Isfahan, and Khurramshahr. It
was the explosive situation in the provinces that convinced them that
a genuine revolution was in progress.

On their return to Washington, Clement, Griffin, and Cohen arranged a meeting with Under Secretary David Newsom to explain the
seriousness of the situation they had witnessed in Iran. The three
officers and Iran desk officer Henry Precht subsequently met with
Brzezinski's deputy David Aaron and NSC Iran-watcher Gary Sick,
both of whom listened to the evidence and eyewitness accounts for
nearly an hour. Aaron, who was a somewhat more liberal version of
Brzezinski, was unimpressed by what he heard. At one point, he reportedly asked Henry Precht, "Tell me Henry, who exactly is the opposition?" "The people, David, the people," Precht acidly responded.
In the end, Aaron simply said, "Well you fellows may be right but we
have no choice but to support the shah." When the State Department
officials asked Gary Sick what he thought, he tersely responded, "I
agree with David."[58]

The sad state of the situation is seen in the fact that Sick has since condemned Sullivan for failing to ask for advice from Washington. Sullivan, on the other hand, has written that he was deeply puzzled and frustrated because he was never provided any instructions from Washington. It seems true that Sullivan's credibility suffered back in Washington because of his earlier consistent optimism about the shah's chances. It is also clear, however, that the major foreign policy-making forces in Washington had determined that the shah was to be supported at all costs and that his regime could be protected through the application of enough military force. Nothing was going to change their minds.

Brzezinski was generally supported in this stance by Harold Brown and the Department of Defense, James Schlesinger and the Department of Energy, and, to a somewhat lesser extent, Stansfield Turner and the Central Intelligence Agency. Furthermore, several powerful American businessmen and Pahlavi supporters such as John J. McCloy, Nelson Rockefeller, and Henry Kissinger were applying pressure on American policymakers to support the shah with whatever it took and at all costs. At a special meeting of high-level decision makers in the situation room of the White House on November 2, 1978, for example, Brzezinski reported that he had received a telephone call from Nelson Rockefeller, who criticized the government for apparently doing little to support the shah.[59]

A seldom-mentioned irony is that the shah himself indicated that further military measures would be counterproductive and would result in such bloodshed that his dynasty would be hated and his family's very existence would be in mortal danger. He would have nothing to do with such measures. The shah was also incredulous when he heard that Brzezinski had vetoed Sullivan's proposal that the United States make direct contact with Khomeini in Paris. After watching his troops kill over ten thousand of his own people in the streets of Iran's cities, the shah determined that violent tactics were doomed to fail. Because of this position, the monarch found himself criticized by Brzezinski as being weak, vacillating, and indecisive. Later, in February 1979, Brzezinski was as disgusted with the Iranian military as he had been earlier with the shah, since "the Iranian military evidently did not have the will to act."[60] Ultimately, in Brzezinski's eyes everyone was vacillating: Ambassador Sullivan, the shah, and the Iranian military itself.

The Department of State-National Security Council tension carried heavy professional and personal costs. As the crisis developed, the White House increasingly cut Henry Precht and his colleagues at State out of the decision-making process. On December 19, 1978, Precht wrote a revealing letter to Ambassador Sullivan in Tehran. This communication was marked "Official-Informal-Secret-Eyes Only" and captured the frustration of an official who, in retrospect, had as good a grasp of events unfolding in Iran as anyone in Washington.

> I presume you are aware of the Top Secret list of questions that was sent out over the weekend for the Shah. I have not been shown the list, such is the level of distrust that exists in the White House towards the State Department (and egotistically, I feel, towards myself). I am afraid that we are losing valuable time and that events may sweep us by, depriving the U.S. of the opporunity to recoup its position in Iran.
>
> I have probably confided more than I should to a piece of paper, but I doubt I have much of a future anyway. I would ask you to protect me for the sake of the education of the young. Whatever the risks, I believe it important to give you my frank assessment of how things are shaping up on the Iranian front these days.[61]

Divided against itself, preoccupied with other international issues, and somewhat restrained in its capacity to do bureaucratic battle by a code of professional ethics, the Department of State watched Brzezinski and his staff arrogantly shape a policy that placed America on the losing side in a revolution. This policy seriously compromised American national interests and was partially responsible for the extremism and anti-Americanism that broke forth in Iran after the revolution.

At the urging of Michael Blumenthal and with the consent of Brzezinski, President Carter called on George Ball to carry out an independent study of the situation and to develop policy recommendations. Ball energetically began his research on November 30, 1978, and sought the advice of a wide network of Iran specialists. On at least one occasion, State Department official George Griffin managed to slip an Iran scholar up the backstairs of the White House and into Ball's office. The NSC staff did not welcome input recommended by the Department of State.

Ball prepared an eighteen-page memorandum for the president entitled "Issues and Implications of the Iranian Crisis." In this hard-hitting report, Ball sharply criticized the basis of the Nixon Doctrine and stated that the United States bore much of the responsibility for the shah's megalomania. He argued that the shah was finished as an absolute monarch. Ball pointed out that military repression was doomed to fail and that it risked turning Iran into another Lebanon. Ball recommended that the shah transfer full power to a government responsive to the people. The mechanism that Ball favored for such a transfer was a Council of Notables composed of responsible individuals carefully selected by the United States. In Ball's view, "I thought this was the only way we could protect it from becoming a government of the shah's own designation."[62] At the same time, Ball urged the president to open a disavowable channel of communication to Ayatollah Khomeini.

Although Ball's proposal was mild, given the lateness of the date, only Acting Secretary of State Christopher gave it unqualified support. Ball submitted the memorandum on December 11, 1978. The next morning he met with Brzezinski, who was very "dubious" and who indicated that he thought a restoration similar to the one of 1953 could be accomplished.[63] Ball went in to see Carter that afternoon, and, to his surprise, "there was Zbig sitting there." Carter told Ball that he liked the report but that he would not accept its recommendations since he would not tell another head of state what to do. Ball replied that Carter would only be responding to a friend's needs, a friend who had sought the president's advice. Partly under the influence of Brzezinski, Carter failed to take George Ball's advice. Brzezinski later admitted that he had made a mistake in seeking the independent opinion because this violated a basic law of bureaucratic tactics: "One should never obtain the services of an 'impartial' outside consultant regarding an issue that one feels strongly about without first making certain in advance that one knows the likely contents of his advice."[64]

According to George Ball, about the only positive result of his activities was that he convinced the president not to send Zbigniew Brzezinski to Tehran. Apparently, Brzezinski felt that his presence in Iran would provide Washington with new insights into the Iranian political scene while bolstering the courage and position of the shah. Ball incredulously told Carter that this plan, "with all due respect is the worst idea I have ever heard."[65] Given the fact that Ball had obviously heard many bad ideas over his long diplomatic career, this statement made an impression on the president, who decided to cancel the Brzezinski trek.

The futile efforts of George Ball were soon replaced by a recommendation by the Department of Defense and supported by Brzezinski to send a high-ranking U.S. military official to Iran as a liaison to the Iranian military forces, who seemed to hold the key to Iran's political future. The man selected was Gen. Robert "Dutch" Huyser, deputy commander-in-chief of the U.S. European Command under Alexander Haig. General Huyser had been traveling to Iran since the late 1960s and had close personal and professional relationships with Iranian military leaders. He has also pointed out that "I had many audiences with the Shah, at which a mutual respect and trust were established."[66] That year he had already visited Iran twice—in April and again in August.

Dutch Huyser arrived in Iran on January 4, 1979. His charge was to hold the Iranian military together and to send a sharp signal that the United States stood behind the current regime. He has said, "In general terms I was sent there by the Government of the United States to stabilize the Iranian military and to encourage the Iranian military to support their legal government."[67] The military was to back Prime Minister Shapour Bakhtiar; if the Bakhtiar government fell, then Huyser was to encourage the Iranian generals to carry out a coup d'etat. According to Huyser, "if that government collapsed, then at exactly the right moment, I was to see that the military took action."[68]

The decision to protect the integrity of the military was closely intertwined with another matter of considerable concern to American officials. It involved the supersecret, sophisticated electronic listening posts at Bihshahr and Kapkan in northern Iran. From these posts the United States had been closely monitoring Soviet missile and space activities. The Kapkan site, located forty miles east of Mashhad, was especially valuable to the United States and was considered irreplaceable. Although the Bihshahr station had been closed in December 1978, Kapkan continued to operate until the local Iranian employees mutinied, demanded their backpay, and held the twenty-two American technicians there captive. In a harrowing, little-known mission, two American military leaders still in Tehran, Capt. H. F. Johnson and Col. T. E. Shaefer, along with two resourceful Iranian employees and 30 million rials, flew to Kapkan in an Iranian C-130 piloted by an unfriendly Iranian air force officer. After paying the local employees, they returned with the twenty-two technicians, who were actually employed by the CIA. This quiet rescue mission saved American lives but left the listening posts in Iranian hands. Huyser and other American officials had hoped to hold the military together in order to ride the revolution out so that, among other things, America might continue to operate these valuable intelligence sites.

Huyser's presence in Iran undercut Ambassador Sullivan's authority; it seemed evident to all that the White House now had its own representative in Tehran. Huyser's mission was a dramatic indication of Washington's two-track, collision-course, contradictory policy toward Iran. Huyser was a direct, competent officer, but he was badly over his head in the Iranian political thicket. Traveling around north Tehran in a bulletproof vest and closeted daily with five or six of the shah's leading generals, Huyser never understood Iran. He has admitted that he never heard Khomeini's name before April 1978 and that he estimated that only 10 to 20 percent of the Iranian population supported Khomeini.[69] Like the myopic military officers he advised, he appeared to believe that the communists were somehow standing behind the religious leaders. While he pointed out that the Iranian generals "saw a Communist behind every mosque,"[70] he also argued "that if Iran became an Islamic Republic, it would eventually end up in the Communist camp."[71]

Over dinner in the evening at the ambassador's residence, Huyser and Sullivan would discuss the day's events. After dinner they would both call Washington from two secure telephone circuits. In Sullivan's words:

> On one line I would speak to Under Secretary of State Newsom or Assistant Secretary Saunders. On the other, Huyser would speak with the chairman of the Joint Chiefs of Staff, David Jones, or with Secretary of Defense Harold Brown. We would then compare notes after our conversations to try to sort out what Washington was attempting to convey to us. There were times when we felt we must have been talking to two different cities.[72]

Since they were both thorough professionals, Huyser and Sullivan respected both one another and one another's opinions, something that was uncommon among American decision makers in Washington. Nonetheless, they disagreed sharply in their assessment of the Iranian military. Sullivan felt it was deeply split, quite demoralized, and would fall apart in the face of the crisis that loomed ahead. Huyser curiously overestimated the strength of the shah's armed forces despite their leaders' personal and professional rivalry, their appalling lack of planning, and their refusal to take responsibility. Huyser witnessed this firsthand every day of the month he was in Tehran.[73] When he drafted a cable to Washington giving his positive assessment of the military's solidarity, he asked for Sullivan's opinion. Sullivan said he did not agree, and Huyser included the dissenting view in the telegram. In a poignant moment after Huyser had left the ambassador's office, Sullivan turned to his deputy chief of mission and said that he strongly believed his assessment to be correct, but "Goddamn, I wish in this case that I am wrong."[74] In the end, Sullivan was proven right; even Huyser came to admit that "Yes, the military did collapse, ten days after Khomeini returned to Iran and seven days after I departed."[75]

Despite this, high-ranking American military advisers who remained in Iran after Huyser left were shocked by the February 1979 collapse of the Iranian military. In retrospect, they explained the collapse in the following terms. First, in a major meeting of four hundred flag and middle-grade officers, a decision was made to permit the civilian and constitutional forces to determine the future of the country. Second, the hard-line senior officers lost their credibility because of intense personal rivalries, infighting (especially in the air force), and clumsy political moves. General Manuchehr Khosrowdad, for example, took himself out of the game by intemperate, frontal verbal attacks on Prime Minister Shapour Bakhtiar, who simply had him removed as commander of army aviation and relegated to the command of a secondary military support group.[76]

In general terms, no one should have been surprised by the collapse of the military. It had been under incredible pressure for months. The rank-and-file soldiers were very religious and naturally susceptible to the ideas and proclamations of their cleric leaders. But even the officer class had been successfully penetrated, and a number of the high-ranking officers began to work quietly with the opposition. These included such officers as Gens. Hatam, Na'ini, and Bakhshazar. The families of important military men were targeted for special attention and extraordinary pressures by the religious revolutionaries. Throughout 1978 and early 1979, thousands upon thousands of soldiers had defected. By the time Gen. Abbas Qarabaghi became chief of staff in early December 1978, defections were numbering one thousand a day and rising.[77]

The Iranian revolutionary opposition considered Ambassador Sullivan much more knowledgeable about the situation in Iran than General Huyser. In their words: "While Sullivan was the best informed American official concerning the Iranian situation, his views were ignored in Washington because they were bad news (*akhbar-i bad*) and therefore unacceptable. On the other hand, everyone eagerly awaited Huyser's report."[78] In the opinion of the Iranian opposition, Huyser had "very little information" because he closeted himself only with the highest-ranking Iranian generals. In his own accounts, Huyser had admitted no contact whatsoever with the opposition forces and has indicated that he spent $4\frac{1}{2}$ to 7 or 8 hours every day (with one exception) with the Iranian commanders.[79]

Besides further dividing the policy-making establishment in Washington, the Huyser mission had profoundly negative effects in the Iranian political context. The opposition forces viewed Huyser's presence as an obvious U.S. attempt to intervene directly and militarily in a last-ditch effort to save the Pahlavi regime. The fact that the United States had chosen to send a high-ranking military emissary rather than an important civilian diplomat hurt the secular moderate opposition and contributed to the extremist climate. The shah himself saw this as a hostile act designed to hasten his exit. And a small group of high-level Pahlavi loyalists in the military viewed Huyser's mission as an attempt to keep them from a bloody coup in order to install a military government.

President Jimmy Carter: The Engineer Responsible

President Jimmy Carter must ultimately be held responsible for the confused and confusing policy that contributed to the disastrous American foreign policy loss in Iran. An honest man of considerable intelligence, he was nonetheless at a distinct disadvantage in the intricate, constantly shifting world of foreign policy. Although he spent many, many hours studying the Iranian situation, he never understood. An engineer with a somewhat tunneled mind-set, Carter had an enormous capacity to store and retain masses of facts and information. He had great difficulty, however, connecting, relating, and interpreting these facts. He could not see patterns or trends and had little sense of history. In the words of one observant White House adviser, he lacked a "reconciling mechanism." The president "did not always make the relevant connections between the information he had just absorbed about Country X and the information about Situation Y that he had so efficiently stored away a month ago."[80]

As a result, he was consistently baffled and frustrated by the emotional, shifting, unpredictable nature of events as they exploded in the context of revolutionary Iran. Brzezinski, also a very bright man, had his own rigid, simplified, Sovietcentric view of the world. Carter chose ultimately to accept the advice of his national security adviser. In so doing, he ignored most of the State Department professionals who had been desperately trying to warn him for some time. He also ignored the advice of his ambassador, a late convert to the idea of the shah's vincibility. And he ignored the wisdom provided by George Ball, a shrewd outside professional with impeccable credentials, whom Carter himself had agreed to bring in for an independent opinion. According to Hodding Carter: "It was difficult to know from afar why and how the President placed so much value on Brzezinski. A second-rate thinker in a field infested with poseurs and careerists, he has never let consistency get in the way of self-promotion or old theories impede new policy acrobatics."[81]

In the eyes of the Iranian masses opposed to the shah, one of Carter's most serious political miscalculations was the timing of his telephone call to the shah after Black Friday. The shah's troops had fired into unarmed crowds at Jalah Square, killing and wounding hundreds of men, women, and children, on September 8, and President Carter took time out from his important Camp David meetings to call the shah early Sunday morning, September 10. Carter told the monarch that he had his personal support and friendship. This publicly announced telephone message convinced the Iranian people that Carter approved of the Jalah massacre and that the United States was now determined to oppose the revolution at all costs.

In Iran, informed political observers severely criticized Carter's policies. One shrewd commentator described the record of the Carter administration as "the good, the bad, and the ugly." In his words: "It began well and deserves credit for pressuring the Shah to open up and thus give movement a chance to get underway. As the inevitable explosion occurred, however, the administration stubbornly and stupidly persisted beyond all reasonable limits in backing first the shah, then Bakhtiar. Now the only way the U.S. can recover any affection and prestige among the mass of Iranians is by stopping this nonsense and backing the Khomeini forces."[82]

But Carter never did this. In fact he vetoed any direct American contacts with Ayatollah Khomeini, contact that was strongly recommended by most knowledgeable American advisers and that was one issue on which both Ambassador Sullivan and General Huyser agreed.[83] After seriously considering approving a mission that was to be headed by former State Department official Ted Eliot to meet with Khomeini in Paris, Carter backed away when Brzezinski, through the means of clever bureaucratic tactics of stalling and intrigue, smothered the idea.

President Carter's task was extremely difficult. Many of his best intelligence sources provided him with a deeply flawed and inaccurate picture of Iran. But Carter did little to improve on this record and repeated the flawed conclusions long after he should have revised his assessments. In August 1977, the CIA concluded a sixty-page study with the statement that "the Shah will be an active participant in Iranian life well into the 1980s" and that "there will be no radical change in Iranian political behavior in the near future."[84] As late as September 28, 1978, the Defense Intelligence Agency reported that the shah "is expected to remain actively in power over the next ten years."[85]

Carter himself kept repeating these rosy assessments. On October 28, 1978: "We have historic friendships with Iran. I think they are a great stabilizing force in their part of the world." On November 30, 1978: "We trust the shah to maintain stability in Iran, to continue with the democratization process, and also to continue with the progressive change in the Iranian social and economic structure. . . . We have confidence in the shah." On December 12, 1978: "I fully expect the shah to maintain power in Iran, and for the present problems in Iran to be resolved. . . . I think the predictions of doom and disaster that come from some sources have certainly not been realized at all. The shah has our support and he also has our confidence." On January 16, 1979, the shah fled Iran, never to return. At a news conference the next day, Carter continued to demonstrate his confusion and misunderstanding in response to a question from United Press International's Helen Thomas, who asked him how he could have been so wrong when a month ago he stated that the shah would maintain power. The president answered by saying that "I think that the rapid change of affairs in Iran has not been predicted by anyone so far as I know."[86] If the president had looked to a number of professionals in his own State Department, he would have found many, including at the end his own ambassador, who had been desperately trying to signal him from behind the barriers imposed by the National Security Council.

President Carter's task was complicated by the sheer amount of conflicting advice that he kept receiving. Waves of influential American officials splashed over Iranian borders throughout 1978. There was a kind of Washington-Tehran air shuttle in operation. The shah spent hundreds of hours in discussion with American influentials during 1978 alone. Earlier in the year, when few Americans were aware of real trouble, individuals from Lady Bird Johnson to Nelson Rockefeller had visited with the shah. As the political crisis increased, so too did the number of American visitors. These included Congressman Stephen Solarz in mid-October, Deputy Secretary of Defense Charles Duncan later that month, Under Secretary of State Richard Cooper and Deputy Assistant Secretary of State Jack Miklos just after the Duncan visit, the State Department team of Clement, Griffin, and Cohen in early November, and Art Callahan, an emissary from Brzezinski, who met with the shah on November 14. This last visit was extraordinary; Callahan was a businessman who had once been CIA station chief in Iran and was now negotiating with the shah's government for a multibillion dollar contract.[87] Not surprisingly, Callahan's conclusions reinforced those of Brzezinski and the NSC staff.

The shah's office in Niavaran Palace must have been especially crowded with American visitors in late November; the following four delegations spent time with him there then: (1) Lt. Gen. Eugene F. Tighe, Jr., director of the Defense Intelligence Agency, and Robert Bowie, deputy director of the Central Intelligence Agency; (2) Secretary of Treasury Michael Blumenthal and a congressional delegation; (3) David C. Scott, chairman of the Board of Allis Chalmers, which was still at this late date seeking a major joint business venture in Iran; and (4) Senate Majority Leader Robert Byrd and staff members. Carter was inundated with conflicting information, much of which was filtered and interpreted by Brzezinski.

At the same time, Carter was bombarded by opinions from many other directions. From Europe, Alexander Haig, who had opposed Huyser's mission to Tehran, ranted at the president for not being tough enough. According to Brzezinski, Haig had "phoned in a state of great emotional outrage and concern. He feels that we are being much too soft, that we should have put an aircraft carrier task force in the Indian Ocean, deployed some aircraft in Saudi Arabia, and indicated firmer support."[88] From within the White House itself, Vice President Walter Mondale began to shift his position as he realized that the shah's fall was inevitable and therefore cautioned the president against attempting to prop up a losing dictator.

In his frustration and anger, President Carter at times lost his cool and berated a number of his own officials. He constantly received conflicting advice and therefore wavered back and forth in his policy decisions. Although the wavering continued throughout the revolution, his general policy followed Brzezinski's advice most closely. "Carter still hoped to preserve the shah's power long after intelligence reports and top foreign policy advisers insisted, as a matter of realism, the United States must assist the orderly transition to whatever political forces were going to displace the peacock throne."[89]

This sad state of affairs was to continue after the shah had left Iran and the United States found itself faced with the necessity of dealing with a robust, xenophobic new government in revolutionary Iran. The Carter foreign policy-making cast remained the same; only the errors differed. They were to be larger and more grievous, traumatizing the United States and searing the consciousness of the American people for 444 days.

8 The Islamic Republic and America: Ruptured Relations and a Venture in Rapprochement

The revolution blew the lid off the Iranian social cauldron, in which a poisonous and explosive brew of personal, political, economic, and religious forces had long been fermenting. This boiling broth included the following ingredients: ethnic and tribal tensions, political repression and police brutality, institutionalized injustice and corruption, economic inefficiencies and inequities, gathering religious extremism, bureaucratic confusion and ineptitude, personal rivalry and persistent cynicism, and deepening class conflict. The forces of modernization, fueled by increasing oil revenues, outdistanced both social improvements and especially political development. As these gaps widened, the pent-up forces increased in explosive potential, and burst following the final overthrow of February 1979.

When the shah left Iran on January 16, 1979, and again in mid-February when the revolution became a reality, millions of Iranians took to the streets in an ecstasy of personal and political celebration that demonstrated the depths of their disaffection. The poison that emanated from this disaffection spewed forth in many forms for years afterwards. The country approached anarchy as hundreds of thousands took weapons in hand and various well-armed political groups sought to reap the rewards of their struggle against the hated Pahlavi government. Students took over the universities, workers the factories, and revolutionary committees the politics. Thousands more took this opportunity to settle personal grudges, and extremism and violence threatened to tear the country to pieces.

Peasants rose against their landlords, sometimes killing them on the spot; mobs demolished symbols of the old system—luxury hotels, banks, cinemas, and liquor stores; soldiers shot their commanding officers and took charge; the shaky new authorities began to arrest, jail, and execute in the name of revolutionary "justice." When the regime attempted to slow these executions and to implement more legitimate trials, the masses demanded retribution. In Isfahan, for example, a large mob took over the central prison and massacred several high-ranking members of the former regime who were being held there. In mid-May 1979, a large delegation (including members of revolutionary tribunals and militias) visited Ayatollah Khomeini and demanded that either the executions continue or they would take matters into their own hands and execute all those held in the various prisons.

Demands for revenge and retribution were deafening. In this emotional political melee, extremists such as Hojjat ol-Islam Sadiq Khalkhali in the revolutionary court system and Haj Asadollah Ladjevardi in the prison system became the tools of vengeance. Khalkhali, later termed "the hanging judge," wrote up execution orders with little concern for legal procedures. In Kurdistan he scribbled execution orders on scraps of paper, and in Tehran he hurried executions before the accused could appeal. In his own memoirs Khalkhali described how he hurried the execution of former prime minister Hoveyda before the moderate government headed by Mehdi Bazargan could get word to the court to stay the execution. And he simply ignored Hoveyda's last plea that he have an opportunity to speak with Ayatollah Khomeini's son, Ahmad. Such are the actions of many who come to the political fore after revolutionary upheaval.[1]

In Iran the arrests and executions began immediately after the demise of the old regime in mid-February. Arrests began February 14, and executions were implemented the next day. The primary targets of this revolutionary justice were those who most represented the instruments of repression of the Pahlavi government. These included leaders in the military, the police, SAVAK, and the prison system, along with political thugs and torturers. During the first four months following the overthrow, the overwhelming percentage of those executed belonged to one of these categories. Of 205 documented executions between February 11 and June 11, 1979, 49 were of military personnel, 45 of police officials, 40 of SAVAK agents, 16 of professional torturers and prison heads, and 7 of political thugs. These categories alone accounted for 83 percent of the executions. The others killed were 19 criminals, 13 members of the shah's political elite, and 2 industrialists.[2]

This revolutionary violence was accompanied throughout by counterrevolutionary terrorism as former members of the Pahlavi system themselves became guerrillas and attacked leaders of the new regime whenever and wherever possible. The real internal war, however, did not begin until 1981, when the revolutionaries themselves confronted one another for control of the revolution. Meanwhile, the central struggle was political in nature and involved the moderate liberals and the extremist clerics. The Iranian revolution, not unlike the French and Russian revolutions, witnessed a brief postrevolutionary period in which the moderates moved to the ascendancy.

The Rule of the Moderates

The first stage of the Iranian revolution lasted from February 5, 1979, when Ayatollah Khomeini announced Mehdi Bazargan as his choice for prime minister, until June 22, 1981, when Abol Hassan Bani Sadr was dismissed from his position as president. This period had been preceded by the prime ministership of Shapour Bakhtiar, whose ill-fated tenure was as short as it was ineffective. An old member of the National Front from Musaddiq days, Bakhtiar was much more popular among American decision makers in Washington than he was in Iran, where even the National Front disowned him when he became prime minister on December 30, 1978. He held his position for less than five weeks before he fled to France. Bakhtiar's experience set the losing tone for the liberal, moderate, Westernized professionals who had entered the postrevolutionary period with high hopes.

Shapour Bakhtiar was born in 1914 to a khan of the Bakhtiar tribe, which produced some of the most influential political leaders in modern Iranian history.[3] He earned a bachelor's degree in political science and a doctorate in law from the University of Paris and returned in 1946 to Iran, where he began work for the Khuzistan Labor Office. Here he supported worker's strikes against the Anglo-Iranian Oil Company and established personal credibility among small groups of laborers. Bakhtiar was a member of the Iran party of the National Front and was deputy-minister of Labor in Muhammad Musaddiq's cabinet. He was a liberal supporter of constitutional monarchy and had a reputation among National Front circles as a man of great personal vanity and even greater political ambition. Over the years he developed personal and political rivalries with such eminent National Front leaders as Allahyar Saleh and Karim Sanjabi.

Bakhtiar was well known in the United States. He maintained close contact with American diplomatic officials in the early 1950s and 1960s. He consistently criticized the shah's regime and sought U.S. support for democratic reforms. The two CIA profiles of Bakhtiar done in 1964 and 1978 present him as "rough, blunt and headstrong," as "politically shrewd and ambitious." In political circles, he was never completely trusted. In a cable of December 1978 to the U.S. Embassy in Tehran over the signature of Secretary of State Vance, Bakhtiar was described by a "well-informed Iranian" as not being "as thoroughgoing an oppositionist as he makes out to be." The day before, Ambassador William Sullivan had cabled Washington indicating that CIA sources in Iran viewed Bakhtiar as an "adventurer who is suspected of secret ties to the shah." Although these characterizations are perhaps exaggerated, there is little doubt that Bakhtiar, although certainly a liberal democrat, was an ambitious political maneuverer, one who was never trusted even among his associates.[4]

Given this record, it is not surprising that Bakhtiar was doomed as prime minister. Ayatollah Khomeini understood this immediately and would have nothing to do with him. Furthermore, Bakhtiar's demeanor was visibly Western; he seemed to be the very caricature of the overdressed, tie-wearing (fukuli), "Western-struck" (gharbzad) dude bitingly criticized in Iranian literature for years. According to the 1964 intelligence report: "Bakhtiar is more European than Iranian in dress and mannerisms and often injects French and English words into a Farsi conversation."[5] Although these characteristics may have attracted the United States to Bakhtiar, they carried the opposite meaning in Iran. He never had a chance to enjoy the fruits of power; the first moderate prime minister to climb to power over the fallen shah was jettisoned after approximately one month in office.

On February 5, 1979, Ayatollah Khomeini named a seventy-three-year-old engineer to the prime ministership. Unlike Bakhtiar, Mehdi Bazargan had impeccable opposition credentials and had spent several years in the shah's prisons. Born in 1906 to a religious family, Bazargan received his degree in thermodynamics in Paris and spent much of his intellectual energy reconciling Islamic doctrine and modern science. He opposed the communist Tudeh party and worked as head of the National Iranian Oil Company during the Musaddiq period. With Ayatollah Mahmud Taliqani, Bazargan organized the Liberation Movement of Iran (Nihzat-i Azadi-yi Iran), which provided the ideas and personnel that played a central role in the revolution and the provisional government headed by Bazargan during nine difficult months in 1979. Taliqani and Bazargan composed an effective team; they were able to bridge the gap between the extremism of the clerics and the liberalism of the Western-trained intelligentsia. Taliqani was an especially critical force in this context because he was held in the highest esteem by the ulama. His death on September 10, 1979, dealt the Bazargan government a severe blow and hastened the defeat of the moderate forces.

Short, balding, and bespectacled, Bazargan had a strong reputation for personal piety and integrity. Despite his small physical stature, he was not easily intimidated and was politically courageous. His government included such individuals as Ibrahim Yazdi (foreign minister) and Abbas Amir Entezam (deputy prime minister), both American-educated technocrats of forceful disposition. Yazdi and Entezam were less experienced politically than Bazargan, and both adopted a form of tough, confrontational, public politics that easily exposed them to the fire of political enemies. Bazargan's approach was quieter and more effective. In the end, Bazargan's revolutionary credibility and mass appeal rested on the support of Ayatollah Khomeini, with whom both he and Taliqani enjoyed excellent relations. Khomeini respected both men because of their steadfast opposition to the shah and their deep religious convictions. But when the struggle intensified between the moderates and the extremists, Khomeini ultimately stood back and watched as the extremists prevailed. After twice refusing to accept Bazargan's resignation, Khomeini finally did so on November 5, 1979, the day after the student extremists took hostages at the American embassy in Tehran.

Whereas Shapour Bakhtiar was willing to take office in a country in which the shah was still the titular head, Bazargan had consistently refused any such form of collaboration. He hoped to build a new government of liberal democratic form, but within a sturdy Islamic framework. This dream failed, and the old prime minister found himself constantly on the defensive as extremist opponents from both left and right sniped at him and his government. Bazargan and his associates were also quite willing to maintain normal diplomatic relations with the United States as long as the United States honored Iran's independence and autonomy. As will be shown below, Bazargan and his closest associates maintained close and direct contact with American governmental officials. With Bazargan's demise, moderates continued to rule under different leadership. Bazargan was replaced by a man who carried Islamic credentials while stressing the need to establish complete independence from the world's imperialism and to create a new Islamic economic system.

Abol Hassan Bani Sadr was born in Hamadan in 1933, the son of a respected cleric in that provincial city. Educated at Tehran University, he traveled to Paris in the early 1960s and studied social science and economics at the University of Paris. Although Bani Sadr deplored the internal repression of the shah's regime, he was especially critical of Iran's dependence on Western powers, and his writings were filled with condemnatory analyses of Iran as an economic client state of the United States. An intelligent, reform-minded intellectual, Bani Sadr saw the answer to Pahlavi tyranny in some form of liberal Islamic state that would throw off the shackles of Western domination. Although he had met Khomeini in Najaf in the early 1970s, he did not begin a close association with the imam until Khomeini arrived as an exile in Paris in October 1978. At this time, Bani Sadr and Khomeini developed a close personal and professional relationship that would endure for thirty-two dramatic months.

In Paris, Bani Sadr knew Sadeq Ghotbzadeh and Ibrahim Yazdi, who were actively involved in supporting Khomeini. Even though the latter two had long been suspicious of Bani Sadr, whom they viewed as a political dilettante and opportunist, all three worked to support Khomeini, who was out of his element in the West. Ghotbzadeh and Yazdi had long experience in the United States, where they had lived and consistently opposed the shah's regime. Ghotbzadeh was an especially fascinating character; in the early 1960s he had carried on a one-man antishah campaign in Washington, D.C., while a student at Georgetown University. Somewhat affectionately known by his American friends as "crazy Sadeq," Ghotbzadeh was always a maverick, a man who marched to his own drummer. Yazdi was a more conventional figure of more serious Islamic convictions who opposed the shah's regime from his job as a pharmacologist with a specialty in molecular oncology in Houston, Texas. Educated in Iran, he received a postdoctoral fellowship at Baylor University and studied nutrition and food engineering at MIT before becoming an assistant professor at Baylor College of Medicine in the Departments of Pathology and Pharmacology. A bright man of courage and conviction, Yazdi had first met Khomeini in the fall of 1964, becoming the imam's representative in the United States in the early 1970s. Whereas Ghotbzadeh was a free spirit, Yazdi was much more intense and hard-driving.

In comparison to Ghotbzadeh and Yazdi, Bani Sadr was an idealist, a bookworm, and a man of Europeanized intellectual tastes. He was the most personally ambitious of all the liberal revolutionaries; his ego was larger than even that of Shapour Bakhtiar. Like the others, he was a representative of the professional middle class and had little rapport with or understanding of the Iranian masses. Nor did he have the skill or patience to build political organizations. In the informed words of Iran historian Shaul Bakhash, Bani Sadr remained "the revolutionary exile of Paris. Even as president, pamphleteering, political journalism, debating, and polemics excited his interest far more than the pedestrian tasks of administration."[6]

Abol Hassan Bani Sadr returned with Khomeini to Iran, and with the imam's support he became a member of the revolutionary council, the assembly of experts, minister of Foreign Affairs, and minister of

Finance before he was elected Iran's first president in January 1980. Having received over 70 percent of the vote in the presidential election, Bani Sadr assumed he had a mandate from the people, failing to understand that his popularity derived mainly from Khomeini's personal support. In the last months of his presidency, he ineffectually and somewhat pathetically attempted to appeal to the Iranian people, who had little in common with a Paris-trained intellectual.

Bani Sadr found himself in deep political trouble from the beginning. He was mistrusted by several members of his own liberal coalition and was considered too Western, too liberal, and too ambitious by the Islamic Republican party (IRP), headed by such powerful clerics as Ayatollah Muhammad Hussein Beheshti. Although Khomeini had appointed Bani Sadr as commander-in-chief of the armed forces after the war with Iraq had begun, the extremist forces of the religious right slowly cut away at Bani Sadr's authority. They did so in an atmosphere where extremism and emotion prevailed. This tensely charged climate was promoted by political acts originating from both within and outside Iran. Most important perhaps was the visceral paranoia of Iranian citizens who believed that the United States was plotting against their revolution in an attempt to once again set in motion political events such as those that occurred during the Musaddiq period in the early 1950s. When the shah was admitted to the United States in October 1979, revolutionary Iranians were convinced that the Musaddiq record was about to be played again. Bani Sadr's presidency was dominated by the hostage crisis, by the Iraqi invasion of September 22, 1980, and by his losing struggle against the religious extremists of the Islamic Republican party. In the end, Khomeini sided with the IRP and the clerics against Bani Sadr.

The depth of class conflict could be seen most clearly in the personalities of Bani Sadr and his prime minister, Muhammad Ali Raja'i, who had won the position through the efforts of his patrons in the IRP. Raja'i and Bani Sadr were the same age. But this was all they had in common. The new prime minister grew up in poverty, worked as an errand boy and street vendor, and somehow managed to graduate from high school and Tehran Teacher's College. Poorly educated, even ridiculed as illiterate by the modern, educated intelligentsia, Raja'i was a quiet, persistent, and extremely stubborn little man. Bani Sadr viewed him with undisguised contempt. But the feelings were mutual, and Raja'i was eventually able to blunt Bani Sadr's political ambitions. He was the instrument of the IRP, which had considerable mass support. In the battle that took place between the lower and lower middle-class religious forces and the Western-educated moderates of the middle and upper middle classes, the former emerged triumphant. It was not surprising that Khomeini threw his critical support behind the ulama and the masses.

In the early months of 1981, the moderate middle-class intelligentsia found itself losing influence fast. The Bakhtiar and Bazargan power centers had already been discredited and excised from the political arena. Bani Sadr, the last hope of the moderate intelligentsia, blinded at times by his own ego, began to move leftward, informally fashioning an alliance with the radical left-wing Islamic socialist group, the Mujahidin-i Khalq. At the same time he worked to establish strong ties with the Iranian military leaders and spent much of his time at the front during the first months of the Iran-Iraq war. Finally, students produced documentary evidence to indicate that Bani Sadr had in 1979 met on several occasions with an American businessman who was in fact a CIA agent. These events alarmed the already alienated religious right, who increasingly portrayed Bani Sadr as a dangerous liberal opportunist. Bani Sadr in turn retreated behind the figure of Khomeini, who acted for a time as his protector.

In late May 1981, the IRP leaders convinced Khomeini that Bani Sadr was in league with the Mujahidin and that the left wing was plotting a coup against the revolution. Khomeini had long been suspicious of the Mujahidin, a group he referred to as the *munafaghin* (hypocrites), and when he became convinced that Bani Sadr had allied himself with this group, Khomeini took action. On June 10, 1981, he dismissed Bani Sadr from his important post as commander-in-chief of the armed forces. Large rallies in Tehran organized by the Mujahidin and the liberal National Front on June 10 and June 15, respectively, only increased the alarm of Khomeini and the IRP. On June 21, the IRP-dominated Majlis voted to declare the president politically incompetent. The prosecutor general then ordered Bani Sadr's arrest, and he was dismissed as president on June 22. Forced into hiding, Iran's first popularly elected president fled Iran with Mujahidin-i Khalq leader Massoud Rajavi on July 29, 1981. His presidency lasted seventeen months. Thus the period of moderation ended in revolutionary Iran.

Besides their personal idiosyncracies, internal quarrels, and political inexperience, the moderates were doomed to failure in Iran for systemic reasons. They were struggling to survive in a climate in which the political winds blew strongly against them, and continually breaking events fanned extremist sentiments. These events included frontal attacks on the leaders of the revolution, threats to the territory of Iran itself, hostile actions by external forces in the regional and international contexts within which Iran acted, and natural deaths of crucial political personalities. These threatening developments clustered around the years 1979–1981—the time frame of the confrontation that was to determine the course of the revolution. These events, selectively listed in the table below, contributed to the paranoia and defensiveness of the revolutionary leaders and gave special credibility to the most extreme elements among them. Since the revolution seemed under attack from all sides, the new leaders who struggled to the top were precisely those with the mentality of tough campaigners.

Points for Paranoia: Events Contributing to the Triumph of Extremism

1979	
Assassination of Gen. Valiullah Qarani	April 23
Assassination of Ayatollah Murtiza Mutahhari	May 1
U.S. Senate condemns Iran for executions	May 17
Assassination attempt on A. A. Hashemi-Rafsanjani	May 25
Assassination of Sayyid Muhsin Bihbihani	July 21
Ezzedin Husseini declares Kurdish war on regime	August 23
Ayatollah Mahmud Taliqani dies	September 10
Muhammad Reza Shah Pahlavi admitted to U.S.	October 22
Bazargan and Yazdi meet Brzezinski in Algiers	November 1
U.S. diplomats taken hostage in Tehran	November 4
U.S. government freezes Iranian assets	November 14
Students release documents on U.S. intelligence	December
Soviet invasion of Afghanistan	December
Assassination of Hojjat ol-Islam Muhammad Mufatah	December 18

1980	
Turkoman rebellion in Northeast Iran	February
Carter breaks diplomatic relations with Iran	April 7
U.S. hostage rescue attempt fails in desert	April 25
Iraqi invasion of Iran	September 22

1981	
First meeting of Gulf Cooperation Council	May 24
Dr. Mustafa Chamran killed at war front	June 21
Bani Sadr dismissed as president	June 22
Assassination attempt on Ali Hussein Khamene'i	June 27
Bombing/assassinations at IRP headquarters	June 28
Assassination of Hassan Ayat	August 5
Assassinations of M. A. Raja'i and M. J. Bahonar	August 30
Assassination of Ayatollah Ali Quddusi	September 5
Assassination of Ayatollah Asadollah Madani	September 11
Airplane crash killing Iranian military commanders	September 28

They expected no quarter and gave no quarter; they were ready to kill and to be killed. In short, they were the extremists, the true believers.

Throughout Bani Sadr's presidency, the moderates' power and credibility seeped down an American-designed drain. Bani Sadr and other liberals were considered far too sympathetic to America, and the hostage crisis only reinforced these perceptions. United States policies, including the disastrous April 1980 Tabas raid, further crippled the more moderate forces, who were fighting desperately for their political survival. Secret documents uncovered in the U.S. Embassy compound compromised the integrity and influence of several important liberal leaders and put them constantly on the defensive. Washington's public support for them only hastened their inevitable defeat. In the first months of 1981, the word "moderate" (*miyanru*, literally "middle of the wayers") became a pejorative term that carried treasonous overtones. The slogans Death to America and Death to Liberals became increasingly intertwined in the chants of the religious masses in the streets of Tehran.

Historian Crane Brinton has described the rule of the moderates who take control immediately after any great revolutionary overthrow and has argued that this group's very moderation is its most critical weakness. In Iran the moderate period lasted precisely twenty-seven months during the leadership of Bakhtiar (five weeks), Bazargan (nine months), and Bani Sadr (seventeen months). In these twenty-seven months, each of the moderate governments became progressively more radical as it fought to survive in an increasingly extremist climate. Bani Sadr survived as long as he did because he was in some ways more radical than moderate. In Brinton's terms, he was one of those moderates who "often behave quite immoderately."[7] In describing Russian revolutionary Aleksandr Kerensky, Brinton may have also written the epitaph for the political career of Abol Hassan Bani Sadr: "The eloquent compromisist leader seems to us a man of words, an orator who could move crowds but could not guide them, an impractical and incompetent person in the field of action."[8] The end of the period of the moderates was marked by full-scale violence and internal war, war that began only one week after the fall of President Bani Sadr.

The Political Strategy of Ayatollah Khomeini

On June 28, 1981, a sixty-pound bomb exploded in the headquarters of the Islamic Republican party, killing over one hundred people, including dozens of members of the Iranian political elite. The dead included the powerful founder of the IRP, Muhammad Hussein Beheshti, four cabinet ministers, six deputy ministers, and twenty-seven Majlis deputies. This shocking event initiated a full-scale internal war as the regime fought back with thousands of arrests and executions. In the ensuing cycle of violence, the opposition groups, primarily directed by the Mujahidin-i Khalq, accelerated their own campaign of guerrilla terror. Their targets were the leaders of the IRP and other influential clerics, including a number of those close to Khomeini himself. On August 30, 1981, the violent opposition carried out an unprecedented assassination in which both the head of government (Prime Minister Muhammad Javad Bahonar) and the head of state (President Muhammad Ali Raja'i) died in a bombing of the Prime Ministry. Many other extremist leaders died violent deaths in 1981, including influential Majlis deputy Hassan Ayat on August 5, prosecutor general Ayatollah Ali Quddusi on September 5, and Khomeini's personal representative in Tabriz, Ayatollah Asadollah Madani on September 11. In response, the Revolutionary Guards (Pasdaran-i Inqilab) went on a rampage and, using every means at their disposal, destroyed the armed opposition to the regime. Ayatollah Khomeini gave his full support to this campaign of repression.

When he first returned to Iran, Khomeini spent only two weeks in Tehran before moving to Qum on March 1, 1979. There is reason to believe that Khomeini fully intended to remain in Qum, from where he could monitor and selectively guide the political system. This was not to be, and after nine months the imam returned to Tehran for reasons of health care and politics. Khomeini's move to Tehran center stage, however, was motivated by reasons other than simple political ambition and personal health. Close associates such as Prime Minister Bazargan persistently called on him to return to Tehran because the political situation was increasingly tenuous. In June 1979, for example, Bazargan wrote a letter to Khomeini outlining the major problems facing the revolutionary government and asking him to come to Tehran, where he could follow events more closely. Bazargan's close associates, Ibrahim Yazdi and Abbas Amir Entezam, also pressed Khomeini to return to Tehran. Politically, he was needed.

In the weeks immediately after the February 1979 overthrow, Iran threatened to collapse into anarchy. Arms were everywhere, and hundreds of factions and groupings with differing goals aspired to power. Most threatening in Khomeini's eyes were the far right and the extreme left. The counterrevolutionary right consisted of many members of the former shah's security, police, and military establishments, individuals who had just lost a revolution and who now had to fight for their survival. Khomeini believed that such groups had readily available foreign support. The left consisted of groups even more extreme than the Mujahidin, such as the Fidayan-i Khalq and the Paykar groups. These political forces had come out of the revolution with great credibility due to their critical role in defeating the shah's Royal Guards in mid-February. Furthermore, they had a fifteen-year history of revolutionary resistance and an organization armed and intact.

Khomeini and his advisers adopted a strategy to slice off these two extremes of the political spectrum. The Fidayan, itself weakened by an internal feud that divided the movement into three parts in 1980, was an easy target since its ideology was largely anti-Islamic in nature. The counterrevolutionary right was also deeply vulnerable because of its past associations with the Pahlavi regime. In 1979 and 1980, these two extremes were largely destroyed. The Mujahidin-i Khalq, however, was a different story. It, too, claimed commitment to Islam and had declared its loyalty to Khomeini. It was also the largest, the most dedicated, and best organized of all the groups vying for power in postrevolutionary Iran. The June 28, 1981, attack on IRP headquarters provided Khomeini and the extremist leaders with the excuse they needed to declare war on the Mujahidin. When the Mujahidin fought back, they only gave the Islamic Republic more martyrs and increased the extremism of a regime that was reminded by the death of every mullah that it was fighting for its very survival. By mid-1982, the Mujahidin were finally broken within Iran; their leader, Massoud Rajavi, had fled to Paris, and their second in command, Musa Khiabani, had been killed in a shootout in Tehran. When Rajavi and his leading Mujahidin followers moved under pressure from Paris to Saddam Hussein's Iraq in June 1986, they lost most of their remaining credibility. In the process of mopping up the Mujahidin, the new ruling clerical elite also effectively and relatively easily destroyed the liberal intelligentsia, who suffocated in an atmosphere of extremism and who maintained a visceral aversion to violence.

Finally, in 1983 Khomeini and the IRP moved against the Tudeh party. Since the revolution, the Tudeh party had pursued a policy of political pragmatism by allying itself with Khomeini and the clerics. Traditionally aligned with the Soviet Union, this national Iranian communist party had long suffered from its Soviet associations. Still, it had a forty-year history in Iran despite the purges carried out against it by the shah's regime. During the first three years of the revolution, it supported Khomeini and the IRP while placing its members in important positions in the bureaucracy. Its members exposed themselves and were well known to the revolutionary regime. When

Vladimir Kuzichkin, a Soviet diplomat and KGB major stationed in Tehran, defected to Great Britain in mid-1982, he provided the British with a list of several hundred Soviet agents operating in Iran. In September the official voice of the Islamic Republic, *Jumhuri-yi Islami*, sharply attacked the Tudeh party and accused it of "throwing a mouse in the soup of the revolution."[9] Kuzichkin's information was shared with the Iranian authorities, who arrested over one thousand Tudeh party members, many of whom had already been under surveillance. Those arrested included Nureddin Kianouri, the influential secretary general of the Tudeh party, who publicly admitted that the party had been guilty of treason and espionage in the service of the Soviet Union. On April 30, 1983, Kianouri reported on Iranian television that he had maintained contact with Soviet agents since 1945 and that Iranian members of the Tudeh party had been delivering top-secret military and political documents to the Soviet embassy in Tehran. On May 4, 1983, the Iranian Foreign Ministry announced the expulsion of eighteen Soviet diplomats for interfering in the internal affairs of the Islamic Republic. This dramatic destruction of the Tudeh party in 1983 completed the dismantling of the Iranian left.

Khomeini and his associates now needed a loyal, effective, and powerful military instrument. After purging the Pahlavi-created military officer corps, the revolutionaries established their own parallel force, the Pasdaran-i Inqilab, or Revolutionary Guards, which Khomeini had decreed into existence on May 5, 1979. This organization fought the guerrilla groups in the streets and alleys of the country. By the spring of 1982, the cleric-rulers had successfully blended the Pasdaran and the regular army into a relatively unified fighting force. After years of fighting both internal opponents and an external invader, the military forces of the Islamic Republic of Iran have become battle hardened and experienced. Khomeini had managed to create a loyal, determined, and experienced fighting force, one that had been baptized in blood and owed its very existence to him.

By 1984 the leaders of the Islamic Republic of Iran had solidified their rule with Khomeini at the center of the system. From there, the shrewd, charismatic ayatollah had presided over the political consolidation of the new regime. His tactics and long-term strategy proved extremely effective. Besides being politically astute, charismatic, impeccably honest, and deeply religious, Khomeini's greatest advantage was his exercise of leadership according to the traditional Shi'i mode. In this tradition, the leader seeks to understand the will of the followers and then to develop his policies accordingly. The followers in turn look to the leader for guidance and pattern their actions accordingly. In Shi'ism, therefore, it is always difficult to determine the point at which the leader leads and the follower follows. Leadership is circular rather than hierarchical. The relationships are formed within a kind of sealed circle where the leader both leads and follows and the followers both follow and lead.[10]

In this system, Khomeini constantly sent out feelers and issued pronouncements while attempting to determine the will of the people. This often resulted both in filtering out personal considerations and in a vindictive, impersonal system of repressive justice during the early years of the Islamic Republic. At times, Khomeini himself sought to introduce some moderation. A case in point was his eight-point pronouncement issued in December 1982 in which he sought to curb the excesses of overzealous, ruthless members of the system of revolutionary justice. Also, he consistently sided with the clerics of the extremist right when, representing the wishes of the deprived masses, they challenged the more secular, moderate left. Thus he ultimately jettisoned Bani Sadr, acquiesced in the execution of Ghotbzadeh, sided with the radical students after they occupied the American embassy, and relentlessly supported the continuation of the war against Saddam Hussein's Iraq.

This form of circular leadership whereby the imam wraps himself into the masses of deprived citizens was reinforced by Khomeini's constant references to the mustaza'fin (deprived, dispossessed), to whom he spoke in their idiom while addressing their needs. The fact that these were the most fervently religious classes provided a powerful reinforcement for this system, a system directed by a faqih, or the most knowledgeable jurisprudent. From a political point of view, this system of leadership was extremely effective; it provided the imam and the new political elite with a large, dedicated constituency. This mass base of support was the primary reason for the survival of the Islamic Republic during the difficult early years of the revolution. Khomeini never forgot that the mustaza'fin constituted the foundation of the revolution, that from these lower classes the bulk of the rank-and-file soldiers were recruited for and died in the war with Iraq. In the words of Khomeini: "To which class of society do these heroic fighters of the battlefields belong? Do you find even one person among all of them who is related to persons who have large capital, or some power in the past? If you find one, we will give you a prize. But you won't."[11] In brief, Khomeini's priorities were always with the mustaza'fin. He clearly stated in September 1982, "We must all make efforts to serve the mustaza'fin who have been deprived throughout history and the government should always give priority to them."[12]

A final Khomeini strategy of political control was negative in nature. Like other major world revolutions, the Iranian revolution found itself immediately under attack from external forces. In Iran's case, these attacks were especially severe because both superpowers, in varying degree, supported Iraq in its war with Iran. Besides this, Iran was opposed by France, Saudi Arabia, Jordan, Egypt, Morocco, the smaller Persian Gulf states and other countries in the region. This unrelenting outside pressure acted as a coalescing force within Iran to rally the citizens around their leaders. In this sense, the external forces that sought to destroy the Iranian revolution in fact contributed to its strength and longevity. Khomeini immediately recognized the political value of these external pressures. In this context, it is important to note that the major slogan of the Iranian revolution has been Neither East nor West. In many speeches, the ayatollah stressed the external threat to Iran: "Today it seems we are left alone as almost all of the West and the East are either directly opposing us or indirectly working against us." He went on to say that Iran would fight these forces "with our bare hands and the weapons of faith."[13]

The leaders of the Islamic Republic maintained a special fear of the superpowers and used American and Soviet actions both during and after the revolution as examples of superpower attempts to defeat and to destroy the revolution. In the case of the USSR, the Iranian regime pointed to the invasion and occupation of Afghanistan, Soviet arms supplies to Iraq in its war with the Islamic Republic, and the revelations of espionage by Tudeh party members as evidence of Soviet hostility. In the American case, the Islamic Republic criticized continued U.S. intelligence activity in Iran both during and after the revolution, congressional condemnations of the Iranian revolutionary government, the admission of the shah into America despite strong Iranian protestations, the economic boycott and actual military invasion associated with the hostage crisis, and the American tilt to the Iraqi side in the Persian Gulf war.

Ayatollah Khomeini used all of this as clear proof of continuing superpower hostility to Iran and its Islamic government. He never relented in his condemnations and exhortations against the United States, which he continued to term "the Great Satan" into the late 1980s. By focusing attention on the superpower threat, he called attention away from many of Iran's domestic problems and toward the threats emanating from "East and West." At the same time, he damaged the reputations of those individuals and groups within Iran who had associations of any kind with the superpowers and thus more easily destroyed their political power. This, in turn, only strengthened his standing among the mustaza'fin, a class with neither the will nor the capacity to develop ties of any kind with outside powers. The United States unwittingly played a critical role in this part of Ayatollah Khomeini's strategy. It did so by its clumsy, misguided, and counterproductive interventionary approach to Iran after the overthrow of the shah.

American Policy and Suffocation by Embrace

The traumatic revolution in Iran left U.S. decision makers shaken and confused. Although bureaucratic conflict eased somewhat after the revolution as Zbigniew Brzezinski and his staff quickly backed away from the issue, an atmosphere of self-justification and finger pointing did develop. Badly discredited, Brzezinski and associates blamed the shah's collapse on officials in the State Department, on the shah himself—on everyone but themselves. Their accusations were supported by two other groups of losers who also felt the need to cover their own footprints of responsibility for the disastrous failure of American and Pahlavi policy. The first group consisted of influential Pahlavi admirers in America led by such figures as Henry Kissinger, Richard Nixon, and the Rockefellers. The second faction was the large Iranian exile community, especially the powerful members of the Pahlavi ruling elite, the former generals, ministers, diplomats, and industrialists. In fact, all three groups were closely related by their efforts to promote and protect the shah's regime and the close relationship of that regime to America. With the shah's overthrow, these groups lost a great deal, not the least of which was their political influence and credibility. Thus, they prepared to fight back.

In the Department of State and in the intelligence community, American professional policymakers began immediately to attempt to develop a new policy toward revolutionary Iran. Several formidable obstacles confronted them. First, the United States was surprisingly ill-informed about Iran; the government did not know the players, nor did it have even a primitive understanding of the dynamics of the revolution. In a letter of July 20, 1979, to Chargé d'Affaires Bruce Laingen in Tehran, Iran desk officer Henry Precht wrote from Washington: "We simply do not have the bios, inventory of political groups or current picture of daily life as it evolves at various levels in Iran. Ignorance here of Iran's events is massive. The U.S. press does not do a good job but in the absence of Embassy reporting, we have to rely on inexperienced newsmen."[14] Almost in desperation, high-ranking State Department officials from Secretary of State Cyrus Vance on down flooded the U.S. Embassy in Tehran with lists of questions and queries.

Second, the Iranian scene was itself impossibly confused and deeply confusing. The political situation was in a state of explosive flux; hundreds of factions were competing for control; and emotionalism and violence were present everywhere. With the possible partial exception of Ayatollah Khomeini, no one, including every major Iranian actor, had any idea of where the revolution was going. The situation resembled a mosaic that had just broken into thousands of tiny fragments, most of which changed constantly in direction and composition. As indicated above, the fact that the lens through which American policymakers viewed this kaleidoscopic array of social forces was itself distorted and clouded only made the task of understanding revolutionary Iran more formidable.

Third, a strong undercurrent of anti-Americanism ran through revolutionary Iran. This undercurrent had been fed by America's close relationship with the shah, whom the revolutionary masses considered a despotic client of America. Although the anti-American feeling differed in intensity from group to group in Iran, it was omnipresent and palpable from the very beginning. American decision makers thus had to work against a distrust in Iran that had been building for twenty-five years. The situation in Iran after the revolution, therefore, was extremely sensitive and required a delicate and creative diplomatic approach. Given the history of America's political involvement in Iran, it was essential that the United States not take any actions that would feed this Iranian paranoia, which had considerable basis in fact.

Finally, newly developing Iran policy had to be fashioned in a Washington world inhabited by powerful Pahlavi supporters. These were angry groups who blamed the Carter administration for the fall of the shah and who were now preoccupied with thoughts of counterrevolution. Such groups sought to discredit the revolution in every way possible, portraying Iranians as uncivilized, the revolutionary leaders as barbaric and fanatical, and the revolution itself as a brief aberration that lacked popular support. A major strategy employed to condemn the revolution was to portray it as communist-inspired and supported, with Khomeini even occasionally portrayed as a "red mullah." One article, widely read by decision makers in the Carter White House, stressed the alleged role of the KGB in the revolution.[15] A more sophisticated version of this argument was presented by uninformed scholar-ideologues who claimed that Khomeini worked closely with the Palestinian Liberation Organization, which had Soviet backing, and that therefore Khomeini had Soviet backing. In the words of Michael Ledeen and William Lewis: "Finally, as the shah and the Americans knew, the entire PLO network that functioned as a support system for Khomeini's movement was itself a piece in the Soviet Union's international chess game." Anxious to demonstrate a Soviet-Khomeini linkage, these writers emphasized alleged crucial support for the revolution by countries such as Syria and South Yemen and even implied a Cuban-PLO-Iran connection, all part of "Khomeini's international connections."[16]

In this overall context, the United States committed a series of major political errors during the first nine months of the revolutionary government's existence. These errors were mutually reinforcing and ultimately ended in the catastrophic hostage crisis, which brought Iran-American relations to an all-time low and left a legacy of ill-will and animosity between the two countries. The most serious policy miscalculation was the U.S. preoccupation with the moderates. Having bet on a losing shah, the United States now placed bets on a series of moderate leaders who quickly moved to positions of power after the shah's overthrow. Although the Department of State primarily developed this policy, the foreign policy-making establishment in Washington also subscribed to it. Ironically, the divisions that had marked U.S. policy-making during the last years of the shah now largely disappeared since most official groups chose to follow the lead of the Department of State in this matter. After all, it was the State Department that had in the end accurately predicted that a true national revolution was in progress and that the shah was finished. A more important reason was that the highest level of foreign policymakers at the National Security Council and White House chose to quickly back away from the glare of failure and leave the mess to the Department of State.

The American preoccupation with the moderates was natural. These were the individuals whose liberal views most closely coincided with American political philosophy. Culturally and politically, they were sympathetic; most of their leaders spoke English, and many had been educated, if not in the United States, then at least in Europe. Other than the obvious examples of the first three leaders of revolutionary Iran (Bakhtiar, Bazargan, and Bani Sadr), they included such individuals as Abbas Amir Entezam, Ibrahim Yazdi, Sadeq Ghotbzadeh, Hedayatollah Matin-Daftari, Nassir Minachi, Hassan Nazih, and old National Front personalities such as Yadollah Sahabi and Karim Sanjabi. All carried impressive opposition credentials and were widely known to have struggled against the Pahlavi regime. Furthermore, the United States had established direct contact with these individuals, and embassy officials in Tehran had held many meetings with them during the late months of 1978.

The United States emphasized the moderates also partly by default. The Shi'i religious establishment resisted meeting with official Americans. Although there were occasional contacts early in 1979, such as when Ambassador Sullivan or other embassy officers met with Ayatollah Beheshti, they dried up that same spring. After that, according to Henry Precht, American officials were largely unable to get in touch. "We tried, but couldn't get to them."[17] Precht himself had more success on his trip to Iran in October 1979 just before the hostage incident. In Tehran, accompanied by Persian speaker John Limbert, he was invited to attend a Friday prayer meeting addressed by Ayatollah Montazeri, with whom the two officers met privately. Precht and Chargé d'Affaires Bruce Laingen also met with Beheshti, and Precht described both meetings as friendly. But these were exceptional, brief interludes. The United States had maintained no contacts with the religious leaders throughout the 1970s and, during this period, had pursued a policy clearly antithetical to the interests of the ulama. Given this background and the dominant national mood of suspicion toward the United States, it is not surprising that the religious leaders were reluctant to respond enthusiastically to American overtures. The moderates, on the other hand, were more easily approached and did hold the government where they were obliged to deal with American officials. Not all secular officials, however, were available to the Americans. Sadeq Ghotbzadeh, head of Iran Radio and TV, refused to see embassy officials.

The State Department's position on the moderates in Iran was reinforced by the American Iran scholars. These academics had excellent reputations because in general they had been ahead of the government in predicting the collapse of the Pahlavi dynasty. They included such individuals as Richard Cottam, who acted as a contact and broker between the Iranian moderates and the U.S. government. Cottam's contacts with the National Front went back to the 1950s, and he was a strong proponent for liberal rule in revolutionary Iran. Other scholars with some credibility among policymakers argued that the Shi'i religious leaders were unlikely to become directly involved in the day-to-day business of government but would most likely remain in the background as general guides and guardians. I was among the leading proponents of this argument, going so far in 1979 as to state in a February 12, 1979, interview in *Newsweek* that "I don't believe Khomeini will be involved formally in the government. He will be influential, especially in the early stages, but he has denied again and again that he will hold office."[18] This view, which was soon proven to be seriously mistaken, was based on the fact that since the year 1501, when Shi'i Islam became the state religion in Iran, no cleric had ever run a government. The shattering, unprecedented nature of the Iranian revolution effectively falsified this historical lesson and confounded many Iran specialists.

The American belief in the moderates led the government to sponsor a policy of cautious support and increased contacts with the shaky new political elite then emerging in immediate post-Pahlavi Iran. The Department of State and other U.S. agencies gradually built a new, if smaller, presence in Iran, beginning in midsummer of 1979. In an attempt to improve on past performance, the latest group of official Americans posted to Iran were determined to get in touch with as many Iranians as possible. Given what had happened in the past, now "there was an enormous thirst for information."[19] They proceeded to develop visible direct contact with the political elite of the government of President Bazargan. On the Iranian side, the new moderate leaders encouraged these contacts and supported close ties with official Americans. There were political reasons for this risky tactic. Among other things, postrevolutionary leaders such as Abbas Amir Entezam believed in the intelligence competence of America and wished to acquire badly needed information from the United States.

Many Iranian revolutionaries watched this mutual embrace sullenly and with growing concern. They believed that the violent revolution against the shah had also been carried out to destroy American influence in the political affairs of their country. Suddenly, Americans were back and active. That U.S. officials were apparently allying themselves with Western-educated liberals concerned them even more. The groups most concerned about the U.S. presence were the radical left and the extremist religious right, with whom the United States had little rapport. In its enthusiasm and desire to rescue itself from a bad situation, the United States failed to reenter Iran cautiously and discreetly. International Cooperation Administration head John Graves recognized this problem and began a September 1979 cable to Washington with the following words: "Too many Americans have been too visible too long in too many aspects of life in Iran."[20] Another diplomat on the spot later argued, "We should have gone back in with six men and a dog."[21]

Despite its new, active political presence in Iran, the United States failed to establish any meaningful relationships with the major extremist religious leaders. Even their contacts with the tame ayatollahs, such as Ayatollah Shariatmadari, were tenuous. This was partially because leading members of the ulama were unenthusiastic about contact with Americans in the absence of any U.S.-Khomeini relations. In Washington there was a stubborn resentment in the White House toward Ayatollah Khomeini, a petulant attitude that resulted in a consistent refusal to approach the central leader of the revolution. Although it is of course questionable whether Khomeini would have been willing to meet with U.S. officials, experienced American foreign service officers later argued strongly that the failure to contact Khomeini was a diplomatic error of major proportions. In the words of Carl Clement, for example, "How could we hope to establish relations with a country by ignoring its leader? It was illusory to attempt to work with the government while at the same time refusing to have anything to do with the imam. The government had no power. Khomeini had the power."[22] The Soviets understood this well, and their ambassador arranged an early meeting with Ayatollah Khomeini. The French ambassador had also met twice with the ayatollah by the fall of 1979.

The failure to develop communication with Khomeini was a carryover from the time when Brzezinski had cleverly blocked plans for American direct contact with Khomeini. After the shah's overthrow, several important American policymakers raised questions about this continuing failure to contact the leader of the revolution. In April and May 1979, Chargé d'Affaires Charles Naas had begun communication with Washington about a meeting with Khomeini. This attempt, approved by Prime Minister Bazargan and apparently by Khomeini himself, had been agreed to by Washington when an ill-considered Senate resolution destroyed it.[23] By September 1979, some U.S. officials continued to exhibit their alarm at what now seemed an obvious American attempt to ignore and even isolate Khomeini. In fact, it was the United States that was isolating itself from the revolution. In a long memorandum entitled "Policy Towards Iran" to Secretary of State Cyrus Vance on September 5, 1979, Assistant Secretary Harold Saunders summarized the situation in the following terms:

> —We have had no direct contact with the man who remains the strongest political leader in Iran. His hostility towards us is unlikely to abate significantly, although there have been fewer venomous statements against us recently. Clearly, a first meeting could be a bruising affair.
> —A meeting with Khomeini will signal our definite acceptance of the revolution and could ease somewhat his suspicions of us. . . .
> —On the other hand, we would risk appearing to cave in to a man who hates us and who is strongly deprecated here and by Westernized Iranians. Thus, we would want to be careful not to

appear to embrace Khomeini and the clerics at the expense of our secular friends. . . .

—The symbolism of a call on Khomeini would not attach to visits to the other religious leaders, but they will not see us until we have seen him. We badly need contacts with Taleghani, Shariat-madari, and other moderate clerics. We want to reassure them of our acceptance of the revolution as their influence may rise in the months ahead.[24]

This revealing memorandum went on to recommend that on his return to Tehran from Washington Chargé d'Affaires Bruce Laingen send a message that he would be willing to meet with Khomeini—or that a meeting with Khomeini be a priority for a new American ambassador. Two months after this memorandum was written, the students took over the U.S. Embassy in Tehran, and any hope for communication with the leader of the Iranian revolution was irrevocably lost. This memorandum demonstrates the extraordinary facts that eight months after the revolution the United States still had no contact with Khomeini, that Washington decision makers were well aware that Iranian revolutionary leaders doubted America's acceptance of the revolution, and that the United States did not in any way want to dilute its credibility with the moderate secularists.

The policy toward Khomeini is symptomatic of the overall attitude of the United States toward the Iranian revolution. A certain bitterness and hostility was evident from the beginning. The acceptance of the revolution was grudging at best, and this was quite clear to the revolutionaries. The evidence went far deeper than the failure to open communication with Khomeini. It began with the refusal of the United States to publicly acknowledge the revolution. Such statements of acceptance were curiously absent from American pronouncements, even though the other major nations of the world immediately proclaimed their support and goodwill to the new government in Iran. In a draft of a cable to Washington in August 1979, Bruce Laingen stressed the need for more positive public American support. Even the moderate Iranian government saw "in the virtual absence on our part of any public statements" of goodwill toward the revolution "a reflection of less than full endorsement." Laingen argued that "an occasional positive and public statement by administration spokesmen about our interest and hopes in the new Iran can help reduce some of the chip on the shoulder, damn you for our gas lines, attitudes towards Iran in the U.S. public that do not help us in pursuing our long-range interests in Iran."[25]

Besides alienating the extremists, the United States ironically also succeeded in deeply disturbing the moderates, the very group that

American decision makers hoped to court and to strengthen politically. If the United States professed to support them, the moderates themselves argued this was indeed a strange sort of support. In their view there had been no strong statements in support of the revolution, no willingness to admit possible past foreign policy errors, no resupply of badly needed spare parts (spare parts already paid for), no willingness to consider extradition of political criminals or the repatriation of Pahlavi funds, and no serious attempt to cooperate with the real leadership of the Iranian revolution. In exasperation, almost desperation, the moderates constantly complained to American diplomats about these unfriendly acts of political omission. On three occasions in early October 1979, Abbas Amir Entezam accused the United States of much friendly talk but no friendly action, of playing a "wait-and-see game" with the objective of interfering in Iranian affairs again in the future. He pointed out that the Soviet ambassador had been to see the revolutionary government "100 times" and "had been kicked out 100 times" but that the Soviets continued to offer concrete assistance. Referring to the U.S. failure to provide badly needed spare parts for which Iran had already paid $400 million, Amir Entezam sharply criticized the "U.S. failure to convey those signals which would indicate U.S. acceptance of the Iranian revolution and a willingness to deal with the revolution on the basis of equality and respect."[26] In a long discussion of American-Iranian relations, Ibrahim Yazdi stated in retrospect with considerable conviction that "the U.S. never really supported us. If so, it was strange support given America's constant refusal of all our requests. They didn't give us one thing. Nothing. They didn't care."[27]

Although positive indications that the United States endorsed the reality of the revolution were few, a number of American actions were easily interpreted to be downright hostile. These errors of political commission seriously harmed U.S. interests in Iran and, among other things, helped destroy the moderate forces. They were especially damaging against the background just described and set the stage for the most catastrophic miscalculation of all, the admission of the shah into the United States on October 22, 1979.

In Washington, influential congressmen who had long maintained especially close relations with the Pahlavi regime gave interviews and sponsored resolutions deprecating and condemning the Iranian revolution and its policies. Two such men were Sens. Jacob Javits and Henry Jackson; both were known in Iranian circles as longtime apologists for the shah and his government. On May 17, 1979, the Senate took up a resolution sponsored by Senator Javits condemning Iran for the revolutionary executions. This resolution was triggered by the execution of a Jewish businessman named Habib Elghanian on May 9. The execution was presented in Washington as evidence of a revolutionary pogrom against Jews, and Javits and others immediately moved to condemn Iran in the strongest possible terms. Actually, Elghanian had been one of twenty-nine executed May 7 to May 11, 1979; he was the only one of Jewish ancestry; and all had been targeted because of their close associations with the shah's regime.[28] Elghanian, who for years had been identified in U.S. Embassy reports as one of the three wealthiest individuals in Iran, was charged with corruption, capitalist exploitation, and treason for close political and economic associations with Israel.

The Javits resolution, which among other things resolved that the Senate "expresses its abhorrence of summary executions without due process" was supported by eighteen senators; ten spoke on the Senate floor in its favor. Senator Robert C. Byrd was especially supportive of the resolution, which he termed "very timely. For as we speak, the killing continues in Iran." Byrd went on to condemn Iran, where "an arbitrary exercise of power is being demonstrated by certain Iranian officials, an arbitrariness that flies in the face of all human sensibilities." Senator Laughton Chiles of Florida added that "too many of us have stood by too long and have been silent too long. . . . We wish to see Iran return to a country of law." And Sen. Abraham Ribicoff of Connecticut stated that "what is going on in that country [Iran] is barbaric and beyond the imagination of all of us." Ribicoff added that "the Shah was a proven and true friend of the United States. The entire world should condemn the excesses now taking place in Iran."[29]

The Senate resolution caused nationwide anti-American demonstrations in Iran and was viewed as evidence of U.S. opposition to the revolution. In the words of Charles Naas, then chargé d'affaires in Iran: "The place went wild."[30] American eyewitnesses to the demonstrations in Mashhad attest to the power of these riots and the fact that they represented an important tilt to overt anti-Americanism after the revolution.[31] Iranian leaders asked why there had been no Senate resolutions during the shah's rule, when thousands had been imprisoned, tortured, and executed. In their words, why the sudden U.S. Senate concern for due process, arbitrary exercises of power, and rule of law in Iran? Khomeini himself used this incident as a prime example of American hypocrisy and hostility toward the revolution.

The May 17 resolution was greeted with great consternation among American diplomats in Iran, who had been working hard to build new relationships with postrevolutionary Iran. Among other things, they had been anxiously awaiting the arrival of the new U.S. ambassador, Walter Cutler, who was ready to leave for Iran as part of the process of normalization. The ill-considered and ill-timed Senate resolution convinced the Iranian leaders of America's hostile views toward the revolution, and the United States was notified that Cutler was not welcome. Meanwhile, Naas's plans for a meeting with Khomeini were laid to rest forever, and Naas, who had been working on Iranian affairs since 1974, left Iran in June in a gloomy and despondent frame of mind. Many believe that this Senate action, promoted by American Pahlavites with especially close ties to the state of Israel, was the first major event leading to the U.S. Embassy takeover five months later. Charles Naas stated that the Javits resolution "really hurt us" and that from then on the Iranians "refused to play ball."[32]

In the fall, another undiplomatic, thoughtless, and counterproductive act by an American senator left a heavy negative imprint on U.S.-Iranian relations. In an interview with "Meet the Press" in October 1979, Sen. Henry Jackson made the statement that the Iranian revolution was doomed to failure and that the country was about to break up into small pieces. This statement was greeted with great concern in Iran, where officials assumed that this public pronouncement by an influential American senator was not only proof of American hostility but also an indication that the United States had plans to help break Iran into little pieces. According to one high-ranking Iranian official who was then in touch with U.S. Embassy officials, Senator Jackson's words "had hit the upper levels of the foreign ministry like a bombshell."[33] Again, in Tehran, American diplomats were horrified. Senator Jackson's statement represented one more milestone along the way to American-Iranian estrangement.

These events took place in a context of a series of counterproductive official U.S. actions. These included two related categories of action: political policies and covert intelligence activities. Politically, after the revolutionary overthrow, U.S. officials worked hard to assist influential members of the Pahlavi regime to escape Iran and to gain entry into America. These included everyone from military officers to SAVAK officials to wealthy industrialists. Personal connections between high-ranking American military personnel and powerful members of the shah's regime played an important part in this process. In one case, the Defense Intelligence Agency used its channels to enable an influential Iranian naval officer in exile to send money to his sister-in-law in Tehran. In another instance, the State Department cabled the U.S. Embassy in Tehran to request visas for the children of the former deputy-administrator of the shah's Civil Aviation Organization, which was known in Iran as a center of financial corruption and a cover for intelligence operations. Employees of the Civil Aviation Organization were in fact given special priority as visa applicants after the revolution.

By the fall of 1979, U.S. officials in Iran were using the visa weapon as a means of gathering intelligence information about revolutionary Iran. Most of the high-ranking members of the ancien regime had been assisted, and now most applications originated from middle-class Iranians. Their only hope for a visa was to provide valuable information to American authorities. This procedure was summarized in a September 18, 1979, memorandum from the U.S. defense attaché: "Visa referrals will only repeat *only* be handled to gain intelligence information useful to the United States government."[34]

Although there were many examples of U.S. intelligence activity in Iran after the revolution, two episodes loomed especially large in shaping the subsequent state of U.S.-Iranian relations. The first was a Central Intelligence Agency plan to develop a liaison with Abol Hassan Bani Sadr; the second was a more general CIA plan designed to establish close working relationships with the moderate faction within the Iranian revolutionary establishment. Both plans were rather crudely designed and heavy handed, and both contributed to the dramatic failure of the moderates and to the final collapse of American credibility in Iran. They became known to the Iranian extremists in late 1979–early 1980 after the student groups gained access to secret documents on occupying the U.S. Embassy in Tehran. These documents then became a powerful political tool used by the revolutionary extremists to bludgeon the moderates, who were now demonstrated to have had close associations with American intelligence officials.

The CIA *and an Attempt to Recruit a Revolutionary President*

In January 1979, a tall, distinguished-looking American in his early sixties approached Abol Hassan Bani Sadr in Paris. At the time, Bani Sadr was one of Ayatollah Khomeini's closest advisers and the Iranian revolution was approaching its conclusion. The American introduced himself to Bani Sadr as Guy Rutherford and indicated that he was an American businessman with influential contacts in Washington. During two meetings in Paris, Rutherford told Bani Sadr that he represented a Pennsylvania company named Carver and Associates and that as an international businessman he valued Bani Sadr's assessments of events in Iran. He pointed out that he intended to spend some time in Iran on a future business trip to the Far East and would appreciate the chance to visit with Bani Sadr during this visit. Rutherford and Bani Sadr established friendly personal rapport during the two Paris meetings.[35]

Soon after these Paris sessions, Bani Sadr returned to Iran as a central figure in the entourage of Ayatollah Khomeini. As one of Khomeini's most trusted advisers, Bani Sadr quickly moved into formal positions of influence, becoming a member of the fifteen-person Revolutionary Council and the seventy-two-member Assembly of Experts. On June 12, 1979, Guy Rutherford telephoned Bani Sadr (allegedly from Brussels), confirming a trip to Iran sometime in the next several weeks. According to the canons of Iranian hospitality, Bani Sadr indicated his willingness to meet with Rutherford in Tehran. Rutherford arrived in Tehran in early August and later met three times with Bani Sadr. During these meetings (August 25 and 29, September 2), Rutherford developed an informed personal evaluation of Bani Sadr and a general assessment of the Iranian economic and political scene as interpreted by Bani Sadr. Rutherford also apparently offered Bani Sadr a consulting fee in order to assure his cooperation.

Guy Rutherford was also sometimes known as William Foster. His real name was Vernon Cassin, and he was in fact employed by the Central Intelligence Agency. Cassin was an experienced CIA agent who had been stationed in the Middle East since the mid-1950s, when he became chief of station in Damascus. There he had been involved in an abortive attempt to rearrange the political system of Syria in 1956. He later became chief of station in Amman, Jordan, and then moved into deep cover positions pertaining to Middle Eastern affairs. Described by a colleague as "a complete professional who went by the book,"[36] Cassin relished intrigue and covert activity. In Tehran, he cooperated closely with CIA chief of mission Thomas Ahern, who was known as Paquin. Bani Sadr's codename was SDLure/1, and he was sometimes referred to simply as L/1. Because of the sensitivity of Cassin's mission, Cassin was to be provided "watertight coverage" with a twenty-four-hour emergency telephone contact number. Cassin was to be in Iran with the "objective of developing L/1 and turning him over to an embassy officer."[37] In his September 7, 1979, final assessment, Cassin concluded that Bani Sadr was a valuable contact and that "efforts should continue to obtain his cooperation. An individual with the access he enjoys should be able to furnish info of value in the period ahead." And he went on to discuss the methodology of "grooming" the subject (Bani Sadr) for further use.[38]

According to the Iranian students who published the documents linking Bani Sadr to the CIA, Bani Sadr had been offered $1,000 per month to act as an "American company advisor."[39] Although there is no evidence that Bani Sadr knew he was being recruited by the CIA, he later recalled that Cassin "offered me $5,000 a month" and that in response "I told him to go away."[40] Four months after the CIA contact, Abol Hassan Bani Sadr was elected the first president of the Islamic Republic of Iran. But it was only one month after this bold contact that extremist students took over the U.S. Embassy and took possession of the documents detailing the CIA-Bani Sadr connection. Once they had laboriously pieced together a number of the documents that had been frantically fed through the paper shredder, they knew of Bani Sadr's American contacts, and they cleverly used this information to discredit the president in the eyes of Ayatollah Khomeini and the extremist clerics. In a July 1981 personal interview, Javad Mansouri, an important member of the Islamic Republican party deeply involved in the embassy takeover, stated that they were 100 percent certain that Bani Sadr was the SDLure/1 referred to in the documents. In his words: "Embassy documents prove that Bani Sadr has committed high treason. Is there a place in the world where a man proved to have committed high treason is President?"[41]

The Central Intelligence Agency's brazen attempt to recruit and to buy information from Bani Sadr backfired badly when the embassy documents exposed the entire escapade. Not only did this completely destroy Bani Sadr's already deteriorating credibility, but it also reinforced the views of Iranian revolutionaries that the United States had every intention of taking control of the revolution itself. In their eyes, this was clear and incontrovertible evidence that the shah's admission into the United States was part of an overall plot to weaken and ultimately overturn the Iranian revolution. The fact that the U.S. Embassy had once before (in 1953) served as a locus for counterrevolutionary activity only convinced them that taking the embassy and holding American diplomats hostage was the patriotic thing to do. In their own words: "The major lesson of the documents is the deep American enmity towards the Islamic revolution and its leader Imam Khomeini. The revolution was so unpalatable to America that it could not for a moment neglect plotting against it in order either to destroy it or to detour it by backing Iranian compromisers."[42]

U.S. Intelligence and Its Crushing Embrace of the Moderates

The major moderate political group that remained in place after the revolution was the Liberation Movement (LM) of Iran, which was led by such individuals as Mehdi Bazargan and Ibrahim Yazdi. The members of this organization were former members of the National Front and the National Resistance Movement (Nihzat-i Muqavimat-i Milli) and stressed nationalism and constitutionalism with a heavy Islamic flavor. Although the United States had information about this movement and its members, it had made very little contact or communication with it. Over the years, the LM had maintained only an informal liaison with Professor Richard Cottam of the University of Pittsburgh, a former U.S. government official who had served in Iran.

In May 1978 the LM and the U.S. Embassy in Tehran began direct contact. The first meeting was held at the El Chico restaurant in Tehran on May 8 and was attended by embassy political officer John Stempel and a LM member known as Mohammad Tavakoli. A heavy shroud of mutual suspicion enveloped this initial contact; Stempel sensed that Tavakoli viewed him as "either a SAVAK fink or CIA agent."[43] In the end, the two developed a working personal rapport and thus began a series of direct meetings that lasted through the year. Although the primary contact was between Stempel and Tavakoli, Mehdi Bazargan himself met with Stempel on three occasions, and Yadollah Sahabi was present twice. American ignorance of the LM is seen in the fact that it was not until December that embassy officials realized that Mohammad Tavakoli was in fact Mohammad Tavassoli, a well-known member of the LM who became mayor of Tehran just after the revolution. Stempel had been meeting for months with an opposition leader whose identity he did not know.

Ambassador William Sullivan had initiated these contacts in an attempt to improve American understanding of the Iranian political terrain. From the beginning, the LM representatives inquired consistently about "what the U.S. hoped to gain" from the meetings. Stempel's response was, "better understanding and appreciation of the movement."[44] For its part, the LM desired some communication with the United States since it was then helpless and exposed before the shah's security forces. Also, like most Iranian political actors, LM members believed in the overwhelming nature of American political influence both in Iran and in the Middle East more generally. For example, LM leaders were convinced that the United States had given the Iraqis the order to place Khomeini under house arrest in Najaf in September 1978. They furiously approached Stempel about this and were not totally convinced when he indicated to them that "it was absurd to think the U.S. would have this sort of influence on Iraq."[45]

After the revolution, the United States decided to take full advantage of its contacts with the LM, many of whose members now found themselves in key positions of political leadership in Iran. The channels of communication that Stempel had established in 1978 became the primary means by which America now sought to keep tabs on the revolution. In the relative absence of any serious contacts with the religious leadership, the focus of attention became the revolutionary moderates of the Liberation Movement. Furthermore, as long as the United States had diplomatic representation in Iran, it had little choice but to deal with official representatives of the Islamic Republic; they, in turn, as the legitimate leaders of Iran, were locked into dealing with U.S. officials. The relationship, however, went further than this and involved American intelligence agents and a great deal of informal contact. It was this contact that later became known to the revolutionary extremists and that contributed to the demise of the moderates in brutal postrevolutionary infighting.

Although the entire CIA detachment had been on the first two planes out of Iran after the embassy takeover on February 14, 1979, agents began to filter back into Iran beginning in late summer. In early fall, station chief Thomas Ahern and an associate were joined by two colleagues, Malcolm Karp and William Daugherty. American chargé Bruce Laingen understood the serious political danger of this kind of CIA presence in Iran, and, while agreeing to it, he warned of "the great sensitivity locally to any hint of CIA activity" and stressed the importance "that cover be the best we can come up with."[46] Laingen argued that for the time being the number of CIA officers at the embassy should be held to no more than four.

The Iranian revolutionary militants later particularly criticized two intelligence briefings provided to Prime Minister Bazargan and his inner circle by CIA officials in August and October 1979. The key Iranian political figure involved in these contacts was Abbas Amir Entezam, who, after serving as Bazargan's deputy prime minister, became Iran's ambassador to Sweden and the other Scandinavian countries. Although very much a loyal Iranian patriot deeply committed to the revolution, Amir Entezam believed that it was in Iran's interest to maintain relations with the United States. Known in the intelligence cable traffic as SD/PLOD/1, Amir Entezam was highly regarded by American officials. When he left Iran for his Swedish post, Bruce Laingen described him to the U.S. ambassador in Sweden: "He is an unusually polished and urbane and westernized Iranian, very much in the inner circle of the revolution here in Iran, but hardly a revolutionary in style or appearance. He has spent considerable time in our country and knows and likes the United States very much. You will like him."[47] Although being polished, urbane, and Westernized may have impressed American diplomats, these characteristics were less important to the extremist religious leaders who represented the interests of the Iranian masses.

The principal American contact was CIA agent George W. Cave, who was later to play a central role in the 1985–86 Iran-Contra affair. Cave was an Iran specialist who had served in Tehran between 1958 and 1963 and had returned for another tour beginning in August 1973. If not outstanding, his knowledge of Iran was considered to be satisfactory. John Stempel flew to Stockholm on August 5, 1979, and met with Amir Entezam for 4½ hours that day and the next. Cave, who happened to be celebrating his fiftieth birthday at the time, also participated and was presented to Amir Entezam only as a "senior briefing officer."[48] At this time, Amir Entezam made a number of suggestions concerning U.S. policy, but at the top of his list was the recommendation that the United States provide Iran with information on any internal threats to the revolutionary government, especially threats that had outside support. This request had already been made by Amir Entezam to U.S. diplomats back in Tehran.

Anxious to establish relationships with the new regime in Iran, American officials agreed to provide briefings to a very select group in Bazargan's government. Although Amir Entezam had also suggested a permanent contact in Tehran, Cave countered with the idea that the United States would provide briefing officers as needed who would fly into Tehran for private meetings. The first such session took place on August 21, 1979, when CIA officer Robert Clayton Ames flew into Tehran and briefed Prime Minister Bazargan, Foreign Minister Yazdi, and Deputy Prime Minister Amir Entezam on the political situation of Iraq, the Palestinians, Afghanistan, and the Soviet Union. The discussions focused on these potential threats to the Iranian government. American officials felt that this intelligence session had been "well-received" by the Iranians.[49]

The second session, well described in the embassy documents, took place on October 15, 1979, and involved George Cave himself, who had flown into Tehran for the briefing. This briefing was particularly noteworthy to the extremist fringe of the revolutionaries since it occurred only one week before the shah was admitted into the United States. Those present included Chargé d'Affaires Bruce Laingen, energy specialist Ron Smith, George Cave, Foreign Minister Yazdi, and Amir Entezam, then ambassador to Sweden. Defense Minister Mustafa Chamran was to have attended but was in Kurdistan at the time. Prime Minister Bazargan was not present. During this two-hour meeting, Smith gave a detailed briefing on the energy situation in the Soviet Union. Yazdi and Amir Entezam indicated deep concern about the Kurdish problem. Yazdi went so far as to imply that the United States and Israel might be directly involved in fomenting this upheaval by working through the Iraqis. Cave and Laingen assured Yazdi that this was not the case since America's interest was in the stability and integrity of Iran. The "essential U.S. interest in Iran is that oil keeps flowing."[50] The American officials commented on Yazdi's deep "paranoia." Yazdi, on the other hand, indicated that perhaps a group within the U.S. government was quietly working to destabilize the Kurdish areas; he specifically volunteered the CIA as the culprit since this agency had a proven record of taking such actions on its own.

From the Iranian point of view, this session was a disaster. Ron Smith's rambling discourse on Soviet energy problems was viewed as a smokescreen by the Iranians present. Yazdi later termed it "a bunch of nonsense" and indicated that the Iranian participants later speculated on what the hidden agenda might have been for this meeting.[51] In a private follow-up meeting with George Cave in Tehran on October 18, Amir Entezam said that the briefing had not been "precisely what [the] Bazargan government needed. . . . Their wants for the moment were basically for tactical information on [the] Kurdish situation and political intelligence on who [was] supporting [the] Kurds and why." Cave argued that the Israelis were definitely not involved. When Amir Entezam asked what could be done to resolve this Kurdish problem, Cave provided some strange and unhelpful advice involving the revival of an old tripartite arrangement including the Turks. Cave reported that "while it may seem incredible, what they really want is for us to devise solutions to their problems."[52]

Just as CIA agent Vernon Cassin's meetings contributed to the demise of Bani Sadr, the Stempel-Cave-Ames meetings with the Bazargan group contributed to the increasingly anti-American climate that dominated revolutionary Iran in the years after the occupation of the U.S. Embassy. Support for the meetings between American intelligence officers and the LM moderate revolutionaries was found on both sides. Having generally lacked effective contact before the revolution, the United States now belatedly sought to make up for lost time. On the Iranian side, Amir Entezam, in particular, pushed hard for increased contact between America and the Bazargan government. The fledgling revolution was under siege and surrounded by enemies; thus, a number of the moderates believed U.S. support to be essential. They especially sought intelligence on enemies from without.

Although Mehdi Bazargan and Ibrahim Yazdi were unenthusiastic about the U.S. linkage, embassy documents reveal that they did acquiesce and participate in a number of the meetings. They clearly did so in order to protect the revolution and their own positions within it. Many LM leaders harbored middle-class fears of the left and were genuinely worried about the prospect of a Soviet takeover. Yazdi argued that it was the United States that continually pressed for the covert contacts and that the Iranian government also had meetings with British and Soviet intelligence officials.[53] There is considerable truth in this; on one occasion, for example, George Cave indicated to Amir Entezam that he had some "important information" for him.[54] It is also certain from the record, however, that the Iranians, especially Amir Entezam, encouraged the U.S.-Iran link.

When these meetings became known to the radical students and to the extremist clerics after the embassy takeover, they were used as valuable political capital in the power game then going on in Tehran. Bazargan, Yazdi, and other members of the old Liberation Movement lost credibility and slid down the slippery and dangerous slope of revolutionary politics. Amir Entezam, barely escaping with his life, was arrested in late 1979, tried for treason, and sentenced to life imprisonment in June 1981. His important role in initiating contacts with American intelligence agents was documented in detail at the trials. Thus, the moderate revolutionary forces were exposed to the withering fire of their extremist enemies.

America and Iran in the 1980s: Hostages, War, and Diplomatic Confrontation

On the night of October 22, 1979, a Gulfstream aircraft landed quietly at La Guardia airport in New York City. The jet carried the shah and empress of Iran and a small royal entourage. Hours earlier, President Jimmy Carter had given the approval for Muhammad Reza Shah Pahlavi to enter the United States for medical treatment. This momentous decision led directly to a new era in Iranian-American relations—an era dominated by extremism, distrust, hatred, and violence. Carter had resisted admitting the shah to the United States for nine pressure-packed months, but he finally relented in the face of formidable pressures, including persistent lobbying for admission by the shah's powerful friends in America, genuine humanitarian considerations, and political calculations involving the forthcoming 1980 presidential elections. Carter later described the circumstances surrounding his decision: "I was told that the Shah was desperately ill, at the point of death. I was told that New York was the only medical facility that was capable of possibly saving his life and reminded that the

Iranian officials had promised to protect our people in Iran. When all the circumstances were described to me, I agreed."[55]

Despite dire predictions by Iran specialists about a swift anti-American response in Iran, the reaction was curiously muted in the first week after the admission became known to Iranian revolutionaries. It seemed to take some days for the significance of this event to sink into the revolutionary consciousness. Meanwhile, other American political actions only heightened the distrust and increased the tension, in particular, Henry Jackson's public attack on the Iranian revolution in October and the meeting in Algiers between National Security Adviser Zbigniew Brzezinski and Mehdi Bazargan, Ibrahim Yazdi, and Mustafa Chamran on November 1. The Algiers meeting, especially, deepened the anti-American paranoia and shortened the political life of the moderates.

Given the paranoia rampant in Iran and the shah's recent admission into the United States, the Algiers meeting was a severe political miscalculation. Both Brzezinski, who was consistently insensitive to events taking place in Iran, and the Iranian officials, who should have known better, erred in participating in this session. On that day, November 1, 1979, huge revolutionary demonstrations with a heavy anti-American flavor took place in Tehran. Approximately two million angry demonstrators shouted "Death to America" and listened to fiery speeches denouncing the United States for harboring "the criminal shah." That evening, Iranian National Television showed pictures of Brzezinski shaking hands with the Iranian delegation. The Iranian extremists interpreted this as evidence of the Bazargan government's collusion with an America that had just given refuge to the shah, whom they held responsible for all their problems.

Years after the revolution both sides still vehemently claim that the other requested the meeting. In his book, Brzezinski flatly states that Prime Minister Bazargan "requested a meeting with me."[56] Former Foreign Minister Yazdi strongly denies this and accuses Brzezinski of a direct lie in order to lessen his own responsibility for the unfortunate political consequences of the act.[57] Secretary of State Cyrus Vance indicates his "surprise" at Brzezinski's participation in the meeting and reports that "he later told us that the meeting had been held at the Iranians' initiative."[58] Yazdi indicates that the fact that Brzezinski came to Bazargan's hotel room is one important indicator that the national security adviser initiated the meeting. Other sources support Yazdi's version of the event. Brzezinski's assistant Gary Sick, for example, writes that the American chargé d'affaires in

Tehran, Bruce Laingen, "had urged that Brzezinski or others in the U.S. delegation meet with the Iranians."[59] John Stempel writes that the United States had been "pressing for a high-level meeting, which took place when Brzezinski met with Bazargan and Yazdi in Algiers on November 1."[60]

The fact that Brzezinski may have erred in his recollections of the event is less important than that in engaging in his own curious style of personal diplomacy he contributed both to the taking of American hostages and to the destruction of moderate influence in the revolution. Bazargan, Yazdi, and Chamran also miscalculated; they were well aware of feelings and social forces at work in their country. On November 4, 1979, less than two weeks after the shah was admitted to the United States and less than three days after the Algiers meeting, a group of nearly five hundred extremist students attacked the U.S. Embassy in Tehran, initially taking sixty-one Americans hostage. For the next 444 days, American citizens watched in helpless anger and horror as Iranian extremists held fifty-two of the American officials hostage in Tehran. American-Iranian relations had sunk to an all-time low.

The hostage crisis has been described and analyzed from the American side in great depth and detail.[61] The Carter administration was preoccupied every waking moment with this situation, and the president himself personalized the episode and devoted all his energy to its resolution. This only exacerbated the confrontation as the Iranians refused to yield to a persistent assortment of U.S. pressures. These included a wide variety of diplomatic tactics, economic pressures and embargos, military threats, and even an abortive, ill-fated military rescue attempt. Back in Iran, the hostage holding was a central part of the postrevolutionary power struggle, and Washington's actions became a daily factor in the complex domestic Iranian political equation.

It now seems certain that the militants had plans to move on the American Embassy in Tehran long before November 4 and that they put their plans into action when anti-American rhetoric and feeling began to peak in the first three days of that month.[62] Although the American Embassy takeover may have been planned in advance in general terms, the actual operation involved different leaders and factions with unclear long-term goals. Ayatollah Khomeini himself at first quietly expressed disapproval of the move but later became a strong supporter when he realized the overwhelming popularity of the act among the Iranian masses. There is evidence that the students themselves were astonished by the responses their action elicited, both within Iran and across the world.

As the Carter administration overreacted and the American mass media turned its complete attention on the event, the student extremists quickly recognized the influence they had suddenly attained. While the American giant shouted and threatened the lawbreakers before the eyes of the world, the extremists stubbornly refused to budge and, in traditional bazaar bargaining style, only increased the price for any accommodation. In Iran, the moderate-extremist struggle intensified, and the former lost ground rapidly. Prime Minister Bazargan resigned on November 6, and the moderates who had communicated with the United States were left powerless. Abol Hassan Bani Sadr was also politically impotent. Deeply upset by the taking of diplomatic hostages, most middle-class Iranian moderates found themselves sitting on the sidelines watching American bluster deepen the international crisis and increase the credibility of the extremists in Tehran.

While National Security Adviser Brzezinski sternly issued threat after threat to the Iranians, President Carter and Ayatollah Khomeini engaged in the construction of a public rainbow of insults. The Iranian position was summarized by Khomeini's statement that if the United States wished to invade Iran, it would have to kill all 35 million Iranians, who would willingly die as martyrs struggling against the Great Satan. Then America could have Iran. Economic sanctions and embargos and military threats made very little impact on this mentality.

The hostage incident occasioned three major political power struggles within Iran. The most general confrontation was the conflict between the extremists and the moderates. The incident demonstrated that the extremists had mass support while the moderates lacked credibility at the grass roots of society. The extremists used the hostage episode to consolidate their hold over the revolutionary political controls. The second struggle overlapped with the first and involved the formal governmental apparatus represented by the Islamic Republican party on the one hand and the student militants within the embassy compound on the other hand. The embassy takeover presented the IRP with a fait accompli. Like Khomeini himself, IRP leaders such as Muhammad Hussein Beheshti were initially ambivalent about the action but soon saw its general popularity and then, always moving with the political winds, used it to help achieve important political ends. Nonetheless, tension persisted between the government and the students. The former privately warned the militants that if any of the hostages were to die, the student captors would themselves pay with their lives. The third and most specific power struggle occurred within the embassy grounds itself, where the students formed various factions that included an important left-right division.

Although the religious extremists outnumbered the students of Marxist inclination, the latter were in many ways more desperate and therefore more likely to take some dramatic retributive act against an American prisoner. There was serious danger, especially during the beginning months, that such an act might occur, thereby forcing military confrontation between Iran and the United States. Such an act would introduce a new level of conflict—war—and would benefit both the radical left within Iran and quite possibly the Soviet Union, monitoring events closely from the north. Partly because of this danger, the left was gradually purged within the student ranks, and the Islamic extremists took control.

The embassy takeover reinforced the extremist phase of the revolution because it continued to radicalize the rules of politics in Iran. The continuing process of radicalization was fed from two directions, from within and from without. The militants were certain in their own minds that the embassy was a center of American espionage, a "nest of spies" (*lanah-yi jasusi*), as they termed it. On taking the embassy, they captured thousands of pages of diplomatic documents and correspondence. They immediately began to piece together the documents that had been shredded and initiated a thorough study of what they had discovered. Not surprisingly, they found in these documents ample evidence for their theories and suspicions. The United States had detailed intelligence concerning personalities and politics of Iran; American diplomats and intelligence agents were in direct contact with a number of postrevolutionary leaders; CIA agents were working out of the embassy, which was referred to in the documents as a Special Reporting Facility (SRF); and at least three of the hostages were clearly identified in the documents as CIA agents.

This kind of information was all the "proof" that the extremists needed of America's continuing intervention in Iran's internal affairs. Arguments that embassies routinely engage in information gathering and that all countries employ intelligence agents were irrelevant to the Iranian revolutionaries, who could point to past examples where such intervention had changed their political system. The evidence that they thought they had found in the U.S. Embassy was enough to reinforce their perceptions that once again America was interfering in Iranian internal affairs, that it was in touch with moderate Western-educated leaders, that it had long intended to admit the shah into the United States, and that it was, therefore, fundamentally hostile to the Iranian revolution.

Less than a month after they occupied the U.S. Embassy, the student extremists began to use the captured documents for internal political purposes. On December 1, they indicated that certain of the hostages were CIA agents, basing their assertion on documentary evidence that implicated Thomas Ahern, William Daugherty, and Malcolm Kalp. They also used the documents to discredit and defeat such moderates as the members of the LM, whom they showed had been in constant contact with American officials. "For three years following the Embassy seizure, the carefully orchestrated publication of screened documents served as an extremely effective weapon in the extremists' drive to discredit the moderates and to neutralize their political influence in the country."[63] The embassy documents shrewdly continued to be used after their discovery; the militants released them slowly and effectively until by 1987 almost sixty volumes had been published.

One series of revelations that contributed greatly to the fear of the revolutionaries was released in fall 1984 and spring 1985. Embassy documents showed that American and Soviet diplomats had been meeting and comparing notes in Tehran restaurants throughout the revolution. Although such meetings had been taking place for years, they increased in frequency in 1978 when Political Officer John Stempel had what he termed a "monthly luncheon" arrangement with Soviet First Secretary Guennady Kazankin. Stempel and Kazankin had been meeting since at least as early as 1976, and although their relationship was marked by underlying political distrust, it was warm enough in personal terms. On one occasion, Stempel and Kazankin met at the American Embassy Caravansarai Restaurant and then "adjourned to the Russian Trade Commission to sample the new sauna . . . which has Finnish sandalwood on the interior and solid wood panelling from Russia in the ante-room and dressing rooms." On another occasion, when Kazankin expressed skepticism that Stempel was "telling him the truth," Stempel "blandly" replied, "Guennady, would I lie to you?" During this period, American diplomat Ralph Boyce was meeting with Viktor Kazakov of the Soviet Embassy, also in Tehran.[64]

Stempel and Kazankin made an interesting pair. Stempel, a lanky, sandy-haired political officer who had been in Iran since 1975, had received a Ph.D. in political science from the University of California at Berkeley in 1965. Conservative and cynical, he had a sharp sense of humor and was perhaps the most knowledgeable American diplomat then in Tehran. Although he was very shrewd, his understanding of Iran did not run especially deep, and at times his personal wittiness substituted poorly for badly needed analysis. Kazankin, too, had a sense of humor, but he also had ulcers and high blood pressure. A graduate of the Foreign Affairs Institute in Moscow, he had served as a Soviet diplomatic official in Afghanistan in the 1960s. Kazankin was not happy with his Iran assignment, and his Iranian contacts were very limited. His intellectual and verbal sparring sessions with Stempel were among the highlights of his residence in Tehran.

The content of the Stempel-Kazankin discussions is very revealing and indicates that both the United States and the USSR were deeply troubled by the unrest in Iran and that neither country was very well informed about what was taking place before their very eyes. When Kazankin asked Stempel what he thought about the January 1978 disturbances in Qum, Stempel indicated that "the whole affair seemed a bit of police overreaction." When at another session Kazankin "cleared his throat and treated Stempel to the rumor that the Shah was reportedly sick from cancer or some other blood disease," Stempel noted parenthetically that "this rumor has abounded in many quarters and may be of Soviet inspiration." Then, when Kazankin returned from a summer vacation in Russia, he asked Stempel on September 11, 1978, to brief him on internal Iranian developments. Stempel pointed out that the shah's government "seemed to have things under control with Martial Law." The Russian went on to say that "the Soviets viewed the Shah as key and that the opposition was not much."

At this September meeting, Stempel rather proudly told Kazankin that President Carter had just phoned the shah a personal message of support. The American diplomat then somewhat sardonically asked Kazankin when Brezhnev planned to do the same. In response, Kazankin stated that "we agree that the Shah is strong especially now that you have shown support for him." A month later, however, Kazankin argued to Stempel that "the U.S. was not doing enough to help the Shah." These documents provided the Iranian religious revolutionaries with what they considered to be incontrovertible evidence that the world's two superpowers had colluded in supporting the shah and in opposing the revolution. Although they never required a smoking gun to support their theories of external interference, the Iranians now felt they had one. That the Soviet finger seemed to have helped the American finger pull the trigger did not lessen anti-Americanism in Iran in the slightest.

Iranian hostility deepened as the Carter administration desperately engaged in numerous activities designed to force Iran to release the hostages. The application of pressure only increased the determination of the hostage holders, whose popularity grew at home in direct proportion to the amount of pressure applied by the United States. As America became mesmerized by and preoccupied with the hostage situation, President Carter found himself under enormous pressure to take decisive action. While a number of his advisers, especially Zbigniew Brzezinski, had been encouraging a military strike of some kind, others such as Cyrus Vance urged caution and patience. Throughout, Carter was torn about his concern for the personal safety of the American hostages and his commitment to America's general foreign policy goals and credibility worldwide. He also had one eye on the public opinion polls, where his popularity had been plummeting.

It is instructive to note that Carter listened especially closely to those advisers most concerned with his diplomatic political future just before he ordered the military rescue mission—his wife, Rosalynn, Walter Mondale, Hamilton Jordan, and Jody Powell. *Time* magazine reported that Carter believed that a successful rescue mission would have assured his reelection. "For all Carter's professed desire to prevent what he saw as the imminent murder of the Americans, he and his staff were not blind to the political benefits that would flow from a bold, dramatic raid."[65] In the end, the ignominious failure of the mission was clearly a factor in Carter's loss to Ronald Reagan in the 1980 election.

Throughout early 1980 the Carter administration debated a rescue mission and strike into Iran. Secretary of State Vance and the Department of State generally opposed the plan, arguing that it would fail, that it could result in the loss of many lives, and that, in the end, it would play into the hands of the Khomeini regime. In this assessment, Vance relied on his Iran experts at State and on leading Iran specialists in American universities. On April 11, 1980, the president held a special meeting of the National Security Council at which it was decided to go ahead with the raid into Iran. Brzezinski argued that it was time "to lance the boil" and that America's honor was at stake. This important meeting took place while Secretary of State Vance was away on vacation in Florida. His place at the meeting was taken by Deputy Secretary Warren Christopher, who had no knowledge of the rescue mission before he attended the session. Vance was not informed of the decision until he returned to Washington from vacation. He again voiced his misgivings and opposition to President Carter. He promised to tender his resignation once the rescue attempt had taken place.

At 7:30 P.M. on April 24, 1980, eight Sea Stallion RH-53D helicopters lifted off from the aircraft carrier *Nimitz* deployed in the Arabian Sea off the coast of southeastern Iran. The helicopters were to fly 600 miles to Desert One, a remote landing strip some 275 miles southeast of Tehran. Here they were to rendezvous with six C-130 Hercules transport planes, and the rescue team was to prepare for another trip to Desert Two, from which the commandos were to board vans and trucks for the 50-mile ride into Tehran. This ill-fated operation named Eagle Claw never proceeded beyond Desert One; it aborted in the early hours of the following morning. In the course of the operation, three of the eight helicopters were rendered inoperable, and one of them sliced into a C-130, setting both crafts aflame and killing eight American servicemen; a hurried exit in the C-130s resulted in the abandonment of helicopters, weapons, maps, and a wide array of secret documents. The entire adventure was an embarrassing tragedy of errors, the details of which remain little known in the United States. Investigations have pointed to dozens of serious mistakes made in the planning and attempted execution of the operation.[66] In short, the American eagle left a broken claw in the deserts of Iran in April 1980.

Many Iran experts believe that the flawed planning extended especially to the Tehran stage of the operation and that in some ways it was fortunate that the mission aborted at Desert One. If the commandos had managed to reach Tehran, there would almost certainly have been massive casualties of both Americans and Iranians. Tehran's citizens lived in packed and crowded circumstances all around the rescue site and would have appeared in large numbers directly in the midst of the operation. Assault leader Charlie Beckwith has been quite outspoken in the methodology of the raid: "When we went into that Embassy, it was our aim to kill all Iranian guards—the people holding our hostages—and we weren't going in there to arrest them; we were going in there to shoot them right between the eyes, and to do it with vigor."[67] If Beckwith needed outside help during the operation in Tehran, he was to call in C-130 transports armed with machine guns and 105-millimeter cannon to "hose down the streets." In fact, besides the C-130s, the plan called for having huge C-141 transport aircraft on call in case there were too many dead and wounded to fit inside the two C-130s.[68] This part of the raid would have almost certainly resulted in the deaths of a number of the American hostages. One hostage was quoted as "thanking God for the sandstorm."[69]

In Washington, having failed in one attempt, Brzezinski boldly and immediately began to make plans for another military adventure. But President Carter appointed Edmund Muskie to replace Cyrus Vance, who had resigned as promised, and now placed all emphasis on diplomatic tactics. Muskie's low-key negotiating approach along with changing political exigencies in Iran ultimately resulted in the release of the hostages on January 20, 1981. The final agreement was complex and involved both political promises and reciprocal economic and international banking arrangements. Although many Americans proclaimed the release and agreement a victory, the hostage episode was, if anything, a serious defeat for American foreign policy. After calling attention to a sign in one of the celebration parades that read "U.S. 52, Iran 0," former hostage Barry Rosen writes that this mentality "expressed the wishful thinking of hundreds of people I talked to, most of whom resented my opinion that we hadn't *won*, or that I myself wasn't proof of this." He concludes that "the entire episode was closer to defeat for both sides, which no amount of celebrating could transform into its opposite."[70]

In the longer run, Rosen's analysis is quite correct. The hostage incident left a legacy of distrust, misunderstanding, and hatred that will plague Iranian-American relations for years. In this sense, both sides are losers. The collapse of American power in the Iranian desert in April 1980 rankled U.S. military and political leaders, who waited for the opportunity to score a dramatic success in their relations with Iran. According to the testimony of NSC officials during the July 1987 Select Committee Hearings on the Iran-Contra affair, it was the lingering embarrassment of this adventure in 1980 that helped promote the ill-fated arms for hostages initiative of 1985–86. Such is the manner in which mistakes of the past smooth the way for policy errors in the future.

Within the short-term context of Iranian revolutionary politics, on the other hand, there is little doubt that the militants and extremists gained a great deal from the hostage episode. They used it effectively to take control of a revolution. The United States became their unwitting ally by publicizing the event far out of proportion to its significance in the world of politics, by personalizing and moralizing, by threatening and posturing, and by attacking Iran in a rescue attempt that was fatally flawed in both planning and execution.

Khomeini had long been warning the Iranian people of an impending American attack. To the Iranians, the failed rescue attempt proved this prediction to be correct and greatly enhanced Khomeini's credibility. Khomeini pointed out that even the mighty United States with all its modern technology had fallen before a God who was acting as Iran's protector. In his words, God had thrown sand into the motors of the helicopters. As Carter and his advisers stepped up the confrontation with Iran, they reinforced the position of the religious extremists. It was only later that Carter had second thoughts about his policies and speculated that a low-key approach may in the end have been the best. "But later, when the press was excluded from Iran, I think the issue would have died down a lot more if I had decided to ignore the fate of the hostages or if I had decided just to stop any statements on the subject. That may have been the best approach."[71]

The hostage-taking served five interrelated purposes for the Iranian revolutionary extremists. First and foremost, as emphasized above, it enabled the extremist factions to gain the ascendancy over the moderates. Second, it provided the religious extremists with the political opportunity and capital to defeat the radical challenge from the left. By taking strong and dramatic action against the United States, the militant religious forces preempted the threat of the radical left. Third, it rallied the masses of Iranian people behind the revolution by providing them with the constant specter of a powerful external opponent. Fourth, it provided the revolutionaries with hostages against the perceived threat of an imminent American act to reverse the revolution. Finally, it provided retribution. A weaker country had taken direct action against a superpower—a superpower whose outcries provided daily evidence of its embarrassment and political impotence.

After national ceremonies of celebration at the return of the hostages, American political leaders wanted to forget the entire hostage episode as quickly as possible. The widely discussed congressional hearings held in March 1981 proved to be nothing but brief, perfunctory exercises involving limited, shallow questions. Certain former hostages who were invited to testify were themselves embarrassed and disturbed by this exercise. Once the hostages were released, even the Department of State chose to ignore what had happened. In the words of John Limbert, an extremely talented Iran specialist and former hostage: "*No one* spoke to any of the Persian-speaking political officers among the hostages to find out what happened and who the captors were. It wasn't until April, 1981 after several of us had urged such a meeting that it was organized. My overall impression is that most officials, with a few exceptions, just didn't care."[72] A serious examination of what had happened and why would certainly have uncovered many unpalatable truths. It would have also done America an enormous favor by providing a badly needed explanation so that errors, oversights, and misunderstandings made in the past may not necessarily have to be repeated in the future.

The Iran-Iraq War

On September 22, 1980, Iraqi troops invaded Iran along a four-hundred-mile front while Iraqi aircraft carried out strikes against a dozen Iranian airfields. When the Iraqis struck, the Iranian revolution was at a low point and intense internal power struggles were in progress in Tehran. The economy was extremely fragile; the Kurds were in revolt in the northwest; and counterrevolutionary forces of all kinds were actively committing punishing acts of terrorism. Also, the hostage crisis was ongoing, and the United States was applying severe international pressure on the Iranian government. While there is little doubt that the Iranian regime was engaging in provocative broadcasts and propaganda against Iraq, it is also true that Iraq invaded Iran and was by any standard of international law the aggressor. Much has been made of the tensions over the Shatt al-Arab waterway, the religious disagreements between Sunni and Shi'i regimes, and longtime Persian-Arab ethnic differences, but the real cause of the war was a political struggle for hegemony of the Persian Gulf. In the process, Iraq hoped to suffocate and destroy the Iranian revolution, a not unappealing goal to such regional states as Saudi Arabia and the Persian Gulf shaykhdoms.

The attack caught revolutionary Iran by surprise. Nonetheless, Iran responded quickly and poured reinforcements into the southwest, where badly outnumbered Iranian soldiers, police, and citizens were fighting a desperate war of defense. After a month of brutal hand-to-hand fighting and very heavy casualties, the city of Khurramshahr fell to the invaders. This was the only major Iranian city to fall to the Iraqis; in May 1982 it was retaken by Iranian forces. Having slowed the invasion and having mobilized and consolidated their forces, the Iranians counterattacked in the fall of 1981 and spring of 1982. In two major battles fought in the area of Dezful in March–April 1982 and in Khurramshahr in April–May 1982, the Iranian troops won important victories, driving the Iraqis off most Iranian soil. In this offensive, the Iranians managed to coordinate the activities of 100,000 regular troops, 30,000 Revolutionary Guards, and another 30,000 members of the popular militia.[73]

During 1983 Iran again went on the offensive, attempting to drive into Iraqi soil and hoping for a breakthrough that would destroy the regime of Saddam Hussein in Baghdad. These invasions were largely failures, and the war degenerated into a campaign of massive Iranian human-wave attacks on fixed Iraqi positions protected by millions of deadly mines and a modern computerized Iraqi defense dug in and covering Iranian advances with overlapping fields of fire. In this struggle of man against machine, the casualty numbers were staggering. With the possible exception of World War I, the casualties as percentages of population figures have been the highest of any war in this century. As the longest Middle East war in recent history, the Iran-Iraq conflict resulted in an estimated 400,000 deaths and 1 million wounded on the Iranian side and 300,000 deaths and 900,000 wounded on the Iraqi side. By 1988 Iran had suffered more battle deaths than the United States in World War II, and Iran had only one-third the population that America had in 1945. Reliable sources indicate that by 1986 the economic costs of the conflict were already as high as $600 billion.[74]

Between 1983 and 1988, Iran changed its military strategy to stress a war of attrition. Unrelenting pressure was put on the Iraqis, who, with a much smaller population, were already stretched very thinly along their line of defense. This new Iranian policy of probing, pushing, and pressuring resulted in two successful limited offenses in February 1984 and February 1986. In the first, Iran managed to take the oil-rich Majnun Islands within Iraqi territory, and in the second Iran captured the southern port city of Fao. In January 1987, Iran mounted successive attacks against Basra, very nearly breaking through to that important city. This was to be the high point for Iran in the war.

Ever since the successful Iranian counterattacks of 1983, the Iraqi regime attempted to convince Iran to participate in peace talks. Iran refused, demanding (1) that Iraq withdraw all its troops from Iranian soil; (2) that Iraq pay reparations for the damage done to Iran; and (3) that Saddam Hussein step down as leader of Iraq. Iran stood by these demands until July 1988, when it accepted a cease-fire as outlined in U.N. Resolution 598.

Iran's acceptance of the cease-fire was partly a result of the sudden Iraqi escalation of the war beginning in the spring of 1988. Outfitting their Soviet-supplied Scud-B missiles with booster packs, the Iraqis fired 160 of these six-ton instruments of death into Tehran. At the same time, they resorted to the indiscriminate use of chemical gases all along the western front, seriously damaging Iranian morale. The fact that both superpowers had moved in unison behind Iraq also contributed to the Iranian decision to accept the cease-fire.

The American presence in the gulf, including the tragic July 3, 1988, accidental shooting down of an Iranian civilian airliner that killed 290 innocent passengers, weighed heavily on the minds of the Iranian leadership. The Soviet role was even more decisive. After the Iranians took Fao in 1986, the Soviet Union began a massive resupply operation to its Iraqi client state, pouring an estimated $9 billion in military aid into the Iraqi war chest. Thousands of Soviet advisers transformed Iraq's static defense into an offensive juggernaut that began to score victories on the battlefield. Iran came out of the war badly hurt, but its overall strength and commitment to its revolution remained strong.[75]

The United States, the Gulf War, and the Secret Attempt at Reentry

From the beginning of the Persian Gulf war, American policymakers were divided over what position the United States should assume in the conflict. For the first two years of the war, America took a position of strict neutrality. With the successful Iranian military campaigns of 1982 and the subsequent offenses against Iraq, policymakers began to fear an outright Iranian victory. Beginning in mid-1983, the United States moved to support Iraq. Those who backed this position included leading State Department officials, such as Secretary of State George Shultz and Assistant Secretary of State Richard Murphy, and, to a lesser extent, Secretary of Defense Casper Weinberger. Deeply concerned about a perceived Iranian threat to Saudi Arabia and with scant knowledge of the Iranian situation, they pursued an active anti-Iranian policy.

In 1982 the United States had removed Iraq from its list of countries considered supportive of international terrorism. High-level American officials began to visit Baghdad in late 1983, and the United States subsequently extended Iraq approximately $2 billion in commodity credits. Beginning in 1984, it became widely known that Iraq was benefiting from intelligence supplied through American sources. Saddam Hussein himself flatly stated in May 1984 that Iraq had the use of intelligence provided by AWACS flown by American pilots based in Saudi Arabia. On November 26, 1984, the United States publicly restored diplomatic relations with Iraq. When Iraqi-fired exocet missiles struck the American frigate USS *Stark* in the Persian Gulf on May 17, 1987, killing thirty-seven American sailors, the Reagan administration quickly accepted the official Iraqi statement that the attack was inadvertent. President Reagan afterwards stated curiously that "Iran is the real villain in the piece," and his administration issued a series of sharp warnings to Iran. In a May 27, 1987, press conference, the president crudely referred to Iran as "this barbaric country" when discussing a hypothetical scenario involving the closing down of international waterways.

These words and deeds understandably increased Iran's alienation from America. To Iran's leaders, the United States was continuing its hostile, counterrevolutionary policy and apparently intended to use every means at its disposal to destroy the Islamic Republic. Iran's leaders often referred to what they considered an obvious American double standard. Why had the United States never condemned Iraq's original attack of 1980 while it consistently criticized Iran's counteroffenses? Why did the United States sharply condemn revolutionary Iranian justice while it said not a word about the brutally repressive regime of Saddam Hussein? Why did America claim its intention to protect shipping in the southern gulf from Iranian attacks while it tolerated the much more frequent Iraqi attacks in the northern gulf? Why had the United States blamed Iran for the blatant Iraqi missile attack on the USS *Stark?*

Iran found itself in the unenviable position of having both world superpowers, the Soviet Union and the United States, supporting its wartime opponent. Besides this, Iraq received enormous military and technological support from France and technical assistance from such countries as Jordan, Morocco, and Egypt. The oil-rich traditional countries, primarily Saudi Arabia, provided Iraq with critical economic aid. With the exception of Syria and the partial exceptions of Libya and Algeria, Iran found itself quite alone. This international isolation, along with the accumulating pressures of the war and the alarming Soviet occupation of Afghanistan next door, led Iranian leaders in 1985–86 to participate in a secret rapprochement involving hostages, spare parts, secret American envoys, and a sordid assortment of international middlemen that broke into a major scandal in November 1986.

Beginning in 1985, a small group of high-ranking National Security Council officials began to implement their own policy toward Iran. With the encouragement of President Ronald Reagan himself and with the cooperation of the CIA, headed by William Casey, these officials sought to sell Iran badly needed arms and spare parts. In return Iran was expected to assist in the release of American hostages held in Lebanon. This program ran directly in the face of State Department policy, but it received the formal approval of President Reagan in the Presidential Finding he signed on January 17, 1986.

The secret, limited rapprochement was spearheaded initially by National Security Adviser Robert McFarlane with the strong backing of William Casey and the CIA. McFarlane's actions were encouraged by consultants such as Michael Ledeen, who maintained intimate Israeli connections.[76] Along with the Israelis, Ledeen urged the NSC to work with Manuchehr Ghorbanifar, an Iranian citizen and private entrepreneur alleged to have been a former employee of SAVAK.[77] Ghorbanifar had been considered unreliable by American intelligence in 1980–82, and he failed a CIA-administered lie detector test in January 1986, showing "deception on virtually all of the relevant questions."[78] Yet, although deeply distrusted, he continued for some time to represent America's line to Iran. Part of the reason concerned his sponsorship by Israel and by Ledeen, who described him as a "wonderful man. . . . almost too good to be true" and "one of those rare individuals who understands not only the subtleties of his own culture but our own as well."[79] Ledeen's confidence notwithstanding, the polygraph report concluded that "Ghorbanifar is clearly a fabricator and wheeler dealer who has undertaken activities prejudicial to U.S. interests."[80]

After McFarlane was replaced in December 1985 as NSC head by Vice Admiral John M. Poindexter, Poindexter and powerful operative Lt. Col. Oliver L. North carried the plan forward. The key event in the project occurred on May 25, 1986, when McFarlane, North, NSC Middle East adviser Howard Teicher, Israeli Amiram Nir, CIA Iran specialist the ubiquitous George Cave, and others flew into Tehran to exchange arms for American hostages. With the partial exception of Cave, who was brought into the project rather late in the game, Iranian expertise was notably absent. Government Iran specialists in the middle echelons of the Department of State had been frozen out of the picture both by Shultz's adamant opposition to any rapprochement with Iran and by the understanding at the NSC that such individuals would only oppose the entire methodology of the project. The plan was cobbled together in an atmosphere of arrogance and ignorance.

Blame for the long string of American tactical blunders must be widely spread through the policy-making system. The shortsighted, anti-Iran position of Shultz only encouraged the NSC caper. The lack of

U.S. expertise on Iran was appalling. American CIA agent George Cave, for example, a man with some Iran knowledge and a healthy skepticism toward entrepreneurs like Ghorbanifar, was presented by American intelligence officials as "an ideal interpreter. He speaks not only Farsi but also Mulla [*sic*] and understands all dialects."[81] Furthermore, NSC operatives actually appeared to believe that as part of the arms for hostages arrangement, Ayatollah Khomeini himself would "step down," reportedly on February 11, 1986, according to Colonel North's "notational timeline."[82]

Although Oliver North presented an attractive picture of a dashing young patriot and freedom-fighter in his appearances before the congressional select committee investigating the Iran-Contra affair in July 1987, his knowledge of Iran was minimal and his tactical judgment highly suspect. His testimony indicated that he was caught up in a cloak-and-dagger adventure that was considerably more complex than he realized. Despite his testimony that CIA director William Casey had portrayed Manuchehr Ghorbanifar as "an Israeli agent," North relied heavily on Ghorbanifar, who, among other things, provided him with the idea of using the funds raised from the sale of arms to Iran for aid to the Contras in Nicaragua. Ghorbanifar reportedly made the suggestion in the bathroom of a London hotel in January 1986. North thought that the suggestion of Iranian arms money for Contra assistance was "a right good idea," "a neat idea," and stated that Casey reportedly referred to it as "the ultimate covert operation." North also testified that it was in the bathroom that Ghorbanifar offered him a $1 million bribe. While admittedly lying repeatedly to the representatives of the government of Iran, North at the same time took at least one young Iranian official ("a brave young man and also a soldier in his country") on a private tour through the White House to "show him the Nobel Prize that was won by Teddy Roosevelt." This foreign policy practiced by a marine lieutenant colonel, therefore, involved fanciful hopes of a Khomeini resignation, ideas floated and bribes offered in bathrooms, private White House tours, widescale lying and deception, and complex exchanges involving arms for Iran, hostages in Lebanon, intelligence from Israel, and Contras in Nicaragua.[83]

Despite profound ignorance and tactical blunders, one might argue that the attempt to develop a line of communication with Iran was in America's strategic interests. A number of complex and interrelated considerations lay behind the decision to approach Iran—seven in all. Two were tactical, three were strategic, and two were external. The tactical reasons involved the hostages and the substance of intelligence reports. The strategic reasons focused on the Soviet challenge, the fear of the forceful exportation of the Iranian revolution to other gulf states, and the issue of petroleum prices. The two external contributing reasons involved support for the plan in both Israel and Iran itself.

One tactical reason involved the personal alarm and political impotence that Ronald Reagan and a number of his advisers felt over the American hostages held in Lebanon. According to Chief of Staff Donald Regan, the president wanted to keep the arms for hostages initiative going "not only for geopolitical reasons but also the fact that we weren't getting anywhere in getting more hostages out. And we were going to spend another Christmas with hostages there, and he is looking powerless and inept as President because he's unable to do anything to get the hostages out."[84] Reagan's preoccupation with hostages was clearly both humanitarian and political. The return of hostage Benjamin Weir on September 15, 1985, just after two Israeli shipments of arms to Tehran, kept the initiative alive. The United States quietly condoned and approved those arms transfers. Although Tehran did not control the extremist Shi'i groups in Lebanon, it did have the capacity to influence them. The hostage issue, however, was only one tiny piece of the decisional mosaic that underlay White House Iran policy.

A second tactical reason for the overture to Iran involved U.S. intelligence reports. In May 1985 Graham Fuller, the CIA's national intelligence officer for the Near East, prepared a memorandum warning that Iran was in severe danger of disintegration, that Khomeini's position was faltering, and that the USSR was poised to take advantage of this possible collapse. NSC analysts Howard Teicher and Donald Fortier reinforced this position in a June National Security Decision Directive (NSDD). These reports represented the fusion of ideas of the CIA and NSC and provided the intellectual rationale for the overture to Iran.[85] The Iran initiative was continued through 1986, when further intelligence studies reportedly indicated that Iran was now gaining the upper hand in the war with Iraq. Given its past tilt to the Iraqi side in the conflict, where would the United States be if Iran should win the war? To hedge its bets the United States pursued a contradictory, two-track policy toward Iran.

The first important strategic reason for the overture to Iran concerned the White House's preoccupation with Soviet power in the gulf region. Teicher's NSDD of June 17, 1985, stressed repeatedly the Soviet threat to Iran and to America's interests in the region.[86] These views were reinforced by influential advisers such as Donald Regan, who argued that the president felt "that we cannot allow Iran to fall into the Soviet camp."[87] The Israelis also shrewdly played on the administration's obsession with the Soviet threat to promote the rapprochement. A pattern of persuasion had already been established in this regard by the same cast of characters (Teicher, North, and so forth) at the NSC. In 1981 the CIA had prepared a fifteen-minute color movie for the president stressing Libyan Muʿammar Qaddafi's links to the Soviet Union.[88] This undoubtedly helped convince Reagan to approve the controversial air attack on Qaddafi's living quarters in Tripoli in April 1986.

The Reagan White House had a second strategic concern, the danger that Iran would export its revolution to neighboring conservative gulf states. America was especially worried about stability in Saudi Arabia, a country with one quarter of the world's proven reserves of petroleum. By 1985 it had become increasingly clear to all but the most obtuse that the Iranian revolution was a fact of life. It was time to work for commitments from the Islamic Republic that it would not attempt to destabilize these oil-rich traditional governments. According to the Reagan administration itself, during the negotiations through most of 1986, there were no Iran-sponsored incidents of terrorism. President Reagan himself referred to this record in his news conference of November 19, 1986, demonstrating the administration's goals in this regard. An integral part of this process was the Iran-Saudi rapprochement that had already begun on May 25, 1985, when Saud bin Faisal, the Saudi foreign minister, paid a surprise official visit to Tehran.

The final strategic reason was essentially economic. Throughout much of 1986, oil prices had plummeted until they bottomed at less than ten dollars per barrel. This occurred primarily as a result of sharply increased Saudi production, production that cut severely into the revenues of the major oil-producing states. In the United States, it badly crippled the economies of the Southwest; in Washington, the cries of the independent oil industry became loud and threatening. Influential national politicians from Texas—Vice President George Bush, Treasury Secretary James Baker, House Speaker Jim Wright, and Sens. Phil Gramm and Lloyd Bentsen—sought to defend the interests of their constituents. In the Middle East, Iran's and America's interests converged on this issue. Within the halls of OPEC, the Islamic Republic had long struggled for lower production and higher prices. The United States, meanwhile, needed prices high enough to protect the domestic oil industry but low enough to placate the consumer. The surprise Saudi-Iranian agreement on lower production in August–September 1986 achieved this goal, and prices rose steadily to the eighteen-to-twenty-dollar level per barrel in 1987. George Bush's trip to Saudi Arabia in the spring of 1986 must be understood in this context. It is significant that Howard Teicher's June 1985 NSDD draft report concluded with a reference to Iran's pricing policy within OPEC.[89] Also, one of the Iranians reportedly involved in the early stages of the rapprochement was Oil Minister Gholam Reza Aghazadeh.

As a major external contributing cause for the U.S. initiative in 1985–86, Israel was of course pursuing its own self-interest. Israel had long been shipping arms and spare parts to Iran on its own. By drawing the United States into the project, the Israelis hoped to gain American legitimacy for their goal of penetrating the leadership of the Islamic Republic of Iran. The centrality of the Israeli effort is seen in the fact that when McFarlane and his cohorts arrived in Tehran on May 25, 1986, to attempt to trade arms for hostages, an Israeli intelligence official, Amiram Nir, was aboard posing as an American. Nir had served as a counterterrorist adviser to Prime Minister Shimon Peres. Although U.S. officials questioned the participation of Nir on such a delicate American mission, Prime Minister Peres himself intervened on Nir's behalf.[90] Other Israelis deeply involved at various stages in this episode included David Kimche, Adolph Schwimmer, and Yaacov Nimrodi. Nimrodi felt he had been muscled out of the action by Nir, who had Oliver North's backing, and stated: "The starling Nir went to the raven North and told him, in the American phrase, 'whatever they can do we can do better.' "[91] Much of the NSC's information on Iran came from Israel, which had its own agenda and was deeply mistrusted by Iran.

The final contributing reason for the American approach to Iran is Iran itself. The arrangement was grudgingly approved at the highest levels of the Iranian government and had the tacit consent of Ayatollah Khomeini, who was genuinely concerned about the survival of the Islamic Republic, given his steadily declining health, Iran's deteriorating internal situation, and the threat of the Soviet Union, now occupying neighboring Afghanistan. From the Iranian side, it was part of a steady movement toward political pragmatism, which had been slowly replacing the ideological extremism dominant since the revolution. When the extremist factions in Iran saw themselves weakened by such developments, a group in their camp responded in October 1986 by leaking the story of the arms for hostages dealings. Only the direct intervention of Ayatollah Khomeini himself held the domestic political situation steady after these revelations. Iran was committed to a new relationship with the United States; after the original Ghorbanifar-Israel channel had been closed down, the Islamic Republic supported a second channel that they considered free from Israeli contamination and that led directly to Khomeini's office.

The reasons for the American overture to Iran are compelling when viewed from a strategic perspective. The American eagle cannot afford to be out of communication with the Iranian lion, the most powerful force in the Persian Gulf. Yet the methodology of the plan to establish this communication was poorly, clumsily, and unprofessionally conceived. It involved the wrong people (McFarlane, North, Teicher) advised by the wrong "experts" (Ledeen, Ghorbanifar) supported by the wrong allies (Israel); they went to the wrong place (Tehran) at the wrong time (during the month of Ramadan and after the United States had tilted to the Iraqi side in the gulf war) carrying the wrong tactical plan. The unprofessional and uninformed nature of this adventure jeopardized the credibility and political survival of both American and Iranian leaders, dealt another serious blow to the fading credibility of the United States in the international arena, and, in the process, threatened to freeze Iranian-American relations for another decade.

On the other hand, Khomeini and other Iranian leaders concluded in the mid-1980s that the Islamic Republic needed relations with the United States. If such relations involved mutual respect for one another's territorial integrity and national autonomy, if the United States retreated from its hostility toward the revolution and adopted a position of strict neutrality in the gulf war, then Iran would accept a normalization of relations. Prodded by their immediate need for arms and spare parts, the Iranians sought lines to the United States in 1985–86.

On the American side, the Islamic Republic of Iran is still largely viewed as a reactionary, repressive government directed by extremists, terrorists, and fanatics. Ronald Reagan's protestations that the United States had evidence that Iran had begun to change its terrorist ways met with disbelief and anger by most American political leaders and by the public. In the words of one Republican strategist: "The American people cannot yet swallow the idea of trading with those nasty Iranians, the same people who burned an American flag."[92] The hostage episode, in particular, has shaped America's views of revolutionary Iran for years to come. The pleas of many informed Americans, including a number of the hostages themselves, such as John Limbert, Barry Rosen, and Charles Scott, that the United States make an effort to understand the Iranian position, have largely fallen on deaf ears. Although the Iranian arms affair demonstrated that American leaders had momentarily begun to rethink the United States's Iran policy, the aftermath of the May 1987 Iraqi missile strike against the USS *Stark* revealed the reality of continuing American hostility toward Iran. As part of this tense atmosphere that developed following the Iran-Contra revelations, the Reagan administration began reflagging Kuwaiti oil tankers in July 1987. In September and October 1987, American helicopters opened fire on an Iranian ship and several patrol boats in the Persian Gulf. The U.S. justified these attacks on the grounds that its forces were retaliating against hostile actions taken by the Iranian navy. This nervous escalation in the gulf reached its climax on July 3, 1988, when the U.S. cruiser *Vincennes* mistakenly shot down an Iranian civilian airbus, killing all 290 people aboard.

On the Iranian side, distrust and anger prevailed as various American plots against the Islamic Republic were sporadically reported in the decade after the fall of the shah. In 1987, for example, it became public knowledge that U.S. intelligence agencies hired a private Texas firm known as Peregrine International Associates to carry out clandestine activities abroad. One of Peregrine's plans involved a 1982 plot to support a military coup against Iran that included the planned assassination of Ayatollah Khomeini. When the key Iranian military operative failed to appear in New York with the $120 million promised to finance the project, the plot died prematurely.[93]

Iran's views concerning the malevolence of America toward their revolutionary government were confirmed by the testimony of Lt. Col. Oliver North in July 1987. In his testimony before the congressional select committee investigating the Iran-Contra affair, North attempted to justify his actions by boasting of the duplicitous manner he used with the Iranian representatives. When questioned about making representations to the Iranians that were inaccurate, North agreed and described them as "blatantly false." In his own words, "I lied every time I met the Iranians."[94] In Tehran, such statements were duly noted, and anti-Americanism reached a fevered pitch after hundreds of demonstrating Iranians were killed by Saudi security forces during the religious pilgrimage to Mecca on July 31, 1987. Iranian leaders blamed the United States both for these deaths and for those that resulted from the July 3, 1988, downing of the civilian airbus.

The tragedy of America and Iran is that each side—the large numbers of Iranians committed to the Islamic Republic and most patriotic Americans—has failed to understand the other's point of view. Meanwhile, the governments of both countries develop their foreign policy in an atmosphere of paranoia, hatred, ignorance, and emotion. The clumsy and costly early attempts by both sides to cautiously re-establish relations have resulted in further misunderstanding and have shaken the credibility of both political systems. Nevertheless, there are signs that deep down both countries feel a common need to communicate and cooperate. Although the 1986–87 revelations followed by direct conflict in the gulf have set the timetable back, there will one day be another attempt. Until that succeeds, both the eagle and the lion will suffer as they confront one another in a tense and tumultuous world.

Secretary of State Cordell Hull, U.S. Ambassador to Iran Louis Dreyfus, Jr., and Foreign Minister of Iran Muhammad Sa'ed meet in Tehran before the 1945 Tripartite Conference in Moscow.

Muhammad Reza Shah Pahlavi and President Franklin D. Roosevelt confer at the Soviet Embassy in Tehran in 1945.

W. Averell Harriman, master diplomat and presidential envoy to Iran over four decades.

Muhammad Musaddiq, nationalist champion and prime minister of Iran, 1951–1953.

Prime Minister Muhammad Musaddiq being greeted
by Secretary of State Dean Acheson in New York in 1951.
Iranian ambassador to the United States
Nazrullah Entezam is pictured in the center.

Ambassador Henry F. Grady at his desk
in the U.S. Embassy in Tehran, March 195

President John F. Kennedy and the shah of Iran on an inspection trip to Camp LeJeune, North Carolina, during the shah's April 1962 visit to the United States. Vice President Lyndon B. Johnson is pictured following the two leaders.

Vice President Lyndon B. Johnson among Iranian villagers during his August 1962 official visit to Iran.

Muhammad Reza Shah with leading military officers during annual greeting ceremonies in Tehran in the late 1960s.

President Richard M. Nixon and the shah of Iran at the White House in July 1973 during the Shah's tenth visit to the United States.

Iranian minister of the economy Hushang Ansary embraces his friend Secretary of State Henry Kissinger during one of their many meetings in the 1970s.

The shah of Iran confers with Secretary of State Henry Kissinger at the shah's summer palace at Noshahr on the Caspian Sea, August 1976.

President Jimmy Carter and First Lady Rosalynn Carter with the shah and empress of Iran on the White House lawn during the shah's last official visit to the United States in November 1977.

Pro- and anti-Pahlavi demonstrators clash near the White House during welcoming ceremonies for the shah, November 1977.

Ayatollah Ruhollah Khomeini arrives by helicopter at Bihisht-i Zahra Cemetery on February 1, 1979, after fifteen years in exile. The ayatollah is greeted by half a million cheering Iranians.

Ayatollah Khomeini prepares to deliver his first speech to the Iranian people after his arrival back in Iran on February 1, 1979.

Ayatollah Hussein Ali Montazeri, a leading member of the Iranian ulama who is often considered the likely successor to Ayatollah Khomeini.

American workers aboard the USS *LaSalle* after having been evacuated from Iran on February 22, 1979, following the dramatic revolution that overthrew the monarchy.

Photo: Ch. Spengler, Sygma.

May 1979 anti-American demonstration in the streets of Tehran.

Aerial view of U.S. Embassy compound in Tehran, 1970.

United States Navy RH-53 helicopters off the deck of the USS *Nimitz* practice formation flying during the early evening on February 5, 1980, before embarking on the ill-fated hostage rescue mission.

Lieutenant Colonel Oliver North testifies on July 10, 1987, before the Senate Select Committee investigating the Iran-Contra arms affair of 1985–86.

PART II

9 Pahlavism in America: The Informal Politics of Foreign Policy-Making

For nearly four decades, the Pahlavi regime in Iran carefully and consciously developed personal and professional ties with the American political and financial elite. These relations expanded and tightened over the years and came to include ties with American leaders in the fields of government, finance, industry, academia, and the mass media. In the 1970s, planeloads of American dignitaries descended on Iran, almost always at the invitation of Iranian leaders in Tehran and often at the insistence of the officials of the Iranian Embassy in Washington. Meanwhile, the shah and his financial advisers and friends had representation and low-key partnerships that extended deeply into the heartland of America. Besides their business arrangements on both coasts, they included activities in Wisconsin, Ohio, Missouri, and Texas.

The Pahlavis' central relationship was with the political and economic interests in New York and Washington. Here, a long-term informal relationship linked Muhammad Reza Shah Pahlavi with perhaps the most powerful financial-political center in the United States. This relationship involved the Rockefeller family and such Rockefeller advisers and clients as Henry Kissinger. Over the years, the Rockefellers (particularly Nelson) consistently promoted the shah of Iran in America. The Shah, in return, cultivated the Rockefeller connection, and the Pahlavis and Rockefellers remained in close personal touch. Nelson, David, and John D. Rockefeller III frequently traveled to Iran to meet with the shah and his highest-ranking officials. These visits continued right up to the revolution. Both Nelson and David Rockefeller made separate trips to Iran in 1976 and 1977; Nelson returned again in the spring of 1978. The Rockefellers were the only American businessmen whose appointments with the shah were arranged before they left the United States. Such appointments were usually made once the American party arrived in Tehran. While David Rockefeller has acknowledged a twenty-year relationship with the shah, Nelson's

Iran connections went back even further. During his many trips to the United States, the shah met with the Rockefellers in New York and in Washington.

As an employee of the Rockefellers, Henry Kissinger easily developed a partiality to the shah. When Kissinger became the most influential foreign policymaker in the United States during the Nixon and Ford presidencies, he not surprisingly strengthened the link between the shah and America. The unprecedented political and economic arrangements between the United States and Iran described earlier in this book were products of Kissinger's influence. As we shall see, the Rockefeller backing of the shah provided much of the bedrock for the uncritical and short-sighted policies that the United States adopted toward Iran. This support transcended political party identifications and presidential administrations in Washington. And it carried with it the active approval of other powerful personalities both inside and outside the government, including Kermit Roosevelt, John J. McCloy, David Lilienthal, William Rogers, and Richard Helms.

The Rockefeller-Pahlavi connection always remained partially hidden. Like most informal political elites who exert enormous public influence privately, the Rockefeller Pahlavites worked hard over the years to exert their influence quietly and unobtrusively. In fact, they seldom had to engage in direct lobbying or public relations for the shah. It was enough that decision makers in Washington knew of their special personal interest in and support for the shah of Iran. They held private dinners and provided forums for the shah when he was in the United States. In Iran, they arranged their meetings with the shah directly, seldom involving official American representatives. When asked about any special connections they may have had with the shah, the American friends of the shah usually chose either to deflect the question or to discuss the relationship in terms of "friendship."

Because of their accessibility to the world's political elite, the Rockefellers stood in a privileged position between heads of state and governments. Over the years, David Rockefeller acted as an influential middleman between many of the most powerful leaders in the world. In the fall of 1964, for example, he met privately for two hours with Premier Nikita Khrushchev in Leningrad and promptly returned to the United States, where he submitted a full report to the Johnson administration. In an extraordinary memorandum filed in the Lyndon B. Johnson Presidential Library, National Security Adviser McGeorge Bundy briefed President Johnson on Rockefeller's meeting with Khruschev. Rockefeller himself was then on his way to visit Johnson in the Oval Office. In Bundy's words: "Rockefeller conveyed to

Khruschev one important message which I had given on a totally-off-the-record basis to Norman Cousins, and which Cousins gave to Rockefeller for Khruschev—namely, that it is important for the Chairman to keep out of the election. Khruschev indicated to Rockefeller that he understood this point and would behave himself." But Rockefeller's business with Khrushchev and Johnson was not only political; it also concerned Rockefeller's own financial interests. Bundy's memorandum to President Johnson stated that "Rockefeller's bank is also having some trouble with the Arabs, but the State Department has been helping him all the way, and I am urging him not to raise this with you."[1] Rockefeller, therefore, had no need to broach this sensitive subject. The matter was already taken care of.

Given this experience and the ideological mind-set of the Soviet Union, it is little wonder that Russian leaders are preoccupied with the idea that the Rockefellers control America. Soviet diplomats in Tehran constantly queried their American counterparts about details of various Rockefeller visits to Tehran. During one luncheon meeting in Tehran in October 1976, for example, the Soviet second secretary asked American political officer John Stempel about a recent visit by David Rockefeller to Iran. He brought the subject up four times during the meal until Stempel "chided him about accepting the traditional Marxist linkage between big capital and big government, and he responded in the same light vein with his usual patronizing words about Americans never being aware of 'fundamental' relationships between big capital and government."[2]

David Rockefeller has seen little "inappropriate" in his extraordinary international political influence:

> I don't see anything that is inappropriate about meeting with heads of state. In the first place, they have the choice as to whether they want to see me or not. I'm not imposing myself on them. And most of them, I think, feel an exchange of views with a businessman who travels a lot and knows a lot can be productive. It gives them a different perspective than they may get merely from talking to diplomats or government officials.
>
> I feel very strongly it would be improper to persuade any country to do anything that would be against the best interest of the United States. In that connection I would point out that almost invariably when I go on trips I talk with people in our government before and after the trip. Not infrequently, they are very happy to get information and perspectives from me that may be a little different from what they're getting from the ambassador in the country.[3]

Although both were committed Pahlavi supporters, David and

Nelson Rockefeller were quite different personalities, and this expressed itself in their relations with Iran. Nelson was personally much closer to the shah, and they maintained an outgoing, frank friendship. David was no less committed, but his loyalty to the Pahlavis was dominated by business considerations. It was David, therefore, who usually led investment missions and who persistently promoted Iranian-American financial ventures of all kinds. Because of Chase Manhattan Bank's deep and obvious financial involvement with Pahlavi Iran, David was more circumspect in his dealings with Iran. Most matters of personal, regional, and international politics involving Iran and America were handled by Nelson until his sudden death on January 26, 1979—ten days after the shah fled Iran and five days before Ayatollah Khomeini returned from fifteen years of exile. His death shifted new responsibilities to David's shoulders. In the struggle that was developing between the Pahlavites and the Carter administration, therefore, Henry Kissinger, representing Rockefeller interests among others, now had to work exclusively with David.

With the coming of the Iranian revolution in 1978–79, the informal political elite of Pahlavi backers were forced into the open. In 1978 the Rockefellers, Kissinger, and others had managed to exert their influence silently, as always. On May 5, Nelson Rockefeller made his last trip to Iran and visited the shah on Kish Island. At the time, Rockefeller, like all American Pahlavites, was confident about the shah's capacity to maintain control. As he often did, Rockefeller assured the shah of America's continuing commitment to him and to his rule. When the domestic political situation in Iran continued to spin out of control, Rockefeller telephoned Zbigniew Brzezinski on November 2, 1978, and urged him to support the shah unconditionally. Brzezinski immediately carried Rockefeller's message to President Carter and the National Security Council. In January 1979, shortly before his death, Nelson Rockefeller met with Iranian ambassador Ardeshir Zahedi in New York. The two discussed the deteriorating situation of the shah and outlined strategies that might save his throne.

With the revolution successful and with Nelson Rockefeller gone, the David Rockefeller-Kissinger group now felt it necessary to move directly to support the exiled shah. Orchestrating this attempt was Henry Kissinger, who applied constant pressure on the Carter administration on behalf of the shah. Although Kissinger's efforts were concentrated on April–June 1979, they had begun in January and continued as late as November, when he was again in touch with Brzezinski. The admission of the deposed shah of Iran into the United States provides an excellent case study of the power of informal actors in

American foreign policy-making. It also explains much about the American-Iranian relationship both before and after the traumatic revolution of 1978–79.

Professional Diplomatic Resistance to the Admission of the Shah

Although there was occasional minor disagreement, the strong consensus of the State Department professionals was that admitting the shah to the United States would be a serious mistake. Iran specialists warned repeatedly that it would be interpreted as a hostile act, that the revolutionaries were watching to see if the United States intended to give refuge to the shah, whom they considered a political criminal. More importantly, in the revolutionaries' eyes such a move would signal the first step in a policy designed to return the shah to the throne in a manner reminiscent of 1953. Although some American observers considered this interpretation to be exaggerated nonsense, Iran specialists argued that what counted in Iran was perceptions and not necessarily realities. Iranians remained paranoid about the Pahlavi-American connection. Objectively, as indicated in chapter 8, U.S. leaders had done little since the revolution to allay their suspicions.

State Department professionals agreed that it would not be in America's national interest to admit the shah into the United States. Henry Precht and Warren Christopher on three occasions wrote memorandums arguing against the admission of the shah. On March 6, 1979, Henry Precht had written a memorandum strongly opposing any admission of the shah to the United States: "Should the Shah come to the US it would be a disaster for US-Iranian relations, for the Western position in the region and would create a severe security problem for our personnel in Tehran and USG officials in Washington. I was not sure that we would be able to maintain an Embassy in Tehran."[4] On July 26, President Jimmy Carter and Secretary of State Cyrus Vance contacted the U.S. Embassy in Tehran about the repercussions of admitting the shah to the United States. In the cable of inquiry, Vance asked specifically about the safety of official Americans if such an action were to be taken. "I would like to have your personal and private evaluation of the effect of such a move on the safety of Americans in Iran (especially the official Americans in the compound) as well as on our relations with the Government of Iran." Although the possibility for admission at some later date was entertained, immediate admission was ruled out. Meanwhile, from Tehran, this opinion was seconded in especially strong terms by Chargé d'Affaires Bruce Laingen and his staff. On July 28, September 2, and September 30,

1979, Laingen and other officials in Tehran recommended that the shah not be admitted to the United States.

In a long response to Vance on July 28, Laingen recommended against admitting the shah anytime soon: "I conclude that for the shah to take up residence in the U.S. in the immediate future, by which I mean the next 2–3 months, would continue as before to be seriously prejudicial to our interests and to the security of Americans in Iran." Laingen indicated that, depending on developments, it might be possible to reconsider sometime in the fall. In brief, "granting asylum to the shah now would negate much that we have achieved to date."[5]

On August 2, Henry Precht responded to Laingen's assessments, indicating his agreement. He did cautiously recommend eventual admission of the shah, perhaps by January 1980. Precht argued, however, that the move would be highly dangerous and that the Iranian government should be told about the tremendous "pressures" that were being applied, that the U.S. government should publicly state its view that any Pahlavi claim to the throne was now invalid, and that the shah should be warned privately against any counterrevolutionary activities. Even this might not be good enough, Precht warned, since "the danger of hostages being taken in Iran will persist. We should make no move towards admitting the Shah until we have obtained and tested a new and substantially more effective guard force for the Embassy." Two weeks later, Assistant Secretary of State Warren Christopher concluded a communication to Tehran with the promise that the shah was not to be admitted to the United States. "You may inform the Iranians, as we have recently done in Washington, that there has been no change in the USG attitude towards a trip by the shah to the U.S."[6]

Twice in September, the U.S. Embassy in Tehran sent messages to Washington recommending against admitting the shah. A September 2 monthly status report on embassy security contained the following warning: "Any decision to allow him [the shah] or his family to visit the U.S. would almost certainly result in an immediate and violent reaction. The ability and/or desire of the PGOI [Provisional Government of Iran] to contain such actions is questionable." Less than a month before the shah was admitted to the United States, Laingen sent another communication to Washington confirming his July 28 communication recommending against the shah's admission. Laingen had received word that the shah was ill and might be admitted for humanitarian reasons. After emphasizing the extremist atmosphere in Iran and the strong anti-shah feeling among the clerics, Laingen responded in a September 30 cable: "Given that kind of atmosphere and the kind of public posturing about the shah by those who control or influence public opinion here, I doubt that the shah being ill would have much ameliorating effect on the degree of reaction here."[7] On October 3 in New York, Secretary of State Vance indicated to Foreign Minister Ibrahim Yazdi of Iran that the shah would not be admitted in the foreseeable future. President Carter supported this position.

In consultations with outside experts on Iran, the Department of State generally received strong recommendations against admitting the shah. In May, for example, I concluded a presentation to the Department of State with the suggestion that U.S. statesmen immediately indicate to the new government in Iran that America had no intention of supporting a counterrevolution such as had occurred twenty-five years before. With this in mind:

> American national interests would be compromised even further in Iran if the shah were to be granted asylum at any time in the United States. Iranians from all walks of life are watching this particular situation very closely indeed. Whether or not the shah will be permitted to settle in the United States has been a leading subject of discussion in Tehran over the past month. Whatever post-revolutionary conflict is going on in Iran today, there is deep consensus in the anger and animosity towards the shah. If he were to come to America, the anti-American feelings and suspicions would deepen dangerously.[8]

Many others, including former ambassador William Sullivan, warned the American government not to admit the shah. Experienced Iranian statesmen also sounded these warnings. On September 17, 1979, for example, Henry Precht met with Ambassador Mahmoud Foroughi in the State Department dining room. Foroughi, a distinguished high-ranking official in the shah's foreign service who had fallen from favor, told Precht that the shah was bitterly hated in Iran and that "it would be very, very bad for the U.S. and for the West if the Shah settled here. Iranians would not understand. They would see our acceptance as an act against Iran and against our own long-term interests. Let the Shah go to South Africa. Everyone knew of his close ties with that regime. He had not been a true friend of the U.S. and had used us for his own advantage."[9]

By late summer, a tiny but widening difference of opinion among professional policymakers on the Pahlavi admission issue was noticeable. As the months of 1979 wore on, State Department officials gradually came under increased pressure to admit the shah. They adopted a stalling tactic, hoping to put off the actual admission as long as possible. The diplomats in Tehran, on the other hand, remained adamant in their opposition to any Pahlavi asylum. The reasons for this growing difference seem quite clear. In Washington, the pressures for admission emanated from several directions. With election year approaching, they originated increasingly from the White House itself. Brzezinski led the charge from the National Security Council. In the background, the Rockefeller-Kissinger group persistently pressed and pushed. In Tehran, Laingen and his staff were on the front lines and in a much better position to judge the realities of the situation. They were also quite aware of their own vulnerability.

When the shah was admitted to the United States on October 22, the diplomats in Tehran reacted in horror and anger. The most sensitive among them and those who knew Iran best were especially outraged. Colonel Charles Scott, for example, strongly believed that long-term American interests clearly took precedence over any rationale for admitting the shah. And he had been promised in briefings in Washington that the shah would not be granted asylum in the United States. When he was told in Tehran that the shah was in fact to be admitted, Colonel Scott "felt that we had been betrayed by our own people. How could they admit the Shah and leave us in Iran to face the angry wolves? It made no sense to me. My mind flashed back to my briefings at the State Department when I was told there were no plans to permit the Shah to enter the U.S. I had been lied to and I didn't like it."[10]

Hostage and Iran specialist Barry Rosen described the reactions of American diplomats when Chargé d'Affaires Laingen told them on October 22 that the shah was that same day to be admitted to the United States: "Total silence followed. In time it was broken by a faint groan. Faces literally went white. I put my hands over my own face and had a good think—not about policy or professional duties but how much I wanted to go home." Rosen's analysis of the situation is worth quoting:

> Despite many strong reasons for preserving our dignity by welcoming the Shah, I was utterly opposed to it. Having failed so often to recognize the power of symbols to the Iranians—and the significance in particular of the Shah as the symbol of evil—to do so again would announce that we understood nothing about the revolution. Those who bruited the possibility probably didn't understand that admission would be a seemingly calculated insult to almost an entire nation. Sooner or later we had to acknowledge that our support of the Shah had been badly conceived and managed. In short, we had to let go of him; preserving our honor at this stage with otherwise expected hospitality simply cost too much hatred. The risk also was too great.[11]

Other hostages agreed. Budget and Fiscal Officer Bruce German, for example, wrote in the *Washington Post* that "the majority of the hostages know that the shah should never have been allowed to enter the United States, regardless of the reasons given." He asked sharply: "Moreover, who made the decision? Kissinger, Rockefeller?" In a letter to his wife, German reportedly warned: "Watch out for Kissinger, Rockefeller, and Helms."[12]

In New York City for the opening sessions of the United Nations in early October, Foreign Minister Ibrahim Yazdi had met with Cyrus Vance. At this meeting Yazdi had bluntly asked Vance if the United States had any intention of admitting the shah. Vance recollected telling Yazdi that "we did not rule out admitting him at some point" and that Yazdi's reaction was "noncommittal." Gary Sick reports that Vance replied that "we had told the shah that we did not believe that he should come to the United States at this time. What the future might hold, he could not say." Yazdi himself has stated that Vance "assured me that the U.S. had no plans to take the shah into the country."[13] Although Vance's response may have been diplomatically tactful and he may have intended to hedge, two things are certain. First, Yazdi was deeply concerned that the United States might give refuge to the shah and, if so, that the position of the moderates in Iran would be seriously compromised. Second, Yazdi himself felt that he had been given the assurance that the United States would not admit the shah anytime in the near future.

Muhammad Reza Shah Pahlavi was suddenly admitted to the United States when the administration was informed that he was seriously ill and that he required medical care available only in America. Physicians close to David Rockefeller had examined the shah and found in late September that he was indeed very sick. On October 18, his illness was diagnosed as cancer and complications thereof. Word was immediately sent to the U.S. government. It was at this point that Secretary of State Vance changed his position and joined Brzezinski, Mondale, Jordan, and others urging that the shah be admitted to the United States for medical reasons.

Like the American diplomats in Tehran, the members of Mehdi Bazargan's government were shocked by the admission of the shah. They too thought that Washington had promised not to admit him. They desperately attempted to control the damage by asking that the shah be treated outside of New York, that he be insulated from the American press, that Iranian doctors have the opportunity to examine him, and that his visit be as brief as possible. They insisted that the Iranian people would refuse to believe that medical arguments were the primary reason for the shah's entry. The U.S. government turned a deaf ear to these requests.

The reaction of the acting chief of the Political Division of the Ministry of Foreign Affairs, Parsa Kia, demonstrates the magnitude of the Iranian regime's desperation. In an October 31, 1979, discussion with Chargé d'Affaires Bruce Laingen at the Foreign Ministry in Tehran, Parsa Kia brought up the subject of the shah in the United States. In a forty-minute "emotional, unofficial, and personal plea," he attempted to convince Laingen of the necessity that the shah leave America immediately. He indicated that the Bazargan government could not control the situation and that the shah's continued presence in the United States could well result in the breaking of relations between Iran and America. Like many others in the United States and Iran, Parsa Kia sensed serious trouble; four days later it came. Iranian extremists overran the U.S. Embassy and took American diplomats hostage.[14]

The Prevalence of Informal Politics: How to Admit a Shah

As the field general in the campaign for the shah's admission to the United States, Henry Kissinger had enormous resources. James Reston noted in early 1979 that Kissinger was "the most influential outside-insider of our time." His resources included, above all else, a wide array of influential contacts both in the United States and abroad. Within the United States, he was an integral part of the Rockefeller organization, having been hired as a consultant and adviser by Nelson Rockefeller himself. Kissinger has referred to Rockefeller as his "friend and mentor" and dedicated the first volume of his massive political memoirs to Rockefeller. Kissinger had become a Rockefeller family counselor in the late 1950s, and he worked hard in Nelson Rockefeller's losing campaign for the Republican nomination for president in 1968. Although both Rockefeller and Kissinger despised Nixon, to his own great surprise, Kissinger ended up as Nixon's national security adviser. After waiting to see if his "mentor" would be offered a cabinet post, Kissinger took the position at Rockefeller's insistence. Kissinger's presence in the White House provided Nelson Rockefeller with a direct pipeline to the center of power.

Kissinger confided in Rockefeller behind Nixon's back, and the two often poked fun at the president, whom they apparently considered crude and unstable. In one exchange of taped telephone calls, Kissinger praised Nixon profusely when the president asked for his opinion on a memorandum he had written describing his China visit. He told Nixon that he had been "very, very clever" and "very, very good." Shortly afterwards, Kissinger spoke to Rockefeller about Nixon's report. The two friends snickered together over the memorandum. After telling Rockefeller that he had read Nixon's report on his China trip, he went on to describe the President as "such an egomaniac. All he wrote was . . ." "His memoirs," interjected Rockefeller. "Just what he said. Nothing what the Chinese said. Practically nothing. A fascinating account of himself," Kissinger sneered. "I love it," Rockefeller responded.[15] This exchange reveals a great deal about Kissinger's methods. It also documents his especially close personal relationship with Nelson Rockefeller.

Henry Kissinger was both a foreign policy adviser and a personal protégé-confidant of the Rockefellers. Besides being a paid consultant for years, he received cash gifts. There was one documented $50,000 gift apparently given him just three days before he joined the Nixon administration and a reported $65,000 trust fund established for him by Nelson. Kissinger also married Rockefeller's aide, Nancy Maginnes. Rockefeller announced the engagement and provided the couple with one of the family planes for the honeymoon. When Kissinger was absent from a ceremony in which he was awarded the Family of Man Medal in 1973, Nelson Rockefeller accepted it in his stead, stating succinctly: "He's never let me down and he's never let the country down." During the early 1970s, Kissinger shipped his personal files to the Rockefeller estate in Pocantico Hills, New York. In brief, Henry Kissinger had close personal and political ties to the Rockefellers.[16]

After Nelson Rockefeller died, Kissinger maintained his connections with the family primarily through David. The campaign to admit the shah put both men in even closer touch as they fought together to help their old friend, political partner, and business associate. The Rockefellers and Kissinger shared similar perspectives on international affairs. In fact, the relationship was intellectually incestuous and mutually reinforcing: Kissinger advised the Rockefellers while working hard to anticipate their opinions. David, whose greatest institutional loyalty had always been to the Chase Manhattan Bank, strongly supported the American intervention in Vietnam until the bitter end. In South Africa, in 1967 he had criticized apartheid while defending major American financial investments there. His arguments were still being repeated by the Reagan administration in the late 1980s; namely, that if American business pulled out, "the greatest impact would fall on blacks," and that South African blacks were "far better off economically than the black people anywhere else in the African continent."[17] In general, the Rockefellers and Kissinger showed a penchant for supporting dictatorial regimes that were both probusiness and anticommunist. The twin evils of many of these regimes—corruption and oppression—were not considered matters of equal concern. They established relationships with the top of the international pyramids of power and not with the social forces that ultimately determine the long-term future of Third World societies—the masses.

Like many American diplomats and policymakers who worked with Iran, the Rockefeller-Kissinger group maintained constant contact with the shah and his small circle of political and financial advisers. The International Basic Economy Corporation (IBEC), created by Nelson Rockefeller in 1947, had a long history of involvement in the construction business in Iran. Chase Manhattan Bank itself established a 35-percent interest in the Iran International Bank, created in 1974. In New York, and especially in London, Chase Manhattan was the recipient of huge deposits made by the National Iranian Oil Company. According to one researcher: "The Shah ordered that all his government's major operating accounts be held at Chase and that letters of credit for the purchase of oil be handled exclusively through Chase. The bank also became the agent and lead manager for many of the loans to Iran. In short, Iran became the crown jewel of Chase's international banking portfolio."[18] Even as late as 1979, NIOC dollars flowed through Chase Manhattan at the rate of $300 million to $500 million per week.[19]

Just as the Rockefeller-Kissinger relations were sealed by financial and personal considerations, Kissinger's relations were similarly reinforced with Pahlavi Iran. Kissinger had close relations with such Pahlavi inner-circle members as Ardeshir Zahedi and Hushang Ansary. Both had been ambassadors to the United States. Ansary was the economic official with whom Kissinger signed the multibillion-dollar trade agreement in 1975. Zahedi was an extremely effective public relations official for the shah in America and reportedly plied Kissinger with gifts over the years. According to Zahedi's former personal secretary, Delphine Blachowicz, these included a jeweled clock and a blue carpet in 1973–74 and the everpresent caviar that Blachowicz reportedly delivered to Kissinger's suite at the Waldorf Towers on one occasion. Published sources indicate that Zahedi gave Kissinger a carpet for his New York City apartment as "kind of a going away present" from one friend to another. Despite the gifts, the Kissinger-

Zahedi relationship lacked somewhat in warmth since Kissinger privately considered Zahedi his intellectual inferior.[20]

Such was not the case with Ansary, who continued close personal and business associations with Kissinger after the fall of the shah. According to a *Forbes* magazine investigation in 1985–86, for example, Ansary had recently purchased a hotel/casino/car rental company in the Netherlands Antilles called SunResorts NV. Ansary, who reportedly became a naturalized citizen of the United States in 1986, planned to use this venture to make a major acquisition. One of the members of the board of directors of the new company was Henry Kissinger himself, who greatly respected his friend "Hushang's" shrewd, uncanny capacity to make money. According to *Forbes*, the price of the stock of SunResorts "took off in April [1986] after Ansary tapped his gilt-edged old-boy network and unveiled a new blue-ribbon board of directors including Henry Kissinger."[21] Ansary had managed to escape to the United States just before the revolution. With the financial fortune he had at his disposal and with the high-level personal connections he maintained with powerful Americans like Kissinger, he quickly found a niche in the American world of high finance. The Kissinger-Ansary friendship easily survived the traumatic revolution intact.

Because of the strong influence and personal ties between the Pahlavis and the Rockefeller-Kissinger alliance, the shah's friends in New York immediately moved to his rescue and sought to cushion his landing when he fell from power. Kissinger himself was especially active, visiting the deposed monarch at Paradise Island, in Mexico, and in New York City. He maintained close contact with both Nelson and then David Rockefeller on the case, and, in the White House, he communicated directly with Zbigniew Brzezinski, a leading pro-Pahlavi partisan within the Carter administration. Brzezinski, too, had Rockefeller connections. While at Columbia University, he had become friendly with David Rockefeller, and in the early 1970s, he was named director of the Council on Foreign Relations. More importantly, after Rockefeller played the key role in the establishment of the Trilateral Commission in 1973, Brzezinski became the commission's first director of research. He bristles when his Rockefeller connection is compared to that of Kissinger: "Henry Kissinger worked closely but also for Nelson Rockefeller. I worked closely but *with* David Rockefeller. I didn't work *for* David Rockefeller. I consider him to be a very close friend. I consider his wife to be a good friend, but he is not my employer, nor was he ever my employer."[22] Brzezinski, in the meantime, was in constant touch with Ardeshir Zahedi, on whom he depended for much of his information on Iran. Zahedi had already visited with Nelson Rockefeller in New York. Such was the nature of this powerful network of influence-wielding.

In the first week of April 1979, Kissinger called first Brzezinski and then President Carter in his campaign to get the shah asylum in the United States. The call to Carter paved the way for a visit by David Rockefeller to the Oval Office two days later (April 9, 1979) as pressure began to build on Carter. Kissinger's call to the president was designed to let Carter know that he, Henry Kissinger, agreed with David Rockefeller about America's deep obligations to the shah. By his own admission, Kissinger made "five private approaches" between April and July 1979 in his attempt to convince the Carter administration to admit the shah into the country.[23] Besides calls to Brzezinski and Carter, these included two personal visits with Secretary of State Cyrus Vance. A graphic representation (see figure 1) of the complex

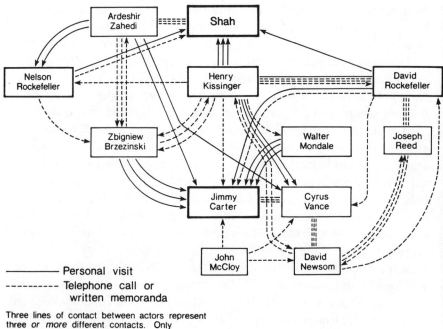

Figure 1 The Kissinger-Rockefeller Campaign for Pahlavi Admission to the United States, 1978–1979.

network of contacts involved in the Rockefeller/Kissinger campaign for admitting the shah to the United States immediately discloses two facts: First, Kissinger played the central role in the campaign; second, President Carter was placed under enormous pressure from many directions.

A little known but especially important part of the campaign to admit the shah involved Vice President Walter Mondale. In June 1979, Brzezinski telephoned Kissinger to indicate that Mondale was wavering in his opposition to the Pahlavi asylum. Kissinger then called Mondale, and the two had a frank discussion, the contents of which are known only to the participants themselves. Shortly after this, Mondale deserted the Carter/Vance alignment and threw his weight behind Brzezinski's position. On July 23, Brzezinski informed Secretary of State Vance and Secretary of Defense Brown of Vice President Mondale's memorandum strongly recommending that the shah be admitted to the United States. Four days later, at a foreign affairs breakfast, Mondale presented his change of heart in dramatic fashion. Even Brzezinski seemed somewhat taken aback by the fervor of Mondale's conversion. In Brzezinski's words: "He even went so far as to compare our refusal to admit the Shah to President Ford's refusal to meet with Solzhenitsyn, commenting that it would play very bad politically."[24] From then on, Mondale joined the Brzezinski group within the White House supporting the Pahlavi admission.

Nelson and David Rockefeller put their own organizations at the shah's disposal. In January 1979, Nelson Rockefeller had sent Robert "Bob" Armao to Tehran as a special messenger to the shah. His charge was to improve the shah's public relations internationally. From then on, Armao served as a powerful and competent chief of staff for the shah and was the main logistics man as the shah travelled from port to port after leaving Iran. A tough, mysterious figure who had acted as Rockefeller's labor adviser and who had held the post of official greeter for New York City, Armao was extremely loyal to the shah. He alienated officials in both the Department of State and the National Security Council. Even Brzezinski's assistant Gary Sick described Armao as "a perfect example of the aide who becomes *plus royaliste que le roi*. He was protective, secretive, combative and decidedly hostile to the Carter administration."[25] President Carter has described Armao as "a troublemaker who wouldn't tell the truth, who made damaging statements to the news media and, I think, caused the Shah a lot of grief."[26] In the struggle that went on between private and public power, it was clear that Armao was a major facilitator in the former camp.

Even more important than Armao, however, was Joseph V. Reed, a very senior aide to David Rockefeller. Like Armao, who had worked for Nelson, Reed, who was David's executive assistant at Chase Manhattan, held loyalties to the Rockefellers and through the Rockefellers to the shah. Reed was placed in charge of the exiled shah's affairs, and it was he who maintained close contact with ranking State Department officials. According to the *New York Times*, Reed visited twenty-six countries in 1979 alone, and in several of them he made inquiries on behalf of the shah, who desperately sought a place of refuge.[27] Reed was an officious individual who enjoyed dealing with monarchs; he later served briefly and ineffectively as United States ambassador to Morocco. Armao, Reed, and other members of the Rockefeller organization were more deeply involved with U.S.-Pahlavi relations than even the United States government. According to Sick: "As time went by, whatever problems the shah encountered were referred first to David Rockefeller and his organization and only secondarily to Washington."[28]

Meanwhile, from the background, other individuals pressed hard for the shah's interests. These included a number of influential congressmen and businessmen both inside and outside the government. The most important of the other Pahlavites was an influential figure very close to the Rockefellers, John J. McCloy. Jack McCloy was eighty-five years old and boasted fifty years of legal, financial, and political influence in America. An extremely able man, McCloy held an exalted position in the Rockefeller network. His posts included chairman of the Chase Manhattan Bank from 1953 to 1960. head of Chase's overseas affiliate, the Chase International Investment Corporation, trustee of the Rockefeller Foundation, chairman of the Council on Foreign Relations, and senior partner in the New York law firm of Milbank, Tweed, Hadley and McCloy, which represented the shah as well as Chase Manhattan. Although McCloy's relations were especially close with David Rockefeller, he also enjoyed the confidence of Henry Kissinger, who consulted him frequently when he first entered the Nixon White House. Kissinger stated, "With the body of a wrestler and a bullet head, John McCloy seemed more like a jovial gnome than a preeminent New York lawyer and perennial counselor of Presidents and Secretaries of State." Kissinger describes McCloy as "always available," "ever wise," and "a reliable pilot through treacherous shoals." Although he rarely provided solutions, "he never failed to provide the psychological and moral reassurance that made solutions possible."[29] In the case of the admission of the shah, this is precisely what McCloy attempted to do.

John McCloy lobbied the Carter administration incessantly in favor of the shah, especially through written communications. He was an old friend of Secretary of State Cyrus Vance, with whom he had served on various high-level political advisory boards in Washington. McCloy inundated Vance with pro-shah letters. In Vance's description: "John is a very prolific letter writer. The morning mail often contained something from him about the Shah."[30] McCloy worked closely with both David Rockefeller and Henry Kissinger in the drive to admit the shah. At one of McCloy's ninetieth birthday parties in the spring of 1985, Rockefeller, Kissinger, and McCloy congratulated one another on their efforts on behalf of the shah. And Rockefeller indicated to friends that if he had to do it all over, he would do the same thing.

The Rockefeller-Kissinger-McCloy pressure in favor of the shah soon became troublesome to President Carter and Secretary of State Vance. Although Vance accepted it in somewhat philosophical fashion, Carter considered it annoying and unprofessional. Within his own administration, he found Brzezinki's hard-line, pro-shah attitude both baffling and exasperating. On several occasions he warned Brzezinski to back off. Most annoying of all to the Carter administration was the shrewd public campaign of Kissinger, who traveled around the United States slyly attacking the Carter administration's Iran policy. It is extremely instructive to note in this context that on the very evening of the day (April 9, 1979) that David Rockefeller had met with President Carter and had made his futile plea for the shah, Kissinger delivered his oft-quoted angry comment at a Harvard Business School dinner in New York City. According to Kissinger, "a man who for 37 years was a friend of the United States should not be treated like a Flying Dutchman looking for a port of call." In a particularly vicious attack on the Carter administration, columnist George Will joined the Rockefeller-Kissinger campaign to admit the shah in an April 19, 1979, column in the *Washington Post*. After praising the shah as a great friend of America, Will sarcastically concluded the column with his view of Carter's reluctance to admit the shah: "It is sad that an administration that knows so much about morality has so little dignity." After the hostages were taken, Kissinger quickly blamed the Carter administration and said that the American people were irate over Iran "because they are sick and tired of getting pushed around and sick and tired of seeing America on the defensive."[31]

Kissinger's self-serving campaign was only partially successful. In a November 25, 1979, interview on "Meet the Press," eminent statesman George Ball bluntly stated that "had it not been for Mr. Kissinger and a few others making themselves enormously obnoxious for the administration, trying to force the Shah into this country, maybe we wouldn't even have done it, even for reasons of compassion."[32] Occasional political commentators and journalists were even more critical. Anthony Lewis, for example, wrote that "the most striking thing about Kissinger's performance in the Iran affair is its cowardice. He urged the Shah's admission to the United States but has taken no responsibility for its result. He has privately assured officials of his support in the hostage crisis and publicly undermined them."[33] Another columnist identified Kissinger as "the principal architect of the current catastrophe in Iran. Working with David Rockefeller, he persuaded a reluctant administration to admit the shah to the United State out of compassion. Now, typically, he is denying that he did it."[34]

In his various attempts to avoid any responsibility for the decision to admit the shah, for the taking of U.S. diplomats hostage, and, ultimately, for the rupture in U.S.-Iranian relations, Henry Kissinger has presented a wide assortment of justifications for his actions. Although he has consistently argued that he and Rockefeller had been quite correct in their activities, he has sought to supplement this position with further explanations. In particular, he has tried to shift all the blame to Carter, arguing that he had not been directly involved after the summer of 1979. In any case, he has argued, the decision was fully the responsibility of the Carter administration. With the benefit of hindsight, Kissinger later offered Carter some advice. "If I'd been consulted, I would probably have recommended they reduce the staff in the embassy." Finally, he told an interviewer that he really did not have such a close relationship with the shah; nothing like the warmth of the relationship he had developed with Sadat, for example. In fact, Kissinger stated, "I met him only eight or nine times."[35]

However history judges Henry Kissinger, a number of conclusions can be stated unequivocally. First, Kissinger, Nelson and David Rockefeller, and John J. McCloy, none of whom held any official governmental position at the time, cooperated in an intensive campaign to influence U.S. foreign policy on a particularly critical issue. This group of influential American Pahlavites had long been involved in Iranian-American affairs through special personal, financial, and political ties that they had maintained with the shah and his closest advisers. The policy preferences of the Rockefeller-Kissinger group ran against those of most State Department professionals in Washington, those of the American diplomats in Tehran, and those of the secretary of State and the president of the United States himself. In the end, through a combination of circumstances, the Rockefeller-Kissinger preferences prevailed, igniting a series of traumatic political events that in many ways compromised the best interests of the United States. This triumph of private power over public interest was unusual in one other important respect. This unofficial, informal elite group moved into the full glare of the public eye in their dramatic attempt to influence policy. Before this they had remained in the background in helping to shape American policy toward Iran. One perceptive journalist has summarized the situation well:

> All this is not to say that Rockefeller interests, whatever they might be, are not legitimate and worth hearing. But the Rockefellers seem to have gotten more than just a hearing. They were allowed to go to the front of the line, to conduct a private and quite secret dialogue as if the issue was a matter strictly between them and the government—as if it didn't have anything to do with you, me, and, of course, the people in the embassy in Tehran. Somehow we all got excluded. A decision was made, a plane allowed to land, and the Shah of Iran got out. There were good reasons to keep him out and good reasons to let him in, but the reasons had nothing to do with his arrival. There was something else instead.
> He had a friend at Chase Manhattan.[36]

In a moment of anger and frustration on October 19, 1979, President Jimmy Carter asked his closest advisers then pressuring him to admit the shah to the United States: "What are you guys going to advise me to do if they overrun our embassy and take our people hostages?"[37] Given this, many observers have questioned why Carter did admit the shah into the United States. Even more baffling is why the Rockefellers, Kissinger, McCloy, and others, all very busy and overcommitted individuals, invested so much of their valuable time and resources on this pro-shah campaign. That the Rockefeller-Kissinger group realized they would be exposed to public scrutiny and criticism yet went ahead with their giant lobbying effort has contributed to the confusion. Having described the "how" of this political campaign, it is now time to analyze the "why."

Reasons for the Carter Decision and the Rockefeller-Kissinger Private Intervention

President Jimmy Carter had four reasons for his ill-advised decision—a decision that contradicted his own good sense and the advice of American diplomats in Iran: (1) Right or wrong, it was strongly argued that the United States owed asylum to the shah since the latter had long been a faithful friend and ally of the United States. This was the central position of such individuals as Richard Nixon, Henry Kissinger, and David Rockefeller. (2) With the shah ill (regardless of the controversy surrounding the nature and seriousness of the illness), there was a genuine humanitarian concern involved. This was especially important to such individuals as President Carter and Secretary of State Vance. (3) Administration officials were deeply sensitive to domestic political ramifications. Failure to admit the shah could have had a strong adverse effect on Carter's chances for reelection. Hamilton Jordan, Jody Powell, and Rosalynn Carter seemed especially aware of this dimension. (4) Most immediately and specifically, enormous pressure for admission had been applied for months by private American Pahlavite forces led by such figures as David Rockefeller, Henry Kissinger, and John J. McCloy.

Even though many of those involved have publicly denied it, there is good reason to believe that the fourth consideration was in the end the most important. This fourth factor brought all the other arguments together. The Rockefeller-Kissinger group consistently argued that nothing less than the honor and credibility of the United States were at stake. Morally, America owed asylum to the shah, an old friend who had come on to hard times.[38] Overlapping this argument was the humanitarian plea based on the shah's illness. The same informal power brokers who had been criticizing the Carter administration for its concern for human rights suddenly became deeply concerned about human rights, in this case, the human rights of a shah.

The Rockefeller-Kissinger "old loyal friend" argument has seldom been analyzed critically. The shah was above all else his own friend, and he acted accordingly throughout his rule. As argued in earlier chapters, he often took actions in direct conflict with the national interest of the United States. The Carter administration's first responsibility was to America and to the representatives of America then serving their country in Iran. As one columnist put it: "The usual justification is that they [the Carter administration] could not turn their back on a loyal ally. . . . Poppycock. Their greater obligation was not to the shah but to national interests. A day seldom passes that the United States doesn't bar undesirables whose presence would not be helpful."[39] Members of the Carter administration were not unaware of these arguments. Another important reason for their decision to admit the shah may have been political.

The Rockefeller-Kissinger group carried enormous influence in domestic political circles in the United States. Their position could be critical when President Carter sought reelection in 1980. This political reality was definitely on the minds of Carter's closest political advisers. Hamilton Jordan, for example, referred to this consideration several times in his book. In the final debate concerning the shah's admission, Jordan described his position as follows: "I mentioned the political consequences [of not admitting the shah]. Mr. President, if the Shah dies in Mexico, can you imagine the field day Kissinger will have with that? He'll say that first you caused the Shah's downfall and now you've killed him."[40] Although neither Carter nor his advisers were as politically crass as much of the mass media indicated during the hostage crisis,[41] there is little doubt that the issue of the forthcoming election was a factor in their thinking.

Perhaps even more important than their influence in domestic politics, the Rockefeller-Kissinger Pahlavites had considerable leverage in important foreign policy goals that Carter was seeking. Not the least of these was his Strategic Arms Limitation Treaty (SALT) initiative. According to the *Wall Street Journal*, Carter officials reconsidered their resistance to the shah's admission "when Kissinger linked a favorable decision to his support for the arms pact. Administration strategists believe his backing essential if they are to win Senate ratification."[42] Kissinger's rather blatant tactic is confirmed by Zbigniew Brzezinski, who referred to a telephone call he received from Kissinger in late July 1979. Brzezinski straightforwardly wrote that "Kissinger in his subtle fashion linked his willingness to support us on SALT to a more forthcoming attitude on our part regarding the Shah."[43]

The overriding commitment of the Rockefeller-Kissinger group to the shah is more difficult to explain. The two most compelling theories can be termed the Old-Boy Network Theory and the Chase Manhattan Financial Theory. The first explanation is primarily personal in nature; the fundamental motivating force in the second is economic. The first is relatively straightforward and is subscribed to by many members of the American political and financial elite. In brief, they argue that the Rockefeller-Kissinger group was in fact the Rockefeller-Kissinger-Pahlavi group. The shah had close personal and social relations with the Rockefeller family for approximately three decades. The Rockefellers and the Pahlavis shared a similar mind-set and viewed their interests as mutual. The mind-set was fundamentally conservative, Republican, anticommunist, and politically authoritarian. As central members of the political elites in each country, they considered their mutual personal interests to be the same as the mutual interests of their respective countries.

In this world of informal international social and political elites, personal loyalty is a cherished value. Individuals often remain committed to their friends regardless of their political fortunes. According to one of his associates, David Rockefeller, for example, was always "very loyal to his friends and he thinks in very personal terms. He is a very decent person this way. He had been the recipient of much warm hospitality from the shah over the years. It would be mean and graceless of him to turn on this friend in a time of need."[44] One Rockefeller associate at the Council on Foreign Relations explained Rockefeller's actions on behalf of the shah as "a personal thing." Kissinger reportedly even suggested that once the shah was in the United States the council should invite him to make a presentation before their membership.[45]

George Ball agrees with this thesis. In his view, the Rockefeller-Kissinger-McCloy campaign for the shah was waged for largely sentimental reasons. The shah was one of their own group; he was one of them. It was a matter of "noblesse oblige"; one should never be in a position of abandoning a friend. John McCloy "liked the shah and thought he had been a sturdy friend." Kissinger "was totally enamoured of the shah and, furthermore, he had staked a certain amount of his reputation on the shah." In Ball's opinion, David Rockefeller saw it as a matter of "standing by a friend." The shah, in turn, understood the value of maintaining close relationships with these powerful Americans and "had a particular hex on them."[46]

The binding effect of personal ties is also seen in the relations of Richard Nixon and the shah of Iran. Although Nixon had his differences with the Rockefeller group, he completely shared their views with respect to the shah. Nixon was furious about Carter's policies toward the shah. A strong reciprocal personal loyalty was involved here. The shah stood by Nixon through the Watergate scandal, and his ambassador to the United States, Ardeshir Zahedi, made a number of personal gestures of support to Nixon both during and after Watergate. Zahedi, like the shah, felt a deep personal commitment to Richard Nixon. He was devastated the day Nixon left office and wrote and visited San Clemente often to indicate his continued support. It is not surprising, therefore, that Nixon, at great discomfort to himself, visited the shah in exile in Mexico and later attended the shah's funeral in Cairo.

Alongside the Old-Boy Network Theory, which emphasizes reciprocal personal loyalties, a new and much more complex theory has quietly developed. The Chase Manhattan Financial Theory stresses the economic component of power and bases its arguments on the fundamental financial interests that bound the shah to the Rockefeller group, witnessed primarily in such institutions as the National Iranian Oil Company and the Chase Manhattan Bank.

The Shah, the Chase Manhattan Bank, and Frozen Assets

Several observers of the Iranian-American debacle and the admission of the shah into the United States have developed a theory that focuses on the financial self-interest of the Rockefeller group as represented primarily by the Chase Manhattan Bank.[47] This theory documents the hostile actions taken by the Islamic Republic toward the Chase Manhattan Bank, which found itself badly exposed in Iran following the revolution. Chase Manhattan was in a relatively weakened state,[48] holding several large, questionable loans totaling well over a billion dollars to official Iranian instrumentalities. As the lead organizer and partner in eleven banking syndicates that had made large loans to Pahlavi Iran, Chase Manhattan's reputation was at stake. This threat was made more serious by the fact that Chase's own Iranian lawyers questioned the constitutional legality of several of the loans negotiated with the shah's regime in the years 1977–1979.

According to this analysis, Chase Manhattan nervously watched the revolutionary government slowly and steadily draw down its sizable deposits in their bank (see figure 2). Chase's confidence was not bolstered by occasional comments made by leaders in the new Iranian government implying that Iran might repudiate some of the shah's debts, especially those involving institutions in which the shah's old friend David Rockefeller had a special interest. In this situation, it is alleged that Chase Manhattan's executives and lawyers began to seek a method to declare Iran in default. As the Iranian financial reserves at Chase fell to levels that came ever closer to the funds Chase had loaned Iran, this search became more desperate. It seemed clear that Iran intended to withdraw all its funds from Chase Manhattan and then perhaps even to repudiate repayment of the loans. Published reports indicate that Chase officials were especially frustrated since the new government in Iran met its interest payments meticulously, thereby providing no pretext for default proceedings.

This theory, therefore, postulates that it was necessary to provoke an incident. Whether intentionally planned or not, there was a provocation. The incident involved the admission of the shah into the United States, which triggered the subsequent taking of American diplomats hostage. On the morning of November 14, 1979, just ten days after the hostages were taken, President Carter, acting on the advice of Secretary of Treasury G. William Miller, froze all Iranian governmental assets in American banks. Like so many other of the key actors, Miller had ties with the Chase Manhattan Bank and with Iran. He had been a

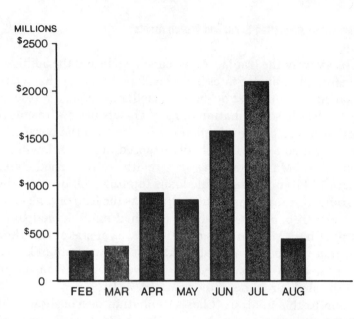

Figure 2   Financial Transfers out of National Iranian Oil Company Accounts at Chase Manhattan Bank, New York, February–August 1979.

SOURCE: Supplemental Affidavit of Alan Delsman in support of motion for a preliminary injunction, The Chase Manhattan Bank, N.A., vs. The State of Iran et al., before the Southern District of New York, Docket #79 Civ.6644; as presented in and adapted from Mark Hulbert, *Interlock* (New York: Richardson and Snyder, 1982), p. 144.

member of Chase's International Advisory Committee beginning in 1976. Also, as chairman of Textron, he signed nearly $1 billion in contracts with the government of Iran to provide that country with Bell Helicopters.

Earlier that same morning, the Department of Treasury had received word that in a press conference in Tehran, Iran's acting foreign minister, Abol Hassan Bani Sadr, had threatened to withdraw Iranian funds from American banks. This was the event the Carter administration used to justify the seizure of Iranian assets a few hours later. It argued that such withdrawals represented a serious threat to U.S. national security and to the economy. Persian sources describe the relevant portions of the press conference as follows:

> Abol Hassan Bani Sadr, Acting Minister of Foreign Affairs, announced in a news conference that Iran has decided to withdraw all [*kulliyah*] of its deposited reserves from American banks. He said that there was no need to worry about the United States government freezing these deposits since most of them were located in

American bank branches located in Europe. Iran has nearly 12 billion dollars deposited in European and American Banks with most sums located in American banks, especially in the Chase Manhattan Bank which is owned by Rockefeller. It should also be noted that the deposed shah was one of the shareholders [*sahmdaran*] of this bank. Bani Sadr reminded the audience that the funds withdrawn will be deposited in banks that have friendly relations with the Islamic Republic of Iran.[49]

Although it seems certain that such withdrawals would be detrimental to the interests of the Chase Manhattan Bank, it also is clear that it did not represent a serious threat either to the American economy or to U.S. national security. The Carter administration did at first use the Bani Sadr statement as the immediate justification for announcing the freeze.

The American banks interpreted the freeze order to include those American branches located in foreign lands, which caused great consternation in the European banking community. Also, the Carter administration made the puzzling decision to permit American banks to "offset" the funds that Iran had deposited in their vaults against the monies that the banks had loaned Iran. This effectively turned control of the frozen assets over to the banks and deprived the U.S. government of much of the leverage it needed to solve the hostage crisis. The Carter administration "relinquished control over Iran's assets. If the banks had not been allowed to take the offsets, the government would have been able to negotiate with the Iranians directly."[50] Meanwhile, throughout the hostage crisis, representatives of the large American banks were deeply and quietly involved in the sensitive negotiations. Citibank, represented by John E. Hoffman of Shearman and Sterling, New York's largest law firm, took the lead in the negotiations. The only other bank secretly informed during the critical early stages of the negotiations was Chase Manhattan, represented by a team of bank finance lawyers from Milbank, Tweed, Hadley and McCloy. Chase was a tense and tough player in this game of high stakes. As Roy Assersohn has written, "Throughout the whole transaction the hardest nosed and most aggressive of all the banks was probably the Chase Manhattan, which reacted quickly and, while staying within the law, was nevertheless quite prepared to push aside all other considerations and other banks to secure what it deemed to be its own targets."[51]

The timing of the freeze announcement was crucial to Chase Manhattan. On November 5 the Iranian Central Bank had telexed Chase instructing them to make the forthcoming interest payment of $4.05 million *due on November 15* from the surplus funds available in their London office. This interest was owed on a $500 million loan negotiated in January 1977 with the shah's government. Chase had been the lead partner in this loan, which involved seven American and four foreign banks. Carter's freeze announcement was made one day before the loan was due to be paid. This conveniently enabled Chase Manhattan to declare Iran in default on the interest payment since the funds in London had just been frozen. It also occurred late enough so that Iran was unable to make other arrangements to honor the interest payment. During the ten days between November 5 and November 15, Chase Manhattan made little attempt to communicate with Iran's Central Bank or even to acknowledge receipt of the telex; it did nothing to enable payment in some currency unaffected by the freeze; it declared the default with unusual speed; it communicated and consulted with its syndicate partners at a sluggish pace; and it declared Iran in default despite the unanimous opposition of the four foreign banking partners in the syndicate.

Once it had declared the $500 million loan in default, Chase Manhattan then used "cross-default" clauses in the contract to declare all other loans to Iran in default. "Chase then seized Iran's deposits to offset these loans. When the dust had cleared, Chase had no loans to Iran left on its books."[52] From that time onward, the entire hostage crisis was complexly entangled with America's bankers and their legal teams. In the end, the resolution of the crisis clearly benefitted the American banking community. "The banks thus emerged from the hostage crisis with compensation for virtually all their major claims against Iran. And some banks did even better than that; those fortunate enough to have the use of Iran's frozen assets for fourteen months were able to turn a profit on the hostage crisis."[53] Chase Manhattan was near the top of the list of those who benefited. In the final settlement, Iran paid off nearly $4 billion in loans it had received from the American banks. When they learned that the loans would be repaid in full, "the bankers nearly fell off their chairs."[54] The inexperience and incompetence of the Iranian negotiators resulted in a huge unexpected financial windfall for the American banks. According to Robert Carswell and Richard J. Davis, two of the highest-ranking officials in the Treasury Department involved in the crisis, "As a class the banks came out well, but those who hold cash usually do."[55]

In brief, the Chase Manhattan thesis is summarized by a congressional committee as a scenario in which "Chase Manhattan engineered a freeze by convincing the government to permit the Shah to come to the U.S., knowing that that act would precipitate violence in Iran and make a freeze inevitable."[56] Those who present this position argue that little short of an emergency situation challenging the security of America itself could have rescued Chase Manhattan from a severe blow to its financial standing and to its credibility in the delicate world of international finance. Some event had to occur that would require the president of the United States to invoke the International Emergency Economic Powers Act to institute the freeze. The provocation was the admission of the shah to the United States. That those individuals who pressed the hardest for the shah's admission were also leading officials in the Chase Manhattan Bank is not coincidence, according to this reasoning. These individuals, who included David Rockefeller and Henry Kissinger, had been repeatedly made aware of the possibility that an admission of the shah could lead to an Iranian seizure of the U.S. Embassy in Tehran. These observers imply that individuals such as Rockefeller and Kissinger lobbied hard for the admission of the shah partly to exacerbate the already strained relations between the United States and a revolutionary Iran that was threatening their financial interests. It was no secret that a freeze had been among the alternative strategies prepared by the Department of Treasury as far back as February 1979 when the shah left Iran.[57] The timing of the freeze and Chase Manhattan's rush to declare Iran in default in the face of a clear Iranian willingness to make its interest payments is used as supporting evidence for the thesis.

The Chase Manhattan thesis became so prevalent in the press at one point that a House committee felt it necessary to respond to the charges. In July 1981, the Committee on Banking, Finance, and Urban Affairs prepared a report that directly but ineffectively attempted to deny the Chase Manhattan thesis. In fact, in many ways it unwittingly lent support to the thesis. For example, in attempting to demonstrate the insignificance of Iranian actions to Chase Manhattan's financial well-being, the report stated that the "existence" of the bank "would not have been threatened" by the withdrawal of Iranian assets. In the same sentence, however, it admitted that these withdrawals would have confronted Chase with "serious earning problems." It failed to address the issue of a possible threat to the credibility of Chase Manhattan in the banking community. The report also spent an inordinate amount of time defending David Rockefeller, whose influence concerning the financial aspects of the hostage crisis "is much overstated" and who, although "personally acquainted with the Shah, was not an intimate associate to the degree that is often assumed." The report admitted that there was indeed a relationship between David Rockefeller and the shah and that this relationship "did influence the placement of NIOC accounts in Chase Manhattan Bank." The report also unconvincingly downplayed the size of the deposits that the shah's government had made at Chase Manhattan.[58]

It is questionable whether David Rockefeller, Henry Kissinger, or anyone else associated with Chase Manhattan Bank pushed for the shah's admission knowing that this would ultimately lead to the default opportunity that they needed. Too many variables could not be foreseen: a successful embassy takeover, a prolonged hostage taking, a presidential freeze of Iranian assets, an administration decision to permit offsetting, a freeze that included Iranian assets in American banks overseas, and a freeze that was perfectly timed to implement effectively a default action. In fact, the major Kissinger-Rockefeller campaign for Pahlavi admission had occurred back in April, May, and June of 1979. This was before the major withdrawals of Iranian funds from Chase Manhattan (see figure 2). In the words of George Ball, this thesis is suspect, if for no other reason than it gives these bankers "too damn much credit. Chase Manhattan Bank is not that bright."[59]

Research, interviews, and a careful reading of the record indicate, however, that Rockefeller and Chase Manhattan were well aware of the special hostility reserved for them by the leaders of revolutionary Iran. Besides the steady financial withdrawals, Iran posed a considerably more serious threat since it could be shown that four of the major loans made to Iran in 1977–78 in Chase-led syndicates had been questionably obtained. In short, Mehran Tavakoli of the Iranian law firm of Ghani and Tavakoli had strongly warned them that the loans could be unenforceable because they ran counter to Article Twenty-five of the Iranian constitution. This article concisely stated that "no state loans at home or abroad may be raised without the knowledge and approval of the National Consultative Assembly." Ghani and Tavakoli, representing Chase, issued an opinion strongly implying that such loans were unconstitutional.[60]

A little-known storm broke over this opinion. Before submitting their formal written opinion, Ghani and Tavakoli were invited to New York to discuss the matter with the bankers' lawyers. Cyrus Ghani, an intelligent, keen observer of the United States, flew to New York in early 1977 to present his firm's conclusions. In two days of meetings at 1 Chase Plaza, Ghani faced some twenty-five lawyers from participating banks. Most major New York law firms were represented. These sophisticated representatives of the nation's largest banks sought to determine the facts and to understand the rationale behind Ghani and Tavakoli's conclusion that the loans were unconstitutional. Roy Haberkern of Milbank, Tweed, which handled Chase's legal affairs, headed Chase's contingent. Bruce Nichols of Davis, Polk & Wardwell representing Morgan Guaranty was a particularly incisive questioner. Tom Cashel of Simpson, Thacher & Bartlett representing Manufacturer's Hanover Trust displayed a willingness to attempt to understand Ghani's reasoning. The central argument of the lawyers for the big banks was that the constitutional authority for foreign loans had been delegated to the Iranian Plan Organization. Ghani and Tavakoli's position was that such power could not be delegated.

In explaining the rationale for his firm's controversial decision, Ghani effectively discussed the realities of Iranian history with the lawyers. He traced the methodology of foreign borrowing of the Qajar rulers in the late nineteenth century. By borrowing huge sums of money from England and Russia, these shahs had placed Iran under the effective economic control of outside powers. The Constitutional Movement of Iran (1905–6) was a reaction to such financial acts; consequently, it was not accidental that Article Twenty-five had been written into the Iranian constitution. The people had to be consulted in the matter of loans to foreign countries in order to insure Iran's independence. The monarch's power, therefore, had to be checked by a legislative body. In these circumstances, it was improper to talk about the delegation of such power to a particular government agency.

On the second day of the meetings, Chase's lawyers sought a compromise and attempted a number of end runs. Chase led an attempt to fulfill notice requirements after the fact by having the speaker of the Majlis acknowledge receipt of the loan agreement; the speaker was willing to indicate that the Majlis's Finance and Budget Committee had approved the loan. Also, the lawyers agreed to seek opinions from the Ministry of Justice and from the chief justice of the Iranian Supreme Court on this matter. These opinions were solicited and concluded, not surprisingly, that the loans were in fact constitutional. Ghani and Tavakoli refused to buckle and stood by their original interpretation, but, despite their advice and considerable hesitation on the part of some of the American lawyers, the banks went through with the loans.

With a new, unfriendly government now in power in Tehran, Chase Manhattan faced the unpalatable possibility that the new regime could declare the Pahlavi loans illegal and simply repudiate them. This would possibly expose Chase to a battery of legal suits on the part of the other syndicate banks for failure of fiduciary responsibility and for ignoring advice of counsel. Although Chase Manhattan could have survived the withdrawal of Iranian deposits, it would have been in considerably more difficulty if Iran challenged the legality of the large loans. To the banking community, credibility is far more important than credit. In fact, credibility is credit.[61]

Given the demonstrated hostility of the revolutionary government in Iran, by late 1979, David Rockefeller and his colleagues at Chase Manhattan had reason to press for the admission of the shah into America. A professional financial incentive reinforced the ties of friendship. Any deterioration in relations between the United States and Iran at this point could only work to the benefit of Chase. While the shah's admission would guarantee this deterioration, Chase Manhattan would now find itself allied totally with the United States government. A dramatic rupture in Iranian-American relations would at the least provide Chase Manhattan with an entire new set of possibilities to protect their financial flanks. And they would now have the powerful United States government on their side. Once the shah had been admitted, leading officials at Chase Manhattan watched for every opportunity to cover permanently their exposed position in Iran. And, as has been shown, they achieved this goal masterfully.[62]

Thus, besides the important old-boy ties of personal loyalty and friendship, underlying economic and financial reasons rested behind the campaign to admit the shah. By this time, there was no doubt that the leaders of revolutionary Iran had identified Chase Manhattan Bank as a particular enemy of the Islamic Republic. And they had begun to act accordingly. Chase Manhattan had everything to gain and nothing to lose by the shah's admission. Although it seems unlikely that Rockefeller, Kissinger, and the bank planned the shah's admission in order to set up the freeze that would enable them to declare Iran in default, it is very likely that they were sensitive to the serious economic needs of their bank and the importance of establishing a political climate that would serve those needs. The admission of the shah into the United States could only contribute to the creation of that climate.

Pahlavism in America: Reinforcing Circles of Influence

The Kissinger-Rockefeller case study analyzed above represents one significant wedge in a system of complex, reinforcing concentric circles of influence that bound the shah's regime to America for almost four decades. A simplified view of this multilayered wheel of influence identifies the ten major Iranian actors and twenty-eight leading Americans who represented the key nodes of the system (see figure 3). They, of course, were only part of the overall network; hundreds of others also reinforced the Pahlavi-American relationship.[63] Each relevant actor also represents particular organizations or institutions identified in the figure. The twenty-eight Americans can be termed Pahlavites because of their strong belief in and support for the shah and his system of government.

The actors are arranged around the shah, who rests at the center of the system surrounded by nine Iranians who over the years maintained especially close ties to America. The five concentric circles that surround this Iranian core are arranged according to relative influence and impact on the American-Pahlavi alliance. The innermost circle of seven Americans is dominated by, but not confined to, the Rockefeller group. The second circle of four may be referred to as the ring of legal expeditors, since three of the four were lawyers with close commitments to the Pahlavis. The third circle, also of four individuals, is composed of leading American business representatives who worked closely with Pahlavi Iran. The fourth circle includes U.S. senators and congressmen who were staunch Pahlavi supporters, while the fifth ring of influence consists of individuals drawn from academia and the mass media.

The Iranian Linkage Figures

Muhammad Reza Shah Pahlavi himself promoted the extremely close ties that came to mark Iranian-American relations. He was assisted, however, by many members of the Iranian political and economic elite who were themselves thoroughly familiar with the United States. Nine particularly important members of this inner circle, all of whom were loyal to the shah and were thoroughly committed to his system of patrimonial rule, are identified in figure 3. Of these nine, the three most influential were Ardeshir Zahedi, Princess Ashraf Pahlavi, and Hushang Ansary. All three were personally acquainted with American presidents, Democratic and Republican, and maintained close friendships with numerous members of the American political elite. Educated at Utah State University, Zahedi maintained the widest network of American contacts; Ansary quietly and selectively built his ties with the financial and economic elite; and Ashraf Pahlavi focused her attention on both the highest-ranking American politicians and the social elite.

For years disliked and condemned by a wide spectrum of Iranian society for her alleged corruption and loose behavior, Ashraf Pahlavi was much more popular in international social and political circles. In Iran, Princess Ashraf was the most criticized member of the royal family and was often accused of drug trafficking, personal immorality,

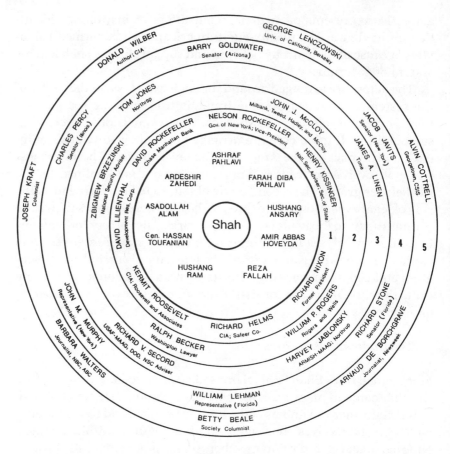

Figure 3

evil influence-wielding, and wasting huge sums of money in the casinos of the French Riviera and the West Indies. Many considered her the leading member of a Pahlavi family that, in the words of British Ambassador Anthony Parsons, hung as "an albatross around the Shah's neck" and from which emanated "a strong smell of corruption."[64] Over the years, U.S. Embassy reports described her in the most unsavory terms.[65] Referred to by observers as the Black Panther, Ashraf was combative, committed, and, in seeking her own political and economic goals, relentless. She was loyal to herself, to her friends, and to her twin brother, the shah of Iran.

Completely at home in Paris or in New York, Ashraf Pahlavi held numerous positions of prestige within international organizations and was associated for sixteen years with the United Nations, where she was especially active on the Human Rights Commission. She met with President Truman in 1947 even before her twin brother made his first trip to the United States. In 1953 she worked directly with American intelligence agents in the plot that resulted in the overthrow of Muhammad Musaddiq. Ashraf discussed international politics with President Eisenhower in the White House in 1956. Her power was such that even after the fall of the shah, she wrote directly to Jimmy Carter on behalf of her brother and received a handwritten response from him.

Ashraf's relationships with the leading American Pahlavites were close. In her words, they were "our personal friends." In particular, she referred to Nelson and David Rockefeller and Henry Kissinger: "Since the days of the Point Four Program, when Nelson Rockefeller had been President Truman's Special Assistant on Foreign Affairs, the Rockefeller family had been close friends." Princess Ashraf referred to Kissinger as "a man I have known and admired since we met at a Washington reception years ago."[66] Indeed, it was at Washington and New York receptions where Ashraf Pahlavi first established contact with many American political, social, and economic leaders.

A typical case in point occurred in June 1969 when the princess received an honorary doctorate of law from Brandeis University and then hurried to Washington to be guest of honor at a reception given by Iranian ambassador Hushang Ansary and his wife. The "glittering event" was attended by political leaders from three administrations, the Supreme Court, the diplomatic corps, and the U.S. Senate and Congress. Vice President Spiro Agnew and his wife, Elinor, attended (their second visit to an Iranian embassy reception in less than a month) along with the following familiar people, among many others: Kermit and Polly Roosevelt, Gerald and Betty Ford, Paul and Rebecca Rogers, Warren and Margaret Magnuson, John and Martha Mitchell, Earl and Nina Warren, and Potter and Mary Ann Stewart. These and other members of the "star-studded guest list" applauded politely when Ansary described Ashraf in words taken from an ancient tribute: "The lightness of a leaf, the glance of a fawn, the gaiety of the sun, the gentleness of a breeze, the hardness of a diamond, the sweetness of money [did he mean honey], the heat of fire."[67]

Earlier that day, Ashraf had also been guest of honor at a luncheon aboard the yacht *Tricia* given by Secretary of Housing and Urban Development George Romney and his wife. Present for this luncheon were high-ranking State Department officials, American business-men, and congressmen, including John Brademas of Indiana. Still later Elinor Agnew gave a tea at the Agnews' Sheraton-Park apartment for the princess; the guests here included Beatrice Aiken, Beatrice Frelinghuysen, Mary Ripley, Polly Roosevelt, and Ann Marie Becker. Although, by Ashraf's own admission, she preferred Republicans, her contacts included many powerful Democrats as well. It is ironic and important to note that Ashraf Pahlavi, the soul of elegance, sophistication, and popularity in the salons of the West, represented a major human symbol against which the Iranian opposition rallied in the revolution that overthrew the shah. Meanwhile, over the years in Washington and New York, she earnestly and effectively polished the image of the Pahlavi government among hundreds of Americans who wielded enormous influence in American foreign policymaking.

Besides Ansary and Zahedi, other loyal Iranians who assisted Princess Ashraf in binding their royal government to America through personal and institutional ties were Empress Farah Diba, Asadollah Alam, Amir Abbas Hoveyda, Hushang Ram, Reza Fallah, and Gen. Hassan Toufanian. Farah's influence and credibility in America developed slowly. A more respected figure than Ashraf, with whom she usually fought losing battles for influence with the shah, Farah made an important visit to the United States by herself in 1977. Here, her unostentatious demeanor and genuine concern for her people acted as effective public relations for the Pahlavi government. A key event in this visit was a luncheon held in New York attended by 650 of that city's leading political and business leaders on July 8. At this luncheon, the Appeal of Conscience Foundation presented Farah with its award for humanitarian service. Important businesses that preferred not to make contributions or to send representatives to this ceremony were prevailed on by both the Iranian Embassy and the U.S. government to participate.

Empress Farah's interests in education, culture, and the arts enabled her to develop strong ties with American academics, artists, musicians, librarians, and writers. But her influence began to widen considerably in the middle-1970s as American politicians and businessmen began gravitating to her sphere of influence. This occurred partly because of her perceived personal integrity. More specifically, it was furthered by her close relationship with the Aspen Institute, through which influential Americans from all walks of life participated in conferences in both Iran and the United States. Strengthening this relationship was a financial grant of $750,000 from the Pahlavi Foundation through the representations of Farah to the Aspen Institute. In an elaborate conference held at Persepolis in September 1975, the Aspen Institute, in cooperation with the empress's office, invited a wide assortment of Americans considered influential. They included fifteen academics (mainly Iran specialists, including myself); educational administrators such as Robert Goheen, Ernest Boyer, and Arjay Miller; businessmen such as Robert O. Anderson of Atlantic-Richfield, Najeeb Halaby of Halaby International/Pan American Airlines, and Philip Caldwell of Ford; pollsters such as Daniel Yankelovich; congressmen such as Les Aspin and William Lehman; and journalists such as Ronald Kriss of *Time*, John B. Oakes of the *New York Times*, and James Hoge of the *Chicago Sun-Times*.[68] From 1975 to 1978, after a long, distinguished career in the Foreign Service, Charles Yost headed the Aspen/Iran program.

Asadollah Alam's American connections were developed primarily from Iran and in Iran. As an early chancellor of Pahlavi University in Shiraz—an Iranian university experiment patterned after American higher education and employing many American professors—Alam worked closely with many Americans.[69] His special forte, however, was establishing close relations with American ambassadors and the U.S. Embassy in Tehran. Prime Minister Hoveyda, although European educated and not as U.S. oriented as his rival, Ardeshir Zahedi, spoke fluent English and developed close ties with many influential Americans, especially in his later years. He made an important official visit to Washington in December 1968 and met with a variety of American leaders. The American Pahlavite elite served as his hosts and clustered about him at official functions. Attending the White House dinner in Hoveyda's honor on December 5, for example, were such individuals as Richard Helms, John J. McCloy, Ralph and Ann Marie Becker, David and Helen Lilienthal, Kermit and Polly Roosevelt, and Tom and Ruth Jones. Between 1971 and 1979, Hoveyda maintained a constant American link—his urbane, cultured brother, Fereydoun, spent those years in New York as Iran's permanent representative to the United Nations.

Hushang Ram was one of the shah's three closest financial advisers. He headed the Pahlavi-controlled Bank-i Omran, which maintained banking connections deep in the heartland of the United States. For years, Bank-i Omran owned a percentage of the First National Wisconsin Bank in Milwaukee. Reza Fallah used his powerful position in the National Iranian Oil Company to negotiate oil and oil-related business with the leaders of many of America's major oil companies. Over the years, Fallah became very rich and was well known to both American and European businessmen.

General Hassan Toufanian was deeply involved in all arms sales between the United States and Iran between 1964 and 1978. In this capacity, he was in constant touch not only with American military leaders but also with the highest-ranking executives in the world of defense contracting, such as Tom Jones of Northrop and G. William Miller of Textron. Toufanian played a determining role in allocating billions of dollars of arms contracts. His ties with American contractors were so close that after the revolution it was widely believed in Iran that U.S. agents helped him escape from prison and spirited him off to America.

Besides these nine elite Iranian linkage figures, many others were closely involved with America. Each figure named, for example, had his or her own satellites who broadened and strengthened the connections. Usually these individuals were young professionals and technocrats who were either educated in the United States or maintained professional ties with America. Many were extremely talented. Princess Ashraf's satellite figures, for example, included Abdol Reza Ansary, Mahnaz Afkhami, and Parviz Radji, Pahlavi Iran's last ambassador to Great Britain. Hushang Ansary's technocratic assistants with strong credibility in America included Hassan Ali Mehran and Farokh Najmabadi, both known to be individuals of competence and integrity.

In addition to this complex system of multistranded links, a few individuals were free-floating forces. In general, these actors had independent bases of power and an autonomy of their own. They refused to become emanations of anyone else. Usually they represented great wealth and old family influence, as did the huge, wealthy, and well-educated Farmanfarmaian clan. The most influential and ambitious Farmanfarmaian was deeply involved in Iran-American affairs. Khodadad was a Colorado-trained economist whose influential American friends often referred to him simply as Joe. Other individuals who were considerably more willing to evaluate the Pahlavi system critically than Joe included such men as Ali Amini, Abol Hassan Ebtehaj, and Mehdi Sami'i. These free-floaters were especially important to the system since they claimed autonomy even from the shah. They often quietly criticized the Pahlavi family and its mode of governance. In official and unofficial American elite circles, these individuals were mistakenly viewed as the real Iranian opposition.

The nine Iranian linkage figures briefly described above often owned property or homes in America. They were thoroughly conversant with American culture, sports, theater, economics, education, and politics. With few exceptions, their English was impeccable. They were smooth, suave, courteous, generous, and sophisticated. With the exception of the free-floaters, they were completely loyal to the shah, whom most of them (Ashraf and Farah partially excepted) approached with dedicated obsequiousness. They carried the shah's message to the American political and industrial elites and used all means at their disposal to increase the growing number of Pahlavites in key positions in America. In this they were enormously successful.

The Inner Circle Seven: The Most Powerful American Pahlavites

The two Rockefellers, Henry Kissinger, Richard Nixon, and their relationships with the shah's Iran have already been discussed in detail. Both Kermit Roosevelt and Richard Helms have also been introduced in various places in this study. Actually, Roosevelt and Helms shared much in common in matters Iranian. Both were key figures in the Central Intelligence Agency; both had long associations with the shah of Iran and with several members of his political elite; both established consulting firms whose clients included members of the shah's political and economic elite; and both remained active in influencing American political and public opinion on Iran long after the revolution had transformed the Iranian polity.

Richard Helms worked for the CIA before he became ambassador to Iran in the critical four years 1973 to 1977. Best described as a professional's professional, he was the consummate bureaucrat. Accused of perjury when he implied in testimony before a congressional committee that the CIA had not been involved in domestic spying, he survived through his dogged professional commitment to the organization that he had served for so many years. More importantly, he was an insider's insider, well connected into the social and political circuit in Washington. In February 1975, according to the *Washington Post*, when Helms was under serious attack for his testimony, a "small circle of influential people, the ones who help shape America's foreign policy and share national secrets" arranged a small, "intimate" dinner party in his honor. Held at the Chevy Chase home of Tom and Joan Braden, the quiet event was attended by such individuals as Henry Kissinger, W. Averell Harriman, Stuart Symington, Robert S. McNamara, Barbara Walters, and Israeli ambassador Simcha Dinitz. Kissinger solemnly termed Helms "an honorable man" as "the established circle drew the wagons up close in his defense." The event was heavily attended by other Pahlavites.[70]

Tall, cool, and unflappable, Helms could be tough in debate and smoothly sardonic in commentary. His effectiveness as ambassador to Iran was hampered by his CIA associations and by the fact that he had to make sixteen trips back to Washington to defend himself before congressional hearings. Although his wife, Cynthia, developed an impressive understanding of Iran and was perhaps the most effective official American first lady in Tehran since the days of Grace Dreyfus, she could hardly be expected to replace her husband. Nevertheless, Helms was always extremely well informed and he did his homework.[71]

On leaving the ambassadorship in Iran, Richard Helms established a consulting firm known as the Safeer Company. After the revolution, he spoke often before a wide range of groups interested in Iran, U.S. foreign policy, and intelligence issues. These groups included *Time* magazine executives, State Department officials, Foreign Service trainees, intelligence operatives, and Defense Department decision makers.

Helms believed that the shah was good for the United States, that America's interests were the shah's interests, and vice versa. It is easy to see why Helms believed that the United States should have resorted to "dirty tricks" to keep tabs on the shah and to help him remain in power. But in his philosophical view, sometimes even dirty tricks do not achieve the desired result. Such was the case of Pahlavi Iran. In a reassessment of the Iranian-American debacle held at the Foreign Service Institute in November 1985, Helms shrugged his shoulders at what had occurred. In his words: "Is it necessary that the United States win every battle . . . that the U.S. run the world? I don't think so. At times things are going to go sour. Let's not go around biting our nails about it."[72]

As head of the CIA, as an ambassador in Iran, but especially in his role as an insider in the Washington political community, Richard Helms knew firsthand the considerable influence that the Pahlavites wielded in America. As a career public servant he was surely more detachedly professional than Pahlavites such as the Rockefellers, and even Kissinger in this case. Yet he well understood the strong commitment that the American political and economic elite had to the shah's regime. Thus, in his view, no matter how effective the Department of State or CIA could have been in their analyses of the Iranian situation, there would have been little chance for significant policy change. With this understanding, Helms has only shrugged his shoulders when others have gathered for assessments and political post mortems about what went wrong in Iran. He understood better than most the strength of the ties that bound the United States to Pahlavi Iran.

Kermit Roosevelt's role in promoting and protecting the Pahlavi-American connection has been mentioned already. After his clandestine role in helping the shah regain his throne in 1953, Roosevelt maintained a long, strong relationship with the shah and the shah's courtiers. Roosevelt traveled to Iran four to five times a year during the 1960s and made an estimated thirty trips to that country before the revolution.[73] His business, which was both political and financial in nature, took him directly to the royal palace. When the shah visited the United States, Roosevelt was consistently on the guest list for receptions and White House dinners. He carried political messages on behalf of the shah to leading American decision makers, often reflecting the shah's ideas and arguing the Pahlavi point of view. In Roosevelt's case, politics and business were closely intertwined, and it was widely reported that his Washington firm, Kermit Roosevelt and Associates, had Muhammad Reza Shah Pahlavi as one of its public relations clients.

The final member of the Pahlavite inner circle is in many ways the most interesting and the most important. David Lilienthal was a liberal, idealistic individual with a deep social conscience and a sensitive intellectual consciousness. Yet he believed completely in the shah and in his methodology of politics. Unlike most other Pahlavites, Lilienthal made many trips to Iran, traveling widely throughout the countryside. He was acquainted with village and tribal life and dedicated himself and his organization, the Development and Resources Corporation, to improving the social and economic conditions of the Iranian lower classes. He believed that he could achieve this goal while also earning a profit for his corporation. When he entered his twenty-three-year association with Iran, Lilienthal convinced himself that the shah of Iran was a good man completely dedicated to the welfare of his people and that the Iranian masses loved and supported him. Despite considerable firsthand evidence to the contrary and a series of misfortunes that plagued his venture in Iran (see chapter 3), Lilienthal never wavered from this view until the very end. Like certain members of the shah's own Iranian inner circle, Lilienthal blamed everyone but the shah for the corruption and repression that marked Pahlavi rule.

Before he died on January 13, 1981, David Lilienthal had been deeply disillusioned and saddened by the revolution that tore through Iran. On December 29, 1978, he wrote in his diaries: "This is surely one of the saddest entries I have ever made in these journals: the Shah is leaving Iran; the long campaign has succeeded. The Communists have registered one of their greatest gains." On January 19, 1979, after the shah had left Iran, Lilienthal wrote that "I felt as if I had been physically wounded." He repeatedly assured himself that "we, D&R, have done a good job in Iran, a constructive human and honest job. We should not become defensive"; and "what we did in Iran was good."

The extraordinary journal entries during and through the revolution are painful to read. After a time of referring to Khomeini as "Old Whiskers," the religious leaders as "savage turbaned hoodlums," and the student revolutionaries as "American-educated twirps," Lilienthal began some deep soul-searching and, as the honest man that he was, asked "some stiff questions about myself. Could I be all that wrong, after all those years of experience in development and particularly in Iran . . . ?" Eight months later, after a meeting with his old colleague, Abol Hassan Ebtehaj in New York, he began to answer these "stiff" questions:

> Listening to Ebtehaj the other day did confirm that the "revolution" was made almost inevitable by the blind greed of the "very best" of the Westernized Iranians. Ebtehaj built one of the most fabulous homes and styles of living I have ever seen . . . development became for him a technical achievement, not a human goal.
> I complained that no one had ever explained to me during all those many years that the 200,000 mullahs I now hear were functioning throughout the country had great political power. He spoke of those mullahs with the greatest disdain. They come from the "lowest" and most ignorant of Iran's people; they know nothing, can run nothing. Moreover, the mullahs, these begging dirty, turbaned characters, are much more corrupt than anything in the days of the Shah.[74]

But David Lilienthal was no longer listening to his old Iranian friend and guide. He knew he had been misled for twenty-three years, twenty-three years in which he had uncritically and unwittingly acted as a powerful voice for the Pahlavi dynasty in America.

Lilienthal's reputation for honesty and integrity made him an especially effective spokesman for the shah. He earnestly delivered his praises of Pahlavism to American presidents and their wives, to the most influential leaders of the mass media, to businessmen and bankers, and to political leaders at all levels of the federal government. Examples abound. After a private session with Henry Luce of *Time* in December 1958 during which time Lilienthal described the shah's rule in superlatives, Luce excitedly concluded: "We want *Time* in on this story as well as *Life*. Matter of fact I would like to go out there myself." A year later Lilienthal argued the Pahlavi case with Edward R. Murrow after the latter perceptively commented: "I would say it is a rather brittle regime." Worried about the Kennedy administration's stance on Iran, Lilienthal cautioned the shah that "there will be many new faces. Quite a few will be from academic life, a rather sheltered existence, who will be brilliant but not always practical nor wise. Many of them have yet to learn how tough the world is by going through rugged experiences, as I have, and as he [the shah] has. (At this he gave a knowing, quiet half-smile)." Not only did Lilienthal lobby Kennedy and Johnson directly about the shah, he also influenced the thinking of their wives. After a State dinner for the shah at the White House in August 1967, Lilienthal privately described the shah to an enthralled Lady Bird Johnson: "I told her what a remarkable man the Shah was."[75]

Although David Lilienthal was a liberal thinker, he was also a member of the American political and economic establishment. His entrance into the Iranian scene was encouraged and backed by the financial genius, Andre Meyer of Lazard Frères. Lilienthal's relationships with the Rockefellers were also close. Besides his important membership on the Council on Foreign Relations, he maintained many other contacts with this influential group he often referred to as "the Family." In early 1971, his Development and Resources Corporation was purchased by the Rockefeller-owned IBEC, now headed by Rodman Rockefeller, Nelson's eldest son. David Lilienthal and Rodman Rockefeller had a close personal and professional relationship even though they at times disagreed on business matters. Lilienthal summarized their philosophical difficulties well in a brief description of Rodman: "He is a frank and explicit worshiper of power, and power over people. So that he would like to use me is understandable, particularly since I am indeed a schmo and 'good guy.' "[76] David Lilienthal and the Rockefeller family admired and supported the Pahlavi regime in Iran. They did business in Iran together and reinforced one another's attitudes about the situation in that country.

The inner circle of Pahlavites was extremely effective in promoting U.S.-Iranian ties. All seven were strong, successful, and independent-minded individuals. Each had quite different reasons for supporting the shah's regime. The economic motivation was undoubtedly critical, but personal, social, and political factors were also important. The inner circle of Pahlavites represented varying shades of political and social opinion: David Rockefeller was conservative; Nelson, a conservative/moderate; David Lilienthal, a political liberal with a genuine social conscience; Henry Kissinger, a political pragmatist with a keenly self-interested conscience; and Richard Helms and Kermit Roosevelt, conservative but loyal official bureaucrats who sometimes appeared to act on the conviction that the end justifies the means.

The Second Circle of Connectors

The second circle of influential American figures consists of lawyers and a national security adviser (see figure 3). Over the years, the shah's government employed a large number of important American law firms, especially in New York and Washington. Although not as intimately involved with Pahlavi Iran as the members of the first circle, these people effectively promoted Pahlavism in America. Their influence provided much of the cement that bound the U.S. establishment to the Pahlavi establishment. One of these professional expeditors (McCloy) was a member of the Rockefeller extended family, while two others (Rogers and Brzezinski) were indirectly associated with "the Family."

Besides John McCloy, who has already been mentioned, another establishment legal figure who represented Pahlavi Iran was former attorney general and secretary of State William P. Rogers. Appearing on the Iranian scene in the 1970s, Rogers was a partner in the New York law firm of Royall, Koegel and Rogers (later simply Rogers and Wells). In 1974, Rogers accompanied Merrill Lynch head Donald Regan to Tehran to open a Merrill Lynch business connection in Iran. Regan, later the powerful chief of staff for President Ronald Reagan, told the Tower Commission in 1987 that "I opened an office in Tehran for Merrill, Lynch and have [sic] very close connections in Tehran in the era of the Shah during the '70s."[77]

William Rogers's law partner, John A. Wells, was a longtime political aide to Nelson Rockefeller and had been his presidential campaign manager in 1964.[78] Rogers and Wells represented the Pahlavi Foundation in the United States, and Rogers himself was a member of the American Pahlavi Foundation's board of directors. According to a New York Times article, Rogers and Wells helped set up the American Pahlavi Foundation as a tax-exempt organization whereby the income from its valuable Fifth Avenue property would be used to send Iranian students to American universities.[79] Rogers himself argued that the idea for the scholarships originated in Iran. "The Iranians wanted to establish more scholarships and asked if they could organize such a foundation. . . . They needed to have a board. . . . There were no meetings or anything. This was a pro forma corporation of a charitable foundation."[80]

On an earlier occasion, Rogers telephoned investigative journalist Jack Anderson three times categorically denying rumors that the shah had been funneling large sums of money into Richard Nixon's presidential campaign by way of Mexico. Rogers and Wells sent a telegram of denial to United Feature Syndicates, which distributes Anderson's columns. Among other things, the telegram stated: "We strongly urge that this story not be published." In response, Anderson said: "We can hardly resist publishing a story that the shah is so anxious to suppress."[81] It is clear that after he left public office William Rogers did become involved in legal and business arrangements with Pahlavi Iran.

In Washington, Lawyer Ralph E. Becker was a consistent admirer of the Pahlavi dynasty. Although an important official in the Republican party, Becker's influence transcended political parties; he received a number of appointments in President Lyndon Johnson's administration. A decorated veteran of World War II and an ambassador to Honduras, Ralph Becker belonged to over one hundred civic, social, and political organizations and received decorations from seven countries. Iranian friends who worked with him were in awe of Becker's influence and often spoke about his "behind-the curtains" (*pusht-i pardah*) political power.

Ralph Becker was president of the five-hundred-member Iran-America Society in the United States from 1964 to 1976. He lobbied hard for the shah and received two important Pahlavi decorations, the Order of Homayoun and the Order of Taj. He demonstrated his influence as a committed Pahlavite in 1968 when he wrote to civil service head John Macy to point out that he was responsible for a number of favorable articles in the *Congressional Record* praising the shah and his government. The copies of the statements he enclosed for Macy included laudatory pro-Pahlavi statements by Rep. Clement J. Zablocki of Wisconsin and Rep. E. Ross Adair of Indiana as well as by Sen. Charles Percy of Illinois, Sen. Howard Baker of Tennessee, and Sen. Clinton Anderson of New Mexico. On July 24, 1968, State Department Iran country director Ted Eliot sent Becker a copy of a *Tehran Journal* article that had reprinted Senator Baker's praise for the shah. In the note, Eliot wrote that he was enclosing a copy of the July 1968 article "reporting Senator Baker's praise of the Shah. Many thanks, as always, for your help." Becker, perhaps better than anyone else, represents the kind of influential American who silently shaped official America's uncritical view of the shah's Iran.[82]

Although not a lawyer, Zbigniew Brzezinski exerted an enormous amount of influence in support of the shah, as noted earlier. He did this almost entirely in his role as President Jimmy Carter's national security adviser. He maintained a special relationship with Ardeshir Zahedi. Because he was a relative latecomer to Pahlavism, he cannot be placed in the first circle of influentials. Yet, due to the critical and concentrated nature of his influence in the late 1970s, he belongs most properly in the second ring of influence.

These men acted as "connectors" in the system by welding the rings of Pahlavite influence through their ties with the shah's Iranian inner circle and other circles of influence. They had especially close ties with the first ring of American Pahlavites, the ring dominated by the Rockefeller family. Another lawyer who might be considered to be a satellite member of this second ring demonstrates this. William E. Jackson was another member of Milbank, Tweed who represented Pahlavi interests in the United States. The son of former Supreme Court Justice Robert Jackson and head of Milbank, Tweed's litigation division, he had graduated from Harvard Law School and had helped to recruit Elliot Richardson for Milbank, Tweed. Referred to by State Department officials as "David Rockefeller's attorney," Jackson also served as the shah's personal lawyer. He represented the interests of the shah and Princess Ashraf after the revolution. An excellent attorney, Jackson's assistance to the Pahlavis demonstrated the double interlocking nature of personalities and institutions—David Rockefeller and the shah, Chase Manhattan Bank and Milbank, Tweed—involving America and Iran.

The Third Circle of Pahlavites: Generals and Businessmen

Among the most crucial connectors in the American-Pahlavi linkage were U.S. government officials, who on retirement from public service were employed by private industry seeking contracts with Iran. Numerous middle- and high-ranking American military officers once stationed in Iran went to work for private businesses and institutes that signed financial agreements with Pahlavi Iran. Although Kermit Roosevelt and Richard Helms were among the most important civilian figures who fit this description, the major contracts were military in nature, and it is here where the relationship had special financial reinforcement. The most visible examples of this relationship involved heads of the various important MAAG missions to Iran. These included powerful ARMISH-MAAG general Harvey Jablonsky, who later went to work as a representative for Northrop; U.S. Air Force MAAG chief Harold Price (Philco-Ford); and U.S. Navy MAAG head Capt. R. S. Harward (TRACOR, Rockwell International). Jablonsky represented the archetypal hard-hitting influential military man become arms salesman. As a trusted confidant of the shah on military matters, Jablonsky was able to whet the shah's technological appetite in ways favorable to Northrop.[83]

A slightly different example of an American military general with important responsibilities in Iran during the shah's rule who later played a central role in U.S.-Iranian relations was Gen. Richard V. Secord. Unlike many of the other retired military men who took advisory positions with U.S. industries seeking Iranian contracts after their service in Pahlavi Iran, Secord did not retire until 1983, after the revolution. His subsequent professional career centered more on contracts with the U.S. government than with Iran. Still, Secord's fate seemed tied to Iran. During the hostage incident in 1980, Secord was reportedly involved in a plan to seize strategic sites in Iran. Later, as an adviser and consultant to Lt. Col. Oliver North and the NSC, he became a principal figure in the Reagan administration's Iran-Contra scandal. North considered Secord to be an accomplished Iran expert, and the two worked closely together during the Reagan administration's Iran initiative. Following a meeting in Brussels in August of 1986, Secord put North and the NSC in contact with an influential Iranian—the second channel of Iranian-American communication during the final stages of the Iran-Contra affair.

Richard Secord first served in Iran as an adviser to the Iranian Air Force in 1963 and then again in 1964 and 1965. He was appointed chief of the U.S. Air Force section of MAAG in Tehran in September 1975 and served there until July of 1978. While in Iran, he acted as chief adviser to the commander in chief of the Iranian Air Force and directed all U.S. Air Force programs in Iran as well as a number of U.S. Army and U.S. Navy security assistance projects. It was in Iran at this time that Secord reportedly became acquainted with Albert Hakim, an Iranian entrepreneur then working with such CIA agents as Frank Terpil.

On his retirement, Secord joined Iranian businessman Albert Hakim in a company known as Stanford Technology Trading Group International. Newspaper reports indicate that Hakim was involved in the sale of $7.5 million worth of electronic surveillance equipment to the Iranian Air Force in 1974–75. According to the *Wall Street Journal*, Secord and a "network" of other former military officers also formed a company, American National Development Corporation, shortly after Secord retired that "began receiving classified government contracts soon after."[84] Secord's influence in shaping Iranian-American relations, therefore, transcended the Iranian revolution.

Although certain military leaders exerted considerable political and economic influence in Iranian-American relations, the members of the American industrial elite were even more important. The chairs of the boards and chief executive officers of major U.S. corporations were the ones who aggressively sought and signed the lucrative contracts in Iran. Two examples were Thomas Jones, president of Northrop and James A. Linen, chairman of Time, Inc. Both visited Iran; both knew the shah and members of his inner circle; both supported and signed major contracts with Iran; and both strongly believed in Pahlavism.

Tom Jones, an accomplished and aggressive salesman for his company, was extremely popular among the inner circle members of the shah's elite, who at times found themselves mesmerized by his dynamism and charm. An important and extremely effective representative for Jones and Northrop in Iran was former public official Jeffrey Kitchen. Kitchen, who had served as deputy assistant secretary of State for politico-military affairs, was one of the most accomplished lobbyists in Tehran in the late 1960s and 1970s.

Jim Linen married Sally Scranton, the sister of Gov. William Scranton of Pennsylvania, and graduated from Williams College in the class ahead of Richard Helms. Helms and Linen worked closely together as heads of the college yearbook in successive years at Williams. Incorruptible and internationally adventurous, Jim Linen had close ties with the Rockefellers and was a leader among those encouraging American investment in Iran. The high-powered May 1970 American business delegation to Iran, for example, was led by Linen but backed by David Rockefeller and Chase Manhattan Bank. The State Department referred to it as the Linen Investment Seminar. Governor Scranton was one of the seminar participants. In fall 1976, Time, Inc. signed a contract to establish a publishing company in Iran. A relatively small project designed to penetrate the mass market while at the same time developing an Iranian editorial staff, this venture carried unusual potential before it was overtaken by the revolution. Jones and Linen are only two examples of the hundreds of powerful American businessmen associated with Pahlavi Iran.

Pahlavism and the United States Congress

The shah's government consciously sought to establish close relationships with members of the Congress. Over the years, several hundred senators and representatives either visited Iran or were invited to social functions sponsored by high-ranking Iranian officials in Washington. The fourth circle of American Pahlavites identified in figure 3 contains the names of six congressmen—four senators and two representatives—who had especially close ties to Iran. These include Senators Jacob Javits, Barry Goldwater, Charles Percy, and Richard Stone, and Congressmen John M. Murphy and William Lehman. Many other influential American lawmakers also had close associations with the shah's Iran, such as Sen. Edward Brooke and Rep. John Brademas.

Senator Goldwater was a strong Pahlavi backer partly because of his conviction that a militarily strong shah would help deflect Soviet challenges in the region. He consistently supported arms sales to the shah. Senator Percy's belief in the shah was enhanced by Princess Ashraf, Hushang Ansary, and Ardeshir Zahedi. By May 1979, Percy was deeply involved in seeking asylum for the shah in the United States. Senators Javits and Stone, along with Congressman Lehman, were unwavering supporters of the shah's regime because of the very close Pahlavi-Israeli relationship. Congressman Lehman of Florida, for example, in a statement on the House floor in February 1979, used the Iranian revolution as an example of "Arab" instability and emphasized the "strategic importance" of Israel to the United States.[85] In a few cases, it would appear that official Americans worked closely with Iran for purposes of personal gain. The special relationships that bound certain U.S. congressmen to Pahlavi Iran can be most clearly seen in two case studies: those of Sen. Jacob Javits and Rep. John M. Murphy.

A liberal, highly respected Republican member of the U.S. Senate, Jacob Javits uncharacteristically supported arms sales to the shah's regime because of his deep commitment to the state of Israel, a country with few allies in the Middle East. The shah's Iran was a rare Israeli ally. Javits maneuvered brilliantly in the Senate, subtly blocking aid to such Arab countries as Saudi Arabia while staunchly supporting military sales to the shah. Three meetings of the subcommittee on foreign assistance of the Senate Committee on Foreign Relations held in September 1976 demonstrate Javits's skill. While supporting a massive arms sales package to Iran, he cosponsored a resolution cutting the number of Sidewinder and Maverick missiles requested by Saudi Arabia from 2,000 and 1,500 to 850 and 650, respectively. Just before the vote on all sales, Javits managed to separate out the Saudi sale from the package and to have it voted on separately. Javits then voted *not* to support a resolution denying the Saudi sale and shrewdly watched while the Saudi sale was disapproved by a vote of 8–6. He voted not to block the Saudi sales because he had to support the resolution in which he had already helped emasculate the Saudi request. Senator Javits knew what the outcome of the vote on the separate resolution would be in any case.[86]

The Javits-Pahlavi connection approached a national scandal in 1976 when it became known that the senator's wife, Marian, had accepted a $67,500 annual retainer from the Iranian government to do public relations for Iran Air. This was part of a $500,000 contract that the Iranian government signed with New York agency Ruder & Finn to promote Iran's image in America. Among other things, the contract provided that the agency was "to act as spokesman to professional men and women and top notch businessmen while making approaches to such publications as the *New York Times, Time* magazine, *Harper's,* and the *Washington Post* with a goal toward the publicizing of articles on key areas of interest in Iran." Despite her contract, Marian Javits was uncomfortable about the oppression of the shah's regime. At an April 1978 luncheon with Parviz Radji, the Iranian ambassador in London, she stated that by backing the shah militarily, America "is part of it." Radji responded: "So are you my dear."[87] Senator Javits himself was enormously embarrassed by the adverse publicity surrounding this affair, and Marian Javits renounced the contract soon afterwards. With the Iranian revolution, Jacob Javits indicated his longtime support for the shah's regime one last time by taking an immediate hostile position toward the new government in Tehran. The Javits resolution (discussed in chapter 8), which seriously harmed American diplomatic efforts in early 1979, is the major example of this hostility.

An oft-decorated veteran of the Korean War, Democrat John M. Murphy represented Staten Island for a decade and half in the U.S. Congress. While a congressman in the mid-1970s, Murphy became involved in a myriad of business negotiations with high-ranking officials in the governments of South Korea, Nicaragua, and Iran. A longtime friend of Gen. Anastasio Somoza, a classmate of his at West Point, Murphy worked to help Burmah Oil establish an oil refinery in Nicaragua. As part of this proposal, Murphy suggested that the oil be provided by Iran. According to the *New York Times,* Murphy at one point went so far as to attempt to arrange a meeting between Somoza and the shah. During these and other negotiations, Murphy traveled often to Iran and developed a network of influential Iranian friends and acquaintances. In 1973–74, Murphy became a member of the Pahlavi Foundation in the United States and shared a position on the board with William P. Rogers and others. In his words, "a personal Iranian friend asked me to be on the board with Bill Rogers. They needed—uh—to have some Americans on the board to advise them on various matters."[88]

Although the John M. Murphy case is surely an extreme example of a national American legislator involved with Pahlavi Iran, it stands as an important historical reminder of the nature of some of the ties that developed between important personalities in both countries. Motivations for strong Pahlavi support differed considerably from one American congressman to another. Most supported the shah because they firmly believed that this was in America's best interest; some did so because it was viewed to be in Israel's best interest; and a few did so because they saw it in their own best interests. Nevertheless, some legislators in Washington were always highly suspicious of the shah and his policies. These included Hubert Humphrey in his earlier days as a congressman and, more recently, John Culver, Gaylord Nelson, Thomas Eagleton, and George McGovern. Despite this, the Pahlavi regime enjoyed a surprising level of consistent support over the years in the Congress. In a revealing overstatement in 1976, the shah reportedly told Iran's representative to the United Nations that Ambassador Zahedi in Washington "has all the American senators in his pocket."[89]

American politicians do not live in a vacuum. Like others, they are influenced by the mass media and by public opinion, which affects them even as they influence it. They are sensitive to the opinions of important businessmen and influential social figures in the country. They also at times consider the words and writings of academics on foreign policy. In the case of Iran, the climate of opinion in which lawmakers operated was heavily pro-Pahlavi in nature. The fifth and outer circle of the reinforcing concentric circles of American Pahlavites was dominated by leading figures in the worlds of scholarship and the mass media.

Public Opinion and Pahlavism

In 1976, Pahlavi Iran, with the approval of the shah himself, hired the services of national polling firm Yankelovich, Skelly and White to survey a number of American opinion leaders concerning their views of the shah and his country. Daniel Yankelovich had himself developed high-level contacts in Iran when participating in the 1975 Persepolis-Aspen conference on development. He was awarded the Pahlavi contract the year after he delivered an extremely flattering statement that concluded the proceedings of the Persepolis conference.[90] Yankelovich sought to interview American "influentials" in order to ascertain their attitudes towards Iran. These influentials were composed primarily of members of the mass media, state politicians, and academics. The survey, the results of which were closely guarded, stands as impressive proof of the shah of Iran's preoccupation with his image in the United States.

Throughout his career, Muhammad Reza Shah closely followed the American mass media's coverage of his rule. He was easily upset about any critical commentary and reacted accordingly. For thirty years, American diplomats were bluntly approached by members of the Pahlavi political elite about articles that the shah disapproved of. In the early 1950s, for example, the Iranian court minister and prime minister approached the U.S. ambassador in Tehran about less than praiseworthy articles that had appeared in *Time, Newsweek,* and *Life.* On one occasion, in a general piece on Iran in February 1951, *Time* made an unflattering reference to Princess Ashraf. The Iranian government insisted that American Ambassador Grady apologize to the princess. The situation was temporarily resolved when the ambassador's wife called on Ashraf and expressed her admiration. This resulted in an article favorable to Princess Ashraf prepared by the United Press representative in Tehran. On several other occasions over the years, the U.S. government was able to influence coverage. In September 1953, for example, Assistant Secretary of State Henry Byroade had lunch with the editors of *Time* and *Life* in New York in order to elicit more favorable coverage of the shah's position in Iran. In his cable back to Tehran, Byroade stated: "Believe *Time* editors now fully understand problem and will make effort slowly correct position in manner which does not make them appear completely inconsistent."[91]

Despite this occasional successful governmental pressure, the American mass media were generally suspicious of this kind of intervention. Incidents such as those described above were the exceptions rather than the rule. Since he ruled Iran with a controlled press, the shah was slow to understand that the U.S. government did not always dictate the articles and editorials that appeared in American newspapers. As he became more sophisticated, the shah recognized that it was really up to him to build good public relations with the American mass media.

The shah was so sensitive to criticism that all members of his inner circle (and many of their subordinates) became preoccupied with the need to see that American opinion leaders viewed Pahlavi Iran in positive terms. The shah generally sent accomplished public relations men as ambassadors to the United States and to Great Britain, a country where he also demanded a good press. The last two ambassadors to these countries, Ardeshir Zahedi and Parviz Radji, did impressive jobs in serving these ends. Zahedi was Americanized; educated at Utah State University, he was hardworking, generous, and down-to-earth. Radji had close ties to Prime Minister Hoveyda and Princess Ashraf. He was suave and articulate and had been educated at Cambridge University. Both Zahedi and Radji spent much of their ambassadorial time cultivating ties with the members of the mass media and fending off sharp queries from Tehran whenever critical articles appeared in the press of the countries to which they were posted.

Over the years, the American mass media presented a very favorable image of Iran and of the shah. Various systematic studies have now documented the pervasiveness of the pro-Pahlavi reporting.[92] With minor exceptions, it was not until deep into the revolution that leading American newspapers and periodicals such as the *New York Times*, the *Washington Post*, *Time*, and *Newsweek* began to raise fundamental questions about the regime. Occasional critical pieces would appear on their op-ed pages, but these were clearly exceptions. Even after the revolution, the establishment press in America continued to distort Iranian political events almost as if it were watching and waiting for another Pahlavi restoration. It is true that the pro-Pahlavi chorus was never without a few weak voices singing critical refrains— Jack Anderson in occasional columns on corruption and oppression, Mike Wallace confronting the shah in interviews, and occasional serious analyses by the *Christian Science Monitor*, the American newspaper with the best overall record for objectivity in covering events in the shah's Iran. But in general the American mass media reinforced the shah's own public relations, and many of its most influential members were especially enamoured by Pahlavi Iran. And so they reported it.

The outer circle of Pahlavites contains the names of four journalists with extremely close ties to Iran (see figure 3). These four individuals, Arnaud de Borchgrave, Joseph Kraft, Barbara Walters, and Betty Beale, shared little in common other than their admiration for and consistent promotion of the shah's rule. De Borchgrave, an influential senior editor at *Newsweek* for years, had direct access to the shah, and his writings consistently praised the shah and his regime. After the revolution, serious allegations were made by an Iranian press office protocol officer named Siamak Zand that he had personally delivered two matched carpets worth ten thousand dollars each to de Borchgrave's room at the Tehran Hilton. Zand claimed these were gifts in return for de Borchgrave's laudatory articles about the shah. De Borchgrave vigorously denied these charges and threatened to sue, to take a lie detector test, and to open his apartment for outside inspection. It is most probable that De Borchgrave, like many ideological conservatives, genuinely believed in the shah and felt that he represented America's best interests in the Persian Gulf. A review of his interviews and writings, however, leaves little doubt of his strong support for the Pahlavi government.[93]

Barbara Walters was extremely close to the Pahlavi royal family and to Ambassador Ardeshir Zahedi. Her television interviews with the shah and the empress introduced the leaders of the royal family to the American public in a very positive light. At one point in 1975 when she was hostess on NBC's "Today Show," Zahedi reportedly sent her back to New York on a private jet he had chartered. Barbara Walters was a central part of the social network that Zahedi established on the East coast and annually received the most expensive gifts that Zahedi provided for members of the mass media. The Iranian Embassy gift list indicated that she was to receive caviar, Cartier silver, and, perhaps the most expensive of the many hundreds of gifts delivered to members of the American mass media between 1975 and 1977, a diamond watch.[94]

The social cement that was instrumental in binding all circles of the shah's most powerful American supporters into one wheel of influence was provided by such individuals as Betty Beale. A noted hostess and influential society columnist, she continuously praised Pahlavi elite members and polished their images. She, too, was a special friend of Ardeshir Zahedi and lamented his disappearance after the revolution: "Unfortunately, the biggest hunk of the glamour, excitement and brilliance of Washington entertaining disappeared with the absence of Iranian Ambassador Ardeshir Zahedi. There has not been in this city in perhaps a half century another host who entertained so many important people with such elegance and such concern for the comfort of his guests."[95] While other favored members of the mass media were the recipients of single bottles of Dom Perignon champagne, the Iranian Embassy provided Betty Beale and her husband with entire cases of both champagne and wine. In this instance, the gifts were multiple and also included Cartier silver and caviar.

The shah's embassy in Washington was a repository for huge supplies of caviar, pistachios, valuable silver, wine, and champagne. The Beluga caviar had a value of $217 a tin while the Dom Perignon champagne was valued at $35 a bottle. Several gift lists were kept at the Iranian Embassy, and on special occasions, such as Christmas, expensive mementos were delivered to influential Americans.[96] A particularly lengthy list was entitled "United States—Mass Media." This 135-page document contained the names of 620 Americans, 285 of whom received gifts between 1975 and 1977. A list of the gifts and the numbers distributed for each of the three years preceding the revolution shows the extent of the giving (see table 2).

These gifts were distributed to individuals employed in the mass media: radio, television, newspapers, magazines, news services, and so forth. They were directed to individuals from the highest executives to cameramen and newsroom personnel. Those considered most influential or special friends received the most expensive gifts. Besides the four individuals referred to above, the special friend category included

Table 2 Iran Embassy Gifts to Members of the U.S. Mass Media,
1975–1977

	1975	1976	1977
Champagne (bottles)	85	59	36
Champagne (cases)	1	3	4
Caviar	61	32	47
Wine (cases)	3	1	1
Cartier silver	41	37	22
Candles/candlesticks	46	11	0
Books	20	136	94
Pistachios	6	9	8
Ties/silk scarfs	6	17	1
Diamond watch	0	0	1
Other gifts	3	6	43
Total	272	311	257

Carl Rowan, Irving R. Levine, Tom Brokaw, and James A. Linen. Of the three major news networks, NBC was considered most sympathetic to the shah. At least twenty-two NBC employees were on Zahedi's gift list. Multiple gifts were provided Julian Goodman, the chairman of the board of NBC and Herbert Schlosser, the president of the company at the time. Schlosser was responsible for hiring Henry Kissinger as a consultant and commentator for a reported five-year $5 million contract. NBC produced little critical material on the shah's Iran.

These gifts were not bribes. They were personal remembrances and mementos that helped build and strengthen human relationships. Zahedi used them largely to reinforce warm feelings that most of these individuals already held toward Pahlavi Iran. Most influential journalists supported Iran for other reasons. They believed in what the shah was doing at home; they were impressed by the representatives of his government; they strongly agreed with his policies supporting Israel and opposing the Soviet Union; and they ultimately considered him a staunch, stable friend of the United States. They held these beliefs more easily because American reporters were woven into the social network developed by Zahedi and associates. They included writers of widely differing political outlooks. Just as de Borchgrave represented a strongly conservative supporter, Joseph Kraft was an example of a more liberal Pahlavite.

Columnist Joe Kraft was an especially close friend of Ambassador Zahedi and would on occasion stay at Zahedi's luxurious home when he visited Tehran. He relished his many private interviews with the shah and even offered the king political advice on occasion. His columns were consistently supportive of the shah and sharply critical of the opposition, which he first described as communist and later as fundamentalist. Until the end, Kraft had no doubt that the shah would prevail; when the monarch inevitably fell, Kraft quickly blamed the Carter administration for everything.

In April 1974, Kraft reported that "what the Shah seems to be doing is preempting the fundamentalist position." A year later, he began a column with the following words: "Leaders all around the world have recently had dramatic ups and downs. Only the Shah of Iran seems to go from success to success." At the end of August 1978, Kraft warned that "the opposition in Iran cannot take over. It is incapable of managing a modernization process that has now gone too far to be reversed." He described the shah's regime as "the only barrier in an ocean of instability" and concluded that "the shah comes close to being indispensable." After the shah's fall in 1979, Kraft, a proven slow learner when it came to understanding the fragility of Middle Eastern dictators whom he considered personal friends, concluded an April 11 column about President Sadat of Egypt with words similar to those he had used to describe the stability of the shah: "Sadat, despite the existence of an opposition in Egypt, is almost sure to be in power for a long, long time."

The Iranian revolution greatly upset Joseph Kraft. He told an audience in Washington, "My sense is that the country does not want to face up to the really tough sacrifices that go with hitting at some way this crazy fluke curve ball—Islamic Fundamentalism—that history has dealt us." In Kraft's mind, President Carter was not swinging hard enough at this Islamic curve. The columnist was bitter about Carter's policy, which he termed a "policy of waffling and accommodation" (December 1979), "appeasement" (March 1980), and "the administration's bootlicking approach" (August 1980). A committed Pahlavite to the end, Kraft only continued to heckle the batter and had little positive advice to offer anyone who might be standing in the on-deck circle waiting to face those tough pitches.[97]

Whereas members of the American mass media failed to provide sensitive or critical coverage of Iran, academia also had a less than impressive record. Despite occasional hard-hitting studies by such scholars as Ervand Abrahamian, Eric Hooglund, and Hamid Algar, most scholarship on contemporary Iran was surprisingly uncritical. Academics were often linked in the Pahlavi connection, and although many may have expressed reservations about the regime privately, they were highly circumspect in their publications. Other scholars, clearly sympathetic to the shah's government, reinforced the views of the Kissingers, Javitses, Krafts, and De Borchgraves. They were located at such places as the Center for Strategic and International Studies associated with Georgetown University (Alvin Cottrell) and included independent researchers and influential writers (Donald Wilber) and distinguished scholars in major universities (George Lenczowski).

Donald N. Wilber, author of *Iran: Past and Present*, which went through nine editions, was an Iran specialist of considerable talent and a recognized authority of Islamic architecture. He first traveled to Iran as a young archaeological student in 1934. He was employed by the OSS in Iran between 1941 and 1946. From 1947 to 1969, he was a member of the CIA, while writing prolifically on subjects Iranian. During these years, he traveled to Iran thirteen times, and in 1952–53 he was a member of Kermit Roosevelt's Operation Ajax team, which helped overthrow Muhammad Musaddiq. Convinced that monarchy was the only political system that could govern Iran, Wilber was a dedicated Pahlavite who was "on friendly terms" with every Iranian ambassador to America since Hussein Ala in the 1940s. Although he knew Iran well and had traveled the countryside extensively, he seemed oblivious to the social and political problems that plagued the country. Thus, he could make the curious statement: "In all my travels, often to places remote from highways and towns, I saw villages without poverty and filth, and met friendly people. I suspect that those who wrote about the plight of the peasants had never visited a village." Wilber's commitment to the shah is seen in his own description of his dislike for Robert Kennedy because, "for one thing, he did not like the Shah of Iran."[98]

Although open to other ideas and a man of integrity and great energy, George Lenczowski was perhaps the leading Pahlavite among American Iran specialists. The author of several important books, Lenczowski edited a large volume entitled *Iran under the Pahlavis*, which appeared in 1978—at about the same time as the Iranian revolution.[99] This poorly timed study was largely uncritical in approach and reinforced the image of Pahlavi stability at the very time the regime was going under. Lenczowski traveled often to Iran; he interviewed the shah and developed close relationships with many members of the Pahlavi elite. It is not surprising that with the revolution, George Lenczowski accepted an assignment with the Rockefeller organization. In his diary entry for March 3, 1980, David Lilienthal noted a call from Professor "Lancowski": "Jack McCloy and David Rockefeller had asked him to put together some of the facts about the constructive things that had been accomplished 'by the preceding regime' in Iran."[100]

The group of unconditional Pahlavi admirers was relatively small among scholars of contemporary Iran. Although there was always a dialogue among Iran specialists, even those most critical of the shah sometimes pulled their punches. The ivy on the halls of much of American academia was greened by the shah's government. Generous grants and contracts were provided to such universities as Harvard, MIT, Princeton, Southern California, Kent State, Georgetown, Howard, and American. A large grant to the University of Chicago was renounced after major opposition from its faculty and students. All in all, fifty-five U.S. institutions of higher education maintained official links with the shah's Iran. Influential Iranians appended to the shah's inner circle even penetrated governing bodies of U.S. universities. Cyrus Ansary, for example, an influential lawyer and brother of Hushang Ansary, served on the board of directors of American University. Over the years, various members of the Pahlavi family received honorary degrees from American educational institutions.

Many members of the mass media along with certain influential scholars provided the intellectual justification for America's close relationship with Iran for four decades. Many Americans thought of the shah as a somewhat stern, Westernlike ruler struggling to bring his country into the twentieth century while giving away his lands to grateful peasants. He was a friend of America with considerable oil and an enemy of the Soviet Union, with which he courageously shared a long border. He was a kind of storybook king with a succession of lovely wives. Like his friends King Hussein of Jordan and Anwar Sadat of Egypt, he was clearly a moderate, civilized force in an area of the world dominated by fanatics and communists. Like Hussein and Sadat, he was friendly with people like Barbara Walters, Henry Kissinger, and Richard Nixon. He was a strong and sturdy ally, appreciated by America and loved by his people. American Pahlavites subscribed to this image. They promoted this benevolent, stable picture of Iran so assiduously that when the Pahlavi pillar collapsed from within Americans everywhere were profoundly shocked.

American Pahlavism Analyzed

The direct political influence wielded by the shah's most powerful American friends on the Carter administration during the Iranian political crisis demonstrates the strength of Pahlavism in America.

Pahlavi supporters' motives were complex and included personal friendship and loyalty, conservative political beliefs, strategic issues involving Israel and the Soviet Union, and, in some cases, economic and financial self-interest. An analysis of the dynamics that energized the various circles of influence presented in figure 3 reveals six important conclusions.

First, cutting through and across this Pahlavi wheel of power in the United States is the preeminent influence of the Rockefellers, of "the Family," in the words of David Lilienthal. The two Rockefeller members of the inner circle were joined there by influential Rockefeller employee Henry Kissinger. Other Pahlavites directly employed by the Rockefellers included lawyers John J. McCloy and William Jackson. David Lilienthal, James A. Linen, and William Rogers all had Rockefeller associations that included membership on the Council on Foreign Relations. Rogers was also a member of the Rockefeller Foundation, and Lilienthal's corporation was absorbed by a Rockefeller corporation. Linen worked with David Rockefeller in promoting American business investment in the shah's Iran. Scholar George Lenczowski, whose views on Iran coincided with those of the Rockefellers, eventually accepted an assignment with them. Other important members of the twenty-eight identified Pahlavi supporters, such as Richard Nixon, Barbara Walters, and Joseph Kraft, were indirectly plugged into this faction through their personal ties with Henry Kissinger. All in all, nearly half of the twenty-eight were directly or indirectly tied to Rockefeller interests.

Second, despite the coalescing and unifying force of the Rockefeller connection, Pahlavi believers in the United States represented a wide variety of individuals and interests. Pahlavites could be found among Democrats and Republicans as well as among liberals and conservatives. And Pahlavi support transcended personal and social rivalries as well. The liberal-conservative division is particularly instructive in this regard. Charles Percy and Barry Goldwater, Jacob Javits and Henry Jackson, David Lilienthal and John J. McCloy, Carl Rowen and Arnaud De Borchgrave—all shared a common pro-Pahlavi perspective. This perspective was also shared by Democrat Lyndon Johnson and Republican Richard Nixon and by personal rivals Henry Kissinger and William Rogers. Even Hubert Humphrey, an early and outspoken liberal skeptic of the shah's style of rule in Iran, in the last decade and a half of his career became a cautious supporter of the shah.[101] It is interesting to note that the Carter administration, so often blamed for the Iranian-American disaster, had little representation in the circles of leading American Pahlavites.

Third, much of the reason for this broad base of support for the shah among American influentials resides in the major effort made by the shah and his sophisticated inner circle to accomplish precisely this goal. The regime emphasized personal rapport and social ties. Ardeshir Zahedi was a proven master at this form of public relations. Crusty and principled Barry Goldwater, therefore, could state on the floor of the United States Senate that Zahedi was "one of the best personal friends that all of us has here in Washington." Goldwater went on to say that "I first met this gentleman many years ago when he came to my hometown of Phoenix to work first as a dishwasher and then a waiter to learn the American free enterprise system."[102] Joseph Kraft put his friendship with Zahedi in the following words: "Zahedi was kind of a friend. He was one of the only interesting guys around here during the Nixon era." And David Brinkley said of Zahedi: "He came to our house very often. He remains a personal friend, though I haven't seen him lately."[103]

Zahedi never forgot a birthday nor failed to send his best wishes to American leaders, whether in or out of office, at a time of personal illness or on the occasion of an important national holiday. As Iran's ambassador to London in 1965, Zahedi sent Lyndon Johnson an orchid tree when Johnson was recuperating at the ranch after an operation; the following year, still in London, Zahedi sent a hospitalized LBJ a vase of chrysanthemums and asters; while serving as Iran's foreign minister in Tehran in the late 1960s, Zahedi periodically sent President Johnson caviar and other remembrances such as an expensive vest pocket watch and an exquisite china box. Others in the first family were not forgotten. In January 1969, for example, Zahedi sent Lucy Johnson four tins of caviar. Zahedi's American personal secretary between 1973 and 1976 viewed Zahedi as "an exceptional individual" who "did his job superbly, and in fact was not given sufficient credit for his astuteness, his party/playboy image masking his real shrewdness." This shrewdness was used every moment to win important American friends for the shah. After describing Zahedi's personal and political finesse, his secretary wrote in October 1977 that "these words are meant to salute his success in playing the Washington game far more effectively than anyone else in town. But it is a game, a very ruthless one masked by the mellifluous overtones of social dalliance. Let us not forget that the stakes may be cataclysmic."[104]

Fourth, the magnificent sustained public relations campaign of the shah and his political elite was assisted by the enormous ignorance of Iran among American influentials. With one exception, none of the American Pahlavites identified in figure 3 spoke Persian. All saw the society from the top down and remained insulated from the masses. In Tehran, they stayed at the Hilton and Intercontinental hotels, occasionally at the Park Hotel. Several were regularly guests in the palatial mansions of the English-speaking Pahlavi elite. Enamoured of the spectacular Persian art, architecture, and handicrafts, they made trips to the countryside to shop and sightsee at Isfahan, Shiraz, Persepolis, Kish Island, and, when time permitted, at the Caspian seashore. Given the glitter and the glamor, it is not surprising that they had little idea of the grinding poverty, the oppression, and the deep disaffection of the Iranian people from their leaders. If they sensed the corruption in the circles that they frequented, they chose to ignore it. Unlike most, David Lilienthal admitted before his death that perhaps he had never really understood Iran at all. And Lilienthal was one of the few Pahlavites who at least had an exposure to the villages and countryside of Iran.

Fifth, there was a very close Pahlavi-Israeli connection. Many influentials who unconditionally supported the state of Israel also strongly backed the shah. This link was especially important in the outer rings of the concentric circles of American Pahlavism. Although it was not operative in the case of such individuals as the Rockefellers, Kermit Roosevelt, and Richard Helms, U.S. senators and congressmen along with many leading members of the mass media attached their support for the shah's regime to their commitment to the state of Israel. Toward the end of his regime, the shah and a number of his advisers felt that the occasional criticism that began to appear in the American mass media occurred because of the monarch's increasing public sympathy for the moderate Arab cause. They maintained that the shah's condemnation of Israel's occupation of the West Bank and his personal and political alliance with such Arab leaders as Anwar Sadat cooled the support that many partisans of Israel had given him. Whether this thesis is true, many important members of the Pahlavi lobby shared an active commitment to Israel, and much of their enthusiasm for the shah concerned his important informal relations with Israel. The Iran arms arrangement of the mid-1980s demonstrated the intense, almost desperate, attempt by the state of Israel to protect the Iran connection after the fall of the Pahlavi dynasty.

Finally, the influence of the American Pahlavites in American foreign policy-making has continued. After the revolution, they immediately took a strong stand against the new government in Iran, which helped poison the well of hope for a new Iranian-American relationship. A decade after the fall of the shah, many of these individuals were still consultants, lecturers, and commentators on Iranian politics and economics, Iranian-American relations, the Iran-Iraq war, and other important foreign policy questions. In September 1986, for example, both Richard Helms and David Rockefeller were invited to participate in a Central Intelligence Agency conference on the Iran-Iraq war.[105] Kissinger and Associates is another excellent example of this kind of continuing influence. With the partial exception of Donald Regan, who was an appendage to the circles of leading American Pahlavites, most of these individuals were not involved in any central decisional capacity in the Iran arms arrangements of 1985–86. Retired general Richard Secord, however, did play a major operational role in the episode. And even Barbara Walters became involved when she passed information from arms dealer Manuchehr Ghorbanifar directly to the White House in December 1986. While events had proven the Pahlavites' past record of Iran analysis to have been less than impressive, they continued to maintain credibility, surviving the Iranian revolution much better than the shah and most of his entourage. This, perhaps more than anything else, attests to the enormous power and influence of the individuals who practiced the informal politics of Pahlavism in America.

10 The United States in Iran: Diplomats, Intelligence Agents, and Policy-Making

Just before Thanksgiving in 1923, a tall young lady who had graduated from college in Wooster, Ohio, arrived in the northwestern Iranian city of Rasht. She had taken a ship to Liverpool and, after a week in England, had sailed from Southampton for Basra via the Suez Canal. In Basra she boarded a train for Baghdad. And from Baghdad she traveled by Model-T Ford overland to Tehran. Helen Augusta Clarke, who was with the Presbyterian Board, had chosen to leave home, to live and work among the Iranian people to whom she dedicated much of her life. Helen Clarke had sole responsibility for establishing the first all girls' school in Rasht in 1924 and continued as principal of that school until 1936. Intermittently thereafter for many more years she was involved in a variety of ways in the teaching of hundreds of young Iranian women, all of whom cherished this gentle American woman. In 1983, Helen Young (she had met and married T. Cuyler Young in Rasht), with sixty years of service to Iran, both there and from her home in Princeton, New Jersey, still remained in touch with her Iranian friends, who considered themselves members of the Young family. Helen Young represented a special type of American woman, one who loved the Iranian people and was loved in return. She and other legendary Western women such as Annie Montgomery of Hamadan, Jane Doolittle, and Grace Dreyfus all left deep positive imprints in the sands of Iranian-American relations.

In the mid-1960s, the ARMISH-MAAG Hospital across the Rumi bridge off Old Shimiran Road employed educated Iranian nurses to supplement their American help. The Iranian workers were not allowed to use the dining area at mealtime and therefore ate in the janitor's room. This policy had been in effect for some time; the dining room itself was reserved for physicians and nurses who were American citizens. The Iranian employees were forbidden from using the Persian language, even among themselves, while in the hospital. One evening in late 1966, a serious automobile accident occurred on the narrow road that wound past the hospital. An Iranian child was severely injured and in need of immediate medical care. The frantic father who raced into the hospital for assistance was told that this hospital was reserved for U.S. military and diplomatic personnel only. The child was refused admittance and care. The Iranian father, the child in his arms, was last seen rushing down the road in search of transportation to a local hospital.

In September 1964, U.S. Peace Corps Volunteer Barkley Moore, a slow-talking, earnest young man, arrived in Iran to teach English in the provincial Turkoman city of Gunbad-i Kavus in northern Iran. The town had no library, and Moore, who had grown up in the hills of Kentucky, soon began a one-man campaign to raise funds to buy books. Working night and day, he collected enough money from 167 townspeople to begin the library. On July 15, 1965, Barkley Moore opened the first library in Gunbad-i Kavus. The books were in Persian and included 10 hardcovers and 263 paperbacks. In 1968, three years after it opened, over 200 people a day were using the library, which had grown to two rooms with forty chairs. Moore's concept spread, and dozens of village libraries mushroomed throughout the region. Moore lived in Iran for over six years and became famous throughout the country as the young American Peace Corps volunteer who created a library out of thin air.

In the 1970s, nearly 10,000 Americans employed by such U.S. private industries as Grumman, Bell Helicopter, and DuPont, took up residence around the lovely traditional city and capital of Isfahan. Ugly incidents abounded. In October 1975, three American women dressed in bikini shorts and halters strolled into the ancient Friday Mosque where, laughing, gesturing, and talking in loud voices, they toured the holy place in their own good time. On at least one occasion, American teenagers drove motorbikes through the lovely Shah Mosque; fashionably dressed American women turned over a table in an elegant restaurant because service had been slow; and, as the revolution was breaking in the late 1970s, an American shot an Iranian taxi driver in the head in a dispute over the fare. In September 1976, a Bell Helicopter employee was arrested in north Tehran for operating a gambling casino out of his home.

In the late 1960s, a slim, young man with a trim mustache and horn-rim glasses worked in the laboratories and fields of Iran as a plant pathologist for the U.S. Department of Agriculture. Walter J. Kaiser had spent two years in Latin America and had come to Iran in 1966 with no area training. Despite his Ph.D. and comfortable apartment in Tehran, he worked in the Iranian countryside from dawn to dusk and in the process befriended large numbers of Iranian villagers and illiterate workers. A man of enormous energy and deep commitment to his work, Kaiser soon learned to speak Persian, the rough, grammatically suspect village variety used by the farmers near Karaj. The workers loved Kaiser, who was their teacher and their supporter. On more than one occasion, peasant friends traveled by bus to Tehran bringing Kaiser and his wife, Louise, small offerings of gratitude that included everything from chickpeas and flowers to chickens and vegetables.

In the midst of Tehran adjacent to the U.S. Embassy stood the commissary, an oasis of American manufactured food, drink, and household items flown into Iran by the tons. Despite important exceptions such as retired military officers on contract in Iran, only American government personnel enjoyed access to the commissary, out of which developed a huge black market of materials sold at tripled prices. American beers and liquors were especially prized. Iranians lacked access to the commissary, and poorly paid Iranian clerks carried hundreds of packages of goods daily to chauffered station wagons for Americans keeping house in north Tehran. There was one Iranian exception to the commissary rule: members of the Pahlavi family had their own commissary cards, and the princes and princesses, or their designated shoppers, often joined the official Americans in doing their shopping. Outside the commissary, curious and sullen Iranian bystanders gathered daily to watch the process.

In the thirty-five years between 1944 and 1979, an estimated 800,000 to 850,000 Americans visited or lived in Iran. The vast majority of them resided in Tehran, and sizeable numbers lived in Isfahan. Between 1970 and 1978 alone, the number of Americans living in Iran increased from fewer than 8,000 to nearly 50,000. This flood of Americans became a severe problem for U.S. Embassy officials in the 1970s. One of the most frustrating issues facing Ambassador Richard Helms in the mid-1970s was the uncontrollable waves of untrained and ill-prepared Americans flowing into Iran. As the gold rush began and the contracts increased, the American presence expanded. The very best and the very worst of America were on display in the cities of Iran. As time passed and the numbers grew, an increasingly high proportion of fortune hunters, financial scavengers, and the jobless and disillusioned recently returned from Southeast Asia found their way to Iran. Companies with billion-dollar contracts needed manpower and, under time pressure, recruited blindly and carelessly. In Isfahan, hatred, racism, and ignorance combined as American employees responded negatively and aggressively to Iranian society. Iranians were commonly referred to as "sand-niggers," "ragheads," "rags," "stinkies," and Bedouins, and their culture was referred to as a "camel culture."[1]

By the mid-1970s, the deportment of many Americans in Iran had become a topic of considerable discussion in the country. As incidents multiplied and Americans, many without preparation or training for life in Iran, increasingly insulted and berated their Iranian hosts, the countrywide network of personal communication began to buzz with critical commentary and expanding anti-Americanism. Reports of American rowdiness, drunkenness, and physical violence began to appear in the Persian newspapers. One newspaper report referred to a "lewd American" (*Amrika'i-yi chishmcharan*) who made advances to an Iranian woman and then started a fight with her husband.[2] This phrase and others, such as "drunken Americans" (*Amrika'iha-yi mast*) and "pleasure-crazed Americans" (*Amrika'iha-yi ayyash*), began to appear regularly in the conversation of Iranians in Tehran and Isfahan.

In December 1984, at the end of sixty years of Iranian-American experience, Helen Young sadly stated that "we did so many stupid things in Iran and deliberately squandered so much good will. So many were small mistakes that mushroomed into great problems over the years."[3] Yet, Helen Young and many Americans like her, including hundreds of Peace Corps volunteers, prove the existence of other groups whose lives in Iran were exemplary. The mixed record of the general American community in Iran was matched by the experience of the official American diplomatic missions there. Although American diplomats worked within a context shaped by the activities of all U.S. citizens resident in Iran, these officials carried special responsibilities. They were models and symbols of the United States abroad and acted as the sensitive nerve endings of the United States in Iran. An understanding of their successes and failures does much to explain the ultimate, wrenching break in Iranian-American relations. As indicated above, the decade of the 1970s brought with it to Iran an influx of Americans who were unprepared and unfit for residence abroad. It is therefore instructive to examine a typical American diplomatic mission to Iran as it existed before the mass immigration of the mid-1970s.

The American Embassy in Tehran: A Profile

In 1970 the U.S. Embassy in Tehran consisted of a diplomatic staff of forty individuals. Besides those with Foreign Service Officer (FSO) diplomatic status, the contingent included a number of employees with Foreign Service Reserve (FSR) and Foreign Service Information Officer (FSIO) status, American staff employees, and a large group of Iranian employees, including secretaries, drivers, guards, administrators, and other functionaries. In late 1969, Ambassador Armin Meyer was replaced by career diplomat Douglas MacArthur II, a sixty-year-old foreign service veteran, nephew and namesake of Gen. Douglas MacArthur, and former ambassador to Japan and Belgium. Although he knew the Far East and Europe well, MacArthur had no background in the Middle East and was especially unsuited for the Iranian post. A sallow, tough campaigner whose capacity to listen and learn was seriously hampered by his animated, nonstop lectures, MacArthur soon got a grip on the embassy that left little room for independent reporting and staff input.

Ambassador MacArthur took charge of the American operation in Iran at the time when the shah increased SAVAK's control of the domestic scene in Iran. He viewed embassy employees as a large family and treated them as children. Some were a bit unruly and were handled accordingly. The ambassador maintained complete control in a situation where he believed the Soviet Union was poised to strike at Iran at any moment. Within this context, MacArthur was a great admirer of the shah. In the words of the leading political officer at the British embassy at the time: "This man MacArthur has really swallowed the supershah myth."[4] MacArthur repeatedly insisted that his job was to promote and protect U.S. commercial interests in Iran. He had no idea what opposition might have existed in Iran and deluded himself into believing that the liberal, English-speaking professionals who frequented embassy social gatherings were the real opposition—and even he could see that they posed no problem to anyone but themselves.[5]

MacArthur was an intelligent man who focused more of his attention on the inside operations of the embassy than he did on the outside situation in Iran. He was not completely unsuccessful in this, since he fought vigorously to limit commissary privileges to those who deserved them and to encourage proper American behavior abroad. He was, however, clearly the wrong man for the job. His own rigid, legalistic ideas failed visibly when applied in the Iranian context. When he left Iran in February 1972 after an assassination attempt, he departed without having advanced America's understanding of the Iranian social and political system. In this, his record was no better and no worse than his predecessors and successors.

The diplomatic profile of the U.S. Embassy in Tehran in 1970 was in many fundamental ways very similar to the profile of any American embassy in Tehran at any time. There were a few superb diplomats, a large number of mediocre officials, and a group of individuals who were ineffective and counterproductive. Douglas Heck, MacArthur's deputy chief of mission, and Donald Toussaint, the political counselor, were intelligent and open diplomats. Both lacked any serious knowledge of Iran. Heck, a fifty-one-year-old dedicated diplomat, had served in India, Nepal, Cyprus, and Turkey. He had no Iranian area training. Toussaint, a quiet man of integrity, held a doctorate in political science from Stanford University. A student of the French, Chinese, and Malay languages, his last diplomatic post had been in Indonesia. In the words of one diplomat who spoke Persian and who served in Iran for many years, these kinds of diplomats represented the "nice guys." These were loyal, honest, dedicated public servants who knew far too little about the countries in which they served. Over the years, many "nice guys" served in Iran.

Among the best and most knowledgeable Foreign Service Officers in Iran then were four individuals. Tom Greene and Michael Michaud were just finishing thirty months' service in mid-1970. Both were in their early thirties, and both were second secretaries (FSO-5s); their views on Iran carried little influence among the senior officers at the embassy. Greene and Michaud had a working knowledge of the Persian language and were frustrated at the lack of communication in the hierarchical structure that MacArthur had put in place. They were also sensitive to the long-term political problems that they thought faced Iran. Greene, who held a Ph.D. from Princeton, was especially troubled by the U.S. government's unwillingness even to discuss possible alternatives to the shah. Neither of these talented officers had contacts with religious figures even though Michaud felt it important to develop such communication. He had been given orders to stay away from the clerics.

Arnold Raphel and John Washburn were two other young officers who made a serious effort in Iran. Raphel was a FSO-6 and was the only U.S. diplomat in Tehran who could be considered fluent in Persian. He had developed a good sense of Iranian society while posted to Isfahan, where he made an in-depth study of the family networks that energized the political and social system of that city. Washburn, who had studied law and English literature at Harvard, was petroleum officer and second secretary. An extremely bright man with an unusual ability to synthesize and analyze, Washburn was well connected with the wealthy liberal intelligentsia. Although his serious contacts were limited to this class of Iranian, he was less than optimistic about the shah's long-term chances. Washburn tactfully attempted to report his doubts in an end-of-tour night letter addressed to Ambassador Richard Helms and mailed to Washington in August 1973.

Other competent American officials then in Iran included selected consular officers (such as Carl Clement in Khurramshahr) and occasional individuals associated with the United States Information Service (USIS), the Iran-America Society. and the various U.S. military missions. Many other officials, however, were of modest talent, considerable ambition, and ethnocentric outlook. Some were cowed by MacArthur, and several reinforced the ambassador's uninformed views in the same way that many of the shah's advisers parroted the Pahlavi perspective. One bright FSO-4 argued that a knowledge of Persian was incidental to any understanding of Iran and spent much of his time currying the favor of the ambassador by defending the shah's rule at every possible opportunity.

On the other side, one young vice-counsel who worked in Tabriz challenged MacArthur frontally by questioning America's policy in Southeast Asia. On October 15, 1969, Murray C. Smith II addressed a petition to President Richard Nixon condemning U.S. policy in Vietnam. The petition was directed to all U.S. government representatives then resident in Iran. It was designed to coincide with the month of antiwar demonstrations then taking place in the United States. MacArthur and the military hierarchy in Iran were apoplectic at Smith's petition, which was eventually signed by nearly eighty Americans, largely Peace Corps volunteers. MacArthur and his deputy chief of mission, Nicholas Thacher, ensured that Smith was unable to distribute the petition and coordinated their approach with Washington. Rather than give Smith cause for a law suit, they tolerated his presence in Tabriz until he was "selected out" of the Foreign Service when his term expired in June 1971.

Murray Smith was an unusual personality in the Foreign Service in Iran. He was a true believer, an average diplomat, and a dedicated idealist who lived to fight for causes. He was quite willing to give up his position in the Foreign Service despite his almost ten years of service. In the end, he was rather shamelessly nudged out through the cooperation of high-ranking State Department officials in Washington, Ambassador MacArthur, and, ironically, political officers Toussaint in Tehran and Greene in Tabriz. Although personally courageous and willing to fight for his political beliefs, Smith was no better informed about Iranian affairs than many of those officers who shared MacArthur's views on the infallibility of the shah. He did have the distinction of being the only diplomat in Iran at the time who had the fortitude to face down the ambassador.[6]

Extensive interviews with the American officials posted to Iran in 1970 provide the following profile of U.S. Embassy operations. As indicated above, the officers themselves were of mixed quality. Mac-Arthur's patriarchal, arbitrary style hampered morale and hindered critical and objective reporting, but the problems ran much deeper than the debilitating personal traits of one man. Persian language skills were surprisingly limited; area preparation before coming to Iran was superficial and in many cases nonexistent; U.S. contacts extended little beyond the Pahlavi political elite and the English-speaking Iranian intelligentsia; administrative rivalry and lack of communication marked the relations between the various offices, bureaus, and missions in Iran; and the embassy reporting system was such that it was difficult if not impossible for dissenting, unorthodox views to find their ways to Washington. The problems were basically systemic and intertwined.[7]

In general, Americans in Iran lived in splendid isolation.[8] With the exception of the Peace Corps, this was in many ways as true of official Americans as it was of American businessmen and contractors. Foreign Service officers scoffed at the military in particular and called it the Golden Ghetto. Actually, an examination of the living patterns of American diplomats reveals an isolationism of their own. Even those diplomats with a rudimentary understanding of Persian lived near other Americans, frequented American clubs, and frankly named other Americans as their best friends in the country. The twenty-six diplomats surveyed in Tehran in 1970 indicated a noticeable lack of regular contact with Iranians. While one diplomat met twice a week with Iranians, nine had meetings once a week, and sixteen *never* met regularly with Iranian citizens. Of twenty-six respondent diplomats, only three had ever traveled outside of Tehran by bus. Not one had a cleric as a friend. While twenty-two individuals felt it "very important" to have contacts with the political elite of Iran and sixteen felt the same about industrialists, only one diplomat indicated it "very important" to have contacts with the clerics. And that one said he had been discouraged from initiating any such contacts.

While in Iran, many Americans found the opportunity to improve their standards of living. In short, they lived far better than they could have in the United States. Huge homes, gardens, servants, drivers, and many other material perquisites enabled them to rise not only above their own social status back home but increased the class differences that separated them from most Iranians. Class and economic differences magnified national differences. Of the twenty-six diplomats surveyed in Tehran in 1970, only one did not employ a servant. Twenty of twenty-six (80 percent) had swimming pools at their Tehran homes. Given this style of life, it is not surprising that the Iranians with whom the Americans interacted and from whom they rented were drawn from the upper-middle and upper classes of society. American attendance at the Imperial Country Club, royal family membership in the commissary, Iran-American elite interaction in such organizations as the Lions and Rotary clubs, and common interest in such sports as skiing, bowling, and golf all served to blend Americans with a tiny, wealthy group of Iranians who rested at the pinnacle of power.

Americans lived in Iran as they might in New Jersey, California, Nebraska, or Massachusetts. Americans imported everything they could from the United States, including the air and atmosphere around them. Air conditioners, humidifiers, and deodorants, as well as American recreation and education, were emphasized to the total exclusion of their local environment. Indeed, many Americans in Tehran seemed to live in cellophane-wrapped clusters. Americans tended to congregate together; almost all lived north of Takht-i Jamshid Avenue, the thoroughfare that passed just in front of the U.S. Embassy in north Tehran. All of the nearly sixty buses that carried students to the American School followed routes that ran north of Takht-i Jamshid.

The American School, founded in Tehran in 1954, admitted only "children with valid American passports." According to the principal: "This is strictly an American school." As such, it was almost alone among American schools abroad, the closest parallels being certain Department of Defense schools in Europe. Efforts by occasional individuals to introduce courses on Persian history, culture, and language were successfully resisted by the majority of parents and by the administration, headed by a powerful superintendent. In the words of one new school board member in August 1970: "Past school boards here pursued one central policy: 'Keep Iran Out.'" In 1970 an experimental Iranian Cultural Studies program was introduced into the elementary school curriculum. The school fielded three football teams, and cheerleading and the drill team were major extracur-

Table 3   Americans in Iran, July 1970

Department of Defense personnel	778
Dependents of Department of Defense personnel	1,297
Other U.S. government personnel	150
Dependents of U.S. government personnel	250
American residents	4,000
American tourists	900
Total	7,375

SOURCE: U.S. Embassy, Tehran, July 1970.

ricular exercises for American youngsters in far north Tehran. Ambassador MacArthur himself somewhat futilely attempted to have the school leadership begin some integration of the school into the Iranian context.[9]

Americans in Tehran demanded all the conveniences that they enjoyed back in the States. The center of the community, therefore, was the commissary, a repository of Americana located adjacent to the U.S. Embassy compound. Not a PX, but carrying some PX goods, the commissary in Tehran was the largest State Department-sponsored operation of its kind in the world. In 1970, its inventory was valued at $250,000, and its sales were over $4 million annually. All of these numbers, of course, increased enormously through the 1970s as the official American community quintupled in size. At the time, the commissary carried 2,000 items while the PX line offered 1,700 items; liquor and cigarettes counted 400 items. The commissary imported #11 long grain rice to Iran, and Americans consumed it at the rate of a ton a month. Although the pistachio nuts were themselves purchased within Iran, they were processed especially for American taste— roasted longer with less lemon. Coca-Cola cost twice as much at the commissary as it did locally, but Americans resisted buying this soft drink locally and complained when it was unavailable at the commissary. In June of 1970 alone, over twelve thousand cans of Coke were sold at the commissary to thirsty Americans.

A major item sold at the commissary was processed cat and dog food. A wide variety of cans, packs, and bags of animal food was flown to Iran from America, including everything from Gaines Dry Burgers to Puss'n Boots Fish. According to commissary records, in the eighteen months from January 1969 through June 1970, Americans living in Tehran purchased $35,703 of processed cat and dog food at the commissary, removing from the shelves 125,178 packs and cans of this pet item. American aircraft lifted seventy-nine tons of processed cat and dog food to Tehran. According to the general manager of the commissary, a third-country national, Americans became especially irate when the commissary ran short of dog food. Iranians quietly noted that there was hunger, and even famine, in the provinces of Baluchistan and Sistan in the east. But as one cynically noted, the American dogs are well fed.

Even Iranians who were decidedly pro-American and who were employed by the United States were bitter about American attitudes and living standards in Iran. One woman who worked in a key position for the USIS for many years noted: "Americans insisted on living here exactly as they lived in the United States. On the other hand when

Iranians go to America, they are expected to live there exactly as Americans live. They are placed in a series of orientation programs and are urged to Americanize. Certainly, this is a double standard. Americans have a definite superiority complex and Iranians know it. Many deeply resent it."[10] Another Iranian, educated in Oklahoma and employed in the Ministry of Education in Tehran, asked why it was that the United States government and industry sent second and third raters to represent America in Iran. He argued that it was his impression that very few of America's "best people" were present in Iran.[11]

> The important conclusion to be drawn is that the large American military advisory presence in Iran was probably counterproductive in the long run. The adverse effects of the strain placed on the society by the advisor's cultural and political value differences clearly outweighed the progress made in modernizing the military. Nor was the advisor equipped to minimize those value differences. He was granted diplomatic immunity and was encouraged to live in a style perceived by many Iranians as extravagant. Furthermore, he had not received the political, cultural, or language training that might have allowed him to do his job and live his life without irritating Iranian sensitivities.[12]

This transplantation of America into Iran established an atmosphere of isolation that severely crippled the capacity of official Americans to understand Iran. The problem was compounded by the gradual encrustation of the embassy itself as American diplomats found themselves encircled by rings of Westernized Iranians who were not representative of their country. In fact, there were two operative rings. The first screened Iranians away from Americans; the second effectively cut Americans off from Iranians.

In the first case, the United States government employed an extremely high percentage of individuals from religious and ethnic minorities in Iran. A particularly high percentage of Armenian Christians worked for the U.S. Embassy and USIS in Iran. Assyrian Christians and Jews were also disproportionately represented. In 1970, for example, out of 247 embassy local employees, there were 102 Muslims, 101 Armenians, and 44 Assyrians and Jews. Almost 60 percent of the Iranians employed by the U.S. Embassy were members of minority groups. An analysis of other selected years indicates that at times this percentage was even higher; in 1968, for example, nearly two out of every three local employees were non-Muslims. In a country where Armenians composed less than .5 percent of the population, they accounted for approximately 50 percent of U.S. government local employees. Besides such cultural factors as facility with the English language, there were practical reasons for Armenian dominance. One of the most influential local employees for many years was an Armenian who held the critical position of senior personnel assistant at the embassy. He served as the key gatekeeper in the determination of local Iranian employees at the U.S. Embassy.[13]

While American officials jokingly referred to this "Armenian Mafia," this minority presence and influence carried two serious negative consequences. First, it alienated many Iranian Muslims who in their first contacts with the United States were confronted with Iranian Christians. This was a particularly severe problem at the consulate, where thousands of Muslims applied for American visas. For years, the key local officials in charge here were Armenians who were often rude, arrogant, and condescending toward Iranian applicants. By the time they met with an actual American to be interviewed, the Iranian applicants had often already been offended.[14]

A second problem of the minority dominance was that American officials formed much of their opinions of Iran through their constant contact with minority groups. These minorities were unrepresentative of Iranians in general. The very fact that they were non-Muslims screened American officials from much day-to-day contact with Islam and Muslims. American officials, therefore, often viewed Islam through the slightly distorted lenses of Iranian non-Muslims. This communal factor, however, was only one force promoting American insulation from Iranian society. Even more important was the issue of class.

American officials maintained contact with a tiny educated English-speaking elite that gravitated to the embassy and its officials. They had little contact with the lower middle class or lower class that constituted the bulk of Iranian society. Americans were not in serious touch with religious leaders, workers, or Persian-speaking professionals and students. Four "contact lists" of leading political officers between 1969 and 1976 listed 104 names; of these, almost one third were found on two or more lists.[15] The clear majority (over 60 percent) were officials of the Iranian government. Only one religious leader was on the lists, an individual known as Ayatollah Qutsi, who "has an exaggerated view of U.S. influence in Iran and has on occasion embarrassed American officers by openly requesting U.S. government financial support for the clergy 'to fight communism in Iran.'" Political Consul Martin Herz's description of Ja'far Sharif-Emami as "probably my most productive contact here" gives an idea of the quality of the contacts. Sharif-Emami represented only the tiny clique that clustered about the feet of the Pahlavi throne. Herz deplored another contact's lack of English. In 1966 he put together a list of young poets and opposition writers and prepared to invite them to a social gathering at his home. When he discovered that none of these opinion leaders spoke English, Herz disgustedly canceled the party.[16]

The descriptions of the Iranians on the contact lists are often both amusing and revealing. Herz described Minister of Health Manuchehr Shahqoli as "hopeless. His blurry eyes—a most extraordinary phenomenon, looking into his eyes produces a blurry sensation—describe the man." Well-known Pahlavi courtier Jamshid Khabir and his wife were "great party-goers. Their famous party of 1967 was distinguished by the fact that over half the guests came down with acute poisoning, apparently because a devout Moslem on their household staff disapproved of merry-making on a mourning day. Too bad that Mrs. Khabir seems to have escaped unscathed."[17]

"Seldom at any U.S. diplomatic post have so many known so few so well." This concise sentence by Ambassador MacArthur's aide in Tehran summarized well the state of American embassy contacts with Iranians.[18] Twenty-six U.S. Embassy invitation lists for receptions and parties given from 1966 to 1971 confirm the limited contacts. Other than Iranian governmental officials, those present included a coterie of wealthy aristocrats and industrialists, a few eminent U.S.-educated Iranian academics, and selected journalists. More important, the lists included the same names year after year as the wealthy Iranian elite clustered about the embassy to such an extent that they became permanent fixtures there. Among the most ubiquitous Iranian American embassy stalwarts were Abdol Reza Ansary, Mehdi Sami'i, Hushang Ram, Jamshid Khabir, Jahanshah Saleh, Ezzedin Kazemi, and Yusef "Joe" Mazandi.

The core of the Iranian contacts consisted of wealthy upper-class families such as the Sami'i, Ladjevardi, Sabet, Batmanglidj, Ardalan, and Farmanfarmaian families. The Farmanfarmaian family operated as a large informal corporation, and its membership boasted individuals, extraordinarily well educated in the West, who were active in industry, banking, goverment, education, and the arts. With their international wealth and sophistication, they provided the best example of the kind of Iranians most closely associated with the American embassy in Tehran. Eleven Farmanfarmaians attended a November 25, 1969, farewell reception at the embassy for departing political officer John Armitage. The May 20, 1970, Linen Seminar reception hosted by Ambassador MacArthur involved the participation of eight couples of Farmanfarmaian citizens. According to diplomat Archie Bolster: "Our ties are too much with the establishment. We see primarily the people who make the decisions and launch the big programs, but we do not know enough of the people working down the line where the shortcomings in plans are readily seen. The men who tell us the big picture are often concerned with maintaining its beauty rather than admitting its warts, so we need a better perspective."[19]

Eight mutually reinforcing considerations fostered this system of limited Iranian contact: (1) the general weaknesses in language and area training; (2) the built-in embassy system of the "passing along of contacts" to successor officers; (3) the inordinate power of internal Iranian employees or gatekeepers over invitation and contact lists; (4) the continual presence of strongly pro-Pahlavi diplomats in key positions in the embassy hierarchy; (5) the reporting and career promotion system, which discouraged independent analysis; (6) the lack of communication and systemic rivalry that marked the various parts of the overall American mission to Iran; (7) the ineffectiveness of American intelligence organizations, whose administration and priorities crippled their capacity to understand Iran; and (8) the policies of the Pahlavi political elite itself, which pursued programs that reinforced the above seven factors.

Language and Area Training

Most American officials in Iran over the years lacked language and area training. The occasional individuals accomplished in these skills only highlighted the inadequacies of most U.S. representatives.[20] No American ambassador ever posted to Iran spoke the Persian language. No deputy chief of mission ever spoke and read the language fluently. The largest concentrations of language/area skills were located in the Peace Corps missions, where many young representatives learned the language in the villages and countryside where they resided. While fewer than 10 percent of American diplomatic personnel in Iran spoke and read Persian fluently in 1970, the comparable figures for the British and Soviet embassies were 45 and 70 percent. The British trained many of their diplomats at the School of Oriental and African Studies at the University of London. Their language exams were extremely stiff and had been prepared by one of the West's leading Iran specialists, Ann Lambton. Several of Britain's leading diplomats were themselves students of Miss Lambton. The Soviets had a policy of recruiting Central Asians who already had a fluency in Persian. Also, they rotated personnel between Afghanistan and Iran thus strengthening their experience in these Persian-speaking contexts.[21]

Persian is a language of great depth and subtlety. Although outwardly grammatically simple, it requires years of study and speaking experience to master adequately. Ironically, not until during and after the Iranian revolution did the United States choose to send a contingent of skilled Persianists to Iran. A number of them were among the hostages and included John Limbert, certainly one of the best Persian linguists who ever served in Iran, Barry Rosen, Victor Tomseth, and Col. Charles Scott. Another excellent linguist who served as U.S. consul in Tabriz under difficult circumstances during the revolution was Michael Metrinko. By the time the revolution broke out, however, it was too late for skilled linguists and Iran specialists.

Passing Along Contacts

In Iran, personal contacts and relationships are the essence of power and authority relationships. In recognizing this fact, leading officials in the U.S. Embassy in Tehran were sensitive to the need to cultivate contacts. One experienced political officer who wrote a memorandum in 1976 on the general responsibilities of the embassy political adviser wrote, "I do not need to tell you that personal contacts are all important in doing your job well."[22] Embassy officers would therefore pass along their lists of Iranian contacts to their successors. This practice, which in itself seemed quite logical, had in the Iranian case two negative results. First, the initial contacts themselves were far too limited and confined to a small socioeconomic Iranian elite. Passing these contacts along carried the mistakes of the past forward into the future. Second, existing contacts gave little incentive for newly arrived officers to establish new relationships with Iranians.

Many middle- and upper-class Iranians worked hard to gain access to the American embassy and eagerly sought to protect those contacts once they were established. Thus, when an American friend and official left the country, Iranians would themselves seek the name of his successor. If the new man failed to contact them after an appropriate interval of time, the Iranian friends of the embassy would themselves often take the initiative. Thus, over the years, Iranian contacts were handed down from political officer to political officer. The system was promoted by both the American official and by the Iranian contact, since each considered the relationship to be in his or her own interest. By the time of the revolution, some embassy Iranian contacts had maintained their ties with the embassy since the 1950s. They had simply moved from link to link in the long chain of professional succession.

Iranian Social Gatekeepers at the United States Embassy

Just as one member of an ethnic and religious minority could control local hiring practices at the embassy, so too could an Iranian social secretary exert enormous influence in determining the names of Iranians invited to embassy functions. In Tehran, one particular Iranian lady was in charge of invitation lists. With an office in the Chancery, she was invaluable because of her intimate knowledge of the changing social relationships that marked high society in Tehran. In short, she made herself indispensable to the embassy. This put the Iranian social secretary into a critical position of influence and control over the all-important guest lists. Because of superior information about the Pahlavi social and political elite, this Iranian gatekeeper's tenure easily transcended those of American ambassadors and diplomats. At least one ambassador unsuccessfully attempted to weaken the social decision-making power of this influential administrator.

With close contacts in the elite herself, this social gatekeeper reinforced the selection of Iranians who were strictly Pahlavi establishment. Meanwhile, her own ties were strengthened with the political elite, since she often attended the very functions for which she drew up the guest lists. The existence of this local social gatekeeper at the embassy ultimately helped limit the distance that the embassy gate would swing open, thereby reinforcing the elite profile of those Iranians who attended embassy functions.

The Persistent Presence of Pro-Pahlavi Diplomats

Many American diplomats were strongly and genuinely committed to the shah and his regime. These individuals were convinced that the shah enjoyed the overwhelming support of his people and that he was in complete control of a politically stable society. The three highest-ranking U.S. officials in Iran were unabashed supporters of the shah. The U.S. ambassador, the chief of ARMISH-MAAG, and the head of the Special Reporting Facility (Central Intelligence Agency) in Iran were the three American representatives who met periodically with the shah.[23] This contact strengthened their commitment to him and shaped their understandings of Iran's political situation. The shah himself injected them with the serum of Pahlavism. The following extraordinary conclusion in the fall 1976 review of American intelligence in Iran demonstrates the American reliance on the shah for information:

> The Shah has ruled for 35 years. In view of our long-standing ties, his consistency (beneath all the stagecraft) and his candor (within the Persian context), we know quite a bit about his aims and tactics. He is likely to see it in his interest to keep us *au courant* in the future. Given the nature of his state, we will remain largely

dependent on his soliloquies and on the ability of our Ambassador and others to pose penetrating questions.[24]

Besides most of the ambassadors who served in Iran, the Pahlavi partisans stretched through the various ranks of diplomatic officials both in Tehran and at the State Department in Washington. Most were solid, dedicated, intelligent officers who simply bought the Pahlavi invincibility thesis. A major case in point was Jack Miklos, a foreign service officer who held particularly influential posts concerning Iran during the critical years of the 1970s.

Miklos was Iran country director at the State Department in Washington between 1969 and 1974; he then traveled to Iran, where he served as deputy chief of mission under Richard Helms and briefly under William Sullivan. All together, Jack Miklos spent thirteen years of his career in Iran-related duties. Among the high-level Iranian contacts on whom he relied for information on Iran were the Farmanfarmaian family and Asadollah Alam.[25] Although he listened to dissenting opinions, Miklos had fixed, unshakable ideas about the Iranian political system, which he fervently believed to be strong and stable. While in Tehran, he operated on the principle that representation, not reporting, was the embassy's charge. Because he moved back and forth between Washington and Tehran, Miklos's opinions on Iran carried special weight in the 1970s. In fact, he became a major force deflecting informed criticism away from the Pahlavi regime. Many other foreign service officers and military officials shared the uncritical ideas of Jack Miklos.

THE EMBASSY REPORTING SYSTEM. Because a strong pro-Pahlavi bias dominated the highest levels of the American embassy, lower-ranking political officers found it difficult to prepare reports that ran against this opinion. In the embassy in Tehran in 1974, the best-informed political officer described the dilemma: "At this embassy, the ambassador is God. The deputy chief of mission is a demi-God. The political counselor who writes up my efficiency reports is also possessed of divine attributes. Who am I to question their wisdom about Iran? When one bucks the views of these three, he is putting his entire career in jeopardy. I am personally unwilling to do this and therefore I am as flexible as I have to be. I am not willing to pay the price."[26] Another foreign service officer complained that at times his reports were screened by four officers—the deputy to the economic counselor, the economic counselor, the deputy chief of mission, and the ambassador himself—before they could be sent to Washington. In his words: "This is a lousy system. The superior who reads your reports writes your efficiency reports. If he does not agree with your assessment, it often damages you professionally."[27] The entire system was stultifying and intimidating. One experienced State Department official stated in the fall of 1978: "More cables have been suppressed out of Tehran than at any other post in the world."[28]

In October 1969 an article appeared in the *Foreign Service Journal* analyzing the fundamental problems of foreign service reporting. It is not accidental that the piece was written by a young diplomat who had been serving in Iran since late 1967. The essence of the argument is captured in the following passage:

> Reporting officers are under pressure from their superiors (and more subtle pressure from Washington) to make their reports conform to the post's previous reporting, and to the views of senior officials. The result is to encourage adherence to the "conventional wisdom" or the "establishment" point of view. Equally unfortunate is that this emphasis requires that differences of opinion be resolved before the report is sent, and that those differences not be shown in the report. The result is often bland reporting which reduces analytical thought to the lowest common denominator, and which may deprive Washington of independent views as to the facts and their significance.[29]

On occasions, enterprising foreign service officers were able to slip their analyses through to Washington. In June 1972, for example, three economic officers prepared a sensitive report on corruption in Iran. They researched and wrote the piece largely between the tenure of two ambassadors. MacArthur had left his post in February, and his successor, Joseph S. Farland, did not arrive until late May of that year. Entitled "Corruption in Iran—A Problem for American Companies," it was submitted as an airgram on June 20, 1972, and was quietly approved by Deputy Chief of Mission Douglas Heck.[30] Also, in the 1960s, young diplomats whose airgrams were suppressed by their superiors at the embassy would sometimes bring copies to Washington when they returned on home leave. Here, they would quietly pass them along to analysts at the Department of State. These unofficial communications were jokingly referred to at the Bureau of Intelligence and Research as "the suppressed airgram file."[31]

Foreign service officers also struggled to develop other means of presenting their ideas. One of the more innovative was the end-of-tour report prepared in letter form. An excellent example was the long letter of embassy second secretary John Washburn to Ambassador Helms on August 11, 1973. Washburn had served in Iran since October 1969 and had developed a number of keen insights into Iran's politics and future. The following selected passages from this communication indicate that extremely competent foreign service officers did serve in Iran. More important, the fact that these insights were never really acted upon by the responsible American officials indicates the seriousness of the reporting problem.

Iranian and outside observers alike all agree that Iran's increasingly sophisticated economic and commercial operations and requirements are overloading the governing capacity of the Shah's private political system. The symptom of this is the enormous growth in the extent and importance of corruption in Iranian government. . . .

. . . It is also too easy for a government employee . . . to believe that he is on short rations because the Shah is squandering billions on American arms. This becomes acute when the government employees in question supply vital social services such as health care and education. . . .

. . . Because of our close identification with him, these dangers to the Shah are dangers to us, unless we either induce him to accept and provide for them, or disassociate ourselves from his efforts to resist them. . . .

. . . The most important such precaution is to establish an identity of our own separate from the Shah in the eyes of those educated and informed Iranians on whom any regime here will have to depend.[32]

The reporting system discouraged independent, objective description and analysis of the Iranian scene. Even when occasional diplomats found occasional ways to submit their ideas, they had very little impact. Both of the above examples were, of course, hampered by limited circulation. It was in response to this kind of situation, especially in Vietnam, that a dissent channel was developed as part of the foreign service reporting system in 1971. In Iran, this new device was too late and had little impact. State Department officials on the Policy Planning staff indicated that diplomats in Tehran seldom availed themselves of this channel because of timidity but, more importantly, because the actual target of any dissent would have been America's entire relationship with the shah's Iran. Dissenting messages concerning any part of the relationship necessarily challenge the entire relationship.

Administrative Rivalry and Division

The American missions and administrative units in Iran existed in a state of persistent rivalry and competition. This characteristic, already demonstrated to have existed as far back as the 1940s, prevailed until the revolution. A particularly deep fault line divided the embassy and the major military mission to Iran. Other than periodic meetings at the very highest levels—the ambassador and the chief of ARMISH-MAAG—contact was limited. Distrust prevailed between diplomats and soldiers. Interaction that did occur at such places as the American school and, occasionally, American clubs was often tense. Since Americans employed in various missions went about their business in relative isolation from their compatriots, it is not surprising that they did not learn much from one another. This internal system of division operated at all levels of the American bureaucracy in Iran. Both the diplomatic and military components had considerable internal tension and rivalry. In 1977, over thirty different American military organizational units were based in Iran; many competed with one another, and many duplicated the functions of one another.

On the diplomatic side, the embassy proper was separated from the operations of the United States Information Service. This division was more than physical in nature. The attitudes and thinking differed in both units. Foreign service officers seldom attended functions organized by USIS; this was deeply resented by USIS officers, who generally themselves had a better record of attendance at embassy functions. In Iran the price for this lack of communication and cooperation was high since it reinforced homogenous, limited contacts.

It was at USIS where Americans were in touch with the younger generation of Iran's opinion leaders. Most of America's serious contacts with the challenging intelligentsia represented by writers, poets, journalists, academics, and students existed through USIS. Although this organization also suffered from limited contacts, USIS officials occasionally developed innovative and impressive programs. One case in point occurred in August 1970 when foreign service information officer Alan Lester, supported by cultural affairs officer Richard Arndt, invited an offbeat American poet to Iran and then sponsored a fascinating night of poetry in which eleven leading Iranian poets read their poems in Persian. Most of these poets, who were among the leading voices of Iran's conscience during those days of tight Pahlavi control, had never before had any contact with Americans. Regular American embassy officials were conspicuous by their absence from this event. Other than sporadic happenings such as this, most USIS contact with a somewhat broader spectrum of Iranians was developed through its English-language program.[33]

The major contact point was the Iran-America Society (IAS), founded in Iran in 1925 and the largest binational center in the world. Headed during the critical years 1967–72 by a dynamic executive director named Lois Roth, the IAS consisted of a cultural center, an academic center, and a student center. Membership in the IAS increased steadily over the years. In 1970, the 1,280 members were composed of 886 Iranians, 123 Americans, and 271 corporate members. Students enrolled in academic center English courses numbered 4,500 to 5,500 in the 1970s. Just before the revolution, the number was 5,000; it decreased to 1,200 in the summer of 1979 but had risen back to 3,600 just before the hostages were taken.[34] Although the IAS's governing board consisted of Iranian elite members, the young people who attended classes sponsored by the IAS were drawn largely from Tehran's middle class. An estimated 7,000 students a month visited the IAS academic center, which was located immediately across from Tehran University. These young Iranians were largely Persian-speaking and primarily because of this had no interaction with Americans. According to the executive director of IAS, "No one really knows what goes on over there."[35] Embassy officials too seldom visited any of the branches of the IAS. In June 1970, Ambassador MacArthur became the first ambassador in over ten years to attend graduation ceremonies at the Academic Center.

Since the IAS was a binational center with a binational board of directors, it had a degree of independence from USIS. This inevitably caused tension. A more important line of tension at USIS, however, divided the cultural and information sections. Built-in rivalry existed between the cultural affairs officer and the public affairs officer. The cultural affairs people were appalled by what they considered the heavy-handed tactics of propaganda that often emanated from the public affairs section. The two sides often worked at cross-purposes. The cultural section was furious, for example, when the information section produced an issue of the USIS Persian publication (*Marzha-yi Naw*) in June 1970 that contained an article entitled "Princess Ashraf Pahlavi: Patroness of Human Rights." The article alienated precisely the group of young Iranian opinion leaders that the cultural section was attempting to court.[36]

At the embassy, the diplomatic officers also worked in an atmosphere of considerable rivalry. Besides the inevitable personal and professional cliques, there was some intraembassy division based on different functional responsibilities. One problem that was especially troubling to foreign service officers was the limited communication that existed between the Central Intelligence Agency and the State Department officials proper. Although some information was shared, the reporting systems tended to parallel one another. State Department officers complained that the CIA jealously kept its information from them. Interviews with foreign service officers in Tehran revealed strong feelings about this.

The U.S. military mission was even more possessive of its knowledge of Iran, especially of the Iranian military organization and capabilities. Not only did it refuse to share information with the embassy, but it resisted cooperating with the CIA. This situation reached such a state early in 1977 that an overall intelligence review of American knowledge of Iran criticized "the reluctance of the MAAG to provide available information to Intelligence Community representatives in Tehran so that this information can get into national intelligence channels."[37] This was the fourth consecutive overall intelligence review that made this criticism of the MAAG mission's uncooperative behavior.

Military personnel in Iran were not encouraged to produce intelligence reports on internal affairs in Iran. All reporting efforts were channeled through the military attaché, who was often ill-prepared for his responsibilities. According to one military source, the assistant chief of staff for intelligence (ACSI) of the Army General Staff was responsible for the nomination and selection of attachés. "This job was usually given to the least competent general officer on the ACSI staff."[38] The attachés received very little information from the military advisers and were themselves expected to limit their reporting to purely military matters. Most of the intelligence reporting, therefore, was by default left to the CIA. Over the years, tension between the CIA and the Defense Intelligence Agency waxed and waned.

Other American agencies and missions in Iran competed with other governmental agencies or private organizations. These included the Peace Corps and the Near East Foundation, GENMISH and ARMISH-MAAG, the U.S. Agency for International Development and the Development and Resources Corporation, and Point Four and the Ford Foundation. A general principle that followed on these rivalries was that if one agency had no knowledge of an activity, it discounted or disbelieved any report from another agency on that activity.

Informed Iranians were well aware of these divisions and whenever possible would attempt to use them for their own personal or political purposes. Even those Iranian politicians with only sporadic relations with Americans commented on the intra-American rivalry. Cagey political legend Sayyid Ziaeddin Tabataba'i, for example, once stated that "the Americans are their own worst enemies. They are constantly fighting one another in our country. We know all about it."[39] One young foreign service officer in Tehran stated: "Here in Iran there is a huge series of communication gaps and lack of cooperative organization between American programs, projects, organizations, sections, and officers. There is even a serious lack of communication *within* programs and sections."[40] This certainly hampered the capacity of American officials to do their jobs effectively while in Iran.

The Crippled Capacity of American Intelligence in Iran

Despite its enormous reputation among Iranians, who considered it the all-knowing force that shrewdly and surreptitiously directed Iranian affairs while pulling the strings of the Pahlavi puppet, the Central Intelligence Agency was surprisingly uninformed and ineffective in Iran. Not only was it plagued by the problems that debilitated other American officials and missions in Iran but it carried one additional burden. Since Iran was contiguous with the Soviet Union, U.S. intelligence organizations were preoccupied with gathering information on the Soviet Union. The CIA, and other American intelligence organizations active in Iran, focused its efforts on Soviet-watching. In so doing, they committed the cardinal error of either ignoring or deemphasizing the situation in the host country itself.

A primary reason for American intelligence blindness to political events in Iran had to do with the two monitoring stations at Bihshahr and Kapkan. In the minds of some in Washington, it was better to be blind to Iranian affairs than to risk overlooking certain Soviet activities. A communication received from an informed American intelligence officer who discussed the importance of the two listening posts reveals this position:

> There is no doubt that their operation was absolutely critical for two decades in enabling the U.S. to detect and properly evaluate Soviet ICBM testing and capacities. Without the data derived from these stations we would have been half-blind. The loss of similar sites earlier in Turkey and Pakistan were serious blows that was offset only by the presence of the Iranian sites. With them gone we are indeed blind again. The slight public comment that was made in this regard was for obvious reasons, optimistic. Don't you believe it. There is no substitute for those sites. . . . For this reason we were concerned that the Shah should not get so mad at us that he closed the sites. Remember, the sites were there only under an oral agreement between the Shah and the Agency and in that sense we were at his mercy. Personally, I always thought that we could have gone a long way toward contacting and collecting information and opinions from opposition elements before the Shah would have gotten mad enough to cut us off. But so far as the policymakers were concerned they could see no purpose in risking absolutely vital information (derived from the sites) for the sake of marginal information

(internal politics) of interest only to analysts. In retrospect this turned out to be wrong-headed but it is worth keeping in mind that for twenty years it was a successful policy.[41]

There were usually ten CIA case officers in Iran at any given time. Of these, six or seven would be primarily concerned with the Soviet Union and China. The other three or four followed Iranian domestic matters with a special emphasis on such issues as economics and oil, nuclear proliferation, and arms absorption. Straight political reporting was a very low priority. In the words of Richard Helms, who was certainly in a position to know: "The Agency didn't do much political reporting in Iran."[42] The CIA officers in Iran, some of whom were fluent in Persian, often worked under transparent covers (such as civil aviation officer) and were well known as "spooks" not only by the American community resident in Tehran but also by the "Armenian Mafia."

Cover was always a problem for American intelligence agencies in Iran. It was made more difficult when the Department of State developed a requirement that all CIA officers be identified as FSRs (Foreign Service Reserve officers) rather than FSOs (Foreign Service Officers). All CIA officers were FSRs, but not all FSRs were with the CIA. Also, until the 1970s, the CIA occupied its own separate block of offices in the embassy compound.

Given the Sovietcentric mind-set that pervaded the American official approach to Iran, even those intelligence officers who followed the local political scene emphasized the leftist groups that challenged the shah's rule. A high percentage of their time was taken in monitoring the activities of organizations such as the Fidayan-i Khalq and the Mujahidin-i Khalq. They relied heavily on the information obtained from SAVAK, the shah's intelligence apparatus. A 1976 major intelligence review proposed by the CIA concluded that "reporting on terrorism has been good, although we remain dependent on information provided by SAVAK."[43]

The close relationship that the CIA maintained with SAVAK was clearly detrimental to the agency's capacity to gain a sensitive and informed understanding of Iranian political affairs. SAVAK itself spent the 1970s preoccupied with the growing challenge of terrorism in Iran. It shared its information on these extremist groups with the CIA. This limited the agency's ability to maintain contact with the wide variety of opposition groups that were forming against the shah's repressive rule. In 1977, for example, the CIA had only one point of contact with the opposition secular nationalist forces. And, of course, there were no such points of contact with the religious leaders.

There has been much speculation about the cooperation between

SAVAK, the CIA, and Mossad, the Israeli intelligence organization. There is no doubt that Mossad and SAVAK cooperated closely, especially beginning in the mid-1960s when both Iran and Israel had a common enemy, Iraq. It was about this time that Mossad began to become relatively more influential with SAVAK, while the CIA's influence abated somewhat. As General Nassiri became more powerful and arbitrary, SAVAK began to cooperate more closely with Israeli intelligence. This was especially true with respect to Department Three, the Internal Security Division of SAVAK. While CIA officials deny that the agency ever encouraged torture or confessions by force, they consistently imply that the Israelis worked with SAVAK on applying "the hard stuff." When asked about SAVAK-Mossad collaboration on torture, one CIA agent who maintained close liaison with SAVAK for many years simply responded: "I wouldn't be surprised."[44]

Like so many other American Iran-watchers, Central Intelligence Agency officers suffered from the supershah myth. This was especially true of those old Iran hands who spent more than one extended tour in Iran. To them, the shah seemed to have been around forever. They had witnessed his many close brushes with disaster and had come to view him as indestructible. They could not envisage an Iran without the shah. Some of these individuals, like George Cave, Herb Ferguson, and Art Callahan, were dedicated, hard-working government employees who knew a good deal about Iran. Although they were extremely well informed about the workings of the Iranian political elite and the shah's governing apparatus, they also knew and appreciated Iranian history and culture. But, like the State Department officials, they lacked contacts with the religious leaders, the Persian-speaking intelligentsia, the worker-immigrants to the large cities, and other social groups that took to the streets in 1978. They lacked what one might refer to as "mosque time"; they never really penetrated opposition *dawrah*s, or informal groups; and they spent too little time on university campuses or in south Tehran. In the end, there was an American intelligence failure in Iran—a general failure that cut across agencies, offices, ambassadors, and missions.

Elite Culture and the Pahlavi Policy of Information Control

The culture and policy of the shah and his political elite reinforced and strengthened official America's isolation from much of Iranian society. The Westernized Iranians circled and sealed the U.S. Embassy extremely effectively. Many of these were liberal thinkers who professed personal commitments to democratic values and persistently criticized the shah's absolute monarchy. Their campaign of whispered opposition led American officials to believe that they were in close contact with the Iranian opposition. As long as this opposition was busy sipping cocktails at embassy receptions or nibbling at caviar and crackers in luxury hotel restaurants, there seemed little reason to believe that the shah could be in any kind of serious trouble. Although American diplomats were well aware of the small, dedicated guerrilla groups that were active in the streets of Tehran, even these groups seemed to pose no real threat to the regime because of their tiny size and their constant confrontations with the shah's security forces.

Upper and upper middle-class social life in Tehran was intense. American diplomats were constantly going to and coming from parties, receptions, dances, picnics, lunches, and ceremonies of all kinds. Here, they repeatedly interacted with those Iranians who were American embassy fixtures. In general, these Iranians were urbane, witty, well informed, and extremely hospitable. They entertained lavishly in their villas and mansions overlooking the mountains in Shimiran in north Tehran. In short, they were delightful company. And they were all deeply interested in political affairs. Their views of Iranian society and politics became America's views. When occasional diplomats broke through this crust of Iranian celebrities, they did so briefly and dramatically in the form of jeep rides to ancient archaeological sites or excursions to tribal territory. Such activities reinforced the false convictions that they were in close touch with the Iranian people.

A more overtly political tactic was the shah's sporadic expressions of concern about American diplomats who sought to establish contact with opposition forces. Although the shah did not strongly pursue this issue, his occasional questions were enough to frighten American ambassadors, who overreacted by discouraging their political officers from such contacts. With the fall of the shah, many observers and former diplomats argued that the shah's strictures were the real reason why American officials had not been in touch. The shah had forbidden it. In fact, the shah never had to forbid such contacts. American diplomatic leaders were so concerned about offending him that they practiced self-censorship and what diplomats sometimes referred to as preemptive capitulation.

The Iranian culture and the shah's political strategies combined to reinforce a number of the problems that contributed to the Americans' limited contact with Iran. The elite insisted on speaking only English, which they seemed to prefer to Persian; the Iranian friends of the embassy consciously worked to preserve their American contacts through time; strategically situated Iranian embassy employees helped to define the kinds of Iranians with whom Americans interacted; influential Iranians close to the embassy knew the tensions and rivalries that often divided American offices and officials; and the Pahlavi political elite itself subtly discouraged the embassy in general and the CIA in particular from probing too deeply into Iranian society.

The insulation of Americans in Iran was, of course, never complete and total. Many enterprising diplomats, including several of those identified above, moved against the flow and broke out into Iranian society. Although their penetrating forays were neither particularly deep nor sustained, they were effective enough to signal trouble and to raise serious questions about the underlying strength of the shah's political system. Sporadic words of warning and occasional hard-hitting reports did find their way back to Washington. One foreign service Iran specialist who tends to overstate the record of diplomats in Tehran in the 1960s does make an important point when he writes that diplomatic area specialists "reported the weaknesses of the Shah's regime, but the policy-makers back in Washington chose to downplay those weaknesses. Good analytical reporting does not necessarily result in wise policy decisions."[45]

The Washington Control Center: The State Department, the National Security Council, and the Central Intelligence Agency

Various organizations in Washington deeply affected the quality of the information transmitted from the U.S. diplomatic nerve-endings in Iran. Besides the Department of Defense, the Department of the Treasury, and the U.S. Congress, among others, the three most important and misunderstood in the making of Iran policy were the Department of State, the National Security Council, and the Central Intelligence Agency. Although the NSC had the greatest decisional policy at crucial times, it lacked direct contact and firsthand data on Iran. Although the Department of State and the CIA had the best information and, relatively speaking, the best understanding of Iran, the NSC increasingly monopolized the formulation of Iran policy.

The U.S. Department of State: Division and Decline

Over the years, most secretaries of State were strong, surprisingly uncritical supporters and admirers of the shah. Exceptions, such as Dean Acheson, were in office during the earliest and least impressive days of the shah's rule. As a presidential appointee, the secretary of State served as the deputy of the chief executive himself in foreign policy. As such, he shared the president's general perspective. Although the secretary of State must always remain open to views of all kinds, he "must also maintain his credibility within the delicate set of relationships that exists at the very top of a government."[46] In the case of Iran, the highest echelons of the Department of State were consistently pro-Pahlavi partisans. They were usually deeply impressed by the shah. Dean Rusk, for example, is reported to have said that the shah of Iran was the best informed man in the world other than the president of the United States. The ambassadors in Tehran reflected the opinions of the particular administration in power in Washington.

The situation at the middle and lower working levels of the Department of State differed somewhat. Here, Iran specialists at times cast a more critical eye on the shah's methodology of control. In the Bureau of Intelligence and Research (INR) and at the level of the country desk, there was, at a minimum, a willingness to entertain expert opinions that challenged the conventional wisdom. The working level at the Department of State, for example, was the one section of the U.S. government that seriously solicited academic expertise. Although the various Iran country directors differed significantly in their attitudes and commitments to the shah's regime, they all requested outside opinion, even if it was unorthodox. Even Jack Miklos, for example, debated academic experts on the question of the stability of monarchical Iran. This debate was often framed in the context of whether the shah needed America more than the United States needed the shah or vice versa. Miklos himself believed that it was America that needed the shah. Policy, therefore, had to be formulated on that basis.

The officials who worked the Iran desk were inundated with responsibilities having to do with day-to-day Iranian-American relationships and had little time for long-term political analysis and pondering the future. Swamped by paperwork, hard-working officers would arrive at their desks with in-boxes piled high and would work all day moving this material to their out-boxes. Often they worked late hours and weekends. Their responsibilities involved everything from issues of rice production and soybean tariffs to visas and congressional tours to Iran. Through the 1970s, these responsibilities escalated as U.S.-Iranian relationships multiplied dramatically. At the very time that specialists at the Department of State needed to be especially sensitive to political developments in Iran, they found themselves preoccupied in unprecedented ways with a myriad of tasks, most of which had very little to do with the state of the political system in Iran.[47]

It was in the Bureau of Intelligence and Research where serious long-term prognoses concerning Iran were carried out. Over the years, INR employed an exceptionally talented team of Middle East specialists. Many of them were "old Middle East hands" who had spent years living and working in the region, especially in Turkey and the Arab world. Although somewhat thin in specialized Iran expertise, the Middle East hands at INR carried a healthy skepticism into their work that served them well when assessing such systems as the shah's Iran. They compensated for their own lack of in-depth Iran expertise by consulting regularly with Iran experts outside the government. Scholars such as Richard Cottam, for example, reinforced the natural skepticism of the "old hands" through their impressive empirical familiarity with Iran.

Two of the most incisive Middle East analysts at INR were Philip Stoddard and David Long. Both came from scholarly backgrounds, and both qualified as old Middle East hands even though they were relatively young in age. Stoddard was a tall, bespectacled, walking beanpole of information on the Middle East; he spiced up his analyses and presentations with a razor-sharp wit and backed them by personal anecdotes that carried clout and credibility. Long, an irascible, irreverent analyst, was more of an academic than a bureaucrat and had an uncanny capacity to cut to the core in his political analysis. Although he failed to endear himself to governmental administrators, he knew the Middle East well. Neither Stoddard nor Long were Iran specialists; but both knew Iran far better than many Iran experts employed by the government. Neither subscribed to the supershah myth. During the Iranian revolution, Long became INR's Iran specialist by default.

Two other especially important Middle East analysts at INR during the last years of the shah's rule were George Harris and George Griffin. Harris was deputy director of the Middle East component of INR between 1975 and 1977 and was a quiet, balanced scholar of Turkey. A man of great intellectual integrity, he never pretended to be an Iran specialist and listened carefully to those who were—both inside and outside the government. Griffin was South Asian Division chief in 1978 and shared Harris's views. During the revolution, he came to an early conclusion that this time the shah was indeed finished, and he did everything he could to warn the Department of State and the White House of the precariousness of Pahlavi power.

Over the years, INR made a number of studies focusing on instability and the long-term political future of Iran. A favorite issue was "Iran after the Shah." In 1975, INR took the initiative in preparing an important National Intelligence Estimate (NIE) on Iran.[48] Written under the competent direction of George Harris, this study was thorough and, in retrospect, impressively prescient. The NIE contained a large section on opposition in Iran and recognized the importance of its religious dimensions. It flatly stated: "Prominent in the opposition are the religious leaders." It placed special emphasis on the growing link between the religious leaders and the secular intelligentsia.

The dynamics of the preparation of this NIE are instructive. A first draft was composed after several days of research and writing and was then debated for several hours in an interagency meeting. The analysts who emphasized the opposition in the shah's Iran were thrown on the defensive by those who subscribed to the Pahlavi invincibility thesis. In the end, the sections on the Pahlavi vulnerability remained intact, and the project skeptics provided in-depth documentation of the serious nature of the growing opposition in Iran.

Since all NIEs must receive the approval of the major governmental components of the intelligence community, the Defense Department carefully reviewed the draft. Here, not unexpectedly, the study met stiff opposition. The State Department and CIA participants fought a vigorous battle to defend the integrity of the study. They were not entirely successful. United States Air Force analysts refused to accept the assertion that any real opposition to the shah existed in Iran. The assistant chief of staff of the U.S. Air Force, therefore, inserted a footnote in the study indicating that the air force considered the section on opposition to be "overstated." Ironically, on May 21, 1975, shortly after the report was submitted, two U.S. Air Force colonels were assassinated in the streets of Tehran.

Although the Pentagon reluctantly accepted the 1975 NIE, leading embassy officials in Tehran sharply criticized it for being far too negative in its assessment of the shah's stability. The highest echelons in the Department of State did not seriously consider the analysis contained in the 1975 NIE. When the Carter administration took office in 1977 and was soon confronted with deep problems in Iran, the 1975 NIE lay unused and unread in government files.

The last NIE on Iran during Pahlavi times was begun in mid-1978, when the shah's government began to collapse. Analysts from various agencies disagreed sharply among themselves concerning the situation in Iran. Of mediocre quality, static in tone, and striking a strange note of optimism, the draft of the document was presented to the National Foreign Intelligence Board in early September 1978. There it was criticized and shelved by Stansfield Turner on the advice of the director of INR, who represented the views of such analysts as Griffin,

Stoddard, and others. Events in Iran soon overtook the ill-fated study, and it was never revised or revived.

NIE sagas concerning Iran teach important foreign-policy lessons. The Department of State occasionally prepared reports that sharply questioned Pahlavi stability. Countervailing forces located somewhere else in the government always blunted their impact. Even if they survived these counterattacks, either the highest-ranking officials in the State Department itself or the White House ignored them. The censorship ran in two directions. The occasional informed critiques that arrived from Tehran were usually smothered in Washington. Or, as this case demonstrates, the critiques that sometimes emanated from Washington were attacked by high-ranking officials in the American embassy in Tehran.

Although intramural difficulties always existed within the Department of State concerning Iran analysis and policy, more serious problems existed outside of the department itself. Pahlavi partisans were especially evident both within the military and, most importantly, at the National Security Council.

The National Security Council and the Iranian Arms Affair of 1985–86

The NSC and the Department of State competed with one another over the formulation and direction of U.S. Iran policy for decades. This competition intensified in the 1970s and 1980s. The 1986–87 Iran-Contra scandal only represented the culmination of the NSC's drive for control. The debilitating tension that existed between the State Department and the NSC during the revolution and the hostage crisis of 1979–80 has been described in chapter 8. The NSC's dominant position helps explain the disastrous nature of Iran policy at that time. Among other things, the NSC suffered from one overriding problem: its massive ignorance of Iranian society and politics. This flaw exposed itself to the world in the 1985–86 Iran arms venture.

During the Carter administration, the NSC lacked any serious Iran expertise. Naval captain Gary Sick was placed in the impossible position of following Iranian affairs with little background in the subject. Sick served as an assistant to Zbigniew Brzezinski and therefore had little opportunity to exert any influence of his own. Unlike the Department of State, the NSC seldom consulted seriously with outside experts on Iran. From its perspective, such advice was not necessary; Brzezinski had already developed his own unshakable interpretation of what was transpiring there. In his book, Sick documents the tense conflict that marked NSC's relations with the Department of State and also unintentionally exhibits the NSC's embarrassing lack of understanding of Iran. At one point, Sick indicates that Brzezinski instructed him to review all the major State Department reports prepared during 1978 on Iran. Although he bitingly criticized the quality of these reports, Sick failed to emphasize the fact that the NSC lacked analyses of its own almost completely. In Sick's words: "The National Security Council does not maintain comprehensive files on each country or issue, relying instead on the various Washington agencies."[49]

Brzezinski, Sick, and the NSC were clearly in over their heads in the complex situation in Iran. Their condescending view of the Department of State harmed any serious attempt to develop a realistic appraisal of events there. While turning his back on the State Department, Brzezinski chose to look to the shah's closest advisers, especially to Ardeshir Zahedi, for his information on iran. At the Department of State, this was referred to as the "Brzezinski-Zahedi channel." In a letter of December 1978 to Ambassador Sullivan, Iran country director Henry Precht described a private meeting he had with Brzezinski:

> I did not tell him [Brzezinski] what I have since tried to convey through Gary Sick: That is that I consider Zahedi to be a disastrous counterpart in dealing with the Iranian crisis. In my view he is utterly self-serving, lacks good judgment and is prone to act quickly on the basis of bad information. I regret that I believe his counsel has been one of the strongest factors working on opinion in the White House.[50]

Brzezinski, like Kissinger before him, formulated U.S. foreign policy toward Iran from a powerful White House platform, but one barren of understanding of Iranian society and politics. This exercise of power without area expertise, therefore, was clearly present in the NSC system long before Ronald Reagan became president. The tendency to rely upon nonexpert staff members (such as Gary Sick) and outsiders with vested interests (such as Ardeshir Zahedi) was also ingrained in the NSC system before Reagan's presidency. From this perspective, it is possible to question the conclusion of John Tower, whose commission issued a report in February 1987 at the request of President Reagan: "The Iran-contra affair was clearly an aberration. The N.S.C. system is alive and has served us well for the 40 years of its existence."[51] Although it is true that the NSC system may still be alive, it is questionable whether it has been serving the American people well.

Although the Iran-Contra foreign policy imbroglio has been analyzed (see chapter 8), it remains necessary to describe the NSC-State

Department bureaucratic interaction that resulted in the scandal that shattered the credibility of the Reagan administration. In general terms, there are clear parallels with the foreign policy-making process of Carter's presidency. The NSC dominated foreign policy-making; the Secretary of State (George Shultz) lacked the will and/or capacity to defend his turf; the National Security head (Robert McFarlane, John Poindexter) played a disproportionate role in making and implementing foreign policy; this official lacked serious knowledge of the country (Iran) with which he was dealing; and in the absence of such expertise, he relied on either uninformed advisers (Oliver North, Howard Teicher) or advisers who were pursuing their own private agendas (Michael Ledeen, Manuchehr Ghorbanifar).

Differences abounded, however, in the two episodes. These differences help explain why the Reagan incident veered completely out of control. First, State Department officials such as Cyrus Vance and William Sullivan fought gamely to resist the NSC schemes of Zbigniew Brzezinski and others. Sullivan struggled so stubbornly that he ultimately lost his ambassadorship and retired from the Foreign Service. Vance resigned from his post on principle after the failed rescue attempt into the Iranian desert. Compare this to the position taken by George Shultz, who opposed the NSC policies of McFarlane, North, and Poindexter but chose to stand aside relatively quietly. Shultz (and Secretary of Defense Weinberger) "distanced themselves from the march of events. Secretary Shultz specifically requested to be informed only as necessary to perform the job."[52]

Second, the position of the president himself was critical. Jimmy Carter monitored everything and everyone very closely. He oversaw all major operations and paid great attention to detail. Ronald Reagan stood somewhat aloof from the day-to-day operations of foreign policy, and, although he certainly approved the Iran initiative, he seldom interfered in its implementation. Finally, an external force played a major role in the deliberations of the Reagan administration. This force, Israel, exerted a direct influence in Reagan's NSC and was deeply involved in the Iran-Contra episode.

NSC adviser Michael Ledeen along with Adolph Schwimmer and Yaacov Nimrodi, all in touch with Colonel North, "had close ties with the government of Israel."[53] Amiram Nir actually traveled with McFarlane and associates to Tehran in May 1986 disguised as an American. More significantly, Prime Minister Shimon Peres himself encouraged the Iranian arms affair. Both Nir and Schwimmer had been special advisers to Peres, and it was Peres who lobbied to have Nir accompany McFarlane on the Tehran trip. Ledeen was a personal friend of Peres and met with Peres about Iran. At key points in the process when U.S. officials sought to retreat or "stand down" from the plan, Peres personally intervened in Washington. According to the Senate Select Committee report, at the end of February 1986, when the United States was reconsidering its arms for hostages policy, "Israeli Prime Minister Peres wrote to President Reagan encouraging him to continue his efforts to gain a strategic opening in Iran and pledging to assist in this effort."[54] Israeli influence was considerably less in the offices of the NSC and the White House during the days of the Carter administration.

Despite these clear differences, the similarity that cuts through the Iran policy fiascos in both the Carter and Reagan administrations is the organizational conflict that marked NSC-Department of State relations. This effectively resulted in administrative compartmentalization that separated analysis from policy, expertise from action, in the Iranian arms affair. The picture is somewhat blurred, however, by the fact that in the Reagan administration the Central Intelligence Agency worked intimately with the NSC. William Casey and the CIA provided the general arguments to justify the venture and encouraged it throughout. The NSC staff, with CIA assistance, undertook the operational responsibilities. The key planning and coordinating operative in the project was Lt. Col. Oliver North, who had the full backing of NSC heads Robert McFarlane and John Poindexter.

The State Department and its pool of Iran expertise played no significant role in the Iran arms initiative for several reasons. First, Reagan's NSC wanted control of the project. The NSC believed that State Department specialists would surely raise questions about both the ends and means of the plan. Furthermore, the NSC operatives felt no need for State Department Iran expertise since they had their own information, provided primarily by consultants such as Michael Ledeen and contacts like Manuchehr Ghorbanifar and others recommended by the Israelis. CIA input was also available, although it was secondary to these outside sources.

The second reason why the Department of State was frozen out of the newly developing Iran policy was self-inflicted. Secretary of State George Shultz opposed any serious rapprochement with Iran and had been a major factor in the American tilt to Iraq in the Iran-Iraq war. Like Secretary of Defense Caspar Weinberger, Shultz maintained a "Saudicentric" view of the region and considered Iran a major terrorist threat to Saudi Arabia. He had consistently pursued an anti-Iran policy by having State Department officials actively seek to dry up arms and spare parts sales to Iran. In brief, Shultz, quite unlike Vance in the Carter administration, helped take his own organization out of the play.

Given his strong feelings on this issue, it is not immediately clear why Shultz did not more strongly confront an administration that had taken a crucial foreign policy issue out of his hands and was pursuing policy that he found objectionable. The answer is found in the Oval Office itself. From the beginning, the president actively supported the Iran initiative. It is quite clear that Ronald Reagan backed and encouraged the plan throughout. According to Robert McFarlane, when Reagan was queried about the dangers of selling arms to what many considered a terrorist state, he reportedly responded that "I will be glad to take all the heat for that."[55] Also, for a president often considered to be little concerned with operational details, Reagan followed the Iran arms story very closely, although he seldom interfered. Shultz and Weinberger understood this; both seemed reluctant to confront the chief executive too frontally on an issue that he supported so strongly. Shultz himself has publicly admitted that Reagan was "rather annoyed at me and Secretary Weinberger, because I felt that . . . he was very concerned about the hostages, as well as very much interested in the Iran initiative."

Also, Shultz and Weinberger were in a minority of two within the presidential inner circle on this issue. CIA head William Casey was a formidable moving force behind the plan, and he was supported by such other powerful White House figures as Chief of Staff Donald Regan. Also Vice President George Bush was apparently more supportive of the Iran venture than the Tower Commission report implies. By his own admission, he certainly did little to impede it.[56] Furthermore, as indicated in chapter 8, this group, which included President Reagan himself, had a number of very good tactical and strategic reasons for supporting the initiative. Shultz and Weinberger had difficulty responding to these arguments.

Ironically, in the strategic sense, the NSC, CIA, and White House itself seemed to have a better grasp of the realities of American long-term interests regarding Iran than did the secretaries of State and Defense. Unfortunately. they implemented that policy against a background of ignorance compounded by misinformation and distorted interpretation provided by biased, uninformed, and self-centered consultants like Manuchehr Ghorbanifar. Even Casey's CIA distrusted the consultant-intermediaries relied on so heavily by North, McFarlane, and Poindexter. George Cave, the CIA Iran specialist who was again called into action in postrevolutionary Iran, consistently warned the NSC planners about the reliability of these consultants.

With the backing of CIA director William Casey, the NSC both made and implemented foreign policy of the most sensitive kind in the Iran arms affair. Ever worried about the challenge of the Soviet Union, personally and politically concerned about the American hostages in Lebanon, and always conscious of an opportunity for the dramatic—foreign policy with a flair—President Reagan promoted and supported the Iran initiative. He turned to the organization he trusted most, the one that he had already used in Grenada, Lebanon, and Libya. He instructed the National Security Council to proceed with its plans.

The unchecked power of an NSC reinforced by presidential approval resulted in the scandalous transfer of monies from the Iranian arms sales to the Contra forces in rebellion against the government of Nicaragua. This adventure, which took place in opposition to the policy preferences of the U.S. Congress and the American people, was especially damaging to the Reagan administration. It indicated what could happen when the NSC, staffed by powerful, ambitious, and misinformed ideologues, became the primary force determining U.S. foreign policy.

The Iran experience reveals the growing relative weakness of the Department of State in the U.S. foreign-policy process. Elliot Richardson traced the strengthening of the NSC at the expense of the State Department to 1970 when Henry Kissinger drew up a new blueprint for the NSC as a kind of superagency to reconcile competing views of the organizations involved in foreign policy. The State Department acquiesced in this, thereby losing its preeminence. This shift began to occur at precisely the time the shah dramatically changed his political tactics in Iran. Richardson referred to this trend as "the politicization of foreign policy by the White House" and summarized its results as follows: "The relative decline in the role of the Department of State and increase in the role of staffs based at the White House have led, and will continue to lead, to a multiplicity of voices in the articulation of policy. This fosters a perception on the part of other countries that the purposes of the United States are neither clear nor steady."[57]

Another sensitive observer has presented an opposing thesis for the decline in the influence of the Department of State. After an in-depth analysis of a number of crises (including the Iranian hostage episode) by close monitoring of the activities of Under-Secretary for Political Affairs David Newsom in 1979–80, Robert Shaplen summarized the situation of the State Department in the following way:

> The fact remains that under the present system the Department no longer takes charge but is simply given the task of coordinating

policy. Within the bureaucracy, it is the navigator of foreign policymaking, and not the pilot; in fact, there no longer is a single pilot in Washington—only co-pilots competing for the controls, often under turbulent or stormy conditions. Decisions are delayed, crises are followed up instead of being anticipated or confronted, and the whole process has become so frustrating and time-consuming that everyone concerned has to keep running faster just to stay in the same place, while at the same time looking over his shoulder to see what some other branch of government is doing.[58]

Actually, Richardson's and Shaplen's theses are not mutually exclusive. The Iranian case study indicates that the NSC took over both functions from the State Department. Due to its proximity to the president and the energetic, aggressive nature of Brzezinski, McFarlane, and North, it became the primary coordinating and centralizing agency, the preeminent voice, in foreign policy. Throughout the Iran crises, the NSC managed to ward off State Department challenges to its authority and formulate policy accordingly. Other relevant units, such as the Department of Defense, usually capitulated to the NSC position, while the Central Intelligence Agency, with a stubborn independence of its own, also often backed the NSC, as it did in the Iran arms initiative. The CIA, then, deserves more detailed analysis.

The Central Intelligence Agency: Image and Reality

Few foreign institutions have dominated Iranian thinking more than the CIA. For over thirty years, Iranians representing all shades of political opinion have been preoccupied with visions of the CIA working behind the scenes in their country, persistently shaping the outcomes of political events large and small. Variations on this theme usually involve the British and the Russians, with the former at times seen as a fiendishly clever hand that rests behind even the CIA. The shah, who held regular meetings with the CIA station chief in Tehran, sometimes worried about the role of this American agency in his country. The CIA was one of the major forces he identified as responsible for his overthrow in 1979. On the other hand, Khomeini and the revolutionaries have believed that the CIA was largely responsible for the shah's long tenure as king and that it supported him steadfastly until the very end. In the decade after the revolution, the leaders of the Islamic Republic of Iran remained wary of the CIA, which they felt continued to lurk somewhere in their governmental shadows waiting to strike again.

The image of the interventionary CIA was developed after its role in the overthrow of Musaddiq and the restoration of the shah in 1953. As the years passed and as the shah's regime became increasingly entwined with the United States, many Iranians saw an expanded role for the CIA, which now lived front and center in the fertile Iranian imagination. Iranians were certain that the CIA was both omnipresent and omniscient. As the shah's intelligence organization, SAVAK, became more active and ruthless, its policies were immediately linked to the CIA, which was considered to be the godfather to SAVAK. In the 1970s, Americans in Iran were automatically assumed to be CIA agents unless they proved otherwise. Their protestations to the contrary were often considered certain evidence of complicity. Those Americans who were best informed and most skilled in the Persian language were especially suspect. Iranians were always chuckling to themselves and smiling wisely when American friends fluent in the language assured them that they were not working for the CIA.

When the CIA clumsily became involved in Iranian affairs after the revolution, Iranians only looked knowingly at one another. All their suspicions were, of course, confirmed in their minds when they gained access to U.S. Embassy documents. These documents indicated that the embassy itself was the Special Reporting Facility in Iran, that several embassy employees were CIA agents, and that the CIA had been involved in briefing moderate Iranian government officials after the revolution. The fact that the CIA was a prime force in the Iran arms controversy of 1986–87 further convinced Iranians of its centrality in the formulation and execution of policy toward their country. It will be many years, perhaps decades, before Iranians change their opinion that the Central Intelligence Agency has been all-powerful and all-intrusive in determining their fate.

The history of the CIA in Iran does not always confirm the Iranian image. In fact, the CIA's record in Iran is not unlike that of the Department of State. It is a record of interests deflected elsewhere, internal divisions, bureaucratic conflict, shallow contacts, uninformed analysis, and very uneven influence in Washington policy-making circles. Like the State Department, the CIA employed a number of highly competent Iran specialists; it also employed many of very modest talent. Although its record was badly blemished by its August 1978 report (actually prepared in 1977) that reached the infamous conclusion that Iran was in neither a revolutionary nor a prerevolutionary situation, it did submit some excellent reports over the years. These dealt primarily with the tribal situation in the countryside, the Iranian political elite, and the state of the Iranian economy. In short, like the Department of State, the CIA's record on Iran was mixed.

The responsibilities for Iran at CIA headquarters in Langley, Virginia, devolved primarily on two dedicated individuals who dominated Iran analysis from the early 1950s into the 1970s. Tall and thin, bespectacled and befreckled, analyst Earnest R. Oney was a scholarly, somewhat disorganized individual who worked on Iran for the agency from 1951 until January 1979. He acted as branch chief for many years and traveled to Iran for field research on a half-dozen occasions. The other major analyst, Charles C. Rudolph, covered Iran for the agency from 1952 to 1973, when he was a casualty of the sharp employee reduction program instituted by James Schlesinger. Ernie Oney had received his doctorate from the University of Chicago in 1950, and Charlie Rudolph had earned his Ph.D. from American University in 1971. Both were extremely talented, and their knowledge of Iran was impressive. This was especially true of Oney, who had not only a deep intellectual understanding of Iranian culture and politics but also that sixth sense and gut feeling so critical to understanding the country. His knowledge of Iran equaled that of any American academic Iran specialist.

With this kind of knowledge and experience on Iran available to the government, it would seem that the United States would have been extremely well informed on the subject. In fact, there were serious problems at the agency. First, both Oney and Rudolph were stronger on retaining facts and describing events than they were in analyzing and interpreting these events. In the words of one younger Middle Eastern analyst, they "not only failed to see the forest but they had trouble seeing the trees. They spent their time examining the bark on the trees."[59] Although there is some truth in this harsh judgment, it is also true that the United States never really knew the trees, the bark, or the soil that composed the Iranian forest-politic. Those experienced analysts who had some of this expertise were routinely ignored. Long before the revolution, Oney proposed an in-depth study of the religious leaders of Iran. His bureaucratic superiors vetoed the idea, dismissing it as "sociology." The work climate was such that he was sometimes condescendingly referred to by others in the government as "Mullah Ernie." It was not until the revolution and after his retirement that he was able to do his study on the force of religion in Iran. He did it for the agency on contract—*after* the force of religion had been felt not only in Iran but by America as well.

The Iran expertise at CIA headquarters was diluted and ignored for four reasons. First, to some extent the analysts were locked into a system whereby they reported what policymakers wanted to see and hear. Although this problem was not as serious in the CIA as at the State Department, it did exist. Iran reports were shaped to the perceived needs of the administration and president in office. The hypothesis of Harry Howe Ransom that intelligence systems tend to report what they think the political leadership wants to hear is clearly confirmed in the Iran case.[60] As Stansfield Turner noted, this encouraged CIA officials, particularly at the higher levels, to be "hung up on the durability of the Shah."[61]

A second administrative problem also concerned the reporting process. The actual mechanics of reporting often resulted in a weak, innocuous product. The Top Secret Current Intelligence Bulletin that was submitted to the president every day typically began its formation in the analyst's office at the CIA. In the branch that included Iran, the analyst wrote the first version, which was sent up through both the branch chief and the division chief, who had the authority to make alterations and revisions. Having now passed through the division, the report was then revised by editors, individuals with no substantive knowledge of Iran or any of the other countries discussed. The now-edited version of the report was next passed along to a final screening panel consisting of representatives of the CIA, Defense Intelligence Agency (DIA), and Department of State. At this final stage of preparation serious differences of opinion often surfaced. The result was a document that represented bureaucratic compromise. It had often been sterilized to such an extent that the analyst who had begun the process at times did not recognize the final report as that originally submitted. In the case of Iran, the sterilization process was especially pronounced given the mind-set at the White House and the vested interests of organizations such as the DIA. The demands for brevity also worked against serious analysis. Before the revolution, Iran (even when it was in the news) only merited a half page to one page in a twelve-page final document.

Third, constant organizational shuffling and reshuffling within the agency badly debilitated Iran analysis. In 1974, for example, Henry Kissinger began to stress the significance of the Persian Gulf. This led the CIA to rearrange its geographical offices at the worst possible time. The Greece/Turkey/Iran (GTI) branch was broken up; a new Persian Gulf/Iran (PGI) branch was established; and Greece and Turkey were shifted to the European context. The senior Iran analyst was simply sidetracked to a "research" position. Iran responsibilities were then taken over by an individual with expertise in the Arab world but with no special knowledge of Iran. Even worse, the CIA chief of current reporting deemphasized area knowledge at the expense of reporting elegance and the proper style of presentation. He told his analysts that no one had "any proprietary rights to any country" and that what he wanted was "the best art form."[62]

This bureaucratic instability occurred at precisely the time when the table was being set in Iran for a revolution. It had disastrous consequences for the agency's capacity to understand Iran. Both old Iran hands were removed from the scene. While the second analyst had been retired in 1973, the longtime branch chief was shunted aside in 1974. Within one fateful year, forty-five years of accumulated knowledge of Iran were lost to the agency. The reorganization dismantled the branch library on Iran and discarded its books. The bureaucratic leadership argued that the library took up too much space, duplicated material in the main library, and contributed nothing to current reporting. This, perhaps more than anything else, symbolized the new approach to analysis of Iran at the Central Intelligence Agency in the mid-1970s.

These local organizational shifts that plagued the Iran branch were part of a fourth, more general, administrative problem. This was the long-standing division in the Central Intelligence Agency between the analysts and the operatives—the Office of Current Intelligence, as opposed to the section involved in covert operations. The two functioned in quite different spheres and met only at the point where information merged with intelligence. The operator and the analyst lived in two different worlds and often had little understanding of each other's milieu. Traditionally, the covert operations section dominated the agency, and this was resented by the analysts. In the case of Iran, this division was seen in the fact that both sides felt the other was holding back information. The analysts were critical of those reporting from the field on both quantitative and qualitative grounds. There is little doubt that there was a definite decline in Iran reporting from the mid-1960s to the mid-1970s. Also, the analysts considered the reports that were submitted from the field to be very weak. At times they felt that surely those officials stationed in Iran must be better informed than their reports indicated. The operatives, on the other hand, did not hold the analysts in particularly high regard, describing them as "bookworms" and "academic types." At the very least, communication between the field officers and the analysts back in the United States was not always good.

At times, the analysts would travel to Iran on fact-finding trips of their own. On one trip, an analyst discovered a valuable file of reports that an Iranian informant had been submitting for years on the Shi'i religious establishment. The informant had been a long-term employee, but no one had bothered to study his reports. He was the only important source of information that the agency had on the Iranian clerics, and his information had been lost in the shuffle. This informant, an old, knowledgeable gentleman, had been "retargeted" to Soviet affairs in the late 1960s, an excellent indication of the agency's priorities in Iran. That the analyst himself had to go to the field to discover these important files is only one indication of the lack of cooperation between analyst and operative in the agency's Iran section.

The many problems that have plagued the CIA in its operations in the foreign-policy process were vividly demonstrated in the Iran-Contra episode of 1985–86. A new generation of Iran specialists, although intelligent and talented, could not hope to understand the complex and elusive Iranian political landscape in the same way as had the former experienced Iran analysts. Partial exceptions included Graham Fuller, the bright and perceptive national intelligence officer for the Near East/South Asia, and former operative George Cave. Brought out of retirement to participate in this ill-planned venture, Cave found himself part of an operation that already had momentum of its own. Moreover, he became a convert to the escapade and took an increasingly prominent role in the operation. Despite Fuller and Cave, the CIA's Iran expertise was regularly overlooked by the White House, where the NSC had its own sources of information. The plans and policy were formulated by NSC staff members who were long on commitment to flamboyant adventure and short on area expertise. Lieutenant colonels such as Oliver North and admirals such as John Poindexter had only a primitive understanding of revolutionary Iran.

The Politics of Intelligence and Policy Failure

An analysis of the Iranian-American story demonstrates that both the Department of State and the Central Intelligence Agency suffered from similar serious ailments. The brainpower and dedication that was sporadically present in both organizations was neutralized by the systems in which they resided. In the field, both the CIA station chief and the American ambassador regularly met directly with the shah. This Siamese political attachment at the top determined the relationship regardless of what occasionally took place at the lower levels of both units. The information that colored the American image of Iran flowed from top to bottom. The occasional streams of dissenting voices were easily washed aside by the Pahlavi-favored and flavored flood of official pronouncements from above. The Iranian revolution was a movement that gathered momentum from the bottom reaches of society. The shah and his highly touted secret police failed either to sense or to see the powerful momentum of this movement. The United States, primarily dependent on the shah and his elite for its information, also quite naturally misunderstood the social and political realities of Iran. The American eagle, wings outstretched protectively, flew along just above the Pahlavi lion, as the lion led the way through the thick and treacherous political underbrush of the international arena.

In Iran, Americans lived in considerable isolation from Iranian society. They intentionally sought one another and were clearly more comfortable in the company of those Iranians who had been "Westernized," who spoke English, and who favored the most modern dimensions of society. They knew the Iran of the boutiques and the discotheques. Official Americans had limited contact with the Iran of the mosques, the villages, and the urban slums. Besides the isolation that promoted misunderstanding, American officialdom in Iran was constantly embroiled in intramural bickering and competition. This strengthened the impulse to look inward and to become preoccupied with intra-American administrative matters. It clearly weakened the capacity to look outward that was essential to any understanding of Iranian society. Finally, the Iranian social and political elite itself promoted the isolation of America in Iran. The Iranian elite of Pahlavi days shared its own shallow understanding of Iran with its American friends. In some ways, despite their isolation, Americans knew more about the society of the Iranian masses than did many members of the Iranian secular, Westernized elite. The simple reason was that Americans often did more traveling throughout Iran.

Despite all this, there were always some Americans who can be termed the "penetrators." They were found in all American organizations in Iran, including even the military, the official U.S. unit most isolated from Iran and most defensive of the shah and his government. Talented language officers were located in various military missions, and for a time in the 1950s and early 1960s before the program was gutted, the U.S. Army had a foreign area specialist program that produced officers who had academic area training and who lived throughout the countryside of Iran. They were not in intelligence but were military officers, generally at the rank of captain, who served the army as genuine Iran specialists. They included Robert Hand, John Batiste, and, later, Charles Scott. Such sensitive Iran observers were also found, of course, in the diplomatic corps, among scholars, and especially among Peace Corps volunteers. Although many of these American specialists were at times socially ostracized and intellectually isolated, their opinions lacked impact as much because of Washington as Tehran.

The close link of the shah with the CIA station chief and the U.S. ambassador in Iran was fashioned and reinforced by the pro-Pahlavi policy that emanated for decades out of Washington. The system that supported this policy, described in detail in chapter 9, was so pervasive that it influenced all levels of all the bureaucracies involved in Iranian affairs. Most important, it adversely affected the reporting processes both in Washington and in Tehran. The State Department and CIA analysts in Washington always worked in the shadow of the "the Pahlavi premise," the powerful assumption in the highest echelons of the executive branch of the government that the pro-American and anticommunist shah was in complete control in Iran. This Pahlavi premise was even more powerful in Tehran, where the shah and his elite were on the spot to reinforce it effectively at every turn. Those diplomats who attempted to question the premise discovered that they did so at considerable risk to their own careers. After all, they worked for an ambassador who subscribed enthusiastically to the Pahlavi premise. In so doing, of course, a typical ambassador to Iran at times came close to becoming a lobbyist for the shah. In earlier chapters we have seen how various U.S. ambassadors, in varying degrees and ways, performed this function. They failed to heed Thomas Bailey's important diplomatic admonition that an ambassador "should not report just 'happy thoughts' or observations that he feels will conform to the 'party line' then being pursued in Washington, with a consequent boost in his promotion and pay."[63] Over the years, the "happy thoughts" approach dominated the official American approach to Iran. Its prevalence both up and down administrative hierarchies as well as across various official foreign policy-making units demonstrates its contagious nature.

In the decade since the Iranian revolution, a debate has developed over whether the Iranian-American imbroglio was a failure of intelligence or a failure of policy. In fact, it was both. And the two failures were mutually reinforcing. Not only did the United States not understand the culture and political power of the Iranian masses, but it even lacked an in-depth understanding of the Pahlavi political elite. How else can one explain the fact that Americans had no idea that the shah had cancer and that he had hidden the fact from the United States for five years? The cancer has been dramatically described as "without question, one of the best-kept state secrets of all time."[64] It was not as if American diplomats and intelligence agents had not been warned of this possibility. Experienced political officer John Stempel sardonically laughed off a suggestion from a Soviet counterpart in July 1978 that the shah was reportedly sick with cancer. Two State Department INR Iran reports prepared before the revolution concluded the following. In May 1976: "Only 55 years old, in good health, and increasingly careful about security, he [the shah] has a good chance to be able to lead Iran for many more years." In January 1977: "At age 57, in fine health, and protected by an elaborate security apparatus, the Shah has an excellent chance to rule for a dozen or more years."[65] Is not this intelligence failure?

But there was severe policy failure as well. Not all Iran reports were off target. As we have seen in this study, hard-hitting reports questioning the strength and future of the shah surfaced sporadically. The 1975 NIE analysis discussed in detail above, for example, indicated that there was serious trouble for Iran in the years immediately ahead. In 1977 a Carter transition team solicited a paper on the shah as an ally. This report, prepared under the direction of Franklin P. Huddle at INR, raised some fundamental questions about the shah's style and stability in Iran. This more critical perspective was reinforced primarily by academics who occasionally made presentations in Washington. Although the government seldom made adequate use of academic expertise on Iran,[66] this analysis was both public and available. The key policymakers at the NSC and other White House locations had no intention of changing Iran policy regardless of the political intelligence reports they received. This sobering fact was demonstrated in the last months of 1978 when Ambassador William Sullivan and his staff in Tehran, the Iran specialists at the Department of State, and academic Iran experts all provided reams of evidence that the shah was going under. Yet, the Pahlavi supremacy premise, promoted and protected by presidential advisers like Zbignew Brzezinski, reigned supreme until there was no longer any Pahlavi about whom to premise.

Over the years, the key policymakers in Washington considered the shah of Iran indispensable and indestructible. These views were, to use again the words of Thomas Bailey, the "party line." They were well known to diplomats and intelligence officials both in the United States and in Iran and served as a powerful deterrent for critical, analytic reporting. The lack of such reporting in turn reinforced the Pahlavi party line, and the spinning circle of distortion and ignorance accelerated over time. The occasional diplomats, officials, and academics who sharply questioned the Pahlavi premise oddly strengthened the party line by providing the system with legitimacy and a sense of false objectivity. That there had always been someone somewhere predicting the fall of the shah also reinforced the arguments of those who subscribed to the Pahlavi invincibility thesis. In the end, the problem was systemic. It involved a complex array of mutually reinforcing factors and forces that composed a system built on misperceptions, misunderstandings, and misplaced self-interest on many sides. The Iranian arms affair of 1986–87 demonstrates that this system has transcended the Iranian revolution and remains stubbornly in place a decade after the crashing fall of the shah.

11 The Politics of Foreign Policy Failure: A System of Reinforcing Errors

The US government has a weakness for lost causes and for persisting in monumental misjudgments. It took Washington seventeen years to recognize the Russian Revolution, and twenty-nine to recognize China's. We still feud with Castro's. Nobody knows how many billions were wasted over the last half century in these Canute-like operations, all of them sheer nonsense since there has not been a major revolutionary regime yet that didn't end up anxious for trade and good relations.
                    —I. F. Stone, *New York Review of Books*, February 22, 1979

Although U.S.-Iranian relations began on a strongly positive note and the eagle and the lion lived well together in their international habitat, the situation deteriorated rapidly after midcentury. The American intervention in support of the shah and against the popular Musaddiq government in 1953 represented an end to the American honeymoon with the Iranian people. Yet it was clearly still possible for America to rehabilitate its image in Iran. Instead, U.S. policy gaffes exacerbated the situation; by 1977, when President Jimmy Carter took office, it had reached the breaking point. Carter's actions only made the traumatic break inevitable. After the revolution, the hostility reached unprecedented levels. Despite a clumsy abortive effort at quiet rapprochement in 1985–86 by officials on both sides, mutual distrust and political tension have remained high.

The chapters in this book have explained this story in great detail. The why and how questions remain to be answered. In attempting to formulate an explanation of the outcome, it is necessary to identify the variables and to relate them one to another. This information can be organized into three categories: interests, ideology, and ignorance. Within each category, it is possible to develop a typology and then to explore the relationships between these typologies. This will better explain the outcome of the Iran-American imbroglio.

The United States Foreign Policy-Making System

Interests

Two quite different but related interests have shaped American foreign policy toward Iran. The first is normal bureaucratic interest in which various organizations and agencies seek to maximize their own power within a complex environment of political bargaining. This type may be referred to as organizational interests. The second type of interest concerns personal, economic, and political interests pursued by various actors in their promotion of a particular foreign policy. This category is referred to as policy interests.

ORGANIZATIONAL INTERESTS. American policy toward Iran was formulated in an environment of considerable bureaucratic conflict between the relevant organizations. In chapter 10 I have analyzed the major line of organizational conflict—the NSC-State Department tension—bureaucratic conflict that broke dramatically to the surface in late 1986 when it was discovered that the two were simultaneously pursuing quite contradictory policies toward Iran. While the Department of State condemned Iran as a terrorist state and engaged in an international campaign to halt arms sales to the Islamic Republic of Iran, the NSC was selling arms to Iran via secret channels of communication. This controversial episode shook the Reagan administration and revealed how bureaucratic conflict in foreign policy-making had transcended even the Iranian revolution.

Although the NSC-State Department division represents the major fault line in foreign policy-making conflict, bureaucratic rivalry has existed everywhere in the system in the U.S.-Iranian case study. It developed within and between private and public American organizations that dealt with Iran; it marked relations between civilian and military governmental units; it was present within civilian and military organizations; and it existed in Washington and in Tehran. The rivalry was both personal and institutional. Although a degree of organizational conflict is present in all bureaucracies, its pervasiveness and intensity were particularly marked here.[1]

Social scientists have documented the personal and institutional rivalries that have infused the Iranian social and political system. On the personal level, it has involved cynicism, insecurity, mistrust, and exploitation.[2] On the institutional level, it has been referred to as a "web-system," a system of balanced tension or institutionalized conflict.[3] As Americans became entwined within the Iranian personal web-system and as U.S. organizations slowly locked themselves into Iranian administrative structures, American patterns and relationships changed. Typical organizational tension developed into a deeper form of bureaucratic conflict. Issues became more personalized. In short, American behavior increasingly took on the characteristics of the society in which U.S. representatives and institutions operated.[4]

Although the considerable literature on bureaucratic politics and foreign policy-making does not focus explicitly on the question of conflict, such rivalry is an important part of the model. According to the bureaucratic politics model, foreign-policy decisions are the result of the interaction of multiple actors with differing perspectives and goals. The ultimate policy results from a compromise reached among these actors.[5] Important practitioners of this model postulate that the nature of bureaucratic conflict changes significantly during a crisis: the conflict itself decreases sharply, informal external actors lose influence, and domestic political considerations have less impact.[6] The Iran case challenges these hypotheses. During the various crises analyzed in this book, such as the revolution itself, the admission of the shah into the United States, and the hostage incident, bureaucratic conflict was extremely intense, the extraofficial actors were deeply involved, and domestic political considerations were a constant part of the calculations of the president and his closest associates.

The system of institutionalized organizational conflict that marked American foreign policy-making toward Iran contributed directly to the general ignorance of Iran and ultimately to the strong commitment to the premise that the shah must be taken as a given. In Washington, the divided nature of the decision-making structure weakened any efforts to question this premise. Those very professional units most likely to challenge the dominant premise—the Department of State and the Central Intelligence Agency—were themselves torn by internal rivalry and differences. That they were in turn locked into competition with the NSC and the Department of Defense further guaranteed a distorted perspective that promoted the Pahlavi premise.

Domestic political considerations also influenced U.S. foreign policy toward Iran by reinforcing commitment to the shah's regime. Key elected officials, most particularly the presidents themselves, tended to support a foreign policy that maximized their own opportunities for reelection. This basic principle of personal political survival shaped the process of bureaucratic politics as those closest to the president recommended foreign policy that would enhance the chief executive's domestic political fortunes. Although this usually meant that the White House staff and the NSC urged policy with a special eye to protecting the image of the president, this has not always been the case. In the 1986 incident, the NSC's actions jeopardized the reputation of President Reagan. In this case, however, reelection was not an issue. In sum, domestic political factors have often threatened the process of strategic professional foreign policy-making.

POLICY INTERESTS. Various American individuals and groups have pursued their own interests or goals in Iran. These interests were maximized by the nature of the Pahlavi political and economic system. Three major types of interests were sought in this context: (1) private personal interests; (2) general public economic interests with private implications; and (3) international political interests. The third category has two subtypes, an offensive protective interest and a defensive containment interest. In the empirical world, of course, these interests overlap and interlock.

In chapter 9 I provided an in-depth analysis of the methods by which leading American businessmen, lawyers, bankers, politicians, and academicians promoted their own interests in Iran. The shah's system was directed by a Western-educated and modern-oriented political and economic elite that encouraged American private involvement of all kinds. By 1978, thousands of American companies, banks, contractors, and consultants were located in Iran. Many were led by honorable businessmen who represented the best that American capitalism had to offer. Others were disreputable financial scavengers who sought to turn a quick profit and who left nothing in return other than their unsavory reputations.

The pro-Pahlavi policy of Washington administrations, whether Democrat or Republican, was, therefore, strongly reinforced by powerful private parties whose personal and financial interests were tightly bound up with the fate of the shah. These individuals often became influential lobbyists for the shah and his regime. Some, like David Lilienthal, were motivated as much by humanitarian as by financial considerations. Others, such as Marian Javits, signed on for a fee. Many had less overt, but quite real, financial interests.

At times, those who sought social and humanitarian goals and those who sought only financial gain clashed. Lilienthal, for example, was horrified and indignant when approached by Marian Javits for contacts and advice on Iran. He described one visit by Marian Javits and her public relations employer to him in Princeton. They asked him for his help in changing Iran's image in America. "I had trouble controlling my temper and didn't entirely succeed." When he angrily asked, "What do you know about Iran?" the response was, "Nothing really; that's what we expected you to provide us." Lilienthal reacted, "No need to recite how I felt about this. It took us years and years. So in a half hour we are expected to inform them about Iran. What Mrs. Javits said was so shockingly ignorant or askew I won't record it."[7]

A second more generalized and public interest, yet bound up with private economic interests, concerned Iran's rich oil reserves. It is not accidental that Americans closely associated with the oil industry—Max Thornburg, the Rockefellers, Herbert Hoover, Jr., Howard Page, Walter Levy, and John J. McCloy—played key roles in U.S.-Iranian relations. As I indicated in chapter 2, oil played a major role in the U.S. political position on the Musaddiq movement. A memorandum of October 10, 1951 describing a meeting between Secretary of State Dean Acheson and Assistant Secretary George McGhee with the heads of the five major American oil companies demonstrates the intimate connection between the government and the industry.

McGhee told the company leaders that the government had "at all times sought to keep in mind both the importance of maintaining the continued independence of Iran and the impact of any action we might take on the U.S. oil interests in the Middle East." The oil company's response was blunt and extraordinary:

> Representatives of the [oil] group emphasized the very grave consequences of giving the Iranians terms more favorable than those received by other countries. They expressed the opinion that if this were done the entire international oil industry would be seriously threatened. The opinion was offered that even the loss of Iran would be preferable to the instability which would be created by making too favorable an agreement with Iran. Other representatives pointed out that not just the oil industry was involved but indeed all American investment overseas and the concept of the sanctity of contractual relations.[8]

The oil issue influenced Iranian-American relations until the revolution. Whereas in the 1950s the struggle focused on the actual control of oil, in the 1960s the debate concerned production, and in the 1970s the major conflict was over price. Throughout this history, the U.S. government and the American oil industry remained in close touch. At the same time, the possession of petroleum enabled the shah to maintain leverage over the United States and to elicit both private and public support in the United States for his regime and his political policies.

Besides these personal and economic interests, American policy toward Iran was directly influenced by two types of international political interests. An offensive protective interest centered on U.S. commitments to the state of Israel, while a defensive containment interest involved American concern about Soviet expansionism. As briefly indicated in chapter 9, there was a very heavy overlap between supporters of Israel and supporters of the shah in America. Israel cultivated what it referred to as the "Iranian connection," which was originally fashioned in the late 1940s. At this time, Israeli and American intelligence cooperated in a joint effort to assist Jews to escape persecution in neighboring Iraq and initiated a campaign to attempt to gain Iran's recognition of Israel. This involved the distribution of huge sums of money to Iranian politicians. Mossad director Moshe Tchervinski said that "it was possible to achieve almost anything in Iran" through bribery.[9] By these and other means, Israel succeeded in establishing a presence in Pahlavi Iran that continued to expand over the years. This presence "went far in creating continuity in relations between the two countries, allowing Israel [sic] representatives to feel the pulse of Iranian politics and take advantage of opportunities to promote Israeli interests as these presented themselves."[10]

The Pahlavi-Israeli relationship developed along political, economic, military, and intelligence lines, with special emphasis on Iran's willingness to supply Israel with petroleum. Most top Israeli leaders secretly visited Tehran at one time or another, including David Ben-Gurion, Moshe Dayan, Golda Meir, Abba Eban, Yitzhak Rabin, and Yigal Allon. Allon himself visited Iran and met with the shah and other Iranian leaders on three occasions. Arrangements were made by SAVAK head Nimatullah Nassiri.[11] Iranian military leaders also shuttled back and forth to Israel to meet with the highest echelons of the Israeli defense establishment concerning arms and military technology. In July 1978, for example, Gen. Hassan Toufanian, the shah's vice minister of war, visited Tel Aviv, where he held a series of sensitive meetings with Foreign Minister Moshe Dayan and Minister of Defense Ezer Weizmann. At these meetings there was much blunt discussion of political and military cooperation between Iran and Israel. Among other things, Toufanian pressed for a joint missile project, criticized American senators for being "unfamiliar in geography and ignorant in world affairs," and proposed that Iran and Israel make an effort "to save Sadat and [King] Hussein."[12]

The Mossad-SAVAK connection was especially close. A CIA study noted: "The main purpose of the Israeli relationship with Iran was the development of a pro-Israel and anti-Arab policy on the part of Iranian officials. Mossad has engaged in joint operations with SAVAK over the years since the late 1950s. Mossad aided SAVAK activities and supported the Kurds in Iraq. The Israelis also regularly transmitted to the Iranians intelligence reports on Egypt's activities in the Arab countries, trends and developments in Iraq, and Communist activities affecting Iran."[13] In 1976, the American embassy in Tehran summarized what it referred to as the "fruitful private relationship" that Iran maintained with Israel. "Senior representatives are resident in each other's country even though diplomatic relations do not formally exist. Intelligence information is exchanged regularly, and several Israeli technical assistance projects in agriculture and other fields are underway in Iran. Despite the Arab oil embargo, Iran has never cut its flow of oil to Israel and today provides 50 percent of Israel's oil requirements."[14]

In the United States, Israeli interests and Iranian interests were mutually reinforcing. According to Richard Helms, the shah told the Israelis that neither Iran nor Israel should want to be alone "in a sea of Arabs."[15] A leading Israeli scholar described Iran as Israel's "strategic decoy" to divert "Arab attention and resources away from Israel's own borders."[16] Due to the persistence of Israeli leaders and the wartime needs of the Islamic Republic of Iran after the shah's overthrow, this Israeli-Iran connection continued to exist, albeit in much modified form. The heavy Israeli involvement in arms supplies to Iran became a matter of public record with the 1986 exposure of the Reagan administration's secret Iran policy.

The second, and somewhat more obvious, general international interest involved the American desire to contain the Soviet Union. Sharing a 1,600-mile border with the USSR, Iran assumed great geostrategic significance in America's plans to halt the expansion of the Soviet empire following World War II. Many of the interventionary activities of the United States in Iran were triggered by its desire to strengthen the Pahlavi regime against any possible encroachment by the Soviet Union. The foundation for this policy was laid in the 1940s and 1950s when the United States supported Iran in its campaign to expel Soviet troops from Azerbaijan and when zealous policymakers in Washington chose to intervene directly to assist in the overthrow of the government of Muhammad Musaddiq.

These interests intersected at numerous points. Individual points of intersection can be seen, for example, in cases such as the Rockefellers and the Javits. The Rockefeller family's relationship with the Pahlavi dynasty involved personal finance and banking, general petroleum policy, and strong opposition to Soviet expansionism. Jacob Javits's support for the shah involved concern about petroleum policy, opposition to Soviet expansionism, and a special appreciation for Pahlavi commitments to the state of Israel. At the same time, Marian

Javits entered into her own personal business relationship with the government of Iran. On the other hand, there were clear examples where the types of interests were not cumulative and reinforcing. Oil company actors, for example, while deeply concerned about production and prices, were quite oblivious to the interests of the state of Israel. Although somewhat more concerned about the Soviet challenge, they basically viewed Pahlavi stability in terms of its importance for access to Iranian oilfields and for the maximization of petroleum profits.

Individuals and organizations promoted these three types of interests through both private and public channels. A number of the most powerful members of the American political and economic elite developed close relationships with the shah and his entourage. Although some of these individuals held public office, others did not. Still others were what Morton Halperin has termed "the ins and outers"—individuals who moved in and out of public office depending on the administration and the time.[17] Since most members of the shah's elite were internationally sophisticated and spoke fluent English, they easily established rapport with Americans. With the important partial exceptions of regimes such as those of Syngman Rhee, Ferdinand Marcos, Anastacio Somoza, Kings Hussein of Jordan and Hassan of Morocco, and, especially, Chiang Kai-shek, no other authoritarian Third World government maintained the same tight personal and professional relationships with the American elite. The Pahlavi and American political and economic elites penetrated one another at numerous points.

The shah and his advisers understood very well these perceived American interests. Using both private and public channels, therefore, they sought to demonstrate that Pahlavi interests coincided with American interests. The shah encouraged private business ventures by major American financiers, industrialists, and contractors; despite occasional spells of independence, at bottom he promoted U.S. petroleum objectives; and he especially sought to prove his loyalty by supporting American foreign policy objectives. He constantly reminded American leaders of his support for U.S. policy in Vietnam and in Israel. He also stressed his opposition to Soviet intervention in the Persian Gulf by assuming military responsibility for the status quo there.

The perceived U.S. interests were major factors in the determination of U.S.-Iran policy, policy that was promoted both privately and publicly, policy that was encouraged by the shah himself.

Ideology

Much of American policy toward Iran can be explained or rationalized in terms of a deep concern about the challenge of communism. This preoccupation is directly related, of course, to the international political interest referred to above—that is, Soviet expansionism. Nonetheless, the driving dynamic of responding to a perceived ideological challenge ran much deeper than the imperialist policies of one particular nation-state. In the case of Iran, this ideological issue remained central because of the continued existence of a native communist party, the Tudeh party, which maintained a presence both within and outside the country.

Just as the shah understood the persuasive power of recognizing the interests important to American leaders, he also sensed the special importance of the ideological factor. He used the specter of communism whenever he felt that American support for his regime might possibly be wavering. American friends of Pahlavism such as Kermit Roosevelt, Nelson Rockefeller, David Lilienthal, and George Lenczowski, along with presidential national security advisers like Walt Rostow, Henry Kissinger, and Zbigniew Brzezinski, were repeatedly warned by the shah of the serious communist menace to his country. If America failed him, he argued, the communists would move in and take over. At the time of the revolution, for example, he insisted to Americans, private and public, that the communists were behind the upheaval. In May 1978 he sounded this warning during a private meeting with Nelson Rockefeller. Rockefeller then spread the message in elite circles in New York and Washington.[18]

But Rockefeller spoke to the already converted. Zbigniew Brzezinski, for example, had long maintained a Sovietcentric view of the world and saw Iran merely as an externally directed pawn in the East-West struggle. His views of developments in Iran were colored by the red-tinted glasses he wore whenever he glanced at the Middle Eastern horizon. With Ardeshir Zahedi as his line to Iranian reality, he and the Pahlavi political elite reinforced one another's mistaken perceptions. But such perceptions were eagerly accepted in the United States, where academicians and journalists accepted and repeated them. This approach had long dominated Iranian-American affairs. In March 1953 the U.S. naval attaché had written a long report on the Musaddiq movement, which he described as "sliding down the roller coaster . . . toward what appears to be certain communism."[19] Seventeen years later, Ambassador Douglas MacArthur II briefed visitors to Tehran about the "Soviet pincers movement" that was about to crush Iran in its jaws.[20] And in 1978, analysts often interpreted Khomeini's revolutionary movement in terms of its relation to the Soviet Union.[21]

Ideology, in this context, must be viewed in two ways. There is ideology perceived as a genuine threat and ideology used as a rationalization. In the former, the communist threat was viewed as a serious challenge to the political and economic system of Iran. Many American decision-makers sincerely believed this was the case. In the latter, ideology was used to justify policies designed in fact to protect other interests. Here, ideological arguments served to mask and cloak narrower, more specific, self-interest. It is at this point that interest and ideology intersect and interact.

The coincidence of the challenges of Soviet expansionism and the ideology of communism is self-evident. Here, there is no incentive for ideology as rationalization. Such also tends to be the case concerning the commitment to Israel. The Pahlavi-Israeli connection was partially fashioned by a common anticommunist stance. Partisans of Israel in America have long argued that Israel was a reliable, anticommunist ally in the Middle East. Therefore, they used the threat of communism both to Iran and to Israel in their arguments designed to promote the Pahlavi regime. Again, although there may be an element of ideology as rationalization involved in this link since the commitment to Israel may for some take precedence over anticommunism, there is nonetheless a heavy coincidence between interest and ideology.

This is much less true in the case of personal financial and general economic interests. In these instances, ideology as rationalization becomes a much more dominant explanatory factor. Those with fundamental economic interests in Iran, for example, often sought to promote those interests by supporting the shah's regime as an anticommunist bastion. Although few instances as stark as the quotation above whereby oil company heads bluntly argue their economic self-interest over even a possible communist takeover of Iran can be documented, it is clear that a priority of interests was involved. Personal financial and general economic interests usually took precedence over ideological considerations. Arms dealers and contractors provide another case in point. Their commitment to the shah's regime was based on the enormous sales and profits they accrued. Due to the nature of their product, it was particularly efficacious for them to base their pro-Pahlavi policy position on an anticommunist ideological platform.

The concern about private financial interests, the national economy and oil, and steady support for such countries as Israel was fueled by both a perceived ideological threat of communism that hovered shadowlike through the Middle East and a related imperial military challenge that could erupt anytime from the North. As I argued in chapter 10, the threat of communism was used constantly throughout the Iranian arms affair to justify the Israeli-American covert initiative to the Islamic Republic of Iran. This complex network of interrelated and mutually reinforcing factors rested behind the deeply rooted American support for the shah and his government in Iran. It emphasized external factors of interest and ideology while deflecting attention away from the social and political issues that confronted Iranian society. The result was ignorance.

Ignorance

It is not surprising that ignorance was a consequence of the interacting dynamics between interests and ideology. This interaction created an atmosphere within which Americans involved with Iran disregarded and ignored many of the key elements and forces that inevitably determined Iran's future. This was one reason that pervasive ignorance characterized American relations with Iran. The emphasis placed on interests such as personal gain, economic goals, Soviet imperialism, and Israeli needs, along with a preoccupation, both real and artificial, with the ideological challenge of communism inevitably brought about a sterility of understanding. The mutually reinforcing dialectics between interests and ideology effectively undercut the need for an in-depth understanding of the objective realities of Iranian society and politics.

This ignorance led to the fundamental proximate cause of the collapse of Iranian-American relations—the Pahlavi premise. This premise was rooted in the soil of interests discussed above, and it grew rapidly in the climate of misunderstanding that surrounded U.S.-Iranian relations. It stressed Pahlavi invincibility and was based on three assumptions: (1) the shah was first and foremost a friend of the United States; (2) the shah was generally loved and supported by the overwhelming masses of the Iranian people; and (3) those who opposed the shah consisted of a few radicals and extremists who were easily controlled by his security forces. These assumptions, based on a misunderstanding of Iran promoted by considerations of interest and ideology, led directly to the conclusion that the Pahlavi regime in Iran was stable and worthy of unquestioned support. Thus, at the highest levels in Washington, descriptions of Iran were liberally sprinkled with terms that denoted order and stability. Iran was an "oasis," "island," or "pillar" of stability.

Every American president, with the partial exception of Kennedy, praised the shah's government in Iran and enacted strong policies in support of that regime. The highest ranking officials in Washington, including the presidents' national security advisers, the National Security Council itself, and the Department of Defense, accepted and promoted this view. Although middle-level analysts in the Department of State and the CIA sporadically questioned it, the leaders of these important organizations also subscribed to it. This Pahlavi premise gained strength with time and became so entrenched that even the voices of those middle-level and outside analysts who dared to question it became fainter through the 1970s.

The Pahlavi invincibility thesis is an excellent example of what one authority on U.S. foreign policy has referred to as the phenomenon of "shared images."[22] These shared images represent conventional wisdom and percolate through the government bureaucracy from the top. In these circumstances, "Participants will have considerable difficulty getting the ordinary administrator or politician to believe facts that go against the shared images. Officials react as all individuals do to evidence which goes against strongly held beliefs. They either ignore the evidence or interpret it so as to change what it seems to mean."[23]

Despite their pervasiveness, shared images are never unanimous. A few voices are always raised in opposition. Their existence is used as an argument by those who propagate this kind of "party line" to deny the very existence of such a line. In fact, the presence of a few notable devil's advocates actually strengthens the dominant shared images because it lends false legitimacy to them. In the case of Iran, the relative absence of countervailing voices demonstrates the unusual strength of the Pahlavi invincibility thesis. George Ball earned his credentials as the establishment's foremost devil's advocate during his criticism of U.S. Vietnam policy. But in the case of Iran, he arrived late on the scene. Within the government itself, William Miller, who had served in Iran in the early 1960s and who maintained close ties with the National Front, was a questioning voice. Also, in 1960–61, a Council on Foreign Relations Study Group on Iran heard informed views of criticism and concern by Iran specialist T. Cuyler Young. Young's arguments were neutralized in an establishment forum that included powerful participants sympathetic to the Pahlavi regime.[24]

Driven by personal and economic interests that were reinforced by ideological considerations, important individuals and groups in

America developed a distorted image of Iran that the centered around the Pahlavi premise. This premise was particularly vigorous due to the manner in which it developed. The shah and his elite promoted it masterfully, while the informal pro-Pahlavi influentials in the United States used their extensive private network in its support. It was extremely difficult for individuals, especially government officials, to present alternative points of view. Opposing opinions had a very short life. The shared images surrounded everyone who worked on Iranian affairs and continually choked off the growth of different and challenging images.

A prime example of ignorance and at the same time a partial consequence of the Pahlavi premise was the startling inadequacy of U.S. Embassy operations in Tehran. Many problems plagued the embassy, including personnel of modest talent, mediocre language and area preparation, limited contacts and an isolation from the culture, and a general malaise of morale that infected the mission over time. With rare exceptions, the ambassadors posted to Iran after World War II were ill prepared for their responsibilities. Those who did have knowledge of Iran were themselves committed carriers of the Pahlavi premise. Their contact pool was extremely shallow.

Startling examples of official U.S. ignorance of Iran abound. In 1974, the best-informed American political officer in Tehran had never heard of Ali Shariati, the Paris-trained intellectual whose speeches and writings in Iran provided much of the inspiration for the revolution. What is worse, in 1977 the foreign service officer with the greatest experience in Iran and the one most knowledgeable about internal affairs there also admitted that he had never heard of Shariati.[25] And these were among the best diplomats that the United States posted to Iran. But the problem was one of both quality and quantity. Organizational chaos and cutbacks exacerbated the situation. In the early 1960s, for example, the embassy employed nearly three times as many political officers as in the late 1970s. In 1961, there were twenty-three political officers in the U.S. Embassy in Tehran; by 1977, this number had dropped to eight. And these few individuals were overcommitted to a range of responsibilities that left them little time to establish contact with the pulse of political affairs.

The Iranian case has spawned a debate about the difficulties involved in maintaining touch with the opposition in countries with authoritarian political systems. Many have argued that it is both imprudent and impossible to initiate contacts with opposition elements in such circumstances. Regarding Iran, certain observers have proposed that little could have been done to establish these contacts since the shah frowned on such activities and the United States dared not risk alienating him. "By virtue of his functions, a diplomatic representative has to associate primarily with members of the government and the ruling establishment. To seek deliberate contacts with the opposition in an authoritarian system is to court disfavor, accusations of double-dealing, and possibly an invitation to leave as a persona non-grata."[26] Unfortunately, this argument, in Iran at least, became a justification for the lack of contact and the resultant misunderstanding that marked the American perspective on the shah's Iran. It has been most ardently presented by precisely those individuals both in and out of the government whose contacts were sharply limited to the Pahlavi elite.

It is, of course, especially difficult to establish contacts with opposition elements in authoritarian systems. On the other hand, it is far from impossible, and it is essential if there is to be any serious understanding of the political system. Ambassador Robert Neumann was quite correct when he stated that the diplomacy of establishing contacts with the opposition is such that "the public underrates the problems—and that the diplomats overrate them."[27] Although it may be true that diplomats must deal "primarily" with the government in power, it is also true that this does not automatically indicate that they cannot contact opposition forces cautiously. This is an important part of what diplomacy is all about, and it has been accomplished by talented American diplomats in many countries at many times.[28]

That such contact was not effectively established in Iran is revealing, especially since, according to a source no less than Richard Helms himself, "the Embassy had no understandings nor made any agreements with him [the shah] on how it would conduct itself. In short, there were no 'deals.'"[29] Ambassador William Sullivan quoted the shah himself to make the same general point. When Sullivan told the shah that Washington had reversed its decision to establish contact with Ayatollah Khomeini, the shah incredulously responded, "How can you expect to have any influence with these people if you won't meet with them?"[30] In the contemporary history of Iranian-American relations, only one American diplomat was even threatened with being declared persona non grata. Yet high-ranking diplomats in Iran behaved as if the shah had ordered them to refrain from developing any broad contacts within Iran and so engaged in a debilitating form of self-censorship.

Hans Morgenthau has written about "the almost instinctive American preference for politically safe contacts favorable to the social and political status quo." He has said that this policy "pays as long as the government of the day remains in power; but when the government loses, the United States loses with it."[31] Such was the case of Iran.

An even more serious problem in Iran was that Americans *believed* they were in touch with the opposition. This institutionalized self-deception is indicated in the words of one Iran specialist who argued that American diplomats "were generally well aware of the sources of discontent and could identify various opposition groups. An extra social hour spent in the company of a well-known dissenter (a poet, a professor) would not have brought any major revelations."[32] This argument, of course, avoids the issue of "less-known" dissenters—the religious leaders, the bazaar workers, the occupants of the south Tehran shantytowns. Sporadic contact with the well-dressed, liberal National Front does not necessarily constitute contact with the opposition. In the extraordinary words of former U.S. political counselor Martin Herz, who served in Iran from 1963 to 1967: "In my own experience, the opposition usually beats a path to the door of the United States Embassy: and if it isn't allowed in through the door it may come through the window; and if it isn't allowed in through the window, it may send messages 'over the transom.'"[33] The liberals who beat a path to the door of the U.S. Embassy during the shah's rule were an opposition quite different from the one that beat a path over the wall of the embassy after the shah fell. It was an opposition the United States knew little about.

Yet some competent official Americans in Iran sporadically attempted to warn Washington. Within the embassy itself, the devil's advocate mechanism operated. But, as in Washington, the mechanism was feeble and its message faint. Pahlavite ambassadors easily converted it into a means whereby they were able to argue the objectivity and build the credibility of their analysis. An excellent example of the manner in which this process operated is a mildly critical report submitted by Martin Herz in the mid-1960s. This was used for years as an example of the kind of hard-hitting, objective analysis that was coming out of the embassy in Tehran. In fact, Herz, an intelligent diplomat with limited understanding of Iran, had more consistently praised and defended the Pahlavi system, a system that he understood primarily through the eyes of personal friends in the shah's own inner circle. Even though the document in question contained some paragraphs of devil's advocacy, its conclusions were optimistic. Despite a section entitled "The Malaise of the Regime," it also argued that "the Muslim clergy, to the extent that it is disaffected, is probably a declining power factor," that "the Shah is probably not widely hated even by his detractors and enemies," and, to those who argued that the shah's regime could not long endure, that, "We do not share this conclusion, first, because the base has been somewhat broadened and, second, because it is difficult to see at present what effective combination of power factors could successfully attack the Shah's regime."[34]

The Pahlavi premise dominant in Washington reinforced the inadequacies of the U.S Embassy in Tehran. Halperin's "shared images" percolated outward from Washington to the diplomats in Tehran, where they were promoted by senior embassy officials. Many of these officials had already been exposed to these dominant images in Washington before they arrived in Tehran. To challenge them would have been not only to reject the conventional wisdom but also to risk serious career penalties. As Under-Secretary of State David Newsom noted, "the credibility of the diplomatic messenger who brings bad news suffers."[35] On the other hand, the fact that diplomats in Tehran were loathe to bring bad news only reinforced the Pahlavi premise in Washington.

Thus, the interaction of interests and ideology produced a climate of ignorance that gave rise to the Pahlavi premise, which in turn explained the foreign-policy outcome of unconditional support for the regime of Muhammad Reza Shah Pahlavi. American decision makers formulated policies designed to provide firm, constant support for an authoritarian political system up to the collapse and disintegration of that system. This traumatic collapse not only destroyed the Pahlavi government but also deeply damaged the power and credibility of the United States in this critical part of the world.

The United States and Iran: Twelve Foreign Policy Lessons

The overall lesson for U.S. foreign policy that follows from an analysis of the Iranian-American imbroglio is that the fundamental problem is systemic. A complex network of interrelated, reinforcing factors resulted in an outcome that seriously damaged American national interests. A summary analysis suggests twelve separate but related recommendations for future American foreign policy-making with respect to the Third World.

1. *Any unquestioned, dominant policy premise in Washington should be treated with skepticism and subjected to careful and continual questioning.* Such "shared attitudes" or "party lines" have a tendency to become entrenched with time, and vested interests provide them with private and public political protection. The longer such premises prevail, the more difficult it is to challenge them. Therefore, the U.S.

position with respect to a particular Third World country should be subject to constant review and reconsideration based on changing political realities. This recurring reexamination should take place at the highest levels of the organizations involved in the formation of U.S. foreign policy. The Iranian-American debacle resulted largely from the Pahlavi invincibility premise that existed in Washington during the administration of every U.S president since John F. Kennedy. In a world challenged fundamentally by forces of change, the United States can ill afford to lock itself irrevocably into a particular policy perspective.

2. *The influence of private interests that seek to promote a particular foreign policy must be exposed and controlled.* As demonstrated by the influential Pahlavite lobby in America, powerful informal political elites can exert critical pressure in making U.S. foreign policy. The reasons for such private pressure may be personal, political, economic, ideological, or emotional. Yet this form of lobbying does not necessarily promote American national interests. Although it is certainly possible that private interests may coincide with national public interests, they often do not. In this situation, foreign policy-making should be determined by public officials professionally qualified to perform this task.

A corollary of this proposition involves private interests within the government itself that link up with external groups in pursuit of shared foreign-policy goals. This "privatization" of foreign policy-making was evident in the Iran-Contra affair when zealous staff members in the NSC such as Lt. Col. Oliver North secretly pursued initiatives that ran counter to policy enunciated by the U.S. Congress and the Department of State.

3. *Important foreign-policy decisions should not be made primarily on the basis of domestic political exigencies.* American political leaders are always sensitive to the need to win reelection, and they often seem to support any foreign policy that they feel will maximize these chances. Whether such a position is itself of benefit to overall American interests or whether it is a wise long-term policy are sometimes considered secondary issues by national leaders. In the case of the president, for example, scholars have argued that key foreign policy decisions are made on the basis of their domestic political utility for the chief executive himself.[36] It was partly because of this danger that John F. Kennedy once stated: "Domestic policy can only defeat us; foreign policy can kill us."[37] During the Carter administration, domestic political considerations played a minor role in the disastrous deci-

sion to admit the shah into the United States and a major role in the policy developed to deal with the hostage crisis. The priority of domestic political considerations is also related to the informal private elite and its promotion of a particular political premise in Washington. This elite has not been above using its considerable influence in the American political scene as leverage for a preferred foreign policy.

4. *In a world of multiple crises, U.S. policymakers must beware of focusing all attention on one or another issue at the expense of other more volatile and strategically more costly crises.* Just as domestic political considerations can be a diverting influence, so too can international crises, which occur increasingly frequently in this interdependent world. As a superpower on the international stage, the United States often finds itself embroiled simultaneously in numerous crises around the world. In attempting to attend to one crisis, U.S. decision makers have a tendency to turn their backs on others, thereby inviting foreign policy disaster in these other contexts. In the case of the Iranian revolution, President Carter and his most experienced and sensitive advisers were deeply preoccupied by the Arab-Israeli issue and the Camp David agreement. By the time they turned their attention to Iran, it was late, and policy decisions had already been preempted by other bureaucratic offices, in this case the National Security Council. Debilitating international diversions can paradoxically reinforce domestic political priorities, since certain international issues are selected for attention because of their domestic American implications.

5. *American policymakers must focus their attention less on the Soviet role in Third World upheaval and more on the deepening class conflict and vibrant new forms of populist religion that increasingly energize much of the Middle East, Africa, Asia, and Latin America.* For years, American policymakers have maintained such a fixation with Soviet intentions and activities that they have presumed Soviet involvement in upheaval whenever and wherever it occurs. This Sovietcentric point of view has resulted in distorted U.S. understanding of social forces at work in much of the Third World. In the Middle East, the Arab-Israeli/Palestinian issue was not created by the USSR; neither Nasser nor Qaddafi was a product of Soviet machinations; Anwar Sadat's assassin was not a communist; the Lebanese imbroglio was not conceived by the Soviet Union. Most pertinently, the Iranian revolution was home-grown. Despite some imaginative early attempts by certain officials and scholars to link Khomeini to the Soviet Union and the extremist student-revolutionaries to a communist-controlled faction of the Palestine Liberation Organization, the Soviet Union had

precious little to do with the revolution. Like the United States, it was caught unaware by the speed and thoroughness of the movement. This Sovietcentric view of the world also contributed to the problem of international diversions as American officials turned their attention especially to crises considered to be specifically related to Soviet aims.

6. *The United States must resist the early resort to military force to administer to crises born of political and economic causes.* Instead, sophisticated, sensitive, and creative new methods of diplomacy are essential to the successful formulation of foreign policy in contexts resistent to the clumsy and sometimes counterproductive application of force. In the Middle East, this lesson is seen in the consequences of the 1982 Israeli invasion of Lebanon, the 1983 disaster of American marines sent into Lebanon, and indeed by the costly Soviet military occupation of Afghanistan. In Iran, the shah's regime, backed by one of the most powerful military machines in the Third World, collapsed in the face of a massive popular uprising in which millions of citizens marched in the streets during a year of generally peaceful demonstrations. The fact that the Pahlavi armed forces were backed by the American military establishment only highlights the limits of military power. Political power in the form of diplomacy, intellectual power in the form of understanding, and ideological power in the form of principles all carry special strengths. In confronting the challenges of Third World societies torn by turbulent change, brainpower is at least as important as firepower. This emphasis on military methods is closely related to the Sovietcentric mind-set discussed above. It is in response to the Soviet challenge that the United States has felt it necessary to respond with an increasing early emphasis on the force of arms.

7. *The United States foreign policy-related organizations must institutionalize an emphasis on language and area studies.* Although the Foreign Service Institute, given its resources, does what it can to prepare diplomats for new assignments, serious inadequacies remain. It may indeed be true that Iran represents an especially severe case of debilitating embassy inadequacies; at the same time, it does expose an area badly in need of fundamental reform. In order to understand other cultures, especially those alien to the American-European system, it is necessary to have both the proper tools and the proper attitude. Although American officials have been quite aware of the problem they term "localitis," they have not always been as sensitive to the basic lack of understanding based on weak area preparation and a narrow range and shallow level of contacts. In this situation, the American eagle, with its increasing concern for a sharpened beak

and talons, risks a weakened capacity to see, hear, sense, and understand when flying in unfamiliar environments. This limited capacity to communicate and understand Third World societies is partially a result of the preoccupation with military power. On the other hand, the distorted understanding of complex social and political forces can at the same time promote the emphasis on physical force. In Iran, by viewing the society from the top down, American officials maintained a somewhat simplistic view of political realities, a view that promoted policy that stressed the efficacy of military force. The United States draped its interests around the royal shoulders of the shah, whose own existence was supposedly guaranteed by his powerful military establishment.

8. *American diplomats must become conversant with all levels and sectors of the societies to which they are posted.* Since all diplomats are charged with the task of remaining informed, it is essential that they throw their information-gathering nets as far as possible across the social and political waters of their host countries. Below-par area training is part of a process that promotes the constricted nature of U.S. contacts in foreign countries. This, of course, must be done carefully, professionally, and tactfully. As indicated in considerable depth in the chapters above, in Iran there was an intelligence failure of considerable proportions. The Iranian-American relationship was largely bound and determined at the very top—it was an elite-to-elite connection. This failure to know and to understand because of limited contacts directly reinforced the area training inadequacies. By associating primarily with selected, English-speaking elites who inhabit the uppermost reaches of the power structures, there is little incentive to spend time in the difficult struggle for language competence and in-depth area understanding.

9. *American diplomats must be carefully, selectively, and professionally chosen for their particular assignments.* This is especially true in the case of the ambassadorial selection, since this personal representative of the president of the United States establishes the style and shapes the perspective of the entire embassy that he or she directs. Also, such selection must carefully consider the sensitivities of the government and peoples of the receiving country. An analysis of the history of Iranian-American relations reveals a number of particularly poor ambassadorial choices choices. Perhaps the most obvious error was Richard Nixon's appointment of former CIA chief Richard Helms as U.S. ambassador to Iran during the critical 1973–77 period. Given the history of CIA activities in Iran and the strong negative feelings

among Iranian citizens from all walks of life about the CIA's real and purported roles in the country, this was a most unfortunate decision. Many Iranians believed that this appointment was an arrogant act by the United States to move the CIA into a position of direct, on-the-spot control of their country. And it was deeply and extensively resented. Helms's competence, which was considerable, was beside the point. An ill-suited ambassador, therefore, can reinforce and even exacerbate the problems of inadequately prepared officials with shallow understanding and limited contacts.

10. *The flawed official understanding of Third World societies can be improved by seriously consulting the analyses available in nongovernmental sources.* There has been a tendency to overemphasize classified materials or materials gathered only through governmental channels. As indicated above, much of this information is flawed by inaccuracies that flow from biased sources. That information is classified does not necessarily mean that it is either more accurate or more valuable than what is available in published sources. On the contrary, scholars, journalists, businessmen, and others carry two major advantages over official observers. First, since they are not government employees, they are generally more trusted and carry more credibility in foreign lands. This enables them to tap a broader range of perspectives and at the same time to gain information that is not necessarily biased in the same manner as that available to government sources. Second, scholars in particular have more time to dig and more space for all-important analysis. Harried diplomats work under heavy time pressure and are often overwhelmed by crises.[38] Former CIA chief Stansfield Turner has written that on taking that important post, he soon realized that "there was excessive use of secret data as opposed to open information." In terms of the Iranian revolution, he has pointed out that "there was relatively little secret information that was pertinent."[39] This reluctance to consult external sources systematically only reinforced the views presented by official sources, sources often inadequate to the task and directed by diplomatic leaders unsuitable for their posts.

11. *American foreign policy-making must increase its emphasis on long-range analysis and institutionalize a planning process that is seriously consulted by leading decision makers.* America lacks theoretical guidelines to enable its policymakers to come to grips with the challenge of fundamental global change. In Iran, the United States failed badly when faced with a genuinely revolutionary situation. In the words of diplomat Charles Naas: "Let's face it, this was a massive

revolution. As individual foreign service officers and certainly as a government as a whole, we had very little experience of how to handle such a situation. As a result, once again we were badly equipped intellectually to move in the post-revolutionary situation."[40] Improved analytic capabilities are essential if the United States is to move beyond crisis management and into the more complex field of crisis avoidance. According to a former director of the CIA, "Analysis, especially political analysis, is the Achilles heel of intelligence."[41] This weakness in analysis cuts across all American foreign policy-making agencies. The roots of problems must be exposed and remedies suggested in this context. Only informed analysis can lead to the development of effective policy that will serve American national interests in the long term. The traditional lack of attention to the external sources that tend to place more stress on analysis, of course, has only exacerbated this problem.

12. *Finally, bureaucratic conflict and rivalry must be moderated in order to insure the more efficient determination of high-quality information and the more sensitive formation of policy.* Professionalism must take precedence over the personal and political struggles to which organizations are so very susceptible. More specifically, the increasingly institutionalized National Security Council-Department of State schism must be repaired. The foreign policy disaster of Iran demonstrates its seriousness. At the time of the Iranian revolution, the NSC, the organization with the least understanding of the forces brewing in Iran, was precisely the group that had most influence on the president's policy preferences. This conflict continued after the revolution until it ruptured publicly with the 1986 revelations concerning the NSC-sponsored arms sales to Iran. In his introduction to the Tower Commission Report, R. W. Apple summarizes the NSC as "led by reckless cowboys, off on their own on a wild ride, taking direct operational control of matters that are the customary preserve of more sober agencies."[42] Yet this problem of bureaucratic conflict pervaded all U.S. governmental organizations that dealt with Iran. Their effectiveness was partially smothered both by their conflict with other organizations and by their own intramural rivalries and feuds. This severe bureaucratic tension contributed greatly to many of the other problem areas isolated and briefly discussed above. Most important, it impeded analysis and weakened the capacity of diplomats and foreign policy-makers to do their jobs.

These twelve problem areas overlap and interlock in a system that highly resists reform. They comprise a linked chain, each twisted link contributing directly to the strength of the one before it. Foreign policy analysts have often called attention to one or several of these problems. The Iran-America case has the peculiar "advantage" of reflecting an unusually broad range of foreign policy weaknesses. Most of the problems that have plagued U.S. foreign policy over the years have made their appearance, to one degree or another, in this story. More important, the Iran case demonstrates how these problems reinforced one another and how they constituted a highly resilient system of errors. This finding has profound implications for any attempts at reform. Revisions or improvements in any one area are unlikely to alter significantly the overall system. Only a conscious attempt to transform the system is likely to yield significant results.

On the other hand, a close examination of the weaknesses indicates that some areas may be more sensitive to reform than others. The denominator most common to the widest range of problem areas—in nine of the twelve—is the fundamental failure of understanding. Whether because of diversionary influences, personal or economic self-interest, or just plain ignorance, the United States failed to understand the culture, religion, and broad range of social and cultural forces at play in Iran. Although U.S. officials generally had adequate knowledge of the shah and his civilian and military elite, they never really understood the orientations, motivations, and fundamental power of the masses. Although understanding does not automatically result in improved policy, it is certainly a necessary beginning. In Iran, if the realities had been grasped, it is considerably more likely that U.S. policy would have been more enlightened and therefore more successful.

Iran is in many ways very special. A Shi'i Muslim society ruled by an absolute monarch, Iran had a long history of foreign intervention into its internal affairs. The manner in which American leaders entangled themselves with the Pahlavi elite approached a degree seldom seen elsewhere. Early blatant interventionary successes (the Musaddiq episode), which set the stage for later failure, were also relatively rare in American diplomatic history. Finally, the system of U.S. foreign policy-making seemed particularly inept and flawed in Iran.

Despite this, at a more general level Iran is representative of many Third World societies: an authoritarian political system in a society with pronounced class divisions confronted by the unsettling challenge of modernization. At a time when the Third World looms increasingly large on the international political horizon, the United States must learn to develop new relationships based on trust and mutual respect with the peoples and classes that will direct these developing societies in the years ahead. In order to create such new patterns, it shall be essential to address the problems identified above. Otherwise, the string of dramatic foreign policy defeats that began with China and continued through Cuba and Vietnam shall not end with Iran.

In a world torn by inequality, weakened by misunderstanding, and convulsed by violence, the American eagle needs to do more than strengthen its wings and sharpen its talons. It must also improve its qualities of perception, its communication skills, and its moral credibility. Its painful experience with the Iranian lion in the Persian Gulf can prove to be a valuable learning experience. If so, the sometimes confused and ruffled American eagle can regain its capacity to soar in respected splendor and dignity across the turbulent international landscape.

Bibliography

BOOKS

Abedi, Mehdi, and Gary Legenhausen, eds. *Jihad and Shahadat: Struggle and Martyrdom in Islam: Essays and Addresses by Ayatullah Mahmud Taleqani, Ayatullah Mutahhari and Dr. Ali Shari'ati*. Houston, Tex.: Institute for Research and Islamic Studies, 1986.

Abrahamian, Ervand. *Iran between Two Revolutions*. Princeton, N.J.: Princeton University Press, 1982.

Acheson, Dean. *Present at the Creation*. New York: W. W. Norton, 1969.

Afkhami, Gholam R. *The Iranian Revolution: Thanatos on a National Scale*. Washington, D.C.: Middle East Institute, 1985.

Afshar, Haleh, ed. *Iran: A Revolution in Turmoil*. Albany, N.Y.: State University of New York Press, 1985.

Akhavi, Shahrough. *Religion and Politics in Contemporary Iran*. Albany, N.Y.: State University of New York Press, 1980.

Alexander, Yonah, and Allan Nanes, eds. *The United States and Iran*. Frederick, Md.: Aletheia Books, 1980.

Algar, Hamid. *Islam and Revolution: Writings and Declarations of Imam Khomeini*. Berkeley, Calif.: Mizan Press, 1981.

———. *Religion and State in Iran, 1785–1906*. Berkeley, Calif.: University of California Press, 1969.

———. *The Roots of the Islamic Revolution*. London: Open Press, 1983.

Amirahmadi, Hooshang, and Manoucher Parvin, eds. *Post-Revolutionary Iran*. Boulder, Colo.: Westview Press, 1988.

Amirie, Abbas, and Hamilton A. Twitchell, eds. *Iran in the 1980s*. Tehran: Institute for International Political and Economic Studies, 1978.

Amirsadeghi, Hossein, and R. Ferrier, eds. *Twentieth Century Iran*. London: Heinemann, 1977.

Amuzegar, Jahangir. *Technical Assistance in Theory and Practice: The Case of Iran*. New York: Praeger, 1966.

Arfa, Gen. Hassan. *Under Five Shahs*. New York: William Morrow, 1965.

Armstrong, Scott, et al., eds. *The Chronology: The Documented Day-by-Day Account of the Secret Military Assistance to Iran and the Contras*. New York: Warner Books, 1987.

Assersohn, Roy. *The Biggest Deal*. London: Methuen, 1982.

Avery, Peter. *Modern Iran*. New York: Praeger, 1965.

Bakhash, Shaul. *The Reign of the Ayatollahs: Iran and the Islamic Revolution*. New York: Basic Books, 1984.

Ball, George W. *The Past Has Another Pattern: Memoirs*. New York: W. W. Norton, 1982.

Banani, Amin. *The Modernization of Iran, 1921–1941*. Stanford, Calif.: Stanford University Press, 1961.

Bashiriyeh, Hossein. *The State and Revolution in Iran*. New York: St. Martin's Press, 1984.

Bayne, E. A. *Persian Kingship in Transition*. New York: American Universities Field Staff, 1968.

Beck, Lois. *The Qashqa'i of Iran*. New Haven and London: Yale University Press, 1986.

Beckwith, Charles A., and Donald Knox. *Delta Force*. New York: Harcourt Brace Jovanovich, 1983.

Beeman, William O. *Culture, Performance and Communication in Iran*. Tokyo: Institute for the Study of Languages and Cultures of Asia and Africa, 1982.

———. *Language, Status and Power in Iran*. Bloomington, Ind.: Indiana University Press, 1986.

Behnam, M. Reza. *Cultural Formations of Iranian Poltics*. Salt Lake City, Utah: University of Utah Press, 1986.

Benard, Cheryl, and Zalmay Khalilzad. *"The Government of God": Iran's Islamic Republic*. New York: Columbia University Press, 1984.

Bharier, Julian. *Economic Development in Iran, 1900–1970*. London: Oxford University Press, 1971.

Bill, James A. *The Politics of Iran: Groups, Classes and Modernization*. Columbus, Ohio: Charles E. Merrill, 1972.

Binder, Leonard. *Iran: Political Development in a Changing Society*. Berkeley and Los Angeles, Calif.: University of California Press, 1962.

Bonine, Michael E., and Nikki R. Keddie, eds. *Modern Iran: The Dialectics of Continuity and Change*. Albany, N.Y.: State University of New York Press, 1981.

Bostock, Frances, and Geoffrey Jones. *Planning and Power in Iran: Ebtehaj and Economic Development under the Shah*. London: Frank Cass, 1989.

Boyle, Francis Anthony. *World Politics and International Law*. Durham, N.C.: Duke University Press, 1985.

Brzezinski, Zbigniew. *Power and Principle: Memoirs of the National Security Adviser, 1977–1981*. New York: Farrar, Straus, and Giroux, 1983.

Butler, William J., and Georges Levasseur. *Human Rights and the Legal System in Iran*. Geneva: International Commission of Jurists, 1976.

Carlsen, Robin W. *The Imam and His Islamic Revolution*. Victoria, B.C.: Snow Man Press, 1982.

Carter, Jimmy. *Keeping Faith: Memoirs of a President*. New York: Bantam Books, 1982.

Carter, Rosalynn. *First Lady from Plains*. Boston: Houghton Mifflin, 1984.

Chaliand, Gerard, ed. *People without a Country: The Kurds and Kurdistan.* London: Zed Press, 1980.

Christopher, Warren, et al. *American Hostages in Iran: The Conduct of Crisis.* New Haven and London: Yale University Press, 1985.

Chubin, Shahram, and Sepehr Zabih. *The Foreign Relations of Iran.* Berkeley, Calif.: University of California Press, 1974.

Cottam, Richard. *Nationalism in Iran.* Pittsburgh, Pa.: University of Pittsburgh Press, 1979.

Diba, Farhad. *Mohammed Mossadegh: A Political Biography.* London and Dover, N.H.: Croom Helm, 1986.

Dorman, William A., and Mansour Farhang. *The U.S. Press and Iran: Foreign Policy and the Journalism of Deference.* Berkeley, Calif.: University of California Press, 1987.

Douglas, William O. *Strange Lands and Friendly People.* New York: Harper and Row, 1951.

Elwell-Sutton, L. P. *Persian Oil: A Study in Power Politics.* London: Laurence and Wishart, 1955.

Enayat, Hamid. *Modern Islamic Political Thought.* Austin, Tex.: University of Texas Press, 1982.

English, Paul Ward. *City and Village in Iran: Settlement and Economy in the Kirman Basin.* Madison, Wis.: University of Wisconsin Press, 1966.

Esposito, John, ed. *Islam and Development: Religion and Sociopolitical Change.* Syracuse, N.Y.: Syracuse University Press, 1980.

Estes, Günther, and Jochem Langdau, eds. *Iran in der Krise.* Bonn: Verlag Neue Gesellschaft, 1980.

Farhang, Mansour. *U.S. Imperialism: From the Spanish-American War to the Iranian Revolution.* Boston: South End Press, 1981.

Fatemi, N. S. *Diplomatic History of Persia, 1917–1923.* New York: Russell F. Moore, 1952.

Ferrier, R. W. *The History of the British Petroleum Company: The Developing Years, 1901–1932.* Vol. 1. Cambridge: Cambridge University Press, 1982.

Fesharaki, Fereidun. *Development of the Iranian Oil Industry: International and Domestic Aspects.* New York: Praeger, 1976.

Fischer, Michael M. J. *Iran: From Religious Dispute to Revolution.* Cambridge, Mass.: Harvard University Press, 1980.

Forbis, William H. *The Fall of the Peacock Throne.* New York: McGraw-Hill, 1981.

Garthwaite, Gene R. *Khans and Shahs: A Documentary Analysis of the Bakhtiyari in Iran.* Cambridge: Cambridge University Press, 1983.

Ghani, Cyrus. *Iran and the West: A Critical Bibliography.* London and New York: Kegan Paul International, 1987.

Goodell, Grace E. *The Elementary Structures of Political Life: Rural Development in Pahlavi Iran.* New York and Oxford: Oxford University Press, 1986.

Graham, Robert. *Iran: The Illusion of Power.* New York: St. Martin's Press, 1978.

Grayson, Benson Lee. *United States-Iranian Relations.* Washington, D.C.: University Press of America, 1981.

Green, Jerrold D. *Revolution in Iran: The Politics of Countermobilization*. New York: Praeger, 1982.

Grummon, Stephen. *The Iran-Iraq War*. Washington, D.C.: Council on Foreign Relations, 1982.

Hairi, Abdul-Hadi. *Shi'ism and Constitutionalism in Iran*. Leiden: E. J. Brill, 1977.

Halliday, Fred. *Iran: Dictatorship and Development*. New York: Penguin Books, 1979.

Halpern, Manfred. *The Politics of Social Change in the Middle East and North Africa*. Princeton, N.J.: Princeton University Press, 1963.

Heikal, Mohammed. *Iran: The Untold Story*. New York: Pantheon Books, 1981.

Helms, Cynthia. *An Ambassador's Wife in Iran*. New York: Dodd, Mead, 1981.

Hendershot, Clarence. *Poltics, Polemics and Pedagogs*. New York: Vantage Press, 1975.

Heravi, Mehdi. *Iranian-American Diplomacy*. Brooklyn, N.Y.: Theo Gaus' Sons, 1969.

Herz, Martin F., ed. *Contacts with the Opposition*. Washington, D.C.: Institute for the Study of Diplomacy, n.d.

Hickman, William F. *Ravaged and Reborn: The Iranian Army*. Washington, D.C.: Brookings Institution, 1982.

Hiro, Dilip. *Iran under the Ayatollahs*. London: Routledge and Kegan Paul, 1985.

Hooglund, Eric. *Reform and Revolution in Rural Iran*. Austin, Tex.: University of Texas Press, 1982.

Hoveyda, Fereydoun. *The Fall of the Shah*. New York: Wyndham Books, 1979.

Hulbert, Mark. *Interlock*. New York: Richardson and Snyder, 1982.

Huyser, Robert E. *Mission to Tehran*. New York: Harper and Row, 1986.

Ioannides, Christos P. *America's Iran: Injury and Catharsis*. Lanham, Md.: University Press of America, 1984.

Jabbari, Ahmad, and Robert Olson, eds. *Iran: Essays on a Revolution in the Making*. Lexington, Ky.: Mazda Publishers, 1981.

Jacobs, Norman. *The Sociology of Development: Iran as an Asian Case Study*. New York: Praeger, 1966.

Jacqz, Jane W., ed. *Iran: Past, Present and Future*. New York: Aspen Institute for Humanistic Studies, 1976.

Javadi, Hasan. *Dandil: Stories from Iranian Life*. New York: Random House, 1981.

Jordan, Hamilton. *Crisis: The Last Year of the Carter Presidency*. New York: G. P. Putnam's Sons, 1982.

Kamshad, Hassan. *Modern Persian Prose Literature*. Cambridge: Cambridge University Press, 1966.

Kapuscinski, Ryszard. *Shah of Shahs*. Trans. William R. Brand and Katarzyna Mroczkowska-Brand. San Diego and New York: Harcourt Brace Jovanovich, 1982.

Katouzian, Homa. *The Political Economy of Modern Iran: Despotism and Pseudo-Modernism, 1926–1979*. New York: New York University Press, 1981.

Kazemi, Farhad. *Poverty and Revolution in Iran*. New York: New York University Press, 1980.

Keddie, Nikki R. *Religion and Rebellion in Iran: The Tobacco Protest of 1891–1892*. London: Frank Cass, 1966.

———. *Roots of Revolution: An Interpretive History of Modern Iran*. With a section by Yann Richard. New Haven and London: Yale University Press, 1981.

———, ed. *Religion and Politics in Iran*. New Haven and London: Yale University Press, 1983.

———, ed. *Scholars, Saints, and Sufis*. Berkeley, Calif.: University of California Press, 1972.

Kennedy, Moorhead. *The Ayatollah in the Cathedral: Reflections of a Hostage*. New York: Hill and Wang, 1986.

Kuniholm, Bruce R. *The Origins of the Cold War in the Near East*. Princeton, N.J.: Princeton University Press, 1980.

Kwitny, Jonathan. *Endless Enemies: The Making of an Unfriendly World*. New York: Congden and Weed, 1984.

Ladjevardi, Habib. *Labor Unions and Autocracy in Iran*. Syracuse, N.Y.: Syracuse University Press, 1985.

Laing, Margaret. *The Shah*. London: Sidgwick and Jackson, 1977.

Ledeen, Michael, and William Lewis. *Debacle: American Failure in Iran*. New York: Alfred A. Knopf, 1981.

Lenczowski, George. *Russia and the West in Iran, 1918–1948*. Ithaca, N.Y.: Cornell University Press, 1949.

———, ed. *Iran under the Pahlavis*. Stanford, Calif.: Hoover Institution Press, 1978.

Lilienthal, David E. *The Journals of David E. Lilienthal: The Road to Change, 1955–1959*. Volume 4. New York: Harper and Row. 1969; *Journals: The Harvest Years, 1959–1963*. Volume 5. New York: Harper and Row, 1971; *Journals: Creativity and Conflict, 1964–1967*. Volume 6. New York: Harper and Row, 1973; *Unfinished Business, 1968–1981*. Volume 7. New York: Harper and Row, 1983.

Limbert, John W. *Iran: At War with History*. Boulder, Colo.: Westview Press, 1987.

Louis, Wm. Roger. *The British Empire in the Middle East, 1945–1951*. Oxford: Clarendon Press, 1984.

Louis, Wm. Roger, and James A. Bill, eds. *Musaddiq, Iranian Nationalism and Oil*. London: I. B. Tauris and Co., 1988.

Lytle, Mark H. *The Origins of the Iranian-American Alliance, 1941–1953*. New York: Holmes and Meier, 1987.

McGhee, George. *Envoy to the Middle World: Adventures in Diplomacy*. New York: Harper and Row, 1983.

Milani, Mohsen M. *The Making of Iran's Islamic Revolution*. Boulder, Colo.: Westview Press, 1988.

Millspaugh, Arthur C. *The American Task in Persia*. New York: Century, 1925.

———. *Americans in Persia*. Washington, D.C.: Brookings Institution, 1946.

Momen, Moojan. *An Introduction to Shiʿi Islam*. New Haven and London: Yale University Press, 1985.

Moshiri, Farrokh. *The State and Social Revolution in Iran: A Theoretical Perspective*. New York: Peter Lang, 1985.

Mottahedeh, Roy P. *The Mantle of the Prophet*. New York: Pantheon, 1986.

Motter, T. H. Vail. *United States Army in World War II—The Middle Eastern Theatre: The Persian Corridor and Aid to Russia*. Washington, D.C.: Department of the Army, 1952.

Nasr, Sayyed Hossein. *Ideals and Realities of Islam*. London: George Allen and Unwin, 1966.

Nirumand, Bahman. *Iran: The New Imperialism in Action*. New York: Monthly Review Press, 1969.

Nobari, Ali-Reza, ed. *Iran Erupts*. Stanford, Calif.: Iran-America Documentation Group, 1978.

North, Oliver L. *Taking the Stand: The Testimony of Lieutenant Colonel Oliver L. North*. New York: Pocket Books, 1987.

O'Donnell, Terence. *Garden of the Brave in War: Recollections of Iran*. New Haven and New York: Ticknor and Fields, 1980.

Pahlavi, Ashraf. *Faces in a Mirror: Memoirs from Exile*. Englewood Cliffs, N.J.: Prentice-Hall, 1980.

Pahlavi, Mohammad Reza. *Answer to History*. New York: Stein and Day, 1980.

———. *Mission for My Country*. New York: McGraw-Hill, 1961.

———. *The White Revolution*. Tehran: Imperial Pahlavi Library, 1967.

Painter, David S. *Oil and the American Century*. Baltimore and London: Johns Hopkins University Press, 1986.

Parsons, Anthony. *The Pride and the Fall, Iran 1974–1979*. London: Jonathan Cape, 1984.

Parvin, Manoucher. *Cry for My Revolution, Iran*. Costa Mesa, Calif.: Mazda Publishers, 1987.

Powell, Jody. *The Other Side of the Story*. New York: William Morrow, 1984.

Powers, Thomas. *The Man Who Kept the Secrets: Richard Helms and the CIA*. New York: Pocket Books, 1979.

Radji, Parviz C. *In the Service of the Peacock Throne*. London: Hamish Hamilton, 1983.

Rajaee, Farhang. *Islamic Values and World View: Khomayni on Man, the State and International Politics*. Lanham, Md.: University Press of America, 1983.

Ramazani, Rouhollah K. *The Foreign Policy of Iran, 1500–1941*. Charlottesville, Va.: University of Virginia Press, 1975.

———. *Iran's Foreign Policy, 1941–1973*. Charlottesville, Va.: University of Virginia Press, 1975.

———. *The United States and Iran: The Patterns of Influence*. New York: Praeger, 1982.

Reeves, Minou. *Behind the Peacock Throne*. London: Sidgwick and Jackson, 1980.

Richard, Yann. *Le Shi'isme en Iran*. Paris: Librairie d'Amerique et d'Orient, 1980.

Roosevelt, Archie. *For Lust of Knowing: Memoirs of an Intelligence Officer*. Boston: Little, Brown, 1988.

Roosevelt, Kermit. *Countercoup: The Struggle for the Control of Iran*. New York: McGraw-Hill, 1979.

Rosen, Barbara, and Barry Rosen (with George Feifer). *The Destined Hour*. Garden City, N.Y.: Doubleday, 1982.

Rosen, Barry M., ed. *Iran since the Revolution*. New York: Brooklyn College Program on Society in Change, 1985.

Rubin, Barry. *Paved with Good Intention: The American Experience and Iran*. New York: Oxford University Press, 1980.

————. *Secrets of State: The State Department and the Struggle over U.S. Foreign Policy*. New York: Oxford University Press, 1985.

Saikal, Amin. *The Rise and Fall of the Shah*. Princeton, N.J.: Princeton University Press, 1980.

Salinger, Pierre. *America Held Hostage: The Secret Negotiations*. Garden City, N.Y.: Doubleday, 1981.

Sampson, Anthony. *The Seven Sisters: The Great Oil Companies and the World They Made*. New York: Viking Press, 1975.

Sanasarian, Eliz. *The Women's Rights Movement in Iran: Mutiny, Appeasement and Repression from 1900 to Khomeini*. New York: Praeger, 1982.

Schahgaldian, Nikola B. *The Iranian Military under the Islamic Republic*. Santa Monica, Calif.: Rand Corporation, 1987.

Scott, Charles W. *Pieces of the Game*. Atlanta, Ga.: Peachtree Publishers, 1984.

Shariati, Ali. *Marxism and Other Western Fallacies: An Islamic Critique*. Trans. R. Campbell. Berkeley, Calif.: Mizan Press, 1980.

Sheehan, Michael K. *Iran: The Impact of United States Interests and Policies, 1941–1951*. Brooklyn, N.Y.: Theo Gaus' Sons, 1968.

Shuster, W. Morgan. *The Strangling of Persia*. New York: Century Co., 1912.

Shwadran, Benjamin. *The Middle East, Oil and the Great Powers 1959*. 2d rev. ed. New York: Council for Middle Eastern Affairs Press, 1959.

Sick, Gary. *All Fall Down: America's Tragic Encounter with Iran*. New York: Random House, 1985.

Simpson, John. *Inside Iran: Life under Khomeini's Regime*. New York: St. Martin's Press, 1988.

Stempel, John D. *Inside the Iranian Revolution*. Bloomington, Ind.: Indiana University Press, 1981.

Stoff, Michael B. *Oil, War, and American Security*. New Haven and London: Yale University Press, 1980.

Sullivan, William. *Mission to Iran*. New York: W. W. Norton, 1981.

Tabataba'i, Allameh Seyyid Muhammad Husayn. *Shi'ite Islam*. Trans. and ed. Seyyid Hossein Nasr. Albany, N.Y.: State University of New York Press, 1975.

Tower, John, Edmund Muskie, and Brent Scowcroft. *The Tower Commission Report*. New York: Bantam Books/Times Books, 1987.

Turner, Stansfield. *Secrecy and Diplomacy*. Boston: Houghton Mifflin, 1985.

Upton, Joseph M. *The History of Modern Iran: An Interpretation*. Cambridge, Mass.: Harvard University Press, 1961.

Vance, Cyrus. *Hard Choices: Critical Years in America's Foreign Policy*. New York: Simon and Schuster, 1983.

Villiers, Gerard de. *The Imperial Shah: An Informal Biography.* Trans. June P. Wilson and Walter B. Michaels. Boston: Little, Brown, 1976.

Walters, Vernon A. *Silent Missions.* Garden City, N.Y.: Doubleday, 1978.

Wilber, Donald N. *Adventures in the Middle East: Excursion and Incursion.* Princeton, N.J.: Darwin Press, 1986.

———. *Contemporary Iran.* New York: Praeger, 1963.

———. *Riza Shah Pahlavi: The Resurrection and Reconstruction of Iran: 1878–1944.* Hicksville, N.Y.: Exposition Press, 1975.

Williams, John Alden, ed. *Themes of Islamic Civilization.* Berkeley, Calif.: University of California Press, 1971.

Woodhouse, C. M. *Something Ventured.* London: Granada, 1982.

Wright, Robin. *Sacred Rage.* New York: Linden Press/Simon and Schuster, 1985.

Yaniv, Avner. *Deterrence without the Bomb: The Politics of Israeli Strategy.* Lexington, Mass.: D. C. Heath, 1987.

Yar-Shater, Ehsan, ed. *Iran Faces the Seventies.* New York: Praeger, 1971.

Zabih, Sepehr. *The Communist Movement in Iran.* Berkeley, Calif.: University of California Press, 1966.

———. *Iran since the Revolution.* Baltimore: Johns Hopkins University Press, 1982.

———. *The Mossadegh Era.* Chicago: Lake View Press, 1982.

Zonis, Marvin. *The Political Elite of Iran.* Princeton, N.J.: Princeton University Press, 1971.

ARTICLES

Abrahamian, Ervand. "The Crowd in Iranian Politics, 1905–53." *Past and Present* 41 (December 1968): 184–210.

———. "The Guerrilla Movement in Iran, 1963–1977." *MERIP Reports* 86 (March–April 1980): 3–15.

Afrachteh, Kambiz. "The Predominance and Dilemmas of Theocratic Populism Contemporary Iran." *Iranian Studies* 14 (Summer–Autumn 1981): 189–213.

Armajani, Yahya. "What the U.S. Needs to Know about Iran." *World Review* 22 (May 1979):13–19.

Ashraf, Ahmad, and Ali Banuazizi. "The State, Classes and Modes of Mobilization in the Iranian Revolution." *State, Culture and Society* 1 (Spring 1985): 3–40.

Bakhash, Shaul. "Who Lost Iran?" *New York Review of Books.* June 26, 1980, pp. 17–22.

Ball, Nicole, and Milton Leitenberg. "The Iranian Domestic Crisis: Foreign Policy Making and Foreign Policy Goals of the United States." *Journal of South Asia and Middle Eastern Studies* 2 (Spring 1979): 36–56.

Beeman, William O. "Devaluing Experts on Iran." *New York Times,* April 11, 1980.

———. "How Not to Negotiate: Crossed Signals on the Hostages." *Nation* 232 (January 1981): 42–44.

Bialer, Uri. "The Iranian Connection in Israel's Foreign Policy, 1948–1951." *Middle East Journal* 39 (Spring 1985): 292–315.

Bolles, Blair. "Egypt, Iran and U.S. Diplomacy." *Foreign Policy Bulletin,* August 15, 1952, p. 3.

Bozeman, Adda B. "Iran: U.S. Foreign Policy and the Tradition of Persian States-craft." *Orbis* 23 (Summer 1979): 387–402.

Cottam, Richard W. "American Policy and the Iranian Crisis." *Iranian Studies* 13 (1980): 279–305.

———. "The United States, Iran and the Cold War." *Iranian Studies* 3 (Winter 1970): 2–22.

———. "The United States and Iran's Revolution: Goodbye to America's Shah." *Foreign Policy* 34 (Spring 1979): 3–14.

Doenecke, Justin D. "Revisionists, Oil and Cold War Diplomacy." *Iranian Studies* 3 (Winter 1970): 23–33.

Dorman, William A. and Ehsan Omeed. "Reporting through the Shah's Eyes." *Columbia Journalism Review* (January–February 1979): 27–33.

Elwell-Sutton, L. P. "Nationalism and Neutralism in Iran." *Middle East Journal* 12 (Winter 1958): 20–32.

Englehardt, Joseph P. "American Military Advisers in Iran: A Critical Review." *Joint Perspectives* (Summer 1981).

Gasiorowski, Mark. "The 1953 *Coup d'Etat* in Iran." *International Journal of Middle East Studies* 19 (August 1987), 261–86.

Hitselberger, James. "Another Look at Mashhad, Iran: A Return Visit from April to June, 1979." *Review of Iranian Political Economy and History* 3 (Fall 1979): 123–47.

Ioannides, Christos P. "The Hostages of Iran: A Discussion with the Militants." *Washington Quarterly* 3 (Summer 1980): 12–35.

Johansen, Robert C., and Michael G. Renner. "Limiting Conflict in the Gulf." *Third World Quarterly* (October 1985): 803–38.

Keddie, Nikki R. "Religion and Irreligion in Early Iranian Nationalism." *Comparative Studies in Society and History* 4 (April 1962): 265–95.

Ladjevardi, Habib. "The Origins of U.S. Support for an Autocratic Iran." *International Journal of Middle East Studies* 15 (May 1983): 225–39.

Lambton, Ann K. S. "The Impact of the West on Persia." *International Affairs* 33 (January 1957): 12–25.

Lenczowski, George. "The Arc of Crisis: Its Central Sector." *Foreign Affairs* 57 (Spring 1979): 796–820.

Lilienthal, David E. "Enterprise in Iran: An Experiment in Economic Development." *Foreign Affairs* 38 (October 1959): 1–8.

Limbert, John. "Nest of Spies: Pack of Lies." *Washington Quarterly* (Spring 1982): 75–82.

Maechling, Charles, Jr. "Coup or Counter Coup in Iran." *Foreign Service Journal* (December 1979).

Mahdavi, Hossein. "The Coming Crisis in Iran." *Foreign Affairs* 44 (October 1965): 134–46.

Mansur, Abul Kasim. "The Crisis in Iran: Why the U.S. Ignored a Quarter Century of Warning." *Armed Forces Journal International* 116 (January 1979): 26–33.

McFarland, Stephen L. "A Peripheral View of the Cold War: The Crises in Iran, 1941–47." *Diplomatic History* 4 (Fall 1980): 333–51.

Michaud, Michael A. G. "Communication and Controversy: Thoughts on the Future of Foreign Service Reporting." *Foreign Service Journal* (October 1969): 23–24, 33, 35.

Miller, William Green. "Political Organization in Iran: From Dowreh to Political Party." *Middle East Journal* 23 (Spring–Summer 1969): 159–67, 343–50.

Mottahedeh, Roy. "Iran's Foreign Devils." *Foreign Policy* 38 (Spring 1980): 19–34.

Pfau, Richard. "Containment in Iran, 1946: The Shift to an Active Policy." *Diplomatic History* 1 (Fall 1977): 359–72.

———. "The Legal Status of American Forces in Iran." *Middle East Journal* 28 (Spring 1974): 141–53.

Ramazani, R. K. "Who Lost America? The Case of Iran." *Middle East Journal* 36 (Winter 1982): 5–21.

Razi, Gholam H. "The Effectiveness of Resort to Military Force: The Case of Iran and Iraq." *Conflict Quarterly* (Summer 1985): 44–57.

Richardson, Elliot L. "The State of State." *Foreign Service Journal* (September 1981): 15–17.

Ricks, Thomas M. "Iran and Imperialism: Academics in the Service of the People or the Shah?" *Arab Studies Quarterly* 2 (Summer 1980): 265–77.

———. "U.S. Military Missions to Iran, 1943–1978: The Political Economy of Military Assistance." *Iranian Studies* 12 (Summer–Autumn 1979): 163–94.

Rose, Gregory F. "The Post-Revolutionary Purge of Iran's Armed Forces: A Revisionist Assessment." *Iranian Studies* 17 (Spring–Summer 1984): 153–93.

Rouleau, Eric. "Khomeini's Iran." *Foreign Affairs* 59 (Fall 1980): 1–20.

Sciolino, Elaine. "Iran's Durable Revolution." *Foreign Affairs* 61 (Spring 1983): 893–920.

Smith, Terence. "Putting Hostages' Lives First." *New York Times Magazine*, May 17, 1981.

———. "Why Carter Admitted the Shah." *New York Times Magazine*, May 17, 1981.

Tehranian, Majid. "Communication and Revolution in Iran: The Passing of a Paradigm." *Iranian Studies* 13 (1980): 5–30.

Thorpe, James A. "Truman's Ultimatum to Stalin in the 1946 Azarbayjan Crisis: Fact or Fantasy?" *Society for Iranian Studies Newsletter* 4 (October 1972).

Walden, Jerrold L. "The International Petroleum Cartel in Iran: Private Power and the Public Interest." *Journal of Public Law* 11 (Spring 1962): 3–60.

Weinbaum, Marvin G. "Iran and Israel: The Discreet Entente." *Orbis* 18 (Winter 1975): 1070–87.

Westwood, Andrew F. "Elections and Politics in Iran." *Middle East Journal* 15 (Spring 1961): 153–64.

Young, T. Cuyler. "Iran in Continuing Crisis." *Foreign Affairs* 40 (January 1962): 275–92.

———. "The Social Support of Current Iranian Policy." *Middle East Journal* 6 (Spring 1952): 128–43.

Zabih, Sepehr. "Change and Continuity in Iran's Foreign Policy in Modern Times." *World Politics* 23 (April 1971): 522–43.

PERSIAN LANGUAGE SOURCES

Afrasiabi, Bahram. *Musaddiq va Tarikh (Musaddiq and History)*. Tehran, 1360/1981.

Al-i Ahmad, Jalal. *Dar Khidmat va Khiyanat-i Rushanfikran (In the Service and the Treachery of the Intellectuals)*. Tehran, n.d.

———. *Gharbzadigi (Western-Mania)*. Tehran, 1341/1962.

Ayat, Hassan. *Darsha'i az Tarikh-i Siyasi-yi Iran (Lessons from the Political History of Iran)*. Tehran, 1363/1984.

Bahar, Dr. Mihdi. *Miraskhar-i Isti'mar (The Heir of Colonialism)*. Tehran, 1344/1965.

Bahar, Muhammad Taqi. *Tarikh-i Mukhtasar-i Ahzab-i Siyasi-yi Iran: Inqiraz-i Qajariyah (A Short History of Political Parties in Iran: The Fall of the Qajars)*. Tehran, 1321/1942.

Bamdad, M. *Tarikh-i Rijal-i Iran (History of Iranian Statesmen)*. 6 vols. Tehran, 1347–51/1968–72.

Bani Ahmad, Ahmad. *Asiya va Diplumasi-yi Amrika (Asia and American Diplomacy)*. Tehran, n.d.

Bazargan, Mihdi. *Inqilab-i Iran dar Du Harakat (The Revolution of Iran in Two Stages)*. Tehran, 1363/1984.

Davani, Ali. *Nihzat-i Ruhaniyyun-i Iran (The Movement of the Iranian Clerics)*. Tehran, 1360/1981.

Davari-Ardakani, Riza. *Nasiunalizm, Hakimiyyat-i Milli va Istiqlal (Nationalism, National Sovereignty and Independence)*. Isfahan, 1363/1984.

Davudi, Mihdi. *Qavam al-Saltanah*. Vol. 1. Tehran, 1326/1948.

Fateh, Mustafa. *Panjah Sal Naft-i Iran (Fifty Years of Persian Oil)*. Tehran, 1335/1956.

Fazil, Javad. *Sukhanan-i Ali (The Sayings of Ali)*. Tehran, 1345/1966.

Ghani, Cyrus, ed. *Yaddashtha-yi Duktur Ghassim Ghani (The Memoirs of Dr. Ghassim Ghani)*. 12 vols. London, 1980–84.

Hidayat, Sadiq. *Hajji Aqa*. 2d ed. Tehran, 1330/1952.

Jamalzadah, Sayyid Muhammad Ali. *Khulqiyyat-i Ma Iranian (The Character of We Iranians)*. Tehran, 1345/1966.

Janzadah, Ali. *Musaddiq*. Tehran, 1358/1979.

Javanshir, F. M. *Tajrubah-yi 28 Murdad: Nazari-yi Tarikh-i Jinbish-i Milli Shudan-i Naft-i Iran (The Experience of the 28th of Murdad: A View of the History of the Nationalization Movement of the Oil of Iran)*. Tehran, 1359/1981.

Kai-Ustuvan, Hussein. *Siyasat-i Muvazinah-i Manfi dar Majlis-i Chahardihum (The Policy of Negative Equilibrium in the Fourteenth Majlis)*. Vol. 1. Tehran, 1327/1949.

Khomeini, Sayyid Rouhollah. *Vilayat-i Faqih: Hukumat-i Islami (Tutelage of the Jurisprudent: Islamic Government)*. Tehran, 1357/1979.

Mahmud, Mahmud. *Tarikh-i Ravabit-i Siyasi-yi Iran va Inglis dar Qarn-i Nuzdahum (The History of Anglo-Iranian Relations in the Nineteenth Century).* 8 vols. Tehran, 1336–41/1957–62.

Makarim-Shirazi, Nasir. *Asrar-i Aqabmandigi-yi Sharq (Secrets of the Underdevelopment of the East).* Tehran, 1348/1960.

Makki, Hussein. *Kitab-i Siyah (The Black Book).* Tehran, 1329/1951.

———. *Tarikh-i Bist Salah-yi Iran (The Twenty-Year History of Iran).* 3 vols. Tehran, 1323–24/1944–45.

Musaddiq, Muhammad. *Asnad-i Naft va Nutqha va Namahha-yi Tarikhi (Oil Documents, Speeches, and Historical Letters).* Tehran, 1349/1970.

Mutahhari, Murtiza. *Bakhsh Darbarah-yi Maraja'iyyat va Ruhaniyyat (Discussions concerning Supreme Religious Leadership and Islamic Clericalism).* Tehran, 1341/1963.

Qarabaghi, Abbas. *Haqayaq-i Darbarah-yi Inqilab-i Iran (Facts about the Iranian Revolution).* Paris, 1984.

Qasimi, Abulfazl. *Tarikh-i Jibhah-yi Milli-yi Iran (History of the National Front of Iran).* Tehran, 1350/1971.

Ra'in, Isma'il. *Faramushkhanah va Firamasuniri dar Iran (Masonic Lodges and Freemasonry in Iran).* 3 vols. Tehran, 1347/1968.

Ravandi, Murtiza. *Tarikh-i Ijtima'i-yi Iran (The Social History of Iran).* 3 vols. Tehran, 1341/1962.

Rawhani, Fuad. *San'at-i Naft-i Iran: Bist Sal pas az Milli Shudan (Iran's Oil Industry: Twenty Years after Nationalization).* Tehran, 1356/1977.

Razi, Muhammad Sharif. *Ganjinah-yi Danishmandan (Treasures of Learned Men).* 8 vols. Qum, 1352–57/1974–79.

Ruhani, Sayyid Hamid. *Barrasi va Tahlili az Nihzat-i Imam Khomeini (An Analysis and Study of the Movement of Imam Khomeini).* Tehran, 1360/1982.

Sadr, Hassan. *Isti'mar-i Jadid (Neocolonialism).* Tehran, 1349/1961.

Sahib al-Zamani, Nasir al-Din. *Javani-yi Purranj (Suffering Youth).* Tehran, 1344/1965.

Shadman, Sayyid Fakhr al-Din. *Tasakhir-i Tamaddun-i Farhangi (The Conquest of Foreign Civilization).* Tehran, 1326/1948.

Shaji'i, Zuhrah. *Nimayandigan-i Majlis-i Shawra-yi Milli dar Bistuyik Dawrah-yi Qanunguzari (The Representatives of the National Consultative Assembly during the Twenty-One Legislative Periods).* Tehran, 1344/1965.

Tunakabuni, Firaydun. *Yaddashtha-yi Shahr-i Shuluq (Memories of a Crowded City).* Tehran, 1348/1970.

Yazdi, Ibrahim. *Barrasi-yi Safar-i Ha'izir Bi-Iran (An Examination of Huyser's Trip to Iran).* n.p., 1361/1983.

———. *Akharin Talashha dar Akharin Ruzha (The Last Endeavors in the Last Days).* Tehran, 1363/1984.

GOVERNMENT DOCUMENTS

Asnad-i Lanah-yi Jasusi. Vols. 1–58. Tehran: Intisharat-i Danishjuyan-i Piru-yi Khatt-i Imam, 1980–87.

Congressional Research Service. Library of Congress, Report Prepared for Committee on Foreign Relations, U.S. House of Representatives. *The Iran Hostage Crisis: A Chronology of Daily Developments.* 97th Cong., 1st Sess.

U.S. Congress, House of Representatives, Committee on Banking, Finance and Urban Affairs. *Iran: The Financial Aspects of the Hostage Settlement Agreement.* 97th Cong., 1st Sess., July 1981.

U.S. Congress, House of Representatives, Committee on Foreign Affairs. *Report of the Special Study Mission to the Middle East, South and Southeast Asia. and the Western Pacific.* 84th Cong., 2d Sess., May 10, 1956.

U.S. Congress, House of Representatives, Committee on Foreign Affairs, Subcommittee on Europe and the Middle East. *General Huyser's Mission to Iran, January 1979.* 97th Cong., 1st Sess., June 9, 1981.

U.S. Congress, House of Representatives, Committee on Foreign Affairs, Subcommittee on the Near East and South Asia. *The Persian Gulf, 1974: Money, Politics, Arms, and Power.* 93d Cong., 2d Sess., July 30, Aug. 5, 7, 12, 1974.

U.S. Congress, House of Representatives, Committee on Government Operations. *Hearings before a Subcommittee on United States Aid Operations in Iran.* 84th Cong., 2d Sess., May 2, 31, June 1, 5, 8, 11–13, 18–19, 25–27, 29, July 16, 1956.

U.S. Congress, House of Representatives, Committee on International Relations, Special Subcommittee on Investigations. *The Persian Gulf, 1975: The Continuing Debate on Arms Sales.* 94th Cong., 1st Sess., June 10, 18, 28, July 29, 1975.

U.S. Congress, House of Representatives, Committee on International Relations, Subcommittee on International Organizations. *Human Rights in Iran.* 94th Cong., 2d Sess., Aug. 3, Sept. 8, 1976.

U.S. Congress, House of Representatives, Staff Report, Subcommittee on Evaluation, Permanent Select Committee on Intelligence. *Iran: Evaluation of U.S. Intelligence Performance Prior to November 1978.*

U.S. Congress, Senate, Committee on Foreign Relations. *Executive Sessions of the Senate Foreign Relations Committee (Historical Series).* 87th Cong., 1st Sess., 1961, vol. xiii, pt. 2.

U.S. Congress, Senate, Committee on Foreign Relations, Subcommittee on Foreign Assistance, Staff Report. *U.S. Military Sales to Iran.* 94th Cong., 2d Sess., July 1976.

U.S. Congress, Senate, Committee on Foreign Relations, Subcommittee on Foreign Assistance. *U.S. Arms Sales Policy.* 94th Cong., 2d Sess., Sept. 16, 21, 34, 1976.

U.S. Congress, Senate, Committee on Foreign Relations, Subcommittee on Foreign Assistance. *Sale of AWACs to Iran.* 95th Cong., 1st Sess., July 18, 22, 25, 27, Sept. 19, 1977.

U.S. Congress, Senate, Subcommittee on Multinational Corporations and United States Foreign Policy. *Multinational Petroleum Companies and Foreign Policy.* 93d Cong., 2d Sess., Feb. 20–21, Mar. 20–21, 27–28, 1974. Pts. 7, 8.

U.S. Congress, Senate, Committee on Foreign Relations, Subcommittee on Multinational Corporations. *Multinational Corporations and United States Foreign Policy: Grumman Sale of F-14's to Iran.* 94th Cong., 2d Sess., Aug. 9, Executive Session, and Sept. 10, 13, 15, 27, 1976. Pt. 17.

Notes

INTRODUCTION

1. The quotations in this paragraph are taken from John Tower, Edmund Muskie, and Brent Scowcroft, *The Tower Commission Report* (New York: Bantam Books/Times Books, 1987), pp. 296, 298, 313. For details and documentary evidence, see Scott Armstrong et al., eds., *The Chronology: The Documented Day-by-Day Account of the Secret Military Assistance to Iran and the Contras* (New York: Warner Books, 1987), pp. 353–91.

2. These two quotations are drawn from Armstrong, *The Chronology*, pp. 375, 380.

3. Personal copy of document.

4. *Washington Post*, December 13, 1978, p. 14.

5. George N. Curzon, *Persia and the Persian Question* (London: Longmans and Green, 1892), 1:480.

6. Arthur C. Millspaugh, *Americans in Persia* (Washington, D.C.: Brookings Institution, 1946), p. 135.

7. Gertrude Bell, *Persian Pictures*, 3d ed. (London: Ernest Benn, 1947), p. 31.

8. William O. Douglas, *Strange Lands and Friendly People* (New York: Harper and Brothers, 1951), p. xiv.

CHAPTER 1. AMERICA AND IRAN: EARLY ENTANGLEMENTS

1. The data in these first two paragraphs are drawn from William E. Strong, *The Story of the American Board: An Account of the First Hundred Years of the American Board of Commissioners for Foreign Missions* (Boston: Pilgrim Press, 1910), and, especially, from the actual *Annual Reports* of the American Board published in Boston by Crocker and Brewster (1834–43) and by T. R. Marvin (1844–61).

2. Rev. Justin Perkins, *A Residence of Eight Years in Persia* (Andover, N.J.: Allen, Morrill and Wardwell, 1843), p. 500.

3. Ibid., p. 506.

4. Personal interview with diplomat, Washington, D.C., Sept. 2, 1980.

5. William O. Douglas, *Strange Lands and Friendly People* (New York: Harper and Brothers, 1951), p. 325.

6. Arthur C. Millspaugh, *Americans in Persia* (Washington, D.C.: Brookings Institution, 1946), pp. 49–50.

7. "Memorandum by John D. Jernegan of the Division of Near Eastern Affairs: American Policy in Iran," Washington, D.C., Jan. 23, 1943, as printed in Yonah Alexander and Allan Nanes, eds., *The United States and Iran* (Frederick, Md.: Aletheia Books, 1980), p. 95.

8. Ibid., p. 97.

9. Ibid., p. 104.

10. George Kirk, *The Middle East in the War*, Survey of International Affairs 1939–1946 Series, ed. Arnold Toynbee (London: Oxford University Press, 1952), pp. 150–51.

11. "Despatch No. 517, The Minister in Iran (Dreyfus) to the Secretary of State," Tehran, Apr. 14, 1943, in Alexander and Nanes, *United States and Iran*, p. 101.

12. T. H. Vail Motter, *United States Army in World War II—The Middle Eastern Theatre: The Persian Corridor and Aid to Russia* (Washington, D.C.: Department of the Army, 1952), p. 167. This official military history is an invaluable source, both well researched and well written.

13. State Department, 891.00/1–2844, memorandum by Acheson, as quoted in Mark Hamilton Lytle, "American-Iranian Relations, 1941–1947, and the Redefinition of National Security" (Ph.D. diss., Yale University, 1973), pp. 103–4. This fine dissertation combines empirical material with analysis. It is now revised and available as Mark H. Lytle, *The Origins of the Iranian-American Alliance, 1941–1953* (New York: Holmes and Meier, 1987).

14. Ibid., p. 51.

15. OSS 61429, Feb. 15, 1944, as quoted in Lytle, "American-Iranian Relations," pp. 209–10.

16. Elliot Roosevelt, *As He Saw It* (New York, 1946), as quoted in Bruce R. Kuniholm, *The Origins of the Cold War in the Near East: Great Power Conflict and Diplomacy in Iran, Turkey, and Greece* (Princeton, N.J.: Princeton University Press, 1980), p. 165. Kuniholm's book is a superb study of American diplomacy in Iran, Turkey, and Greece in the 1940s.

17. "Despatch No. 480, The Minister in Iran (Dreyfus) to the Secretary of State," Tehran, Mar. 9, 1943, in Alexander and Nanes, *United States and Iran*, pp. 99–100. One scholar flatly states that Dreyfus was removed because of his criticism of British policy. "When some of Dreyfus's reports were accidentally given to the British Foreign Office, British diplomats were so angry that they successfully pressed for his removal" (Barry Rubin, *Paved with Good Intentions: The American Experience and Iran* [New York: Oxford University Press, 1980], p. 20). This interpretation oversimplifies a complex situation and overstates the British influence in this event.

18. "Memorandum by the Adviser on Political Relations (Murray)," Washington, D.C., Aug. 3, 1942, in Alexander and Nanes, *United States and Iran*, pp. 109–10.

19. "Despatch No. 480, The Minister in Iran (Dreyfus) to the Secretary of

State," Tehran, Mar. 9, 1943, in Alexander and Nanes, *United States and Iran*, pp. 99–100.

20. "Despatch No. 602, The Minister in Iran (Dreyfus) to the Secretary of State," Tehran, July 4, 1943, in Alexander and Nanes, *United States and Iran*, p. 115.

21. For an excellent and detailed discussion of the politics of this period, see Ervand Abrahamian, *Iran: Between Two Revolutions* (Princeton, N.J.: Princeton University Press, 1982), pp. 169–280. See also Habib Ladjevardi's important study of the politics of labor in Iran, *Labor Unions and Autocracy in Iran* (Syracuse, N.Y.: Syracuse University Press, 1985).

22. Muhammad Musaddiq, speech in the Majlis, as quoted in Keyvan Tabari, "Iran's Policies toward the United States during the Anglo-Russian Occupation, 1941–1946" (Ph.D. diss., Columbia University, 1978), p. 121, which helps provide the domestic Iranian perspective of the rapid-moving events of the 1940s.

23. Hussein Kai-Ustuvan, *Siyasat-i Muvazinah-i Manfi dar Majlis-i Chahardihum (The Policy of Negative Equilibrium in the Fourteenth Majlis)*, vol. 1 (Tehran, 1327/1949), p. 123.

24. Earl Curzon to Sir P. Cox (Tehran), no. 85 (191069/150/34), Foreign Office, Apr. 10, 1920, in Rohan Butler and J. P. T. Bury, eds., *Documents on British Foreign Policy, 1919–1939* (London: Her Majesty's Stationery Office, 1963), pp. 466–67.

25. This exchange is easiest retrieved in Kuniholm, *Origins of the Cold War*, p. 184.

26. The words of Sir Frederick Godber as reported in Public Record Office, FO 371, Sept. 23, 1943, in Michael B. Stoff, *Oil, War, and American Security* (New Haven and London: Yale University Press, 1980), p. 104. See also Lytle, "American-Iranian Relations," p. 125.

27. See Kuniholm, *Origins*, p. 193n.

28. Lytle, "American-Iranian Relations," p. 107.

29. Tabari, "Iran's Policies," p. 111.

30. Ibid., p. 140.

31. This important point is made in passing in Abrahamian, *Iran: Between Two Revolutions*, p. 211.

32. See Lloyd Gardner, *Economic Aspects of New Deal Diplomacy* (Madison, Wis.: University of Wisconsin Press, 1964); Gabriel Kolko, *The Politics of War: The World and United States Foreign Policy, 1943–1945* (New York: Random House, 1968); and Justin D. Doenecke, "Revisionists, Oil and Cold War Diplomacy," *Iranian Studies* 3 (Winter 1970): 23–33.

33. Richard W. Cottam, "The United States, Iran and the Cold War," *Iranian Studies* 3 (Winter 1970): 3, 4.

34. Lytle, "American-Iranian Relations," p. 146.

35. Ibid., p. 168.

36. Tabari, "Iran's Policies," pp. 210–11.

37. Peter Avery, *Modern Iran* (New York: Praeger, 1965), p. 385.

38. Great Britain, Public Record Office, FO 371/20837, Seymour to Eden, Apr. 12, 1937, p. 51.

39. Avery, *Modern Iran*, p. 382. For an informed and detailed discussion of Qavam as a political actor, see Abrahamian, *Iran*, pp. 225–50. Abrahamian is less willing than Avery to credit Qavam for any shrewd overall plan calculated to neutralize the Soviet threat to Iran. My own interpretation more closely approximates that of Peter Avery.

40. General Hassan Arfa, *Under Five Shahs* (New York: William Morrow, 1965), p. 325.

41. As quoted in George Lenczowski, *Russia and the West in Iran, 1918–1948* (Ithaca, N.Y.: Cornell University Press, 1949), pp. 310–11.

42. Avery, *Modern Iran*, p. 394.

43. See, for example, the important research results of James A. Thorpe summarized in Thorpe, "Truman's Ultimatum to Stalin on the 1946 Azarbayjan Crisis, Fact or Fantasy?" *Society for Iranian Studies Newsletter* 4 (October 1972). An Aug. 16, 1965 memorandum by Edwin M. Wright to Herbert Fine describes in detail Wright's recollection of these events. "Events Relative to the Azerbaijan Issue— March 1946" stresses that Under Scretary of State Dean Acheson made the statement that the United States should let the Soviet Union "know that we are aware of its moves" but "leave a graceful way out if it desired to avoid a showdown." Wright, then the leading Iran analyst in the Department of State, feels that Truman was referring to the telegrams of March 5 and 8 when he made the statement in 1952 that he had issued an "ultimatum" to the USSR. For the text of the telegram of Mar. 5, 1946, sent by Secretary of State James Byrnes to Soviet Foreign Secretary Vyacheslav Molotov, see Alexander and Nanes, *United States and Iran*, pp. 162–63.

44. Stephen L. McFarland, "A Peripheral View of the Cold War: The Crisis in Iran, 1941–47," *Diplomatic History* 4 (Fall 1980): 333–51.

45. George V. Allen, "Mission to Iran," manuscript, George V. Allen Papers, Harry S. Truman Library, Independence, Mo., pp. 37–38, as quoted in Richard Pfau, "Containment in Iran, 1946: The Shift to an Active Policy,"*Diplomatic History* 1 (Fall 1977): 361–62.

46. Habib Ladjevardi, "The Origins of U.S. Support for an Autocratic Iran," *International Journal of Middle East Studies* 15 (May 1983): 231, carefully traces American support in the 1940s for monarchical authoritarianism in Iran. "One would have thought Great Britain and the United States, being themselves democracies, would have expressed sympathy for constitutional government in Iran. But they decided that a 'stable autocratic monarchy' better protected their interests in Iran than an 'unstable constitutional monarchy'" (p. 236).

47. George V. Allen to John D. Jernegan, Jan. 21, 1948, Record Group 84, Box 2257, File 800, Washington National Records Center, as quoted in Ladjevardi, "Origins of U.S. Support," p. 232.

48. For an excellent discussion of Thornburg and his role in Iran in the late 1940s, see Thomas M. Ricks, "U.S. Military Missions to Iran, 1943–1978: The Political Economy of Military Assistance," *Iranian Studies* 12 (Summer–Autumn 1979): 163–93.

49. Rouhollah K. Ramazani, *Iran's Foreign Policy, 1941–1973* (Charlottesville, Va.: University of Virginia Press, 1975), p. 157. Like Kuniholm's study, this is an indispensable source that probes the details of great-power diplomacy in Iran.

50. *Department of State Bulletin*, June 26, 1950, p. 1048.

51. As quoted in Lytle, "American-Iranian Relations," p. 179.

52. Ibid., p. 12.

53. Kuniholm, *Origins of the Cold War*, p. 155.

54. Sir Reader Bullard, *The Camels Must Go* (London: Faber and Faber, 1961), p. 236.

55. Millspaugh, *Americans in Persia*, p. 206.

56. Bullard, *The Camels Must Go*, p. 278.

57. Millspaugh, *Americans in Persia*, pp. 209–10.

58. Motter, *Persian Corridor*, p. 435.

59. "Despatch No. 579, The Minister in Iran (Dreyfus) to the Secretary of State," Tehran, June 10, 1943, as printed in Alexander and Nanes, *United States and Iran*, p. 131.

60. "Despatch No. 591, The Minister in Iran (Dreyfus) to the Secretary of State," Tehran, June 24, 1943, as printed in Alexander and Nanes, *United States and Iran*, p. 132.

61. Lytle, "American-Iranian Relations," p. 196.

62. FO 371, 40164, E 1987, General Smith to CIGS, Mar. 16, 1944, as quoted in Lytle, "American-Iranian Relations," p. 200.

63. Lenczowski was the press attaché for the Polish Embassy in Tehran, 1942–45. He later became an American citizen and a leading scholar of Iranian affairs.

64. Secretary of State Cordell Hull to President Franklin D. Roosevelt, "American Policy in Iran," Washington, D.C., Aug. 16, 1943, as printed in Alexander and Nanes, *United States and Iran*, pp. 103–4.

65. Motter, *Persian Corridor*, p. 480.

66. Mihdi Davudi, *Qavam al-Saltanah*, vol. 1 (Tehran, 1326/1948), p. 204.

CHAPTER 2. PETROLEUM POLITICS AND THE AMERICAN INTERVENTION OF 1953

1. Much of the material presented in this chapter will also appear in Wm. Roger Louis and James A. Bill, eds., *Musaddiq, Iranian Nationalism and Oil* (London: I. B. Tauris and Co., 1988).

2. Quoted in George McGhee, *Envoy to the Middle World: Adventures in Diplomacy* (New York: Harper and Row, 1983), p. 73.

3. Interview with American diplomat then stationed in Tehran, Washington, D.C., Nov. 11, 1981.

4. See, for example, Muvarrikh al-Dawlah Sipihr, "Sipahbud Razmara an tawr ki ta Kunun Nashinakhtahid (General Razmara: The Man You Had Not Known until Now)," *Khandaniha*, 3 Mihr 1341/25 Sept. 1962. In a note in *Nationalism in Iran* (Pittsburgh, Pa.: University of Pittsburgh Press, 1979), Richard Cottam mentions that discussion of Dooher's activities "made almost a daily appearance in the Tehran press" during Razmara's premiership (p. 209, n. 7).

5. See Hussein Fatemi's editorial in *Bakhtar-i Imruz*, 30 Urdibihisht 1330/20 May 1951, for a description of one such episode.

6. See n. 3, above.

7. Persian and English sources disagree considerably concerning Musaddiq's birthdate. The years given range from 1879 to 1885, with at least one source presenting each of the seven years in this span. Many Persian sources indicate 1879 (1258 by the Iranian calendar), while the other extreme of "about 1885" is the date given in the British Foreign Office biography. Based on a survey of the sources and discussions with members of Musaddiq's family, I believe the birthdate to be the 1882 date given above, which is 29 Urdibihisht 1261 according to the Persian calendar. See Ali Janzadah, *Musaddiq* (n.p., 1358/1979), p. 5. This book, which contains Musaddiq's autibiographical notes in his own handwriting, is the most reliable source I have located on Musaddiq's life.

Given the calendar differences and the somewhat casual nature of much of the historiography of Iran, inconsistencies in dates occur constantly for even the most significant political happenings. I note, for example, a half-dozen different dates given in a half-dozen different sources for the Iranian severance of diplomatic relations with Great Britain in the fall of 1952. In this study, I have made a special effort to be as accurate as possible with dates. Despite this, some error seems inevitable.

8. Muhammad Musaddiq, speech, Majlis, Mar. 7, 1944, as printed in Hussein Kai-Ustuvan, *Siyasat-i Muvazinah-i Manfi dar Majlis-i Chahardihum (The Policy of Negative Equilibrium in the Fourteenth Majlis)* vol. 1 (Tehran, 1327/1949), p. 35.

9. Gerard de Villiers, *The Imperial Shah: An Informal Biography*, trans. June P. Wilson and Walter B. Michaels (Boston: Little, Brown, 1976), pp. 156, 170.

10. Cf. Ibid., p. 168, and Leonard Mosley, *Power Play: Oil in the Middle East* (Baltimore, Md.: Penguin Books, 1973), p. 199.

11. *New York Times*, Mar. 6, 1967, p. 33.

12. Great Britain, Public Record Office, FO 371/20837, Seymour to Eden, Apr. 12, 1937, p. 32.

13. Interview with Hidayatollah Matin-Daftary, Tehran, June 26, 1974.

14. Henry F. Grady, "The Real Story of Iran," *U.S. News and World Report*, October 19, 1951, 14.

15. Donald N. Wilber, *Contemporary Iran* (New York: Praeger, 1963), p. 89.

16. Musaddiq, speech, Majlis, Mar. 7, 1944, as printed in Kai-Ustuvan, *Siyasat-i Muvazinah-i Manfi*, p. 34.

17. Personal interview, Austin, Tex., Apr. 18, 1976.

18. As quoted in Janzadah, *Musaddiq*, p. 230.

19. Ibid., p. 241.

20. Many sources treat the history of British-Iranian oil relations. The most authoritative analysis from the British side is R. W. Ferrier, *The History of the British Petroleum Company: The Developing Years, 1901–1932*, vol. 1 (Cambridge: Cambridge University Press, 1982). From the Iranian side, the two best sources are Fereidun Fesharaki, *Development of the Iranian Oil Industry: International and Domestic Aspects* (New York: Praeger, 1976), and Mustafa Fateh, *Panjah Sal Naft-i Iran (Fifty Years of Persian Oil)* (Tehran, 1335/1956). Fateh's book (in Persian) is indispensable. Mustafa Fateh received his degree from Columbia University in 1918, went to work for the AIOC in 1923, and for three decades was the highest-ranking Iranian in the company. Fateh wrote a second volume that continued with the fall of Musaddiq and analyzed the politics of the 1954 consortium agreement. The Iranian government confiscated the manuscript and imprisoned Fateh, putting him in solitary confinement for twenty-six days in 1957. Another valuable source is Benjamin Shwadran, *The Middle East, Oil, and the Great Powers 1959*, 2d rev. ed. (New York: Council for Middle Eastern Affairs Press, 1959), chaps. 1–6.

A hard-hitting book that sharply presents the Iranian position in its conflicts with Great Britain over oil is L. P. Elwell-Sutton, *Persian Oil: A Study in Power Politics* (London: Laurence and Wishart, 1955). The brief for the AIOC is presented in Henry Longhurst, *Adventure in Oil: The Story of British Petroleum* (London: Sidgwick and Jackson, 1959), and in S. H. Longrigg, *Oil in the Middle East: Its Discovery and Development*, 3d ed. (London: Oxford University Press, 1968).

21. Winston Churchill, *The World Crisis, 1911–1914* (New York: Charles Scribner's Sons, 1923), p. 134, as quoted in Fesharaki, *Development of Iranian Oil Industry*, p. 9.

22. Fesharaki, *Development of Iranian Oil Industry*, p. 11.

23. For detailed documentation of the outrage expressed in Iran toward the 1919 Anglo-Persian agreement, see N. S. Fatemi, *Diplomatic History of Persia, 1917–1923* (New York: Russell F. Moore, 1952). For an unusual defense of the 1919 agreement, see Peter Avery, *Modern Iran* (New York: Praeger, 1965), pp. 202–8.

24. Ferrier, *History of the British Petroleum Company*, p. 588. The quotation is repeated on p. 592 in the same book.

25. Ibid., p. 595.

26. Information provided by Denys Cadman, son of Sir John Cadman, in interview with author, Austin, Tex., Dec. 17, 1984.

27. Interview with Mustafa Fateh, Tehran, Dec. 14, 1966. Fateh acted as the translator between Sir John Cadman and Reza Shah.

28. Fateh, *Panjah Sal Naft-i Iran*, pp. 289–90.

29. As quoted in Ferrier, *History of the British Petroleum Company*, p. 626.

30. Fateh, *Panjah Sal Naft-i Iran*, p. 291.

31. The fascinating untold story of Cadman's successful bargaining with Reza Shah is contained in Cadman's personal diary, in the possession of his son, Denys Cadman, in Austin, Tex. I wish to thank Denys Cadman for permitting me to read this diary. The entries of Apr. 11, 24, 28, and 30, 1933, make reference to the shah's decision to cooperate with the British. Iran's acting minister of the Interior at the time, Ali Asghar Zarinkafsh, has recollected that Reza Shah gave way before British pressure and that the AIOC benefited most from the 1933 agreement. (Interview with Zarinkafsh, Tehran, Sept. 10, 1966.)

32. Hussein Makki, *Kitab-i Siyah (The Black Book)* (Tehran, 1329/1951), p. 153.

33. Ronald W. Ferrier, "The Development of the Iranian Oil Industry," in Hossein Amirsadeghi, ed., *Twentieth-Century Iran* (London: Will Heinemann, 1977), p. 106.

34. Richard Funkhauser, "September 10, 1950 Background Paper," in Senate Committee on Foreign Relations, Subcommittee on Multinational Corporations, *Multinational Corporations and United States Foreign Policy*, 93d Cong., 2d sess. on Multinational Petroleum Companies and Foreign Policy, Feb. 20–21, Mar. 27–28, 1974, pt. 7, p. 126.

35. Saleh in *U.N. Security Council Official Record*, 6th Year, 563d Meeting, 15 (S/PV 563, 1951), as quoted in Jerrold L. Walden, "The International Petroleum Cartel in Iran: Private Power and the Public Interest," *Journal of Public Law* 11 (Spring 1962): 70. Another source indicates that the AIOC stated its total royalty payments to Iran as of the end of 1950 to be about £150 million. See Shwadran, *Middle East, Oil, and Great Powers*, p. 159.

36. Walden, "International Petroleum Cartel," p. 70. Both Musaddiq and later the shah made this point often. See *The Speech of H. E. Dr. Mossadegh concerning the Nationalization of the Petroleum Industry in Iran* (Tehran, 1951), p. 31. According to the shah: "The company knew of our irritation due to the high percentage paid in corporation taxes to the British Government; these taxes in fact greatly exceeded the royalties to Iran." Mohammed Reza Pahlavi, *Mission for My Country* (New York: McGraw-Hill, 1960), p. 90.

37. Anthony Eden, *Full Circle* (Boston: Houghton Mifflin, 1960), pp. 214–15.

38. Julian Bharier, *Economic Development in Iran, 1900–1970* (London: Oxford University Press, 1971), p. 160. The figures on the workforce are drawn from p. 162.

39. Geoffrey Jones, *Banking and Empire in Iran: The History of The British Bank of the Middle East* (Cambridge: Cambridge University Press, 1986), pp. 316–18.

40. Longrigg, *Oil in the Middle East*, p. 157.

41. Avery, *Modern Iran*, p. 423.

42. Vernon A. Walters, *Silent Missions* (Garden City, N.Y.: Doubleday, 1978), pp. 247–48. This is a fascinating account of the Harriman-Musaddiq negotiations.

43. Great Britain, Public Record Office, FO 371/20837, Seymour to Eden, Apr. 12, 1937.

44. Charles W. Hamilton, *America and Oil in the Middle East* (Houston, Tex.: Gulf Publishing, 1962), p. 47.

45. The words of Edmund Stevens reporting for the *Christian Science Monitor*, Apr. 16, 1951.

46. Christopher T. Rand, *Making Democracy Safe for Oil* (Boston: Little, Brown, 1975), p. 133.

47. John M. Blair, *The Control of Oil* (New York: Vintage Books, 1978), p. 79.

48. Ervand Abrahamian, *Iran between Two Revolutions* (Princeton, N.J.: Princeton University Press, 1982), p. 321. Abrahamian's study contains the best detailed analysis in English of the various political organizations active in Iran during these years. A second excellent source is Cottam's *Nationalism in Iran*.

49. Abrahamian, *Iran between Two Revolutions*, p. 322.

50. See Mohammed Reza Pahlavi, *Answer to History* (New York: Stein and Day, 1980), p. 71.

51. Elwell-Sutton, *Persian Oil*, p. 195. A definitive biography of Kashani is contained in Haj Shaykh Muhammad Sharif Razi, *Ganjinah-yi Danishmandan (Treasures of Learned Men)* (Qum, 1352/1973), 1:267–70. See also Yann Richard, "Ayatollah Kashani: Precursor of the Islamic Republic?" in Nikki R. Keddie, ed., *Religion and Politics in Iran* (New Haven and London: Yale University Press, 1983), pp. 101–24.

52. One of the few observers who recognized the significance of the Islamic linkage to the nationalist movement was Ann K. S. Lambton, who in an article in *International Affairs* (January 1957) argued that it was only when the religious classes came to the support of the movement that it acquired widespread support. This article has been quoted in support of this thesis by both Rose L. Greaves and Wm. Roger Louis. See Greaves, "1942–1976: The Reign of Mohammad Reza Shah," in Amirsadeghi, ed., *Twentieth-Century Iran*, p. 73, and Louis, *The British Empire in the Middle East, 1945–1951* (Oxford: Clarendon Press, 1984), p. 661.

53. Homa Katouzian, in his hard-hitting, opinionated, but extremely informative book, argues that Musaddiq's movement was a democratic and not a nationalist movement. By Musaddiq's own admission, it was both. The nationalist element for a time helped to pull together many disparate groups. Katouzian's point, however, is an important one, since it emphasizes the democratic goals that Musaddiq and many of his followers hoped to achieve. See Katouzian, *The Political Economy of Modern Iran: Despotism and Pseudo-Modernism, 1926–1979* (New York: New York University Press, 1981), p. 171.

54. For interesting insights into the personality and political ideas of Fatemi, see Sepehr Zabih, *The Mossadegh Era* (Chicago: Lake View Press, 1982), pp. 128–35. These pages contain a report of a long interview the author had with Fatemi in The Hague on July 25, 1953.

55. Richard Funkhauser, "The Problem of Near Eastern Oil," Lecture to National War College, Dec. 4, 1951, in Senate Committee on Foreign Relations, *Multinational Corporations*, p. 170.

56. Louis, *British Empire*, pp. 596, 656.

57. Ibid., p. 653. For Grady's views on Iran, the British, and Musaddiq, see Grady, "Real Story of Iran," pp. 13–17.

58. Interview with American diplomat, Washington, D.C., Nov. 11, 1981.

59. Funkhauser, "Problem of Near Eastern Oil," p. 170.

60. Shepherd to Furlonge, Confidential, May 14, 1951, FO 371/91535/EP 1531/356, as quoted in Louis, *British Empire*, p. 654.

61. Louis, *British Empire*, p. 739, n. 5.

62. As quoted in Anthony Sampson, *The Seven Sisters: The Great Oil Companies and the World They Made* (New York: Viking Press, 1975), p. 120. This extraordinary memorandum is worth reading in its entirety.

63. As quoted in Louis, *British Empire*, p. 650.

64. David S. McLellan, *Dean Acheson: The State Department Years* (New York: Dodd, Mead, 1976), p. 387.

65. Memorandum describing telephone call from Secretary of Defense Lovett to Secretary of State Acheson, Sept. 25, 1951, President's Secretary's Files, Harry S. Truman Library, Independence, Mo.

66. Dean Acheson, *Present at the Creation* (New York: W. W. Norton, 1969), p. 506.

67. Eden, *Full Circle*, pp. 216–17.

68. Interview with Walter Levy, New York, Jan. 3, 1985. Some of the material in the following paragraphs is drawn from this interview. For Levy's competent overview of Musaddiq and the oil crisis of 1951–53, see his "The Present Situation in Iran," which contains a transcript of a speech delivered by Levy at a conference sponsored by the Middle East Institute and held at Georgetown University, Dec. 12, 1953. Sections of this commentary are printed in Walter J. Levy, "Economic Problems Facing a Settlement of the Iranian Oil Controversy," *Middle East Journal* 8 (Winter 1954): 91–95.

69. The summary of the content of this working proposal is taken from McGhee, *Envoy to the Middle World*, pp. 400–402.

70. Ibid., p. 403.

71. Ibid.

72. Memorandum of discussion at the 132d meeting of the National Security Council, Feb. 18, 1953, NSC Series, Box 4, Dwight D. Eisenhower Library, Abilene, Kans.

73. Ibid., p. 337.

74. Ibid., p. 322.

75. For an excellent discussion of the collaboration efforts of the American oil companies during the Musaddiq period, see David S. Painter, *Oil and the American Century* (Baltimore and London: Johns Hopkins University Press, 1986), chap. 8.

76. Arthur Krock, *Memoirs* (New York: Funk and Wagnalls, 1968), p. 262.

77. Memorandum of conversation, Ahmad Human (deputy minister of Court) and John H. Stutesman (second secretary, U.S. Embassy), Nov. 6, 1951, Record Group 84, Box 29 (1950–52), National Archives, Washington, D.C.

78. Louis, *British Empire*, p. 685, n. 26.

79. For an informed and thoroughly researched discussion of American intelligence operations in Iran following World War II, see Mark J. Gasiorowski, "The 1953 *Coup D'Etat* in Iran," *International Journal of Middle East Studies* 19 (August 1987): 261–86.

80. An example of the level of the reporting can be seen by listing a few of the titles of the articles that appeared on Iran at the time: "Portrait of a Man Dreaming up a Coup: Great Ham Act Goes to Waste," *Life*, Nov. 23, 1953, pp. 37–39; "Crackdown in the Middle East: Red-Inspired Iranians Retreat," *Newsweek*, Nov. 23, 1953, pp. 40–42; "Iran: In the Red," *Newsweek*, Sept. 21, 1953, p. 49; and "Iran: Mooo," *Time*, Nov. 30, 1953, p. 40.

81. "Iran: Whose Ox Is Nationalized?" *Time*, Mar. 26, 1951, p. 31.

82. Memorandum, Byrnes to Roosevelt, Oct. 15, 1943, in Senate Special Committee Investigating the National Defense Program, Hearings, pt. 41, Petroleum Arrangements with Saudi Arabia, 80th Cong., 1st Sess., 1948. Fateh also refers to the Byrnes letter in *Panjah Sal*, p. 500. See also Michael B. Stoff, *Oil, Water, and American Security* (New Haven and London: Yale University Press, 1980), p. 131.

83. McGhee, *Envoy to the Middle World*, p. 322.

84. For details on these proposals, see Department of State, Memorandum of conversation, Oct. 8, 1952, Papers of Dean Acheson, Harry S. Truman Library, Independence, Mo., and Department of the Interior, confidential memorandum, "Iranian Oil Problem," Charles Rayner to C. S. Snodgrass, Oct. 22, 1951, Papers of Dean Acheson, Harry S. Truman Library, Independence, Mo.

85. B. S. McBeth, *British Oil Policy, 1919–1939* (London: Frank Cass, 1985), p. 75.

86. Senate Committee on Foreign Relations, *Multinational Corporations*, p. 99.

87. The testimony of Leonard J. Emmerglick, who was special assistant to the attorney general in 1952, in ibid., p. 109.

88. Ibid.

89. Sampson, *Seven Sisters*, p. 126.

90. Both Harriman and Walters explicitly expressed deep disappointment in their ineffectiveness in dealing with Musaddiq, and each indicated that he was not used to diplomatic failure. See Walters, *Silent Missions*, pp. 258–59, 263. George McGhee found the British as intransigent as Musaddiq and was extremely disappointed by his inability to effect an agreement: "My real regret in leaving the department when I did in December 1951 was that I had not been able to solve the Iranian crisis" (*Envoy to the Middle World*, p. 17).

91. Walters, *Silent Missions*, p. 250.

92. Acheson, *Present at the Creation*, p. 510.

93. Interview with Dr. Hassan Alavi, member of the Majlis Oil Commission, Tehran, Feb. 1, 1966. In a subsequent conversation on Oct. 12, 1985, in Austin, Tex., Alavi explicitly confirmed this important recollection.

94. Eden, *Full Circle*, p. 221.

95. Ibid., p. 224.

96. Kermit Roosevelt, as quoted by Robert Scheer in the *Los Angeles Times*, Mar. 29, 1979, p. 1.

97. Department of State, incoming telegram, David Bruce (Paris) to secretary of State (Washington), Nov. 10, 1951, Papers of Dean Acheson, Harry S. Truman Library, Independence, Mo.

98. C. M. Woodhouse, *Something Ventured* (London: Granada, 1982), p. 117. Woodhouse stresses this strategy, writing in an earlier place that "I was convinced from the first that any effort to forestall a Soviet *coup* in Iran would require a joint Anglo-American effort. The Americans would be more likely to work with us if they

saw the problem as one of containing Communism rather than restoring the position of the AIOC" (p. 110).

99. For details, see Gasiorowski, "1953 *Coup d'Etat.*" Donald Wilber confirmed the specifics of such activities in an interview with the author, Princeton, N.J., Jan. 13, 1981.

100. The oft-quoted exception is Richard and Gladys Harkness, "The Mysterious Doings of CIA," *Saturday Evening Post*, Nov. 6, 1954, pp. 66–68. For President Eisenhower's personal account of the Musaddiq episode and the American intervention, see Dwight D. Eisenhower, *Mandate for Change, 1953–1956* (Garden City, N.Y.: Doubleday, 1963), pp. 159–66.

101. See Woodhouse, *Something Ventured*, and Kermit Roosevelt, *Countercoup: The Struggle for the Control of Iran* (New York: McGraw-Hill, 1979). Although accurate in its general thrust, the latter is very careless in the matter of particulars and must be used with extreme care. One example will suffice. In attempting to downplay the mass participation of Iranians in the Musaddiq movement, Roosevelt writes that Dean Acheson reported several hundred people killed and twenty injured in demonstrations when U.S. emissary W. Averell Harriman arrived in Tehran on July 15, 1951. According to Roosevelt: "This seems a curious proportion of killed to injured and is as great an exaggeration as most other estimates of Iranian casualties during this period" (p. 90). This bizarre charge reverses Acheson's actual statement, which described a demonstration "in which several hundred people were injured and twenty were killed" (*Present at the Creation*, p. 508).

102. Personal communication with one of the analysts.

103. Thomas Powers, *The Man Who Kept the Secrets: Richard Helms and the CIA* (New York: Pocket Books, 1979), pp. 43–44. Helms was then considered to be critical of the use of covert operations.

104. Letter to the author from an American diplomat who served with Henderson in Iran, Jan. 4, 1985.

105. Roosevelt, *Countercoup*, p. 18.

106. Leonard Mosley, *Dulles* (New York: Dial Press/James Wade, 1978), p. 269.

107. Roosevelt, *Countercoup*, p. 8.

108. Woodhouse, *Something Ventured*, p. 125.

109. Eden, *Full Circle*, p. 237.

110. Asadollah and Seyfollah Rashidian are identifiable in the Roosevelt book as Nossey and Cafron, "Laughing Boy" and "The Mad Musician," respectively. Seyfollah Rashidian was indeed a pianist and musician; he was anything but mad. The "Boscoe Brothers" mentioned in the book refer to another set of brothers.

111. Roosevelt, *Countercoup*, pp. 183–84.

112. Ibid., pp. 41, 78–79, 127.

113. Interview with Kermit Roosevelt, Washington, D.C., Nov. 12, 1981.

114. The Roosevelt-"Black" relationship was the first major case in which the U.S. government used knowledgeable American Iran experts to achieve policy goals that were developed without heeding the advice and recommendations of these experts. Journalists were used even more blatantly. In the case of the 1953 countercoup, see Kennett Love's unpublished paper entitled, "The American Role in the Pahlevi Restoration." Love was a *New York Times* correspondent in Tehran at the time of the countercoup.

115. Interview with Donald Wilber, Princeton, N.J., Jan. 13, 1981. Just as Amer-

ican operatives (such as Kim Roosevelt) like to claim complete credit for the venture, so too do British officials overstate their roles in the intervention. British intelligence has alleged, for example, that "Roosevelt really did little more than show up in Iran with CIA funds to encourage agents the British had organized and then released to American control" (Christopher Andrew, *Her Majesty's Secret Service: The Making of the British Intelligence Community* [New York: Viking, 1985], p. 494).

116. Woodhouse, *Something Ventured*, p. 130.

117. U.S. Department of State, Office of Intelligence Research, *Iran's Political and Economic Prospects through 1953*, Intelligence Report Number 6121, esp. p. 10. Personal copy of report.

118. These statistics have been calculated and provided to me by Fereidun Fesharaki in a personal communication of Feb. 13, 1981.

119. Statement by Congressman B. Carroll Reece. See House of Representatives Committee on Government Operations, Hearings before a Subcommittee on United States Aid Operations in Iran, 84th Cong., 2d Sess., May 2, 31, June 1, 5, 8, 11–13, 18–19, 25–27, 29, July 16, 1956, p. 796.

120. William O. Douglas, "The U.S. and Revolution," in K. E. Boulding et al., *The U.S. and Revolution* (Santa Barbara, Calif.: Center for the Study of Democratic Institutions, 1961), p. 10.

121. Painter, *Oil and the American Century*, p. 198.

122. Kashani, as quoted in *Shahid*, no. 535, 3 Azar 1330/24 Nov. 1951.

123. Telegram, Abassador Loy Henderson to secretary of State, Nov. 12, 1951, Record Group 84, Box 29 (1950–52), National Archives, Washington, D.C.

124. The Rashidian name appeared in the U.S. Senate Hearings on the Grumman sale of F-14s to Iran, in which the Lavi brothers, agents for Grumman, admitted that of $3.1 million in Grumman commissions, $2.48 million was paid over to International Services, an organization in which the Rashidians were the principals (Senate Committee on Foreign Relations, Subcommittee on Multinational Corporations, *Multinational Corporations and United States Foreign Policy: Grumman Sale of F-14's to Iran*, 94th Cong., 2d Sess., Aug. 9, Sept. 10, 13, 15, 27, 1976, pp. 133–34).

125. Harlan Cleveland, "Oil, Blood and Politics: Our Next Move in Iran," *Reporter*, Nov. 10, 1953, p. 19.

126. Interviews with Khomeini representatives, Tehran, Nov. 26–Dec. 1, 1978.

CHAPTER 3. THE POLITICS OF REACTION AND PAHLAVI
RETRENCHMENT, 1954–1961

1. For this quotation and an excellent overview of SAVAK, see Earnest R. Oney, "The Eyes and Ears of the Shah," *Intelligence Quarterly* 1 (February 1986): 1–3. For other reliable discussions of the practices of SAVAK, see the journal *Seven Days* (April 1980): 14, 20, and Jonathan Randal's *Washington Post* article of Dec. 13, 1979. Richard Savin provides a grim firsthand view of the inside of a SAVAK prison in his *Vakil Abad Iran: A Survivor's Story* (Edinburgh: Canongate/Q Press, 1979). Savin spent two and a half years (1976–78) in Vakil Abad prison, near Mashhad.

2. The names and numbers in this paragraph are drawn from Zuhrah Shaji'i, *Nimayandigan-i Majlis-i Shawra-yi Milli dar Bistuyik Dawrah-yi Qanunguzari (The Representatives of the National Consultative Assembly during the Twenty-One Legisla-*

tive Periods) (Tehran, 1344/1965), p. 176, and Bahram Dihnad, *Parliman-i Iran: Sharh-i Zindigani-yi Shakhshi va Ijtima'i-yi Nimayandigan-i Dawrah-yi Nuzdahum-i Majlis-i Shawra-yi Milli va Dawrah-yi Duvvum-i Majlis-i Sina (The Iranian Parliament: The Personal and Social Biographies of the Representatives of the Nineteenth Majlis and the Second Senate)* (Tehran, 1335/1956). The percentages of landed representatives to these Majlises reported by Ervand Abrahamian (based also on the Shaji'i study) are somewhat less than what my calculations indicate. See Abrahamian, *Iran: Between Two Revolutions* (Princeton, N.J.: Princeton University Press, 1982), p. 421.

3. Homa Katouzian, *The Political Economy of Modern Iran: Despotism and Pseudo-Modernism, 1926–1979* (New York: New York University Press, 1981), pp. 193–94.

4. An excellent discussion of this ill-fated experiment in political party formation from above is presented in Andrew F. Westwood, "Elections and Politics in Iran," *Middle East Journal* 15 (Spring 1961): 153–64.

5. Interview with Iranian physician and longtime colleague of Eqbal, Austin, Tex., Oct. 12, 1985.

6. As quoted in Margaret Laing, *The Shah* (London: Sidgwick and Jackson, 1977), p. 231.

7. Interview with Alam associate, Tehran, July 30, 1970.

8. For a thoroughly researched study of the British-American positions concerning the oil agreement, see Wm. Roger Louis, "Musaddiq, Oil, and the Dilemmas of British Imperialism," in Wm. Roger Louis and James A. Bill, *Musaddiq, Iranian Nationalism and Oil* (London: I. B. Tauris and Co., 1988).

9. Fatollah Naficy, communication with the author, July 10, 1985. Then chair of the Iran Oil Company, Naficy served as secretary of the Iranian delegation to the consortium negotiations. He also served as chair of Iran's Technical Committee, which advised the negotiating committee. Naficy explained the details of the negotiations to me in long letters of Apr. 30 and July 10, 1985.

10. Anthony Sampson, *The Seven Sisters: The Great Oil Companies and the World They Made* (New York: Viking Press, 1975), p. 135.

11. Charles W. Hamilton, *Americans and Oil in the Middle East* (Houston, Tex.: Gulf Publishing, 1962), p. 59. Actually, the AIOC was not quite a wreck to be salvaged. It still had considerable production in Iraq and Kuwait, promising prospects in Abu Dhabi and Qatar, and was busy building refineries in Aden and Australia as partial replacements for Abadan.

12. Senate Committee on Foreign Relations, Subcommittee on Multinational Corporations, *Multinational Corporations and United States Foreign Policy*, 93d Cong., 2d Sess. on Multinational Petroleum Companies and Foreign Policy, Feb. 20–21, Mar. 27–28, 1974, pt. 7, p. 298.

13. Christopher T. Rand, *Making Democracy Safe for Oil* (Boston: Little, Brown, 1975), p. 25.

14. Great Britain, Public Record Office, FO 371/20837, Seymour to Eden, Apr. 12, 1937, p. 7.

15. Fereidun Fesharaki, *Development of the Iranian Oil Industry: International and Domestic Aspects* (New York: Praeger, 1976), p. 50.

16. Communication with the author, July 10, 1985.

17. This entire incident was related to me by the retired chancellor himself. Interview with Ali Akbar Siyassi, Tehran, Apr. 29, 1967.

18. Jerrold L. Walden, "The International Petroleum Cartel in Iran—Private Power and the Public Interest," *Journal of Public Law* 11 (Spring 1962): 51–52

19. Benjamin Shwadran, *The Middle East, Oil, and the Great Powers 1959*, 2d rev. ed. (New York: Council for Middle Eastern Affairs Press, 1959), p. 188.

20. Fesharaki, *Development of the Iranian Oil Industry*, pp. 59–60.

21. Senate Committee on Foreign Relations, *Multinational Corporations*, p. 289.

22. Minute by Thomas Belgrave (petroleum adviser in Foreign Office), Nov. 19, 1953, FO 371/104643, as quoted in Wm. Roger Louis, "Musaddiq, Oil, and the Dilemmas of British Imperialism," in Louis and Bill, *Musaddiq, Iranian Nationalism and Oil.*

23. Senate Committee on Foreign Relations, *Multinational Corporations*, p. 290.

24. The texts of these important letters are reproduced in ibid., pp. 249–52.

25. United Nations, Department of Economic and Social Affairs, *Economic Developments in the Middle East, 1959–1961* (New York: United Nations, 1961), p. 146. These revenue figures are similar to those given in Shwadran, *Middle East, Oil, and Great Powers*, p. 190. The revenues calculated by Homa Katouzian, *Political Economy of Modern Iran*, are somewhat different. According to Katouzian, the $10 million in 1954 became $88 million in 1955 and $364 million in 1960 (p. 206).

26. Enrico Mattei had personal and political reasons for concluding this agreement with Iran. An independent and colorful entrepreneur, he had uncharacteristically chosen to cooperate with the AIOC during the 1951–53 embargo. Like the American independents, Mattei expected to be included in the 1954 consortium agreement as a reward for his loyalty to the oil fraternity. When the major companies cut him out of the deal, he was furious and vowed to make his own arrangements. Mattei died in a mysterious airplane crash on Oct. 27, 1962. Many observers, including the shah of Iran, publicly stated that they did not believe Mattei's death was an accident.

27. Mohammad Reza Pahlavi, *Answer to History* (New York: Stein and Day, 1980), p. 22.

28. The text of this letter is reproduced in Yonah Alexander and Allan Nanes, eds., *The United States and Iran* (Frederick, Md.: Aletheia Books, 1980), pp. 252–53.

29. Ibid., p. 253.

30. This Sept. 5, 1953, press release is reproduced in ibid., pp. 253–54.

31. "United States Policy towards Iran: A Report to the National Security Council by the N.S.C. Planning Board," Dec. 21, 1953, in ibid., p. 267.

32. "The Present Situation in Iran: A Statement Made before the Middle East Conference," Washington, D.C., Dec. 12, 1953, in ibid., pp. 259–63.

33. "Joint Chiefs of Staff Joint Intelligence Committee Memorandum for the Joint Strategic Plans Committee and the Joint Logistic Plans Committee [Enclosure Draft]," Apr. 13, 1955, in ibid., p. 273.

34. House of Representatives Committee on Foreign Affairs, *Report of the Special Study Mission to the Middle East, South and Southeast Asia, and the Western Pacific*, 84th Cong., 2d Sess., May 10, 1956, p. 57. Other than Zablocki, the following five representatives were part of the study mission: E. Ross Adair of Indiana, Robert C. Byrd of West Virginia, Marguerite Stitt Church of Illinois, John Jarman of Oklahoma, and Walter H. Judd of Minnesota.

35. *Washington Post*, Nov. 15, 1977, p. B3.

36. "Agreement of Defense Cooperation between the Government of the United

States of America and the Imperial Government of Iran," Mar. 5, 1979, in Alexander and Nanes, *United States and Iran,* pp. 306–7.

37. See "Iran on a Dangerous Path," *International Affairs* (Moscow) 4 (April 1959): 47–52.

38. Dwight D. Eisenhower, "Address to the Members of the Parliament of Iran," Dec. 14, 1959, in Alexander and Nanes, *United States and Iran,* pp. 309–11.

39. David E. Lilienthal, *The Journals of David E. Lilienthal,* vol. 4: The Road to Change, 1955–1959 (New York: Harper and Row, 1969), p. 26.

40. As quoted in E. A. Bayne, *Persian Kingship in Transition* (New York: American Universities Field Staff, 1968), pp. 188–89n.

41. David E. Lilienthal, *The Journals of David E. Lilienthal,* vol. 5: *The Harvest Years, 1959–1963* (New York: Harper and Row, 1971), p. 174.

42. Ibid., p. 339. For Lilienthal's summary of the Khuzistan project, see his "Enterprise in Iran: An Experiment in Economic Development," *Foreign Affairs* 38 (October 1959): 1–8.

43. *Kayhan International* (Tehran), Nov. 14, 1961, as quoted in Marvin Zonis, *The Political Elite of Iran* (Princeton, N.J.: Princeton University Press, 1971), p. 67.

44. House of Representatives Committee on Government Operations, *Hearings before a Subcommittee on United States Aid Operations in Iran,* 84th Cong., 2d Sess., May 2, 31, June 1, 5, 8, 11–13, 18–19, 25–27, 29, July 16, 1956, pp. 797, 998. The information contained in the following paragraphs of the text has been drawn from this document.

45. Ibid., p. 999.

46. "Conclusion of the Investigation on United States Aid Operations in Iran by the Foreign Operations Subcommittee of the Committee on Government Operations, U.S. House of Representatives," Jan. 28, 1957, in Alexander and Nanes, *United States and Iran,* pp. 295–96.

47. House of Representatives Committee on Government Operations, *Hearings,* p. 197.

48. Senate Committee on Foreign Relations, *Report of the Special Study Mission,* p. 211.

49. Interview with Sayyid Muhammad Baqir Hijazi, Tehran, Oct. 3, 1966. Hijazi had been imprisoned with Qarani. General Qarani became chief of the Joint Staff of the Iranian Armed Forces for a short time following the Iranian revolution of 1978–79. He was assassinated by a terrorist group on Apr. 23, 1979.

50. See, for example, Katouzian, *Political Economy of Modern Iran,* pp. 199, 209–10.

51. L. P. Elwell-Sutton, "Nationalism and Neutralism in Iran," *Middle East Journal* 12 (Winter 1958): 29.

52. Ibid., p. 31.

53. T. Cuyler Young, "Iran in Continuing Crisis," *Foreign Affairs* 40 (January 1962): 291–92. On June 24, 1961, the *Nation* concluded an analysis of American policy in Iran with the following: "It should be obvious that the American ideal, if it is ever to be persuasive, if it is ever to have validity, must find loftier expression than the gun of the secret police chief clasped in fingers stained by many a dirty buck. It must concern itself with people, not with rulers; it must help the broad mass of the people; it must offer both freedom and hope, not oil profits and graft" (p. 551).

54. A. H. Ebtehaj, "A Program for Economic Growth," paper presented at the International Industrial Conference, San Francisco, Calif., Sept. 1961, p. 4.

CHAPTER 4. AN INTERLUDE OF REFORM: JOHN F. KENNEDY AND IRAN, 1961–1963

1. Quoted from "The Inaugural Address of John Fitzgerald Kennedy," Jan. 20, 1961, in George W. Johnson, ed., *The Kennedy Presidential Press Conferences* (New York: Earl M. Coleman Enterprises, 1978), p. 40.

2. See Jim F. Heath, *John F. Kennedy and the Business Community* (Chicago and London: University of Chicago Press, 1969), p. 106. For a provocative and fascinating book that argues that John Kennedy was "a determined counterrevolutionary," see Bruce Miroff, *Pragmatic Illusions: The Presidential Politics of John F. Kennedy* (New York: David McKay, 1976), esp. pp. 110–66.

3. Walter Lippmann, *The Coming Tests with Russia* (Boston: Little, Brown, 1961), p. 16.

4. Ibid.

5. See Arthur M. Schlesinger, Jr., *Robert Kennedy and His Times* (New York: Ballantine Books, 1978), p. 469. For a detailed account of Justice Douglas's travels in Iran, see William O. Douglas, *Strange Lands and Friendly People* (New York: Harper and Row, 1951).

6. J. W. Bowling, U.S. Department of State, NEA/Greece, Turkey, Iran, "The Current Situation in Iran," pp. 8–9. Personal copy of document. This document is reproduced in part in Yonah Alexander and Allan Nanes, eds., *The United States and Iran* (Frederick, Md.: Aletheia Books, 1980), pp. 315–22.

7. J. W. Bowling, U.S. Department of State, NEA/Greece, Turkey, Iran, "Political Characteristics of the Iranian Urban Middle Class and Implications Thereof for U.S. Policy," pp. 7–8. Personal copy of document. Reproduced in part in Alexander and Nanes, *United States and Iran*, pp. 322–29.

8. Ibid., p. 8.

9. Personal copy of letter from T. Cuyler Young's papers.

10. Senate Committee on Foreign Relations, *Executive Sessions of the Senate Foreign Relations Committee (Historical Series)*, 87th Cong., 1st Sess., 1961, 13, pt. 2:159.

11. Ibid., p. 160.

12. Ibid., pp. 160–61.

13. *U.S. News and World Report*, Mar. 6, 1961, pp. 64–65.

14. *U.S. News and World Report*, Jan. 27, 1969, p. 49.

15. See Mohamed Heikal, *Iran: The Untold Story* (New York: Pantheon Books, 1981), p. 72.

16. Information provided in interview with Iranian statesman who was with the shah when the latter received word of the Kennedy assassination, Tehran, January 1967.

17. William O. Douglas, *The Court Years, 1939–1975* (New York: Random House, 1980), p. 304.

18. Dean Rusk, "Memorandum for the President," Mar. 17, 1961, personal copy.

19. Memorandum to U.S. Department of State, "Discussion with the Iranian Ambassador." Personal copy. Although the author of this informative memo is unnamed, it is probably a high-ranking U.S. Point-Four official who worked closely

with Ardeshir Zahedi in Iran beginning in 1950–51. All the quotations and information in this paragraph are drawn from this document, which is reproduced in part in Alexander and Nanes, *United States and Iran*, pp. 329–31.

20. "Message from United States Ambassador to Tehran (Holmes) to the President and Secretary of State on Chester Bowles's Visit to Iran," Feb. 19, 1962, as reprinted in Alexander and Nanes, *United States and Iran*, pp. 345–48. See also *Kayhan International* (Tehran), Feb. 15, 1962, p. 12.

21. *New York Times*, Apr. 13, 1961, pp. 1–2; *Philadelphia Inquirer*, Apr. 13, 1962, p. 3.

22. Central Intelligence Agency Memorandum, Abbot E. Smith to the Director, Aug. 16, 1962, Vice Presidential Security File, Vice Presidential Travel, V.P. Johnson's Trip to the Middle East, August–September 1962, Box 2, Lyndon B. Johnson Presidential Library, Austin, Tex.

23. Memorandum, "Substantive Points to Make to the Shah," in ibid.

24. Telegram, Ambassador Julius Holmes to Department of State, Aug. 25, 1962, p. 3, in ibid.

25. Ibid., p. 2.

26. As reported in *Iran Almanac, 1963* (Tehran: Echo of Iran, 1964), p. 173.

27. Eric Hooglund, *Reform and Revolution in Rural Iran* (Austin, Tex.: University of Texas Press, 1984), p. 171.

28. As quoted in E. A. Bayne, *Persian Kingship in Transition* (New York: American Universities Field Staff, 1968), p. 191.

29. Armin Meyer, in Abbas Amirie and Hamilton A. Twitchell, eds., *Iran in the 1980s* (Tehran: Institute for International Political and Economic Studies, 1978), p. 382. Meyer's comments were made at an October 4–6, 1977, symposium held in Washington, D.C. This volume contains the published proceedings of this symposium. In Tehran, Amini immediately challenged Meyer's assertion. Meyer was U.S. ambassador to Iran, April 1965–May 1969.

30. Interview with the author, Tehran, Nov. 3, 1966. I had numerous private meetings with Arsanjani between August 1966 and May 1969, when he died suddenly of a heart attack. Much of the material in this section is drawn from notes taken during those meetings. As incredible as it may seem, certain Western scholars of Iranian land reform were somehow able to write about the subject without ever mentioning Arsanjani's name. See, for example, D. R. Denman's fifty-page article in George Lenczowski, ed., *Iran under the Pahlavis* (Stanford, Calif.: Hoover Institution Press, 1978), pp. 253–303.

31. Personal copy of Farhad letter.

32. Homa Katouzian, *The Political Economy of Modern Iran* (New York and London: New York University Press, 1981), p. 221.

33. Bayne, *Persian Kingship*, p. 50.

34. Katouzian, *Political Economy*, p. 216.

35. Firaydun Tunakabuni, *Yaddashtha-yi Shahr-i Shuluq (Memories of a Crowded City)* (Tehran, 1348/1970), p. 150.

36. This and all other quotations in the paragraph are taken from Memorandum, William H. Brubeck to McGeorge Bundy, Jan. 21, 1963, Vice Presidential Security File, Government Agencies, State Department, 1961–1963, Box 12, Lyndon B. Johnson Presidential Library, Austin, Tex.

37. David E. Lilienthal, *The Journals of David E. Lilienthal*, vol. 5: *Harvest Years, 1959–1963* (New York: Harper and Row, 1971), p. 258.

38. Research Memorandum, "Soviet-Iranian Exchange of Notes on Exclusion of Foreign Missile Bases in Iran," Sept. 21, 1962, Department of State, Bureau of Intelligence and Research, Roger Hilsman to Secretary of State Rusk, Vice Presidential Security File, Government Agencies, State Department, 1961–63, Box 12, Lyndon B. Johnson Presidential Library, Austin, Tex.

39. Miroff, *Pragmatic Illusions*, p. 131.

40. Hamid Algar "Introduction," in Imam Khomeini, *Islam and Revolution* (Berkeley, Calif.: Mizan Press, 1981), p. 17.

CHAPTER 5. COUNTERREFORM, LYNDON JOHNSON, AND PAHLAVI RETRENCHMENT, 1963–1970

1. "Proposed Statement by Vice President Lyndon B. Johnson Before the House Foreign Affairs Committee, June 5, 1961," Vice Presidential Security File, Vice Presidential Travel, Visit to Southeast Asia, May 9–24, 1961, Lyndon B. Johnson Presidential Library, Austin, Tex., pp. 7, 10. This library is hereafter referred to as LBJ Library.

2. Ibid., p. 5.

3. Lyndon Baines Johnson, *The Vantage Point: Perspectives of the Presidency, 1963–1969* (New York: Holt, Rinehart and Winston, 1971), p. 68.

4. Hugh Sidey, *A Very Personal Presidency: Lyndon Johnson in the Presidency* (New York: Atheneum, 1968), pp. 140–41.

5. Hugh Sidey uses this term in the first chapter of his book (ibid., p. 23).

6. Ibid., p. 147.

7. United Nations, *Treaty Series*, vol. 776 (1971), nos. 11051–64, "Exchange of Notes concerning an Agreement between the Government of the United States and the Government of Iran," Mar. 19, 1962, no. 423, p. 290.

8. Ibid., Dec. 18, 1963, no. 299, p. 296. For the text of this important note of Nov. 17, 1963, see ibid., p. 295.

9. Richard Pfau, "The Legal Status of American Forces in Iran," *Middle East Journal* 28 (Spring 1974): 141. For another rare discussion of this important turning point in Iranian-American relations, see Rouhollah K. Ramazani, *Iran's Foreign Policy, 1941–1973* (Charlottesville, Va.: University of Virginia Press, 1975), pp. 361–63.

10. Interview with the author, Feb. 15, 1966, Tehran.

11. T. Cuyler Young, "U.S. Policy in Iran since World War II," paper presented at seminar, Problems of Contemporary Iran, Harvard University, Cambridge, Mass., Apr. 17, 1965, pp. 22–23. Although ignored by American decision makers, this paper was translated into Persian, and within days five thousand copies were circulated in Tehran.

12. Young, classroom lecture, Princeton University, February 1965.

13. "Text of the Declaration of Imam Khomeini," 4 Aban 1343/26 Oct. 1964, in Jalal Al-i Ahmad, *Dar Khidmat va Khiyanat-i Rushanfikran (In the Service and the Treachery of the Intellectuals)* (Tehran, n.d.), p. 13.

14. Personal copy in Persian. Translated by the author.

15. Personal copy of the declaration, Apr. 16, 1967, in Persian. Translated by the author.

16. Marvin Zonis, *The Political Elite of Iran* (Princeton, N.J.: Princeton University Press, 1971), p. 98.

17. U.S. Department of State, Bureau of Intelligence and Research, *Studies in Political Dynamics: Iran* 13 (December 1966), personal copy.

18. During a private interview in a tiny office in the Ministry of Information in late 1970, Nikkhah warned that unless Iran began to introduce basic political development there would be a massive "explosion." He had been released from prison earlier that year after he had recanted and admitted the error of his ways on Iranian national television (interview, Nov. 1, 1970, Tehran). Parviz Nikkhah was executed following the 1978–79 revolution.

19. For an excellent analysis of the origins and goals of these organizations, see Ervand Abrahamian, "The Guerrilla Movement in Iran, 1963–1977," *MERIP Reports* 86 (March–April 1980): 3–15.

20. Zuhrah Shaji'i, *Nimayandigan-i Majlis-i Shawra-yi Milli dar Bistuyik Dawrah-yi Qanunguzari (The Representatives of the National Consultative Assembly during the Twenty-One Legislative Periods)* (Tehran, 1344/1965), p. 238.

21. U.S. Embassy, Tehran, to Department of State, "Decision-making in Iran," July 22, 1976 *(Asnad, 7:121)*. *Asnad (Documents)* refers to the papers that were confiscated and published by the students who occupied the American embassy in Tehran in November 1979.

22. Ibid.

23. Interview with Hoveyda, Tehran, Aug. 4, 1970. This political portrait of Hoveyda is based on many hours of private discussions with him between May 1967 and June 1974.

24. Jabra I. Jabra, *Hunters in a Narrow Street* (London, 1960), as quoted in *A Middle East Reader*, ed. Irene L. Gendzier (New York: Pegasus, 1969), p. 114.

25. George W. Ball, *The Past Has Another Pattern: Memoirs* (New York: W. W. Norton, 1982), p. 435.

26. Most of the facts presented in this paragraph are drawn from Nessim Shallon, "Annual Report for 1970 for the Inter-Agency Consultative Board," United Nations Development Program, March 1971, mimeograph. For a rare early incisive critique of the shah's land reform program, see Hossein Mahdavy, "The Coming Crisis in Iran," *Foreign Affairs* 44 (October 1965): 134–46. A study analyzing the political strategy and predicting the political failure of the Pahlavi reform programs is James Alban Bill, *The Politics of Iran: Groups, Classes and Modernization* (Columbus, Ohio: Charles E. Merrill, 1972).

27. Department of State, *Studies in Political Dynamics: Iran*, p. 29.

28. W. Averell Harriman was originally selected to lead this delegation.

29. Memorandum, George Carroll to the Vice President, July 27, 1966, LBJ Library, EX FO 5, 6/30/66–8/31/66, Box 42. The information in the following paragraph is also taken from this revealing document.

30. The information in the above two paragraphs has been drawn from *Asnad*, 8:1–20. United States Embassy (Tehran) report, "The Current Reorientation of Iran's Military Procurement: A Summary Report of U.S. Efforts to Create a New Relationship," Aug. 6, 1966.

31. E. A. Bayne, *Persian Kingship in Transition* (New York: American Universities Field Staff, 1968), p. 215n.

32. Senator J. W. Fulbright to the President, Oct. 18, 1966, and Memorandum, W. W. Rostow to the President, Nov. 8, 1966, both in LBJ Library, Confidential File, FO 3–2 (January–March 1966), Box 48.

33. Memorandum, Robert S. McNamara to the President, Feb. 9, 1967, ibid.

34. John D. Stempel, *Inside the Iranian Revolution* (Bloomington, Ind.: Indiana University Press, 1981), p. 68.

35. Memorandum, Harold Saunders to Douglass Cater (special presidential assistant for Health, Education and Welfare), July 26, 1968, LBJ Library, GEN CO 122, Box 41.

36. Interviews with American diplomats, Tehran, Iran, 1966–67.

37. Memorandum, W. W. Rostow to the President, May 17, 1967, LBJ Library, Confidential File, CO 123, Box 9.

38. President Johnson to Ambassador Armin H. Meyer, June 27, 1968, LBJ Library, GEN CO 122, Box 41. The other quotations in the paragraph are taken from letters found in GEN CO 122 and 123, all in Box 41.

39. This letter and the related correspondence are found in LBJ Library, Confidential File, CO 123, Box 41.

40. Both letters are found in ibid.

41. Personal papers of T. Cuyler Young. Cuyler Young admitted that he was himself much to blame for the council's decision. His moderately critical views of the shah's rule, however, troubled the council. In his August 9, 1970, response to the rejection letter, Young emphasized that the fundamental differences lay in their opposing views on "the dictatorship": "I recognize that in this regard I am in a minority amongst most Americans concerned with recent Iranian affairs; but in the long view I still am of the opinion that this is the tough, gutty central problem of Iran in its modernizing efforts, and for this reason it is of central importance in longterm U.S.-Iranian relations."

42. For Johnson's special relationship with Israel, see the study by Lou Gomolak on Lyndon Johnson and the Middle East forthcoming from the University of Georgia Press.

43. David E. Lilienthal, *The Journals of David E. Lilienthal*, vol. 6: *Creativity and Conflict, 1964–1967* (New York: Harper and Row, 1973), p. 48.

44. Extensive lists of gifts are contained in records deposited in LBJ Library, GEN CO 122, Box 41.

45. Dr. Mihdi Bahar, *Miraskhar-i Isti'mar (The Heir of Colonialism)* (Tehran, 1344/1965). Translated by the author. The *Tehran-i Musavvar* articles appeared on 7, 21, and 28 Murdad and 4 and 11 Shahrivar, 1345/1966. Other information in this paragraph is based on interviews with Bahar, Nov. 29, Dec. 8, 1966. A physician, Bahar was a bright and hard-working researcher.

46. Habib [pseud.], "America, Iran and Development," *Bamshad*, 6–13 Azar 1345/1967, p. 42. In Persian. Translated by the author.

47. Memorandum, CAS to Chief, Political Section, "Recent Anti-American Statements of Allahyar Saleh," Dec. 6, 1966 (*Asnad*, 21, pt. 2:109–10).

48. Tunakabuni, *Yaddashtha-yi Shahr-i Shuluq (Memoirs of a Crowded City)*, p. 200. Translated by the author.

49. *Khabarnameh*, Shahrivar 1349/September 1970, as quoted in Hamid Algar, "The Oppositional Role of the Ulema in Twentieth Century Iran," in Nikki R. Keddie, ed., *Scholars, Saints, and Sufis* (Berkeley, Calif.: University of California Press, 1972), p. 251.

50. I was in Tehran at the time of Sa'idi's murder. The information concerning his death is taken from my field notes. The quotation is from "Martyr Ayatollah Sa'eidi: Remembered and Revered," *Message of Revolution* 19 (June–July 1983):

68. A detailed account of his life is provided in Ali Davani, *Nihzat-i Ruhaniyyun-i Iran (The Movement of the Iranian Clerics)* (Tehran, 1981), 5:309–23.

CHAPTER 6. IRAN, AMERICA, AND THE TRIUMPH OF REPRESSION, 1971–1977

1. *Time*, Oct. 25, 1971, p. 32.
2. This figure is a personal estimate based on an examination of various sources, including interviews with both Iranian and foreign participants. Under heavy criticism for the expenditures, Minister of Court Asadollah Alam called a press conference on October 24 and announced the celebration expenses at $16.8 million. *Time* put the figure at $100 million, "more or less." The shah described critics who alleged the celebration had cost $2 billion as "not of sound mind." In any case, he added, Iran "couldn't care less." *Kayhan International* (Tehran), Oct. 16, 1971, p. 1.
3. *Kayhan International* (Tehran), Oct. 16, 1971, p. 1.
4. Interview, *Le Monde*, carried in *Guardian/Le Monde*, English ed., Oct. 16, 1971.
5. *Iran Report*, Autumn 1971, p. 1, as quoted in Thomas M. Ricks, "Contemporary Iranian Political Economy and History," RIPEH 1 (December 1976): 48.
6. Interview, *Le Monde* Oct. 16, 1971.
7. Gérard de Villiers, *The Imperial Shah: An Informal Biography* (Boston: Little, Brown, 1976), p. 259.
8. Quotations from William J. Butler and Georges Levasseur, *Human Rights and the Legal System in Iran* (Geneva: International Commission of Jurists, 1976), p. 22, and the *Observer*, May 26, 1974. For sources that judiciously document the severity of secret police tactics in Iran at this time, see Amnesty International, *Annual Report, 1974–75* (London, 1975); House of Representatives Committee on International Relations, Subcommittee on International Organizations, *Human Rights in Iran* (Washington, D.C.: Government Printing Office, 1977); and Philip Jacobson, "Torture in Iran," *Sunday Times* (London), Jan. 19, 1975, p. 9. For a shocking, firsthand account of the details of SAVAK torture in Pahlavi prisons, see Reza Baraheni, *The Crowned Cannibals: Writings on Repression in Iran* (New York: Vintage Books, 1977).
9. Michael M. J. Fischer, *Iran: From Religious Dispute to Revolution* (Cambridge, Mass.: Harvard University Press, 1980), p. 120.
10. For a detailed discussion of this memorandum, see the excellent study by Shahrough Akhavi, *Religion and Politics in Contemporary Iran* (Albany, N.Y.: State University of New York Press, 1980), pp. 135–37.
11. After attending this lecture, which was delivered before an audience that I estimated to be 2,500 people, I spent three hours in private discussion with Shariati. In this discussion, Shariati, at the time hounded by SAVAK, strongly condemned the Iranian government for its blatant attempt to use Islam as a cloak of legitimacy for its repressive and irreligious rule.
12. For the standard account of Ghaffari's life, see Ali Davani, *Nihzat-i Ruhaniyyun-i Iran (The Movement of the Iranian Clerics)* (Tehran, 1981), 6:210–24.
13. Interview, Tehran, Sept. 4, 1970. Many studies of Shi'i Islam and the Iranian ulama have been published in recent years. Other than the Fischer and Akhavi volumes referred to above, four studies stand out above all others: Hamid Algar,

Religion and State in Iran, 1785–1906 (Berkeley and Los Angeles, Calif.: University of California Press, 1969); Hamid Enayat, *Modern Islamic Political Thought* (Austin, Tex.: University of Texas Press, 1982); Farhang Rajaee, *Islamic Values and World View: Khomeyni on Man, the State and International Politics* (Lanham, Md.: University Press of America, 1983); and Roy Mottahedeh, *The Mantle of the Prophet: Religion and Politics in Iran* (New York: Pantheon, 1986).

14. This is an estimate provided me at the time by the U.S. Embassy in Tehran.

15. Ervand Abrahamian, *Iran: Between Two Revolutions* (Princeton, N.J.: Princeton University Press, 1982), p. 480.

16. These data are drawn from two special reports prepared by the U.S. Air Force Office of Special Investigations in December 1975. Entitled "Terrorist Movements in Iran" and "Anti-American Terrorism in Iran," these documents provide detailed lists of all acts of anti-Americanism reported in Iran between 1970 and 1975. Personal copies of reports obtained through Freedom of Information Act.

17. Reza Baraheni, "The Death of the Poet," in *God's Shadow: Prison Poems* (Bloomington, Ind.: Indiana University Press, 1976), p. 42.

18. Conversation with taxi driver, Tehran, June 28, 1974.

19. Mohammad Reza Pahlavi, *Mission for My Country* (New York: McGraw-Hill, 1961), p. 45.

20. See W. Howard Wriggins, *The Ruler's Imperative: Strategies for Political Survival in Asia and Africa* (New York: Columbia University Press, 1969).

21. E. A. Bayne, *Persian Kingship in Transition* (New York: American Universities Field Staff, 1968), p. 139.

22. Ibid., p. 186.

23. *Kayhan International* (Tehran), Mar. 3, 1975, p. 2.

24. Ibid., Oct. 19, 1971, p. 8.

25. *Newsweek*, Aug. 23, 1976, p. 52.

26. Senate Committee on Foreign Relations, Subcommittee on Foreign Assistance, Staff Report, *U.S. Military Sales to Iran* (Washington, D.C.: Government Printing Office, 1976), pp. viii–ix.

27. Memorandum, Henry A. Kissinger to the Secretary of State and Secretary of Defense, "Follow-up on the President's Talk with the Shah of Iran," July 25, 1972 (*Asnad*, 8:44).

28. Ibid., p. 45.

29. Senate Committee on Foreign Relations, Subcommittee on Multinational Corporations, *Multinational Corporations and United States Foreign Policy: Grumman Sale of F-14s to Iran*, 94th Cong., 2d Sess., Aug. 9, Sept. 10, 13, 15, 27, 1976, pp. 176–79.

30. Barry Rubin, *Paved with Good Intentions: The American Experience and Iran* (New York: Oxford University Press, 1980), p. 261.

31. Senate Committee on Foreign Relations, *U.S. Military Sales*, and *Christian Science Monitor*, Jan. 20, 1978, p. 5.

32. Senate Committee on Foreign Relations, *U.S. Military Sales*, pp. viii–x.

33. Senate Committee on Foreign Relations, *Multinational Corporations*, p. 191.

34. Senate Committee on Foreign Relations, Subcommittee on Foreign Assistance, *U.S. Arms Sale Policy*, 94th Cong., 2d Sess., Sept. 16, 21, 24, 1976, p. 13.

35. Henry Kissinger, *White House Years* (Boston: Little, Brown, 1979), p. 1261.

36. As quoted by Jim Hoaglund, "Thousands of Kurds Flee following Revolt's Collapse," *Washington Post*, Mar. 24, 1975, p. A7. Hoaglund was an eyewitness to

the flight of the Kurds, and his articles disturbed Kissinger and State Department officials, who referred to them in their diplomatic correspondence.

37. This report became known as the Pike Report for the committee chair, Rep. Otis G. Pike of New York. Although never formally released to the public, the report was reprinted in large sections by a number of leading American newspapers. See, for example, *New York Times*, Jan. 26, 1976, pp. 1, 14. The *Village Voice* carried the reports in a 24-page special supplement in its Feb. 16, 1976, issue. Both quotations are from p. 71 of this supplement.

38. As quoted in William Safire, "Son of 'Secret Sellout,'" *New York Times*, Feb. 12, 1976, p. 31.

39. William Safire, "Mr. Ford's Secret Sellout," *New York Times*, Feb. 5, 1976, p. 31. Almost alone, Safire kept the plight of the Kurds before the American public. His columns analyzing the Kissinger-Nixon-Ford use of the Kurds appeared on Feb. 5, 12, Dec. 13, 1976, Dec. 19, 1977, Mar. 12, 1979, and Oct. 20, 1979. See Safire, *Safire's Washington* (New York: Times Books, 1980), pp. 82–88, 330–36.

40. As quoted in Edmund Ghareeb, *The Kurdish Question in Iraq* (Syracuse, N.Y.: Syracuse University Press, 1981), p. 140. Another excellent source explaining this episode is Ismet Sheriff Vanly's article in Gerard Chaliand, ed., *People without a Country: The Kurds and Kurdistan* (London: Zed Press, 1980), pp. 153–210.

41. Kissinger, *White House Years*, p. 1265. On this page, Kissinger promises to explain the White House decisions concerning the Kurds "in a second volume." In fact, he fails to mention the Kurds in his 1,283-page second volume, *Years of Upheaval*.

42. As quoted in *Washington Star*, Apr. 18, 1978. This article on Barzani was inserted in the May 8, 1978, issue of the *Congressional Record*, vol. 124, pt. 10, pp. 12890–91, by Sen. William Proxmire.

43. *Austin American-Statesman*, Aug. 7, 1976, p. E22.

44. Kissinger, *White House Years*, p. 1265.

45. For information on these contractors and their activities in Iran, see Senate Committee on Foreign Relations, *U.S. Military Sales*, p. 59; *Middle East Economic Digest*, Feb. 7, 1975, pp. 8, 26–27; and the investigative articles in *New York Times*, Feb. 20, Apr. 14, 1975.

46. AmEmbassy (Tehran) to Department of State, "Corruption in Iran—A Problem for American Companies," June 20, 1972, Annex E (*Asnad*, 17:70).

47. *New York Times*, Feb. 11, 1976, p. 66. For an early balanced study of Grumman's international activities, see Louis Kraar, "Grumman Still Flies for the Navy, but It Is Selling the World," *Fortune*, February 1976, pp. 78–83, 142, 144, 146.

48. *New York Times*, Feb. 15, 1976.

49. Senate Committee on Foreign Relations, *U.S. Military Sales*, p. 48.

50. Rubin, *Paved with Good Intentions*, p. 165.

51. Kermit Roosevelt, *Countercoup: The Struggle for the Control of Iran* (New York: McGraw-Hill, 1979), p. 173.

52. Carl T. Rowan's disappointing "Our Crisis in Iran" was aired on Oct. 29, 1978. I attended a special premier viewing of this film at the Washington-Hilton Hotel on the evening of October 27. Although the revolution was then in progress, this showing, attended by several hundred members of the Iranian and American elites, had an unreal festive air about it.

53. These data have been compiled by AT&T. I wish to thank Fred Weismuller and Frank Mullen especially for their assistance. The statistics refer only to outgo-

ing traffic and not to calls originating from Iran. The actual volume of telephone messages would in fact be slightly more than twice the numbers presented here.

54. *Department of State Bulletin*, Nov. 10, 1969, pp. 397–98.

55. For these quotations, see Robert Sam Anson, *Exile: The Unquiet Oblivion of Richard M. Nixon* (New York: Simon and Schuster, 1984), pp. 210–11, 224–25.

56. Discussion with General Fish, Washington, D.C., Oct. 5, 1977. In November 1977, Fish was reportedly removed from his position after a disclosure that the administration had underestimated arms sales for the fiscal year 1977 by $1.4 billion. See *New York Times*, Nov. 24, 1977, p. 32.

57. Embassy of Iran (Washington), *Persian Panorama* 1 (Winter 1974): 40.

58. Interview, Tehran, May 27, 1974.

59. Interview, U.S. Embassy, Tehran, June 30, 1974.

60. Ibid.

61. U.S. Department of State, Bureau of Intelligence and Research, "Iranian Outlook," May 4, 1976, Report no. 411. Personal copy of report obtained through Freedom of Information Act.

CHAPTER 7. AMERICA AND THE IRANIAN REVOLUTION, 1977–1979

1. Robert Graham, "Economic Policy under the Shah," in Gunther Estes and Jochem Langdau, eds., *Iran in der Krise* (Bonn: Verlag Neue Gesellschaft, 1980), p. 145. For Graham's thoughtful in-depth analysis of the economic backdrop to the revolution, see his *Iran: The Illusion of Power* (New York: St. Martin's Press, 1978).

2. As reported by Parviz C. Radji, *In the Service of the Peacock Throne* (London: Hamish Hamilton, 1983), p. 208.

3. Comments by Walter Levy at Aspen Institute/Persepolis Symposium, Persepolis, Sept. 15–19, 1975; personal notes of Levy commentary.

4. From personal copy of Hoveyda's budgetary presentation for the year 2536 (Mar. 21, 1977–Mar. 20, 1978).

5. Personal interview, Isfahan, Oct. 12, 1977.

6. Ambassador William Sullivan to Secretary of State Vance, "Straws in the Wind: Intellectual and Religious Opposition in Iran," July 25, 1977 (*Asnad*, 8:174–81).

7. Barry Rubin, *Paved with Good Intentions: The American Experience and Iran* (New York: Oxford University Press, 1980), p. 193. In fact, in a June 1, 1978, airgram, "Iran in 1977–78: The Internal Scene," U.S. diplomats flatly stated that "the Shah's basic commitment to liberalization made its appearance in mid-1976." (*Asnad*, 12, no. 2:116).

8. Interview, Tehran, June 30, 1974.

9. Samuel P. Huntington, *Political Order in Changing Societies* (New Haven and London: Yale University Press, 1968), p. 137. In his book, Huntington is particularly impressed by "modernizing monarchs" (pp. 101, 153–57) and "revolutionary emperors" (p. 158).

10. Memorandum, William J. Butler to International Commission of Jurists on "Private Audience with the Shah of Iran on May 30, 1970," June 17, 1977, and Aide Memoire, Butler to Prime Minister Amir Abbas Hoveyda on "Summary of Discussions between His Imperial Majesty the Shahanshah Aryamehr and William J. Butler at Shiraz on May 2, 1978," June 8, 1978. Copies courtesy of William J. Butler.

11. Mohammed Reza Pahlavi, *Answer to History* (New York: Stein and Day, 1980), p. 150.

12. Jerrold D. Green, *Revolution in Iran: The Politics of Countermobilization* (New York: Praeger, 1982), p. 60.

13. Interview, Tehran, Oct. 10, 1977.

14. The information and quotations in this paragraph are drawn from the Iranian press.

15. *Kayhan International* (Tehran), Jan. 29, 1977, p. 1.

16. Homa Katouzian, *The Political Economy of Modern Iran: Despotism and Pseudo-Modernism, 1926–1979* (New York: New York University Press, 1981).

17. Interview with William J. Butler, New York, Oct. 8, 1986.

18. Cyrus Vance, *Hard Choices: Critical Years in America's Foreign Policy* (New York: Simon and Schuster, 1983), p. 317.

19. This important point is made forcefully by John Stempel, who was then an influential political officer in the embassy in Tehran. See John D. Stempel, *Inside the Iranian Revolution* (Bloomington, Ind.: Indiana University Press, 1981), p. 79.

20. Interview with U.S. Embassy official in Tehran, Oct. 11, 1977.

21. As observed in Tehran, Oct. 9–12, 1977.

22. Vance, *Hard Choices*, p. 319.

23. Senate Committee on Foreign Relations, Subcommittee on Foreign Assistance, *Sale of AWACS to Iran*, 95th Cong., 1st Sess., July 18, 22, 25, 27, Sept. 19, 1977, pp. 3–5.

24. Ibid., p. 7.

25. Interview, Washington, D.C., Oct. 5, 1977.

26. Vance, *Hard Choices*, p. 320.

27. Rouhollah K. Ramazani, *The United States and Iran: The Patterns of Influence* (New York: Praeger, 1982), p. 49. This valuable little book presents an informed and incisive summary of U.S.-Iranian relations.

28. Senate Committee on Foreign Relations, *Sale of AWACS to Iran*, p. 86.

29. Ibid., p. 5.

30. Jimmy Carter, *Keeping Faith: Memoirs of a President* (New York: Bantam Books, 1982), p. 434.

31. Hamilton Jordan, *Crisis: The Last Year of the Carter Presidency* (New York: G. P. Putnam's Sons, 1982), pp. 88, 89.

32. Carter, *Keeping Faith*, p. 437.

33. Vance, *Hard Choices*, p. 321.

34. Interview with Charles Naas, Washington, D.C., May 20, 1986.

35. Ahmad Rashidi-Mutlaq [pseud.], "Iran va Isti'mar-i Surkh va Siah" ("Iran and Red and Black Colonialism"), in *Ittili'at*, 17 Day 2536 (January 7, 1978), p. 7.

36. Speech, Ayatollah Khomeini, Najaf Feb. 19, 1978, forty days after the demonstrations and deaths in Qum on Jan. 8, 1978, as translated by Hamid Algar, ed., *Islam and Revolution: Writings and Declarations of Imam Khomeini* (Berkeley, Calif.: Mizan Press, 1981), p. 224.

37. For examples of those who name Homayoun as the author, see Stempel, *Inside the Iranian Revolution*, p. 90, and Rubin, *Paved with Good Intentions*, p. 206.

38. An analysis of monies distributed to families of martyrs by the Foundation of Martyrs (Bunyad-i Shahid) indicates that 1,500 Tehran families received aid. According to our estimates, this number represents approximately 60% of those who were killed in Tehran during the overthrow of the shah in 1978–79. The 2,500 Tehran deaths are estimated at 23% of those killed throughout Iran during the period. This percentage is based on a detailed examination of 577 documented

cases of individuals killed during the revolution. Of this number, 135, or 23%, died in Tehran. According to this method of calculation, 10,870 persons throughout Iran died violent deaths in resisting the shah's government in 1978–79. For the data referring to funds distributed by the Foundation of Martyrs, see *Jumhuri-yi Islami*, 21 Bahman 1359/10 Feb. 1981, p. 12. For the lists and brief biographies of those killed during the revolutionary upheaval, see Organization of Islamic Services, *Lalahha-yi Inqilab: Yadnamah Shuhada (The Tulips of the Revolution: Remembrance of the Martyrs)*, which was published in Persian in 1980. The tedious calculations were carried out by Ahmad Farokhpay, who suggested this manner of determining the death toll.

39. Anthony Parsons, *The Pride and the Fall: Iran, 1974–1979* (London: Jonathan Cape, 1984), p. 150.

40. "Iran in 1977–78: The Internal Scene," June 1, 1978 (*Asnad*, 12, no. 2:121).

41. Sayyid Hamid Ruhani, *Barrasi va Tahlili az Nizhat-i Imam Khomeini dar Iran (A Review and Analysis of the Movement of Imam Khomeini in Iran)* (Tehran, 1361/1982), pp. 42–49. This source lists the names of 189 leading religious figures educated and trained by Khomeini. The list is headed by Ayatollah Hussein Ali Montazeri. This valuable source was called to my attention by William Royce.

42. The quotations in this paragraph are drawn from Khomeini's speeches delivered on Feb. 19, Aug. 21, and Sept. 6, 1978. See Algar, ed., *Islam and Revolution*, pp. 225, 232, 235.

43. Fereydoun Hoveyda, *The Fall of the Shah* (New York: Wyndham Books, 1979), p. 49.

44. Interview, Tehran, Nov. 29, 1978.

45. Rubin, *Paved with Good Intentions*, p. 210.

46. William H. Sullivan, *Mission to Iran* (New York: W. W. Norton, 1981), p. 164. In the next sentence, Sullivan repeats the strange American myth that he "enjoyed a reputation for Islamic piety."

47. Zbigniew Brzezinski, *Power and Principle: Memoirs of the National Security Advisor, 1977–1981* (New York: Farrar, Straus, and Giroux, 1983); Gary Sick, *All Fall Down: America's Tragic Encounter with Iran* (New York: Random House, 1985); Jimmy Carter, *Keeping Faith;* Rosalynn Carter, *First Lady from Plains* (Boston: Houghton Mifflin, 1984); Hamilton Jordan, *Crisis;* Sullivan, *Mission to Iran;* and John Stempel, *Inside the Iranian Revolution.* For a rare example of an official who frankly admits his failure of understanding in Iran and who refuses to engage in apologetics, see Parsons, *The Pride and the Fall.*

48. Scott Armstrong, "Carter Held Hope Even after Shah Had Lost His," *Washington Post,* Oct. 25, 1980, p. A12.

49. Personal copy of paper delivered at U.S. Department of State, Mar. 10, 1978.

50. Personal copy of paper delivered at U.S. Department of State, Oct. 27, 1978.

51. Comments of State Department official who participated in briefing Ambassador Sullivan, Washington, D.C., May 19, 1977.

52. Stempel, *Inside the Iranian Revolution,* p. 79.

53. Personal copy of Sullivan letter of December 11, 1977, to William J. Butler. Butler points out that his missions to Iran were carried out solely at ICJ's initiative and not at the suggestion of the U.S. government (interview, New York, Oct. 8, 1986).

54. W. Sullivan to Secretary of State Vance, "Inspection Memorandum," May 4, 1978 (*Asnad*, 1–6:545). Sullivan openly admits his failure to see the revolution

coming. In his own words in a communication of Apr. 8, 1986, to the author, he writes: "As you are aware, I have never claimed prescience about the shah's downfall and have always used my November 9 cable as the date of my own epiphany."

55. Statement at Foreign Service Institute conference, "Revolution in Iran," Washington, D.C., Nov. 12, 1985.

56. George W. Ball, *The Past Has Another Pattern: Memoirs* (New York: W. W. Norton, 1982), pp. 457–58.

57. The words of Hodding Carter III, "Life inside the Carter State Department—Memoir," *Playboy*, February 1981, p. 214. Carter served as press secretary for Secretary of State Vance.

58. Scott Armstrong recounts the Aaron-Precht exchange in the *Washington Post*, Oct. 28, 1980, p. A10. Sick's opinion is recalled by Stephen Cohen in two personal communications. The particulars of the trip and meeting have also been checked in personal interviews with Carl Clement in Washington, D.C., on May 21, 1986, and with Henry Precht in Austin, Tex., on Nov. 2, 1986.

59. Brzezinski, *Power and Principle*, p. 363.

60. Ibid., p. 393.

61. Henry Precht to Ambassador William Sullivan, Dec. 19, 1978 (*Asnad*, 13:17–18).

62. Interview with George Ball, Princeton, N.J., Dec. 5, 1986. I have also had the opportunity to read Ball's memorandum.

63. The information in this paragraph is drawn from my Dec. 5, 1986, interview with Ball.

64. Brzezinski, *Power and Principle*, pp. 370–71.

65. Ball, *The Past Has Another Pattern*, p. 461.

66. Robert E. Huyser, *Mission to Tehran* (New York: Harper and Row, 1986), p. 7.

67. House of Representatives Committee on Foreign Affairs, Subcommittee on Europe and the Middle East, *General Huyser's Mission to Iran, January 1979*, 97th Cong., 1st Sess., June 9, 1981, p. 2. Important details of the Huyser mission are made available in this hearing.

68. Huyser, *Mission to Tehran*, p. 88.

69. See ibid., pp. 12, 74. Huyser is not altogether consistent on this point. In one instance, he admits that Khomeini "had a good portion of the masses on his side" (p. 259). He also writes that "the vocal masses were certainly for him [Khomeini], though the solid majority might be against" (p. 268).

70. Ibid., p. 116.

71. Ibid., p. 267. For a similar statement by Huyser, see p. 98. For the military leaders' preoccupation with the communist threat, which they saw as the driving force of the revolution, see pp. 29, 34, 36, 39, 46–50, 83, 92, 112, 116, and 145. Huyser's less extreme views on the same subject are provided on pp. 221, 235, 274, and 291–92.

72. Sullivan, *Mission to Iran*, p. 230.

73. Huyser himself repeatedly emphasizes the lack of planning among the Iranian military leaders, who were disorganized and unprepared to mount any kind of coup attempt. See Huyser, *Mission to Tehran*, pp. 69, 79, 93, 103, 105, 132, 156. At one point, Huyser goes so far as to state that "Iran's military leadership was in a totally helpless state" (p. 69).

74. Interview with Charles Naas, Washington, D.C., May 20, 1986.

75. Huyser, *Mission to Tehran*, p. 289.

76. Information provided by Gregory F. Rose, who was in Iran at the time. Also, conversation with Rear Admirals Paddock, Lyons, and Collins, Pentagon, Washington, D.C., Sept. 4, 1979.

77. The information presented in this paragraph is drawn partially from General Abbas Qarabaghi, *Haqayaq Darbarah-yi Inqilab-i Iran (Facts About the Iranian Revolution)* as reprinted in *Iran Times*, Apr. 18, 1986, pp. 11–12. In Persian. This book is filled with important data about the Iranian military and the revolution. It was published in 1984 by Suhayl Publications in Paris. In English, see Gholam R. Afkhami, *The Iranian Revolution: Thanatos on a National Scale* (Washington, D.C.: Middle East Institute, 1985), chap. 4. Afkhami relies heavily on Qarabaghi in this chapter, which is easily the best part of his book.

General Huyser disagrees with these assessments, estimating that defectors numbered not 1,000 a day but "more like a hundred a a day" or "probably 100 to 200" daily (*Mission to Tehran*, pp. 105, 160).

78. Ibrahim Yazdi, *Barrasi-yi Safar-i Ha'izir Bi-Iran (An Examination of Huyser's Trip to Iran)* (n.p., 1361/1983), p. 28.

79. See House of Representatives Committee on Foreign Affairs, *General Huyser's Mission*, pp. 15–16.

80. The observation of Hedley Donovan, presented in "The Enigmatic President," *Time*, May 6, 1985, p. 26.

81. The words of Hodding Carter III in "Life inside the Carter State Department," p. 214.

82. Ambassador William Sullivan to Secretary of State Vance, Report of February 6, 1986, Conversation of Iranian Professional with U.S. Embassy Political Officer David Patterson, Feb. 8, 1979. Personal copy of document.

83. See, for example, Huyser, *Mission to Tehran*, pp. 74, 89, 102, 113, 134, 141.

84. House of Representatives, Permanent Select Committee on Intelligence, Subcommittee on Evaluation, Staff Report, *Iran: Evaluation of U.S. Intelligence Performance Prior to November 1978* (Washington, D.C.: Government Printing Office, 1979), p. 6.

85. Ibid.

86. A record of President's Carter's statements about Iran during the Fall of 1978 is contained in the February 1979 issue of *Afro-Asian Affairs*. The exchange with Helen Thomas was viewed on CBS News Special Report, "Showdown in Iran," January 23, 1979, narrated by Walter Cronkite.

87. Sullivan, *Mission to Iran*, pp. 193–94.

88. Brzezinski, *Power and Principle*, p. 378.

89. Scott Armstrong, *Washington Post*, Oct. 25, 1980, p. A12.

CHAPTER 8. THE ISLAMIC REPUBLIC AND AMERICA: RUPTURED RELATIONS AND A VENTURE IN RAPPROCHEMENT

1. *Iran Times*, Feb. 28, 1986, p. 15.

2. These data were compiled by the author from lists published in the Persian press after the revolution.

3. For an excellent historical account of the Bakhtiari tribe, see Gene R. Garthwaite, *Khans and Shahs: A Documentary Analysis of the Bakhtiyari in Iran* (Cambridge: Cambridge University Press, 1983).

4. These quotations are drawn from *Asnad*, 20, pt. 1. The two CIA profiles are published on pp. 73–74 and 94–96.

5. Ibid., p. 74.

6. Shaul Bakhash, *The Reign of the Ayatollahs: Iran and the Islamic Revolution* (New York: Basic Books, 1984), p. 144. This is an excellent, objective, well-documented account of the first two years of the Islamic Republic of Iran. It is an indispensable source.

7. Crane Brinton, *The Anatomy of Revolution*, rev. ed. (New York: Vintage Books, 1965), p. 123.

8. Ibid., p. 145.

9. *Iran Times*, Oct. 1, 1982, p. 1.

10. For a superb analysis of the concept of leadership in Shi'i Islam, see Murtiza Mutahhari's article in Mutahhari, *Bakhsh-i Darbarah-yi Marja'iyyat va Ruhaniyyat (Discussions concerning Supreme Religious Leadership and Islamic Clericalism)* (Tehran, 1341/1963), pp. 165–98.

11. *Tehran Times*, Feb. 10, 1982, p. 6.

12. Ibid., Sept. 19, 1982, p. 1. Although the term, *mustaza'fin*, has come to refer to most supporters of Khomeini and the Islamic Republic regardless of class, it most specifically and basically refers to the economically deprived, the lower classes.

13. *Tehran Times*, July 26, 1982, p. 1.

14. Henry Precht, Director of Office of Iranian Affairs, to L. Bruce Laingen, Chargé d'Affaires a.i., American Embassy, Tehran, July 20, 1979 (*Asnad*, 15:127). Mailed "Official-Informal Confidential."

15. Robert Moss, "Who's Meddling in Iran? The Telltale Signs of Soviet Handiwork," *New Republic*, Dec. 2, 1978, pp. 15–18.

16. Michael Ledeen and William Lewis, *Debacle: American Failure in Iran* (New York: Alfred A. Knopf, 1981), p. 117. This book, rushed into print and filled with unsubstantiated assertions, is thoroughly unreliable. In the introduction, the authors admit that "there are not many notes in the text" since much of the material came from "individuals who requested, and were promised, anonymity." The book is filled with numerous factual errors, raising serious questions about the reliabili- of the controversial interpretations that abound in the study.

17. Interview with Henry Precht, Austin, Tex., Nov. 2, 1986. The information in this paragraph has been confirmed by Precht.

18. *Newsweek* (international ed.), Feb. 12, 1979, p. 52. This view was strongly shared by the Iranian moderates. Deputy Prime Minister Amir Entezam, for example, flatly stated in August 1979 that "Khomeini is a good man who does not believe in 'Akhoundism'" (*Asnad*, 10:53 [pages in vol. 10 numbered from left to right by writer]).

19. The words of Henry Precht, interview with the author, Austin, Tex., Nov. 2, 1986.

20. J. Graves to USICA Washington, "A Major Public Affairs Concern," Sept. 4, 1979 (*Asnad*, 16:65).

21. Interview with John D. Stempel, Washington, D.C., Sept. 2, 1980.

22. Interviews with Carl Clement, Washington, D.C., Nov. 12, 1985, May 21, 1986.

23. Interview with Charles Naas, Washington, D.C., May 20, 1986.

24. Harold H. Saunders to Secretary of State Cyrus Vance, "Policy towards Iran," Sept. 5, 1979 (*Asnad*, 16:72).

25. L. Bruce Laingen to Secretary of State, "Iran: Policy Overview," Aug. 20, 1979 (*Asnad*, 16:48).

26. These accusations and others like them are contained in *Asnad*, 10:25, 34–35, 41. The criticisms were made by Amir Entezam in Stockholm and Tehran during discussions he had with American officials.

27. Interview with Ibrahim Yazdi, Houston, Tex., June 1, 1986. In these discussions, Yazdi was clearly astounded by the proposition that the United States had in any way supported the moderates in Iran.

28. For the names and dates of those executed (in Persian), see *Iran Times*, May 11, 1979.

29. For a complete text of the resolution and the quotations taken from the Senate discussions supporting the resolution, see U.S. Congress, *Congressional Record*, Proceedings and Debates of 96th Cong., 1st Sess., May 10–17, 1979, pp. 11674–76.

30. Interview with Charles Naas, Washington, D.C., May 20, 1986.

31. Conversations with James Hitselberger, who was in Mashhad at the time, Austin, Tex., May 1986. For his published account of the situation in Mashhad, see J. Hitselberger, "Another Look at Mashhad, Iran: A Return Visit from April to June 1979," *Review of Iranian Political Economy and History (RIPEH)* 3 (Fall 1979): 123–147.

32. Remarks at conference, "Revolution in Iran," Department of State, Foreign Service Institute, Washington, D.C., Nov. 12, 1985.

33. B. Laingen to Secretary of State, "The Shah in the U.S.," Oct. 28, 1979 (*Asnad*, 7:290).

34. Colonel Thomas E. Schaefer to USDAO Tehran Personnel, "Visa Referrals," Sept. 18, 1979 (*Asnad*, 1–6:121).

35. The information in this and the following four paragraphs is drawn from *Asnad*, vol. 9. The eleven documents published in this volume provide the detailed evidence of the Bani Sadr (SDLure/1) plan. For another reconstruction of this event, see Scott Armstrong, "CIA Tried to Recruit Bani Sadr, Confiscated Documents Reveal," *Austin American-Statesman*, Jan. 31, 1982, p. 1. This story had first appeared in the *Washington Post*. Another source that provides additional information about this extraordinary event is Christos P. Ioannides, *America's Iran: Injury and Catharsis* (Lanham, Md.: University Press of America, 1984), pp. 64–66.

36. Wilbur Crane Eveland, *Ropes of Sand: America's Failure in the Middle East* (London and New York: W. W. Norton, 1980), p. 143. Cassin's intelligence career in Syria is discussed in some detail in this source.

37. Document of July 24, 1979 (*Asnad*, 9:68).

38. Document of Sept. 9, 1979 (ibid., p. 51).

39. Students' introduction in Persian (ibid., p. 7).

40. Armstrong, "CIA Tried to Recruit Bani-Sadr."

41. As quoted in Ioannides, *America's Iran*, p. 66. This is the same Mansouri who was arrested, tried, and jailed for complicity in the Marble Palace assassination plot of April 1965. This attempt on the life of the shah is described in chap. 5.

42. Students' introduction in Persian (*Asnad*, 9:4).

43. Memorandum of Conversation, John D. Stempel, May 8, 1978 (ibid., 24:3). This volume of the U.S. Embassy documents contains detailed memoranda of the

various meetings embassy officials had with leading members of the LM throughout 1978.

44. Ibid., p. 5.

45. Memorandum of Conversation, John D. Stempel, Sept. 25, 1978 (*Asnad*, 24:29).

46. L. Bruce Laingen to Secretary of State, "SRF Assignments," Aug. 9, 1979 (*Asnad*, 1–6:111). Secret cable through "Roger Channel."

47. L. Bruce Laingen to Rodney Kennedy-Minott, American Ambassador to Sweden, July 10, 1979 (*Asnad*, 10:69). "Confidential-Official-Informal" letter.

48. Secretary of State Vance to American Embassy Tehran, "Exchange of Information with PGOI," Aug. 8, 1979 (*Asnad*, 10:60). Secret cable, special encryption through "Roger Channel." This important document summarizes the results of the Stempel-Cave meetings with Amir Entezam and is worth reading in its entirety.

49. Harold H. Saunders to Secretary of State Vance, "Policy towards Iran," Sept. 5, 1979 (*Asnad*, 16:75).

50. L. Bruce Laingen to Secretary of State Vance, "Briefing of Yazdi and Entezam," Oct. 18, 1979 (*Asnad*, 10:28). This important document is Laingen's summary of the Oct. 15 briefing given to the Iranians by George Cave and Ron Smith. Other intelligence documents summarizing this meeting are reprinted on pp. 17–21.

51. Interview with Ibrahim Yazdi, Houston, Tex., June 1, 1986.

52. Both quotations are from "Adlesick" [George Cave] to Director, Oct. 18, 1979 (*Asnad*, 10:18).

53. Interview with Ibrahim Yazdi, Houston, Tex., June 1, 1986.

54. "Jaumotte" to Director, October 1979 (*Asnad*, 10:7).

55. As quoted in Terence Smith, "Why Carter Admitted the Shah," *New York Times Magazine*, May 17, 1981, pp. 36–37. A detailed analysis of the politics involved in the admission of the shah to the United States is presented in chap. 10.

56. Zbigniew Brzezinski, *Power and Principle* (New York: Farrar, Straus, and Giroux, 1983), p. 475.

57. Interview with Ibrahim Yazdi, Houston, Tex., June 1, 1986.

58. Cyrus Vance, *Hard Choices* (New York: Simon and Schuster, 1983), p. 373.

59. Gary Sick, *All Fall Down* (New York: Random House, 1985), p. 189. Sick later muddies the waters somewhat by writing: "When the Iranians arrived in Algiers, they suggested a private meeting and Brzezinski agreed" (p. 189). The key word in this sentence would seem to be "private."

60. John D. Stempel, *Inside the Iranian Revolution* (Bloomington, Ind.: Indiana University Press, 1981), p. 306. Henry Precht also favors this interpretation (interview, Austin, Tex., Nov. 2, 1986).

61. An excellent, reliable overall source written by senior foreign policy advisers themselves is Warren Christopher et al., *American Hostages in Iran: The Conduct of a Crisis* (New Haven and London: Yale University Press, 1985). Among the many books written by the hostages themselves, two are worthy of special attention: Barbara and Barry Rosen (with George Feifer), *The Destined Hour* (Garden City, N.Y.: Doubleday, 1982), and Charles W. Scott, *Pieces of the Game* (Atlanta, Ga.: Peachtree Publishers, 1984). Both Barry Rosen and Charles Scott spoke Persian and had a special interest in Iranian history and culture. As such, they are especially keen observers and commentators. For a detailed chronology of the hostage episode, see Congressional Research Service, Library of Congress, Report

Prepared for Committee on Foreign Relations, U.S. House of Representatives, *The Iran Hostage Crisis: A Chronology of Daily Developments*, 97th Cong., 1st Sess. (Washington, D.C.: Government Printing Office, 1981).

For an important, interesting assessment of the hostage incident from the point of view of international law supporting the Iranian position, see Francis Anthony Boyle, *World Politics and International Law* (Durham, N.C.: Duke University Press, 1985), esp. pp. 183–92. Boyle, a rather lonely voice on this issue, postulates that "a fairly compelling argument could be made that the seizure and detention of the American diplomats was a legitimate exercise of Iran's right of self-defense under article 51 of the U.N. Charter." Boyle cites "the doctrine of anticipatory self-defense" in support of this position: "Yet viewed from the Iranian perspective, the American diplomats were justifiably seized and detained in order to forestall another decisive and perhaps fatal coup d'etat sponsored by the United States government operating in explicit violation of international law" (p. 189).

62. See Ioannides, *America's Iran*, pp. 114–16. This is a very valuable source; the author had considerable firsthand knowledge of the hostage incident, covering the event in Tehran for the Greek newspaper *Mesimvrini*. While there, he had the unique opportunity to become personally acquainted with a number of the student leaders involved in the seizure. This volume contains a transcript of some of the interviews Ioannides had with the student militants (pp. 217–40). See also Scott, *Pieces of the Game*, pp. 21, 53, 153.

63. Ioannides, *America's Iran*, p. 129.

64. The 1978 Stempel-Kazankin meetings in Tehran took place on Jan. 1, 9, Feb. 5, Mar. 19, May 16, July 18, Sept. 11, and Nov. 13. The two may also have met on July 27 and Oct. 2. The information contained in this paragraph and the following two paragraphs is largely drawn from memoranda of conversation written by John Stempel and reproduced in *Asnad*, 48:65–81.

65. Paul B. Ryan, *The Iranian Rescue Mission: Why It Failed* (Annapolis, Md.: Naval Institute Press, 1985), p. 105.

66. Although the entire story of the rescue mission remains to be told and many sources remain classified, the following sources provide enough detail for informed judgment. An important first source is the 78-page sanitized study prepared by the Special Operations Review Group, headed by Adm. J. L. Holloway III, entitled "Rescue Mission Report" and published in April 1980. This report clearly softens criticism; nonetheless, it lists twenty-three areas of misjudgment or error. A more hard-hitting and comprehensive study is Paul Ryan's *Iranian Rescue Mission*. See also Charlie A. Beckwith and Donald Knox, *Delta Force* (New York: Harcourt Brace Jovanovich, 1983), and the valuable articles in *Aviation Week and Space Technology*, May 5, 12, 1980.

67. As quoted in Ryan, *Iranian Rescue Mission*, p. 60.

68. *Washington Post*, May 4, 1980, p. A30.

69. As quoted in Ryan, *Iranian Rescue Mission*, p. 127.

70. Rosen and Rosen, *Destined Hour*, p. 311.

71. As quoted in Terence Smith, "Putting Hostages' Lives First," *New York Times Magazine*, May 17, 1981, p. 101.

72. Letter to the author, May 22, 1982.

73. These and other useful statistics on the Iranian army and military offensives are contained in William F. Hickman's useful monograph *Ravaged and Reborn: The Iranian Army, 1982* (Washington, D.C.: Brookings Institution, 1982).

74. See Gholam H. Razi, "The Effectiveness of Resort to Military Force: The Case of Iran and Iraq," *Conflict Quarterly* (Summer 1985):50. This excellent piece of scholarship destroys a number of prevalent myths about the Iran-Iraq war. Razi argues, for example, that observers too easily stress the ancient history of animosity between Iran and Iraq when in fact these two countries have had long periods of cooperation. Razi also makes the important point that the two countries have important cultural and religious affinities. Another rare and important source on the war is Robert C. Johansen and Michael G. Renner, "Limiting Conflict in the Gulf," *Third World Quarterly* (October 1985): 803–38.

75. These conclusions are based on a fact-finding trip I made to the Islamic Republic of Iran in August 1988.

76. John Tower, Edmund Muskie, and Brent Scowcroft, *The Tower Commission Report* (New York: Bantam Books/Times Books, 1987); hereafter referred to as *Tower Commission Report*. Michael Ledeen was a consultant to the NSC from November 1984 to December 1986. Ledeen, like Ghorbanifar, was not entirely trusted by U.S. officials. The Tower Commission Report indicates that Oliver North told Poindexter that Amiram Nir suspected "there is probably a secret business arrangement" among Schwimmer, Ghorbanifar, and Ledeen (p. 237). There was even discussion of having Ledeen take periodic polygraph tests. On one message, North wrote: "Gorba got 13,200/missile   Gets $260 missile   Gives $50 missile to Ledeen" (p. 253). For Ledeen's own account of his role in the Iran arms arrangement, see *Washington Post*, Jan. 25, 1987, p. B1.

77. *Tower Commission Report*, p. 106.

78. Ibid., p. 206.

79. Ibid., p. 203; *Wall Street Journal*, Mar. 2, 1987; and *Washington Post*, Jan. 25, 1987, p. B2.

80. *Tower Commission Report*, p. 208.

81. Ibid., p. 258.

82. Ibid., p. 244.

83. The information and quotations in this paragraph are drawn from the following sources: *New York Times*, July 9, 1987, pp. A10–12; July 11, 1987, p. 6; July 15, 1987, p. A12; *Washington Post*, July 9, 1987, p. A1, A25–26; July 15, 1987, p. A7. See also the complete published testimony of Oliver North in *Taking the Stand: The Testimony of Lieutenant Colonel Oliver L. North* (New York: Pocket Books, 1987), esp. pp. 152–53, 203, 397, 702–3. North's account is challenged by Ghorbanifar, who was provided little opportunity to respond in the American mass media. The *New York Times*, July 11, 1987 (p. 5), did carry Ghorbanifar's reaction to the reported bathroom diplomacy: "If Mr. Ghorbanifar, an Iranian, made one of your President's most important policies up in a bathroom, I'm sorry for the United States. Imagine it! I'm supposed to have taken a man who is chief of operations for the National Security Council and said 'Come to the bathroom, screw me, overcharge for the weapons, finish me in Iran, and then send the money to your friends, the contras.' Honest to God, this is the biggest joke I have ever heard in my life. I was never alone with him."

84. Ibid., pp. 201–2. In the words of the chief of the Near East Division of the CIA: "And there is a lot of fear about the yellow ribbons going back up and that this President would have the same problems that the last President had with Iranian hostages, Iranian control" (p. 261).

85. Ibid., pp. 112–21.

86. Ibid., pp. 116–18. The Tower Commission Report is filled with references to the Soviet factor as a crucial element in the Iran initiative. See, for example, pp. 112–15, 226, 261–65, 268, 271, 273, 275.

87. Ibid., p. 226.

88. Seymour M. Hersh, "Target Qaddafi," *New York Times Magazine*, Feb. 22, 1987, pp. 19, 22.

89. *Tower Commission Report*, p. 117.

90. Ibid., p. 45.

91. *New York Times*, Jan. 12, 1987, p. 4.

92. *New York Times*, Jan. 15, 1987, p. 12.

93. For the details of this plot, see *Philadelphia Inquirer*, Apr. 26, 1987, p. A01. See also *Iran Times*, May 1, 1987, pp. 1–2.

94. *New York Times*, July 10, 1987, p. A8, and July 11, 1987, p. 7; *Washington Post*, July 11, 1987, p. A13.

CHAPTER 9. PAHLAVISM IN AMERICA: THE INFORMAL POLITICS OF FOREIGN POLICY-MAKING

1. Memorandum, McGeorge Bundy to the President, Sept. 11, 1964, National Security File, NSC Staff File, 6/64–2/65, Lyndon B. Johnson Presidential Library, Austin, Tex.

2. Memorandum, John D. Stempel Conversation with Guennady Kazankin, Oct. 18, 1976 (*Asnad*, 47:77). In April 1976, Kazankin had questioned Stempel about what Nelson Rockefeller had been "up to at Kish Island" (p. 65).

3. *Wall Street Journal*, Mar. 27, 1981, 2:1.

4. Precht, "Shah's Travel and DGA," Mar. 6, 1979 (*Asnad*, 7:266).

5. The Laingen memorandum is available in *Asnad*, 7:272–75. See L. Bruce Laingen to Secretary of State, "Shah's Desire to Reside in the U.S.," July 28, 1979.

6. Precht to Laingen, "Planning for the Shah to Come to the United States," Aug. 2, 1979 (*Asnad*, 1–6:10–13), and Christopher to Laingen, "Inquiry for PGOI Concerning the Shah," Aug. 16, 1979 (*Asnad*, 7:280).

7. Regional Security Officer to Department of State, "Monthly Status Report for August 1979," Sept. 2, 1979 (*Asnad*, 16:62). Laingen's September communication is published in *Asnad*, 1–6:101. See Laingen to Secretary of State, "The Shah of Iran," Sept. 30, 1979.

8. J. A. Bill, "Post-Pahlavi Politics: Chaos and the Construction of a New System," paper prepared for the U.S. Department of State, Washington, D.C., May 18, 1979, p. 6. Two other participants in the session, Richard Helms and William Miller, for quite different reasons, argued that the shah be admitted.

9. Henry Precht, "Memorandum of Conversation," Sept. 17, 1979 (*Asnad*, 28:79).

10. Charles W. Scott, *Pieces of the Game* (Atlanta, Ga.: Peachtree Publishers, 1984), pp. 171–72. For Scott's other references to his strong objections to the admission of the shah, see pp. 11–12, 23, 36, and 146.

11. Barbara and Barry Rosen, *The Destined Hour* (Garden City, N.Y.: Doubleday, 1982), pp. 101–2.

12. *Washington Post*, Feb. 13, 1980; *Middle East*, (December 1980): 31.

13. For these quotations: Vance, *Hard Choices* (New York: Simon and Schuster, 1983), p. 371; Sick, *All Fall Down* (New York: Random House, 1985), p. 189; and Yazdi, interview, Houston, Tex., June 1, 1986.

14. Laingen to Secretary of State, "Shah in U.S.," Oct. 31, 1979 (*Asnad*, 7:289–90).

15. William Shawcross, *Sideshow: Kissinger, Nixon and the Destruction of Cambodia* (New York: Simon and Schuster Pocketbooks, 1979), pp. 74–75.

16. For the information in this paragraph, see Peter Collier and David Horowitz, *The Rockefellers: An American Dynasty* (New York: Signet, 1977), esp. p. 454n; Joseph Persico, *The Imperial Rockefeller: A Biography of Nelson A. Rockefeller* (New York: Simon and Schuster, 1982), esp. p. 249; and Philip H. Burch, Jr., *Elites in American History: The New Deal to the Carter Administration* (New York: Holmes and Meier, 1980), p. 287, n. 31.

17. Collier and Horowitz, *The Rockefellers*, p. 419.

18. Mark Hulbert, *Interlock* (New York: Richardson and Snyder, 1982), p. 85. The thrust of this important quotation is correct, but it is unlikely that Chase "exclusively" handled "all" of Iran's oil accounts.

19. House of Representatives, Committee on Banking, Finance, and Urban Affairs, *Iran: The Financial Aspects of the Hostage Settlement Agreement*, 97th Cong., 1st Sess., July 1981, p. 8.

20. See Eugene L. Meyer, "When the Iranians Bore Gifts," *Washington Post*, Dec. 1, 1979, p. A8, and Nicholas Burnett, "Zahedi's Affairs," *Harper's*, September 1979, pp. 101–4. The information provided in these two sources has been confirmed and expanded in a series of personal communications with Delphine Blachowicz in the summer of 1980. Although there were allegations that Zahedi dispensed financial bribes and arranged wild parties and orgies for American congresspersons, Blachowicz has indicated her grave doubt that any such activities ever took place.

21. *Forbes*, June 2, 1986, p. 123. Telephone interviews with *Forbes* researcher, May and August 1986.

22. As quoted in Robert Scheer, "Brzezinski—Activist Seeker of World Order," *Los Angeles Times*, Jan. 24, 1977, pp. 3, 13.

23. If anything, this is a minimum estimate. In examining the record, it is possible to document two Kissinger calls to Brzezinski, one to Carter, two visits with Vance, one call to Mondale, and another telephone conversation with Brzezinski in which the latter initiated the exchange. Between late July and November, Kissinger retreated somewhat from his extensive lobbying for the shah. In November, however, he again became involved by his own admission.

24. Brzezinski, *Power and Principle* (New York: Farrar, Straus, and Giroux, 1983) p. 474.

25. Sick, *All Fall Down*, p. 179.

26. As quoted in Terence Smith, "Why Carter Admitted the Shah," *New York Times Magazine*, May 17, 1981, p. 40.

27. *New York Times*, Nov. 18, 1979, p. 14.

28. Sick, *All Fall Down*, pp. 179–80.

29. Henry Kissinger, *White House Years* (Boston: Little, Brown, 1979), pp. 22–23. A valuable biography of McCloy is being prepared by Kai Bird and Max Holland.

30. As quoted in Terence Smith, "Why Carter Admitted the Shah," *New York Times Magazine*, May 17, 1981, p. 44.

31. As reported in *Daily Texan*, Nov. 21, 1979, p. 1.

32. *Washington Post*, Nov. 26, 1979.

33. *New York Times*, Nov. 11, 1979.

34. Mary McGrory, *Washington Star*, Nov. 27, 1979.

35. The quotations are from Anthony Sampson, "The Moves Behind the Shah's Visa," *St. Louis Post-Dispatch*, Nov. 10, 1980, p. 17A.

36. Richard Cohen, "Rockefeller Keys Open Doors for Sick Shah," *Washington Post*, Nov. 20, 1979, p. C5.

37. Hamilton Jordan, *Crisis: The Last Year of the Carter Presidency* (New York: G. P. Putnam's Sons, 1982), p. 32.

38. This same honor and credibility argument was used again for promoting a policy of military action after the American diplomats were taken hostage as a direct result of admitting the shah. The same individuals who had used it to welcome the shah now attempted to present it as a reason to attack Iran.

39. Jack Anderson, "Carter was Advised Not to Admit the Shah," *Washington Post*, Dec. 11, 1979, p. E11.

40. Jordan, *Crisis*, p. 31. Throughout the hostage crisis as well, Jordan and Jody Powell interpreted events and made policy recommendations on the basis of how they would affect Carter's reelection chances; see pp. 36, 45, 53, 80, 119, 122, and especially p. 127, where Jordan admits: "Yet somehow the hostages and the election were woven together in my mind."

41. For a discussion of mass media distortion claiming that the primaries and reelection were the first and last motivating force for President Carter, see Jody Powell, *The Other Side of the Story* (New York: William Morrow, 1984), esp. pp. 209–22.

42. *Wall Street Journal*, Nov. 23, 1979, p. 1.

43. Brzezinski, *Power and Principle*, p. 474.

44. Interview with Rockefeller associate, Mar. 21, 1986.

45. Telephone interview, Feb. 11, 1985.

46. Interview with George Ball, Princeton, N.J., Dec. 5, 1986.

47. The Chase Manhattan theory has been presented with greatest care and in greatest detail by Mark Hulbert in *Interlock* (New York: Richardson and Snyder, 1982). The central propositions in the theory have also been outlined in the following sources: Bill Paul, "Chase Bank and Others Face Court Challenges on Huge Loans to Iran," *Wall Street Journal*, Mar. 28, 1980, pp. 1, 31; Robert Ball, "The Unseemly Squabble Over Iran's Assets," *Fortune*, Jan. 28, 1980, pp. 60–64; Anthony Sampson, "Iran's Threat to American Banks," and "U.S. Banks React on Hostages," *St. Louis Post-Dispatch*, Nov. 11, 12, 1980, pp. 13A, 15A; Jonathan M. Winer, "The Iranian Assets Grab," *Nation*, Jan. 17, 1981, pp. 43–46; and L. J. Davis, "Hostages for Chase Manhattan," *Penthouse*, December 1980, pp. 76ff. The most systematic response to the arguments presented in these sources has been prepared by a committee of the House of Representatives. See Committee on Banking, Finance, and Urban Affairs, *Iran: The Financial Aspects*. Despite this report, at least one member of the committee, Congressman George Hansen of Idaho, subscribed to the Chase Manhattan theory.

48. For an informed discussion of the Chase bank's declining position and severe financial problems of the mid-1970s, see *Financial Times*, Jan. 30, 1980, p. 8. According to this article, between 1975 and 1978 the bank was forced to write off close to $1 billion of loan losses.

49. *Ittili'at*, 24 Aban 1358/15 Nov. 1979, p. 2.

50. See Hulbert, *Interlock*, p. 196.

51. Roy Assersohn, *The Biggest Deal* (London: Methuen, 1982), p. 273. This is a

valuable source. For two other fascinating accounts of the complex maneuverings of the large U.S. banks and law firms during the hostage crisis, see Paul Hoffman, *Lions of the Eighties* (Garden City, N.Y.: Doubleday, 1982), pp. 311–34, and James B. Stewart, *The Partners* (New York: Simon and Schuster, 1983), pp. 19–52. According to Hoffman, the banks were not the only beneficiaries of the settlement. So too were the law firms. In his words, the hostage incident "was a bonanza for the bar, generating millions of dollars in legal fees for more than one hundred major law firms" (*Lions of the Eighties*, p. 313).

52. Hulbert, *Interlock*, p. 156.

53. Ibid., p. 204.

54. Hoffman, *Lions of the Eighties*, p. 327.

55. Carswell and Davis, "The Economic and Financial Pressures: Freeze and Sanctions," in Warren Christopher et al., *American Hostages in Iran: The Conduct of a Crisis* (New Haven and London: Yale University Press, 1985), pp. 229–30.

56. House Committee on Banking, Finance, and Urban Affairs, *Iran: The Financial Aspects*, p. 56.

57. According to the Congressional banking committee report, the bankers knew about this possible action before it occurred due to extensive telephone contacts between the Treasury Department and the Federal Reserve Bank. See Ibid., p. v. Carswell and Davis, therefore, may be technically correct when they write that "as far as the authors know, prior to the decision to freeze Iran's assets, no person outside the U.S. government was told that such a freeze was under consideration or had been decided" ("Economic and Financial Pressures," p. 176). It was not necessary to tell what was clearly known.

58. *House Committee on Bank, Finance, and Urban Affairs, Iran: Financial Aspects*, pp. v–vi, 8, 56.

59. Interview with George Ball, Princeton, N.J., Dec. 5, 1986.

60. The information in this paragraph and the following three paragraphs has been provided by major participants in these negotiations (telephone interviews, Nov. 17, 22, and 28, 1986). Chase continued to retain the services of Ghani and Tavakoli because of the great integrity and reputation of the Iranian firm. Although Cyrus Ghani himself argued the firm's case in New York, two other members of the firm were especially skeptical about the constitutionality of the loans. Given the repressive political climate in Iran at the time, the position taken by Ghani and Tavakoli in this incident is extraordinary.

61. For documentation, see Bill Paul's fine *Wall Street Journal* investigative article, "Chase Bank and Others Face Court Challenges."

62. Some scholarly studies that have analyzed the syndicated loans and subsequent freeze have tended to dismiss the Chase Manhattan thesis out of hand. They have also failed to address the important issue of the legality of the loans in the first place. See, for example, Edward Gordon and Cynthia Lichtenstein, "Current Legal Developments: The Decision to Block Iranian Assets—Reexamined," *International Lawyer* 16 (Winter 1982): 161–86, and Benjamin J. Cohen, *In Whose Interest? International Banking and American Foreign Policy* (New Haven and London: Yale University Press, 1986), pp. 147–76.

63. The list of the individuals presented in figure 3 and discussed in this section is in no way exhaustive. It does, however, identify a central core of actors who were among those Iranian and American linkage figures who played key roles in binding the two countries together politically, economically, and socially.

64. Anthony Parsons, *The Pride and the Fall: Iran, 1974–1979* (London: Jonathan Cape, 1984), p. 28.

65. In one of the milder characterizations, a 1976 CIA report describes the princess as follows: "The Shah's twin sister, *Ashraf*, has a near legendary reputation for financial corruption and for successfully pursuing young men" (Central Intelligence Agency, Office of Political Research, *Elites and the Distribution of Power in Iran*, February 1976 [*Asnad*, 8:27]).

66. Ashraf Pahlavi, *Faces in a Mirror: Memoirs from Exile* (Englewood Cliffs, N.J.: Prentice-Hall, 1980), pp. 211–12.

67. The material in this and the following paragraph is drawn from Donnie Radcliffe, "Glittering Event for Princess of Iran," *Evening Star* (Washington, D.C.), June 10, 1969, p. C1.

68. On Sept. 30, 1975, John Oakes wrote a thoughtful, critical article in the *New York Times* questioning the underlying stability of the shah's government. In retrospect, this sensitive piece stands out as an exceptional and prescient statement, given the conventional wisdom of the time.

69. For an analysis of the cooperation and conflict that marked Iranian-American efforts at Pahlavi University in its formative years, see J. A. Bill, *The Politics of Iran: Groups, Classes and Modernization* (Columbus, Ohio: Charles E. Merrill, 1972), pp. 78–87.

70. *Washington Post*, Feb. 2, 1975, pp. A1, A20–21.

71. Cynthia Helms has written a very useful book describing Iran before the revolution. See *An Ambassador's Wife in Iran* (New York: Dodd, Mead and Co., 1981).

72. In a *Time* magazine-sponsored symposium in March 1979, Helms urged that "we go back to some of those good old dirty days when we had an arsenal of things that we used to do around the world" (*Time*, March 12, 1979, p. 31). The other quotations in the paragraph are taken from my personal notes of Helms's comments at the Nov. 8, 1985, Foreign Service Institute presentation.

73. Interview with Kermit Roosevelt, Washington, D.C., Nov. 12, 1981.

74. Helen M. Lilienthal, ed., *The Journals of David E. Lilienthal*, vol. 7: *Unfinished Business, 1968–1981* (New York: Harper and Row, 1983), p. 762, other quotations on pp. 734–35, 739, 742, 744, and 753. This volume contains the revealing account of the bewilderment and disillusionment of an honest man who had seriously misread Iran from the beginning.

75. For the four quotations in this paragraph, see D. E. Lilienthal, *Journals*, vol. 4: *The Road to Change, 1955–1959* (New York: Harper and Row, 1969), p. 294; Lilienthal, *Journals*, vol. 5: *The Harvest Years, 1959–1963* (New York: Harper and Row, 1971), pp. 21, 173; and Lilienthal, *Journals*, vol. 6: *Creativity and Conflict, 1964–1967* (New York: Harper and Row, 1973), p. 485.

76. Lilienthal, *Unfinished Business*, p. 394.

77. John Tower, Edmund Muskie, and Brent Scowcroft, *The Tower Commission Report* (New York: Bantam Books/Time Books, 1987), p. 227.

78. Burch, *Elites in American History*, p. 286, n. 27. John A. Wells died in 1980.

79. Ann Crittenden, "The Shah in New York," *New York Times*, Sept. 26, 1976, sect. 3, pp. 1–2. When asked about this article, Rogers said the article was "all wrong. There is nothing to that at all." He stated that "Punch" Sulzberger wrote him a personal letter of apology about the article (telephone interview with William P. Rogers, Dec. 3, 1986). On Oct. 3, 1976, the *New York Times* printed the

following under the heading "Corrections": "Any implication in a Business and Finance Section article, 'The Shah in New York,' published last Sunday, that William P. Rogers, former Secretary of State, or his law firm, Rogers & Wells, acted improperly in representing the American interests of the Pahlavi Foundation of Iran was unintended. The Times regrets any such inference drawn."

The author of this important investigative article, Ann Crittenden, points out that neither Rogers nor the *New York Times* formally questioned any of the facts presented in her article. Crittenden also argued that this "correction" piece was an apology and clearly not a retraction. Once the article was published, Rogers, who had refused to meet with Crittenden, complained directly to Sulzberger (telephone interview with Ann Crittenden, Jan. 14, 1987).

80. Telephone interview with William P. Rogers, Dec. 3, 1986.

81. Jack Anderson, "Shah Link to Nixon Campaign Hinted," *Washington Post*, June 10, 1974, p. B13.

82. The information on Ralph Becker has been drawn largely from interviews with Iranian officials and from the Macy files, Box 34, Lyndon B. Johnson Presidential Library, Austin, Tex. In his *Who's Who in America* profile, all references to Becker's Iran activities were gradually deleted after the revolution.

83. Some of the information in this paragraph has been drawn from Barry Rubin, *Paved with Good Intentions* (New York: Oxford University Press, 1980), p. 164.

84. *Wall Street Journal*, Feb. 13, 1987, p. 42. The other information in the paragraphs on Secord is drawn from his official U.S. Air Force biography and from articles by Charles Babcock in the *Washington Post*, Nov. 8, 1986, and by Associated Press writer Joan Mower in the *St. Louis Post-Dispatch*, Dec. 5, 1986. For relationships between Secord, Hakim, and former CIA officials Theodore Shackley and Thomas Clines, see Peter Maas, "Oliver North's Strange Recruits," *New York Times Magazine*, Jan. 18, 1987, pp. 20–22, 52, 55, 60. See also Scott Armstrong et al., eds., *The Chronology: The Documented Day-by-Day Account of the Secret Military Assistance to Iran and the Contras* (New York: Warner Books, 1987), esp. pp. 2, 9, 12, 23, 28, 451–52.

85. House of Representatives, William Lehman, "Israel's Strategic Importance Must be Recognized," Feb. 15, 1979, *Congressional Record*, (Washington, D.C.: Government Printing Office, 1980), p. 2678.

86. Senate Committee on Foreign Relations, Subcommittee on Foreign Assistance, *U.S. Arms Sales Policy*, 94th Cong., 2d Sess., Sept. 16, 21, 24, 1976.

87. The two quotations in this paragraph are taken from the *New York Times*, Jan. 15, 1976, p. 4, and Parviz C. Radji, *In the Service of the Peacock Throne* (London: Hamish Hamilton, 1983), p. 165.

88. Crittenden, "The Shah in New York," *New York Times*, pp. 1–2. The rest of the Murphy story is reported in the *New York Times* on Oct. 26, Nov. 27, 1977, Apr. 4, 1978, July 3, 1979, Dec. 4, 1980, Mar. 12 Sept. 4, 1982, and July 16, 1983. In a telephone interview of Dec. 3, 1986, William Rogers said he had met Murphy but once. In 1980, John Murphy was found guilty of receiving an unlawful gratuity from a fictitious Arab in the Abscam operation. In July 1983, he entered prison for a three-year term.

89. Fereydoun Hoveyda, *The Fall of the Shah* (New York: Wyndham Books, 1979), p. 110.

90. After referring to certain tensions that existed in Iran, Yankelovich euphor-

ically stated: "Among nations, human history records relatively few acts of creativity that bring forth a new model of the good society appropriate to its time, place, and circumstance. I feel we have had the rare privilege this week of catching a glimpse of such an act of creativity in the making—something new and unprecedented under the sun." See Jane W. Jacqz, ed., *Iran: Past, Present and Future* (New York: Aspen Institute for Humanistic Studies, 1976), p. 6. The Aspen Institute/Persepolis Symposium was attended by over one hundred dignitaries from fourteen countries. I was one of the fifteen American scholars present at the conference.

91. For the information and quotation presented in this paragraph, see C. V. Ferguson, Department of State, Outgoing Telegram to Amembassy, Tehran, Feb. 3, 1951; Ambassador H. Grady, Amembassy Tehran, Telegraph no. 1766 to Secretary of State, Washington, Feb. 7, 1951; Grady, Telephone no. 1789 to Secretary of State, Washington, Feb. 9, 1951; and Byroade to Amembassy Tehran, Sept. 15, 1953; all in National Archives, Washington, NND 832934, Record Group 59, Box 4115, 788.1/2-151–788.11/12-3054.

92. The major study is William A. Dorman and Mansour Farhang, *The U.S. Press and Iran: Foreign Policy and the Journalism of Deference* (Berkeley, Calif.: University of California Press, 1987). See also William A. Dorman and Ehsan Omeed's important article, "Reporting Iran through the Shah's Eyes," *Columbia Journalism Review*, January/February 1979, pp. 27–33. For a well-documented survey of the glaring weakness of coverage and interpretation of the *New York Times* and the *Washington Post* of Iran between 1971 and the revolution, see Martin Walker, *Powers of the Press: Twelve of the World's Influential Newspapers* (New York: Pilgrim Press, 1983), pp. 342–93. Walker concludes that *Le Monde* was clearly superior to either American paper in its coverage of Iran during this period. Other major world newspapers were also sadly lacking.

93. For the basic report outlining Zand's allegations concerning de Borchgrave, see R. W. Apple, Jr., "Iranian Names Four He Says Took Gifts," the *New York Times*, Nov. 17, 1978, p. A6. *Newsweek* carried the Zand charges in an unusual footnote format on p. 57 of its Nov. 27, 1978, issue.

94. When questioned about the diamond watch, Walters indicated that she had returned the gift, which in her words was "a pretty watch with a diamond at either end." Concerning caviar, she said, "At one point or another I think probably everybody received caviar." Maxwell Glen and Cody Shearer, "Top Journalists Took the Shah's Champagne," *Los Angeles Herald Examiner*, Aug. 9, 1980, p. A19. For documentation concerning the chartered jet episode, see Burnett, "Zahedi's Affairs," p. 104.

95. As quoted in Burnett, "Zahedi's Affairs," p. 103.

96. As a scholar researching Iran in the 1960s and 1970s, I can attest firsthand to the Iranian embassy's policy of gift giving. During the Christmas season on two occasions in the mid-1970s, I received in the mail Rosenthal China cigarette boxes sent from the Iranian embassy. Each box had a portrait of the Royal Family on the cover. On another occasion, Ambassador Zahedi gave two colleagues and me tins of caviar when we visited the Iranian embassy in Washington.

97. Besides the various syndicated columns written by Kraft, see his speech, "A Decade of Problems," LTV Washington Seminar, *American Foreign Policy in the '80s* (Dallas: LTV Corporation, 1980), pp. 60–69. The baseball analogy appears on p. 66.

98. The quotations in this paragraph are drawn from Donald N. Wilber, *Adven-*

tures in the Middle East: Excursions and Incursions (Princeton, N.J.: Darwin Press, 1986), pp. 229, 139, and 207, respectively. A list of the many publications of Wilber is provided on pp. 237–49.

99. Lenczowski, ed., *Iran under the Pahlavis* (Stanford, Calif.: Hoover Institution Press, 1978).

100. Lilienthal, *Unfinished Business*, p. 776.

101. At a press conference in January 1978, Iranian ambassador to Washington Ardeshir Zahedi announced that the shah of Iran had donated $250,000 to the Hubert Humphrey Foundation. The chairman of the fundraising committee was Henry Kissinger (*Kayhan International* [Tehran], Jan. 29, 1978, p. 3).

102. Senate, Senator Goldwater, "Address by Ardeshir Zahedi, Ambassador of Iran," introductory comments by Goldwater, *Congressional Record*, Sept. 17, 1974, S 16769.

103. Glen and Shearer, "Top Journalists," p. A19.

104. The quotations are from a June 6, 1980, personal communication from Delphine Blachowicz and her letter to the editor of the *Miami Herald*, Oct. 16, 1977. The Zahedi gifts to the Johnsons are enumerated in great detail in GEN CO 122, Indonesia, Box 41, Lyndon B. Johnson Presidential Library, Austin, Tex.

105. Helms participated in the conference; Rockefeller did not.

CHAPTER 10. THE UNITED STATES IN IRAN: DIPLOMATS, INTELLIGENCE AGENTS, AND POLICY-MAKING

1. Martie and Robin Sterling, *Last Flight from Iran* (New York: Bantam Books, 1981), pp. 30, 34, 40, 59, and 68. This is an unpleasant little book that describes the experience of Bell Helicopter (BHI) in Isfahan. According to the authors: "Since it is BHI's job to modernize, civilize, machanize, and 'aeronize' this nation of nomads, we do our damnedest. But it takes a lot out of all of us" (p. 34).

2. *Ittili'at*, 27 Day 1354/27 Jan. 1976, p. 22. For other articles in the Persian press containing items on flagrant American misbehavior in Iran, see *Ittili'at*, 29 Bahman 1352/9 Jan. 1974, p. 14; 22 Tir 1354/1 June 1975, p. 22; 1 Tir 1354/21 Oct. 1975, p. 26; and 11 Bahman 1354/10 Feb. 1976, p. 26. For a powerful Persian short story sharply criticizing the crude and exploitative American in Iran, see Gholam Hussein Sa'edi's "Dandil," trans. Hasan Javadi, in Sa'edi, *Dandil: Stories from Iranian Life* (New York: Random House, 1981), pp. 1–28. This story was first published in Persian in 1968.

3. Telephone interviews with Helen Young, Dec. 21, 27, 1984. She died on May 18, 1985.

4. Interview, Tehran, Aug. 28, 1970.

5. Interview with Ambassador Douglas MacArthur II, Tehran, June 29, 1970. I spent six months in 1970 studying the American embassy and Americans living in Tehran.

6. Personal copies of documents and letters gathered in Tehran and Tabriz in 1970 concerning the Murray Smith case. For the published story, see the two investigative articles by Tom Dowling in the *Washingtonian*, September, October 1971.

7. These conclusions and the materials presented in the following sections are based on intensive interviews carried out in Tehran over six months from June to December 1970 with 26 official Americans then posted to Iran. Those interviewed

included 15 FSOs, 7 FSIOs, and 4 staff/military officials. The results of these interviews have never before been published.

8. The American living patterns described in this chapter do not differ substantially from the manner in which Americans have lived in many other overseas settings. For three excellent sources on this subject, see Harlan Cleveland, Gerard J. Mangone, and John Clarke Adams, *The Overseas Americans* (New York: McGraw-Hill, 1960); Charlotte Wolf, *Garrison Community* (Westport, Conn.: Greenwood Publishing, 1969); and Dennison Nash, *A Community in Limbo* (Bloomington, Ind.: Indiana University Press, 1970).

9. The information contained in this paragraph is drawn from interviews with parents, students, and administrators of the American school in Tehran in August–September 1970. The American School in Tehran enrolled 1,200 students in grades 1–12 at the time. Approximately half of the students were dependents of military personnel, and 40 were the dependents of embassy officials. Most of the others were the children of American businessmen. Two other schools that enrolled a mix of Americans, Iranians, and third country citizens were the Community School and the International School.

10. Interview, Tehran, Aug. 11, 1970.

11. Interview, Tehran, Aug. 12, 1970.

12. Joseph P. Englehardt, "American Military Advisors in Iran: A Critical Review," *Joint Perspectives* (Summer 1981): 36. The artwork accompanying this article reinforced Englehardt's point. Iranians are portrayed in Arab headdress and robes! Englehardt wrote a strong letter to the commandant of the Armed Forces Staff College calling attention to this embarrassing mistake. In his words, this artwork "demonstrates precisely the lack of sensitivity for foreign cultures that the article heavily criticizes" (copy of Aug. 17, 1981, letter signed by J. P. Englehardt).

13. This pattern was not particular to Iran. In Turkey, for example, local embassy employees included Greek Christians, Armenians, and Austro-Hungarians. For years, the U.S. Embassy in Cairo employed a disproportionate number of Christian Copts.

14. Because of the numerous complaints in this regard, in 1970 I quietly accompanied Iranian acquaintances who were applying for visas to the consulate in Tehran. The local personnel were indeed rude and arrogant—until they discovered that I was an American. The American consular officials with whom we met were unfailingly polite, but the damage had already been done.

15. These contact lists are printed in *Asnad*, 17:1–24, 31–36, 56–65. They are the lists prepared by Martin Herz (9/9/67), Larry Semakis (4/26/69), John Armitage (11/26/69), and Archie Bolster (7/25/76). Semakis and Bolster were both highly competent diplomats with a facility for the Persian language. I have no basis on which to judge John Armitage.

16. For the two direct quotes in this paragraph, see *Asnad*, 17:12, 23.

17. Ibid., pp. 7, 11.

18. Interview with Tom Hutson, Tehran, Nov. 16, 1970. Hutson resigned from the Foreign Service in April 1980.

19. Memorandum, Archie M. Bolster to the Ambassador, "A Brief Look Back," July 26, 1976, p. 2. Document provided by Archie Bolster.

20. Among the most talented Foreign Service officers who served in Iran in the 1960s and 1970s were Franklin Crawford, William Miller, Archie Bolster, William

Clevenger, Charles Rassias, Larry Semakis, and Stanley Escudero. And there were others.

21. The data in this paragraph were obtained from the British embassy in Tehran in July 1970. The Soviet figures are estimates provided by American and British diplomats in Tehran at the time.

22. Memorandum, A. M. Bolster, "Duties of Embassy Political Advisor," Mar. 28, 1976 (*Asnad*, 17:54).

23. Department of State, Office of the Inspector General, Foreign Service, "Inspection Report on the Conduct of Relations with Iran," October 1974, p. 9 (*Asnad*, 8:91).

24. Department of State, Assessments Subcommittee, "FOCUS Iran, Part II: Action Review," Dec. 27, 1976, p. 2 in section entitled "The Shah as a Source of Information" (*Asnad*, 8:150).

25. Interview with Jack Miklos, Tehran, June 3, 1974.

26. Interview with political officer, Tehran, June 21, 1974.

27. Interview with FSO-5, Tehran, June 24, 1970.

28. The words of Philip Stoddard, Bureau of Intelligence and Research, U.S. Department of State, Washington, D.C., Oct. 27, 1978. Later, Stoddard amplified his conclusion when asked for reaffirmation and explanation: "I'm talking about cables and airgrams that could not be cleared for sending to the Department by Embassy officials." The embassy hierarchy had a strong "grip" on what was being reported. "If they didn't like it, you didn't get it" (Telephone interview, Nov. 7, 1986).

29. Michael A. G. Michaud, "Communication and Controversy: Thoughts on the Future of Foreign Service Reporting," *Foreign Service Journal* (October 1969), p. 24.

30. This revealing report is reproduced in *Asnad*, 17:74–89.

31. Telephone interview with Philip Stoddard, Nov. 7, 1986. According to Stoddard, in the 1960s Greece was another country that shared with Iran severe embassy reporting problems.

32. Personal copy of the Washburn letter. The letter is available both in Persian and in indecipherable English in *Asnad*, 8:47–57 (in English), 64–81 (in Persian).

33. The author attended this evening of poetry, which was held at the Abraham Lincoln Library in Tehran. The Persian press carried articles on the event. See, for example, *Firdawsi*, 2, 9 Shahrivar 1349/24, 31 Aug. 1967, p. 23 in both issues.

34. Interview with former hostage William Royer, Austin, Tex., Feb. 20, 1981. Royer had been working for USIS in Iran for only six weeks before he was taken hostage.

35. Interview with Lois Roth, Tehran, July 16, 1970.

36. Interview with Richard Arndt, Tehran, July 1, 1970.

37. Acting Director of the Central Intelligence Agency to Jack C. Miklos, Chargé d'Affaires, American Embassy, Tehran, Jan. 26, 1977 (*Asnad*, 8:133).

38. The words of a military officer with considerable Iran expertise who served both in Iran and in the office of the assistant chief of staff for Intelligence (personal communication, Nov. 9, 1986).

39. Interview with Sayyid Zia, Saʿadatabad, near Vanak, Iran, Apr. 18, 1967.

40. Interview, Tehran, July 3, 1970. This particular officer left the Foreign Service shortly after his Iran assignment.

41. Former CIA official to the author, June 16, 1982. Since this was written, a site in China has picked up some of this coverage.

42. Statement at Foreign Service Institute presentation, Nov. 8, 1985.

43. David H. Blee, National Intelligence Officer for the Middle East, to Ambassador Edward S. Little, Chairman of Human Resources Committee, Central Intelligence Agency, "Reporting Assessment—FOCUS Iran," Nov. 4, 1976 (*Asnad*, 8:140).

44. Interview with CIA official, Washington, D.C., Sept. 2, 1980.

45. Archie M. Bolster, "Persian-Speaking Diplomats," *Brown Alumni Monthly*, September 1980.

46. This statement refers to Secretary of State Vance's belief in the shah's invulnerability even when provided with contrary evidence by his own State Department analysts. It was made at the Foreign Service Institute's conference "Revolution in Iran," Washington, D.C., Nov. 12, 1985.

47. In 1970, I spent a week working at the Iran Desk as part of an innovative scholar-diplomat program designed to acquaint academics with the realities of policy-making. Even then, diplomats were harried and harassed by a heavy workload.

48. I have firsthand knowledge of this report. The information in the following paragraphs has been confirmed in interviews at Department of State, Bureau of Intelligence and Research, Sept. 3, 1980, Nov. 5, 12, 1981.

49. Gary Sick, *All Fall Down* (New York: Random House, 1985), p. 91. Sick, who points out that he reviewed the files under the "baleful" eye of Henry Precht, reports that he only found one piece of reporting that stressed the serious nature of the opposition in Iran. He cannot resist pointing out that this was written "during the period when Ambassador Sullivan was on his extended home leave." But then in a footnote he admits that the report, written by political officer George Lambrakis, was in fact prepared sometime before June 1. Sullivan was in Tehran at the time. See pp. 92, 348.

50. Henry Precht "Official-Informal, Secret-Eyes Only" to Ambassador William H. Sullivan, Dec. 19, 1978 (*Asnad*, 13:16).

51. *New York Times*, February 27, 1987, p. 6. For the complete text of this investigation, see John Tower, Edmund Muskie, and Brent Scowcroft, *The Tower Commission Report* (New York: Bantam Books/Times Books, 1987). Hereafter cited as *Tower Commission Report*.

52. *Tower Commission Report*, p. 82. Shultz himself disputes this interpretation. In his July 23, 1987, testimony before the congressional select committees investigating the Iran-Contra affair, he argued that had waged a "battle royal" against such powerful advisers as NSC head John M. Poindexter and CIA director William J. Casey. See *New York Times*, July 24, 1987, pp. A1, A6–8; *Washington Post*, July 24, 1987, p. A1, A6–8.

53. *Tower Commission Report*, p. 83.

54. Senate Select Committee on Intelligence, Select Committee on Secret Military Assistance to Iran and the Nicarguan Opposition, "Report on Preliminary Inquiry," Jan. 29, 1987, p. 22. Hereafter cited as *Select Committee Report*. For other references to Peres's role in this venture, see pp. 2–3, 33, and 35 of this report. See also *Tower Commission Report*, pp. 25, 45, 109–10, 215–16.

55. *Tower Commission Report*, pp. 27, 148. For President Reagan's involvement throughout, see pp. 27–29, 35–39, 42–48, 51, 132, 147–48, 157–58, 182–83, 219,

224, 227–28, 261, 287, 295. See also *Select Committee Report*, pp. 5–7, 11, 13–14, 16, 27, 37.

The following quotation in this paragraph is taken from Shultz's testimony before the congressional select committees on July 23, 1987. See *New York Times*, July 24, 1987, p. A7.

56. Vice President George Bush's name is conspicuously absent in much of the *Tower Commission Report*. When it is mentioned, it usually appears only as "the Vice President." It is clear that Bush was present at crucial White House meetings in which decisions concerning the Iranian arms deal were made. Although he has pointed out that he was at the Army-Navy football game during a White House meeting of December 7, 1985, he was present at important meetings on December 11, 1985, and January 7, 1986. While in Israel on July 29, 1986, Bush received a thorough briefing on the Iran arms affair from Amiram Nir. See *Tower Commission Report*, pp. 219–25, 384–89. For reference to Bush's role in the Iranian arms affair, see also *Select Committee Report*, pp. 2, 6–7, 16–17, 32, 39. For Bush's position that he was unaware of strong arguments against the Iran arms sales and that he was "not in the loop," see *Washington Post*, Aug. 6, 1987, p. 1.

57. Elliot L. Richardson, "The State of State," *Foreign Service Journal* (September 1981): 17.

58. Shaplen, "Profiles: Eye of the Storm, David Dunlop Newsom," *New Yorker*, June 2, 1980, pp. 84–86.

59. Personal interview with CIA officer, Washington, D.C., Nov. 29, 1982. The material presented in these sections on the CIA and Iran is based on numerous interviews with CIA officials who worked on Iran in one capacity or another over the years.

60. Ransom, "Being Intelligent about Secret Intelligence Agencies," *American Political Science Review* 74 (March 1980): 141–48.

61. Turner, *Secrecy and Democracy: The CIA in Transition* (Boston: Houghton Mifflin, 1985), p. 115.

62. The PGI arrangement itself last only two years before there was another reshuffling and Iran became part of the South Asian division.

63. Thomas A. Bailey, *The Art of Diplomacy: The American Experience* (New York: Appleton-Century-Crofts, 1968), p. 65.

64. Sick, *All Fall Down*, p. 182.

65. On Stempel's exchange with Soviet diplomat Guenneday Kazankan, Memorandum of Conversation, J. D. Stempel, "Afghanistan Coup and Disturbances in Iran," May 16, 1978 (*Asnad* 48:76). Stempel writes the following in response to Kazankan's thesis on the shah's cancer: "This rumor has abounded in many quarters and may be of Soviet inspiration."

The INR reports are "Iranian Outlook," Report no. 411, May 4, 1976, and "The Future of Iran: Implications for the US," Report no. 704, Jan. 28, 1977. Acquired through Freedom of Information Act.

66. Former State Department Iran Country Director Henry Precht has made the following point with respect to academicians and the Iran episode: "We spent very little time with them relative to their value. . . . It's too bad that the government doesn't make better use at higher levels of the people who really know the countries that we're dealing with" (Foreign Service Institute Conference, "Revolution in Iran," Nov. 12, 1985).

CHAPTER 11. THE POLITICS OF FOREIGN POLICY FAILURE: A
SYSTEM OF REINFORCING ERRORS

1. For an interesting discussion of the way in which groups struggle with one another over the formulation of foreign policy, see Barry Rubin, *Secrets of State: The State Department and the Struggle over U.S. Foreign Politics* (New York: Oxford University Press, 1985). For a more general overview, see Douglas Yates, Jr., *The Politics of Management* (San Francisco, Calif.: Josey-Bass, 1985).

2. Marvin Zonis, *The Political Elite of Iran* (Princeton, N.J.: Princeton University Press, 1971).

3. James A. Bill, *The Politics of Iran: Groups, Classes and Modernization* (Columbus, Ohio: Charles E. Merrill, 1972), and Bill, "The Plasticity of Informal Politics: The Case of Iran," *Middle East Journal* 27 (Spring 1973): 131–51.

4. The influence cut both ways, of course. Iranian behavior was influenced by American bureaucratic style, which was more formal, legalistic, and boundaried and less personal, flexible, and fluid. According to the ground-breaking work of Manfred Halpern of Princeton University, the dominant mode of human relations in the United States and the Western world is termed "boundary management." In Iran, the major modes of human interaction are "emanation" and "direct bargaining." For a sample of Halpern's work, see M. Halpern, "Four Contrasting Repertoires of Human Relations in Islam: Two Pre-Modern and Two Modern Ways of Dealing with Continuity and Change, Collaboration and Conflict, and the Achieving of Justice," in L. Carl Brown and Norman Itzkowitz, eds., *Psychological Dimensions of Near Eastern Studies* (Princeton, N.J.: Darwin Press, 1977), pp. 60–102.

5. See Graham Allison, *Essence of Decision: Explaining the Cuban Missile Crisis* (Boston: Little, Brown, 1971), and Morton H. Halperin, *Bureaucratic Politics and Foreign Policy* (Washington, D.C.: Brookings Institution, 1974).

6. John Spanier and Eric M. Uslaner, *How American Foreign Policy Is Made* (New York: Praeger, 1974).

7. Helen M. Lilienthal, ed., *The Journals of David E. Lilienthal*, vol. 7: *Unfinished Business, 1968–1981* (New York: Harper and Row, 1983), pp. 569–70.

8. Department of State, Memorandum of Conversation, "Iranian Oil Problem," Oct. 16, 1951, Papers of Dean Acheson, Harry S. Truman Library, Independence, Mo. The oil company executives present were Eugene Holman, president of Standard Oil of New Jersey, R. G. Follis, chairman of the board of Standard Oil of California, Sidney A. Swensrud, President of Gulf Oil, Brewster B. Jennings, President of Socony-Vacuum, and W. S. S. Rogers, chairman of the Texas Company.

9. Uri Bialer, "The Iranian Connection in Israel's Foreign Policy, 1948–1951," *Middle East Journal* 39 (Spring 1985): p. 299n.

10. Ibid., p. 315.

11. Uri Lubrani, "The Iranian-Israeli Relationship," in Itamar Rabinovich and Jehuda Reinharz, eds., *Israel in the Middle East* (New York: Oxford University Press, 1984), pp. 342–48. For another important source that examines Iranian-Israeli relations, see Avner Yaniv, *Deterrence without the Bomb: The Politics of Israeli Strategy* (Lexington, Mass.: D. C. Heath, 1987), esp. pp. 93–95, 157–58, 220–23.

12. *Asnad*, 19:17, 20 (numbered from left by writer). This volume contains two extraordinary memoranda of conversations between Toufanian on the one hand

and Dayan and Weizmann on the other. See "Minutes from Meeting held in Tel-Aviv between H. E. General M. Dayan, Foreign Minister of Israel and H. E. General H. Toufanian, Vice Minister of War, Imperial Government of Iran," July 18, 1977, and "Meeting: Minister of Defense, Gen. E. Weizmann, and Gen. Tufanian, of Iran—Also Present: Mr. Uri Lubrani, Dr. Suzman, Director-General, Mr. A, Ben-Yosef, Col. Elan Tehila," July 18, 1977.

13. Central Intelligence Agency, *Israel: Foreign Intelligence and Security Services* (March 1979), p. 24. This revealing document of an American assessment of Israeli intelligence operations is published in *Asnad* 11:1–47. When the U.S. mass media reported on some of the contents of this document, Israeli officials were furious. Iser Harel, former head of the Mossad, reportedly described the CIA report as "amateurish and superficial" in its content and "niggardly and ungrateful" to Israel in its thrust. Harel argued that the fact that such a document was present in the U.S. Embassy in Tehran and had not been destroyed was irresponsible. At the CIA, he felt that "a house cleaning is in order" (*Christian Science Monitor*, Feb. 10, 1982).

14. John Stempel, "Political Section Summary" of a more comprehensive report on the state of Iran, June 22, 1976 (*Asnad*, 7:94–95).

15. Statement at Foreign Service Institute Presentation, Nov. 8, 1985.

16. Yaniv, *Deterrence without the Bomb*, p. 158.

17. Halperin, *Bureaucratic Politics and Foreign Policy*, pp. 89–90.

18. In a session on Iran held at the Chase Manhattan Bank in fall 1978, Rockefeller strongly argued that the communists were behind the revolutionary upheaval in Iran (Personal interview with Chase employee, New York, fall 1986).

19. Office of Naval Intelligence, Information Report, "Iran: Some Basic Motivations of Iranians which Concern the Present Situation," Tehran, Mar. 18, 1953, p. 5. This document has been provided me by Paul O'Dwyer and Gary Silverman, who represented the Islamic Republic of Iran in a postrevolutionary suit against the shah.

20. Interview with Ambassador MacArthur, Tehran, June 29, 1970.

21. See Robert Moss, "Who's Meddling in Iran? The Telltale Signs of Soviet Handiwork," *New Republic*, Dec. 2, 1978, pp. 15–18.

22. See Halperin, *Bureaucratic Politics and Foreign Policy*, pp. 150–55.

23. Ibid., p. 151.

24. The Iran Study Group met eight times between February 1960 and October 1961. The participants most sympathetic to the Pahlavi regime included Kermit Roosevelt, Donald Wilber, David Lilienthal's associate Gordon Clapp, and Council Middle East specialist John C. Campbell. Those who tended to support Young's analysis included journalist Kennett Love and scholar Richard Cottam (Work Papers of Iran Study Group in possession of the author).

25. Interviews in Tehran with the two diplomats, June 30, 1974, Oct. 11, 1977.

26. George Lenczowski, "The Arc of Crisis: Its Central Sector," *Foreign Affairs* 57 (Spring 1979): 811.

27. Robert G. Neumann, in Martin F. Herz, ed., *Contacts with the Opposition* (Institute for the Study of Diplomacy, Washington, D.C.: Georgetown University, n.d.), p. 15.

28. See the comments of the various former ambassadors in ibid.

29. Helms, in ibid., p. 23.

30. As reported by Sullivan in ibid., p. 4.

31. Morgenthau, in ibid., pp. 4–5.

32. Lenczowski, "The Arc of Crisis," p. 811.

33. Herz, *Contacts*, p. v–vi.

34. See Amembassy Tehran to Department of State, "Some Intangible Factors in Iranian Politics," No. A-702, June 15, 1964, drafted by M. F. Herz and published in *A View from Tehran* (Institute for the Study of Diplomacy, Washington, D.C.: Georgetown University, n.d.).

35. David D. Newsom, "Diplomats—Bearing the Message," *Christian Science Monitor*, Mar. 10, 1986.

36. Bernard Cohen, *The Public's Impact on Foreign Policy* (Boston: Little, Brown, 1973); James Rosenau, *The Scientific Study of Foreign Policy*, rev. ed. (New York: Nicols Publishing, 1976); and the important case study, F. O. Hampson, "The Divided Decision-Maker: American Domestic Politics and the Cuban Crisis," *International Security* 9 (1984/85): 130–165.

37. See Arthur M. Schlesinger, Jr., *A Thousand Days: John F. Kennedy in the White House* (Boston: Houghton Mifflin, 1965), p. 426.

38. The fact that scholars, for example, carry certain advantages unavailable to official observers provides them with fewer excuses for the sometimes shoddy and biased work that some of them produce.

39. See Stansfield Turner, *Secrecy and Diplomacy* (Boston: Houghton Mifflin, 1985), pp. 116–17.

40. Naas, statement at conference on "Revolution in Iran," U.S. Department of State, Foreign Service Institute, Washington, D.C., Nov. 12, 1985.

41. Turner, *Secrecy and Diplomacy*, p. 271.

42. John Tower, Edmund Muskie, and Brent Scowcroft, *The Tower Commission Report* (New York: Bantam Books/Times Books, 1987), p. xv.

Index

Bakhtiar, Shapour, 70, 100, 240, 254, 256, 263–64
Bakhtiar, Teymour, 99, 114, 127, 138, 143, 162
Ball, George, 168, 244, 249, 252–53, 257, 335–36, 340, 436
Bangladesh, 199
Bani Sadr, Abol Hassan, 263, 265–68, 270, 286–88, 296, 342–43
Baqa'i, Muzaffar, 67, 69
Baraheni, Reza, 192
Barzani, Mulla Mustafa, 205, 206–8
Baskerville, Howard, 17
Bayat, Murtiza Quli, 33
Bazaar, 25, 68, 71–72, 99, 144, 161–62, 217, 238, 242, 250, 296, 439
Bazargan, Mehdi, 70, 100, 262, 263, 264–65, 271, 288, 292–93, 294–95, 296, 327, 328–29
Beale, Betty, 369, 370
Becker, Ralph E., 361
Beckwith, Charles, 301
Beheshti, Ayatollah Muhammad Hussein, 267, 271, 279, 296
Bevin, Ernest, 74
Bihbihani, Ayatollah Muhammad Musavi, 101
Blumenthal, W. Michael, 244, 252, 259
Bolster, Archie M., 176, 391, 503nn15, 20
Bowling, John W., 133–34
Brademas, John, 213, 351, 364
Brezhnev, Leonid, 150
Britain. See Great Britain
British Bank of Iran and the Middle East, 64
British Petroleum–AIOC, 106, 111
Brooke, Edward, 364
Brown, Harold, 230, 244, 251, 333
Browne, Edward G., 43
Brzezinski, Zbigniew, 226, 433; and fall of shah, 243–60 passim; and postrevolutionary Iran, 276, 294–95; and hostage rescue mission, 300–303; and admission of shah to U.S., 331–33, 339, 361; and NSC, 409–10, 411, 415
Bukhara'i, Muhammad, 161–62
Bullard, Sir Reader, 43
Bundy, McGeorge, 140, 175, 177, 178, 320
Bureaucratic conflict. See Organizational conflict
Bureau of Intelligence and Research (U.S. State Dept.), 214, 245, 406–9
Burghe'i, Ayatollah Muhammad, 190
Burujirdi, Ayatollah Muhammad Hussein, 69, 101, 142, 152, 238
Bush, George, 2, 311, 413, 506n56
Business, U.S.: interests in Iran, 177–78, 180–81, 203, 204, 209–10, 360, 363, 364, 366, 428, 434–35; and admission of shah to U.S., 319, 320–21, 329–30,

331, 337, 340–48. See also Petroleum
Butler, William J., 223, 226, 487n53
Byrd, Robert, 229, 260, 284
Byrnes, James, 34, 80
Byroade, Henry, 116, 368

Cadman, Sir John, 59, 60, 468n31
Callahan, Art, 259, 403
Capitulations Agreement, 156–61
Carroll, George, 170–71
Carter, Hodding, 257
Carter, Jimmy, 3, 6, 215–21 passim, 226–34, 243, 252, 253, 257–60, 442; and hostage crisis, 295–96, 300–301, 303; and admission of shah to U.S., 323, 332, 335, 337–40, 441–42; and Iranian assets, 341, 342, 344; administration's differences from Reagan's, 411–12
Carter, Rosalynn, 231, 232, 243, 300, 338
Casey, William, 308, 309, 413, 414
Cassin, Vernon ("Guy Rutherford"), 286–88
Cave, George, 1–2, 291–92, 293, 308, 309, 403, 422, 492nn48, 50, 52
CENTO, 115, 117–18
Central Intelligence Agency. See CIA
Central Treaty Organization. See CENTO
Chamran, Mustafa, 291, 294, 295
Chapin, Selden, 123
Chase Manhattan Bank, 120, 180, 322, 329–30, 334, 337, 339, 340–48, 362, 364, 497n48, 498nn60, 62, 508n18
China, People's Republic of, 199
Christianity, in 19th-century Iran, 15–16
Christopher, Warren, 244, 245, 253, 300, 323, 324
Church, Frank, 136
Churchill, Winston, 28, 59–60, 85, 90
CIA, 213, 355, 394, 399–400; Iranian view of, 3, 86, 401, 444–45; and 1953 intervention in Iran, 79, 86–94 passim; and Kurds, 205, 207; and SAVAK, 210–11, 402–3, 416; and Iran policy, 244, 251, 258; and Iran listening posts, 254; Iran activities after revolution, 286–93; hostages as agents of, 297, 298; and Iran-Contra arms affair, 308–12 passim, 412, 413–14; ineffectiveness in Iran, 401–3; activities, problems analyzed, 415–20, 420–24
Clapp, Gordon, 120, 122, 123–24, 126
Class issues: conflicts, 25–26, 145–46, 390–92, 393–94, 403–5
Clement, Carl, 245, 250, 385
Clerics. See Religious right; Shi'is
Cohen, Stephen, 250, 488n58
Cold War, 30–31, 37–38
Communism, Iranian, 83; in Azerbaijan, 34, 36; U.S. preoccupation with, 52,

Iranian Central Bank, 343, 344
Iranian Oil Exploration and Producing Co., 108
Iranian Oil Participants, 108
Iranian Oil Refining Co., 108
Iranian revolution of *1978–79*, 233–43; influence of *1953* intervention on, 94, 96–97; roots of, 163; number of casualties in, 236, 486–87*n38*; U.S. in, 243–60; aftermath of, 261–63, 271–72; groups opposed to, 271–73; external threats, 275; U.S. hostility to, 276–85. *See also* Hostages, U.S. Embassy
Iranians, attitudes to Americans: to CIA, 3, 86, 401, 415–16; early positive feelings, 16–18, 42; respect for Dreyfus, 21; resentment of Millspaugh, 26–27; ambivalence, 46–48; resentment of *1953* intervention, 86, 94–97; links to shah seen as elitist, 123; alienated by aid, 126–30; Kennedy's appeal among masses, 137; response to LBJ, 140; reaction to SOFA, 157–61; alienation, hostility of, 179–80, 181–82, 190, 234, 314, 381, 382, 388–89, 390; anti-Americanism in revolution, 234, 239, 241, 256–57, 257–58, 277, 284, 294; and hostage crisis, 295–306 *passim;* and Iran-Iraq war, 307; positive responses to individuals, 379, 380, 381; goodwill squandered by U.S., 382
Iran-Iraq war, 274, 275, 304–6, 314, 494*n74*
Iran Novin party, 164, 167
Iran party, 70
Iraq, 104, 117, 198; signs treaty with USSR, 199; and Kurds, 205–6; and war with Iran, 274, 275, 304–6, 494*n74;* U.S. resumes relations with, 306–7, 314
Iricon group, 111
Islam. *See* Islamic activism; Shi'is
Islamic activism, 238; against Musaddiq, 66, 71–72; and nationalization, 83; and shah, 101–2, 142; resents U.S., 128–29; reaction to White Revolution, 148, 152–53, 168; reaction to SOFA, 159–61; in Mansur plot, 162–63; opposes investment group, 181–82. *See also* Shi'is
Islamic Nations party, 162
Islamic Republican party, 267, 270–71
Islamic Republic of Iran: violence in, 261–63, 270–73; moderates in, 263–70, 278–80; extremist forces in, 267–70 and table; Khomeini's system of control, 273–76; and Iran-Contra affair, 312–15; and assets, bank loans, 341–48; attitude to CIA, 415
Israel: and SAVAK-Mossad connection, 98, 403, 430, 508*n13;* shah supports, 171, 177; receives Iranian oil, 204; assists

Kurds, 205; ships arms to Iran, 312; as reason for backing shah, 365, 377; and Iran-Contra arms affair, 411–12, 435; and "Iranian connection," 429–31

Jablonsky, Gen. Harvey, 362
Jackson, Henry, 283, 285
Jamah'i Mujahidin-i Islam, 68
Javits, Jacob, 213, 283–84, 364, 365–66, 431
Javits, Marian, 365–66, 428–29, 431–32
Jernegan, John, 43
Johnson, Lyndon B., 139–41, 154–56, 169–70, 176–77
Jones, Thomas, 353, 363, 364
Jordan, Hamilton, 243, 244, 300, 327, 338–39, 497*n40*
Jordan, Samuel Martin, 17
Justice, U.S. Dept. of, 82

Kaiser, Walter J., 380–81
Kalp, Malcolm, 298
Kashani, Ayatollah Abul Qassim, 66, 68, 69–70, 71–72, 94–95, 101
Kavtaradze, Sergei, 28
Katouzian, Homa, 225, 475*n25*
Kazankin, Guennady, 298–99
Kennedy, Edward (*1940s* diplomat), 43
Kennedy, Edward (senator), 211
Kennedy, John F., 120, 130, 131–33, 137–40, 152–53, 221, 441
Kennedy, Robert, 133, 373
Khabir, Jamshid, 391
Khalkhali, Hojjat ol-Islam Sadiq, 262
Khamene'i, Ali Hussein, 189
Khomeini, Ayatollah Ruhollah, 70, 96–97, 128; *1963* antishah actions, 148, 152; reaction to SOFA, exiled, 159–61; condemns investment conference, 181; condemns shah's extravaganza, 185; plan to discredit, 188; returns from exile, 216, 242–43; reaction to Carter, 243; and Iranian revolution, 238–40; support underestimated, 254–55; Carter vetoes contract with, 258; and power struggle after revolution, 263–70 *passim;* political strategy of, 270–76; perceived as communist, 277–78, 442–43; U.S. ignores, 281–82; and hostage crisis, 295, 302–3; and Iran-Iraq war, 306; and Iran-Contra arms affair, 312–13
Khomeini, Sayyid Ahmad, 262
Khosrowdad, Gen. Manuchehr, 236, 256
Khrushchev, Nikita, 132–33, 320–21
Khunsari, Ayatollah Muhammad Taqi, 69
Khuzistan province project, 120–21, 122–23

Kia, Gen. Alavi, 127
Kia, Parsa, 328
Kianouri, Nureddin, 273
Kissinger, Henry, 165, 351, 414, 418; and
    arms sales to shah, 200–202, 204, 209;
    ties with shah, 203, 212, 319, 320, 322–
    23, 502n101; and Kurds, 206–8,
    484n41; and Iranian policy, 244, 251,
    276; and admission of shah to U.S.,
    328–40 passim, 345, 496n23
Kitchen, Jeffrey, 364
Khiabani, Musa, 272
Komer, Robert W., 175, 177
Koob, Kathryn, 16
Kosygin, Aleksey, 171
Kraft, Joseph, 369, 371, 375
Kurdistan, 36
Kurds, 204–8, 292
Kuzichkin, Vladimir, 273

Laingen, Bruce, 276, 279, 282, 290, 291–
    92, 295, 323–25, 326, 328
Lambton, Ann K. S., 43, 392
Landlords, 145, 164
Land reform, 144–46, 162, 164
Lazard Brothers, 120
Leavell, Col. John, 30
Ledeen, Michael, 308, 313, 411–12,
    494n76
Leggett, Sir Frederick, 75
Lehman, William, 364, 365
Lenczowski, George, 48, 373–74, 375,
    433, 466n63
Lester, Alan, 398
Levy, Walter, 45, 76, 217, 470n68
Lewis, Anthony, 336
Liberalization, of late 1970s, 219–26
Liberation Movement of Iran (LM), 264,
    288, 298
Lilienthal, David, 120, 121, 122, 123–24,
    126, 178, 181, 203, 320, 357–59, 428–
    29
Limbert, John, 16, 279, 303, 313, 393
Linen, James A., 180–81, 203, 363, 364,
    371, 375
Lippmann, Walter, 132–33, 135
Long, David, 407
Longrigg, Stephen, 64
Lower classes, workers: strike oil fields,
    51; percentages of oil-field labor force
    in 1935–48, 63; as Tudeh party mem-
    bers, 67; discontent with shah, 115,
    142, 168; and Mansur plot, 162–63;
    foreign work force, 217; support for
    Khomeini, 274; Americans' lack of con-
    tact with, 390, 403, 405

MAAG (Military Assistance Advisory
    Group), 39, 362, 394, 400
MacArthur, Douglas, II, 191, 383, 399,
    433–34, 502n5

McCloy, John J., 244, 251, 320, 334–35,
    336, 340, 429, 496n29
McFarlane, Robert, 1–2, 308, 312, 411,
    415
McGhee, George, 72–73, 77, 78, 79, 83,
    84, 429, 471n90
McGovern, George, 367
McNamara, Robert S., 173, 355
Madani, Ayatollah Asadollah, 271
Mahdavi, Fereydoun, 220
Majlis: and issue of oil, 29, 62–63, 65;
    1947 elections for, 37; 1954, 1956 elec-
    tions for, 99; dissolved by shah in
    1961, 143; and SOFA, 156, 157, 159;
    revived in 1963, 163–64
Makki, Hussein, 61, 71, 76
Maliki, Khalil, 69, 71, 195
Mansouri, Javad, 288, 491n41
Mansur, Hassan Ali, 161–62, 164
Marxist Democratic Movement, 34
Mattei, Enrico, 112, 113, 475n26
Media, American: belittle Musaddiq, 55;
    and preoccupation with communism,
    80, 471n80; criticize shah's extrava-
    ganza, 185; admire shah, 200; and
    Pahlavism, 366, 367–74, 501nn92, 94;
    and the Kurds, 484n39
Media, Iranian: proliferate in 1949, 51;
    campaign against APOC, 60; anti-U.S.
    articles under shah, 178–79, 214; crit-
    icism of shah, 225; attack on Kho-
    meini, 233–35; attack on Tudeh party,
    273; comment on Americans in Iran,
    382
Medicine: U.S. medical workers in Iran,
    17; U.S. aid for, 124, 126
Mehran, Hassan Ali, 218, 354
Memoirs of a Crowded City (Tunakabuni),
    180
Metrinko, Michael, 393
Meyer, Armin, 172, 173, 174, 478n29
Michaud, Michael A. G., 384
Middle classes: as Tudeh party members,
    67; composition of, in 1950s, 68–72; as
    supporters of shah, 99; discontent un-
    der shah, 114–15, 117, 142; shah urged
    to cultivate, 134, 135; opposed to
    Amini, 146; reaction to White Revolu-
    tion, 148, 151; and Marble Palace plot,
    163; in revived Majlis, 163–64
Migration, rural-urban, 217
Miklos, Jack, 201, 259, 395, 406
Milani, Ayatollah Hadi, 129
Military, American, in Iran: 1940s mis-
    sions, 19–20, 39, 40–41, 45, 46; troops
    create problems, 47; and extrater-
    ritoriality, 156–58, 389; limits of, 443
Military, Iranian, 18, 19, 45; U.S. aid for,
    40–41, 50, 113, 114, 115, 170–73, 200–
    202, 208–10, 226, 227, 228–32, 365; as
    shah's instrument of power, 98–99,